An Illustrated Book of
Know-How for the Camp Worker

CAMP

Illustrated by IDA B. CRAWFORD *and* HELEN B. DAVIDSON

A. VIOLA MITCHELL, A.B., M.A.

Missouri Valley College, Marshall, Missouri

IDA B. CRAWFORD, A.B., M.A.

Former Art Supervisor, Winthrop College, Rock Hill, South Carolina

COUNSELING

THIRD EDITION

W. B. SAUNDERS COMPANY

Philadelphia and London

W. B. Saunders Company: West Washington Square,
Philadelphia, Pa. 19105

12 Dyott Street
London, W.C.1

Reprinted February, 1962, June, 1963,
September, 1964, September, 1965

August, 1966, April, 1967 and August, 1968

Camp Counseling

To an Old Camper

You may think, my dear, when you grow quite old
　　You have left camp days behind,
But I know the scent of wood smoke
　　Will always call to mind
　　　Little fires at twilight
　　And trails, you used to find.

You may think some day you have quite grown up,
　　And feel so worldly wise,
But suddenly from out of the past
　　A vision will arise,
　　　Of merry folk with brown, bare knees
　　And laughter in their eyes.

You may live in a house built to your taste
　　In the nicest part of town,
But some day for your old camp togs
　　You'd change your latest gown,
　　　And trade it all for a balsam bed
　　Where the stars all night look down.

You may find yourself grown wealthy,—
　　Have all that gold can buy,
But you'd toss aside a fortune
　　For days 'neath an open sky,
　　　With sunlight on blue water
　　And white clouds sailing high.

For once you have been a camper
　　Then something has come to stay
Deep in your heart forever
　　Which nothing can take away,
　　　And heaven can only be heaven
　　With a camp in which to play.

—MARY S. EDGAR

From *Wood-Fire and Candle-Light*
Published by The Macmillan Co.

Preface to the Third Edition

IN THIS AGE of fabulous miracles, camping, like all of our ways of life, has undergone tremendous changes to the extent that it seemingly makes advisable a complete revision of *Camp Counseling*. The reader will find that most of the chapters have undergone extensive changes and that many have been entirely rewritten. Much new material has been added and the old has been revised and modernized in keeping with developments in the field. For any improvements made, much credit must be given to the several users who have kindly devoted time and thought to making constructive suggestions; their comments are always welcomed and deeply appreciated.

New substance has been added to the first section of the book, making a division into an additional chapter desirable. In response to the request of several, an additional chapter has been added to the second section pertaining to the camp counselor and his duties. All chapters have been revised and enlarged. Several short chapters have been combined so that the book still contains the original number of thirty-two.

Obviously, it is not possible in a single volume to make an exhaustive treatment of the many facets of camping which are discussed in the book. However, the reader will find a completely revised and comprehensive bibliography at the end of each chapter to guide him to source material should he wish to pursue any phase more thoroughly. The listings and descriptions of films pertaining to camping and allied fields have also been brought up to date.

The reader will note the addition of thirty-three photographs pertaining to all phases of camp life. There are also 128 new drawings to clarify old and new techniques, to help identify subject matter discussed in the text, or to add what we hope will be "spice." In addition to the many suggestions for program in the chapter so entitled, hundreds of other possibilities will be found in both written word and illustration scattered throughout the book.

The index is complete and includes cross-indexes which, the author hopes, will enhance the usefulness of the book. There is also an alphabetized listing of publishers with their addresses as well as a supplementary list of general books pertaining to camping.

As in previous editions, an attempt has been made to keep this book completely in line with the recommendations of the American Camping Association as to the content of courses for prospective counselors. Our aim has constantly been to make *Camp Counseling* ever more useful and usable. We sincerely hope that you will find it so.

VIOLA MITCHELL

References for the Instructor in Counseling

Bibliographies of Studies and Research in Camping. A.C.A., Revised, 1958, 27 pp., 30¢.

Camp Administrative Forms and Suggested Procedures in the Area of Personnel. A.C.A., 1956, 30 pp., 35¢.

Counselor-in-Training Course. Camp Fire Girls D-230, 1956, 33 pp., 60¢.

Counselor-in-Training Program Aides Course. Camp Fire Girls.

Cumulative Index to Camping Magazine. A.C.A., 35¢, Subject Index, Vol. I, No. 1, March–April 1926, to Vol. XXX, No. 8, Dec., 1958.

Hamilton, Fanchon: *Training for Outdoor Leadership in Troops and Camps.* Girl Scouts, 55 pp., $1.00.

Hammett, Catherine T.: *A Camp Director Trains His Own Staff.* A.C.A., 1948, 32 pp., 50¢.

Hartwig, Marie, and Peterson, Florence: *Camp Counselor Training Workbook.* Burgess Publishing Co., 1960, Revised.

Joy, Barbara Ellen: *Annotated Bibliography of Camping.* A.C.A., 1961, Revised.

Joy, Barbara Ellen: *Outline of Course in Camp Administration and Organization.* Camp Publications, No. 37, 4 pp., 55¢.

Joy, Barbara Ellen: *Outline of Course in Camp Craft and Pioneering.* Camp Publications #38, 6 pp., 70¢.

Joy, Barbara Ellen: *Outline and Procedures for In-Camp, Pre-Season Counselor Training Course.* Camp Publications #39, 6 pp., 60¢.

Klein, Alan F.: *Role Playing in Leadership Training and Group Problem Solving.* Assn. Press, 176 pp., 1956.

Knowles, Hulda, and Malcolm: *How To Develop Better Leaders.* Assn. Press, 1955, 64 pp., $1.00.

Koskey, Thomas A.: *Baited Bulletin Boards.* Baited Bulletin Boards, 30 Clareview Ave., San Jose 27, Calif., 32 pp., $1.00.

Resident Camp Program Aide Course. Camp Fire Girls #D-231, 1956, 39 pp., 60¢.

MAGAZINE ARTICLES

Adee, Don, and Crawford, Don: *Camping for College Credit.* C.M., Dec., 1957.

Allen, Hugh D.: *Here's a Way to Better Counselor Training.* C.M., Feb., 1950.

Chapman, Frederick M.: *Classes in Camp Aid Outdoor Education.* C.M., June, 1956.

Coombs, Fred M.: *A Camp Comes to the Campus.* Recreation, Sept., 1955.

Dimock, Hedley G.: *Role Playing—A Workable Approach to Better Camp Leadership.* C.M., May–June, 1956.

Dimock, Hedley G.: *Role Playing—An Aid to Learning and Developing Leadership Skills.* C.M., May–June, 1956.

Kessel, J. Bertram: *Role Playing Vitalize Pre-Camp Training.* J.H., P.E., and R., Jan., 1957.

Klein, Alan F.: *Improved Staff Means Improved Performance.* C.M., Feb., 1956.

Lowes, Barry: *Pre-Camp Training Assures a Job Well Done.* C.M., Feb., 1956.

Martin, George W.: *Camping With Confidence.* J.H., P.E., and R., Feb., 1956. (Mountaineering Class at Olympic College)

Martin, George W.: *College Outdoor Living.* J.H., P.E., and R., Oct., 1955. (Mountaineering Class at Olympic College)

Counselor-in-Training (C.I.T.) Programs

Brown, Harry E.: *How We Operate a Successful JC Program.* C.M., Feb., 1956.

Clark, Leslie S.: *Teen-Age Camp Counselor Trainees.* J.H., P.E., and R., June, 1954.

Dudley, Charles M.: *How Our Junior Guide Program Helps Us Keep Senior Campers Enthusiastic.* C.M., Jan., 1957.

Hower, Marjorie A.: *How One Camp Organized a Successful Program For Counselors In Training.* C.M., Mar., 1953.

McMullan, Jean G.: *A CIT Program That's Really Professional.* C.M., April, 1955.

Report Made On C.I.T. Survey: C.M., Feb., 1954.

Sinn, Mrs. B. A., and Pels, Mrs. Herbert: *Good Counselors Are Made In Camp.* C.M., Feb., 1950.

Preface and Suggestions for Use

IT IS HOPED that this camping manual will prove useful as a basic source book for both experienced and inexperienced camp counselors. It is obviously impossible to include in one volume all the materials camp workers need to fit them for carrying on the broad and varied program of a modern summer camp, but as much material as seems practicable has been treated in some detail. Since some important aspects have only been touched upon, extensive bibliographies have been included at the end of each chapter to supplement the materials of the text.

This book is designed to meet the needs of at least five classes of persons: (1) college students taking courses in camp leadership or camp counseling; (2) prospective camp counselors enrolled in the between-season training courses given by various organizations; (3) counselors participating in precamp training courses at camp; (4) counselors on the job in camp; and (5) camp directors who are conducting precamp or in-training programs.

The Counselor, since he occupies such an influential position with youngsters, needs to be a well-rounded and well-adjusted person. He must have as a working background some knowledge of the history, philosophy and objectives of camping. He must understand people and be able to appreciate their varying personalities and characteristics—both the older ones who will be his staff associates and the youngsters who will be his campers. He needs to have personal skill in one or more camp activities and must have the "know how" of teaching others. Above all, since camping is carried on mainly in an outdoor environment, he must have the camping and woodcraft knowledge and skills necessary to live comfortably, happily and safely in the out-of-doors.

The ideal counselor training course would have an enrollment of around sixteen and would be carried on in a camping situation, with children of camp age in attendance. In such a laboratory, prospective counselors could see the things discussed put into practice under actual camp conditions. Unfortunately, such a Utopian set-up is rarely possible, and the majority of courses must be carried on under classroom limitations. A resourceful instructor, however, will make opportunities for at least a few excursions out-of-doors on cook-outs, overnight sleep-outs, weekend camping trips, and perhaps a four-to-ten-day camping trip to climax the end of the course. Diverse teaching methods keep interests alert and make for thorough learning as they appeal to the visual-minded, the auditory-minded, and those who learn best by "doing" or actually experiencing a thing. The following techniques are suggested:

1. Study of the text, amplifying it by demonstrations, experimentation, discussion, testing, and so forth.
2. Supplementary reading—no course can be adequate which does not acquaint the student with the wealth of materials available on various phases of camping:
   (a) Certain readings specified for the entire group.
   (b) Special reading for those interested in some particular phase, such as nature study, dramatics, waterfront, or arts and crafts.
3. Round-table, panel or class discussions growing out of talks, outside readings, or topics assigned for special study.
4. Special reports made by groups or individuals.
5. Teacher, group or individual demonstrations.
6. Special projects, such as collecting camp poetry or songs, making articles of camp equipment, waterproofing matches, making spatter prints, and so on.
7. Bringing in visiting consultants such as camp directors, Boy or Girl Scout leaders, Red Cross waterfront or first aid workers, and school personnel in such related fields as sociology, nature study and home economics.
8. Bulletin board displays, changed frequently and on schedule by members of the group. Attention drawn through the use of colored mounting paper, colored thumb tacks, printed topical headings, and other means.
9. Use of the many good slides and movies now available. (See pages 395–400.)

10. Check lists used to record the specific achievements of class members.
11. Exhibits of camp bulletins, pamphlets, books, model camp-sites, arts and crafts projects, nature lore, camping and wood-craft skills, tools, and the like.
12. Scheduled laboratory periods for practicing campcraft skills. Field trips, overnight or weekend trips. Sponsoring such trips for neighborhood children.
13. Preparing annotated bibliographies. One important phase of a training course is browsing through the literature of camping and allied fields to acquaint the student with sources so that he can quickly find what he wants when he wants it.
14. Writing term papers on chosen topics or those pertaining to the job the student expects to have in camp next season.
15. Planning and participating in cook-outs, overnight trips and weekend trips. This affords opportunity for democratic practice in planning program, food, equipment, duty charts, menus, food lists, and so on, as well as gives actual practice in camping techniques.
16. Making a loose leaf camping notebook or scrapbook.

Though there is a continuing and rapid growth in the quality and quantity of the training in camping colleges are giving, it continues to lag far behind what is needed for approximately 400,000 camp staff members who are hired every year. Approximately 50 colleges own or have access to camp facilities and 280 give courses in camping, some of them on "campsites."*

Obviously no practical course in camping can be carried on without a minimum of camping equipment such as knives, hatchets, files, cooking utensils, blanket pins, tents, and so on. Students may be asked to buy their own, or equipment may be loaned or rented to them by the sponsoring agency.

Most groups will find the list of additional readings at the end of each chapter too extensive for the time available. These lists are purposely left so that the instructor can go through them, eliminating any books or pamphlets unavailable in his particular situation and selecting according to the particular needs and interests of his group. To avoid repetition, only skeletal information is given at the ends of chapters for sources referred to in several chapters; complete data are in the bibliography given on pages 389 and 390.

VIOLA MITCHELL
IDA B. CRAWFORD

* McBride, Robert E.: *Camping at the Mid-Century,* page 4.

Acknowledgments

SINCERE THANKS are given to Misses Barbara Ellen Joy and Marjorie Camp for their always helpful encouragement and comment and also for several of the photographs which appear in the third edition. The kind interest and suggestions of Mr. Gerard A. Harrison, Assistant Executive Director of the American Camping Association and Mr. and Mrs. Charles C. Alford of Crystal Lake Camps, Hughesville, Pa. have been deeply appreciated. Thanks are also due to the Misses Joyce Hammond and Lee Abbott of State University College of Education, Oneonta, New York for photographs and other help rendered; and also to Mr. and Mrs. H. H. Hanson for helpful comments and permission to use the poem by Mr. Hanson; to Agathe Deming Arnn; to Mrs. Elizabeth Cumming, Davidson College, N.C., for help in obtaining the poem by Charles Mitchell.

Grateful acknowledgment is made to the following publishers who have generously given their permission for the use of quotations. To The Bobbs-Merrill Co., Inc. for use of the work of James Whitcomb Riley; to Coronet Magazine for the quotation of Carl Schurz; to Houghton Mifflin Co. for use of the works of Longfellow and Thoreau; to Doubleday-Doran and Co. for the poem by Walt Whitman; to The Chilton Greetings Co. for use of the poem from THE FRIENDSHIP BOOK; to Charles Scribner's Sons for the use of the work of Robert Louis Stevenson; to The House of Hubbard for *Elbert Hubbard's Epigram;* to the Indianapolis News for *Yours;* to

The Macmillan Co. for Mary S. Edgar's poems; to the Open Road Publishing Co. for the poems of Deep River Jim; to Reilly & Lee Publishing Co. for permission to use the poem of Edgar A. Guest; to the American Camping Association and CAMPING MAGAZINE for *What is a Camper* by Louis C. Kuehner; to Silva, Inc. for the photograph of the Silva Compass; and to Abingdon Press for the prayers from MEDITATIONS UNDER THE SKY.

To the countless publications from all fields of camping, we express our indebtedness for help they have given us in suggesting ideas and furnishing information. To the many individuals whose helpful suggestions and constructive criticism have, we hope, helped us to improve and make more functional this new edition.

To Mrs. Helen A. Davidson we express thanks for her painstaking care in the drawing of the new pictures which appear in this third edition and to Mrs. Ralph Kichline, Brenda Bailey, Lynne Kilvington and Georganne Weller for their cooperation in the preparation of the manuscript.

We wish also to express our regret at not being able to give recognition for the use of some of the material. In spite of diligent search and the writing of many letters, it has been impossible to trace some of the quotations and ideas for camp "fixings" to their original sources.

Contents

I. Growth and Objectives of Camping

1. *Camping*.   3

2. *History of Organized Camping*.   19

3. *The Objectives of Camping*.   29

II. The Camp Counselor

4. *The Camp Counselor*.   37

5. *The Counselor on the Job*.   48

6. *The Counselor Must Understand People*.   68

xvii

7. *The Counselor as a Leader*   82

8. *Some Problems You May Meet*   91

III. Camp Activities

9. *Planning the Program*   101

10. *Dramatics*   116

11. *Music*   124

12. *Arts and Crafts*   130

13. *Literature in Camp*   145

14. *Nature and Conservation*   155

15. *Aquatics*   173

16. *Spiritual Life*   183

IV. Camp Craft and Woodcraft

17. *Some Camp Pests*   191

18. *Ropes and Knotcraft*   199

19. *The Weather*   209

20. *Getting About in the Out-of-Doors*   222

21. *Hiking, Trailing, and Stalking*   240

22. *Tincancraft*   248

23. *Knifemanship and Toolcraft* 255

24. *Axemanship* 266

25. *Fires and Fire Prevention* 273

26. *Tents and Shelters* 292

27. *Duffel for Camping and Trips* 305

28. *Sleeping in the Open* 326

29. *Keeping Food Cool and Safe* 333

30. *Cooking Devices* 339

31. *Foods and Outdoor Cooking* 348

32. *Trip Camping* 365

Selected General Bibliography 389

Directory of Publishers and Organizations 391

Films and Slides Pertaining to Camping 395

INDEX 401

I

Growth and Objectives
of Camping

"THE CAMPERS ARE HERE
AGAIN — LET'S HIBERNATE"

1

Camping

FAMILY CAMPING

A Booming Trend

Were you one of the millions of citizens of the United States who, in 1960, took to the highways and byways to go from here to yonder? It is estimated that 40,000,000 of those Americans who set forth to "see America first," or one out of every three or four spent from one night to two or more weeks under a tent or other rustic form of shelter. This constitutes an astonishing increase of over ten times the number who ten years ago were reverting to camp life, somewhat more but mostly less like the life our ancestors lived centuries ago. The Conestoga wagon has been supplanted by many horsepower, harnessed under the hood of an automobile or station wagon with a car top carrier and/or a trailer to carry hitherto unheard of outdoor conveniences for the comfort and safety of wayfarers. This array of equipment has changed so dramatically that a pioneer's eyes would literally "bug out" in astonishment, incredulity and perhaps even a touch of disgust at the softness of the modern two legged creature known as man.

Not since the days of the gold rush has America seen such a feverish haste to leave home and scatter to the four winds. This thirst for the rustic life has mounted each year to the point of causing custodians of public and private lands to struggle fruitlessly to keep up with the demand

"Are you sure you brought everything on the check list, Pa?"

for campsites and the few facilities essential to fit them for human habitation. During the peak months of June, July, and August, wise campers make reservations ahead in some of the popular spots for some must be turned away and others limited to a stay of only a few days. The National Forests alone expect to be called upon to accommodate 66 million individuals by 1962 and the National Park Service is bending all its efforts to meet the demand as it tries to provide 30,000 additional campsites that will accommodate 90,000 campers. A prominent mail order house reports that four times as many tents were sold in 1958 as had been sold a mere nine years earlier; another estimates that its sales of camping equipment alone will total over 20 million dollars in one year. The sales of the popular station wagon increased six fold in a mere seven years and, though most of these wagons were being put to daily use in family living, many were purchased with a direct view to usefulness during the summer vacation camping trip; in fact, at least one prominent automobile manufacturer has designed its wagon especially to fit the needs of family camping. More power to this trend for we believe that it is really true that "a family that plays together stays together."

Causes for the Camping Boom

Who can say why this huge growth in outdoor living has taken place? All we can do is speculate about what irresistibly draws a person toward a more or less simple life full of inconveniences in lieu of his luxurious home. Here he need only press a button to flood the room with light, walk into a public dining room to be served excellent food, move a gadget to regulate the temperature, or flip the TV dials to bring in a favorite Western hero who rides the range and roughs it for him as he sits comfortably by in an easy chair. It doesn't make sense, does it?

Nevertheless the urge for such a life is there, compelling and demanding. Perhaps its roots in many men spring from their experiences in the armed forces as they lived under primitive conditions and were trained in survival methods in case they should be marooned in unfriendly territory or become the unfortunate victims of an airplane mishap in the region of nowhere. Possibly the love of camping results from a desire to emulate the lives of heroes of the past or to live the life of adventure and self-reliance, which Western movies and novels dazzle temptingly before us. School camping has been increasing by leaps and bounds and has no doubt sparked a flame as it opens new vistas and ways of life to those boys and girls fortunate enough to experience it. The displays of intriguing and challenging new equipment on the dealers' shelves and in his windows are hard to resist. Longer vacations and a short work week have left us with the necessary time and some of us undoubtedly join the parade because "it's the thing to do." Others are attracted because neighbor Jackson and his family have talked of little else since the glorious two weeks they spent camping last summer. Last, but not least, a great deal of it must be due to the wonderful experiences millions of children and counselors have had and are continuing to have in the many organized camps sponsored by various agencies and private individuals throughout the country. The Boy Scouts alone claim to have trained over 27,000,000 boys and men in the skills of the camper since 1910. In any field, the more we know about a thing and the more skills we have developed in it, the more we enjoy doing it. What is more natural, then, than for former campers to betake themselves and their children off to try to recapture some of the peace and happiness of camp days?

Camping brings a wonderful opportunity to relax and relieve tensions, built up by too many people, alarm clocks, office hours, business lunches, jangling telephones, and appointments with the hair dresser. Here we can meet new people and enjoy their companionship, yet just as easily retire into our little shells and get away from bothersome people and things when the mood dictates. Instead of falling asleep to the accompaniment of screeching tires, barking dogs, nocturnal cats and Junior's still watching TV in the living room, it's a relief to drift off to unconsciousness in the peacefulness of our native environment, be it forest, mountain, lake, desert or plain. We're free to feast our senses to the hilt as we gaze at the last embers of a campfire under a canopy of stars, listen to a distant loon, smell the pungent aroma of pine needles and wild honeysuckle, and taste the unparalleled goodness of food cooked over an open fire and ministered to a large appetite produced by a busy, active day in the out-of-doors.

Perhaps this freedom, to do what we want to do when we want to do it, is one of the reasons we find the transient life so enchanting, for we can head the family car in any direction down the thousands of miles of superhighways recently created and soon be "lost" in a completely new environment. There we can stay a night and then move on to new horizons or we can remain as long as we wish if the fishing is good or other attractions live up to our expectations. We may, instead, be one of those systematic individuals who works out a careful itinerary, leaving a mimeographed copy behind so that relatives and friends can reach us with a friendly note and the latest news from the old home front. Most people, however, prefer to wander as the spirit dictates, for what could be finer than to feel perfectly free to follow the whim of the moment. One of the charms of such blissful existence lies in the activities that are naturally a part of camping for you can hike, canoe, bicycle, swim, ride horseback, fish, climb mountains or collect rocks, shells or anything else of interest. Perhaps you will prefer to establish a main camp as a base and forage out on daily excursions to places accessible only on foot or by canoe. If you want to go into wilderness areas where human traffic just isn't, and where there are no well marked paths, you will find experienced guides at your service and pack animals to transport your gear.

The trend in modern American life is toward larger families and younger parents who still have the love of adventure and desire for the new so prevalent in youth. What is more logical, then, than to round up the children and start out together? An additional advantage to the young couple, still not well established financially, is the economy of a camping expedition. A family of four would spend $10–$15 a day to stay at a motel; access to a national or state forest or park campsite costs as little as 50¢ to $1.00 and $5 to $10 a day additional can be saved by cooking your own food. One family reported a twenty-day trip, covering 7,000 miles at a cost of only about $150 and, had they elected to stay put at a site nearer home, the cost would have been substantially less, for automobile expenses constitute an important part of trip expenditures. In fact, after a family has acquired the necessary equipment for camping, this mode of life costs little more than staying at home. Adequate equipment for a family of four can be acquired for as little as $175, even less, if you are willing to settle for used or surplus items. It is possible to spend much more if you wish but beware of becoming the victim of an overzealous salesman who insists on selling you plush items in a quantity and quality neither necessary nor desirable. In truth, when starting out, you may be smart to rent your equipment at one of the outlets available in most cities; in that way, you can test it out and learn what you really want by your own experience and conversations with others you meet at various stopping points. Begin with a minimal outfit and add extras as your bank account and growing knowledge dictate.

Camping gives people a new sense of self-respect as father gains stature as true head of the family by erecting the shelter, chopping the wood and building the fire for the family meal. He is showing his masculinity by contriving various outdoor conveniences to keep the family comfortable. Mother, too, assumes new dignity and status in her own eyes as she serves up tasteful and attractive meals from the dehydrated and concentrated foods available on her grocer's shelves. If she wishes, she can procure whole meals or even a whole week's menu for from two to five people packed in a compact, light parcel,

"And would you care for an electric shaver with our finest half mile extension cord?"

ready for adding water and cooking; best of all, the meals taste just as good or better than those at home. Truly the old days of "the three B's, beans, bacon, and bannock"* are gone for today's campers.

No doubt the new equipment has contributed a great deal to camping's popularity for most of the arduous work formerly associated with it has been removed. Lightweight tents of new materials literally pop into place in as little as ninety seconds in the hands of an experienced person and some are supported by "ribs" or inflated rubber tubes, partially or completely dispensing with the old bothersome tent poles. Even inexpensive tents now come with water resistant floors and nylon screening, often on several sides, to admit a cooling cross breeze. Some have a coating of aluminum to insulate against the heat and models are available in almost any size, shape, and type the human heart could desire. "Car top" tents that open up against the side of a car or end of a station wagon provide for family living with maximum privacy.

Sleeping bags, though not actually essential, are a convenience. Those made of dacron or similar light materials roll up into a very light compact bundle and, when combined with air mattresses and pillows, and perhaps a collapsible cot, bring all the sleeping comfort of home.

New gasoline stoves are almost foolproof and permit you to cook or bake anything you could do at home. Gasoline and propane lanterns adequately light your premises; it is possible even to get a tent light that plugs into the cigarette lighter socket of your car. Featherweight portable refrigerators keep your food cold and nested aluminum dishes are available in any size for cooking and eating. One can rough it as much or as little as you like; comfortable living is possible with skeleton outfits, yet there are many refinements and "gadgets" for those who want them—a folding toaster, a camp rotisserie, a portable latrine or shower, an electric fan and hi-fi set, to mention a few. No doubt still other contrivances will be

on the market before this book comes off the press, for camping has become "big business" and manufacturers are exerting their best efforts to find better ways to cater to the whims of converts.

Perhaps the above discussion will have summed up at least some of the reasons for this almost phenomenal growth in family and adult camping. But here, we must pause in our ramblings for they have taken us somewhat afield and away from the primary purpose for which this book was written.

ORGANIZED CAMPING

What is Organized Camping?

An organized camp is one set up and run primarily for young people, a place in which they live more or less in a world of their own, working, playing, worshipping, and carrying on the various activities of living under the watchful eye of a staff of adult counselors and other staff personnel. Usually the camp is located in a spot of rustic beauty in a remote and somewhat isolated area; however, quite successful camping can be and has been done in the city park of a busy metropolitan area where the youthful inhabitants become so engrossed in what they are doing that they are almost oblivious to the teeming life around them.

There are various types of organized camps but we shall concern ourselves at the moment with the type known as a *resident camp* where campers spend their sleeping as well as waking hours for a period of several nights, weeks, or months.

Any camp has a personality all its own and is consequently not exactly like any other camp in existence. Nevertheless most of them have certain points of similarity. In a large and elaborately equipped camp, we usually find acres of trees, paths through the trees, and some sort of water, a lake, river, or ocean. There

* Whelen, Townsend, and Angier, Bradford: *On Your Own in the Wilderness.*

would probably be rustic cabins, tepees, Adirondack shacks, or tents on wooden platforms for the campers to live in. There would also be a common dining room, a lodge or recreation building, a handicraft shop or workshop, sanitary facilities including showers, well-equipped kitchen, a camp office, tool houses and sheds for the caretaker. Various other buildings would be scattered about to provide shelter for the health center, trading post, counselors' retreat, nature museum, library, and supplies and equipment for trips out of camp.

In the open, we might find a large riding ring, ranges for archery and rifle, an outdoor chapel, an amphitheatre, a council ring and several outpost campsites where campers could go to sleep and cook out. There is probably a stable for horses and an outdoor swimming pool unless natural waterways provide suitable facilities for swimming and diving. At the waterfront will be found an array of canoes, sail boats, row boats, and perhaps power boats with all their accompanying accessories. We may find fields and courts for such organized sports as tennis, archery, badminton, horseshoes, golf, baseball, basketball, and even some with a trampoline tucked away somewhere. In some camps, it is possible even for youngsters to delve into such interests as ballet dancing, electronics or nuclear physics.

This sounds like quite a thriving community, doesn't it? Indeed it is just that, for a modern, fairly large camp represents an investment of tens or even hundreds of thousands of dollars and the total value of camps in 1959 was estimated at $600 million. Yet, as with most great institutions, camping began on a very modest scale, and it will be interesting to trace back through the years to see how and why this marked development has taken place.

Present Status of Organized Camping

Organized camping was "born and reared" in solid, austere New England,

as were many of America's progressive ideas, and the majority of camps are still located in that area. Heavy concentrations of camps are found in New York and Pennsylvania in the East and Washington and California in the West. It was a Yankee "notion" which, in the approximately hundred years since the birth of organized camping in 1861, has resulted in the establishment of an estimated 16,000–18,000 camps of different kinds serving from five to six million boys and girls each summer. It is estimated that about 12 per cent of youngsters of school age now enjoy an experience at some camp during the summer. Boys outnumber girls about two to one and the majority of campers range in age from nine to fourteen years.

About 15,000 persons find year round occupation in camping while an additional 175,000 or more are added during the peak camp season; the majority of the latter are college graduates or college students seeking remunerative employment for the summer. The camps themselves vary greatly in size, some having as few as eight campers while others accommodate over 1,000. The average, however, probably handles from eighty-five to 125 campers. Around 275 to 300 colleges now give courses in camp counseling and serve as a valuable source of trained personnel for camp directors.

The booming growth in number of children of school age that has kept school boards hustling to provide enough classrooms and teachers has likewise hit the camps and we find some with quotas completed by April; late registrants are forced to apply elsewhere or be placed on waiting lists.

WHY THE SUMMER CAMP?   Each summer, as the last ties of school are broken, youth equips itself with a heterogeneous assortment of duffel and hies itself off to summer camp. Collectively, it is the annual exodus from the hot, stuffy, smelly, noisy city and away to the open spaces of good old Camp Wahoo, but, individually, it is infinitely more. Each camper has some secret and deep-seated longings which he hopes camp will satisfy for him; each parent has visions of the return of a better adjusted, healthier and happier child, made so by his summer's experiences.

Yes, this is *Camp,* the great melting pot of childhood, where youth has a chance to live in a youth's world populated with persons from diverse regions, creeds and sometimes even nationalities and races. What an opportunity for the development of true democracy and the real understanding which alone can lead to the establishment of "One World"! As Mr. Watson B. Miller has stated, "Camping, at its best, really practices what we preach about democracy."*

A wise person once said, "There is nothing new under the sun" and camping is certainly no exception. Only the concept of it has changed, but it will continue to vary as it keeps pace with the changing needs, desires and philosophies of society.

Early Campers

Early peoples needed no wooden houses, for they were nomadic by nature and traveled about according to the seasonal movements of game and other sources of food and clothing. They actually "camped" 365 days of the year. The Indians were the first great American campers, and experts they were at it, for they have left us vast stores of wood lore and camping "know how," developed by their understanding hearts, their seeing eyes, and their sensitive, intelligent hands.

The moment the Pilgrim Fathers landed on American shores they, too, became campers in every sense of the word, for their very existence depended upon their ability to wrest a living from the elements. The history of America is rich in the lore of its early explorers and frontiersmen who matched wits with Nature in a constant struggle for clothing, food and shelter. Their deeds of valor and courage play an important part in our development, and our hearts beat high with

excitement and pride as we read of the prowess of such American campers as Kit Carson, Daniel Boone, Theodore Roosevelt, Daniel Beard and Ernest Thompson Seton. Early pioneers had to be self-reliant and ingenious, for there was no supermarket where "Junior" could pick up a pound of hamburger, no department store to supply a pair of jeans, and no hardware store to furnish a ten-penny nail. Almost every growing thing had value as a source of food, medicine, clothing or shelter. The pioneers *had* to know and understand nature, for there was no time for mistakes when selecting proper wood for an axe handle or the best herb to use for sickness and pain. Hunting and trapping animals to supply furs, food and clothing necessitated an intimate knowledge of animal ways of life.

It is human nature to forget the disagreeable and recall only the pleasant; thus the glamorous, exciting exploits of our forefathers have largely blinded us to the privations, dangers and hardships which were the very core of their daily lives.

LIFE WAS MAINLY RURAL. At the time of the signing of the Constitution our national population was 98 per cent rural, but with the coming of the machine age and the increasing tendency to cluster about concentrated areas of employment, this percentage has decreased. Now only about 36 per cent of our people live in what could be classed as rural areas with only 10 per cent living on "farms" as classified by the 1960 census. This trend toward urban existence has had a marked influence upon the American way of life, particularly for the youthful members.

Let us, like Alice, step through the looking glass into a typical farm scene of several generations ago. There we find boys and girls whose knowledge of nature seems almost innate, for, as with the pioneers, each plant, animal and tree had

* From Proceedings, 1947, of the Southeastern American Camping Association.

some utilitarian value. Theirs was a manner of life in which manual training, arts and crafts, and home economics, though not known as such, were simply accepted as an essential part of everyday living. They "learned by doing" under the personal tutoring of parents and other adults. Formal school training in readin', writin' and 'rithmetic was confined to the few winter months when the services of the children could best be spared from farm tending, harvesting and other duties.

Chores about the farm furnished vigorous exercise, and the whole countryside provided ample room in which to run and jump and shout during leisure time. Nor was there a lack of social contacts, for families were large and closely knit, and members enjoyed the companionship of brothers and sisters of approximately the same age as they worked and played together. Visitors, even though strangers, provided welcome diversion and were urged to make an extended stay, for distances were too great and traveling too hazardous and uncomfortable to warrant brief overnight visits or a casual evening of bridge. For close neighbors, there were numerous social affairs such as cornhuskings, bellings, house and barnwarmings, taffy pulls, spelling bees, and singing schools.

Modern Urban Life

Now let us move forward to take a look at the modern urban child. He spends a long nine or ten months in an overcrowded school geared to meet college entrance requirements and consequently seemingly oblivious to his needs and wishes. His life is regulated by schedules and bells, and he is subjected to the formal teaching methods made necessary when large numbers of students must meet course and credit standards.

Camping has no quarrel at all with formal education, which is undoubtedly striving valiantly to do its best in the situation in which it finds itself. But camping can and does furnish a way to supplement formal school education by supplying a type of education best carried on in the informal atmosphere of the summer camp where youngsters sleep, work, eat and play with counselors and fellow-campers in an atmosphere of friendly rapport and camaraderie. Here the child can know nature, including human nature, at its best.

The present economy does not encourage the large families of a former day, and the child often lives entirely with adults in a small cottage or apartment where there is no room to run, jump, climb and throw. When he indulges his perfectly normal craving for action, his antics are likely to end unhappily as his ball crashes through the Kwality Grocery plate glass window, he tramples in Mrs. Jones' prize petunia bed, or his noise drives old Grandma Finkelstein to bellicose retribution. For engaging in what should be the birthright of every child, he is likely to receive a good "bawling out," physical punishment, or even disciplinary measures as a juvenile delinquent. Can we wonder that he is puzzled and sometimes rebellious? Our modern knowledge of childhood shows us how irritating and warping it can be to live amidst the constant "do's" and "don'ts" of people crowded in on all sides like sardines in a can on a grocer's shelf.

Both parents are often employed outside the home, and spend their free time in pursuits which continue to segregate them from their offspring. There is too little time for recreation or even being together. Instead of giving themselves in companionship, understanding and sympathy, parents try to substitute with liberal allowances for movies, funny books, baby sitters, TV shows, and other make-shifts which are supposed to buy happiness. The child has large quantities of leisure time, since his existence in the modern push-the-button age of labor-saving devices makes chores practically nonexistent.

Children quickly fall into the pattern set by their parents and become afflicted with "spectatoritis," depending on commercial organizations to supply them with ready-made entertainment and recreation, which are all too often merely time consuming busywork. It is easy to understand the elation such a child derives from struggling and sweating to build a bean-hole or a lean-to, for this activity fulfills the universal desire to do something constructive and useful, to display something *he* has made with *his* own hands. Children work like little beavers on camp projects and do not consider it work at all, for, as Sir James Barrie said, "Work is only work when you would rather be doing something else."

Many parents realize the shortcoming of city life, and nostalgic memories of their own rural upbringing or days in camp, make them determined to give their children a taste of it through summer camping even though it means sacrificing and scrimping through all the other months of the year.

TYPES OF CAMPS

Many organizations have recognized in camping an excellent opportunity to further their objectives and so have estab-

lished their own camps, each tailored to meet the purposes of the sponsoring group. It would be virtually impossible to list all the types of camps in the shifting panorama of camping, but they fall roughly into three main groups according to sponsorship: (1) private, (2) agency, and (3) municipal.

Private Camps

Private camps are sponsored by individuals who, while usually quite mindful of the best interests and welfare of their campers and of the importance of their work as a service to humanity, still must look upon camper fees as the direct means of earning a livelihood.

In general, they charge a somewhat higher fee, ranging from around $450 to $1,000 for an eight week season. This ordinarily limits their patronage to the children of the upper middle class or well-to-do, and the greater finances available sometimes enable them to provide more in the way of equipment and facilities than other camps do.

Much pioneering in camping has taken place in the private camps, where the long term of eight or ten weeks affords enough time for the camper to make real progress toward realizing definite camping objectives. Most private camps draw their clientele from various areas, thus providing a change of environment and the broadening influence of association with campers from other regions. There are about 2,700 private resident camps in the United States.

Agency Camps

Agency camps are usually nonprofit and are supported by the public through the United Fund, public tax or private subscription. Examples are the camps of the Boy and Girl Scouts, Boys Clubs, and YMCA. The small fee, usually ranging from $2 to $4 a day, makes camping possible for children from even low-income families and camperships are often available for those who cannot pay even this small fee. The large number of campers handled during a season necessitates a rapid turnover, so that the average child can be accommodated for only a week or two. Although this is undoubtedly a handicap in achieving camping objectives, it is not nearly so great as it would seem, for the camping period is often but a continuation of the yearly program of the winter carried on by the regular staff.

Agency camps constitute a whopping 80 per cent of the total camps in existance. They are usually located near the homes of the campers whom they serve, so that transportation costs are cut to a minimum. They have had a tremendous effect upon camping and continue to do excellent work in the field.

BOY SCOUTS.   The Boy Scouts were organized in England by Lord Robert Baden-Powell and furthered in the United States by Daniel Beard and Ernest Thompson Seton. Their first camping here was carried on at Camp Becket in 1909, and camping has occupied an important place in their program ever since. In 1949, they operated 831 resident camps in addition to much day and troop camping.* They now carry on camping activities on a larger scale than does any other organization in the United States. They have contributed much to the development of new camping techniques and their low-priced literature is outstanding in the field.

GIRL SCOUTS.   The Girl Scouts were chartered in 1912, and this same year, their founder, Juliette Low, established Camp Lowland for the Girl Scouts of Savannah Georgia. Camping has always been a vital part of their program and their inexpensive and very worthwhile literature has made an invaluable contribution to the field. Their standards as set up for various phases of Girl Scout camping have many times led the way for all. This organization has been active in stressing the pioneering type of activity.

CAMP FIRE GIRLS.   Mr. and Mrs. Luther Halsey Gulick organized and es-

tablished the Camp Fire Girls in 1912, largely to meet the needs of their own seven daughters. The organization's first camp was at Lake Sebago, Maine. It was called Wohelo, a word formed from the first two letters of Work, Health and Love, and since adopted as the watchword of the Camp Fire Girls. The group's symbol is "fire" around which the first homes were built, and their motto is "Give Service." Effectiveness of their program is heightened by the ceremony, legends, Indian lore, poetry and music upon which the program is based.

THE 4-H CLUBS.   4-H Club Camps are promoted for rural boys and girls who have been selected to receive extra training to better fit them for leadership in their own home communities.

WELFARE AGENCIES AND SOCIAL SETTLEMENTS.   These pioneers in the camping movement directed their efforts primarily toward supplying camping opportunities for those financially unable to pay any or more than a small part of their own expenses. Some of their early ventures were known as Fresh Air Farms or Fresh Air Camps, since many of their protégés came from crowded tenement districts where grass and trees are novelties and the sun's rays shine between the tall buildings only for a short time each day when the sun is directly overhead. Many suffer from malnutrition, so that good nourishing food and other health

* Benson and Goldberg: *The Camp Counselor*, page 5.

measures occupy a prominent place in the program.

Mothers and babies as well as older children are sometimes included in the program, which supplies a much needed and worthwhile service.

Y.M.C.A. AND Y.W.C.A.   Both these organizations early recognized the possibilities in camping as a new approach to character-building and both promote it as an important part of their all-year program. They have made valuable contributions to camping. The Y.M.C.A. now operates about 641 camps in the United States and the Y.W.C.A. about 200.* The Y.M.C.A. often holds camping periods for girls when the area is not served by the Y.W.C.A.

OTHER GROUPS.   Among other groups which sponsor camping are Pioneer Youth, Boys' Clubs of America, Girls' Clubs, Salvation Army, Catholic Youth Organization, United Fund, Federation of Protestant Welfare Agencies, Jewish Welfare Board, welfare agencies, churches, labor unions, various fraternal groups, and other organizations.

Public Camps

Public camps are generally free or inexpensive to their users, since they are supported by taxes or other fees assessed from the general public.

MUNICIPAL.   The growth of municipal camping progressed slowly at first, since most cities were concentrating on equipping and maintaining the playgrounds they had already started. The public is notoriously loathe to give financial support to recreation, taking the short-sighted stand of preferring to spend money on jails and other correctional institutions which might largely be dispensed with were a good program of character training and recreation provided for youth. The greatest growth of municipal camping has been in the field of day camping and it will no doubt continue to stride rapidly forward in the future.

THE UNITED STATES FOREST SERVICE AND THE NATIONAL PARK SERVICE.   These encourage family camping by offering sites and facilities in government-owned areas. They also often have areas and facilities available for rent to youth organizations not having their own campsites.

Day Camps

A resident camp is one in which campers remain for at least a week, while a day camp is ordinarily located near the homes of its campers so that the children can sleep and eat their morning and evening meals at home. The patrons of day camps arrive by bus or private car at about 9:30 A.M. and spend the day in camping activities, going home again about 4:30 P.M. They often bring the ingredients for a noon cook-out with them. Day camps usually operate from one to five days a week and their convenience and low cost bring camping to many who are too young or financially unable to participate in resident camping. Day camping was originated by the Girl Scouts in 1922 and is now sponsored by such other organizations as Boy Scouts, Y.W.C.A., Y.M.C.A., Camp Fire Girls and the like, as well as by cities and private individuals. One of the most recent spurts in camping has been in the realm of day camping and there are now well over 1,000 privately operated in the United States as well as 3,000 sponsored by groups. These fulfill a real need for it is possible to do almost anything at a day camp that could be done at a resident camp except for the night time activities. Some of the day camps work in even a bit of this by arranging for campers who wish to stay over a few nights and sleep outdoors; arrangements can be made to borrow or rent tents or use the shelter houses of a public park for inclement weather. The program in a day camp must be especially attractive each day so that the campers feel it worthwhile to come back the next.

* Benson and Goldberg: *The Camp Counselor*, page 4.

School Camps

School camping, or "outdoor education," has seen a phenomenal growth within the past twenty-five years or so. The greatest development has been in Michigan which now has over seventy-five school districts incorporating it as a part of the regular school curriculum. Many other states are experimenting in this field; among them are California, Florida, Illinois, Indiana, Missouri, New York, North Carolina, Ohio, Texas and Washington. One of the big drawbacks is, of course, the increased cost which is sometimes as much as two or three times that of regular school.

OBJECTIVES.   The objectives of school camping are very much the same as those of camping in general and the idea of having school sponsorship is to bring the benefits of outdoor living to all or nearly all children of school age, instead of to only about 12 per cent who now enjoy them. The main aim is to leave to the classroom those subjects which can best be taught there and take to the campsite other subjects which can better be demonstrated in the outdoor environment. It is often possible to elaborate on and make more meaningful to the child, subject matter he has already studied in the classroom. Learning starts from the time the child begins to pore over a map to trace the route of the school bus to camp and to work harmoniously with his group to plan equipment lists, procedures and program. As in any camping, the whole experience is one of democratic living where the child learns self-reliance and develops his own ingenuity in adapting himself to a comfortable, yet simple, life. Often he learns for the first time to be on his own, as he accepts responsibility for dressing himself, caring for his living quarters, and sharing in the planning of his own program. He finds ample opportunities to put into practice things he has learned in theory and he will be motivated to investigate and learn still more in order to fulfill his felt needs. Many areas of learning are naturals for camp living; among these are homemaking, woodworking, nature study, arithmetic, health education, arts and crafts, conservation, social science, dramatics, music, moral and spiritual values, physical education, worthy use of leisure time, and the social graces and amenities of living happily and cooperatively with others. What the child doesn't already know, he avidly seeks to learn as his interests are aroused and he sees how helpful and satisfying such information or skills really can be.

ORGANIZATION AND ADMINISTRATION. Schools acquire facilities for school camping in many and varied ways. In some cases, grounds and buildings are donated or loaned by service organizations and public-spirited individuals. In others, properties are rented from public or private owners and in a few instances schools purchase land and construct their own camp buildings. A big opportunity being increasingly used is for schools to arrange to use the grounds and the facilities of an organized summer camp already in existence. This is of mutual advantage since the school gets the shelters and outside acreage it needs at a minimal cost and the camp owner or sponsor receives income from his investment which ordinarily lies idle at this time of year. Some schools utilize the opportunities offered by local, state or national parks. Some colleges arrange to rent or borrow a campsite as a training ground for prospective teachers and invite the school campers in to provide a realistic situation.

In most instances a school starts its program on a modest basis with one or two grades day-camping for from one to sev-

eral days or sometimes staying only overnight. The next year, the same grades may do resident camping for a week or two in the fall or spring. As rapidly as possible the experience is extended to more and more grades, each camping for one or two weeks, so that several schools now keep their camps open for the entire school year. Some substitute or supplement school year camping with summer camping.

Usually the money for group equipment and the general running of the camp comes out of regular school funds, as for any other school activity, with the participants paying for various personal items such as their own food. Campers are often encouraged to earn or save out of their allowances for their expenses. The cost is cut to a minimum by having the pupils help plan, cook and serve their food, wash dishes and engage in general camp tasks. Participation in camping is usually optional.

Most often it is members of the fifth and sixth grades who engage in this new method of education (40 per cent), with those of the seventh and eighth grades next (26 per cent), while an appreciable number of communities sponsor school camping for both younger and secondary school pupils. A few communities conduct camp for atypical groups, such as the handicapped and those who have dropped out of school.

In order to best integrate school with camp life, the regular teachers accompany their students and help carry on what they have jointly planned back in the classroom. When the camp is only conducted for a few months out of the year, the camp director and other staff personnel are often employed in other capacities about the school for the rest of the year. Communities holding camp for several months usually hire a full-time camp director and a few counselors who remain on the campsite to supplement the regular classroom teachers. Personnel from the State Department of Conservation and from the Audubon Society, other consultants and local volunteers often help out. In some cases, State Departments of Instruction and Conservation share the problem of providing leadership.

Classroom teachers are trained by a variety of techniques to play their strategic role in the whole process and one of the needs is for colleges which train teachers to provide more instruction in school camping. Such courses should include training in campcraft techniques and comfortable living in the out-of-doors as well as training in ways to make the regular classroom courses come alive as they are actually experienced and made use of during the camping period. Some take summer or winter school courses as a part of their teacher training program. Often, the school camping experience is conducted as laboratory or field training, or as an extension or in-service course. National School near Sussex, New Jersey, under the leadership of L. B. Sharp, is a pioneer in the training of leaders for school camping.

PLANNING. The worth of the whole experience depends largely upon skillful and thorough planning with both parents and children actively participating. The first step is often to call a mass meeting of all interested parties followed by a general discussion and the appointment of committees to begin the consideration of various phases of the plan. It is necessary to carefully interpret the proposed program to parents and community and to show them that it is not just another frill but an investment of tax money which can and does pay big dividends. By their enthusiastic understanding and support, parents and community workers can aid in many ways such as securing facilities, supplies, finances, needed work at the campsite, transportation, and proper physical and psychological preparation of the youngsters. In addition, teacher-student planning and evaluation before, during, and after the excursion are likewise important.

Special Types of Camps

Besides general camps which usually feature such activities as woodcraft and campcraft, nature, arts, crafts, aquatics, sailing, riding, and sports and games, there are a number of special camps for those with special interests or needs. Some, such as salt-water camps, ranch camps, mountain-climbing camps, and pioneer or trip camps, capitalize upon their particular environments. Others, such as hockey, tennis, aquatic, horseback riding, dramatic, music, dance, religious education, tutoring, language, nature, and research camps, appeal to specialized interests. Still others minister to the needs of such handicapped persons as cardiac, diabetic, epileptic, crippled or "problem" children. Still others are coed, family, adult or golden age (for those over sixty) camps.

American Youth Hostels

Though American Youth Hostels does not have organized camps, it fosters a way of life which is very much in accord with the spirit of camping. Originating in Germany in 1910, it was brought to America in 1934 and there are now some 120 hostels scattered throughout the New England, Middle Atlantic, Great Lake, and West Coast States. The hostels are overnight stops, usually at farms, where, for a fee of 75 cents a night, the hosteler is furnished blankets, mattress, a bed in a dormitory, cooking utensils, stove and fuel, usually refrigeration, and a common kitchen and "rumpus room." Hostelers cook and prepare their own meals and this whole very simple way of life is possible for a cost of from $2.50 to $3.50 each day. Each hostel is under the direction of houseparents. There are only a few simple rules designed to safeguard everyone concerned such as arrival between 4 and 8 P.M., lights out at 10 P.M., rising at 7 A.M., breakfast and on the way by 9:30 A.M. Transportation, except to and from the take-off points, must be under your own power (canoe, bicycle, horse-back, ski, or hiking). AYH is a nonprofit organization and offers equipment, maps and information appropriate to camping at low cost. Anyone from four to ninety-four years may participate and individual membership fees, which include a "pass" to stay at hostels, are $3 for those under eighteen, $5 for those eighteen to twenty, and $6 for those over twenty-one. Groups, such as campers from an organized camp, may obtain a special organization pass to include not over ten with one or two leaders. AYH also furnishes leadership and sponsors trips at minimum cost over the United States, Canada and some of the other thirty countries that are members of International Youth Hostel Federation. For further information, contact American Youth Hostels, Inc., 14 West 8th St., New York 11, New York.

ADDITIONAL READINGS*

General

Benson, Reuel A., and Goldberg, Jacob A.: *The Camp Counselor.*

Bezucha, R. D.: *The Golden Anniversary Book of Scouting.* Golden Book, 1959, 165 pp., $4.95. (Boy Scouts)

Bogardus, La Donna: *Planning the Church Camp for Juniors.* ACA, 1955, 96 pp., $1.00.

Burns, Gerald: *Program of the Modern Camp.*

Dimock, Hedley S.: *Administration of the Modern Camp.*

Directory of ACA Member Camps. ACA, 1959, 275 pp., 50¢.

Directory of Camps for the Handicapped. ACA, 1959, 77 pp., 50¢.

Family Camping. Pasadena Dept. of Recreation, Pasadena Casting Club, Recreation Department, Pasadena, California, 1957, 77 pp.

Geal, Sid: *Report on Camp Visits.* A.C.A., 1959, 25 pp. (mimeographed).

Goodrich, Lois: *Decentralized Camping.*

Guide for Group Camping. Camp Fire Girls.

Irwin, Frank L.: *The Theory of Camping.*

Jacobs, Eveline: *A Guide to Standards for Resident Camps for Crippled Children.* Nat'l Society for Crippled Children and Adults, 1954.

Joy, Barbara Ellen: *Camping.*

---

* In this and succeeding chapters, only the author's name and the name of the publication are given in the list of additional readings. Complete information will be found in the general list of books at the end of the text.

Lyle, Betty: *Camping, What Is It?* A.C.A., 1947, 8 pp., 30¢.

Morgan, Barbara: *Summer's Children.* Morgan and Morgan, 1951, $5.00.

Osborn, Ernest: *How to Choose a Camp for Your Child.* Public Affairs Committee, 22 E. 38th. St., N.Y., 1956, 22 pp., 25¢.

Peterson, Doris T.: *Your Family Goes Camping.*

Resident Camp Standards. A.C.A., Rev. 1956, 11 pp., 10¢.

Resident Camp Standards. Camp Fire Girls, (#D-319), 75¢.

Roehn, Ralph D.: *Better Camping.* Assn. Press, $1.50.

Standards for Girl Scout Camping (#19-520). Girl Scouts, 1958, 32 pp., 30¢.

Sunset Ideas for Family Camping. Sunset Books, Lane Publishing Co., Menlo Park, Calif., $1.75.

Webb, Kenneth B., and Susan H.: *Summer Magic.* Assn. Press, 1953, $2.50.

Webb, Kenneth B., Ed.: *Light from a Thousand Campfires.*

Wells, G. S. and I. C. S.: *Handbook of Auto Camping and Motorists' Guide to Public Play Grounds.* Harper and Brothers, 1954.

Whelen, Townsend and Angier, Bradford: *On Your Own in the Wilderness.*

Wilson, George T.: *Family Camping and Places to Camp in the North Central States.* 112 pp., $1.00.

MAGAZINE ARTICLES

Crawford, Mary Eidson: *Your Help and Understanding Can Provide the Handicapped with a Rich Camp Experience.* C.M., Dec., 1956.

Daubert, Russell B.: *Evaluating the Recreational Camping Program.* Recreation, Mar., 1958.

David, Lester: *Which Camp for Your Child.* Coronet, June, 1959.

Dimock, Hedley S.: *Coeducational Program in Brother-Sister Camps.* C.M., Feb., 1953.

Greene, C. Owen and Catherine G.: *The Value of Co-Ed Camping.* C.M., Feb., 1957.

Isserman, Ruth: *Careful Pre-Grouping Leads to Happy Cabin Mates.* C.M., Dec., 1952.

Klusmann, Wes: *And So To Camp.* C.M., June, 1953.

Sanford, Jean A.: *Hosteling—Inexpensive Travel for Fun.* J.H., P.E. and R., May-June, 1955.

Day Camping

The Church Day Camp, by Committee of Children's Work and Special Committee on Camps and Conferences. Nat'l Council of Churches of Christ, 257 4th Ave., New York, N.Y., 1955, 48 pp., 60¢.

Day Camp Standards. A.C.A., 1956, 7 pp., 10¢

Guide for Day Camping. Camp Fire Girls (D-320), 65 pp., 50¢.

MAGAZINE ARTICLES

Carolan, Patrick J.: *The Personal Touch in Day Camping.* Recreation, Mar., 1957.

Mason, James G.: *Baylor University's Summer Day Camp.* J.H. and P.E., Oct., 1954.

Pattern for Day Camping—As Conducted by the Chicago Park District. Recreation, Mar., 1954.

Wilson, George T.: *Day Camps—from City Streets to Woodland Trails.* C.M., Mar., 1959.

School Camping (Outdoor Education)

Clarke, James M.: *Public School Camping.* Stanford University Press, Stanford, Calif., 1951, 182 pp.

DeWitt, R. T. and Wilson, G. M. (Editors): *School Camping at Peabody.* Peabody College, 1953, 71 pp.

Donaldson, George W.: *School Camping.* Assn Press, 1952, 140 pp.

Friet, Edwin R., and Peterson, Del G.: *Design for Outdoor Education.* P. S. Printers, Inc., 128 S. 2nd Ave., Yakima, Wash., 1956, 34 pp., 50¢.

Gilliland, John W.: *School Camping,* A Frontier of Curriculum Improvement. Assn for Supervision and Curriculum Development, Washington, D.C., 1954, 58 pp.

Guide to School Camping in Wisconsin. Dept. of Public Instruction, Wisconsin, 1956.

Macmillan, Dorothy Lou: *School Camping and Outdoor Education.* Brown Book Co., 1956, 160 pp., $3.00.

Manley, Helen and Drury, M. F.: *Education Through School Camping.* The C. V. Mosby Co., 1952, 340 pp.

Outdoor Education. A.A.H.P.E.R., 1956, 32 pp. (Elementary School)

Outdoor Education for American Youth. A.A.H.P.E.R., 1957, 150 pp., $2.50. (Teenagers)

Outdoor Education through School Camping. Indiana State Dept. of Public Instruction and Indiana State Board of Health, 1958.

Smith, Julian, *Outdoor Education.* A.A.H.P.E.R., 1956, 32 pp., 75¢.

Teacher's Guide—Frederick County Outdoor School. Board of Education of Frederick Co., 115 E. Church St., Frederick, Md., 1958, 120 pp.

Vannier, Maryhelen, and Foster, Mildred: *Teaching Physical Education in Elementary Schools.* W. B. Saunders Co., 1958, $4.75.

MAGAZINE ARTICLES

Brimm, R. P.: *What are the Issues in Camping and Outdoor Education.* C.M., Jan., 1959.

Carlson, Reynold E.: *Family Camping Boom.* J.H.,P.E. and R., May-June, 1959.

Clark, Leslie L.: *A Winter Vacation Camp.* J.H. and P.E., Mar., 1956.

Donaldson, George W., and Donaldson, Louise E.: *Outdoor Education—A Definition.* J.H. and P.E., May-June, 1958.

Donaldson, George W., and Lambert, Hope A.: *School Camp—Outdoor Laboratory for Enriched Learning Experiences.* C.M., May, 1956.

Hammerman, Don: *Just What is School Camping.* C.M., Feb., 1958.

Hammerman, Don: *What! Teach Outside the Classroom.* J.H. and P.E., Nov., 1954.

Harrison, Paul F.: *Education Goes Outdoors.* J.H.,P.E., and R., 1953.

Holland, Barbara: *About Our Outdoor School.* J.H. and P.E., May-June, 1955.

Klinger, Hubert F.: *Financing School Camping.* J.H. and P.E., Dec., 1955.

Margulis, Jonah D.: *Why Don't You Sell Your Camp to Schools?* C.M., Mar., 1959.

Meaning of Outdoor Education. J.H. and P.E., Oct., 1958. (Report from first National Conference on Outdoor Education.)

Otto, C. Lucille: *Our Winter Outdoor School.* J.H. and P.E., Dec., 1957.

Reich, William C.: *Camping is an Integral Part of the Complete Education of the Child.* C.M., April, 1958.

Smith, Julian W.: *Adventures in Outdoor Education.* J.H. and P.E., May-June, 1955.

Squires, John L.: *Standards in Public School Camping.* J.H. and P.E., Sept., 1954.

Taylor, Edgar A., Jr.: *School Camping is Rewarding for Retarded Children.* J.H. and P.E., May-June, 1957.

Young, Jean M.: *Classrooms Move Outdoors.* J.H. and P.E., Dec., 1959.

2

History of Organized Camping

TO PRESERVE CHILDREN

Take: 1 large grassy field
Half dozen children
2 or 3 small dogs
A pinch of brook and pebbles.

Mix children and dogs well together and put them in the field, stirring constantly. Pour brook over pebbles; sprinkle field with flowers; spread over all a deep blue sky and bake in the sun. When brown, remove and set to cool in a bath tub.

AUTHOR UNKNOWN

PIONEERS IN THE CAMPING MOVEMENT

The First School Camp (1861)

Frederick William Gunn, who is generally accorded to be the *Father of Organized Camping,* was the founder and head of the Gunnery School for Boys in Washington, Connecticut. With the coming of the Civil War, his students, boylike, wanted to live like soldiers and were sometimes permitted to march, roll up in their blankets and sleep outdoors. The Gunnery School continued to run throughout a part of the summer, and in 1861, yielding to the wishes of the boys, Mr. and Mrs. Gunn packed the entire student body up for a gypsy trip to Milford on the Sound, four miles away, where they spent two weeks in boating, sailing, tramping and fishing. The experiment proved so successful that it was repeated in 1863 and 1865 with some of the former students returning to join in the excursion.

A new site was later selected at Point Beautiful on Lake Waramauge, seven miles from the school, and the name was changed from Camp Comfort to Gunnery Camp. Mr. Gunn's camp was really the beginning of school camping which is gaining prominence today, for he simply moved his already organized school outdoors for a brief session, a custom which he continued until 1879. However, the objectives of school camping as we know it today are somewhat different.

19

The First Private Camp (1876)

Dr. Joseph Trimble Rothrock, a practicing physician of Wilkes-Barre, Pennsylvania, combined his interests in forestry and conservation with his desire to do something for frail boys by establishing a "North Mountain School of Physical Culture" where these children could improve their health by living out-of-doors in tents while continuing their education. The school, which was located on North Mountain in Luzerne County, Pennsylvania, lasted from June 15 to October 15 and had twenty pupils and five teachers. The student paid $200 tuition for the four months, but the income failed to meet expenses, and Dr. Rothrock abandoned the idea in favor of spending the next year on an Alaskan expedition. Various attempts to revive the school under different leadership were likewise financially unprofitable, and it was permanently closed within a few years.

The First Church Camp (1880)

The Reverend George W. Hinckley, of West Hartford, Connecticut, saw in camping an opportunity to know his boys more intimately and so have a more lasting influence upon them. In 1880 he took seven members of his church on a camping trip to Gardners Island, Wakefield, Rhode Island. The results must have been gratifying, for he later founded The Good Will Farm for Boys, at Hinckley, Maine. His schedule called for a "sane and sensible" religious and educational morning program with afternoons spent in such activities as swimming, baseball and tennis, and evenings devoted to singing, talks and various other forms of entertainment.

The First Private Camp Organized to Meet Specific Educational Needs (1890)

In 1880, while traveling on Asquam Lake near Holderness, New Hampshire, Ernest Berkely Balch chanced upon Burnt Island, which apparently was unowned.

It seemed a perfect spot for carrying out his plan to provide a place where boys from well-to-do families could come to avoid idling away the summer at resort hotels. A year later he returned with five boys and erected a small frame shanty which they christened "Old '81." The group was somewhat surprised, no doubt, by the arrival of a man who claimed to be the owner, but they were certainly not outdone, for they purchased the entire island for the sum of $40. They called their island retreat Camp Chocorua because of its superb view of Chocorua Mountain, thirty miles away, and it continued to exist until 1889.

From the first, the boys had a camp uniform of gray flannel shorts and shirts with scarlet belt, cap, and shirt lacing. All camp work was done by the boys, who were divided into four crews, each with a leader, called the "stroke." One crew was off duty each day while the other three spent about five hours as kitchen, dish or police crews. Spiritual life was carefully planned, and the services must have been quite impressive as the boys came singing through the woods, dressed in cotta and cassock, to the altar of their chapel, which was set deep in a grove of silver maples.

The camp had an average of five staff members and twenty-five boys who com-

peted in tennis, sailing, swimming, diving and baseball. Winners were awarded ribbons bearing their names, the event and the date. Definite objectives for Camp Chocorua were the development in the boy of (1) a sense of responsibility, both for himself and for others, and (2) an appreciation of the worthwhileness of work. The Camp Chocorua silver pin was given annually to the two or three campers best incorporating qualities of "manliness, justice, truth, and conscientiousness." It was intended as a symbol of recognition for innate qualities and not as a reward to be worked for; in fact, those who consciously set out to win it were said to stand little chance of doing so, and no award at all was made in the years when none were judged worthy.

The First Institutional Camp (1885)

Summer F. Dudley, a young resident of Brooklyn, was associated with his father and brother in the manufacture of surgical instruments. His first venture in camping was to take seven members of the Newburgh, New York, Y.M.C.A. on an eight-day fishing, swimming and boating trip to Pine Point on Orange Lake, six miles away. Since the boys had had their heads shaved close in what they deemed proper preparation for the trip, their camp was appropriately dubbed Camp Bald Head.

Dudley spent the next several years in conducting other camping trips for boys and entered the Y.M.C.A. as a full-time worker in 1887. He died in 1897 at the untimely age of forty-three. His last camp on Lake Champlain near Westport, New York, was renamed Camp Dudley in his honor, and is the oldest organized camp still in existence.

Camping for Girls (1892 and 1902)

In 1891 Professor Arey of Rochester, New York, established Camp Arey as a Natural Science Camp, and a year later he lent it for a month's use by girls. Mr. and Mrs. Andre C. Fontaine took over the camp in 1912 and from that time on conducted it as a camp exclusively for girls. The first camp founded expressly for girls was Camp Kehonka for Girls at Wolfeboro, New Hampshire, which was established by Laura Mattoon in 1902.

THE PERIODS OF CAMPING

Organized camping, during its comparatively brief life cycle, has been classified by Dimock* as passing through three stages of development as to its main emphasis. These are (1) the recreational stage, (2) the educational stage, and (3) the stage of social orientation and responsibility. As with any movement, no sharp line of demarcation can be drawn between these periods, for the changes were gradual and overlapping, and at no time was there perfect unanimity of opinion among leaders or uniformity as to the programs and practices of the various camps.

The Recreational Stage (1861–1920)

Early experiments in camping were fostered by public-spirited men who saw in them an opportunity to provide a better way for boys to spend the summer than in loafing about in idleness or harmful pursuit in the city. The main idea was to provide wholesome, healthful fun while

* Dimock, Hedley S.: *Administration of the Modern Camp*, page 24.

"roughing it" in the out-of-doors. High moral and spiritual values were ever held in high esteem, but were supposed to be "caught" like mumps or measles from mere association with fine, upright leaders. There was no thought of financial gain from the project, and this very lack of adequate monetary backing caused the early demise of many camps.

It was common for one or two adults to start out on a trip with as many as forty or fifty boys and a meager supply of equipment. The expeditions were, almost without exception, built around the strong personality of a man who kept the respect and admiration of the boys by his unselfish motives, sympathetic understanding, tactful leadership, and sound principles of the intermixture of work and play. Ralph Waldo Emerson's statement that "Every institution is but the lengthened shadow of a man" certainly applies to these early camps.

The movement was slow to "catch on," for there were probably no more than twenty-five to sixty camps in existence in 1900.

The Educational Stage (1920–1930)

History has repeatedly demonstrated that bursts of energetic change and development inevitably follow wars, and one example is found when, in the years following World War I, there was a decided increase in the number of organized camps and a corresponding alteration in their methods and program. "Progressive education," with its foundation of psychology and mental hygiene, was stressing the individual needs of the child, and camps responded by adding a variety of activities such as dramatics, arts and crafts, dancing and music to their repertoire. Thus it became an objective of camping to supplement and carry on certain phases of the enlarged school curriculum. New testing methods had demonstrated that personality, character and spiritual growth were *not* inevitably

"caught," but must be "taught" and planned for if optimum results were to be obtained.

The Stage of Social Orientation and Responsibility (1930——)

Continued research in testing methods and evaluation showed that camps were not always measuring up to the high aspirations held for them, but, as always, ever-resourceful camp directors proved equal to the occasion and progress continued to be made.

Proponents of camping were shocked by a 1930 study of over a hundred camps which revealed that instead of inevitably being healthful as everyone had assumed, camping was sometimes actually detrimental to health and that the longer a child stayed in camp the more likely his health was to suffer. Camps sought to remedy the situation by adding physicians, nurses and trained dietitians to their staffs and by engaging in more healthful practices including cutting down on the general tempo of camp life.

We know that a society is only as strong as its individual citizens and that only by grounding each in the principles of democracy can we guard our American people against the infiltration of communism and other "isms." Camping, which deals with individual campers during their most formative years, accepts its share of this responsibility as it provides an opportunity for each person to live democratically in a democracy. Ideally, camping is an experience in group living at its best where the individual camper can develop independence, self-control and self-reliance as he helps to plan and accept responsibility for his own way of life throughout the day. Camps are trying to adapt themselves to the needs of the child instead of remolding the child to fit into the ways of the camp.

This period has also seen a phenomenal growth in the amount of camp literature produced so that individuals can share their best experience and thinking.

THE ORGANIZATION OF THE CAMPING PROFESSION

In the early days of camping, camps varied greatly with each setting its own standards and solving its own problems as it best saw fit. Realizing the mutual values of associating and discussing with others of like interests and problems, camp directors and other interested parties began to meet and plan cooperatively. The first such formal meeting was held in Boston in 1903 and was attended by about a hundred men and a sprinkling of women.

The Camp Directors' Association of America was founded in 1910 with Charles R. Scott as its first president, and the National Association of Directors of Girls Camps began in 1916 with Mrs. Charlotte V. (Mrs. Luther Halsey) Gulick as president. The Mid-West Camp Directors' Association was founded in 1921. The three organizations joined forces as the Camp Directors' Association, with George L. Meylan as president, in 1924. In 1926, it began to issue a magazine called *The Camp Directors' Bulletin.*

The American Camping Association

The name of the above organization was changed to the American Camping Association in 1935 and the group has grown remarkably, having a membership of over 8,000 in 1960. It represents camping of all types and includes in its membership camps, individuals and representatives of organizations and institutions interested in the development of organized camping. Many members are from such related fields as sociology, psychology and education.

ITS OBJECTIVES. The objectives of the American Camping Association as stated in its Constitution* are:

1. To further the welfare of children and adults through camping.
2. To extend the recreational and edu-cational benefits of out-of-door living.
3. To provide for the exchange of experiences and successful practices, and for the development of materials, standards and other aids for the progress of camping.
4. To serve as the voice of camp leaders in national and local affairs.
5. To interpret camping to related groups and to the public.
6. To stimulate high professional standards of camp leadership.
7. To give emphasis in camping to citizenship training in keeping with the principles and traditions of American democracy.

During its 1948 and 1950 national conventions, the American Camping Association adopted standards for camps covering personnel, program, campsite facilities and equipment, administration, health, sanitation and safety. All camps which want to be certified as members of the American Camping Association and use the membership seal must be approved in compliance with these standards by a visitation team approved by the Association.

THE ORGANIZATION. The American Camping Association is composed of forty-two sections which are arranged in seven regions. Many sections are further divided into local districts. National Conventions are held every two years with Regional Conventions in the intervening years. The national headquarters of the association are located at Bradford Woods, Martinsville, Indiana.

MEMBERSHIP. Memberships are open to organized camps and to individuals, including a special membership for students. Individual fees for a year are ten dollars with a special student rate of four dollars. Camp membership fees are based upon the gross income of the camp. Each type of membership includes a subscrip-

---

* Constitution of the American Camping Association, Revised, Jan., 1955.

tion to the publication of the organization, *Camping Magazine,* which is published monthly except during July, August, September and October.

SERVICES.   The Association sponsors conferences, workshops, and the writing and publishing of books and pamphlets pertaining to camping. It also publicizes camping to the general public and constantly works to help camps improve their programs. It encourages studies and research pertaining to camping and attempts to secure legislation favorable to camp interests. It develops leadership training course outlines and encourages colleges to improve the quality and quantity of their leadership training courses. Several local sections, since 1957, have been sponsoring instruction in campcraft leading to a certificate as "campcrafter" or "advanced campcrafter," when additional skills have been mastered. These are open to anyone over eighteen years of age and interested parties should contact their local section for details. Many local sections serve as a go-between to help counselors obtain positions and camp directors find counselors.

The Association of Private Camps

This organization was founded in the Northeastern and New England states in 1940 and is a strong organization with a membership representing some 250 private camps. Its headquarters are at 55 West 42nd Street, New York City and annual meetings are held in that city. It issues a newsletter, sponsors research and study groups, maintains a counselor placement service, aids in educating the public about camping, and serves as a clearing house for matters pertaining particularly to private camps.

MODERN CAMPING TRENDS

Decentralization

As camping grew in popularity, the attendance at individual camps increased from the original seven to ten campers to an average of 100 to 200 or even more. To meet the demands of such numbers, camps adopted what might be called a *centralized plan* with buildings arranged Army-style in formal, straight lines on either side of a central street or in a hollow square or circle with such buildings as the mess hall and main lodge in the center. Sleeping quarters, like Army barracks, had long rows of cots for campers and counselors. More and more activities were added to the program, each under the direction of a specialist or head. However, experience convinced many camps that a child subjected to this mass type of camping was sometimes lost in the shuffle, for the methods used were often the very ones he had left the city to escape.

In an effort to accommodate large numbers yet give individuals the advantages of living and working in small groups, nearly all camps have now instituted some form of *unit* or *decentralized* camping. This type, first promoted by the Girl Scouts, consists of breaking up the large group into small units of from twelve to twenty-four campers who live in a more or less segregated area where they plan their own daily activities just as though they constituted a small camp of their own. The groups are variously called units, sections, divisions or villages. Members are more or less homogeneous, being grouped according to age, camping experience, and general development.

Each unit has its own buildings, close enough to the main dining room and lodge for convenience, yet sufficiently secluded to permit carrying on most activities independently. These usually consist of a unit house for group meetings, a latrine and bath house, and an outdoor kitchen. Of course, the unit members take most of their meals at the main dining room and participate in many all-camp activities so that there is a happy blending of living in a small group yet sharing in the life of a big group.

The decentralized plan of camping is particularly popular in the short-term camps such as those sponsored by agencies and schools. Private camps, which usually have the campers for from four to ten weeks, often prefer a system in which campers choose their own activity groups on the basis of mutual interests, skills and physical ability.

Program

The early centralized program was rigidly scheduled with activities arranged like school classes and each camper required to participate in those selected as "good for him." He was supposed to come "bug-eyed" with curiosity to nature study at 9 o'clock and maintain this state of blissful attention for exactly an hour, then magically change into an equally enthusiastic tennis student. The program was planned by the camp or program director, sometimes with the assistance of a few chosen counselors, and was intended to absorb every waking moment of the day. Often tutoring in school subjects or special instruction in music, dramatics or dancing was included at the request of parents.

A program is no longer considered a schedule of activities offered each day or week, but rather the sum total of every experience the child has from the time he enters camp until his final "good-bye." This allows much more flexibility and freedom for the camper to choose where he will go and what he will do. Campers, counselors, and general staff are assuming increasing responsibility for helping to plan the camp program.

Motivation

To motivate the old program, elaborate systems of achievement charts and awards were set up, and competition was sometimes sadly overstressed. Some camps have

reacted so violently to this practice that they now refuse to use anything resembling a check list or awards of any type. Some of the reasons given for their aversion are: (1) Campers become so intent on working for awards that they miss the real values inherent in the activities themselves. (2) Regardless of the care taken in planning any system of awards, some campers or groups seldom win and thus acquire a hopeless "what's the use of trying" attitude. Others win too frequently and become insufferably "cocky." (3) The extreme competitive spirit engendered leads to petty bickerings and jealousies which are entirely contrary to the atmosphere camp is trying to create. The desire to win sometimes becomes so keen that it leads to such regrettable incidents as sprinkling sand on another cabin's floor to keep it from winning a neatness award. (4) The motivating power of the awards is so great that lazy counselors can lie down on the job and exert themselves no more than if they were watching dogs chase a mechanical rabbit at a dog race.

Modern camps tend to minimize awards and make them a result of what is done rather than a definite goal to be worked for and obtained. High camp morale, tradition, a word of commendation from sincere and enthusiastic counselors, the self-satisfaction the individual attains, and the impetus of group approval should furnish enough reward to carry along activities which have natural appeal and worth for youngsters. Campers are encouraged to compete against their own records rather than against the records of others.

Planning for Individual Differences

The modern camp tries to learn the wishes and needs of each camper and set up a wide range of possibilities for meeting them. Units in a decentralized system usually plan their activities around their own living needs. The unit is small enough to permit the close knit atmosphere of family life, with each camper recognized as a personality whose opinions are respected and needs considered by understanding fellow-campers and counselors.

At one time it was customary to assign campers to their cabins without making any effort to determine how they would "fit." In fact, a deliberate attempt was often made to separate friends and break up cliques so that campers would be forced to form new friendships. We now know that a child benefits from camp in direct proportion to his happiness in it, and every effort is made to fill cabins and units with persons who are already congenial or who can learn to adjust themselves to a happy life together.

Leadership

The first camp counselors were often college athletes, selected because of their reputations in sports with their primary appeal coming from their prowess on field or gridiron. They often knew little and cared less about the needs, desires and natures of children.

With the change in camp philosophy and program, has come a demand for counselors who love children and are interested in them and whose sympathy with child nature enables counselor and camper to live together in mutual confidence and friendly rapport. Program specialists are still often employed for such activities as campcraft and trips, swimming, crafts and dramatics, but the trend today is largely to hire general counselors of good character, with wide interests and skills and, most important of all, a deep understanding of children.

The ratio of counselors to campers has changed from the one counselor to sixteen campers of the early days to one counselor for each six to eight campers today.

Nearly all good camps now prefer to hire counselors already certified in campcraft skills and they may also ask them to read chosen materials before coming to camp. It is almost universal practice to hold a precamp training period of one or two weeks on the campsite before the arrival of the campers. There is also a continuation of training during the season through staff meetings as well as observation and conferences with individuals and groups as needed.

Healthful Practices

Health has always been claimed as a main objective of camping, but early camps deluded themselves that good nourishing food plus living in the out-of-doors would add up to good health as inevitably as night follows day. After the 1930 study had exploded this theory, great changes came about in camp health practices and programs. One innovation has been the requiring of a complete health examination for every camper and staff member (1) to prevent the importing and spreading of contagious diseases and (2) to learn of individual weaknesses which need to be corrected or at least protected by a modified program. Trained nurses, doctors and dietitians are a part of the regular camp staff.

Camp personnel now realize the serious error of scheduling every moment so that campers engage in a feverish round of overstrenuous activities from reveille to taps. Serenity and calm are at last winning due recognition, and campers, with careful guidance, are being more often left to follow their own interests even though it occasionally be no more strenuous than sitting under a tree day-dreaming or watching a colony of ants as they carry on their particular form of social living. The rest hour following lunch is inviolate, and campers are encouraged at all times to strike a sane balance between active and inactive pursuits, making sure there is enough vigorous exercise to keep them strong and produce a pleasant, healthful tiredness by nightfall.

There is a growing tendency for the various states to set up regulations and require licenses for camps operating within their jurisdiction.

Indigenous Program and Facilities

The literature of a camp once flamboyantly proclaimed its broad and beautiful acreage, its elaborate equipment and its mammoth main lodge. The wide array of town sports provided required an elaborate outlay of balls, bats, headgear, masks, uniforms, and so forth, together with a collection of level playing fields, swings, slides and teeters. Camps now largely omit town sports, concentrating instead on those activities which are natural to the camp environment and can be done better in camp than in town. Campcraft and woodcraft skills, trips and outpost camping have largely crowded out city and school activities in the better camps.

Camp acreage is still broad and lovely, but it is largely the beauty with which nature has endowed it rather than man-made additions dictated by artificial city standards. Buildings are adequate but not overelaborate, and campers are urged to carry on simple construction to fulfill their own needs for living simply and comfortably. They are encouraged to use native materials for the construction of their temporary or semipermanent improvements.

The Back-to-Nature Movement

Teaching campers to know and love nature has been another constant aim of camping, but efforts often produced lip service with little real feeling and appreciation back of it. Nature study was likely to consist of a casual stroll by disinterested campers to pluck an occasional flower or cage an unlucky bug which happened to flit across the path, then a saunter back to camp to kill and mount the "haul" and carefully label it with a botanical jawbreaker. The amount of true nature appreciation thus developed is certainly open to question.

In a present-day set up it is hard for a camper to escape nature, for he lives right in the midst of it as members of his group carry on a large share of their activities in the out-of-doors. It is almost impossible for him to spend so many hours smelling, hearing, touching, tasting and seeing the wonders of nature without becoming a saner, finer, and stronger self, and developing a deep and abiding love for all nature. How can he help knowing nature after selecting native wood for a sundial, shelter, bridge or dam and locating and preparing barks, roots and berries for dyeing what he has made?

Camping for Everyone

Younger and older campers are attending camps now, and persons of all ages are being urged to stay for a longer season to provide more time for being integrated into the environment and for reaping richer benefits. The rapid growth of low-cost agency camping has brought the experience within the realm of possibility of nearly all, but the percentage of children participating in organized camping is still small. School-age children do 97 per cent of camping, with the ages of nine to fourteen years being the most common in organized camps.

There has also been a great development in such phases as work camps, church camps of all denominations, golden age camps (for those over sixty), adult camps, day camps, school camps, year-round camps, brother-sister camps and coed camps. Family camping is growing tremendously.

Discipline

The word "discipline" comes from disciple and originally meant "to develop by instruction and exercise," but usage has made such a horrible thing of it that its sound strikes fear to the hearts of campers, counselors and camp directors alike. This misapprehension is largely unfounded, for a good camp is a happy place where good will and consideration for others are the order of the day and where the spirit of good rapport makes serious problems largely disappear.

Our increased knowledge of problem children reveals that they are often reacting to "problem" situations and that shortcomings cease to rear their ugly heads when environments are improved. We know, too, that it is seldom safe to judge people by what they "appear" to be, for their overt acts are often mere pretense used to cover up their true feelings. We now realize what a personal tragedy it is for the cocky camper when we take him "down a peg" by making him run the gauntlet or by letting a bigger boy "knock some sense into his head;" his braggadocio is really only a disguise for an underlying inferiority complex and such treatment but further irritates his sore spots. Much better results follow when we learn to search for and eradicate causes instead of launching a direct attack upon symptoms.

We must not get the idea from this discussion that camp is a thoroughly unbridled place where each person does exactly as he pleases. On the contrary, when skillfully conducted, it is a place of superior discipline, for it brings about the best control of all, the kind which comes from within the person and makes him *want* to do what is right because his better nature demands it. A minimum of camp rules are necessary and agreed upon by all as we look on them as "ways we have found to work best."

The Promotion of One World

Someone has said that "We must remember that it takes both the black and the white keys on the piano to play *The Star-Spangled Banner,* and many camps, realizing the importance of furthering better relationships between races, nationalities and creeds, have made a definite effort to provide broadening contacts for campers.

ADDITIONAL READINGS

General

Benson, Reuel A., and Goldberg, Jacob A.: *The Camp Counselor.*
Burns, Gerald: *Program of the Modern Camp.*
Dimock, Hedley S.: *Administration of the Modern Camp.*
Goodrich, Lois: *Decentralized Camping.*
Irwin, Frank L.: *The Theory of Camping—An Introduction to Camping in Education.*
Joy, Barbara Ellen: *Camping.*
Joy, Barbara Ellen: *Camping's Challenge Today.* Camp Publications (#17), 6 pp., 30¢.
McBride, Robert E.: *Camping at the Mid-Century.* A.C.A., 1953, 41 pp., $1.00.
Webb, Kenneth B., Ed.: *Light from a Thousand Campfires.*

MAGAZINE ARTICLES

Burns, Gerald A.: *A Short History of Camping.* C.M., Feb.-Mar.-Apr., 1949.
Gibson, H. W.: *History of the Organized Camp.* C.M., Jan.-Feb.-Mar.-Apr., 1936.
Thayer, J. A.: *Let's Put the Country Back Into the Boy.* Recreation, May, 1956.

3

The Objectives
of Camping

Every little boy has inside of him an aching void which demands interesting and exciting play. And if you don't fill it with something that is interesting and exciting and good for him, he is going to fill it with something that is interesting and exciting and isn't good for him.

THEODORE ROOSEVELT, JR.

WHAT FACTORS have caused the phenomenal growth of camping within less than a century? What makes camping so attractive to youngsters that they eagerly look forward to it throughout the long months of winter? What does it offer to parents that they are eager to finance a share in it for their children? Why are camp directors, counselors and other staff members willing to devote their summer months to it? The answer cannot be summed up in one terse, clear-cut sentence, for camping has many facets to account for its popular appeal.

Camp Provides an Ideal Learning Climate

Someone has said that "boys and girls do not go to camp to be educated but that they cannot camp without being so." Though this may not be literally true in the mental gymnastics sense of education, it is true in the broader sense, for the better camp offers the ultimate in opportunity to develop the mind, heart, eyes, ears, coordinations, appreciations, and even the soul of youth. Montaigne has said, "It is not a soul, it is not a body we are training up; it is a man, and we ought not to divide him into two parts."

If the above claims seem impossible to achieve in a brief period of two months at the most, let us consider life in a summer camp a bit more closely. Camp possesses a camper entirely. Here he eats, sleeps, works, talks and plays twenty-four hours a day, seven days a week with scarcely any outside influences to distract him. Camp is home, school, gang, church

(Joy and Camp.)

and playground to him in contrast to his city "assembly line" existence, where he passes along as on a conveyor belt to have spiritual development screwed on at one spot, a few nuts and bolts in his mind adjusted at another, then home for refueling and repairs, and off with the gang for some rounding out as to the "facts of life." Counting hours, two months spent in camp are the equivalent of a whole year in school.

In camp, the child lives in a realm of youth, in a true laboratory where he actually practices helping to plan by democratic processes for his own health, work and recreation. Camp program is not bound by tradition, a necessity to meet course and graduation requirements, but can be altered freely to satisfy the inner drives and needs of the participant. His attendance is voluntary, and this very lack of compulsion puts him in the mood to enter wholeheartedly into what he is doing, for he himself has helped to select it. Staff personnel are sympathetic and

understanding, and the camper learns to appreciate them as real people who can laugh and play and enjoy carrying on camp activities just as he does. The informal, good-natured, mutually helpful atmosphere is a true revelation to the unfortunate camper who comes from a home full of tension and petty bickering. Contrary to those who feel that the efficacy of a medicine can be measured only by its bitterness, camp "climate" proves to be just right for nurturing unhampered growth and development.

A camper learns because he is dealing with things which have real meaning and interest for him. We all know how easy it is to emerge entirely unscathed from a boresome lecture, for we have a neat little trick of closing our eyes to unwelcome sights and our ears to information which has no meaning for us. But what camper can fortify any of his senses against the instruction he needs for next week's canoe trip or the wood lore which will enable him to select good firewood or berries and bark to stain the belt he has just knotted?

Camp is Chuck Full of Fun

To the camper, the main reason for coming to camp is to have fun, the fun which comes from adventure, learning new things, being with old friends and acquiring new ones, and cramming time with a glorious assortment of new accomplishments, friendships, and memories to last his life through.

Fun is the cornerstone for building children's ideals, as is so beautifully expressed in:

THE BIRTHRIGHT OF CHILDREN*

All children should know the joy of playing in healthful mud, of paddling in clean water, of hearing birds sing praises to God for the new day.

They should have the vision of pure skies enriched at dawn and sunset with unspeakable glory; of dew-drenched mornings flashing with priceless gems; of the vast night sky all throbbing and panting with stars.

They should live with the flowers and butterflies, with the wild things that have made possible the world of fables.

They should experience the thrill of going barefoot, of being out in the rain; of riding a white birch, of sliding down pine boughs, of climbing ledges and tall trees, of diving headfirst into a transparent pool.

They ought to know the smell of wet earth, of new mown hay, of sweet fern, mint, and fir; of the breath of cattle and of fog blown inland from the sea.

They should hear the answer the trees make to the rain and the wind; the sound of rippling and falling water; the muffled roar of the sea in storm.

They should have the chance to catch fish, to ride on a load of hay, to camp out, to cook over an open fire, tramp through a new country, and sleep under the open sky.

They should have the fun of driving a horse, paddling a canoe; sailing a boat. . . .

One cannot appreciate and enjoy to the full extent of nature, books, novels, histories, poems, pictures, or even musical compositions, who has not in his youth enjoyed the blessed contact with the world of nature.

HENRY TURNER BAILEY

Camp Teaches Us New Skills and Ways of Spending Leisure Time

Wouldn't it be wonderful to receive the keys to a pastry shop and be told, "Help yourself—it's all yours"? Can you imagine the delight of punching a finger through a crusty cherry pie, pinching off the corner of a chocolate fudge cake or plunging both hands deep into the cookie jar and stuffing your mouth with the goodies? Camp gives such an opportunity, figuratively speaking, through its chance for exploration and experimentation in the social, manual, aesthetic and spiritual fields. It affords the time and tools to acquaint a person with varied interests, to contribute vocationally and avocationally to his present and future happiness.

He learns the self-respect and pride which come from doing a job well. Terminology changes from a dictatorial "do" to a suggestive "let's," and emphasis is placed on self-reliance, "stick-to-it-iveness" and thoroughness. Cleaning the unit house, slicing onions, or repainting the canoe become minor obstacles to be hurdled for the satisfaction of living in an orderly place, eating a delicious stew, or going on that canoe trip which is just around the last slap of the brush. No amount of salary or blue ribbons can compensate either camper or counselor for a lack of real purpose in what he is doing. Proudly he displays his badge of accomplishment won by hard work done with a will and with heroic good humor.

The courage to think, the daring to create, and the heroism to be original have marked explorers, scientists, and thinkers from the beginning of time. So, with definite intent, camps instill in the camper a belief in himself and a desire to express himself creatively, for no one laughs at him or thinks him queer if he dares to be different and to stand for what he really thinks and feels.

Camp teaches that time is not so many

* From Proceedings for 1946 of the National Education Association of the United States; reproduced by permission.

suitcases to be stuffed to overflowing with carelessly chosen this and that all rolled together in a jumble. Instead, it is a continuous interlude in which the thoughtful camper can find time and space for everything really worth while from his early morning dip to a stroll to the ridge to watch the sunset. Camp experiences afford him the resourcefulness to use leisure time beneficially and not regard it as a period to be dreaded because "I've nothing to do." The happiest people are those whose lives and minds are so crammed with projects and things that they are waiting to do that the day never holds enough hours. It is trite but true that there is really nothing boring—only bored people.

Camp Adjusts Us Socially

The universe is balanced and adjusted so that each part works in harmony with all the others. The earth is held in its orbit by its relationship to other planets, and moon, sun and tides all behave as they do because of their pull and push on each other. We take their orderly synchronization for granted, but we can imagine the chaos that would result should one part decide to act up a bit. Camp, like the universe, is a cooperative community where people react on each other and where the actions of one have an effect upon all the others. Each person is accepted as an individual with powers as well as responsibilities equal in importance to everyone else's. The ideal in camp education is to give campers an approach to life which is individual and creative, yet also cooperative; to make people independent and self-reliant, yet harmonious and disciplined.

A camper learns that he may have a voice in making decisions, but not always his own way; that he has a right to his views, but that he must concede that same privilege to others.

When we place a number of jagged rocks in a smooth spherical container and

shake them continuously for a time, they eventually become smooth and fit together compatibly. So it is with human relationships. Maladjusted, selfish and conceited campers, when put in a wholesome environment and guided by the loving hand of understanding adults, usually lose their rough edges and become socially adjusted, well-behaved youngsters with that inner sense of security and acceptance they have been so ardently seeking in their misguided ways.

Camp Develops Good Habits and Good Character

In introducing herself, Maggie Owen, twelve-year-old autobiographer, writes, "I resolve to be a noble woman but 'tis hard to be noble in a house along with people not noble."* This offers a potent argument for placing children in an environment of high traditions and ideals.

Camp is a place where neatness of person, belongings, cabin and grounds is the expected thing and is brought about by the camper's own efforts as he wields a broom, plies a needle, or uses enough determination to wash—even behind his ears.

Camp is a place where the camper shoulders responsibility for his own welfare and happiness as well as that of his comrades. One taste of having the boat drift away because *he* failed to tie it properly or of having the whole group go to bed hungry because *he* forgot the food he had volunteered to bring, will cure him permanently of such misguided notions as "what I do is my own business."

Camp is a place where a camper must learn to stand on his own two feet, for counselors, although fond of him and anxious to help, are impartial and will not intercede for him as his parents may have done each time he got into difficulties.

*From *The Book of Maggie Owen*, by Maggie-Owen Wadelton, copyright 1941. Used by special permission of the publishers, The Bobbs-Merrill Company.

Living with nature and being guided by nature's rules teaches him resourcefulness, originality and self-reliance. He learns to consider well before starting a project, but, having once started, to pursue it zealously to the end instead of leaving a clutter of half-finished undertakings about him, discarded like hot potatoes at the first waning of enthusiasm. He has a chance to develop qualities of leadership as well as followership; to be modest in winning, as well as courageous in defeat. He learns that many of the richest values in life have no monetary value at all. In fact, in a *good* camp he will be exposed to stimuli and opportunities for the development of almost every trait exemplified in the great.

Camp Keeps Us Safe and Healthy

The instinct to protect its young is a characteristic of every animal, and the bear, the fox or the deer is willing to give its very life for that purpose. Parents, likewise, want the security and peace of mind which come from confidence that their children are well and happy and in trustworthy hands. This desire figures prominently in the mind of the camp administrator as he carefully plans safety precautions and time for eating, sleeping, resting, working and playing. These elaborate safeguards, together with vigorous physical life and a serene, yet exciting, daily existence, can do much to bring about glowing mental and physical health.

Camp Develops an Interest in and Love for the Out-of-Doors

One can scarcely realize the lack of interest in and love for the out-of-doors many city children have until one sees a group of them turned loose with nature. Incredible though it may seem, even college students who aspired to be counselors have shown so little vision and curiosity about anything beyond their city experiences that the mere thought of existing through a weekend camping trip without benefit of radio or a game of bridge was enough to produce visions of dullest boredom. Appreciations come from the heart more than the mind; correspondingly, an appreciation of nature comes about only through living with it and making its intimate acquaintance.

Camp Has Great Spiritual Values

In addition to formal and informal worship services, camp provides the experience of Christian living in a group. Camp is a suspended bit of time where one can *live* the experiences of nature, may listen to the wisdom of the elements, and hear God speak; a place where one may feel His touch in the soft breeze and see His handiwork in the intricasies of a spider web bejeweled with dew.

ADDITIONAL READINGS

American Camping Association Standards. ACA, 1953, 8 pp.

Benson and Goldberg: *The Camp Counselor.*

Burns, Gerald: *Program of the Modern Camp.*

Dimock, Hedley: *Administration of the Modern Camp.*

Dimock, Hedley S., and Statten, Taylor: *Talks to Counselors.*

Doty, Richard S.: *The Character Dimension of Camping*

Goodrich, Lois: *Decentralized Camping.*

Irwin, Frank L.: *The Theory of Camping—An Introduction to Camping in Education.*

Joy, Barbara Ellen: *Camping.*

Joy, Barbara Ellen: *Simple Living in the Outdoors.* Camp Publications (#7), 3 pp., 20¢.

Ledlie and Holbein: *The Camp Counselor's Manual.*

Roehm, Ralph D.: *Better Camping.* Assn. Press, $1.50.

Webb, Kenneth B., Editor: *Light from a Thousand Campfires.*

Webb, Kenneth B., and Susan H.: *Summer Magic.* Assn. Press, or ACA., 1953, 159 pp., $2.50.

MAGAZINE ARTICLES

Feinberg, Daniel: *Some Basic ABC's for Evaluating Your Camp Program.* C.M., Apr., 1957.

Henderson, Frank and Lucile: *8 Things Parents Want from Camp—Does Your Camp Provide Them?* C.M., March, 1959.

II

The Camp Counselor

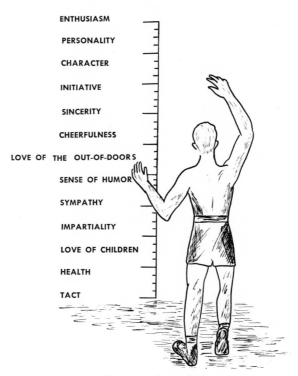

ENTHUSIASM

PERSONALITY

CHARACTER

INITIATIVE

SINCERITY

CHEERFULNESS

LOVE OF THE OUT-OF-DOORS

SENSE OF HUMOR

SYMPATHY

IMPARTIALITY

LOVE OF CHILDREN

HEALTH

TACT

The Camp Counselor.

4

The Camp
Counselor

Ideals are like the stars; you will not succeed in touching them with your hands, but like the sea-faring man on the desert of waters, you choose them as your guides, and, following them, you reach your destiny.

CARL SCHURZ*

CAMP COUNSELING provides a fascinating summer occupation for the thousands of people who return to it summer after summer but, as with any field of endeavor, not everyone is suited to it. Only when there is a mutual admiration society between the counselor who likes almost everything about camp and the camp which likes nearly everything about the counselor can there be that happy blending which makes the days fly by all too quickly. Therefore, in this chapter, we shall try to consider some ways to predetermine how one would fit into the camping picture.

CHARACTERISTICS OF A GOOD COUNSELOR

Liking for People

A real liking for people and sincere enjoyment of being with them is one of the most important determinants for camp counselors since camp life involves associating with people of many types practically twenty-four hours a day. The first consideration of the counselor will be fellow staff members who will probably range from a majority of those of college age to older members of varying ages; there will be a contrast of personalities and interests. You must be versatile and adapt yourself to everyone, maintaining a cordial working relationship with each. A counselor will have frequent contacts with each staff member; he works with the camp nurse in regard to his

* Reproduced by permission of Coronet Magazine.

(H. Armstrong Roberts.)

campers' health, the dietitian to plan cook-outs, the waterfront director, the handy man, the camp director, and others. Your tastes must be so cosmopolitan that you can find things to appreciate in everyone, accepting their quirks and idiosyncrasies just as you hope they will accept yours. On the whole, you'll probably find a pretty fine group for that is the type of person who is ordinarily attracted to a summer camp. Among them you'll likely find several who are very congenial and become lifelong friends. Obviously, you must be a person who would rather work with people than with things or ideas, though you will be called upon to do plenty of the latter, too.

Secondly, the counselor must sincerely enjoy the company of children, even when they are noisy, uncooperative, impulsive, or demanding. You must not like just certain children but must spread your affection over the whole assortment. In fact, it is the unattractive, socially inept child who needs the counselor most of all for

he often hungers most for the bit of affection and appreciation you can give. You must be able to tolerate children in large and frequent doses with continued patience and good humor for you will be their foster parent, teacher, friend, confidante, taskmaster and model. The counselor must be able to see the hidden possibilities in the ungifted child, who seemingly is "all thumbs" and must see behind the "front" of the misfit and maladjusted who are but trying in their immature way to find a place in a society too complex for them.

Granted, the counselor must indeed like children but not to the point of being mawkishly sentimental about them; you will sometimes have to be stern with them when it becomes a question of their welfare or a clash with camp objectives and policies. Yet withal, you must maintain good-will and respect as you skillfully weld young people into a community, learning to live together peacefully, cooperatively and happily.

Liking the Out-of-Doors

Even the most luxurious camp usually consists of more or less rustic surroundings and facilities and any good program will include many hours in the open for both counselors and campers. The counselor should be the sort who enjoys rambling down a woodland path, lolling in the sun on the beach, just sitting on a hill watching the sunset in a blaze of color or joining a group on a cook out around a campfire. You must like the rain, even when you are caught in it, and must enjoy working, as well as playing, in the wide open spaces. Does this discourage you? Don't let it unless you have already tried outdoor living and know for sure that you won't like it; many a counselor has come to camp as green as the greenest camper only to find himself completely captivated by outdoor living before the season is over. If you've never tried it, why not give it a chance?

A Leader and Model

A counselor must be a leader who exemplifies by his own habits and conduct the ideals and objectives of the camp. An ability to attract youngsters is an almost priceless asset but it would be much better to stay at home if the example you set is not of the best; your very attractiveness will then but make your influence the more harmful. Campers pick up bad habits and become boisterous, slangy, vulgar, complaining or boastful, as the counselor sets the pattern.

Pretense and sham are soon spotted in the intimacy of camp life. You might as well face it; everything you are and say and do will be carefully observed by your bright-eyed youngsters who will be quick to detect and equally quick to dislike hypocrisy. They will soon see through an attempt to cover up sloppiness by "Oh, I just never could keep my room straight," or a weak-kneed excuse as, "I just didn't have time," is similarly revealing.

Youth is the period of hero worship, and a child's heart is full of faith and love. Consequently, there is nothing in the world more painful or demoralizing to him than to discover that his beloved idol has feet of common clay and that the first favorable impression he made was only a thin veneer. Every prospective counselor must ask himself if he is willing to live like an inspiring rather than a disillusioning model.

Youthful in Spirit Yet Mature in Judgment

Camp directors demand counselors with mature judgment. This is one of the reasons why the American Camping Association has set nineteen as the minimum desirable age for a counselor. But mature judgment is not always a matter of chronological age, for some attain it early, while others live to be ninety-seven without ever having demonstrated a particle of it. Campers are too precious to entrust to those whose actions are determined by capriciousness and whim. Yet, along with good judgment, a counselor must retain that youthfulness of spirit which keeps you forever curious and craving the new, so that, regardless of passing birthdays, you can still enjoy wading in a babbling brook, hunting the hiding place of a frog, or digging for pirates' gold with your campers.

Camping Skills

A counselor must also take stock of his skills. What can you do? Is there any skill in which you excel? Is your tennis, camp cookery, swimming or woodcraft of such quality that you could teach it to someone else? Can you step into a group which is unduly alarmed over a snake and, by looking at it, assure them that it is harmless and indeed quite essential to nature's well balanced plan? Can you start a fire in a steady downpour to dry out sopping campers? Can you oversee packing a canoe so that it rides properly in the water? Can you tell poison ivy from Virginia creeper?

Even a program specialist needs a general backlog of wood lore and camping skills, for camping is essentially an outdoor process and a modern camp coordinates the many facets of program into one grand experience in out-of-door living. It isn't enough to "just love" nature; one must also know something about it. Can you imagine a doctor saying, "Nurse, look on page 199 in 'Surgery' by Dr. Cutsomemore and see if I'm to tie this thing to that?" An admittedly absurd example; but, if you think you can get away with anchoring a canoe with a French love knot, you are being equally impractical. A camper likes to feel that *his* counselor excels at some one thing be it diving, telling a good story, or being the kindest, most considerate person in camp.

The Counselor's Dream.

As a counselor you may get along beautifully with children and your personality may just burst through at all points, but, unless you can *do* something, your charming smile will soon wear thin. You need not despair if you do not already know camp skills, for the main requirement is a willingness to learn, and there are numerous organizations and books to teach you if you really want to know. Many an excellent counselor has acquired nearly all of his skill and knowledge while on the job in camp.

Persistence

A counselor must be able to find happiness in doing a job well and in serving others without thought of personal gain or self-aggrandizement. You must like hard work and plenty of it, for, except for brief periods of "time off," you will be on duty twenty-four hours a day. You must have enough persistence and will power to replace your wishbone with a backbone and must realize that genius is but 1 per cent inspiration mixed with 99 per cent perspiration. If you are still convinced that you want to spend a summer where you can do something and be something worth-while, then blessings on you, for in you and those like you lie the hope and future of summer camping. Every director knows and admits deep in his heart that, no matter how elaborate his outlay of buildings and equipment or how good his preplanning has been, the real success of his camp depends upon the quality of his counselors.

HOW DO YOU RATE?

If you would like to know your possibilities for success and enjoyment as a counselor, you may get some idea by rating yourself on the tests which follow. Remember that there is nothing to be gained by "cheating" on them for the real proof comes when you begin working with fellow staff members and campers on the job.

Check each trait in the proper column; then connect them with a solid line to indicate your "profile." Note where your weaknesses lie as the line slumps off to the left and also assess your strengths as the line bears triumphantly to the right.

HEALTH	Poor	Below Average	Average	Above Average	Superior
	1	2	3	4	5
1. Stamina enough to last through a strenuous day					
2. Well-balanced meals eaten regularly					
3. Regular sleep in sufficient quantity					
4. Smoking, not at all or moderately and in an appropriate place					
5. No intoxicating liquors (can't be tolerated at camp)					
6. Sufficient vigorous exercise each day					

ACCEPTABILITY TO OTHERS	Poor	Below Average	Average	Above Average	Superior
	1	2	3	4	5
7. Pleasing and neat appearance					
8. Cleanliness of person and clothing					
9. Graciousness and mannerliness					
10. Tact (speak truthfully, but without unnecessarily offending or hurting others)					
11. Cooperativeness (even when carrying out the plans of others)					
12. Cheerfulness (no sulking or moodiness)					
13. Sense of humor (even when the joke's on you)					
14. Good English (no excess slang or profanity)					
15. Warmth (a friendly personality that attracts others to you)					
16. Poise (even in emergencies or embarrassing situations)					
17. Appreciation of the beautiful in deed, music, nature and literature					
18. Sincere liking for children (even unattractive and "naughty" ones)					
19. Enjoyment of hard work (even when it means getting yourself and your clothing dirty)					
20. Skills and knowledge of outdoor living (in rain, as well as sunshine)					
21. Adaptability (can happily change plans to fit in with others or the weather)					
22. Can "take" as well as "give" orders					

	Poor	Below Average	Average	Above Average	Superior
	1	2	3	4	5
23. Love of fun (can see possibilities for enjoyment in almost any situation)					
24. Interested in many things					
25. Specialization (ability to "do" at least one camp activity well)					
26. Initiative (ability to start without outside prodding or suggestion)					
27. Promptness at all appointments and in performing all tasks					
28. Dependability (do *what* you say you will *when* you say you will)					
29. Industry (want to be constantly up and doing)					
30. Persistence (finish what you start with dispatch and thoroughness)					
31. Curiosity (want to know about many things just for the sake of knowing)					
32. Neatness (keep own living quarters neat and clean)					

EMOTIONAL MATURITY

"When I was a child, I spake as a child, ... but when I became a man, I put away childish things" is not necessarily true of adults, who sometimes unconsciously cling to childish ways of thinking and acting. A person who harbors such childish traits is said to be emotionally immature, and, though frequently at a loss to understand why, he is often unhappy, for his behavior keeps him at constant odds with himself and his associates. He often feels mistreated and deprived of his just dues. Camp directors look upon a counselor's degree of emotional maturity as one of the surest indices of his probable success for he can scarcely expect to fulfill his job of helping his campers mature unless he can set an example.

Your physical and mental maturity tell nothing of your emotional maturity, for the fact that you are strong as an ox or fleet as a deer does not indicate that you have learned to face up to life squarely and solve your problems in an adult way. Indeed, you may be a straight "A" student at school and still be unable to apply any of your intelligence to solve your own problems and help you deal more effectively with people.

How often we hear some exasperated person say to another "Why don't you grow up?" Well may we ask what actions and attitudes determine why one person is labelled mature, yet another immature. First of all, a mature person has awakened to the fact that every person around him has wants and needs similar to his own and he therefore cannot always have his own way. For instance, if he has set his heart on doing something with a particular buddy on his day off, he doesn't sulk, try to get even, or throw a tantrum if he finds his pal has made other plans or that unforseen developments have made it necessary for one of them to remain on duty in camp. He tries to persuade others to his way of thinking but he does it by reasoning with them, not by pouting, wheedling, flattering or making himself so disagreeable that others give in rather than suffer the consequences.

When someone with obviously good intentions criticizes something about him, he is smart enough to analyze the remark and profit by any truth there is in it instead of flaring up pig-headedly at the thought that another should even hint that he is anything less than perfect. Accepting deserved criticism is what he might check off as "growing pains." He has pride and faith in himself yet displays a becoming modesty and doesn't feel it necessary to alibi for every shortcoming. He isn't a doormat who lets everyone walk over him at will; he may even on occasion rise up in righteous anger or resentment about things important enough to really matter.

He enjoys the feeling of being able to influence others but doesn't misuse this ability. He exercises it only to lead in right directions but avoids carrying it to the point where he makes willing slaves of others and has them groveling at his feet. He doesn't try to run peoples' lives but, instead, tries to do a good job of running his own. He organizes his daily living with a good balance of work, play, laughter, seriousness and all other components of the good life. He can fit easily into the routine of camp living, accepting reasonable camp rules cheerfully because he knows they are meant to protect the best interests of all. Most of all, he is ever thoughtful of others and considerate of their needs and wishes.

The real criterion is that the emotionally immature person governs his actions by his emotions whereas the mature person keeps his reasoning power instead of his emotions in the driver's seat at all times.

EMOTIONAL MATURITY	Poor 1	Below Average 2	Average 3	Above Average 4	Superior 5
1. Can you accept criticism without undue anger or hurt, acting upon it if justified, disregarding it if not?					
2. Are you tolerant of others and willing to overlook their faults?					
3. Do you feel genuinely happy at the success of others and sincerely congratulate them?					
4. Do you refrain from listening to and repeating undue gossip about others?					
5. Do you converse about other things and persons? Test it by checking your conversation to see how frequently you use "I."					
6. Are you altruistic, often putting the welfare and happiness of others above your own?					
7. Do you refrain from emotional outbursts of anger, tears, etc.?					
8. Do you face disagreeable duties promptly and without trying to escape by playing sick or making excuses?					
9. Can you stay away from home a month or more without undue homesickness?					
10. Can you weigh facts and make decisions promptly, then abide by your decisions?					
11. Are you willing to postpone things you want to do now in favor of greater benefits or pleasure later?					

	Poor	Below Average	Average	Above Average	Superior
	1	2	3	4	5
12. Are you usually on good terms with your family and associates?					
13. When things go wrong, can you objectively determine the cause and remedy it without alibiing for yourself and blaming it on other people or things?					
14. When disagreeing with another, can you discuss it calmly and usually work out a mutually satisfactory agreement without hard feelings?					
15. Can you enter into informal social events of many types wholeheartedly?					
16. Do you really enjoy doing little things for others, even though you know they will likely go unknown and unappreciated?					
17. Do you dress neatly and modestly without tendency to gaudiness or overdress?					
18. Can you dismiss past sins and mistakes that can't be remedied now without dwelling on them?					
19. Can you make decisions regarding others objectively, disregarding your personal dislike or resentment of them?					
20. As a leader, do you work democratically without dictating or forcing your will on others?					
21. Are you loyal to your friends, minimizing or not mentioning their faults to others?					
22. Are you free from "touchiness," so that others do not have to handle you with kid gloves?					
23. Do you act according to your honest convictions regardless of what others may think or say about it?					
24. Do you have a kindly feeling toward most people, a deep affection for some, and no unhealthy attachments to any?					
25. Do you feel that you usually get about what you deserve? Are you free from a feeling that others "have it in for" you?					

In order to make a rough estimate of your over-all emotional maturity, total all scores and divide by 25 (the number of items rated). If you have proceeded honestly and objectively, an average of 4 or 5 means you are quite acceptable, 3 indicates you are average, and a 1 or 2 shows that you are below average and should "grow up." Here are some suggestions to help you attain emotional maturity:

1. Face your deficiencies frankly and resolve to eradicate them just as quickly and completely as possible.

2. Set out to acquire definite skills and interests which have social rather than selfish or personal values.

3. Make it a point to associate with a number of emotionally mature people. Observe them and try to determine why they are so.

4. If you feel a need for help, seek someone qualified and discuss the problem frankly and openly with him. Be willing to act on his recommendations even though they're not flattering.

5. Get wrapped up in causes so big and worth-while that they completely absorb you, making you forget yourself and your troubles.

REWARD FOR THE COUNSELOR

The foregoing traits characterize an ideal couselor and have no doubt convinced you by now that no camp director need waste his time looking for such a paragon of virtue on earth. Certainly no one but an angel with a halo cocked over one ear and strumming on a harp of gold could qualify! Do not despair, however, for there is hope for anyone who scores fairly high on the tests and sincerely wants to score higher.

Let us see what rewards you may expect for your summer's work. If you have had no experience and little special training, your money reward may be meager and you could likely make more by being a waitress at a summer resort or serving customers at the gas station. But you must realize that, in addition to the dollars you receive, your board and room is worth several dollars, and the privilege of being in an environment that costs campers several hundred dollars should not be passed over lightly. Camps sometimes pay a part or all of your transportation expenses, and some provide for doing part or all of your laundry. There are few needs and little temptation to spend money in camp, so that whatever cash you receive is largely clear.

As a leader, you will have almost unlimited opportunity and stimuli to achieve the objectives of camping for yourself; you will be spending your time in the same out-of-doors, under the same sun, and in the same friendly, cooperative atmosphere as do the campers.

You will gain close friends of all ages and will have an unparalleled opportunity to acquire the techniques of happy group living and develop into an emotionally mature person. You will have a chance to improve your own skills in camp activities and to secure practice in leadership and group work, which may later prove a decided professional advantage. You will also derive the satisfaction that comes to all good teachers—the knowledge that you have made a real contribution to the growth and development of the youth of America.

GETTING A JOB

Making Application

When you have decided you want to be a counselor, investigate a number of camps, diligently reading their booklets and talking with former counselors and others who know about them. Select three to five which especially appeal to you because of location (a different section of the country will broaden your horizons), length and dates of season, general policies, program, objectives, and types and ages of children served. It is well to select those that are members of the American Camping Association for you know that they have met high standards of camping practice. Write a letter of inquiry to each, using a good quality stationery and your best handwriting or typing. Camp directors receive hundreds of applications each season, and those which are messy, incomplete or not clearly expressed land in the wastebasket where they rightfully belong. You must remember that you are trying to sell yourself and that merchandise always sells better when attractively packaged.

Make your letter sincere and human, rating yourself honestly and claiming only what you can live up to, for you will be the loser if you step into a job you can't adequately fill. Make the letter brief (not more than one single-spaced typewritten page) and supplement it with a data sheet including such information as your name, address, date of birth, education, present occupation, work experience, exact dates available, special camp training (courses in camp counseling, sociology, psychology, education, physical education, mental health, first aid, aquatics, art, music, journalism, creative writing, geology, astronomy, dramatics, nature study, and so on). Many camps prefer to have this information on their own form, and, if interested in you, will send back an application blank for you to fill out. Give names of three persons (teachers, ministers, employers and the like) who know you well and can speak knowingly of your qualifications; be sure to secure their permission before using their names. If the distance is not too great, indicate a willingness to go for an interview, for a face-to-face talk greatly helps both you and the director decide how well you would fit into the particular situation. Include a stamped self-addressed envelope for the reply.

If an interview is granted, appear neat, well-groomed, and on time to the minute. Enter in a poised, friendly manner, wearing your most sincere smile. Noisiness, overfamiliarity and boisterousness are most objectionable. Answer questions frankly and sincerely, and feel free to ask what information you wish about the camp and its policies. When the interviewer signifies that the interview is over, leave promptly.

*Whispering wind in the tree tops,
Shimmering sun on the lake,
From all of the world's occupations
A life in the open I'd take.**

*From *Deep-River Jim's Wilderness Trail Book*. Permission by The Open-Road Publishing Co.

Accepting a Position

Do not accept a position until you feel reasonably sure that the camp fits with your philosophy of life well enough for you to give it utmost loyalty and devotion. Make sure you have a definite understanding as to remuneration, the exact dates you are expected to serve, your responsibilities and duties, rules regarding smoking, time off, and so forth. Now is the time to clear up all questions and doubts, for after you have once accepted a job, you must not quibble or "weasel" out of obligations. Answer all correspondence promptly, and do not leave your acceptance or rejection of an offer dangling unduly, for the director may lose other desirable applicants while you are trying to make up your indecisive mind. A signed contract is your word of honor that you will arrive on schedule, prepared to carry out all responsibilities agreed upon to the best of your ability.

THE COUNSELOR'S DUFFEL

After you have accepted a job, you will in all probability receive various pieces of literature from the camp. Read them carefully to fix pertinent details in your

mind. When you have ascertained your duties, start intensive preparation to assume them. If possible, take, or at least audit, helpful school courses. Look for general camping books or books on special fields in your school and public library. You may want to start your own camping library and will find many worth-while books available at small cost. One of the most helpful things a prospective counselor can do is to start a camping notebook in which he jots down every bit of useful information and every helpful idea that comes his way. A loose-leaf cover, holding sheets 3¾ by 6¾ inches, is suggested, for it is convenient to take to camp where it fits into your pocket or duffel. Get as much experience as possible in working with groups of children.

ADDITIONAL READINGS

Benson, Reuel A., and Goldberg, Jacob A.: *The Camp Counselor.*

Burns, Gerald: *Program of the Modern Camp.*

Camp Administrative Forms and Suggested Procedures in the Area of Personnel. ACA, 1956, 30 pp., 35¢.

Dimock, Hedley S., and Statten, Taylor: *Talks to Counselors.*

Good Counselors Make Good Camps #19–530. Girl Scouts, 48 pp., 35¢.

Goodrich, Lois: *Decentralized Camping.*

Irwin, Frank L.: *The Theory of Camping*—An Introduction to Camping in Education.

Joy, Barbara Ellen: *Camping.*

Joy, Barbara Ellen: *Professional Relationships in Camp.* Camp Publications, #6.

Ledlie, John A., and Holbein, F. W.: *Camp Counselor's Manual.*

Ott, Elmer F.: *So You Want To Be a Camp Counselor.*

Tobitt, Janet E.: *Program in Girl Scout Camping.*

Webb, Kenneth B., Editor: *Light from a Thousand Campfires.*

Welch, Emily: *It's Fun To Be a Counselor.* Assn. Press, 1956, 63 pp., $1.00.

MAGAZINE ARTICLES

Camps Share Staff Salary Information. C.M., Apr., 1959.

Doherty, J. Kenneth: *Counselor Rating Scale.* C.M., Feb., 1950.

Hawkes, Alfred L.: *Choosing Your Camp Naturalist.* C.M., Feb., 1957.

Healy, Edward M.: *Leadership—Some Aims for the Future.* C.M., Feb., 1956.

Klein, Alan F.: *Counseling is Channel One.* C.M., June, 1959.

Link, Robert E.: *What Makes a Good Counselor.* C.M., Jan., 1951.

MacPeek, Walter: *The Counselor I Want for My Son.* C.M., Feb., 1953.

Ransom, John E.: *A Good Basis for Counselor Evaluation.* C.M., Jan., 1952.

Rubin, Larry: *The Camper's View.* C.M., Apr., 1957.

What Campers Want in a Counselor. C.M., June, 1953.

5

The Counselor
on the Job

A great deal of the joy of life consists in doing perfectly, or at least to the best of one's ability, everything which he attempts to do. There is a sense of satisfaction, a pride in surveying such a work—a work which is rounded, full, exact, complete in all its parts—which the superficial man, who leaves his work in a slovenly, slipshod, half-finished condition, can never know. It is this conscientious completeness which turns work into art. The smallest thing, well done, becomes artistic.

WILLIAM MATHEWS

CAMP ORGANIZATION

IN THIS CHAPTER, we will survey some of the general aspects of a counselor's duties. You will find the chart on page 49 helpful in gaining an overall view of the general set up and lines of responsibility in a typical camp.

Camp Director

The highest authority at camp is the camp director, who, in the final analysis, is responsible for everything that goes on in camp. Each member of the staff is accountable to him even though immediately supervised by someone else with delegated responsibility. The camp will likely have set up general policies regarding routine procedures, but in any other case, no important decision involving the camp as a whole or the welfare of any person in it may be made without the director's knowledge and consent.

Assistant Camp Director

The person second in command may be called assistant director, head counselor, or program director and serves as the contact man or coordinator of the whole camp program. He is accountable to the camp director and works directly with program specialists, unit heads, and often their assistants. He is the mainspring of the whole camp and its morale, as evidenced by both campers and staff, is largely dependent upon him. His specific duties vary according to the size and general set-up of the camp.

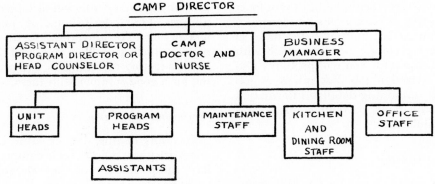

A Typical Camp Organization.

Program Specialists or Department Heads

Program specialists or department heads are usually found in larger numbers in long-term camps or those tending more toward a centralized system, though all camps have a few such as the camp nurse, waterfront director, and so forth. They head such phases of the camp program as tennis, campcraft, arts and crafts, nature, sailing, trip camping, music or dramatics; each may have assistants to help carry on his particular activity. The program specialist may schedule hours when his work area is open to all who wish to come; he may schedule definite periods for certain groups, or give his time and facilities as individuals or groups request. He may or may not be assigned regular cabin duties depending on the philosophy of the camp and how heavy his special program is. The program specialist will usually be responsible for requisitioning the supplies he needs; for seeing that his quarters and equipment are kept in good condition; and at the end of the season, for turning in an inventory, listing supplies needed, and making recommendations for the following year.

Unit Heads and Assistants

A unit head, sometimes called a village or section head, presides over a living unit of four to six cabins or tents. In charge of each cabin is an assistant, usually called an assistant unit head or cabin counselor, who works intimately with the four to nine campers living therein. A unit head works closely with his assistants, helping them plan a unit program suited to the needs and interests of the campers. He arranges with his assistants such matters as division of unit duties and time off and serves as liaison with the head counselor. He must see that his unit program coordinates with the overall program of the entire camp.

BEFORE THE CAMPERS COME

Staff Manual and Job Description

Most camps have a staff manual which will either be sent to you before camp opens or given to you early in the pre-camp training period. You will find many questions of interest answered in the manual and should read it carefully; save it for reference during the season. In it, such topics as the history and philosophy of the camp, organization, including the personnel and their responsibilities, living units and facilities, camp customs, rules, and the skeleton program are discussed. In the manual will be found information pertaining particularly to counselors such as time off, the use of equipment and facilities, rules regarding counselor guests, smoking, the use of automobiles, staff meetings and means of in-camp training. If some questions are still unanswered, be sure to ask specifically about them for it is necessary to have a clear understanding of important matters beforehand so that you can comply wholeheartedly with what is expected. You will probably also have received a job description or job analysis containing detailed information concerning your particular duties and responsibilities.

Precamp Training

Most camps conduct a precamp training period of from seven days to two weeks. This gives the staff a chance to get acquainted with each other and the camp site and learn camp customs and traditions. Here will be given further details about duties and a chance to plan as a group for the entire season. Also it will be possible to meet in small groups to plan for the individual phases of the program for which you are responsible and to receive much information about how to deal with your campers and plan with them for a worth-while summer. During

precamp training, you will also be doing all sorts of campcraft skills from making a bean hole to bedding down for an overnight, which will give you confidence about meeting the campers and preparing for a good summer with them.

Previewing Your Campers

In many camps, unit or cabin counselors are given a list of their campers before camp opens and they should try to learn just as much as possible about each one. The camp will probably have on file, various materials concerning the campers. Since some of the information is confidential, unlimited access to it may be denied, but pertinent information about each one will be given. Be sure to respect the confidential nature of this information. For instance, if a camper has been in camp before, there will be records of his previous accomplishments as well as reports on his personality, social adaptability, adjustment to adults and fellow campers, and improvements noted by his

(Joy and Camp.)

cabin counselors and other staff. There will also be past health records and, of special interest to you, will be the report from his home physician based on the examination given just prior to camp opening. It is important to note any observations regarding swimming or diving, strenuous sports, out-of-camp trips, allergies, food idiosyncrasies; it will be the counselor's responsibility to see that such recommendations are carried out. Young campers usually feel rather strange and insecure for at least a short period after camp opens, even though they are veterans of other summers, and it helps to put them at ease and get started off on the right foot if one can call them by name and immediately show some familiarity with their background.

Personal Adjustment

Try to adjust quickly and happily to camp ways, for, though the change may seem striking at first, you will probably heartily approve of it once you grow accustomed to it. The door has voluntarily been closed on the old days of formal dances and afternoons at the corner drug store and you are on the threshold of what can be a new and thrilling way of life; it will become so only as you lend your best efforts to it. Camp counseling may well turn out to be one of your very best experiences ending with the sense of a job well done and the knowledge that you have won the genuine love and respect of a group of "small fry." Your greatest re-

ward will come when some grubby little paw is placed trustingly in yours and a small voice says, "Hey, you'll be back next summer, won't you? 'Cause I don't wanna come if you don't."

RELATIONSHIPS WITH STAFF MEMBERS

With the Camp Director

A camp director has usually spent long months preparing for the impending season and naturally is very concerned about its success. Ultimately, he is responsible for the health and welfare of every person in camp from staff on down to the tiniest camper. It is true, he has delegated many responsibilities to others but he can not shrug off responsibility for any mistakes of judgment they make. Obviously, the camp director has many problems on his mind and grave responsibilities on his shoulders. You should see that you do not unnecessarily add to his responsibilities by cheerfully and promptly dispatching all tasks assigned to you in the most efficient way you can.

Bear the aims and objectives of the camp foremost in mind and gear your efforts toward their accomplishment; after all, if you don't approve of them, you shouldn't have accepted the job in the first place. Be conscious always that the good of the camp and campers comes first and must supersede any self-centered or selfish desires of an individual or group. One should neither ask for nor expect special favors, for the director must remain impartial. You must obey the spirit as well as the letter of camp rules and regulations. File all required reports promptly and completely to the last detail. Bear in mind how costly equipment is and never waste or mistreat it but keep it bright and shining and in good repair.

One of the most difficult questions will be when to make decisions yourself and when to seek help and advice. On the one hand, you have been hired because you purportedly have a level head and mature judgment and will therefore be expected to make many minor decisions instead of piling them in the laps of others; on the other hand, you must be quick to recognize problems that are of more than minor importance. Those out of your jurisdiction must be taken to your unit head, the camp nurse or doctor, or head counselor. Very serious problems should be taken directly to the Camp Director.

With Staff Members

The esprit de corps of the staff group largely determines camp morale, for counselors cannot do their work well when laboring under tension and vague feelings of insecurity and frustration. Campers are quick to perceive lack of unity in the staff and will probably comment on it among themselves and eventually take sides with ensuing disharmony. It therefore behooves each counselor to exert himself to fit in with the group and do his part to keep it harmonious and cooperative.

A morsel of petty gossip or a careless comment can cause the first break in staff morale, so avoid criticizing or commenting about those whose ways differ from yours. Variety is the spice of life, and anyone who learns to accept the bad with the good in others will lead a much happier life. When you make a disparaging remark about another, he usually hears of it, and with human frailty, is apt to bolster

his ego by retaliating in kind. Soon you find yourself involved in ill feeling and a real "feud." Before we can develop tolerance in campers, we must master it ourselves.

> Do not look for wrong and evil—
>   You will find them if you do;
> As you measure for your neighbor
>   He will measure back to you.
> Look for goodness, look for gladness—
>   You will meet them all the while;
> If you bring a smiling visage
>   To the glass, you meet a smile.
>
> —AUTHOR UNKNOWN

Camp is a blending of many different activities and experiences and any good must be accomplished from the sum total of them rather than from any single part. Counselors must bear in mind that activities are not ends in themselves but are merely means to an end—the tools with which to accomplish the objectives. This is sometimes hard to remember, for any counselor worthy of his hire becomes absorbed in making a success of his particular part of the program and tends to become self-centered and oblivious to the whole picture. Program specialists, in particular, sometimes forget that their job is to fit themselves into their "niche" in camp life instead of setting themselves up on a "pedestal," particularly if their activity is one which easily catches the fancy of campers. Immature counselors sometimes vie with each other in an attempt to bolster their own egos by building up the greatest camper clientele. This, of course, is very selfish and quite detrimental to the overall good of the camp and campers.

Recall that one of the previously stated marks of a good counselor is a broad interest in many things, and a counselor who belittles other activities is but boorishly showing his ignorance. When there is another activity about which you know little, you will be gaining a double reward if you pay a fellow counselor the subtle compliment of asking him to help you learn something about it. You will be acquiring a new friend as well as a new field of interest. Be modest about your own accomplishments for conceit is never an endearing trait.

Try, also, to understand the positions of the maintenance man, the kitchen staff, the camp nurse and other specialists, and fit your requests for help in with their busy routines.

Cooperate and help out whenever you can and be the first to volunteer for special duties, even the unpleasant ones or the ones which involve hard and even dirty work. It is said that when a piano is to be moved, there are usually several volunteers but always a few who hang back and offer to carry the stool. Be a pusher, not a stool carrier.

Make friends with many and avoid cliques or special pals for these are bad for camp morale and eventually make the participants suffer. The most fun comes by mingling in various groups, canoeing, reading, singing, chatting or going off to visit the town during your time off. It is usually best neither to borrow nor lend clothing, money or other personal possessions for such practices usually cause misunderstandings and hard feelings sooner or later.

Take your job (but not yourself) seriously and keep the objectives of good camping ever before you. Everyone wants popularity but you will definitely get nothing worth-while by sacrificing your principles to be "one of the gang." Popularity built on such a foundation is like building on shifting sands and you will soon fall into disrespect, left sitting alone to lick your wounds.

SETTLING-IN YOUR CAMPERS

As a cabin counselor, you will be living intimately with the small group in your charge somewhere near twenty-four hours a day and will come to know them and they to know you very, very well; recall that decentralized camping came into being to provide just such a small group-living situation and it is your job to make

it a homey, congenial, happy one. Think of yourself and your campers as a little family, enjoying the closely knit relationship of family life, yet like any well adjusted family, engaging in frequent "community" activities with other unit "families" and also with the whole camp group. You will already be acquainted with your campers through your study of their records and will have planned for them in all-camp staff and smaller unit staff meetings. Quite a little thought has been given to just what you will do and how you will do it during the first few days after the campers arrive. These first contacts are of great importance in determining the kind of experience the summer will bring and also in establishing a desirable relationship between you and the campers.

Some camps do not assign campers to cabins until they arrive; others feel that there are advantages in making assignments ahead of time. When going into a new environment, youngsters have a greater sense of security when they know there is a definite bed in a definite room ready and waiting for them. Some camps even ask counselors to dash off a brief note to each camper. The few moments used for this pay off in big dividends; it assures the camper that a definite person is expecting him and has gone to this trouble to welcome him. Of course, this practice, as well as the various others we will be discussing, must be adapted to the age of the camper; different techniques are necessary when he is sixteen instead of six.

The Campers Arrive

If the campers arrive simultaneously by bus or other conveyance, the process of settling them into camp differs from when they arrive singly or in small groups. All staff are on hand, for many hands are needed to take care of a multitude of details. Where campers dribble in a few at a time, unit staff may remain in the quarters to act as hosts and see that no camper is left alone; program specialists and other staff act as guides to welcome the new arrivals and escort them to their quarters. To decide how to take care of the new-comers, imagine yourself a small child, leaving parents and familiar surroundings, perhaps for the first time. Obviously, the most important thing is to make the child feel welcome in his new home. Give him the feeling that you and his fellow camp-ers are friendly, congenial people with whom he can have all the FUN he antici-pated and more.

Introduce yourself to him, using your camp name. Learn what his name is, par-ticularly the one by which he wants to be known in camp, and start calling him by it right away. Nothing is so flattering to anyone as to show him that he matters to you enough to make his name stick with you. Incidentally, avoid letting him get "stuck" with an uncomplimentary name such as, "Horse Face," "Fatso," or "Dumbo" for even though he gives no outward sign, he inwardly resents it and his personality may be permanently scarred. Introduce campers to each other and to other staff members; provide prominent name tags to make remember-ing easy; speak to every camper you see, whether you know him or not.

Help him select his bed and make it, using the mitered corners he will continue to use daily and help him stow his things away so that he will feel all settled in for a long stay. Let him get into his comforta-ble camp clothes and show him where the latrine and washroom are. If he has an inventory of his possessions, check things off against it as he unpacks to avoid future trouble about something on the list which was never actually included; report dis-crepancies at the camp office immediately. See that each item is marked with his name.

In most camps, all campers' medicines and first aid equipment are collected and turned over to the nurse or doctor for it is preferred that anyone needing atten-tion, no matter how minor, be referred to the professional person in charge. Even counselors do not render any sort of treat-ment except in case of emergency. Collect

return trip tickets, money, and other val-uables and store them at the camp office.

Camps usually have all campers check in with the doctor or nurse and meet with the waterfront staff for classification and preliminary instruction in waterfront pro-cedures. Be sure that your group fits in with the established routine in a way most helpful to these busy staff members.

Think of ways to break the ice and start your campers off on a friendly basis; see that all are drawn into the conversa-tion, giving extra encouragement to any who seem shy. Request a timid camper to do some little task for you to make him feel needed or ask an old camper to take him to see the council ring, the water-front, the nature house; to feed the pet rabbits; or to fasten up the cabin sign, which has loosened since last year. As soon as most of your group has arrived, start the important process of weaving them into a congenial group by doing "fun" things together. Have the children pair off with buddies who do everything together; in this way each gets the feeling that he already has at least one good friend. Hold a brief, informal discussion in the cabin or under a shady tree and plan some of the things you are going to do that will be fun; ask the children for suggestions. Play a get-acquainted game; have a marshmallow roast; select a cabin name and yell; or go on a tour of the campsite. Plan something specific and mutually exciting to look forward to the next day or that afternoon, if there is still time, so that no one would even think of going home.

Before the first meal, go over the high

lights of dining room procedures and hold a little forum on good table manners and proper dining-room conduct. Children may come from homes where they have not learned these things and are easily embarrassed if they make a mistake. Stress the importance of cleanliness and neatness at all times, especially when in the dining room. Assign old campers to wait on tables and to carry on other duties until newcomers have a chance to get into the swing of things.

A child whose parents have not brought him to camp should write a card to go out on the first mail telling of his safe arrival. It is a friendly gesture on the counselor's part to write a short note to the parents within the first day or two, telling them your name and giving them some little personal contact with you.

At some time during the day, bring out some of the main points of camp life such as mail call and the main camp rules and discuss why they are necessary for the general welfare of the camp family. Campers don't resent reasonable rules when they understand the "why" of them so approach them from that angle. Ask the children to figure out the reasons for the rules; you'll be surprised at how well they do. It isn't hard for Tommy to see that if he doesn't wash his share of the dishes, someone else will have to work overtime; if he doesn't bring his canoe back on time, another who is waiting will be cheated; or that he will be too tired to enjoy the cook out planned for tomorrow if he doesn't go to sleep on time tonight. It is also good psychology to let the children help formulate some of the rules within their province. Don't try to tell them everything at once, just the most important; save details for later on.

The First Night

Some camps have an all-camp council ring or other mass meeting the first night so that the whole group can see themselves and have the entire staff introduced to them. The staff may put on a skit or entertain in some other way to further identify themselves as persons. In other camps, it is considered better practice to arrange for unit campfires on the theory that a camper should get well acquainted in his own small group before tackling the large one.

Arrange for an early bedtime; the newcomers will be more tired than they think from the emotional strain and excitement. The counselor may want to get teeth brushed, faces washed, pajamas on, and other evening rituals attended to before it gets dark. Then you can meet in the coziness of your cabin for a short evening program of discussion, quiet games or a good bed-time story before you accompany them on a last trip to the latrine. Explain the procedure for rising and breakfast in the morning and that, after "taps," there is to be no more noise or talking so that all can go to sleep promptly and be all rested and fresh for a day of fun tomorrow. Assure them that you'll be very near all night and that they are to call you if they need to go to the latrine or are *really* frightened; remember that city children may never have heard an owl before and even the small rustlings of wild things out hunting their suppers, a tree creaking in the wind or a twig falling on the roof may be very alarming to them in the unaccustomed stillness of the outdoor environment.

A TYPICAL DAILY SCHEDULE

Camp schedules are variable. Here is a sample one:

```
 7:00  Reveille
 7:30  Breakfast
 8:00  Clean up cabins and camp grounds
 9:00  Activities
11:15  Recreational swimming
12:00  Dinner
 1:15  Rest Hour
 2:15  Activities
 4:15  Recreational swimming
 5:45  Supper
 6:45  Evening activities (all-camp, unit, or cabin)
 8:45  Cabin call. Get ready for bed
 9:00  Taps (may be later for older campers)
```

The First Few Days

What happens during the first few days is important for first impressions are lasting. Homesickness is prone to raise its ugly head and one of the best ways to forestall it is to keep individuals busy every minute; plan exciting things for the future so that there is something constantly in the wind to look forward to. Stick with the children closely the first few days and work hard at welding them together in a feeling of "oneness" for you are laying the foundation for the success of the whole season.

Seize on opportunities for informal chats, individually, in small groups, or as a whole group so that all of you become old friends and can act perfectly natural with each other. Try especially hard to draw in the "loners" and spot the mischief makers and misfits.

Don't try to tell them too much at once but gradually introduce camp "kapers" (camper duties) and work out a system for keeping cabins and unit quarters neat and clean as well as doing a share toward the upkeep of the whole camp. Information is most readily absorbed when they meet a situation where it is needed. Camp traditions and programs, special events, camp government and how it works, waterfront procedures, fire drill, safety and health practices, sick call, and such pertinent matters will all come in for their share of attention as the days pass by.

One of the first things campers will want to do is get settled and make their living quarters comfortable and attractive. By all means let them help in planning what is to be done so that the work becomes a fascinating self-propelled activity to keep them busy and happy for hours. You may strip the cabin quite bare to provide the pleasure of furnishing it with a bedside table or dresser made from crates, lashed wooden clothes pegs and rustic clothes hangers, plaques to decorate the wall, and so forth. The unit grounds should come in for attention, too; the children can remove such hazards as glass, pieces of tin and roots that might trip someone. Trash cans can be painted in bright colors so people won't miss them and clutter up the grounds. Stones make a decorative border for paths, and many other "improvements" will be suggested once they put their thinking caps on.

Before long, you'll want to plan a menu and program for a cook out and if *you* have chosen the spot well, the children will soon notice how perfect it would be for a unit outpost camp and, this, interspersed with their many other camp activities, will happily solve your program problem for some time to come.

CAMP HOUSEKEEPING

Since one of camping's principal objectives is to teach a camper self-reliance, he must learn to keep his own personal belongings in trim. "A place for everything and everything in its place" must be the order of each and every day; since many campers have learned virtually nothing of housekeeping practices at home, you will need to demonstrate and give specific help with correct techniques. Keep a watchful eye until proper housekeeping becomes routine.

Right after breakfast, the entire cabin should straighten possessions and help tidy the abode and adjacent grounds. They will probably also share in putting the unit and whole camp back in order. Check lists should be made for each duty so that each group will know just what is expected of it. The attitude of the counselor is important here, for, if you enjoy work and show it by pitching in with a will, your campers will follow suit and will soon learn how nice it is to live in a clean, orderly cabin. Try to be especially happy and cheerful as you go about your tasks and see how time flies when the whole group enters into singing old favorites or learning a new song. Discourage bickering and grumbling, and encourage banter and light hearted chatter. No job is irksome if you're having fun while you do it.

On rainy mornings, make up beds right away to keep out dampness. On sunny days, turn back or hang out sheets and blankets to air, bringing them in before five o'clock to avoid evening dampness. Air and turn mattresses and put on fresh linen each week, making up beds with square, hospital-style corners.

Each person should hang or fold his clothing neatly away, tidy his personal effects, and collect his soiled clothing in a bag, ready to send to the laundry. Plying a needle prevents a rip from becoming a tear, and a button sewed on now may prevent later embarrassment or inconvenience. Most camps have tent or cabin inspection one or more times a day, at varying times and unannounced. This assures keeping the cabin orderly rather than just tidying up for inspection. Reward a cabin or unit with some trifling award such as a brightly colored cardboard broom or mop to be displayed all day when they have earned it. Group pressure will soon bring backsliders into line.

Toilet articles and towels are never borrowed and other borrowing is discouraged and never without the express permission of the owner; "borrowing" isn't the correct name for such practice.

In many camps, campers help with various chores, sometimes in an effort to cut down expense and thus make it cheaper for them to attend camp, and always to create in them an appreciation for the dignity and respectability of work. Such duties may include keeping unit showers, latrines, cabins, unit houses, and main lodge in order, collecting and disposing of trash, helping prepare vegetables and fruit, setting tables, waiting on tables, and washing dishes. Counselors should help so that the work is done thoroughly and should cooperate in devising ways to do it more quickly and efficiently.

Stress the importance of placing all waste in conveniently located receptacles and point out how ludicrous it is to throw trash on the ground today where they or a fellow camper who is serving as grounds keeper must pick it up tomorrow.

Let campers help you work out a rotating kapers (duties) chart, using some such scheme as shown below.

Another way to decide who will do kapers is to draw names out of a hat. A little thought will help you find some interesting way to turn these into exciting adventures instead of dreaded chores.

The most careful plan for sanitizing dishes can be totally lost by improper table setting. See that hands are washed clean with soap and water on the way to set tables and that they do not touch parts of the dishes that will contact food or a camper's mouth (edges of glasses and cups, "business ends" of forks, spoons, knives, and the like).

	Mary	Helen	Jean	Sarah	Peggy	Joan	Mary
Clean-up squad—sweep cabin floor...............	Su	M	Tu	W	Th	F	S
Woodsmen—clean out ashes in fireplace, bring in wood	M	T	W	Th	F	S	Su
Table setters—set tables and help prepare vegetables.	Tu	W	Th	F	S	Su	M
Hoppers—wait on and clear tables..............	W	Th	F	S	Su	M	Tu
Ground keepers—clean up campsite.............	Th	F	S	Su	M	Tu	W
Kitchen police—help do dishes..................	F	S	Su	M	Tu	W	Th
Unit duty—help at the Unit house...............	S	Su	M	Tu	W	Th	F

Dish Washing

Campers often wash their dishes, the people at each table being responsible for their own. Plenty of lively singing and joking can make dishwashing fun instead of a nuisance. Rotate the several duties as in a kapers' chart, or let the campers draw lots each time.

NO DISHWASHER *!!!*
OH, NO *!!!!*

Detail one counselor to see that water is heating, ready for use as soon as the meal is over; dishes wash much more easily where there is no time for food to dry on them. A counselor should handle all hot water; campers are too likely to scald themselves or someone near. Here is a suggested list of assignments:

1. First scraper—uses rubber scraper to remove food from dishes.
2. Polisher—supplements efforts of first scraper, using paper napkins; separates dishes into piles of plates, cups, etc., for washing.
3. Dish washer—washes dishes and wipes off tables.
4. Rinser—arranges dishes in long-handled, wire dish-drains or net bags with trays to catch excess water and carries them to the sterilizer.
5. Sterilizer (a counselor)—lowers dishes, still in container, into boiling water (170° to 180° F.) for one to two minutes or into warm water with sanitizing agent added.
6. Sweeper—cleans around tables after dishes are covered or put away.

Hot, soapy water is best for the washing, which should take place in the following order: glassware, silver, dishes and, finally, pots and pans. Have enough hot water available to replace the dishwater as it becomes greasy or cold. It is more sanitary to immerse dishes in scalding water and let them air-dry as they stand in the racks, than to use dish cloths to dry them, with the exception of silverware and pots and pans which might rust.

Ride herd on the job to see that dishes are really clean. Wash towels and dish-cloths used on dishes after each use and boil them at least once a day.

OTHER CAMP ROUTINES

Cleanliness

Being at camp is no excuse for disregarding personal cleanliness for various skin disturbances and infections can be traced directly to this. A swim does not substitute for a daily or at least three times weekly warm soap bath, which can be taken from a wash pan if no other facilities are available. Hair should be washed at least every week or two, with counselor help if necessary. See that campers use fresh towels and wash cloths as needed and, of course, they never use anyone else's. Hang towels and wash cloths out to air and dry after use. Make a daily inspection for cleanliness, scanning particularly the ears, elbows and neck.

One of civilization's unwritten laws is that hands must be washed before meals and after going to the toilet. See that teeth are brushed in the morning and again before retiring; toothbrushes should be hung in an airy place to dry.

Urge girls with long fingernails or toenails to clip them for they are inappropriate for camp life. They catch on everything; they collect dirt; they may scratch the camper or others; and eventually they get jaggedly broken off anyway. Everyone's fingernails should be inspected for proper trimming and cleanliness.

See that your campers put on fresh clothing from the inside out and that soiled clothing is stored properly, ready for periodic laundering. If soiled garments are sent to a laundry, see that the camper gathers his into an appropriate bag, lists it, and deposits it at the appointed place on time. Each item must be marked with his name.

Cabins, units or whole camps often enjoy a special clean-up day when everyone washes his clothes, helps to clean up the cabin and grounds, and then finishes off with a shampoo and hot bath for himself.

WASHING CLOTHING. It isn't too hard to wash clothes by hand and it becomes a necessity on a trip. Soak the clothes for thirty minutes in a bucketful of hot soapy water and then douse them up and down until the water has gone through them several times or, better still, use a rubber plunger on them. Scrub especially soiled parts with a brush and extra soap. Rinse thoroughly and hang them out to dry on a rope hung between two trees or on bushes or branches. If you are in a hurry for them to dry, wring them out just as dry as you can and turn them over every half hour or so.

Clothing

Campers should wear clothing appropriate to the weather and the activity. Since mornings and evenings are usually cool, extra clothing is needed then. Shoes should be worn at all times, and campers should be completely "waterproofed" when venturing out on rainy days.

Clothing should be hung up or neatly folded and kept in the proper place; any damp items such as bathing suits should be hung out on a line to dry before ever bringing them into living quarters.

Trading or selling personal possessions is banned, for parents often fail to share in the enthusiasm of the campers for the "bargains" they have made.

HEALTH AND SAFETY

One of a counselor's important responsibilities will be to cooperate with the health staff in protecting and furthering the health of campers, for his close contact with a group is a particularly advantageous position for helping in this respect.

A set of scales was once considered the best yardstick for measuring the benefits of camping; a gain in weight was assumed to represent a corresponding gain in health. We now know this to be in error, for any gain beyond normal for a growing child would benefit only the underweight. For the average child, it indicates merely a superabundance of sweets and starches, adding healthful weight to none and burdening the already overweight with additional pounds.

Another far too prevalent idea was that, in order to be and look like a real camper, one must get as sunburned and weather beaten as possible and prove his toughness by scorning attention to such minor (?) details as scratches, blisters and mosquito bites. Early campers displayed their scratched, flea-bitten appearance with pride, for, to their warped reasoning, these scars of battle were evidence that they had been "roughing it" and could take it.

During precamp training the counselor will have learned the health set-up of the camp. Most camps have one or two nurses on duty and a physician in residence or on call. The headquarters of the health department is in the infirmary or health lodge, where there is space to take care of campers needing extra food, rest or special treatment.

Daily Care

Each morning, while campers are dressing, eating breakfast or doing cabin clean-up, scan them for signs of ailment or injury. Note such symptoms as headache, sore throat, indigestion, sneezing, cough, fever (as indicated by a hot, flushed skin), pimples, skin rashes, swell-ings, cuts or other irritations, and signs of fatigue such as listlessness, irritability, excitable talking, undue noisiness, loss of weight, or paleness. Refer a suspect to the nurse immediately, escorting him there if necessary, for campers sometimes shy away from the infirmary lest they be banned from swimming or other favorite activity. Show him the wisdom of taking a few moments now to forestall what might develop into an illness of days or even weeks if neglected. Some camps require counselors to turn in health reports each morning so that the nurse can note and call in any campers needing further attention.

When signs of fatigue are rather widespread in a group, it indicates an overstrenuousness of the whole tempo of life, and a light schedule is advisable for a few days with extra time provided for rest and sleep. Prevent fatigue by alternating quiet and active pursuits, seeing that competition is not carried to the point of overstimulation, and insisting on proper observance of hours for rest and sleep.

Sunburn can be serious as well as a painful thing. Teach campers to acquire their deep chocolate-brown gradually using a good sun tan lotion but, most of all, working up to exposure gradually with ten to fifteen minutes the first day and a few more minutes added daily. Set a good example by not going out to fry yourself once-over lightly in one concentrated dose. Sun bathers should wear sun glasses or cover their eyes with a towel.

If you are in tick-infested country, everyone, including yourself, should be inspected twice a day. The Public Health Service says there is little chance of being infected with Rocky Mountain Spotted fever if virulent ticks are removed within four to six hours; don't try to pull them loose or crush them in your fingers but touch a lighted match or heated wire to them and they'll back out right away.

Campers who are tired should forego swimming and no one should go in the water immediately after eating. They should wear shoes and robes of some sort both to and from the swimming area and should not loiter about in wet suits.

See that extra clothing is worn on cool mornings and evenings. Your attitude toward health should be one of proper consideration without becoming over-solicitous or fussy.

Friends in the Infirmary

Most camps send a camper home or to the hospital if his illness is likely to last more than a few days or if it is of a serious nature. However, minor illnesses may detain him in the infirmary for what may seem like wearisome hours. Thoughtful friends can make the time pass faster by such little remembrances as a round-robin letter, a diary or account of what they are doing, a home-grown poem, a handmade gift from the arts and crafts shop (particularly one with his name on it), or a serenade. A visit during visiting hours is welcome if the nurse permits it; if not, just waving to him through the window helps. With the approval of the nurse, keep him supplied with puzzles, a radio, light reading matter or come in and tell or read him a story. If he's able, he'll enjoy working on a crafts project, his scrapbook, making favors for a group party, or labels for the nature trail. Keep him reminded that all of you miss him and are anxious to have him back again.

DINING ROOM PROCEDURES

Counselors and campers must arrive spic and span and on time for meals. Singing helps pass the time while waiting. Having a prearranged seating plan cuts down pushing and crowding to get favored places, and in some camps, campers sit with their regular counselors; in others they rotate to enlarge their circle of acquaintance. Campers stand quietly behind their benches until counselors seat themselves at the head and foot of the table. Open the meal with a grace, either sung, said in unison, said by one individ-

ual, or silently. Counselors serve as hosts, serving the plates family style.

Camps pride themselves on their carefully planned and well-cooked menus, but it is of little avail if campers are permitted to pick and choose what they eat. Food allergies must be allowed for, but you should ascertain from the health staff that they are genuine and not just a way to avoid eating foods for which the camper has a real or imagined dislike. Serve each plate, allowing individuals to ask for only small portions of things they do not care for; then insist that each cleans up his plate. Making a game of eating by admitting those who clean their plates into a "Jack Spratt Club" accomplishes this painlessly and many campers learn to like foods they never would have eaten otherwise. Seconds and even thirds are available for those who wish them, but save portions for the slower eaters so there is no incentive to gulp down the first serving as rapidly as possible.

A crowd of girls usually includes a few "reducers," for as Mr. Franklin P. Jones has said, "Women are never satisfied. They are trying either to put on weight, take it off, or rearrange it." Overweight campers may be encouraged to cut down *sensibly* on their intake of fattening foods; the majority of reducers, however, should be discouraged in their attempts, for camp life is so strenuous that large quantities of energy-yielding foods are needed. The problem may sometimes be handled best by a group study of dietetics including the values of a varied and well-balanced diet. When youngsters understand the importance of each item, they usually become quite cooperative about their eating. Some camps maintain special diet tables for those with idiosyncrasies or those who need to gain or lose weight.

The dining room atmosphere should be one of easy relaxation, with quiet, though sprightly, conversation and no pushing, reaching, loud laughter or talking. Try to bring everyone into the conversation and do not let anyone monopolize it. No one begins to eat until all have been served and the host has taken his first bite. Talking to those at another table is always in poor taste, and no one except "hoppers" or those with urgent reasons who have been excused by the head may leave the table until all have finished. Obviously, nothing should be scheduled immediately after the meal, lest it cause campers to race to get through in time for it.

Observe all the precepts of good table manners, such as talking only when the mouth is empty, breaking bread into quarters and buttering only one portion at a time, cutting meat a piece at a time, proper handling of knife and fork, and the like. Comments about the food and griping or bickering of any sort are not conducive to good digestion and are strictly off limits. Do not embarrass a camper who has violated a rule of etiquette by making a public scene; take it up with him privately later; his misdemeanor is more likely to be due to lack of ease, desire for attention, or just not realizing the implications than to a desire to misbehave. Keep your eye on the head table and see that campers remain silent for announcements. When through eating, campers pass their dishes up to the head who scrapes them and stacks them neatly. He then gives a signal to the "hoppers" to clear the table.

Singing songs, especially those requiring movements, distracts the slower eaters and retards clearing tables, washing dishes, and putting the food away. Many camps follow the practice of having the singing led by a stipulated song leader after everyone has finished eating.

Eating Between Meals

Camp meals are planned to include enough sweets to satisfy normal needs, and campers are therefore not encouraged to supplement them with soft drinks, candy and other goodies, which may greatly counteract the good effects of the carefully planned diet. If permitted at all, set a limit on the daily amount of such items, and rigidly enforce it.

Despite requests to the contrary, many parents seemingly must demonstrate their love by sending their children "gooey" knickknacks from home. Camps sometimes solve the problem by warning parents before camp that such food will be returned unless enough is sent to substitute for a regular dessert for the whole cabin group. Others simply save the individual packages until enough have accumulated to make a treat for all. Parents may be appeased by suggesting that they send their child fruit, a piece of camp equipment, or things other than food as a token of their affection. Campers readily understand the reasons for not keeping or eating food around living quarters when you point out to them the ants, flies, mice and other unwelcome guests that will be attracted by the crumbs.

I'LL NEVER MAKE IT TOMORROW

REST AND SLEEP

Rest Hour

As Sancho Panza said, "God Bless the man who first invented sleep," and busy camp life makes campers and counselors breathe a sigh of thankfulness for the rest hour which usually comes right after lunch to rejuvenate them for the remainder of the day. It is a siesta when everyone either sleeps or engages in some quiet activity so that others may sleep. There is no reason why either counselors or campers should object for it is permissible to read, write letters, mend, or go out under a tree to tell stories, play quiet games or work on a craft project. Stay with your campers to see that they observe this period and set an example by observing it properly yourself for you need to recharge your own batteries. Your camp may choose an individual name for the rest hour, such as siesta or FOB (Feet On Bed and Flat on Back).*

Sleep

Camp life is so strenuous that only those who get plenty of sleep can keep up and enjoy it to the fullest. Administering to this need constitutes one of your main responsibilities. The following amounts of sleep (in addition to the one-hour rest period) are recommended:

Ages	Hours of Sleep
6–7	11
9–11	10½
12–14	10
15–17	9
Staff	8

* Smith, Billie F.: *How 40 Camps Handle Rest Hour.* C.M., Dec., 1952.

Campers do not eat in cabins??

Children, like adults, differ in their reactions to the excitement and "busy-ness" of camp life, so some may need rest over and above this amount.

As previously mentioned, a common mistake has been to try to crowd too many activities and periods of excitement into the camp day. This is especially true as the last weeks of camp draw near and each counselor grows intent on squeezing some highlight of his particular activity into a last "round-up" of water carnivals, arts and crafts exhibits, horse shows, and what not. The wise camp tries to adopt the saner practice of spreading these special events throughout the entire summer so that campers can leave camp rested and healthy instead of completely frazzled out.

Children sleep better when healthily fatigued, but moderation is advisable in all things, and too much excitement and tiredness make sleep fitful and restless.

Taps

The time just before taps is usually one of the choice periods of the day. Everyone washes, brushes his teeth and makes his final trip to the latrine so that there are a few moments left for group planning, evening devotions, discussion, inactive games, a quiet bedtime story, star gazing, singing or listening to soft music before "lights out." Since it isn't fair to expect campers to change from one mood to another too suddenly, no roughhouse, horseplay, exciting adventure or ghost stories are permissible.

As with all rules, you must be firm about enforcing the time for lights out and quiet. Set the standard from the first night in camp. Do not dash out of the cabin at breakneck speed the instant the last camper hits the bed, but wander leisurely about with a special "goodnight" for each, seeing that he is tucked in and using blanket pins for very small tots who tend to squirm about and expose various odds and ends of their anatomy. Counselors usually take turns on cabin duty in the unit so that some may get away for a little free time. When it is your turn to be on duty, stay there, for if you make a practice of leaving as soon as you think the campers are asleep, they'll play possum until you are gone and then pandemonium will break loose. Your campers need assurance that you are near, ready to help if they become frightened or need you; this is especially important during a thunder or lightning storm. Night raids on other cabins and impromptu moonlight excursions are definitely out; night trips to the latrine should be quick and quiet, for there must be no disturbance of any kind until reveille.

Reveille

The rising signal should sound long enough before breakfast to allow ample time for a last stretch, washroom procedures and putting bedding outside or turning it down to air. When the rising signal sounds, you should be the first out of bed. See that all arise promptly. This will be no trick at all during the first few days in camp for some campers will be so excited they'll wake at the crack of dawn and will need to be restrained so others can sleep. If you're going out extra early for a bird walk, don't wake the whole camp as you go by.

You may need to help younger campers manipulate buttons and hairbrushes, but should encourage them to do it themselves as soon as they can. A morning dip may be permitted, but it should certainly not be required for many people react unfavorably to cold water and exercise so soon after rising. For the same reason, a compulsory "daily dozen" before breakfast is frowned upon.

OTHER DETAILS

Visitors' Day

Visitors are a more or less disturbing factor to the smooth-running routine of camp, so that there are usually specified hours and days when they are welcomed. Inform your own prospective guests of the exact hours when you will be available to visit with them.

Too frequent visits from a camper's parents are prone to take his attention from camp activities and often tend to make him homesick; they also defeat the important objective of emancipating him from his possibly too doting or domineering parents. Therefore, most camps encourage only a minimum of them.

When visiting day arrives, everything from the camp grounds down to Joe's elbows must be looking their best. Campers must be neat and clean and on hand to greet their parents and show off the camp. You, yourself, are a host and must be cordial, friendly and helpful to all and available for a few moments' conversation with the parents of each of your particular campers. Put your best foot forward, for parents will be much happier if favorably impressed by their child's counselor. When talking to them, remember that you have one thing in common—the welfare of the camper. Avoid gushing and insincere praise, for parents are fully aware that their children fall far short of being angels. Comment casually on good points or signs of improvement you have noticed, but never let yourself be drawn into severe unfavorable comment. If parents persist in trying to engage you in

such a discussion, refer them to the camp director or head counselor.

This is a time for campers, too, to learn to be good hosts or hostesses. Encourage them to spare a few moments to be gracious to the parents and guests of other campers as well as to their own.

Avoid showing favoritism and share your time with all the parents. Follow camp policy in regard to accepting money or expensive gifts from parents.

Records and Reports

You will doubtless be asked to keep various records concerning campers, including those mentioned early in the chapter. Although these often seem like odious chores and a waste of time, in reality, they usually take only a few moments if you keep up with them. They are very important since they serve several purposes. They provide the only means for the busy director and head counselor to really get an accurate picture of what is happening all over camp; they also furnish a written record of what occurred and when in case any question arises about it later. Records help summarize your efforts and evaluate your work. Camps vary a good bit in the records they request but most require that accurate health records be kept and usually that you keep some sort of "diary" concerning your program. Accounts of individual campers and their activities, reactions, growths, and problems are also requested. These often build up a picture of the camper, which helps you understand his needs and decide how to meet them. They also serve as a basis for reports to parents or to the sponsoring agency at the end of the season. Do them completely and thoroughly. In addition, you will probably be asked to turn in an inventory and recommendations for next year at the end of the season.

Time Off

All camps give counselors some time

off—usually an hour or two each day, and a longer period each week or two weeks. You probably learned the particulars of this when you signed your contract. This interlude can and should be of great benefit to both you and the camp. Dealing in such intimacy with many personalities exacts a severe toll in nervous and emotional energy and causes patience to grow short, emotions to boil over at trifles, and the sense of humor to forsake its owner completely. Counselors are sometimes unaware of this gradual accumulation of emotional and nervous fatigue and become so attached to their jobs as to be loathe to leave them, even when given time off. Such zealous overdevotion to duty is a sad mistake and sooner or later will produce a dull, cross, bearish person who cannot possibly do his job effectively.

It is important for you to get your mind off camp and everything pertaining to it. You may write letters, make fudge, do your laundry or mending, or go off with a companion or two to roller skate, dance, attend the movies, or take a canoe trip; you may engage in any other favorite pastime which will temporarily erase camp from your mind. When out in public you must remember that you represent your camp and must conduct yourself so that your actions reflect creditably upon it.

Many small towns do not regard shorts favorably and so it is better to wear ordinary street clothes, although slacks are usually acceptable for women counselors. Drinking in public, driving recklessly and any sort of boisterous or socially unacceptable conduct are in very poor taste. Treat the citizens of the town courteously and fairly, in fact, the same way you expect them to treat you.

Permission to use camp equipment may be arranged for, and a good workout on the tennis courts or a boat trip will relax those kinks in your brain and emotions. Use all the time you have, but do not start getting ready to leave several hours ahead of time, return late, or spend the day after your return in recuperating and talking about the big time you had.

Personal Habits

Most camps request that counselors who smoke do so at designated times and in designated places, never in front of campers. Such requests are not based on moral issues but rather upon the fire hazard created by indiscriminate smoking in rural areas with only simple fire-fighting equipment. The use of intoxicants is prohibited on the campsite and often on time off, for even parents who themselves indulge are likely to object to placing their children in charge of counselors who do.

Loyalty

You owe loyalty first, last and always to your camp and camp director. You have chosen this camp above all others because it seems most nearly to fit your objectives and ideals, but, as in any situation, you will find things unpleasant to you. When this occurs, think it over a few days without mentioning your feeling to anyone, and you will likely eventually see the reason for the situation as camp life unfolds. If not, don't grouse about it or talk to others who are as unable as you to interpret things or do anything about them. If your problem still looms as important, go to someone who can give you the right answer, even the director himself if necessary. If you still do not approve of the situation and your dissatisfaction is so great that you cannot adjust yourself happily, consider asking for a release, for both you and the camp will be better off if you part company. Never under any circumstances criticize to outsiders or other counselors and, of course, never before campers. Even when started as good-natured banter, griping will sooner or later prove ruinous to camp morale and also reflect personally on you, the griper. You should bear in mind the story of the man who was entrusted with a secret and, thinking to burst wide open if he did not tell it, dug a hole in the ground and whispered the secret into it. When the grass grew on the spot, the wind blowing through it broadcast his secret abroad. So it is with gossip and criticism.

Note Taking

Carry your camp notebook and pencil as regularly as you wear your shoes, for the worst lead pencil in the world is better than a good memory and many a conscientious, well-meaning counselor has failed because he "forgot." Add to your notebook constantly, jotting down games, program material, that new recipe for clam chowder, the sure way to keep Jackie's shoestrings from coming undone, and refresher notes about the needs, interests, accomplishments and signs of improvement on the part of your campers. You should drop in at the camp library now and then for new ideas or ways of doing things.

ADDITIONAL READINGS

Benson, Reuel A., and Goldberg, Jacob A.: *The Camp Counselor.*
Berg, B. Robert: *Psychology in Children's Camping.*
Burns, Gerald: *Program of the Modern Camp.*
Camp Administrative Forms and Suggested Procedures in the Area of Personnel. ACA, 1956, 30 pp., 35¢.
Dimock, Hedley S.: *Administration of the Modern Camp.*
Dimock, Hedley S., and Statten, Taylor: *Talks to Counselors.*
Doty, Richard S.: *The Character Dimension of Camping.* Assn. Press, 1960, 192 pp., $4.75.
Goodrich, Lois: *Decentralized Camping.*
Hammett, Catherine T., and Musselman, Virginia: *The Camp Program Book.*
Hood, Mary V.: *Outdoor Hazards, Real and Fancied.*
Irwin, Frank L.: *The Theory of Camping—An Introduction to Camping in Education.*
Joy, Barbara Ellen: *Camping.*
Joy, Barbara Ellen: *It's Fair To Expect.* Camp Publications, #15, 2 pp., 25¢, or Camping Magazine, Feb., 1949.
Joy, Barbara Ellen: *Professional Relationships in Camp.* Camp Publications, #6.
Joy, Barbara Ellen: *Suggestions for Good Table Practice and Dining Porch Procedures.* Camp Publications, #8, 6 pp., 35¢.
Joy, Barbara Ellen: *Suggestions for Responsibilities of Counselors for Care of Campers.* Camp Publications, #9, 6 pp., 35¢.
Ledlie, John A., and Holbein, F. W.: *Camp Counselor's Manual.*
Ott, Elmer F.: *So You Want To Be a Camp Counselor.*
Raymer, Mrs. Ralph H.: *The Counselor's Job at Camp.* Ontario Camping Assn., 5 pp.
Tobitt, Janet E.: *Program in Girl Scout Camping.*
Webb, Kenneth B., Editor: *Light from a Thousand Campfires.*
Wentzel, Fred D., and Schlingman, Edward L.: *The Counselor's Job.* Assn. Press, 61 pp., 75¢. (church camp)

MAGAZINE ARTICLES

Gold, Martin: *What Do We Want in Leadership.* C.M., Nov., 1958.
Hyman, Milton: *Points to Consider in Arranging Cabin Groups.* C.M., Apr., 1958.
Lane, Howard A.: *Your Role in Camper Development.* C.M., Mar., 1956.
Smith, Billie F.: *How 40 Camps Handle Rest Hour.* C.M., Dec., 1952.
Yawger, Richard: *What Makes Good Camp Staff Morale.* C.M., May, 1953.

Health and Safety

American Red Cross, First Aid Text Book. A.R.C., or local chapter, 75¢.
First Aid. Boy Scouts, #3238, 25¢.
Health, Safety and Sanitation, Woods Safety Education. Maine Dept. of Educ. and Maine Dept. of Inland Fisheries and Game, Augusta, Maine, 1956, 43 pp.
Holden, John L.: *The Canoe Cruiser's Handbook.*
Joy, Barbara Ellen: *Health and Safety in Organized Camps.* Camp Publications, #3, 7 pp., 35¢.
Joy, Barbara Ellen: *Some Thoughts on Camp Health.* Camp Publications, #14, 2 pp., 15¢.
Live for Tomorrow. Boy Scouts, 39 pp., 30¢.
Safety. Boy Scouts, #3347, 25¢.
Safety-Wise. Girl Scouts, #19–502, 82 pp., 20¢.
The Camp Nurse. ACA., 1956, 25 pp., 50¢.

MAGAZINE ARTICLES

Carlson, Agnes M.: *Your Dishes—Are they Washed Really Clean?* C.M., Nov., 1950.
Dirks, Ruth Upton, R.N.: *Your Camp Nurse on Duty.* C.M., Feb., 1953.
Ebbs, J. H., M.D.: *Fatigue—A Major Health Problem in Camps.* C.M., Mar., 1955, or Ontario Camping Assn., 3 pp.
Hudson, Henry W., Jr.: *Plan for a Healthy Camp.* C.M., Dec., 1951.
Payne, Elizabeth C., R.N.: *The Important Role of the Camp Nurse.* C.M., Jan., 1952.
Scott, Ruth Boyer: *What Your Camp Nurse Will Want to Know.* C.M., Dec., 1953.
What's Your Health and Safety I.Q.? C.M., Nov., 1954.

WHAT IS A CAMPER

"Immediately following that period known as school, an incredible creature known as a camper appears on the scene.

A camper is a rare combination of natural freshness, alarming frankness, unpredictable thoughts and actions, tangled hair, boisterous belly laughs, and unbelievable sincerity and enthusiasm.

Campers are found everywhere—in cabins, lagging behind on the trail, smoking in the latrine, hanging by their feet in a tree house, discussing problems with their counselor on a bench, on the bottom of the swimming pool, squeezing furry animal necks, running away from camp, and, on hot, humid days, hanging affectionately on their counselor.

A camper is innocence with mud on his face, a ball of enthusiasm in T-shirt and jeans, a sun-tanned personality with problems.

Just so you remember him every minute of the day, he sings in a high-pitched voice, makes noises like the mating call of a whip-poor-will, flaps his wings in hawk-like fashion, throws a temper tantrum occasionally, playfully pushes his best friend over the stump in front of the dining hall, gets himself stung by angry wasps, or becomes an entanglement of mixed emotions which finds relief in a fist fight or crying jag.

He likes animals of any size, shape or description, to chew two sticks of bubble gum at a time, to be awakened by the latest hit record, to be captain of the team, to get dressed up like an Indian or pirate at any time, and to hear his name at mail call.

He dislikes rest hour, carrying his bedroll, cold showers, getting up in the morning, seeing his counselor go on leave, and letting his pet frog go at the end of the camp period.

Nobody can spend as much time eating, exploring the creek bed, reading comic books, arguing over who's kicking whom at the table, ordering supplies at the camp store, or just sitting around a campfire having a glorious time dreamily singing favorite camp songs.

Nobody can be so illogical at so many times yet so warm and grateful the next minute. Nobody can cry so conveniently and become equally as effervescent when the occasion demands.

A camper is a magical creature, possessing two arms, two legs, a head and torso, all bursting with the breath of life, all anxious to explore the camp and counselor, most of which is attempted the first day of camp.

And when the last note of Taps sounds and he's tucked securely under the covers and looking up at you wistfully, there's nothing in the world like the feeling of knowing that this camper is a real friend who wants your guidance and who has spent a truly wonderful day with you."

From an article by Louis C. Kuehner, SHERWOOD FOREST CAMPING SERVICE, in Camping Magazine, June, 1957.

6

The Counselor Must Understand People

No one really understands humans except a dog and a sophomore psychology major. MARY L. NORTHWAY

Without halting, without rest,
Lifting better up to best;
Planting seeds of knowledge pure,
Through earth to ripen, through
*   heaven endure.* EMERSON

OBJECTIVES AND HOW TO OBTAIN THEM

FOR ANYONE to be happy in this world, he must live in harmony with his associates. The person who says he doesn't care what people think of him or whether they like him or not is either an odd ball or, ninety-nine times out of a hundred, is playing sour grapes and covering up a deep disappointment and sense of frustration by pretending scorn for what he can't get. This certainly applies to your own sense of well being as a counselor, as we have pointed out, and in addition, you may be sure that you can achieve little worth-while in influencing campers unless you first gain their respect, admiration and friendly cooperation. There are three possible camp facets with which to touch a camper and bring about desirable changes in him. These are the camp environment or facilities, the camp program or what is done in camp, and the camp personnel. The latter is by far the most important of the three for, not only do camp staff affect campers by their words and deeds but the facilities and program contribute only as they are manipulated by people who understand campers and their needs and how to meet these needs. Indeed, without such an awareness, these factors may be misused and have decidedly undesirable effects. For instance, a camp which offers overelaborate furnishings and services and has someone to perform all disagreeable tasks for campers will be turning out helpless, dependent little snobs instead of independent, self-

(Joy and Camp.)

reliant Americans. A camp which motivates its program wholly by elaborate awards, public acclamation, and publicity in the home-town paper may be teaching the participants that winning is the important thing, no matter at what cost or by what means, and that those who "fight the good fight" yet fall by the wayside are to be brushed aside as insignificant also-rans. Thus you must, first of all, be fully aware of what you are trying to accomplish and these objectives must be definite, concrete and specific. It avails little to merely give lip service to a group of high sounding platitudes unless you can spot them individually as good and bad ways of living when met face-to-face in the lives of campers. Secondly, you must understand campers and how to produce desirable changes in their actions and attitudes.

Influencing Others

Let us assume, now, that you have a quite definite mental picture of what you want to accomplish and proceed to consider how you can bring it to fruition. There are just two ways to get another person to do what you want him to. One is to force him to do it by ordering him, or by threatening to punish him, or withholding something he wants such as his dessert, his period in swimming, or his free time if he dosen't do it. Though any of the above may produce the desired action, no lasting improvements are likely, for, as soon as the force is removed, he will probably revert to his former ways or even show his resentment by acting worse than before. He has also learned to dislike authority, and will rebel, inwardly now perhaps but outwardly later on as his bitterness builds up and he feels old enough or big enough to dare it. He may eventually come to hate the act since it is associated with the unpleasantness of the whole procedure.

Therefore, let us turn to the other and better way, which is to get him to act as we wish because he wants to do so. When you stop to think of it, everything we do is in answer to some want. We go to bed because we want to rest; we eat because we want the taste of food or to allay hunger pangs; we practice long hours on the basketball court because we want the school letter and social prestige of playing on the team. We must, therefore, dispel the idea that we can get anyone to do something because *we* want him to, for he couldn't care less; like everyone else, he is primarily interested in what *he* wants. Let us own up to the unpleasant fact that everyone is much more interested in himself than in anyone else. We can successfully bring about lasting changes in his conduct only by showing him that the new way will satisfy one of *his* wants. Suppose he very much desires to pass his endurance tests in swimming so that he can qualify to go on a canoe trip. He'll eat his oatmeal manfully and ask for more and be the first one in his bunk and asleep when he once sees that good eating habits and rest are the only true paths to swimming endurance. How much better the results and the spirit than when you nag at him and try to force him to do it; now, he'll likely get angry at you if you try to prevent him from doing it. Suppose your cabin group dawdles and finds excuses for putting off cabin clean-up after breakfast. Can you imagine the whirlwind of activity

set loose if a choice activity is dandled, like sugar before a horse, for the first cabin group through (with requirements for thoroughness, of course)? This illustrates a positive rather than negative approach to a problem and embodies a very important principle of getting people of any age to do what "is good for them." It really works but of course the technique must be well disguised and used with skill. People heartily dislike the feeling that others are manipulating them. Let us repeat this important point: *get people to do what you want them to by leading them to see that doing so will satisfy one of their wants!* Now, let us consider what people want.

The Fundamental Wishes

Though it is quite obvious that people are different, nevertheless they are also alike in many ways, among them the five desires or wishes which are present in every normal person. Though these vary in intensity, they are there and so strong and demanding that we can understand almost anything a person does when we picture it as an attempt to satisfy one of these desires. As we shall see, a well adjusted person finds a way to fulfill his wishes in socially approved ways but when he can't or thinks he can't do this,

"Ah, ha! a cattail for my torch!"

he may resort to unapproved ways; compelling inner demands require fulfillment, no matter how. When carried to extremes, he becomes stamped as a misfit, juvenile delinquent, or even a hardened criminal.

THE WISH FOR AFFECTION.   One powerful wish is to be accepted and regarded affectionately by one's group. The sense of inner contentment a camper feels when comrades select him for a tent mate or greet him with a friendly word and smile when he enters the cabin door, and the thrill he gets when his cabin mates choose him to represent them on the Camp Council all stem from the fulfillment of this basic desire. The longing to be loved, appreciated, needed and missed is universal. When fulfilled, it produces a feeling of well-being and contentment; when unfulfilled, it brings unconsolable loneliness and unhappiness. A couple of grains of salt should be taken with the camper who says, "I don't wanna go on their old cook out 'cause I don't like them" as he goes off to read a book or stroll through the woods in solitude; the chances are he is really miserable and desperately longing to be accepted as part of the group. You may need the utmost tact and persistence to penetrate the wall he has built around himself but the resulting happier, better-adjusted camper will amply reward you.

Your efforts from the first day to build cabin morale and a feeling of group unity and friendly camaraderie are aimed at helping each newcomer feel wanted and accepted. You may need to take special pains with those who are shy and retiring or who aren't the type others readily take to. This explains why pairing them up or getting an old camper to take them in tow is so effective. The naturally unattractive camper will challenge you especially to search for his good points and help him fit in. A wise father, consoling his befreckled little daughter, said, "I love every one of your freckles because they are *you*." Find out why a camper is disliked or ignored, then set out diligently to remedy the situation.

See that your program is broad and varied enough to provide for every youngster's interests and abilities, be he athletic, musical, a social introvert, a book worm or any other species of young mankind. Be especially aware of the quiet, retiring youngster who tends to be overlooked because he isn't a nuisance and yet may be hiding a deep sense of loneliness.

Countless little ways can be found by a thoughtful counselor to satisfy campers' desire for affection. A friendly "hello," a willing ear to listen to their achievements, a pat on the back and a "well done," a bed time story, or a moment spent seeing that each is tucked in snug for the night will do the trick.

When you detect a child who needs help, it is best to spare his pride by using an indirect approach and unobtrusively devising ways to draw him in. Occasionally it may be best to approach the problem directly and have a man-to-man talk with him, impressing him with the fact that you really like him and consider him a very worthwhile person. Lay your cards on the table and lead him, by his own discussion, to discover how his own selfishness and lack of consideration for others, his boasting, shirking of responsibility, or crude manners and general boorishness are the real reasons others don't accept him. In other situations, you may deem it best to choose a time when he is absent and discuss the situation with his mates, for they can often help most of all by simply taking him back into the group and giving him a chance to start anew with them. Most children are at heart sympathetic and warmhearted, and, when shown how their thoughtlessness is hurting another, are only too glad to help him turn over a new leaf. Tolerance and forgiveness for the shortcomings of others are certainly desirable traits to cultivate, and any improvement in the fellow camper will be a cause for rejoicing as his comrades claim their rightful share of the credit. Helping others is one of the most satisfying ways to fulfill other of our fundamental wishes for recognition and power, as we shall see.

A serious case of maladjustment or continued failure to fit in may call for referral to the camp director or head counselor; more harm than good often follows tampering by those with insufficient training and experience to handle the situation. Sometimes it may be best to transfer the camper to another cabin but this should be a last resort for it will bring him much more satisfaction and lasting good to lick a situation rather than just walk out on it.

THE WISH FOR POWER.   The desire to control or show power over oneself, other persons or things is also universal. A camper knows this satisfaction when he masters the crawl, fashions an outdoor cabinet or table from some string and sticks, works a hard problem in arithmetic, or propels a canoe down the river. He also demonstrates power over himself when he cures such a bad habit as procrastinating or keeping an untidy room, or when he disciplines himself to do a good job of cleaning up a section of the waterfront or constructing a new foot bridge across a stream. He shows power over others when, as chairman of a committee, he steers it to a successful completion of its duties, or when he can sway others around to his way of thinking during a cabin discussion, or when he talks his pal, Joe, out of some proposed misdeed.

A camper suffers frustration and disappointment when he competes with those of superior age, experience or ability; this is one fault of carrying competi-

tion to extremes for consistent winners get inflated egos while consistent losers tend toward inferiority complexes. A good substitute is to have an individual compete against himself as he tries to better a former record. Again, a broad and varied program will provide something in which each camper can experience a satisfactory degree of success.

A misdirected sense of power may explain the bully who controls others through fear, the leader of the gang who dominates and does the thinking for his weaker followers, the individual who enjoys capturing and torturing helpless animals, or the speed boat or automobile driver who goes roaring down the way without regard for the comfort or safety of others or even of himself.

THE WISH FOR SECURITY.   Every person wants to feel safe and secure in his surroundings and with his associates. Campers, particularly when away from home for the first time, miss their familiar routines and ways of life. They find camp ways new and living with such a number of other children odd, especially so if the camper is an only child. A camper can predict with some certainty how his parents and home playmates will react to what he does and has often become quite adept at "getting around" or wheedling what he wants out of one or both parents. Now he is associated with several entirely strange adults as well as new youngsters of his own age and doesn't know what to expect from them. A cross remark or out-

TABLE TOP CAN
BE ROLLED FOR
EASY CARRYING

A Roll-Top Table.

burst of temper in his direction hurts his ego and he may fly back at the person, run to someone else for sympathy or retreat into his shell and brood. The experience may well set the stage for a bad case of homesickness.

There are several things you can do to satisfy a camper's desire for security. He should be assigned to living quarters quickly; the practice of waiting to make cabin assignments until campers arrive inevitably leads to some delay and adds further to the uneasiness of already confused youngsters. Giving out a name tag, calling a camper by his camp name (hearing his own name is always music to anyone's ears), putting his name on his bed and storage compartment, the early tour of the campsite, the pre-acquaintance with dining room and other camp procedure, all add to his sense of security.

Be friendly and pleasant, yet firm when the need arises, but above all, be consistent, for the counselor who is kindly and full of fun one minute yet goes off into sulking, crankiness, or temper tantrums another is certainly no one to lend security to his young charges.

Encourage your campers to chatter freely to you and feel flattered when one discloses secrets to you; never betray his confidences or let him overhear you discussing his personality or problems with others. Make yourself a never failing bulwark to which your campers always feel free to bring their fondest hopes and dreams as well as their worries and problems.

A camper's sense of security must include freedom from fear of harm, both physical and social. Fear of being hurt or ridiculed even interferes with physical coordination and explains the superior results obtained by the modern swimming counselor who works his swimmers hard but gives praise and encouragement when due instead of using the old method of throwing a nonswimmer into deep water and letting him sink or swim. Children who are anxious and afraid of being ridiculed may react by stuttering, bed-wetting, retiring into a shell, fighting back, criticizing others, or engaging in malicious gossip.

THE WISH FOR NEW EXPERIENCES.   To do something different and try one's wings in unconquered fields is the reverse of the desire for security, and denying it too long results in boredom, bad temper, and misbehavior just to create a little excitement. Varying camp routines and work and letting campers help plan their own programs so that they can include new exciting things that interest them helps to satisfy this wish.

Keeping campers busy at things which give them a feeling of accomplishment is one of the secrets of camp happiness. Trips, cook outs, "special days," work projects as in camp construction or on a neighboring farm or truck patch, a hobby display, a camp play, building a tree house, rustic bridge, or nature trail, folk dancing, a visit from a camp neighbor with interesting experiences to relate all help to meet the demand for new experiences.

THE WISH FOR RECOGNITION.   Each camper has a deep-seated desire to stand out as an individual and do at least one or several things better than others. He will consequently work like a beaver to run faster, swim better, swear more fluently, earn higher school marks, make more noise or recognize more birds than his cabin mates. From his early days, this deep urge drives him from one field of endeavor to another in a search for activities in which he can excel. Often his reluctance to engage in a suggested activity is based on an inner abiding fear that he does not or cannot do it well; John's excuses for not going in the water during his swimming period may stem from his self-consciousness about his lack of ability, heightened by the unthinking but unkind remarks of some fellow camper or counselor in that respect. His attitude may well change to one of tolerance or even enthusiasm when a wise counselor searches out some good point to compliment him on or offers help to improve his technique. To work successfully with youngsters, or in fact persons of any age, you need to remember how much better are the results from praise rather than criticism, for it is indeed true that "many more flies are caught with honey than with vinegar." Use a word of praise frequently, but avoid overdoing it or giving it when it is not deserved; others are quick to detect insincerity and will consequently lose faith in and respect for you. Yet the person doesn't exist who doesn't thrive on a bit of sincere praise. He likes the person who gives praise and willingly falls in with his wishes.

Fat Sue's disinclination to join the group in hiking may be based on her inability to "keep up" and fear of cruel comments on her physical stature from other hikers. If her problem goes unsolved, she may learn to snap back and make herself disagreeable just as a tethered dog does when mischievous children tease it. She may fall back on a headache or other excuse and will probably compensate for her inner unhappiness by indulging herself in eating more and exercising less. A tactful talk with her may arouse her interest in bringing her weight down to normal. In the meantime, encourage her to capitalize on her strong points such as her ready wit which keeps her tent mates in stitches or her ability to float better than anyone else.

Bill, who rows poorly and knows it, may be so overwhelmed by the thoughtless taunts and jeers of others that he loses what little coordination he has and flails the water in a truly ludicrous way. You may help him most by unobstrusively suggesting a little private coaching in a remote spot where he can concentrate on his technique without worry about what others are saying or thinking.

A youngster's eagerness to stand well with his peers demands that he receive recognition from them for something he does well. Oftentimes you may even find it worth-while to rearrange the program to make use of some talent not called for by the regular routines. Quiet, socially inept Jane may really shine as her ability to draw well and make attractive posters fills an urgent need to advertise the all-camp fair or circus. We are reminded of a story about a camper whose lone outstanding trait seemed to be an ability to make more noise than anyone else. Her counselor, realizing that her frequently annoying breaches of good conduct were in reality an unrecognized and perfectly unconscious attempt to get the personal attention she could get in no other way, decided to stage a contest to see who could yell the loudest. Of course Jean won as was anticipated and thus achieved her place in the limelight.

A camper would prefer to have *approved* distinction if he can get it. However, his desire for recognition is so strong that he will go to almost any length to satisfy it, even compromising for unfavorable attention if necessary. The constant troublemaker or camp mimic may be explained in this way for he has at least achieved some distinction and would rather be known as bad than consigned to nonentity.

Nevertheless, this camper has a gnawing sense of inadequacy and unhappiness and will be rendered a real service by a counselor who shows him how to achieve distinction in a more satisfactory way. No quick cure can be expected, however, and there will likely be occasional discouraging relapses along the way.

Be especially alert to help the shy, retiring camper find successful achievements. "The child who feels inferior can usually be helped to develop abilities which will in time make him truly superior along certain lines. All genuine superiority grows out of a sense of inferiority which has served as a spur to unusual effort."*

When Wishes are Thwarted

Children are a combination of a lot of

---

* Henry C. Link: *The Rediscovery of Man*, 1938, by The Macmillan Company and used with their permission.

good spiced by a bit of bad, and those who long for the perfectly behaved child should remember this little poem:

> Tommy does as he is told!
> No one ever has to scold!
> Quick! Drag him by the wrist
> To see the psychoanalyst!
> —AUTHOR UNKNOWN

Let us summarize, then, by recalling that when a child is "bad," it is usually because he has not found a satisfying way to fulfill one or more of his basic needs. Therefore, when trouble arises, seek and eliminate the cause. Basic wishes are strong and will be fulfilled by fair means or foul, but children are loath to sacrifice social approval if they can avoid it and still satisfy their desires.

THE WELL-ADJUSTED PERSONALITY

The wish for good mental health is universal for, although most of us would fail miserably if asked to tell just what the term means, we all recognize that it involves a general sense of well-being and of living at peace with oneself and the world. A well-adjusted person has stopped reaching for the moon by attempting things beyond his capabilities, yet, at the same time, he has picked out his strong points and developed them to a high degree of efficiency. He has learned to expect and take the bitter with the sweet in the events of life and has kept his sense of humor strong so that he can laugh at himself when he stumbles, yet pick himself up and try once or many times again. He likes people and has learned how much more important it is to dwell upon their good traits rather than pick out their faults and magnify them out of all proportion. He is friendly and outgoing, yet not a back-slapper or hail-fellow-well-met whose shallowness soon shows through. He is cheerful and optimistic, yet recognizes and meets problems and takes constructive steps to solve them to the best of his ability instead of dashing hither and yon in ineffective worry and indecision. Perhaps, most of all, his distinguishing mark is that he has largely supplemented juvenile interests in self alone with thoughts of others and of how he may best use his time and talents to serve them and so make the world a better place in which to live.

CHARACTERISTICS OF CHILDREN

As previously pointed out, individuals are too different to classify and fit into pigeonholes with the proper recipe for understanding and handling each neatly catalogued in a nearby file. Each has a unique personality brought about by his own heredity and all the bits of learning he has absorbed like a sponge from his particular background and environment. We cannot truthfully say that there is such a thing as an average child but only averages of children. Nevertheless, it will prove helpful to understand these averages since they represent a basic structure upon which each child's own individual characteristics are superimposed.

The Camper From 6 to 8

This period might be termed the *individualistic period,* since, although not as completely egocentric as he was, the child's thoughts are still largely centered upon himself and his interest in others is mostly superficial and transitory. A friend of the hour may be completely spurned or disliked a short time later, then accepted again as a boon companion. In fact, a child of this age shows more interest in pleasing adults than in pleasing his contemporaries and thus it is easy to motivate him to desirable conduct by a bit of praise or other sign of approval from you.

He tends to be incessantly active and cannot be kept physically quiet for long. His interests are keen but fleeting and you must be prepared for him to sud-

denly drop a project or game in which he has been absorbed and clamor for something entirely new and different. He is quite impulsive and highly unpredictable.

His imagination knows no bounds and he goes into a whirlpool of activity as he clears his cabin dooryard and lines a path with rocks to the door of the "White House" or pioneer's cabin where he and his camp mates bunk. He loves to try to creep silently through the woods, stalking in the best manner of Daniel Boone or a fierce Cherokee brave, yet a few moments later, a few touches of costume have transformed him into a handsome fairy prince holding sway over his subjects.

It is very important at this time to encourage him to try out his skills in many fields so that he can sample everything and find out where his true interests and abilities lie. However, his coordination is not dependable and his control over his finer muscles is so poor that he finds concentration on painstaking, exacting techniques wearisome and unsatisfying. Simple, large-muscle activities are best. He needs to be protected against overexcitement and fatigue which tend to interfere with his getting sufficient rest and sleep.

The Camper from 9 to 11

A camper of this age is beginning to value the approval of those of his own age group and may need help to achieve it successfully. Encourage him in his awakening interest in working in a group in such projects as planning a campfire skit or program, a simple gypsy trip, outdoor meal, or a clean-up project for unit or cabin. His imagination still runs rampant and activities are much more fun when he can imagine himself as a forty-niner, a historical figure, or a character from a well-loved story.

He needs help to develop a sense of self-reliance, industry, regularity and dependability. With his increasing muscular control, his interests turn to experimentation with various sports, crafts, and the use of simple tools. He tends to lack confidence in himself and even when he seems boastful and assertive, he is often really masking an underlying sense of insecurity. Beware of using ridicule or sarcasm with him because of this underlying lack of confidence.

He tires easily when activities involve long-continued efforts and his tendency to overdo makes mandatory rigid observance of the rest period and sleeping hours at night. He must still be protected against overfatigue and overexcitement.

The Camper from 12 to 15

This age is referred to as the *gang age* because self-interests are now being supplanted with a deep loyalty to the group or gang, often to the extent of sacrificing self for them. Desire for the approval of his group is becoming so strong that to be different or stand out from the rest is a major catastrophe. All must act and dress as nearly alike as possible even to the extent of cutting off and fringing their jeans, engaging in minor acts of vandalism and disobedience, or wearing long fingernails or a crew haircut. Don't forcibly try to buck this tendency but rather try to channel group approval into the right direction where it will become a tremendous force to keep campers in line. The sense of gang loyalty is not usually quite as strong in girls as in boys.

Loyalty to and enthusiasm for working as a group plus a growing power to discuss and see several sides of a question make this an ideal time to learn to work together in planning program and working out common problems. Use camper leadership, as you inconspicuously slide into your role of leader, big brother and counselor. Encourage individuals and committees to assume responsibilities and strive to develop a social consciousness wherein each camper realizes his own responsibility for and obligations to others.

This is the age of acute hero worship and the choice of the right heroes can be a most potent force for good. Campers are thrilled by examples of thoughtfulness, self-sacrifice, valor and honesty in their models and they themselves, even though loudly protesting, really want to be held to high standards, with reasonable rules and regulations consistently and fairly, but not over-rigidly, enforced. Above all avoid the fatal error of striving for personal popularity by over-leniency or trying to be "just one of the boys." These youngsters will take every advantage of over-leniency they can, but will lose respect for you in the process.

It is difficult to tell whether this period, with its rapid turnover of moods, interests, and general reactions to life, is harder on the individual or on those who associate with him. Rapid physical changes bring profound unrest, making the girl extremely self-conscious about her changing physical appearance and keeping the boy in constant anguish as his voice ranges without warning from treble to bass. Arms and legs are lengthening and hands and feet increasing rapidly in size, leaving the owner embarrased as he tries to maintain control over their changing proportions. Puzzled by these rapid physical, emotional and social changes, the youngster often covers up his lack of ease by loud talk and laughter and general boisterousness.

The Camper from 15 to 18

This period may be one of continued embarrassment as rapid growth changes continue. The youngster is still struggling to achieve a place of status and acceptance within the group. In fact, acceptance by his peers, a growing need for independance from older people, and recognition as a thinking, self-reliant "adult" have become so great that this camper is inclined to resent any suggestion or advice from anyone older or in a position of authority. Hence, it is mandatory to recognize his budding powers of self-direction by letting this camper share in as much planning of his own program and camp government as possible. Wise guidance is still necessary since our untried "adult" is inclined to fluctuate between flashes of new-found maturity and returns to his former immaturity.

This is a period of idealism and of increasing interest in and curiosity about a wide variety of topics often extending even to those of national and international scope. Group discussions and informal "bull sessions" are very popular and participation by older persons who have been places and done things is welcome. A sense of values and standards is rapidly taking form now.

Camps should provide a progressive program for campers who return year after year so that they do not have to keep "doing the same old things" and what they consider "kid stuff." Enlist their help in planning longer and more rugged trips, more elaborate unit improvements and outpost activities, occasional co-ed activities, and opportunities to explore and satisfy individual interests and increasing skills. Many camps have found that a Counselor-In-Training (CIT) program works nicely for campers of this age.

CAMPERS ARE INDIVIDUALS

We have now noted a number of ways in which individuals are alike and yet we know that in reality there is no one in the whole world exactly like anyone else. Each is the result of both his heredity and environment and everyone, during even a short lifetime, has been in contact with thousands of people, situations, and experiences, each of which has left a stamp of influence on him. Age, too, gives us only generalizations, for changes are gradual and a person doesn't miraculously change from a ten-year old into an eleven-year old on his eleventh birthday. In fact, changes occur at different rates of speed in different individuals and even in various traits of the same individual. A twelve-year old may well be as physically mature as a fourteen-year old, have a ten-year old mentality, a social adaptability level of nine and an emotional development of only eight.

Campers are usually separated into living groups according to such factors as age, camping experience, and so forth, but it is easy to see that within your group, you will undoubtedly find quite a bit of diversity.

It would be impossible as well as undesirable for us to try to eliminate these individual differences for society needs a variety of personalities since the butcher, the baker, and the candlestick maker each has his part to play. We tend to notice and perhaps give more homage to the spectacular, effervescent, extrovert leadership type of child, yet the quiet, plodding, conscientious introvert plays an important role, too. You must bear these differences in mind and respect each child's individuality and handle him accordingly.

For instance, not everyone is geared to the same speed, and constantly admonishing a naturally slow person to hurry may

frustrate him until he becomes uncoordinated and extremely nervous. Campers differ in vital capacity or stamina, and the large, husky child isn't necessarily "goofing off" when he protests at carrying the heavy pack or hiking over the miles a small, wiry companion can take with ease.

The problem becomes one, then, of determining just how much pressure to exert to bring an individual up to what you deem an acceptable level. On the one hand, you must challenge him to live up to what is the peak possibility for him; at the same time, you must avoid overpressurizing him to attempt attainments beyond his capacity. Thus you must become adept at curbing with one hand while pushing with the other and must use all of your wits to determine the proper proportion of each.

You must keep a cool head and a steady hand at the helm. Your prayer might well be, "Dear God, give me the strength to accept with serenity the things that cannot be changed. Give me courage to change the things that can and should be changed and wisdom to distinguish one from the other." *

LEARNING TO KNOW YOUR CAMPERS

It becomes evident that, in order to treat campers as the individuals they are, you must learn just as much as you can about each. Here are some of the possible sources of information:

1. The parental information blank, filled in by parents before camp begins.
2. The camper information blank, filled in by the camper. Keep both eyes open when you study this, for, unless questions are skillfully stated, the answers may be what the camper thinks he should say rather that what he actually feels. For instance, we can be suspicious when a camper states as his objective for coming to camp that he "wants to learn to be more socially acceptable."
3. Organizational records compiled by the sponsoring group such as the Boy or Girl Scouts.
4. Records from the previous summer if he is a returning camper. These may include health records,

activities records, and anecdotal or other "profile" records compiled by former counselors and other staff members.
5. The current health examination report from his home physician.
6. Chats with the boy himself. These should usually be informal and brought about by the counselor so that they seem spontaneous and thus put the camper at ease and in a mood to talk freely.
7. Observations of the camper as he participates in activities and the routines of group living.
8. Observations of the reactions of other campers to him and comments gleaned by just listening to their conversation.
9. Studies such as the use of the sociogram explained below.

The Sociogram

The *sociogram* is designed to tabulate or organize information pertaining to how members of a group feel toward each other. For instance, if you want to find out how each member rates as a potential leader in the eyes of the others, you could give each a piece of paper and ask him to write down the name of the cabin mate he feels would make the best tent captain as well as his second and third choices. When all of the slips are in, make a chart such as the one on page 80, listing on it the names of each member of the group and inserting lines to indicate his choice according to the following key:

———————→ First choice
——— – ——→ Second choice
— — — — — → Third choice

For instance, John's first choice was Gordon, his second was Howard, and his third was Frank. It seems from inspection that Gordon rates highest with his cabin mates, having received three first places, a second and a third place; Allan rates lowest having received only one third place vote.

If you wish, you may carry the analysis still further by assigning 3 points for a first place vote, 2 for a second, and 1

* George Sessions Perry and Isabel Leighton: *Where Away.* Whittlesey House.

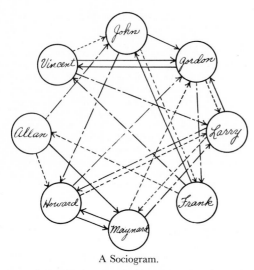

A Sociogram.

for a third. The boys would then stand as follows: Gordon, 12 points; Howard, 8; Maynard, 7; Larry and John, 6; Vincent, 5; Frank, 3; and Allan, 1. In similar fashion you can obtain ratings on any desired trait.

Obviously, when skillfully used, a sociogram can reveal much about group opinion or acceptance of an individual. Repeating the ratings later in the season will show where improvements have been made. The counselor can thus better know who needs help and where, as well as who is liked and respected and can therefore help with leadership.

However, this technique is fraught with danger when used unwisely or interpreted incorrectly. It is not significant when used with people who do not already know each other so should not be given too early in the camp period unless the group comes intact from an in-town situation. However, Doty* reports that campers are able to size up one another with considerable speed and accuracy so that a sociogram would probably be significant as early as the third or fourth day of camp.

One danger is that campers may take the procedure lightly and choose their best friends or engage in a log rolling process of, "I'll vote for you if you'll vote

for me" instead of considering who best exemplifies the quality being voted on. Counselors should use great discretion in deciding how much if anything to tell an individual about how he was rated by the group and, of course, should assure him that the results will not be divulged to others inside or out of the group and then keep his promise.

ADDITIONAL READINGS

Benson, Reuel A., and Goldberg, Jacob A.: *The Camp Counselor.*

Berg, B. Robert: *Psychology in Children's Camping.*

Burns, Gerald: *Program of the Modern Camp.*

Camping—Blue Bird Style. Camp Fire Girls, 1954, 11 pp., 25¢.

Children Are Our Teachers. Children's Bureau Publication #33, revised, 20¢.

Dimock, Hedley S.: *Administration of the Modern Camp.*

Dimock, Hedley S., and Statten, Taylor: *Talks to Counselors.*

Doherty, J. Kenneth: *Solving Camp Behavior Problems.*

Doty, Richard S.: *The Character Dimension of Camping.*

Goodrich, Lois: *Decentralized Camping.*

Grossman, Jean Schick, and Le Shan, Eda J.: *How Children Play for Fun and Learning.*

Fedder, Ruth: *A Girl Grows Up.* McGraw-Hill Book Co., 3rd Ed., 1957, $3.40.

Gruenberg, Sidonie Matser, Editor: *The Encyclopedia of Child Care and Guidance.* Doubleday and Co., 1956, $7.50.

Hurlock, Elizabeth B.: *Adolescent Development.*

Hymes, James L.: *A Pound of Prevention: How Teachers Can Meet the Emotional Needs of Young Children.* New York State Society for Mental Health, State Charities Aid Ass'n., 105 E. 22nd St., New York 10, N.Y. 25¢.

Hymes, James L. Jr.: *Teacher Listen: The Children Speak.* New York State Society for Mental Health.

Irwin, Frank L.: *The Theory of Camping—An Introduction to Camping in Education.*

Joy, Barbara Ellen: *Camping.*

Laird, Donald A., and Laird, Eleanor C.: *The New Psychology for Leadership.*

Landis, Paul H.: *Understanding Teen-Agers.* Appleton-Century-Crofts Inc., 1955, 246 pp., $3.00.

Ledlie, John A., and Holbein, F. W.: *Camp Counselor's Manual.*

Lindgren, Henry Clay: *Effective Leadership in Human Relations.*

Mary and You. Camp Fire Girls, D-299. 30¢. (Understanding girls 7–9)

---

* Doty, Richard S.: *The Character Dimension of Camping.*

Menninger, Dr. William C., et. al.: *How To Be a Successful Teen-Ager*. Sterling Publishing Co., Inc., 256 pp., $2.95.

Menninger, Dr. William C., et. al.: *How You Grow Up*. Sterling Publishing Co., Inc., 160 pp., $2.95.

Morris, C. Eugene: *Counseling With Young People*. Assn. Press, 1954, $3.00.

Moser, Clarence: *Understanding Boys*.

Moser, Clarence: *Understanding Girls*.

Murray, Janet P., and Clyde E.: *Guide Lines for Group Leaders*.

Ott, Elmer F.: *So You Want To Be a Camp Counselor*.

Redl, Fritz: *Preadolescents—What Makes Them Tick*. (Reprint) Child Study, 7 pp.

Roberts, Dorothy M.: *Leadership of Teen-Age Groups*.

Study of Adolescent Boys. National Council, Boy Scouts, 183 pp., $2.00.

Teicher, Joseph: *Your Child and His Problems*. Little, 1953., $3.75.

The Adolescent in Your Family. Children's Bureau Publication #347. 25¢.

Understanding Our Children. Series of 9 pamphlets, Educ. Service Dept., Educators Mutual Life Insurance Co., Lancaster, Pa., 1957.

Webb, Kenneth B., Editor: *Light from a Thousand Campfires*.

Welch, Emily: *Talks for Teenagers*. Burgess Publishing Co., 1959. 84 pp., $2.25.

Wittenberg, Rudolph: *Adolescence and Discipline, A Mental Hygiene Primer*. Assn. Press, 1959, 320 pp., $4.95.

Wittenberg, Rudolph M.: *How To Help People*. Assn. Press, 1953, $1.00.

Working with the Handicapped—A Leader's Guide. Girl Scouts, 1954, 127 pp., 75¢.

Your Child from 6 to 12. Children's Bureau Publication #324, 20¢.

MAGAZINE ARTICLES

Flynn, Eansythe Rowley: *Camping for 5 to 8's—it Presents It's Own Challenge*. C.M., May, 1956.

Friedrich, John A.: *Sociograms Provide Graphic Picture of Camper Group Relations*. C.M., Jan., 1953.

Goodrich, Lois: *Age Level Charcteristics of Campers*. Recreation, Mar., 1959.

Ivan, John J.: *Rating Camp Behavior:* C.M., Feb., 1951.

Lane, Howard A.: *Your Role in Camper Development*. C.M., *Mar., 1956*.

On Understanding Your Children. C.M., June, 1958.

Rapp, Helen: *Adolescence Will be Like This*. Recreation, Feb., 1957.

Rehwinkel, Jeanne: *Hearing What Campers Say*. C.M., Jan., 1952.

Roth, Dr. Charles: *How Bend the Twig*. C.M., Feb., 1954.

Weiss, Carol H.: *Know Your Adolescents*. Recreation, Nov., 1957.

Wells, Kenneth A.: *How to Use an Activity Observation Record*. C.M., Mar., 1956.

7

The Counselor as a Leader

The democratic (?) leader.

Silent prayer of the old preacher:
"Lord, fill my mouth with wonderful stuff,
Then nudge me when I've said enough."

LEADERSHIP

The boss drives his men; the leader coaches them.
The boss depends upon authority; the leader on good will.
The boss inspires fear; the leader inspires enthusiasm.
The boss says, "I"; the leader says, "We."
The boss assigns the tasks; the leader sets the pace.
The boss says, "Get here on time"; the leader gets there ahead of time.
The boss fixes the blame for the breakdown; the leader fixes the breakdown.
The boss knows how it is done; the leader shows how.
The boss makes work a drudgery; the leader makes it a game.
The boss says, "Go," the leader says, "Let's go."
The world needs leaders; but nobody wants a boss.*

KINDS OF LEADERS

THERE ARE three kinds of leaders: (1) the autocratic leader, who rules by force and fear of consequences; (2) the laissez faire leader, who operates on the theory that campers should be let do as they please without adult interference; (3) the democratic leader, who can use discipline when necessary, but who customarily leads the group through his ability to command their respect and work and plan cooperatively with them.

The Autocratic Leader

The autocratic leader seemingly considers his own opinions so superior that he is justified in forcing them willy-nilly on his charges. His "big stick" methods of control brook no lapse of discipline or questioning of his authority, and he threatens drastic and certain punishment

* Dodge, Dora E.: *Thirty Years of Girls Club Experience.*

(H. Armstrong Roberts.)

for all dissenters and nonconformists. Unfortunately, his high-handed tactics accomplish little permanent good, for, as we have previously noted, exemplary conduct evoked by fear lasts only while the leader is present—then the lid blows off like Pandora's box of troubles. Some succumb to him and render cringing, boot-licking subservience, becoming so dependent that they are totally incapable of making any decisions for themselves. Others rebel against the autocratic leader and acquire an unreasonable distaste for discipline and authority of any sort from any source.

The autocrat often demonstrates his own emotional immaturity by meeting misdemeanors and resistance with loss of temper, violent tongue lashings, physical punishment or acts of retribution. Bossing others seems to compensate him in some measure for his own deep-seated feelings of inadequacy; he is an example of satisfying one's desire for power in an unhealthy way.

The Laissez Faire Leader

The laissez faire leader is the opposite of the autocratic leader and asserts no authority at all in a mistaken belief that a group can develop independence and self-reliance only by practicing *complete* self-direction. He realizes that campers should be happy, but is laboring under the delusion that his easy-going, wishy-washy methods of control will bring happiness about. He tries to play the good sport and always falls in line with whatever his group suggests, but they soon become bored with his lack of force and the resultant pointless and unchallenging program. The group either sinks into complete indifference or engages in heated arguments among themselves to overcome boredom, or struggle for control of the group. The leader even fails to achieve the popularity he craves, for campers soon lose all respect for a spineless person who lacks the courage of his convictions.

The Democratic Leader

The democratic leader is a combination of the other two, for he is a "good sport" and a champion of fun and good times, yet he can be firm and exercise control or administer swift and just discipline when necessary.

He can relax and have a good time with his group, yet knows where to draw the line when things are dangerous or against camp policies and objectives. He encourages members to express their views and participate in self-government and program planning insofar as their ages and abilities permit. He realizes that a new group, which has been working under an autocrat, may kick up its heels and be as undisciplined as a spring colt at first and that he must persistently train them to accept responsibility and take over the reins as they prove able. The democratic process is slow, for explanations, discussions and group action take time and the leader is often tempted to cast it to the four winds for he could usually do the job much more quickly and better himself. Yet he realizes that his campers can grow and improve only by solving problems for themselves and that the results will be worthwhile in the long run.

In the best sense of the word, a democratic group is one which has learned to live together in comparative harmony while initiating, conducting and evaluating its own program; it is willing to abide by the results of its own decisions.

Citizens in a democracy must learn to be good "choosers," and each must cheerfully accept group decisions and pitch in to do his share toward carrying them out. The leader acts as a friendly counsel and guide, helping where he is most needed and seeing that responsibilities and privileges are distributed equitably.

Many counselors give lip service to democratic camper planning but actually merely go through the motions as they carry on perfunctory sessions with their groups. A leader should think back over his meeting to see how many of the ideas or details of planning actually came from the campers and how many were simply acceptances of his own proposals. When true democratic proceedings exist in a camp, every person has a chance to express himself in his cabin group and is then represented by the one or two cabin mates who serve on the Unit Council. In turn, the unit sends a few members to the All-Camp Council.

MARKS OF A GOOD LEADER

1. A good leader leads by example.

2. He has a good sense of humor and exercises it to avert crises and keep molehills from becoming mountains.

3. His thoughts are not inverted toward himself and how he will be affected by each situation, but rather outwardly toward the greater "we."

4. He capitalizes on the power of suggestion and subtly plants ideas to sprout and grow to the favorable results he has in mind. He merely drops a vague hint and is seemingly not too concerned about the outcome; this leaves the group free to pick up the hint and proceed to enthusiastically carry it out in the belief that it

is their own, improving and altering it as many minds will when pooled toward a common goal.

5. He tactfully avoids serious misunderstandings and feuds with others and sincerely attempts to see their side of the question as well as his own. He realizes that if he once arouses another's antagonism, he has probably lost all chance to influence him in the future.

6. When there is work to be done, he is in the midst of it, sleeves rolled up and hands just as dirty as anybody's.

7. He understands the force of group pressure and group opinion but also realizes that there is danger in letting campers entirely rule themselves for they still have immature judgment and can be cruel and go to extremes when judging each other. Hurting people is sometimes necessary, but it is a two-edged sword and must be used only when other methods fail.

8. He is ever-mindful of the value of "fun," for happy campers seldom become problems. If he is teaching a new skill, he is thorough, but patient and understanding, and proceeds by an informal, friendly manner. He knows the value of a laugh and always has time for a good joke. He devises ways to make chores fun instead of irksome tasks.

9. He knows that campers, no matter how much they complain and grouse, do not really enjoy slovenly, careless standards of conduct and that they will soon lose respect for a leader who tolerates such laxness. He recognizes that a request gets better response than an order but that, when orders have been found necessary, they must be enforced.

10. He gives praise freely and can see good in nearly everything and everybody. He realizes that insincere praise or that which is overused is quickly detected and discounted. He avoids nagging and excessive fussiness about detail, for he knows that such tactics are inclined to take the heart right out of people and make them stop trying. He seldom if ever resorts to sarcasm or ridicule.

11. He foresees an impending crisis and tries to avert it if he can. If Johnny is chanting how much he dislikes spinach, he does not wait until the whole table is lamenting their pet dislikes, but quietly reminds Johnny, "We talk about only pleasant things at the table."

12. He shuns public scenes whenever possible. A "bawling out" before others hurts a camper's pride and makes him react by (1) giving up and crawling off to stop trying, or (2) growing resentful and intent on revenge. He knows that emotional hurts are even more serious than physical ones. He gives the erring camper a chance to "save face" by seemingly ignoring his misdemeanor in public but later takes it up with him privately in a frank and friendly manner. He knows that "badness" often results from embarrassment or not knowing just what is the right thing to do. He rejects bad conduct but not the camper guilty of it.

13. He seldom tells a camper what to do, but instead, discusses the problem with him, drawing out from him, by his own discussion, what the correct solution is. He never sends a camper away dejected and hopeless but leaves him realizing that the counselor still has faith in him and feels sure he will do better in the future.

14. He never uses physical punishment for it seldom brings about the desired result, is usually against camp rules, and might involve him or the camp in legal difficulties.

15. He uses disciplinary measures sparingly and only when he is convinced that

it is in the best interests of the culprit and, not done vindictively or in an effort to save his own pride. Punishment is so easy to administer and gets such quick and sure results (outwardly, at least) that it is often misused or overused. The superior counselor handles his group so skillfully that serious disciplinary problems seldom occur, but, even so, sooner or later the day will come when action can no longer be postponed. He will find that children are usually good sports about accepting punishment which is deserved and not based upon partiality and/or spite. When discipline is necessary, it should follow as closely as possible on the heels of the misdemeanor and should bear some relationship to it if possible; for instance, depriving a camper of his dessert would be appropriate only for a dining room misdeed. Using work as a punitive measure belittles it and drags it down from the place of honor it ought to hold, though it may be appropriate for a camper who has cluttered up the grounds, thrown food around the dining room, or otherwise created extra work that someone must do.

16. He knows that people usually live up to what is expected of them and that the best way to get a camper to climb to new heights is to show that he expects him to do just that. Issuing a challenge is a very potent force.

17. He does not take a camper's bad conduct as a personal affront, realizing that it is more likely to be a reaction from a past experience or an outside worry. A camper's rebellion at even a reasonable amount of discipline may be caused by having had too much of it at home or school.

18. He satisfies his own basic desires in a healthy way. For instance, he does not secure needed affection by encouraging an unhealthy attachment from a camper. He does not unduly encourage campers to bear tales or slavishly serve him.

19. He seldom bursts forth in momentary anger but instead waits through a "cooling off" period to get the facts and consider all angles so that he can approach it with a cool head and sound judgment.

The democratic counselor could well use the characteristics of the successful teacher as given by H. Q. Cooper:

> The education of a college president.
> The executive ability of a financier.
> The craftiness of a politician.
> The humility of a deacon.
> The discipline of a demon.
> The adaptability of a chameleon.
> The hope of an optimist.
> The courage of a hero.
> The wisdom of a serpent.
> The gentleness of a dove.
> The patience of a Job.
> The grace of God—And
> The persistence of the devil.*

THE USE OF SOCIODRAMA

Sociodrama or play acting lends itself well to use by older campers and can even be used successfully with young ones. It consists of having members of the group act out roles, using dialogue which is either, (1) spontaneous or, (2) written out in advance. It adds spice and variety to the usual proceedings and makes situations much more realistic. It often involves a humorous touch as the impromptu actors inject their own personalities into the act. A discussion period usually fol-

* H. Q. Cooper, quoted by Jackson R. Sharman in *Introduction to Physical Education.* Copyright 1934 by A. S. Barnes and Company, Incorporated.

lows to tie the whole thing into a meaningful whole. It can be used for a variety of purposes such as:

1. To solve a problem. A real or fancied problem is proposed by or to the group and various members then volunteer or are appointed to act out what they think would be the correct solution. For instance, Jack takes the role of a camper who won't observe quiet during rest hour or after taps or shirks on his share of cabin duties. The others then discuss or act out what they deem to be the best way to handle the situation.

2. To bring awareness of others' feelings (develop *empathy*). Individuals take the part of a "new camper," a child of another nationality or race, or a camper who is not well liked. Others may then act out what they feel would be the best way to help him find his place in the group. They then evaluate the various ways.

3. To learn to evaluate. Here, a situation is posed, such as how to serve as tent leader and get others to cooperate in cleaning up the cabin and grounds. Various individuals then demonstrate their conception of how the good cabin leader would act and the group evaluates the various methods portrayed.

4. To consider ways of desirable and undesirable behavior. The group may be asked to show examples of good conservation practices as well as bad or examples of outdoor vandalism such as cutting

initials on trees and indoor surfaces, leaving garbage at the campsite or dumping it in the lake, etc. Other examples might be to act out good and bad behavior in the dining room or how to entertain camp guests.

Obviously, there are many possible variations such as cueing an individual and then asking the group to pick out the good and bad points about what he does, secretly instructing one individual, unknown to the group, to conduct himself as a certain type all day and then have the group try to guess who it was, or letting an individual use his own ingenuity to carry on an activity such as building a campfire or packing his pack sack while the group evaluates his performance. It is often wise to ask the group for suggestions as to topics they would like to consider or let a committee or the Cabin Council suggest problems they think might be helped by such a technique.

LEADING A DISCUSSION

Unto those who talk and talk,
This proverb should appeal,
The steam that blows the whistle
Will never turn the wheel.
—AUTHOR UNKNOWN

Discussing is such a favorite American pastime that it is difficult to imagine two or more people together for even a few moments without engaging in it. Campers, being human, discuss, too, and this interchange of opinion is an important phase of their growing up. Besides the informal discussions which go on perpetually in camp, there are also planned discussions (though the campers may not always be aware of this) which are more or less scheduled as to time and place, and often arise out of the needs or wishes of the group. Such discussions fit naturally into rainy days, late afternoons after swimming, or the period just before taps. It is usually best to keep the atmosphere quite relaxed and informal in the camp situation.

Reasons for Discussion

Discussions often arise merely from a desire to exchange opinions or acquire information about anything under the sun. Such topics as college life, vocations, love and marriage, Indians, fishing, camping techniques, cheating, religion, or Alaska interest boys and girls and serve to help them achieve mature interests and ways of thinking.

Discussions may serve as clearing houses for such problems as how to divide cabin duties and so eliminate "work horses" and "shirkers," campers who lie, steal, or gossip, or why all must be in bed by taps. Often they serve as healthful ways to let off steam and act as safety valves to relieve undercurrents of tension or resentment. It is always better to get such matters out in the open where each has a chance to hear the other's viewpoint; often, ill will vanishes like a bubble as everyone sees that the whole situation was mostly built on imagination and hearsay anyway. Encourage campers to suggest topics they want discussed.

Discussion is the best and most democratic way to plan a group project such as an overnight hike, a three-day canoe trip, a cabin name and slogan, a camp safety week, a stunt for stunt night, or ways of beautifying unit grounds.

Current events prove interesting, too, and being in camp should not isolate a person so that he will appear like Rip van Winkle awakening from a long sleep when he returns to "civilization."

Conducting a Planned or Semiformal Discussion

The how, when and what of a planned discussion are important considerations. Groups of six to eight, never more than fifteen, work best, for they are small enough to permit speaking up without embarrassment and stage fright and the group is closely knit so that each may hear and be heard, an important consideration in an out-of-door situation.

Either a counselor or capable camper may act as leader or chairman and his function is to launch the discussion, then retire into the background; if conversation starts to lag, he must revive it with a thought-provoking comment or question designed to bring about a lively response. Though it may occasionally be wise to let the group stray from the topic at hand, it is the leader's job to determine just when and how far this should go and tactfully steer the conversation back again at the proper time. If needed, appoint a secretary to take notes on the proceedings.

Be informal but exercise enough control to keep things moving toward the objective. Maintain order and see that no one person monopolizes an undue share of time. Campers who are busy with their hands, whittling or working on some arts and crafts project, are often more relaxed and ready to enter into a friendly give and take.

Characteristics of a Good Discussion Leader

A good discussion leader is like a good basketball referee: he keeps the situation well in hand, yet keeps himself in the background. You are entitled to express your opinions like anyone else, but should never use your office as an excuse to force your will or overrule majority opinion. Keep the discussion between the members of the group, not between you and the group.

Use democratic procedures and encourage *every* person to participate, for the quiet individual who spends his time thinking instead of talking often has a most worth-while contribution to make. Be particularly attentive to the unpopular camper whose every opinion is scoffed at just because it is *his*, for if others are permitted to dash cold water on his efforts, he soon stops trying to contribute and fit in with the group.

Keep things moving, for discussions should be forceful and lively, yet avoid undue haste for it may cause some to feel hurried and unable to express themselves fully.

Be friendly and informal, yet maintain the dignity of your office. Do not try to cover up embarrassment or ineptitude by giggling or making wise cracks.

Be broad-minded and able to see all sides of a question and remember that thinking people deem it no dishonor to change their minds. Above all, don't take advantage of your position by sneering, wise cracking or laughing at any ideas seriously expressed by others.

Why Discussions Fail

You may find some groups unable to carry on a worth-while and satisfying discussion, for, even with good leadership, it requires some practice to do so successfully. With beginners, one of your early sessions might well center about "How to Participate in a Discussion."

Make each member of the group feel it is his duty to contribute, for those who say nothing, add as little as the perpetual talkers whose ideas apparently originate in their mouths instead of their brains. Members should refrain from garrulousness, for, as George Eliot said, "Blessed is the man who, having nothing to say, abstains from giving us wordy evidence of the fact." For these, we would like to recommend the "South African treatment," which limits a speaker to what he can say while standing on one foot, with his speech automatically ending the instant he touches his other foot to the ground.

Some want their specific problems solved, apparently feeling that, like an automat, it ought to be possible to drop in a question, push a certain lever, and get an answer like magic. A group can do no more than open up various lines of thought for others to use as tools in arriving at their own solutions.

Every group is likely to contain biased, opinionated persons or "know-it alls" who look upon discussion merely as a sounding board for displaying their own pearls of wisdom before the hungry multitudes of the ignorant. Such is the intolerant camper or counselor who "only listens when *he* speaks" and furiously attacks any who dare to differ with him. They should recall the Chinese saying that getting angry is a sign one has run out of arguments.

Benefits of a Discussion

Although the discussion method is a slow and somewhat inefficient way to solve problems, it is a democratic procedure, for each person has the privilege of expressing his own thoughts and feelings and so minimizes the danger of hearing only the most outspoken. Each also has the opportunity to ask questions and get further information about any points not clear to him, and the very act of participating tends to keep people alert, interested, and more willing to accept decisions made. This is particularly important with youth which resents having ideas and opinions crammed down its throat by older people. Increased understanding and appreciation result when one learns to respect the opinions of others even though not endorsing them. A wise person has said, "I defend with my very life your right to say what you believe though I do not agree with a word of it." We are often astonished and delighted at the deep and interesting thoughts lurking in the minds of our everyday companions. You, as a counselor will certainly gain new insights about your little brood, as they come also to understand you better as a person.

ADDITIONAL READINGS

Benson, Reuel A., and Goldberg, Jacob A.: *The Camp Counselor.*

Berg, B. Robert: *Psychology in Children's Camping.*

Burns, Gerald: *Program of the Modern Camp.*

Dimock, Hedley S.: *Administration of the Modern Camp.*

Dimock, Hedley S., and Statten, Taylor: *Talks to Counselors.*

Doherty, J. Kenneth: *Solving Camp Behavior Problems.*

Doty, Richard S.: *The Character Dimension of Camping.*

Goodrich, Lois: *Decentralized Camping.*

Hurlock, Elizabeth B.: *Adolescent Development.*

Irwin, Frank L.: *The Theory of Camping—An Introduction to Camping in Education.*

Joy, Barbara Ellen: *Camping.*

Joy, Barbara Ellen: *Cooperative Committee Plan in Camps.* Camping Publications.

Klein, Alan F.: *Role Playing in Leadership Training and Group Problem Solving.* Assn. Press, 1956, 176 pp., $3.50.

Laird, Donald A., and Laird, Eleanor C.: *The New Psychology for Leadership.*

Ledlie, John A., and Holbein, F. W.: *Camp Counselor's Manual.*

Lindgren, Henry Clay: *Effective Leadership in Human Relations.*

Morris, C. Eugene: *Counseling with Young People.* Assn. Press, 1954, $3.00.

Moser, Clarence: *Understanding Boys.*

Moser, Clarence: *Understanding Girls.*

Murray, Janet P., and Clyde E.: *Guide Lines for Group Leaders.*

Ott, Elmer F.: *So You Want To Be a Camp Counselor.*

Roberts, Dorothy M.: *Leadership of Teen-Age Groups.*

Ross, Murray J., and Henry, Charles E.: *New Understandings of Leadership.* Assn. Press, 1957, 158 pp., $3.50.

Teicher, Joseph: *Your Child and His Problems.*

Trecker, Audrey R., and Harleigh B.: *How To Work With Groups.* Assn. Press, 1952, 167 pp., $3.50.

Webb, Kenneth B., Editor: *Light from a Thousand Campfires.*

Wittenberg, Rudolph: *Adolescence and Discipline, A Mental Hygiene Primer.*

Wittenberg, Rudolph M.: *How To Help People.*

MAGAZINE ARTICLES

Dean, Kay: *Camper Planning.* C.M., May, 1957.

Dimock, Hedley G.: *Role Playing—a Workable Approach to Better Camp Leadership.* Part I, C.M., May, 1956. Part II, C.M., June, 1956.

Friedrick, John A.: *Techniques for Handling Large Groups.* Recreation, Sept., 1955.

Kessel, J. Bertram: *Role Playing Vitalizes Pre-Camp Training.* J.H., P.E., and R., Jan., 1957.

Leading A Discussion

Bucher, Charles A., Editor: *Methods and Materials in Physical Education and Recreation.*

Grumme, Marguerite: *Basic Principles of Parliamentary Law and Protocol.* Author, 3830 Humphery St., St. Louis 16, Mo., 68 pp. $1.00.

Hammett, Catherine T., and Musselman, Virginia: *The Camp Program Book.*

How To Lead a Discussion. Adult Education of the U.S.A., 1955, 60¢.

McCall's Pocket Book of Parliamentary Pointers. McCall Publishing Co., 32 pp., 25¢.

Menchofer, Joseph D., and Sponberg, Harold E.: *Rules for Parliamentary Procedure.* Mich. State, 1951, 80 pp., $1.00.

Peterson, Harold C.: *Guide for Chairmen.* Northwestern Press, 45 pp., 60¢.

Thurston, La Rue A.: *Complete Book of Campfire Programs.*

Tilson, John Q.: *How to Conduct a Meeting.* Oceana, 50¢.

Trecker, Audrey and Harleigh: *Committee Common Sense.* Assn. Press, 1954, 158 pp., $2.95.

Wheelock, Margaret W.: *A Primer of Parliamentary Procedure.* Publications Services, Y.M.C.A., 27 pp., 10¢.

8

Some Problems You May Meet

He drew a circle that shut me out—
Heretic, rebel, a thing to flout.
But Love and I had the wit to win,
We drew a circle that took him in.

EDWIN MARKHAM*

ALL OF US are occasionally "problem children," for few are sufficiently wise and disciplined to consistently meet thwarted desires with controlled emotional reactions.

Good mental health allows us to act in a way satisfactory to ourselves and our associates so that we have a sense of inner calmness and well-being (*euphoria*). However, such a state is hard to maintain constantly, for the world is full of people, each striving to satisfy his own personal desires, and conflict between individuals is almost inevitable. One's reactions and adaptability to conflict and the demands of nature and circumstance largely determine his degree of mental health.

Counselors Must Develop Insight

Campers meet with such conflicts and problems, too, and sometimes go off on a wrong tack in socially unapproved conduct which, if unchecked, will sooner or later cause them to be dubbed "problem children." Their efforts to satisfy inner urges are often so well disguised as to fool even themselves as well as others concerning their real needs and dissatisfactions; for instance, a bullying, loud braggart may be unconsciously trying, by his spluttering and noise, to hide from himself and others a deep underlying sense of insecurity and inadequacy. Our first reaction to his obnoxious conduct is to give him a good "bawling out" or a "sound thrashing" but when we understand what is behind it, we see how harmful such treatment would be.

* Used by permission of Virgil Markham.

Undesirable behavior is only a symptom and is rarely overcome by direct treatment, for repressing it in one place makes it break out with greater force in another. Like the surgeon, we must find the underlying cause and remove it in order to get the symptom to subside. A camper is not likely to understand why he is "bad," for self-diagnosis is notoriously fallible, and we might as well tell him to stop his tooth from aching as to order him to quit being homesick or noisy. His behavior difficulties are based upon a cause as genuine as is his toothache, and willpower avails but little in either case. Everything he does is for the purpose of meeting some need, even though he himself may not actually be aware of what it is. If his method is objectionable to others, the solution is not to condemn him, but to help him find an acceptable substitute. Like a surgeon or dentist, a counselor must look beyond conduct to its underlying causes; this presents a real challenge, for emotional pains are even harder to diagnose than physical ones. Incidentally, practice in understanding others should help a counselor understand and better direct himself.

So-called "problem" campers are usually the products of problem environments or associates and many arrive in camp with cases already full blown. Conscientious but overdoting parents may have spoiled the child so that he expects the same undue attention in camp where he is surrounded by others, each entitled to his own share of recognition. A child used to living in a household of adults who center all their attention and affection on him, is at a loss when placed with others of his own age. On the contrary, we also find the child who is suffering from lack of love or who may be jealous of the family esteem for a brother or sister, or who feels his parents sent him to camp to get rid of him while they enjoy a trip or other exciting adventure without him. Such a child will understandably demonstrate an abnormal desire for the love denied him at home. Camper difficulties sometimes arise for the first time in camp, or, if already present, get worse when subjected to unwise camp procedures which fail to recognize and meet the real issue.

Emotionally stable persons meet problems and frustrations honestly. Those who are emotionally unstable meet them, (1) by evasion or withdrawing or, (2) by aggression. The strategy and cunning exhibited by the subconscious mind as it attempts to cover up the real trouble, even from the person himself, makes it hard to get at the source and find a solution for the trouble. Counselors with little training and experience may grievously aggravate the situation and should not attempt to handle serious problems or those getting out of hand but should refer them to the camp director, head counselor or counseling expert. There is no such thing as a never-failing remedy or magic recipe, for each situation is complex and individual in itself. Consequently an unskilled counselor is likely to be "mistreating" the patient.

THE CAMPER WHO WITHDRAWS OR EVADES

The timid, apologetic camper often goes unrecognized as a problem, but psychologists realize that his very failure to demand attention and his apparent happiness in pursuing his solitary way often indicate a serious trend. On the other hand, the aggressive person makes himself so obnoxious that he is likely to bring down upon his head the very attention he needs to help him conquer his difficulties while they are still in the early stages.

The evading camper's actions, like the aggressor's, are based upon an inner feeling of dissatisfaction, insecurity or inadequacy, and his behavior may take one of many forms.

Daydreamers who keep their reveries within limits often find wholesome relaxation in them; in fact, when kept under control, day dreaming is beneficial. A great doer is always a great dreamer but only when his dreams prove so stimulating as to make him get up and start changing them into reality. When daydreaming becomes an end in itself and furnishes complete satisfaction for the dreamer, it is harmful, for no one can be kept warm and well fed in an air castle. *Wishful thinkers* persist in believing what they want to believe despite all evidence to the contrary, and escape having to face unpleasant facts by simply ignoring them.

Sorry-for-themselves retreat into an inner sanctum where they dwell moodily upon how misunderstood and mistreated they are until they become literally obsessed with the idea. They may picture themselves as cold and silent in death while those who have wronged them stand by in sorrow and contrition or even morbidly play with the idea of suicide to hasten the processes of nature. When faced with the cold fact that the old world expects them to act like normal human beings with no special humoring or pampering, some want to *run home to mother,* to have their aches and bruises kissed away; others develop a convenient *illness* when faced with unpleasant tasks, while still others become *self-worshipers* to compensate for their lack of status in the eyes of others. Some youngsters who have

failed to secure affection and recognition from those of their own age become abnormally attached to an adult who has been kind or at least tolerant of them. They claim to be completely bored with their peers.

Others crowd out the unhappiness of inability to fit in with their peers by turning to such strictly solitary pursuits as reading, drawing or boating, and thus eliminate the necessity of having to tailor themselves to group acceptance.

Those who have had their suggestions and remarks jeered at or ignored may avoid further hurt by degenerating into *"yes men"* who need show no initiative and can retire into the background and avoid attention to themselves.

Some, when bothered by their own consciences or the accusations of others, try to evade blame and responsibility for their acts by *rationalizing,* or finding plausible excuses for everything they do and thus make their actions seem reasonable. A form of rationalization is found in those who assume the *"sour grapes"* attitude by pretending a disdain for the unattainable. Thus they dismiss as "high brow" those who like good music or literature; those good in sports are "brainless wonders"; good students are "greasy grinds," and those with ambition and initiative are "eager beavers." Some *alibi* or *project* the blame onto outside persons or things, explaining their failures by saying that people have it in for them or won't judge them fairly. The umpire cheats them out of winning or the teacher fails to pass them because he has "pets." They are afraid to face the facts and admit that they, like all humans, have faults and weaknesses.

Pollyannas close their eyes to all unpleasantness and difficulty and refuse to worry about anything at all, expressing confidence that everything is predestined to turn out for the best. This frees them from any responsibility for doing necessary work, or recognizing and correcting their own faults. Though sometimes happy and carefree themselves, their unwillingness to pull their share on the oars leaves a disproportionate amount for others to do.

Some, failing to achieve success in a coveted field, "forget it" by *overcompensating* in another. Thus the girl who is not blessed with physical beauty may become an outstanding student, seamstress or tennis player. The boy without the coordination and physical stamina to gain athletic prowess may become a skilled violinist, a great scientist or a famous writer. Obviously, *substitution* or *compensation* at its best can be a great force for good and a study of the lives of some of our foremost Americans shows that disappointments or feelings of inferiority along some lines have spurred them on to achieve their great distinction in another. But when such feelings distort the personality and cause the person to retire from human companionship, or strive to be the biggest undesirable something such as trouble maker, liar, gang leader, or hoodlum, it is an equally potent force for evil.

THE CAMPER WHO RESPONDS WITH AGGRESSION

The *braggart,* the *bully,* the *smarty,* and the *tough guy* who swagger about in an attitude of pretended fearlessness and assurance are, in reality, covering up their failure to attract attention by legitimate means. The youngster who *smokes* or *drinks* to excess or who uses *foul language* or *swears* is likewise indulging in a misguided effort to gain status as an individual. *Bossy, domineering* people exercise power in the only way they can—by making themselves so unpleasant that others would rather give in than resist.

The *boisterous,* the *show-off,* and the girl who goes to *extremes in dress and make up,* would prefer to find their niche by other means if they but knew how. The antics of the *mimic,* the *cut-up* and the *practical joker* have at one time brought the attention desired, but so far unattained in other ways, and so have been adopted as standard conduct.

The *constant babbler* who monopolizes the conversation subconsciously envies his quiet, more socially acceptable companion who can feel secure of his place without constantly having to occupy the limelight. People *who eat the fastest, most or least,* and those with numerous *food dislikes* or *idiosyncrasies,* are in the same category with those who bask in the "individuality" of *poor health,* an *unusual ailment* or an *artistic temperament.*

The person who *cries* at the drop of a hat or becomes *hysterical* and throws a *temper tantrum* has probably found these methods effective in getting his own way in the past and so continues his tactics.

The *quarrelsome, stubborn or rebellious* person is so unsure of himself that he uses loud words and violent action to drown out his own misgivings and discourage others from questioning him.

The *intolerant* person who "knows all the answers" is, in spite of his dogmatic statements, really distrustful of his own beliefs and is loathe to listen to others lest they show up his inferior reasoning. The *overcritical* person calls attention to little flaws in others in hopes they will make him seem superior by comparison.

Campers who form little *cliques* of two or more are demonstrating insecurity and a fear of inability to make a place for themselves in the larger group. Forcibly breaking up the alliance may cause acute misery as the attention forces their egos down still further; a better solution is to lead them gradually into general group participation so that they will no longer need the consolation of their little band. Some resort to *regression* or reverting to behavior of an earlier period such as baby talk or complete dependence, hoping to be sheltered and excused for childish behavior and shortcomings as they were at that age.

CAMPERS WHO ARE HOMESICK

Campers who give up and want to go home are true problems, for their feelings may prove contagious and, if once allowed to succumb to it and leave camp, it becomes increasingly hard for them ever to sever family ties. Homesickness may be furthered by too many telephone calls or letters of the wrong sort from "child sick" parents. For this reason, camps frequently counsel parents in advance about the type of letters to write and discourage them from calling except in cases of urgency.

Candle Holder

A child who has never been away from home before may be overwhelmed by a sea of strange faces and unfamiliar surroundings. He may be so painfully shy that it is hard for him to meet or even accept friendship, and having to wash and dress before others may be excruciatingly embarrassing. He may be afraid of the quiet strangeness of the woods, particularly at night when the rustlings of animal life are magnified a hundredfold by his unaccustomed ears.

Spells of homesickness reach their peak about the third or fourth day of camp and are strongest at mealtime, in the evening around bedtime or on Sundays. (Note that these are relatively inactive times when the camper has a good deal of time to think about himself.) Homesickness has its basis in fear, such as fear of strangers, of surroundings, or of not being accepted, and is best forestalled by the methods suggested to make the

camper welcome and at home. It may help to let him "talk it out," assuring him that such feelings are perfectly natural and are experienced by nearly every one when he first stays away from home. It also helps to have some adult, preferably someone to whom he seems naturally attracted, spend a great deal of time with him the first few days. Getting him busy at some activity in which he excels such as drawing some pictures for the camp paper, helping with an outdoor fireplace or decorating the tables in the dining room helps add to his feeling of belonging. He might also be given some special job such as stamping letters for the director or making a lanyard for his counselor to add to his feeling of importance and indispensability. Sometimes a challenge to his pride to stick it out for a certain number of days with the promise that he may go home at the end of that time if he still wants to appeals to him. Realize that you are fighting for more than just another camper on the camp roster; you are, in reality, making an important contribution to speed a youngster on his way toward emotional maturity.

ADMONITIONS FOR THE COUNSELOR

1. Avoid snap judgments for human behavior is too complex to solve by a single formula or rule of thumb. Learn all you can concerning a camper who is giving you concern; observe him carefully but without letting him know it. Do not take his previous record too seriously for a change in environment often produces a change in behavior and the child

who has been labeled "bad" at home may completely reverse his conduct when subjected to the new faces, new influences, and new activities of camp.

2. Remind yourself again of all the ways to help each camper satisfy his fundamental desires and attain a feeling of security in his litle cabin family. Vary the program so that each child's interests and abilities can find recognition in some part of it.

3. Recall that misbehavior is usually a bid for attention, an expression of insecurity, or a feeling of being unloved and unwanted, and that public reprimand or punishment ordinarily only aggravates the situation. No one is really more miserable, no matter how skillfully he hides it, than the "bad" or "problem" child and our happiness at helping him "fit in the groove" is but a drop compared to what he will experience.

4. Try inconspicuously to draw aggressive or retiring campers into activities which afford them a true feeling of success and achievement. Their distress automatically disappears as it is swallowed up by socially approved answers for their needs and wishes. It is hard to conceive of any youngster who would willingly continue to "get in peoples' hair" if he could otherwise get the attention, affection and recognition he craves.

5. Make a particular effort to get close to the camper who seems to be creating a problem for himself or others. This may be tedious, for those most needing help are often too timid or proud to ask for or even accept it when offered. Thus, a casual approach through a seemingly accidental canoe ride or hike is better than a formal conference by appointment. Cultivate the ability to be a good listener, for the problem camper's veneer of bravado usually cloaks an aching hunger for a trusted older person in whom he can confide, and skillful handling soon finds him chatting busily about all his secret hopes and aspirations. Once you have won his confidence and

A Chair You Can Make.

friendship, you are well on the way to your goal.

6. Seldom give advice; instead use discreet questioning and suggestion to enable the camper to work out his own solution.

7. Do not heap coals of fire on a camper's head for his misdeeds. This only produces rebellion or causes him to rationalize or project the blame on others, and so he further blinds himself to any real insight into his problem. It also kills any possibility of building up the desired status of friendship and trust between counselor and camper.

8. You may occasionally find it necessary to hurt a camper who persistently refuses to recognize and accept his share in the responsibility for his difficulties. Use it only when all kindlier treatment has failed and never to relieve your own feelings of anger or incompetence.

9. *Enuresis* (bed wetting) is said to occur at some stage in nearly every child. Since there may be a physical cause, the doctor or nurse should first be consulted. Usually, however, the cause is likely to be psychological and is simply a different manifestation of a child's inability to find the emotional satisfactions he needs. In the meantime, such precautions may be taken as providing him with rubber sheets and restricting his liquid intake after 5 o'clock. He should go to the latrine just before retiring and be awakened to go again three or four hours later. Provide him with a flashlight and compan-

ionship if he needs to go during the night. Above all, do not add to his already wounded ego by shaming him but let him know that his trouble is not at all unique. As usual, try to find out what is worrying or bothering him and eliminate it.

Strong Friendships

I do not love thee, Dr. Fell.
The reason why I cannot tell;
But this I know, and know full well
I do not love thee, Dr. Fell.
THOMAS BROWN (1663–1704)

For reasons that we often cannot explain, all of us are attracted to some people and repelled by others, but the truly well-integrated person learns to adapt himself and carry on pleasant relationships with almost everyone. Nevertheless, all of us are privileged to find a few harmonious persons who seem to be natural affinities and with whom doing almost anything at any time is fun. Such mutual attractions are real blessings for they offer life's best experiences and do no harm as long as they do not exclude normal participation in group activities.

Many perfectly wholesome friendships have been condemned as *crushes* by an ill-advised counselor or other person. Most so-called crushes of a camper on a coun-

selor are but a normal attempt on the part of an adolescent to find an object for his ardent admiration and hero worship. Often, he has failed to receive the affection every child needs from parents and friends of his own age and so turns his emotional hunger toward some counselor who has been kind to him. This sometimes creates a delicate situation, for irreparable harm can result from wrong handling and it is easy to obliterate what little confidence the camper has by pointedly ignoring or "squelching" him.

The emotionally mature counselor welcomes this sincere esteem as a rare opportunity to help an adolescent grow and fulfill his personal needs in a wholesome manner. Youth should idealize, and being the object of such admiration should be a challenge to any good counselor to try to prove himself worthy of it. Treat the camper with impersonal but cordial friendliness but without favoritism or partiality. Perseverance and understanding will usually turn the situation into a perfectly healthy and worth-while relationship. Sometimes an emotionally immature counselor takes advantage of this hero worship and uses it to fulfill his own need for recognition and affection; he may then do much harm to the camper.

As previously mentioned, it is humanly impossible to avoid being more attracted to some campers than to others, but a good counselor keeps such preferences a deep, dark secret. He tries to remain objective at all times and keeps himself above showing petty dislikes and differences of opinion. He must remember that the child who is unattractive to him probably affects others in the same way and so, most of all, is likely to be lonesome and in need of affection and attention.

ADDITIONAL READINGS

Benson, Reuel A., and Goldberg, Jacob A.: *The Camp Counselor.*

Berg, B. Robert: *Psychology in Children's Camping.*

Dimock, Hedley S., and Statten, Taylor: *Talks to Counselors.*

Doherty, J. Kenneth: *Solving Camp Behavior Problems.*

Doty, Richard S.: *The Character Dimension of Camping.*

Facts about Fears. Series of 9 pamphlets. Educators Mutual Life Insurance Company, Lancaster, Pa., Free.

Hurlock, Elizabeth B.: *Adolescent Development.*

Laird, Donald A., and Laird, Eleanor C.: *The New Psychology for Leadership.*

Ledlie, John A., and Holbein, F. W.: *Camp Counselor's Manual.*

Moser, Clarence: *Understanding Boys.*

Moser, Clarence: *Understanding Girls.*

Ott, Elmer F.: *So You Want To Be a Camp Counselor.*

Roberts, Dorothy M.: *Leadership of Teen-Age Groups.*

Soloman, Ben: *The Problem Boy.* Oceana Publications, 96 pp., $1.50 (cloth $2.50.)

Statten, Dr. Taylor: *Homesickness.* Ontario Camping Assn., 11 pp., 15¢.

Teicher, Joseph: *Your Child and His Problems.*

Wittenberg, Rudolph: *Adolescence and Discipline, A Mental Hygiene Primer.*

Wittenberg, Rudolph: *How To Help People.*

MAGAZINE ARTICLES

Friedrich, John A.: *Understanding the Camp Group.* C.M., April, 1952.

Josselyn, Dr. Irene: *Psychological Needs of the Overprivileged Child.* C.M., June, 1952.

Leonard, A. T., and van Hartesveldt, Fred: *How Understanding Child Behavior Can Improve Counselor—Camper Relationship.* C.M., Jan., 1957.

Singer, Richard E.: *Counselor's Understanding Helps the Camper Solve the Problem of Enuresis.* C.M., March, 1959.

Strean, Herbert: *What is Homesickness?* C.M., April, 1959.

III

Camp Activities

9

Planning
the Program

Planning is forethought. It pervades the realms of all human action. Whether a man plans a business, a career, a house, or a fishing trip, he is looking into the future in order to arrange his affairs so that they will work out to the best advantage. Applied to our everyday world, planning is nothing but common sense.

C. EARL MORROW*

WHY PROGRAMS DIFFER

IT IS VERY HARD to summarize programs for there are as many different sorts as there are camps. This is not difficult to understand when we realize how many variable factors enter into determining the programs. The following are prominent among them.

The objectives of the camp or of the sponsoring organization

Naturally the activities chosen for the program will be those which best carry out the objectives of the particular camp. We would expect a church camp to lean heavily toward activities of a spiritual nature, a school camp to emphasize particularly the acquiring of school information, and an agency camp to work toward its stated objectives. Special camps such as those featuring dance, music or activities for the physically handicapped will obviously have their programs largely circumscribed.

The philosophy and abilities of the camp director and program director

Those responsible for setting up the program will almost unconsciously sway it in the direction of the activities which interest them most or in which they feel most competent. An avid fisherman will likely see that poles and tackle and time on the program are adequate for his be-

* From *Planning Your Community*. Reproduced by permission of Regional Plan Association, Inc.

loved recreation; a person with a love of music will set the stage for his interest; while a person who likes the sedentary, country-club type of activity will not be likely to promote a strong campcraft and trips program. The better leaders, however, try not to ride their hobbies too hard, and so end up with well-rounded, versatile programs.

The abilities of the staff and resource personnel

Staff members are usually hand picked by the person responsible for hiring them to head the activities he wants to sponsor; thus they may really reflect the wishes of the director or program director. Other executives hire only a minimum of specialists with most of the staff designated as general counselors, but they, in turn, bring with them an assortment of their own particular skills and interests which contribute to a broad and well-balanced program. The danger in having too many specialists is that, at their worst, they may go all-out in efforts to outdo each other in the promotion of their own particular parts of the program instead of cooperating as a team to produce a unified whole. This is the exception, rather than the rule, however, and may be due to a feeling that rehiring and good recommendations depend on their ability to secure camper patronage. A well-rounded specialist with diverse interests or a general counselor who is skillful, for example, with his knife may bring samples of his work and so inspire others to copy his craft. Another counselor soon has the whole camp singing as he accompanies his work with a merry lilt, while still another seems to have a gift for locating some of nature's creatures up to queer and fascinating antics and he soon transmits his ability to see fascinating things in nature to many others.

The nature of the campsite.

Obviously, mountain-climbing will be supplanted by arts and crafts or water-front or some other activities if the camp is built on a plateau, and no one will be weaving with honeysuckle if it does not grow in the environment. A widely separated unit in a decentralized camp can build its outdoor kitchen right near its own backyard whereas a centralized unit will have to explore the wildwood to locate a private nook for its members, but that may be a blessing in disguise as it gets the group out into previously unexplored acres.

The equipment and facilities

A camp with an elaborate outlay of waterfront equipment may produce excellent boat-handling skills and fancy regattas while the camp without enough equipment to go around may find campers and staff busily learning how to use tools and build rafts in order to supply the deficiency. Swimming is almost synonymous with camping to many, yet camps without facilities for it have put on wonderful programs of all too frequently neglected items of program to the benefit and satisfaction of all concerned. Imagination and an outgoing approach can turn a lack of archery equipment into a challenge for Robin Hood and his Merry Men to make their own, again necessitating skill with tools and a knowledge of methods and materials before practice in the skills of the particular sport can be pursued.

The climate

Camps in hot areas will have their campfire programs without benefit of fire and may schedule an extra long siesta and quiet activities during the heat of the day. Camps with cool mornings and evenings will lean more toward vigorous activities, scheduling swimming toward the middle of the day, and making other appropriate adjustments.

Location and terrain

When interesting historical sites abound

in the vicinity, a camp will wisely capitalize on them and plan several trips to visit them. Paul Bunyan Country will be filled with story-telling and special events built around this favorite character. A seaside camp will plan visits to fish-processing plants and fishing vessels. In one camp with a fairly steep hillside, enthusiasm over skiing and tobogganing on pine needles reigned, spurred on by a local resident who had enjoyed these activities as a boy. In another there was a meandering, babbling brook where campers loved to wade and ferret out the secrets of animal and plant life within and around it.

Adirondack Shack.

equipment and worked like little beavers to complete it (with help on the heavy work from some older men); another undertook to clear a vista through the underbrush down to the lake. A group of girls planned an exhibit of dolls dressed in the native costumes of various countries and displayed against papier-mâché relief maps of the respective native lands.

The campers

The ages, previous experiences, skills, financial status and social backgrounds of the campers are very influential in determining programs. A camper who has seen his grandparents do a lively Lithuanian dance can teach it to the others while another contributes a German folk song and still another demonstrates the chip-carving his art-teacher mother has taught him. Farm boys and girls may be far ahead of city cousins in naturelore but lag far behind in executing fancy dives and swimming strokes.

The length of the camping period

Campers who come for only a week or two will need more or less simple projects which they can complete in a short time. Others doing short-term camping will be putting into practice skills and knowledges acquired under the sponsoring agency back in the city. In short-term camps it will be a question of choosing how much and what can be accomplished in the time available. Eight-week camps can approach the program in a little more leisurely fashion and lay long-term plans which build up to a climax of accomplishment at the end of the season. One group of campers decided they needed a log cabin to shelter their arts and crafts

Ratio of counselors to campers

Many children and relatively few counselors mean a preponderance of group activities with little opportunity for small-group and individual instruction.

CHANGING PROGRAM EMPHASES

Early camps felt that filling every moment of a camper's day was the best way to keep him out of mischief and prevent homesickness and boredom. The camper was registered in a number of activities, selected because they were "good for him" or because of parental request, and, if he found himself in one he heartily disliked, it was just too bad, for the schedule and rules were rigid and permitted no change, forcing the child to keep on in a grim death struggle to see whether he or the summer would come to an end first. Activities were scheduled like school classes with attendance carefully checked each day. Motivation came through achievement charts, testing programs, intense competition between individuals and groups, and elaborate systems of awards. In some cases, regimentation and scheduling were carried to such a degree as almost to obliterate the one thing the camper most wanted—to have fun.

As with most customs in the history of mankind, this period was followed by an equal and opposite reaction which, at its worst, went to the extreme of scheduling nothing at all, leaving the camper free to do whatever he chose the livelong day. This practice was apparently based on the assumption that the best way to teach anyone to make choices and govern himself is to give him an entirely free rein and let him learn by the trial-and-error method. The fallacy in this line of thinking is evident, for the theme song of the school of experience is "ouch" and its path is filled with many pitfalls and side lanes which may lead to undesirable learnings. Programs planned exclusively by campers or those not planned at all but which, like Topsy, "just grow," lack continuity and are likely to degenerate into worthlessness and eventual boredom. Best results come from tempering the impetuosity and daring of youth with the sobering influence of experience and greater maturity, as occurs when campers and counselors cooperatively plan the program.

THE NEW CONCEPTION OF PROGRAM

Such camp activities as dramatics, swimming and archery are indeed important parts of camp program, but we no longer look upon them as *the* program. Mary's development does not begin with arts and crafts at 8:30, stop for lunch at 11:30 and continue again at 2:30 with nature study, to cease entirely after her 4:30 horseback-riding period. Instead, program is everything that happens to Mary throughout the day, for each single incident, no matter how trivial, is a potential influence for good or bad. Even bedtime hours from taps to reveille have importance, for they are (we hope) teaching her to stay quiet out of consideration for others and because she herself realizes the need of adequate sleep. Can we argue convincingly that archery, weaving, campcraft or canoeing will be of more ultimate worth to her than forming habits of orderliness, cooperativeness and punctuality? Mary's senses remain impressionable at all times, and we can be sure that

(H. Armstrong Roberts.)

An Outdoor Shower.

she is constantly learning something, be it good or bad, from every experience that comes her way. She cannot be closed up like a book and placed on the shelf at 4:30 to remain unopened until 8:30 the next morning.

Program and activities are not ends in themselves, but are the means by which camping objectives are brought to fruition in the lives of campers. Whereas learning to play tennis may bring Tommy hours of pleasure throughout life, we cannot ignore the equal or greater importance of such concomitant learnings as persistence in mastering a difficult task, good sportsmanship, and respect for someone who can play better.

HOW CAMP PROGRAM IS PLANNED

The new camp program in the better camps is flexible so that it can be altered to fit the changing needs and wishes of those who are to participate in it. This quality makes it readily adaptable to the craving of youth for variety and the need to be up and doing, yet it is by no means haphazard and unplanned, for indeed it takes superior planning of such a program to avoid conflicts over facilities, equipment and the services of the few or many specialists who are on the staff.

Certain hours, as for rising, going to bed, eating, rest hour, swimming, and so on, which affect the whole camp, must be scheduled or at least definitely arranged for so that groups will not interfere with each other. Beyond that, the program of individuals and groups is left pretty much to individual choice within the realm of the possibilities the camp offers.

The program for the entire camp is usually coordinated under one person who may be called the program director, the assistant camp director, or a head counselor. Occasionally, particularly in small camps, the director himself may serve as program director, but it is more common for him to act in an advisory capacity to another who has been allocated this particular responsibility.

In long-term private camps, campers usually largely decide upon their own activities irrespective of what the rest of their living unit may be doing. Various schemes are used for doing this, a common one being to have the program director announce at the end of a meal, breakfast, for example, what activities will be available for the ensuing period; campers then indicate by a show of hands the ones in which they wish to participate. Duplicate lists are made with the original going to the counselor in charge of the particular activity while the carbon is retained in the camp office so that the location of any camper or counselor is always available. It makes for better instruction if participants are classified as to degree of skill, as sailing for beginners only or fire-building for those who have passed their preliminary tests in the use of the knife and hatchet. In other variations offering still freer choice, the program director simply opens the field for suggestions and, when Jack requests an activity such as fishing, the program director asks how many would like to join him in this project.

The foregoing type of scheduling programs by individual choices seems to be the most prevalent in long-term camps which believe that it (1) really centers attention on the individual rather than the activity, (2) widens the circle of friendships as the campers participate with first one, then another, in mutual interest groupings, (3) allows the campers to do what they actually want instead of being coerced into following the wishes of the majority of their living unit and (4) relieves the boredom and animosities which may develop over a period of eight weeks of continuous eating, sleeping and doing everything with the same companions.

The trend in most short-term and many other camps is to operate on the plan of having the living units plan their own programs. Here the thought seems to be that a camper, especially during a short stay in camp, can get better acquainted and feel more at ease if he carries on nearly all of his activities with a small group of his peers. In this small "family" he is recognized as an individual and has more chance to voice his opinions.

Under both plans of programming, it is customary to hold a number of all-camp events during the period, here again the number and character of them varying with the particular camp. Most camps sponsor some sort of camp council in which representative counselors and campers from the various living units meet with the program director to plan such events. Care must be exercised to see that the group consists of many more campers than counselors for campers usually hesitate to speak up if they feel the group is counselor-dominated.

As wide a diversity of activities as facilities and the talents of the staff permit should be offered to provide each child with a chance to try out his own potentialities in many different fields. Who knows but that the little camp orchestra may fire the spark of a future Fritz Kreisler who heretofore has never experienced being on the producing end of music? One of the finest things camp can do is to introduce youngsters to a variety of hobbies from which they may select those which will become lasting sources of joy to them or even financially profitable vocations or avocations.

HOW PROGRAM DEVELOPS

The modern trend in camping is to have the program director, counselors, and campers join in a democratic process of program planning. Counselors act as consultants and advisors, not as dictators, and must avoid superimposing their own ideas yet must guide and control the situation so that wise choices are made. Younger campers need much suggestion, particularly during their first few days in camp for many of them have been quite dependent on radio, movies and television for their entertainment and are at almost

a total loss when called upon to make decisions as to how to spend their time. Even older campers often don't really know what they want to do and are inclined to limit their choices to what they already know and are really rather bored with, because they have so little vision of other possibilities. Here is a golden opportunity for you as a counselor to tactfully broaden their interests and open new vistas as you throw in a hint now and then or pick up and help along one of their own. Even when a suggestion is not adopted in its totality, it will stimulate others until the group "catches fire" on something and is off to a truly thrilling experience together. You can often divert impossible or unwise suggestions into something more suitable by coming forth with a still more exciting substitute.

Best practice calls for having a skeleton plan for the day, week or season in the back of your mind or posted on the bulletin board and plenty of possibilities on deck ready to fill in gaps if campers don't supply them. Your sketchy presentation serves as a springboard or take-off point to be altered and elaborated on as your group takes hold and carries the ball. Working out a definite program is extremely important as it keeps the group thinking and anticipating, and details are added little by little with the complete plan usually formulated only about a day or half day ahead of time. Thus you can continuously evaluate and reconsider as you go along.

With youngsters who feel at ease and free to express themselves, proposals literally fly back and forth and it becomes your job to help separate the wheat from the chaff and settle on a few things which give promise of lasting satisfaction. It is an invaluable experience for campers to learn to plan carefully before starting out on an undertaking and to constantly appraise and evaluate what they are doing. Hindsight is notoriously superior to foresight, but a serious attempt at foresight pays big dividends in preventing costly mistakes and disappointments.

It is a tendency of youth to leap breathlessly into anything that sounds new and exciting, then want to drop it without ceremony as soon as the new has worn off or another attraction appears on the stage. Try to lead your group to estimate before it starts whether or not a project has enough true interest to last to a successful completion. Help them see that a good workman does not leave an assortment of half-finished jobs behind him.

Above all, let your campers in on the plan for it just doesn't work to present programs planned from higher up and try to press them willy-nilly on youngsters; the result is rarely more than half-hearted support. When the campers actively have a hand in the planning, they become so excited they can scarcely contain themselves and your worries about discipline problems and problem campers can largely be forgotten.

You must develop keen ears and quick insights to catch program leads. Often just listening to your group chatter will furnish interesting possibilities. If Jim is describing how his uncle worked on the construction of a city bridge, it may lead to a general discussion of the principles of bridge-building and a suggestion that the group build a bridge across a ravine to save the many steps necessary to go around it. If Susan complains about the brush and rough stones on the way to the waterfront, it's a good time to start a crusade to clear the path. When the Limberlost Unit has just completed a deluxe outdoor shower, promote an invitation for your group to visit it and ten to one you'll soon be helping with plans for a still more luxurious one.

Several stories describe the camping experiences of boys and girls—why not start one during the story hour and watch the account crystallize into action? Step-by-step analyses of how to do things posted in easy-to-read form on a central bulletin board or samples and models placed in conspicuous places ferment brainstorms in young heads. Take a walk and casually mention how certain areas of the campsite could be improved by filling in a muddy place or planting cover crops to control erosion. Make yourself a clothes pole, a no. 10 tin-can cooking outfit or tan a poisonous snake skin and convert it into a belt and watch the interested eyes and eager minds that come to learn. If a canoeing trip is spoiled by a rainstorm that comes up after the hard work of packing, it's a good time to set up a weather bureau and start flying weather flags.

If there is a demand in a field of activity unfamiliar to you, do not discourage it, for research in the camp library will help you, and your fellow counselors will usually be flattered if you ask their help. If you really want to learn new facts and acquire new skills, you can do so, for it is never necessary to remain like the blind leading the blind.

Deciding upon a Program

Some projects arise spontaneously, such as the decision to spend the afternoon in cabin clean-up and decoration when rain has spoiled a proposed supper hike. Others, such as a five-day horse-back trip, the camp birthday party, or the stunt for the All-Camp Stunt Night, require long-term planning for the "big event." The pleasures of an undertaking consist of (1) planning for and dreaming of it, (2) actually doing it, and (3) reminiscing over it and basking in the pride of accomplishment.

Facts which in themselves are dry as a bone become alive and fascinating when learned for a definite purpose. It is righteous rebellion when a child objects to learning the technical jargon of sail boating, knowing full well that it will be months or even years before he can pass the tests enabling him even to set foot in one. His attitude does a complete flip-flop when he is learning a salty vocabulary to use as he actually helps to manipulate the vessel.

The Indigenous Program

Most camps now favor what is known as an indigenous program, based upon the resources and unique personality of the camp involved and using native materials for as many camp activities as possible. In arts and crafts, native woods are used for whittling, native vegetation for dyeing, and local grasses for weaving. The folk songs and ballads of the region comprise the singing, and the dances are those of the local inhabitants. Stories, dramatics, pageants and original songs find their basis in the folk lore, legends and history of the locality. Residents of the area are consulted and brought into camp freely, and the town librarian is consulted for clippings and other materials in her files.

Nature study is an investigation of the flowers, trees and butterflies found on the camp grounds. Star lore, wildlife and forest conservation of the area vie with local lore and history as topics for "program," making it a living, pulsating, vital thing in the daily life of the camper. It is evident that no two indigenous programs would be quite the same, for no two communities offer identical natural resources or historical background.

The Test of a Good Program Activity

Activities which bear up well under the following tests are likely to be good ones and make a real contribution to the objectives of camping.

A Rustic Sign.

1. Is the activity in accord with the idea of simple outdoor living? Does it further an understanding and love of the out-of-doors?

2. Does it answer youth's longing for fun, adventure and dramatic suspense? Do campers *want* to do it or are they merely going through with it to satisfy the whims of adults? Is it interesting in itself without thought of award or other outside inducement?

3. Does it foster camper initiative, resourcefulness and creative expression, or is it a cut-and-dried process where campers follow instructions to cut along the dotted line, then join points A and B?

4. Does it broaden interests and appreciations and help youngsters to see with Stevenson that

> The world is so full of a number of things,
> I'm sure we should all be as happy as kings.

5. Is it free from actual physical danger? Does it contribute to the greater health and vitality of the campers?

6. Could it be done just as well or better in the camper's home community? (This is one of the most important tests and largely rules out the city type of arts and crafts and organized sports such as basketball and baseball if the camper has access to them in his home community.)

7. Does it have carry-over value for use in other situations or after camping days are over?

8. Does it help to develop group consciousness and adaptability to group living?

9. Does it fulfill fundamental desires and help the camper achieve a high state of mental health?

10. Can it be made a true group project to which every member can feel he has contributed, or are all the places of importance usurped by a few of the more aggressive or talented?

POSSIBLE PROJECTS

Construction Work

Since a great deal of camp interest is centered around the actual process of camp living, it is only natural that constructing camp fixin's should occupy an important position.

Among possible projects are making a:

Rustic entrance for unit, cabin or camp
Totem pole
Outdoor kitchen
Outdoor theater
Campfire circle
Log cabin
Nature exhibit
Rock garden
Campcraft exhibit

Rustic furniture
Dam up a creek
Rustic bulletin board
Nature aquarium
Green cathedral—outdoor chapel
Improvised camping equipment
Repair of boats, riding tack, tennis courts
Outdoor kitchen
Weathervane
Outpost camp
Tree house
Lean-to
Council ring
Clearing a path
Bows and arrows
Sun dial
Bridge across the creek
Indian tepee
Soil erosion control
Pottery kiln
Nature trail
Fernery
Rock garden
Shelves, tables, benches
Sun dial
Cleaning up the campsite

Evening Activities

Miscellaneous program of games, singing, stunts, and
  the like
Informal dramatics
Folk, square or round dancing
Parties—hard times, pioneer, Indian, gypsy, formal
  (in couples), plantation, masquerade
Old singing school
Spelling matches
Progressive games
Village night (invite the camp neighbors in)
Barn dance
Amateur night
Hay ride
Camp banquet
Moonlight hike
Star hike or study
Lantern party
Poetry, stories
Shadow plays
Torchlight or candlelight parade while singing
Quiz show
Discussion groups
Liar's club (see who can tell the biggest whopper)

In many camps the occasional evening
campfire program is a tradition dear to
the hearts of the campers and can and
should be varied enough to lift it above
mere routine and anchor it as one of the
most meaningful events of the summer.
It assumes a more romantic and inspiring

air when conducted in beautiful surroundings remote from everyday paths, and
many camps have worked out elaborate
fire-lighting ceremonies for use with it.
Physical comfort warrants attention, for
no one can sit in rapt attention to a program while subjected to a fierce bombard-
ment from voracious mosquitoes. Evening
programs should be tapered off to a quiet,
sleep-inducing conclusion and should end
on time even though some part must be
omitted. Symbols, though simple, mean
much to campers and can be used to
stimulate their imaginations and loyalties.
Hammett and Musselman* suggest having a town crier call campers together for
the Fourth of July program instead of
having them just saunter in, and crown-
ing the winner of a swimming meet with
a wreath of "laurel leaves" rather than
just announcing that he won.

Special Days

County or state fair
Camp Birthday
Mardi Gras
Gypsy day
Dude ranch rodeo
Circus day
Holiday of some other nation (costumes, food, dances,
  games, songs, and so on)
Staff day (when campers and staff interchange roles)
Western barbecue day
Regatta day
Water pageant
Local pageant day
Birthday of some famous person
Clean-up, paint-up day
Story book day (theme of Robin Hood, Paul Bunyan,
  Robinson Crusoe or other book carried out through
  the day)
Village day when neighbors from the village visit
Gift day when campers or groups present a gift of
  something they have constructed to the camp

Rainy-Day Activities

Rainy days always present a problem
to the unimaginative counselor, and a
steady downpour of several days' duration is enough to tax the ingenuity and

* Hammett, Catherine T., and Musselman, Virginia:
  The Camp Program Book, page 203.

resourcefulness of even the doughtiest leader and reduce his spirits to a state of drippy dilapidation. Nevertheless, campers must be kept busy and happy for spells of homesickness are especially likely to sail in with the storm clouds. An A-1 counselor can help his charges turn such an occasion into one of the most satisfying and enjoyable experiences of the summer. If you are a wise leader you will keep the threat of rain ever in the back of your head and steer your group toward outdoor activities which take advantage of balmy weather, literally saving up certain especially appropriate activities for those inevitable rainy days. Here are some possibilities:

Plan a carnival or puppet show
Take a slicker hike in the rain
Compose a cabin or unit yell, song, symbol, slogan, or the like
Learn new songs and sing the old
Work on scrap books and stamp or snapshot albums
Make candy or popcorn, or serve "tea"
Play charades and other indoor games
Plan an open house with simple refreshments for another cabin or unit
Plan stunts for the next all-camp program
Hold discussions
Read or tell stories
Write letters
Listen to recorded music
Plan a future trip, a nature trail, or outpost camp
Toast marshmallows
Hold a convention of the Biggest Liar's Club
Compose a cabin or unit newspaper to be read at supper
Organize a harmonica band or other musical group
Have folk or square dances and singing games
Plan a banquet (with candles or some little extra item of food and program)
Organize Fireside Clubs where small groups can gather in front of available fireplaces to pursue special interests
Arrange a hobby show or other display
Plan a stunt night (keep it on a high level)
Make posters for the bulletin board
Have a pet show—display stuffed animals, etc.
Make puppets or work on a play
Practice campcraft skills such as knots, tincancraft, and so forth
Work on arts and crafts, plan an exhibit
Whittle or carve objects
Mend clothing and get the cabin in apple-pie order
Work on costume box in readiness for the next play
Hold a spelling bee or quiz program
Read or write camp poetry

Make indoor games and play them
Write a dramatic production and prepare to produce it
Make improvised camping equipment such as trench candles and water-proofed matches
Study weather, make weather flags, barometer, and so forth
Play active games to relieve the tension of inactivity
Mark tools and put them in good repair—sharpen knives, axes, and others
Work on riding tack, archery tackle, etc.
Get some extra sleep or rest
Fish, boat or swim in the rain (if no lightning)
Beautify living quarters by block printing curtains, using natural dyes for materials, adding rustic furniture, and so forth
Hold instruction and practice in Red Cross first aid techniques, study rules for tennis, etc.
Have a talent show
Play indoor nature games or get ready for your next nature hike

You will find other suggestions for programs throughout other chapters of this book and in the program sources listed at the ends of several of the chapters.

ADDITIONAL READINGS

Archery

Archery. Boy Scouts #3381, 25¢.
Burke, Edmund H.: Archery Handbook. Arco Publishing Co., 1954, 142 pp., $2.50.
Colby, Carroll B.: First Bow and Arrow: How To Use It Skillfully for Outdoor Fun. Coward-McCann, 1955, $2.00.
Hochman, Louis: The Complete Archery Book. Arco Publishing Co., Inc., 1957, 144 pp., $2.50.
Hunt, W. Ben, and Metz, John J.: The Flat Bow. Bruce Publishing Co., Revised, 1939, 72 pp., 90¢.
Improve Your Archery. Athletic Institute, 1958, 22 pp.
Reichert, Natalie, and Keasey, Gilman: Archery. The Ronald Press Co., 1940, 95 pp., $2.95.
Whiffen, Larry C.: Shooting the Bow. Bruce Publishing Co., 1946, 96 pp., $2.50.

MAGAZINE ARTICLES

Linsey, Ruth: Adventures in Archery, J.H., P.E., and R., Mar., 1958.
Metcalf, Harlan G.: Field Archery is Fun. J.H.,P.E., and R., Sept., 1955.
Shaler, Alan: Making Archery Fun for Campers is Time Well Spent. C.M., Feb., 1958.
Uhrhammer, Gerald H.: Add Interest to Archery. C.M., May, 1955.

Fishing

Brooks, Joe: The Complete Book of Fly Fishing. Popular Science, 1958, 352 pp.

Bucher, Charles A., Editor: *Methods and Materials in Physical Education and Recreation.*

Burns, Eugene: *Fresh and Salt Water Spinning.* The Ronald Press Co., 1952, 96 pp.

Casting and Angling. Julian W. Smith, editor. AAHPER, 1958, 47 pp.

Colby, Carroll B.: *First Fish: What You Should Know To Catch Him.* Coward-McCann, Inc., 1953, 48 pp., $2.00.

Evanoff, Vlad: *How To Make Fishing Lures.* The Ronald Press Co., 1959, 108 pp., $3.50.

Evanoff, Vlad: *Surf Fishing.* The Ronald Press Co., 2nd Ed., 1958, 120 pp., $3.50.

Fishing. Boy Scouts #3295, 25¢.

Hammett, Catherine T., and Musselman, Virginia: *The Camp Program Book.*

Holden, John L.: *The Canoe Cruiser's Handbook.*

Knight, John Alden: *Modern Fly Casting.* G. P. Putnam's Sons, Inc., 80 pp., $3.75.

Leonard, J. Edson: *Bait Rod Casting—Techniques, Lures, Tackle.* The Ronald Press Co., 1953, 64 pp., $2.95.

Leonard, J. Edson: *Fly Rod Casting—Techniques, Lures, Tackle.* The Ronald Press Co., 1953, 95 pp., $2.95.

Rodman, Oliver H. P., and Janes, Edward C.: *The Boy's Complete Book of Fresh and Salt Water Fishing.* Little, Brown and Co., 1949, $4.50. (Ages 12–15)

Sell, Francis E.: *Fresh Water Fishing.* The Ronald Press Co., 1959, 160 pp., $5.00.

Sharp, Hal: *Sportman's Digest of Fishing.* Barnes & Noble, Inc., 1953, 253 pp., $1.50.

Sharp, Hal: *Sportman's Digest of Spin Fishing.* Barnes & Noble, Inc., 160 pp., $1.00.

Sharp, Hal: *Spin Fishing.* Barnes & Noble, Inc., 1955, $1.00.

The Fisherman's Handbook. Fisherman Press, Inc., 3rd Edition, 1956.

Wulff, Lee: *Let's Go Fishing.* J. B. Lippincott Co., Revised, 1955, 101 pp., $2.50.

Zarchy, Harry: *Let's Fish: A Guide to Fresh and Salt Water.* Alfred A. Knopf, Inc., 1952, $3.25.

MAGAZINE ARTICLES

Recommended Fishing Tackle Specifications. J.H., P.E., and R., May-June, 1957.

Games

Active Games For Live Wires. NRA, 32 pp. 50¢. (Ages 6–14)

Borst, Evelyne: *The Book of Games for Boys and Girls: How To Lead and Play Them.* The Ronald Press Co., 1953, 277 pp., $4.50.

Borst, Evelyne, and Mitchell, Elmer D.: *Social Games For Recreation.* The Ronald Press Co., 2nd Ed. 1959, 420 pp., $5.50.

DePew, Arthur M.: *The Cokesbury Game Book.* Abingdon Press, Revised, $2.95.

Donnelly, Richard H., Helms, William G., and

Mitchell, Elmer D.: *Active Games and Contests.* The Ronald Press Co., 2nd Ed. 1959, 672 pp., $7.00.

Forbush, William Bryan, and Allen, Harry R.: *The Book of Games for Home, School, and Playground.* The John C. Winston Co., 1946, 358 pp., $2.50.

Frankel, Lillian, et al.: *Giant Book of Games.* Beckett Sterling, Ltd., 1956, 640 pp., $4.95.

Games for Boys and Men. NRA, 104 pp., $1.25.

Games for Children. NRA, 184 pp., $3.00.

Games for Girl Scouts. Girl Scouts, 78 pp., 35¢.

Games for Quiet Hours and Small Spaces. NRA, 59 pp., 75¢.

Handy Games. Coop. Rec. Service. Available in ring binder ($3.00) or in shelf box ($2.00).

Harbin, E. O.: *Game of Many Nations.* Abingdon Press, 1954, $1.95.

Harbin, E. O.: *Phunology.* Abingdon Press, Revised, 1958, 450 pp., $2.50.

Hindman, Darwin A.: *Handbook of Active Games.* Prentice-Hall, Inc., 1951, 436 pp., $5.50.

Hunt, Sarah Ethridge, and Cain, Ethel: *Games the World Around.* The Ronald Press Co., Revised, 1950, 269 pp., $4.00.

Kraus, Richard: *Play Activities for Boys and Girls.* McGraw-Hill Book Co., 1957, 250 pp., $4.95. (Ages 6–12)

Macfarlan, Allan A.: *More New Games for Teen-Agers.* Assn. Press, 1958, 237 pp., $3.50.

Macfarlan, Allan A.: *New Games for 'Tween Agers.* Assn. Press, 1952, $3.00.

Mason, Bernard S., and Mitchell, Elmer D.: *Party Games for All.* Barnes & Noble, Inc., 1946, $1.00.

Millen, Nina: *Children's Games from Many Lands.* Friendship Press, Revised, 1951, 214 pp., $2.95.

Mitchell, Elmer D., Editor: *Sports for Recreation.*

Moorehead, Albert H., Frey, Richard L., and Mott-Smith, Geoffrey: *The New Complete Hoyle.* Doubleday, and Co., Inc., Revised, 1956, 740 pp., $3.95.

Mulac, Margaret E.: *The Game Book.* Harper and Brothers, 1946, $3.50.

Mulac, Margaret E.: *Hobbies.* Harper and Brothers, $3.95.

Reiley, Catherine C.: *Group Fun.* Girl Scouts, Dodd, Mead, and Co., Inc., 1954, $3.95.

Richardson, Hazel A.: *Games for the Elementary School Grades.* Burgess Publishing Co., Revised, 1951, $2.50.

Ripley, G. S.: *The Book of Games.* Assn. Press, 1952, 236 pp., $3.00.

Smith, Bob: *The Boy's Entertainment Book.* T. S. Denison and Co., 367 pp., $3.95.

Smith, Charles F.: *Games and Recreational Methods.* Dodd, Mead, and Co., Inc., Revised, 704 pp., $4.75.

Thurston, La Rue A.: *Complete Book of Campfire Programs.*

Vannier, Maryhelen: *Methods and Materials in Recreation Leadership.*

Young, William P., and Gardner, Horace J.: *Games and Stunts for All Occasions.* J. B. Lippincott and Co., Revised, 1957, 120 pp., $2.50.

General Program Planning

Burns, Gerald P.: *The Program of the Modern Camp.*
Duran, C. A.: *The Program Encyclopedia.* Assn. Press, 1955, 630 pp., $7.95.
Eisenberg, Helen and Larry: *How To Help Folks Have Fun.* Assn. Press, 1954, 64 pp., $1.00.
Eisenberg, Helen and Larry: *Omnibus of Fun.*
Goodrich, Lois: *Decentralized Camping.*
Guide for Group Camping: Camp Fire Girls, #D-232, 1958, 111 pp., $1.00.
Hammett, Catherine T., and Musselman, Virginia: *The Camp Program Book.*
Handbook for Guardians of Camp Fire Girls. Camp Fire Girls, 1952.
Irwin, Frank L.: *The Theory of Camping.*
Joy, Barabara Ellen: *Campcraft.*
Joy, Barbara Ellen: *Camping.*
Joy, Barbara Ellen: *The Progressive Camp Program.* Camp Publications #5, 6 pp., 35¢.
Kraus, Richard: *Recreation Leader's Handbook.*
Tobitt, Janet E.: *Program in Girl Scout Camping.*

MAGAZINE ARTICLES

Armand, Ball Jr.: *Challenging Work Projects Draw Teen-agers to Camp.* C.M., Dec., 1958.
Bronstein, Arthur J.: *Tree—Choice Programming.* C.M., Dec., 1957.
Cole, Florence: *How to Make Inexpensive Awards.* J.H., P.E., and R., Jan., 1958.
Joy, Barbara Ellen: *And Gladly Would He Learn.* J.H., P.E., and R., June, 1953, or Camp Publications #16, 3 pp., 30¢.
Joy, Barbara Ellen: *And Let the Camper Choose.* C.M., May, 1951.
Loren, Harold: *Construction as a Camp Activity.* C.M., Mar., 1957.
Vickers, Willa: *Conversation Creates Good Program.* C.M., Apr., 1953.
Vinal, William Gould: *Let's Take Camping Back To Nature.* C.M., June, 1950.
Wells, Kenneth A.: *How to Use an Activity Observation Record.* C.M., Mar., 1956.

Horsemanship

Hope, C. E. G.: *Horseback Riding.* Thomas Y. Crowell Co., 1954, $2.00.
Hope, C. E. G., and Harris, Charles: *Riding Technique in Pictures.* Pitman Publishing Corp., 1957, $6.50.
Horsemanship. Boy Scouts (#3298), 25¢.
Jaeger, Ellsworth: *Land and Water Trails.*
Jasper, Mrs. A. William: *Horsemanship.* Boy Scouts, 1958, 68 pp., 25¢.
Moore, Elaine T.: *Winning Your Spurs.* Little Brown and Co., 1954, $5.00.
Orr, Jennie M.: *A Manual of Riding.* Burgess Publishing Co., Revised, 1957, 35 pp., $1.75.
Self, Margaret Cabell: *Horsemanship.* A. S. Barnes and Co., 1952, $6.50.

Self, Margaret Cabell: *Horses, Their Selection, Care and Handling.* A. S. Barnes and Co., 1943, $4.50.
Self, Margaret Cabell: *Riding Simplified.* The Ronald Press Co., 1948, 77 pp., $2.95.
Slaughter, Jean: *Horsemanship for Beginners.* Alfred A. Knopf and Co., 1952, $3.75.

MAGAZINE ARTICLES

Drachman, Albert I.: *How Good is Your Riding Program?* C.M., April–June, 1948.
Lee, Marion H.: *A Practical Camp Riding Program.* C.M., Mar., 1957.

Indian Lore

Buttree, Julia: *The Rhythm of the Red Man.* The Ronald Press Co., 1930, 280 pp., $5.00.
Gorham, M.: *The Real Book About Indians.* Garden City Publishing Co., 1953, $1.25.
Hammett, Catherine T., and Horrocks, Carol M.: *Creative Crafts for Campers.*
Hindman, Darwin A.: *Handbook of Indian Games and Stunts.* Prentice-Hall, Inc., 1955, 384 pp., $4.95.
Hofsinde, Robert: *Indian Games and Crafts.* William Morrow and Co., 1957, 127 pp., $2.50.
Hofsinde, Robert, (Gray-Wolf): *Indian Picture Writing.* William Morrow and Co., 96 pp., $2.50.
Hofsinde, Robert, (Gray-Wolf): *The Indian's Secret World.* William Morrow and Co., 1955, 94 pp., $4.50.
Hunt, W. Ben: *Indian and Camp Handicraft.* Bruce Publishing Co., 1945, 180 pp., $3.00.
Hunt, W. Ben: *Indiancraft.* Bruce Publishing Co., 1942, 124 pp., $3.25.
Hunt, W. Ben: *Indian Crafts and Lore.*
Indian Hand Craft. Bureau of Indian Affairs, Supt. of Documents, Washington, D.C.
Indian Lore. Boy Scouts (#3358), 25¢.
Indian Lore in a Boy's Club. Boys Clubs, $1.00.
Jaeger, Ellsworth, *Woodsmoke.*
Laubin, Reginald and Gladys: *The Indian Tipi.* U. of Oklahoma Press, Norman, Okla., 1957, 208 pp., $3.95.
Leach, Maria: *America Folk Tales and Legends.* World Publishing Co., 1958, 319 pp.
Lynn, Gordon: *Camping and Camp Crafts.*
Macfarlan, Allan A.: *Book of American Indian Games.* Assn. Press, 1958, 284 pp., $3.95.
Mason, Bernard S.: *The Book of Indian Crafts and Costumes.* The Ronald Press Co., 1946, 118 pp., $5.50.
Mason, Bernard S.: *Dances and Stories of the American Indians.* The Ronald Press Co., 1944, 269 pp., $5.50.
McGuire, Frances: *Indian Drums Beat Again.* E. P. Dutton and Co., Inc., 1953, 123 pp., $2.50.
Norbeck, Oscar E.: *Book of Indian Life Crafts.* Assn. Press, 1958, 253 pp., $5.95.
Ressler, Theodore Whitson: *Treasury of American Indian Tales.* Assn. Press, 1958, 310 pp., $3.95.

Solomon, Julian H.: *Book of Indian Crafts and Indian Lore.* Harper and Brothers, 1928, $3.95.

Wiley, Farida, Editor: *Ernest Thompson Seton's America.* The Devin-Adair Co., 1954, 413 pp., $5.00.

MAGAZINE ARTICLES

Cassell, Sylvia E.: *Try an Indian Pow Wow.* C.M., June, 1955.

Hauwiller, Mary: *How Your Campers Can Follow the Trail of the Redman.* C.M., Dec., 1956.

Miscellaneous Activities

Brown, Paul: *Croquet.* D. Van Nostrand Co., 1957, 60 pp., $4.25.

Downer, Marion: *Kites: How To Make and Fly Them.* Lothrop, Lee, and Shepard Co., Inc., 1959, 64 pp., $3.00.

Fowler, H. Waller: *Kites—A Practical Guide to Kite Making and Flying.* The Ronald Press Co., 1953, 96 pp., $1.95.

Harbin, E. O.: *The Fun Encyclopedia.*

Jaeger, Ellsworth: *Council Fires.*

Kettlecamp, Larry: *Kites.* NRA, William Morrow and Co., Inc., 48 pp., $2.75.

Mason, Bernard S.: *Roping.* The Ronald Press Co., 1940, 138 pp., $2.95.

Mulac, Margaret E.: *The Playleaders' Manual.* Harper and Brothers, $3.00.

Ripley, G. S.: *Fun Around the Camp Fire.* Boy Scouts #3694, 106 pp., 50¢.

Webb, Kenneth B., Editor: *Light From a Thousand Campfires.*

MAGAZINE ARTICLES

Berthold, Beatrice: *Summer Skiing on Pine Needles.* C.M., June, 1938.

Garrison, Joy, and Doren, Milly: *Lumey Sticks.* J.H., P.E., and R., Mar., 1956.

Johnson, C. Walton: *Woodmen's Roleo Combines Skills, Competition and Fun.* C.M., Nov., 1958.

Kirchner, Irene R.: *Flag Ceremony.* Recreation, Mar., 1957.

Organize a Spring Top Spinning Contest. Recreation, Mar., 1955.

Parties and Special Activities

Anderson, Clara J.: *It's Fun To Give a Pageant.* Educational Publishers, 16 pp.

Douglas, George W.: *The American Book of Days.* The H. W. Wilson Co., Revised, 1948, 697 pp., $6.00.

Hacker, Fred, and Eames, Prescott: *How To Put on an Amateur Circus.* T. S. Denison and Co., 112 pp., $2.50.

Handy Folklore. Coop. Rec. Service, Available in ring binder, $3.00 or shelf box, $2.00.

Hazeltine, Mary E.: *Anniversaries and Holidays.* A.L.A. 2nd Ed., 1944, 336 pp., $6.00.

Joy, Barbara Ellen: *All-Camp, All-Skill Contest—A Plan for an Afternoon of Team Competition in All Camp Activities.* Camp Publications #13, 6 pp., 40¢.

Keene, Frances W.: *Fun Around the World.* Seahorse, 1955, 128 pp., $2.95, (paper) $1.00.

Macfarlan, Allan A.: *Campfire and Council Ring Programs.*

Spicer, Dorothy Gladys: *Folk Party Fun.* Assn. Press, 1954, 320 pp., $3.95.

Successful Play Activities. NRA., 96 pp., 75¢.

MAGAZINE ARTICLES

Cole, Florence: *How to Make Inexpensive Awards.* J.H., P.E., and R., Jan., 1958.

Photography

Frankel, Godfrey: *Short Cut to Photography.* Sterling Publishing Co., Inc., 1954, 128 pp., $2.50.

Freeman, Mae and Ira: *Fun with Your Camera.* Random House Inc., 1955, 55 pp., $1.50. (grades 4–7)

Gottlieb, William: *Photography.* Alfred A. Knopf, Inc., 1953, 44 pp., $1.75. (grades 2–6)

Gowland, Peter: *How To Take Better Home Movies.* Fawcett Publishing Co., 1955, 144 pp., 75¢.

Hoke, John: *The First Book of Photography.* C. A. Watts and Co., Ltd.), 1954, $1.95. (grades 5–10)

Kesting, Ted: *The Outdoor Encyclopedia.*

Kjelgaard, James Arthur: *Wildlife Cameraman.* Holiday House, 218 pp., $2.75.

Langer, Don: *My Hobby Is Photography.* Hart Publishing Co., Inc., 1956, 128 pp., $3.95. (grades 5–9)

McCoy, Robert A.: *Practical Photography.* McKnight and McKnight Publishing Co., 1958, 240 pp., $4.00.

Marshall, Lucile R.: *Photography for Teen-Agers.* Prentice-Hall, Inc., 2nd Ed., 1957, 180 pp., $3.95.

Mayall, Robert, N., and Margaret L.: *Skyshooting, Hunting the Stars with Your Camera.* The Ronald Press Co., 1949, 174 pp., $4.00.

Photography. Boy Scouts #3334, 25¢.

Photography in Camp—A Manual for Counselors. Eastman Kodak Co.

Picture Taking in Camp. Eastman Kodak Co., 32 pp. (Camper's Manual)

Shumway, Herbert D.: *Nature Photography Guide.* Greenberg Co., 1956, 125 pp., $1.95.

Sussman, Aaron: *Amateur Photographer's Handbook.* Thomas Y. Crowell Co., 5th Ed., 1957, 400 pp., $4.95.

The Brownie Book of Picture Taking. Eastman Kodak Co.

Zim, Dr. H. S., and Burnett, R. Will: *Photography.* Golden Books, 1956, 160 pp., $2.50. (grades 5–7)

MAGAZINE ARTICLES

Hammett, Catherine T., and Musselman, Virginia: *Camp Photography.* Recreation, Mar., 1958.

Photograms—Easy Craft with Camper Appeal. C.M., June, 1953.

Picture Taking is Important Too. C.M., March, 1954.

Shooting and Firearms

Basic Rifle Marksmanship. Nat'l Rifle Ass'n., 1956, 33 pp.

Basic Rifle Marksmanship, Instructor's Guide. Nat'l Rifle Ass'n., 1956, 20 pp.

Camp Reference Issue and Buying Guide. Issued annually by American Camping Ass'n.

Colby, Carroll B.: *First Rifle: How To Shoot It Straight and Use It Safely.* Coward Publishing Co., 1954, 48 pp., $2.00.

Daisy Air Rifle Instruction Program. Daisy Industries, 1958, 12 pp., Free.

Damon, G. E.: *Gun Fun with Safety.* Stackpole Co., 1947, 206 pp., $6.00.

Elliott, Russ: *Your Shotgun Vs. You.* Brown-White-Lowell Press, Inc., Kansas City, Mo., 1955, 117 pp.

George, Jack F.: *Shooting and Firearms Instructor's Guide.* AAHPER, 1956, 61 pp.

Janes, E C.: *A Boy and His Gun.* A. S. Barnes and Co., Inc., 1951, 207 pp., $3.50.

Marksmanship. Boy Scouts #3338, 25¢.

Shooting and Hunting. AAHPER, 1959, 96 pp., $2.00.

Shooting's Fun for Everyone. Prepared by Wilding-Henderson, Inc., Detroit, for Sporting Arms and Ammunition Mfrs. Institute, Sportsman's Service Bureau, 250 E. 43rd St., N.Y., 1957, 19 pp.

Woods Safety Education. Maine Dept. of Inland Fisheries and Game, Augusta, Maine, 1956, 43 pp.

MAGAZINE ARTICLES

Air Rifle Program. C.M., May, 1957.

Cardinal, Paul: *Easy Ways to Improve Your Rifle Range.* C.M., April, 1951.

Fremault, George: *Your Camp Riflery Program.* C.M., March, 1954.

Hicks, Marjorie: *Air Rifle Shooting.* C.M., May, 1953.

Keister, William H.: *From Juniors Through Seniors They All Love Riflery.* C.M., Dec., 1955.

Sure Fire Safety in Riflery. Recreation, Sept., 1957.

Stocker, Stanley W.: *An Improved Riflery Program.* C.M., Dec., 1956.

Stunts and Skits

Brings, Lawrence M.: *The Master Stunt Book.* T. S. Denison and Co., 1957, 431 pp., $3.95. Pantomimes, skits and stunts.

De Pew, A. M.: *Cokesbury Stunt Book.* Abingdon Press, Revised, $2.95.

Easy Stunts and Skits. NRA, 32 pp., 50¢. 16 stunts and skits easy to produce.

Eisenberg, Helen and Larry: *Fun with Skits, Stunts and Stories.* Assn. Press, 1955, 256 pp., $2.95.

Eisenberg, Helen and Larry: *Handbook of Skits and Stunts.* Assn. Press, 1953, 254 pp., $2.95. (over 400 stunts of all sorts.)

Green, Allen V.: *Simple Tricks for the Young Magician.* Hart Publishing Co., 1955, 189 pp.

Howard, Vernon: *Pantomimes, Charades, and Skits.* Sterling Publishing Co., Inc., 1959, 128 pp., $2.50.

10

Dramatics

Of all people, children are the most imaginative.
MACAULAY, *ESSAYS:*
MITFORD'S *GREECE*

THOUGH ALL OF US like to pretend, it is in youth particularly that we find this desire most urgent. From very tender years on we see Suzie being the grown-up lady as she dresses up in Mother's high heels, hat, pocketbook and over-commodious dress and holds sway over her make believe home with doll "children" who must be washed, fed, and disciplined. At the same time, Johnnie is out "shootin' em up" as his big six-gun mows down Indians or "bad men" as if they were clay pigeons at a carnival. Notice the use of the word "be" instead of "play" above for children show one of the most important prerequisites of a good actor; they step out of themselves and actually *are* the people they portray. Imagination, make believe, the urge to imitate, and complete lack of self-consciousness are abundant in most children and need only to have the reins released to burst forth spontaneously. In a trice, our hero becomes successively the cop on the beat, the pilot zooming his jet plane through the air, the duck quacking on the pond, or a railroad train chugging and chooing its way across trestles and up mountains.

FORMAL AND INFORMAL PLAYS AND SKITS

Time was when most self-respecting camps put on at least one full length drama a season, replete with rented costumes, elaborate props, and fancy sets as

116

(H. Armstrong Roberts.)

the young Thespians strutted forth to display their accomplishments to an admiring assemblage of parents, grandparents, brothers, sisters, aunts and cousins who had been especially invited for the occasion. Of course there had to be a real-for-sure testimonial bouquet for the heroine and plaudits, and a present for the hero. All of this was no doubt merited by the young actors and actresses who had spent long hours memorizing lines and mastering gestures and techniques as they strove for faultless perfection. Many of their neighbors, however, refused to come indoors for the production for the squirrel was still chattering in the tree tops, the brook was babbling away outside, the birds were merrily singing on the bushes, the sun was methodically rising and setting in its usual splendor, and the mountain still stood majestically a short distance away, all unnoticed and unsung by our youngster who was spending long hours indoors doing the same things he could do all winter and seeing only mountains, birds, brooks, and a sun as they appeared painted on a set. For most campers, who have neither the ability nor the desire to be professional actors, what should be spontaneous fun and one among many earnest, yet more or less casual, camp activities had taken on the characteristics of a major, all-engrossing opus.

It is true that play-acting and watching rightfully become absorbing interests for many children and adults and, when honestly desired, should be made a part of any well-rounded camp program but the production should be carefully selected and administered so that it becomes *one of many,* not *the* activity of the summer. Long plays can be cut, and one act and short plays, especially adapted to a setting in the out-of-door camp atmosphere, are available and fit nicely into a well-balanced program.

Costumes and Props

Plays for camp should be full of action with no slow, stuffy scenes and no elaborate scenery necessitating long waits for a change of sets. Children's strong sense of imagination and make believe render elaborate costuming unnecessary, for the knight, striding forth in his stew pan helmet, his painted cardboard shield and lashed sword, with his coat of mail improvised from shiny oilcloth is perfectly satisfying to a youthful audience. The necessary trees and grass can be real-for-sure ones in a nearby natural amphitheatre, and the castle in the background can be made from discarded packing boxes, labeled so that no one can fail to know what it is. The princess, who is waiting for her true love to rescue her, can be most enchanting in her "old curtain" dress with a train, braided tresses of frayed rope, jewelry made from seeds, nuts, and shells, and a crown which first came to camp as a tin can and is jewelled with some acorns covered with Mystic or reflector tape. The villain wears a too-big hat and a tailed coat out of the costume box as he twirls his dyed rope mustache and flashes his painted cardboard watch on the end of its "knife" chain suspended prominently across his chest. "Charming" animals with burlap bag bodies, paper bag heads, pipe cleaner whiskers, rope tails and cardboard ears cavort in and out. The old crone has an "old mop" wig above a mouth noticeable for its missing teeth, blacked out with "Black Jack" gum, wears a frowsy burlap bag dress, mended by numerous colorful patches; her gnarled hand grasps a crooked stick cane to help her on her decrepit way. The sofa consists of a few pillows on three chairs, the whole covered with a tastefully draped light green tarp. A little imagination, a discerning eye to seek out odds and ends of furniture, some bits of cloth, a few items purchased from the variety store, a survey of personal and camp property, and a trip to the camp costume box provide the simple things needed and everybody will have had more fun since their own ingenuity is on display rather than ready-made articles shipped from a costumer.

A paper bag that just fits over your head can be converted by a little paint into a false face, with holes for eyes and mouth and paper ears and nose pasted on. Pillow-slip aprons, handkerchief collars, sheet or curtain angel robes, burlap bag Indian costumes with fringe, pirate or gypsy earrings made from curtain rod rings, and a Turkish towel or bathrobe oriental costume serve remarkably well. Bright bits of cloth or old odds and ends add color as gay sashes, scarves or head dresses. Bright objects, such as sheriffs' stars, belt or shoe buckles, jewelry or a flashing sword can be made from flattened tin cans or cardboard covered with aluminum foil or Mystic tape. Guns can be fashioned from wood and painted. Such devices will transform campers as magically as Cinderella's godmother changed mice into horses.

Home Grown Productions

The most enjoyed plays and skits are usually those that counselors and/or children make up themselves, for here again self-expression holds sway and imagination can run riot. Often a whole group or a committee functions, and, though initial ideas may be slow in coming, once a central plot is decided upon, suggestions for developments, scenes and action will usually tumble out all over themselves until it becomes a matter of sifting out the best and assembling them into some semblance of a logical whole; but don't let the fact that it isn't *too* sensible bother you for children love best the things that are illogical and implausible. If somebody knows some good jokes, rearrange the script to work them in. Plays on words, favorite expressions, or peculiarities of camp personnel add hilarity and pleasure for even the subject if tastefully done.

Every character should be played to the hilt with the hero the wisest, most charming and honest man that ever existed in contrast to the villain who is the most underhanded, despicable creature that ever drew a breath. Virtue of every sort must be lavishly rewarded and evil must be as unfailingly punished.

The action should be brisk and colorful and each act should end in a semiclimactic bit of humor, excitement, or grandeur with the audience hissing the villain, applauding the hero or collapsing in a state of laughter. Audience reaction of this sort is good in moderation but shouldn't be allowed to get out of hand. Children love all kinds of animals, so some can be worked in to provide anything from walk on parts to star roles. Incidentally, shy children often lose their timidity when concealed behind a mask or when walking about on all fours under the "fur" of some animal. Don't be afraid to exaggerate, both as to action and plausibility. End your production on a happy note with all the "good" characters attaining what they most desire and the "bad" ones groveling in their just deserts. Work in some dances as the cowboys and gals, in boots, chaps, colorful bandanas, and Colts in holsters, engage in a spirited cowboy dance. Include favorite or new songs with the audience joining in on the chorus. After all, the purpose of the whole thing is to have fun and the true measurement of results is in the good that comes to the participants. This last, of course, rules out anything smacking of bad taste or slap stick.

Many People Take Part

As always, the more the merrier, and everyone can find something to do that fits his interests and abilities. For those who want to act but have no parts, new characters can be added. People will be needed to type up copies of the script, prompt, design sets, plan make-up and costumes, arrange extension cords for footlights and spotlights of Christmas tree lights, flashlights, or candles with tin can or aluminum foil reflectors. Others can arrange seating, prepare programs and posters, act as the town crier to invite all to the affair, serve as ushers, or write an account of the whole thing for the camp paper. Though the above implies that productions are always planned for an audience, this is not at all true for some of the most fun-filled and worth-while performances are spontaneous affairs which are born

and die right in a little cabin or unit group which is trying to entertain itself on a rainy day or programless night. But it is also true that such a group often becomes so absorbed in its project and is so pleased with the results that it wants to expand the initial effort and invite outsiders. Eventually, the whole may end up in a performance at a camp council fire or for guests on visitor's day.

Source of Original Productions

Ideas can come from anywhere. A whole group or one or more individuals can produce them from their heads and set them down on paper for others to carry out. They may revolve around favorite nursery rhymes, Mother Goose tales or putting a well-liked story into words and action. Historical or current events, Bible stories, or the local history of the community or camp may serve as the theme. Best liked of all are probably take-offs on camp situations as campers lampoon the terrible tyrant counselors and other staff, or the staff plays turn about and gives a counselor's eye view of the campers. Campers often like to depict themselves as others see them and contrive to work in many of the hilarious events of the summer. These are fine, if done with discretion, but the utmost care must be used lest elements creep in which might hurt people or wound their pride. Thus "take-offs" on local personnel must be in a spirit of good natured fun and not attempts to express animosities or prejudices. We must be careful, too, not to use dialects or references to color, nationalities, or religions that might offend.

Values of Dramatics

As previously mentioned, dramatic activities give children a chance to indulge their natural love of imitating, pretending, imagining and exaggerating. It gives practice in group cooperation and shows how the talents and interests of many can be compatibly welded into a common, satisfying whole. It requires self-discipline and self-direction and teaches poise, good enunciation and proper voice projection. It often informs us concerning how and where others live and work, now or in former days, and may bring about an appreciation of still another type of worth-while literature, the drama. It opens insights into a form of recreation highly enjoyable for many and often discloses talents even the individual himself didn't know he had for it is true there is a bit of the "ham" in all of us. Most of all, it's fun!

DRAMATIC ACTIVITIES

Many activities which are not actually plays have the elements of play acting in them. Usually, individuals participate in them simply because it is fun, and they would be astonished and perhaps even withdraw if you suggested that there was any connection between what they were doing and dramatics; they would be convinced that they have absolutely no ability along that line. Yet these pastimes do satisfy our often unrecognized wish to pretend and frequently reveal talents and interests no one, least of all the individual himself, suspected that he had.

MUSICAL COMEDIES AND OPERETTAS. These combine music, dramatics, and dancing. Those of Gilbert and Sullivan are old favorites and there are also many other good ones. Then, too, there is always the possibility of making up your own.

READING PLAYS. Those who don't want to take the time and trouble to put on a play can find a satisfactory substitute by having individuals read the parts. All degrees of participation are possible ranging from a simple one-performance affair to one where characters familiarize themselves with their parts until they can read them realistically and even carry out the action called for. This is often a good way to introduce actual play acting for it is an easy step to then go on to commit the lines to memory.

PAGEANTS.   Outdoor portrayals of local lore, camp history or historical events.

FOLK FESTIVALS.   Customs, traditions, costumes, and national characteristics of one or several other countries.

STUNT NIGHT.   A traditional camp fun night with campers and staff displaying their talents at anything from roping a "broncho," performing feats of magic, putting on a skit, or playing in the harmonica, kitchen utensil, or "paper over comb" band. Better have some responsible person act as master of ceremonies and tactfully guide the group or it may degenerate into something utterly boring or undesirable.

PANTOMIME WITH READING.   Actors act out parts as someone reads a well chosen ballad, story or original skit. A few rehearsals improve the performance immensely.

CHARADES.   An old game in which one team or individual pantomimes the syllables of a word such as "dandie-lyin' " or idolatry (eye-doll-a-tree) while the others try to guess what the word is. Other categories to act out are Mother Goose rhymes, book titles, story book characters, advertising slogans, famous present-day or historical people, or professions.

A variation is to have a team choose a word and whisper it to a member of the other team who must then act it out as best he can to help his group guess what it is. Continue, alternating groups, until each participant has had his turn at acting. Keep a record of the total time consumed by each team in guessing the words. The winner is the team that requires the least time.

DUMB CRAMBO.   This is the opposite of charades. One team selects a word and tells the other team what it rhymes with; the second team then acts out various guesses until they finally hit on the right one.

NEW ORLEANS.   An old childhood favorite.

PAPER-BAG DRAMATICS.   Each group is handed a bag full of simple properties and costumes, which they must use to produce a skit.

SEALED ORDERS.   A number of humorous situations are written on slips of paper and placed in a hat; each participant draws a slip and must act out the situation while the others attempt to guess what it is. Group chooses the best presentation. Suggested situations: "timid old lady caught in middle of busy street with the traffic light changing, Uncle Neddie trying to sneak in the house late and go up to his room without being heard, the little camper who is afraid to get in the pool for his first swimming lesson," etc. Other categories such as those mentioned in Charades may be used for acting out.

BURLESQUES.   These are take offs on camp life (or any other desired topic). Subjects might be "the camp unit's first overnight trip; cabin clean up; a camper's version of a camp staff meeting," or "visiting day at camp." Again, beware of hurt feelings.

ALBUM OF FAMILIAR PICTURES.   Arrange a "curtain" of blankets and turn off the lights as a group behind the curtain poses itself as a picture out of grandmother's album, the ladies' bridge club, scene in the camp dining room, etc. Turn on the lights and see what you have. Exaggerate and make it ludicrous.

SHADOW PLAYS.   Stretch a curtain (it works better if it's wet) tightly and place bright lights far enough behind it to leave a miniature stage just behind the curtain. Turn out all the other lights. Actors, staying very close to the sheet so their silhouettes will be sharp and clear, act out a skit, story, ballad, or burlesque. Only a suggestion of costume is necessary and settings and props can be cut from cardboard or old packing boxes and glued together. Give the audience only a brief description of the situation or read the whole script as you act it out. Accompany it with "mood music" if you wish.

CHORAL SPEECH.   This is an old activity which is being revived. It consists of reciting poetry, Bible quotations, stories or whatever is desired in unison. The voices are grouped as to low and high, heavy and light, and the performers are usually arranged in a semicircle around the leader who gives inconspicuous directions for starting, stopping, emphasis, pauses and such. Participants should know the selection well enough to give close attention to the director. Various ways to add variety are to assign solo parts or to have groups recite alternately, antiphonal style. Poems which the group really enjoys, which swing along with a marked rhythm, and are full of repetition work out best. This makes a good program for devotions or a camp fire program.

MARIONETTE AND PUPPET SHOWS. These characters vary all the way from creations fashioned in a few moments from sacks, socks or other materials and intended to be slipped over the hand and manipulated by the fingers (puppets) to elaborate creatures controlled by from one to fifteen strings attached to control sticks which the operator holds (marionettes). They combine various skills and interests since the more elaborate productions need people to design and dress the puppets, operate them, make the stage sets and props, arrange the lighting, write or arrange the script, read the script or story being acted out and furnish musical accompaniment if it is desired. Children greatly enjoy them and they're well worth trying.

ADDITIONAL READINGS

Dramatic Activities

Allstrom, Elizabeth: *Let's Play a Story.* Friendship Press, 1957, 165 pp., $1.95.

Bailey, Howard: *ABC's of Play Producing: A Handbook for the Nonprofessional.* McKay Publishing Co., 1955, 276 pp., $3.95.

Berk, Barbara: *The First Book of Stage Costume and Make-Up.* C. A. Watts and Co., Ltd., 1954, 45 pp., $1.95.

Berk, Barbara, and Bendick, Jeanne: *How To Have a Show.* C. A. Watts and Co., Ltd., 1957, 64 pp., $2.95.

Bucher, Charles A., Editor: *Methods and Materials in Physical Education and Recreation.*

Buerki, F. A.: *Stagecraft for Nonprofessionals.* University of Wisc., 1956, 131 pp., $1.50.

Burger, Isabel B.: *Creative Play Acting.* The Ronald Press Co., 1950, 224 pp., $3.75. (ages 8–18, includes 3 plays).

Carlson, Bernice Wells: *Act It Out.* Abingdon Press, 1956, 160 pp., $2.00, (grades 3–5).

Children's Theatre Manual. Seattle Junior Programs, Comp. NRA, 56 pp., 75¢.

Corbin, H. Dan: *Recreation Leadership.*

DeMarche, Edythe and David: *Handbook of Co-Ed Teen Activities.* Assn. Press, 1958, 640 pp., $7.95.

Dramatics. Boy Scouts #3367. 25¢.

Dramatics and Ceremonies for Girl Scouts. Girl Scouts, 206 pp., $1.50.

Durland, Frances C.: *Creative Dramatics for Children.* Antioch. Press, 181 pp., $1.50.

Elicker, Virginia Wilk: *Biblical Costumes for Church and School.* The Ronald Press Co., 1953, 160 pp., $3.00.

Hake, Herbert V.: *Here's How.* Row, Peterson, and Co., Revised, 128 pp., $3.40.

Hammett, Catherine T., and Horrocks, Carol M.: *Creative Crafts for Campers.*

Hammett, Catherine, and Musselman, Virginia: *The Camp Program Book.*

Knapp, Jack Stuart: *How To Produce a Play.* NRA, 32 pp., 50¢.

Kraus, Richard: *Recreation Leader's Handbook.*

Lease, Ruth and Siks, Geraldine: *Creative Dramatics in Home, School, and Community.* Harper and Brothers, 1952, 306 pp.

Leeming, Joseph: *The Costume Book for Parties and Plays.* J. B. Lippincott Co., 1938, 123 pp., $3.25.

Melvill, Harold: *Complete Guide to Amateur Dramatics.* Citadel Press, 310 pp., $7.50.

Musselman, Virginia: *Informal Dramatics.* NRA, 32 pp., 50¢.

Siks, Geraldine B.: *Creative Dramatics: An Art for Children*. Harper and Brothers, 1958, 472 pp., $6.00.

Vannier, Maryhelen: *Methods and Materials in Recreation Leadership*.

Walker, Pamela Prince: *Seven Steps to Creative Children's Dramatics*. Hill and Wang, Inc., 1957, 150 pp., $3.00.

Ward, Winifred: *Playmaking with Children*. Appleton-Century-Crofts, Inc., 2nd Ed., 1957, 341 pp., $4.00.

Webb, Kenneth B., Editor: *Light from a Thousand Campfires*.

White, Alice: *Anthology of Choral Readings*. Girl Scouts #23-466, 50¢.

Zirner, Laura: *Costuming for the Modern Stage*. U. of Illinois, 1957, 47 pp., $3.00.

Books Containing Plays, Activities, Etc.:

Anderson, Walter W., et. al.: *Indian and Famous Scout Plays*. T. S. Denison and Co., 166 pp., $1.00.

Burack, A. S., Editor: *100 Plays for Children*. Plays, Inc., 1949, $5.95. (grades 2–6)

Casey, Beatrice M.: *Good Things for Everyday Programs*. T. S. Denison and Co., 201 pp., $1.00.

Eisenberg, Helen and Larry: *The Handbook of Skits and Stunts*. Assn. Press, 1953, 254 pp., $2.95.

Eisenberg, Helen and Larry: *Omnibus of Fun*.

Eisenberg, Helen and Larry: *Skits, Stunts and Stories*. Assn. Press, 1955, 256 pp., $2.95.

Gullan, Marjorie: *The Speech Choir; American Poetry and English Ballads for Choral Reading*. Harper and Brothers, 1937.

Harbin, E. O.: *The Fun Encyclopedia*.

Hark, Mildred, and McQueen, Noel: *Modern Comedies for Young Players*. Plays, Inc., 1951, $4.50. (grades 8–12)

Hark, Mildred, and McQueen, Noel: *Teen-Age Plays*. Plays, Inc., $5.00. (grades 7–11)

Howard, Vernon: *Pantomimes, Charades and Skits*. Sterling Publishing Co., Inc., 1959, 128 pp., $2.50.

Howard, Vernon: *Short Plays for All-Boy Casts*. Plays, Inc., 1954, $3.50. 30 royalty-free plays.

Huber, Louis J.: *Easy Arena Plays*. Northeastern Press, 120 pp., $1.00.

Kamerman, Sylvia E.: *Little Plays for Little Players*. Plays, Inc., 1952, $4.00. (grades 1–4)

Macfarlan, Allan A.: *Campfire and Council Ring Programs*.

Miksch, W. F.: *Teen-Age Sketches*. Northwestern Press, 134 pp., $1.00.

Miller, Helen Louise: *On Stage for Teen-Agers*. Plays, Inc., 1948, $5.00.

Miller, Helen Louise: *Prize Plays for Teen-Agers*. Plays, Inc., 1956, $5.00.

Paradis, Marjorie B.: *One-Act Plays for All-Girl Casts*. Plays, Inc., 1952, $3.50. (grades 8–12)

Plays for Children. Children's Theatre Press, 83 pp., 10¢.

Severn, Bill and Sue: *Let's Give a Show*. Alfred A. Knopf, Inc., 1956, $2.75. (ages 8–12.)

Six More Dramatic Stunts: NRA, 36 pp., 50¢.

Six New Dramatic Stunts. NRA, 32 pp., 50¢.

Tobitt, Janet E., and White, Alice: *Dramatized Ballads*. E. P. Dutton and Co., 1937, $2.95. (grades 7–10)

Very, Alice: *Round-the-Year Plays for Children*. Plays, Inc., 1957, 279 pp., $3.75. (grades 2–6)

Ward, Winifred: *Stories To Dramatize*. Chldren's Theatre Press. 1952, 389 pp., $4.75.

MAGAZINE ARTICLES

Booth, Judy: *Camp Dramatics—A Performance for Stars Or A Creative Experience For All?* C.M., June, 1951. (Also reprinted in Webb, Kenneth B., Editor, *Light from a Thousand Campfires*.)

Breeser, Betty: *Fantasy in Camp Programs*. C.M., Dec., 1953.

Harbor, Betty: *Emphasize Fun in Camp Dramatics*. C.M., Mar., 1953.

Perry, Charlotte: *The Creative Approach to Camp Dramatics*. C.M., March, 1955.

Strawbridge, Edwin: *Do Your Plays For Not To The Children*. Recreation, Oct., 1954.

Marionettes and Puppets

Batchelder, Marjorie: *Puppet Theatre Handbook*. Harper, 1947, $3.75.

Batchelder, Marjorie, and Comer, Virginia Lee: *Puppets and Plays—A Creative Approach*. Harper and Brothers, 1956, 241 pp., $4.00. (Not only how to make puppets but how to use them as a means of creative self-expression.)

Cassell, Sylvia: *Fun with Puppets*. Broardman, 1956, 87 pp., $1.50. leader's edition $2.50. (grades 4–7) (Puppets, stages, sets, scenery, how to dramatize stories, etc.)

Ficklen, Bessie H.: *Handbook of Fist Puppets*. J. B. Lippincott and Co., 1935, $3.50.

Jones, Josephine M.: *Glove Puppetry*. Sportshelf, 94 pp., $2.75.

Lanchester, Waldo S.: *Hand Puppets and String Puppets*. Charles A. Bennett Co., Inc., 1957, 54 pp., paper, $2.50.

Lewis, Roger: *Puppets and Marionettes*. Alfred A. Knopf, Inc., 1952, $1.75. (ages 7–11).

Lewis, Shari: *The Shari Lewis Puppet Book*. Citadel Press, 61 pp., $1.95.

Musselman, Virginia: *Simple Puppetry*. NRA, 28 pp., 50¢.

Osgood, Mildred M.: *Marionettes*. School Products, 19 pp., 75¢.

Pratt, Lois H.: *Puppet Do-It-Yourself Book*. The Exposition Press, 1957, 75 pp., $3.00. (A book simple enough for the beginner yet also includes advanced techniques.)

Rasmussen, Carrie, and Storck, Caroline: *Fun-Time Puppets*. Children's Press, 1952, 41 pp., $2.80. (grades 3–4)

Tichenor, Tom H.: *Folk Plays for Puppets You Can Make*. Abingdon Press, 1959, 96 pp., $2.25.

Vannier, Maryhelen: *Methods and Materials in Recreation Leadership*.

11

Music

Music washes away from the soul the dust of everyday life.
AUERBACH

It is the most natural thing in the world for happy campers to sing whenever and wherever they are; conversely, campers who sing just naturally can't keep from being happy. Song should burst forth as spontaneously as mushrooms after a rain, for the miles fly by while hiking, dishes seem almost to dry themselves and a group of paddlers can proceed in perfect rhythm when there's a song in the air. Good music is a great morale booster, for few fail to succumb to a catchy tune, a strong rhythm, or the sheer beauty of a lovely melody. No camper should return home without a complete repertoire of good new (to him) songs in his head.

Kinds of Songs

Most songs can be divided roughly into three types, each having a definite place in camp.

1. *Folk songs* such as "Louisiana Lullaby" and "Walking at Night" cannot be traced to any one composer, for they have been handed down from one generation to the next and sung for many years before anyone ever got around to putting them into writing. They must have had real meaning and worth, for only songs which speak the language of the people can survive for so long. *Ballads,* such as "Barbara Allen" and "The Old Woman's Courtin'," tell a story, and can therefore be dramatized. The *sea chanteys* of sailors such as "Blow the Man Down,"

124

(Joy and Camp.)

various *work songs,* as "Roll the Cotton Down," and the French *voyageur* songs were used to shorten long hours of labor. All types of folk songs, including lullabies, singing games, Negro spirituals, plantation songs, cowboy songs and mountain ballads, hold even more fascination when the singers know the story behind them and the customs, occupations and manner of life of the peoples who originally sang them.

2. In *rounds* or *canons,* the group is subdivided into two or more groups who carry the same tune, but start singing at spaced intervals. Each sings the song through an agreed number of times (usually as many as there are parts), so that they end the song in reverse order. "White Coral Bells" and "Dona Nobis Pacem" are well known examples.

3. *Art songs* are compositions of the masters and are surprisingly often based on old folk songs. They are lovely and offer unlimited possibilities in the way of bringing about a deeper appreciation of really good music. "Prayer" from "Hansel and Gretel" is of this type.

Should a General Counselor Lead Singing?

There is a far too prevalent feeling that only counselors with special talent and training in music should lead or teach songs, but this will rob both you and your group of much pleasure. Any person who can carry a tune can learn to teach songs which will be influential in drawing his group together in happiness and good fellowship. Some successful leaders do not even try to join the singing but merely "mouth" the words in good rhythm as they spur their singers on to a worthy rendition. An enthusiastic person with a little musical knowledge can keep a group together and sometimes gets better results than a professional musician who kills spontaneity and joy by his insistence on perfection.

How Should You Present Songs?

1. You will need tact and patience to wean campers' tastes away from the inferior doggerel and popular tunes of the juke box and transfer them to the abundance of really good music available. It may be wisest to join them at first in the songs they already know, gradually introducing short, catchy new ones, and eventually leading up to more complicated ones. It is surprising how soon the right approach finds campers requesting more new songs and resinging the ones just learned for they find a new source of satisfaction when they learn to sing good songs well.

2. It is easiest to teach songs to a small group whose members can then be used as the nucleus to teach them to others.

3. Know the tune and words thoroughly before trying to teach them. Sing it several times to yourself, perhaps practicing your arm movements for leading in front of a mirror. You may not need arm movements at all, or at least only simple ones, if your group is small for you need only keep them in unison; in fact, it is really detrimental to the spirit of camp singing to use gesticulations approaching those of a symphony conductor. Use your left hand to regulate volume and indicate when certain groups are to start or stop as in rounds. Keep the rhythm with your right hand. A crisp manner on your part will bring a like response from your singers, whereas a lackadasical, spiritless manner will be similarly reflected. Your right arm movements may follow the pattern below.

Have some signal to start as "ready," draw in a breath on the next beat, and then give a brisk downstroke of your right arm for the first word or make an upbeat, pause and start the group with a vigorous downbeat. Be sure to hold your hands high enough for everyone to see. Let the vigor of your hand movements show how much volume and accent you want; hold your hand in a fixed position to indicate a held note, and chop it off at the end of the song so all will stop together.

4. Some camps mimeograph or print song books of their own particular favorites or you may print the words of a new song to be learned in large characters on rolled wrapping paper which can be hung where all can see. Most song leaders, however, feel that singers put more thought and feeling into a song if they sing the words from memory and that this also allows them to watch you and so keep together in the pride and thrill of singing in perfect cadence.

5. When teaching a new song, sing it through to give a general idea of the tempo and spirit and set a good mood for learning. If it seems desirable, call attention to the story or background of the song or the sequence of events as you repeat the words and give little cues to help the singers remember. If the chorus is particularly catchy, teach it first, then present the verses one at a time, coming back to the now familiar chorus each time. Watch carefully and present additional parts of the song as fast as the group is ready for them, but don't rush things too much.

6. Iron out mistakes in timing, phrasing, words or pitch before they have become habits and stress good performance and pride in singing well. A good technique is to occasionally send a few of the group a short distance away to make a

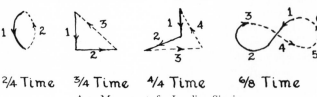

2/4 Time   3/4 Time   4/4 Time   6/8 Time

Arm Movements for Leading Singing.

critical evaluation of how well the rest sing.

7. Have plenty of lively funful singing but never boisterous noise-making with little thought for anything except volume.

8. When starting an already familiar song, sing a line to give the intended tempo and key. It is good to use piano, guitar, accordion, or other instrument occasionally, but tones are truer and singing more spontaneous when groups are accustomed to singing *à capella* (without instrumental accompaniment).

9. As a leader, you should enjoy singing and show it, for temper and grumpiness are disheartening and fatal to a joyful spirit. Don't be afraid to give a word of commendation for good performance.

10. A variety of songs—happy, sad, plaintive, rollicking, thoughtful, sentimental, nonsensical, and just plain lovely—and such devices as antiphonal singing, part singing, and descants (tenor air carried along by a few high voices) add color and diversity. Try letting one group hum harmonizing chords as another sings and encourage good part singing. Never repeat a song too often, and bring the singing period to a close while enthusiasm is still running high. If a song has been sung to the threadbare, boresome stage, have a mock funeral and "bury it"; then plant a dandelion over the grave and let no one thereafter disturb the body.

11. The mood of a group dictates the singing. Quiet, thoughtful songs are best for vesper programs, Sundays and quieting activities before taps, while happy, rollicking ones fit better for other occasions.

12. Organize glee clubs, solos, duets, trios, quartettes, octettes, and so on, for enjoyment or to perform for special occasions. A choir, approaching tunefully through the woods on the way to the Outdoor Chapel, adds greatly to vesper or Sunday services.

13. Use music just before taps, while waiting to go into the dining room, for graces, campfire programs, serenades and antiphonal singing in which one group answers another from an adjoining hill or from canoes out on the water. There should also be periods when campers can listen to the recordings of the best in music.

14. Encourage campers to bring and play their own instruments. Rhythm orchestras are easy and inexpensive to organize and have a particular appeal for younger campers. Campers can make their own instruments, such as shepherd's pipes and ocarinas as described in the sources at the end of the chapter; some camps have orchestras playing camper-made instruments.

15. Let campers compose their own songs for their groups or units or try to fit a new tune to a favorite poem. Surely it is more fun to be original rather than adopt or paraphrase a song from a school or some other camp.

16. Most informal song sessions should be a mutual give-and-take with both campers and counselors sharing in the choice of what to sing.

17. Don't teach too many songs at once; intersperse the old with the new.

ADDITIONAL READINGS

Dancing

Buttree, Julia: *The Rhythm of the Redman*. The Ronald Press Co., 1930, 280 pp., $5.00.

Dugan, Anne Schley, Schlottmann, Jeanette, and Rutledge, Abbie: *The Folk Dance Library*, 5 volumes: *The Teaching of Folk Dance, Folk Dances of Scandinavia; Folk Dances of European Countries; Folk Dances of the British Isles; Folk Dances of the U.S. and Mexico*. The Ronald Press Co., 1948, $4.50 per volume or $20 for set.

Durlacher, Ed.: *Honor Your Partner*. The Devin-Adair Co., 1949, 286 pp., $10.00.

Eisenberg, Helen and Larry: *Omnibus of Fun.*

Flood, Jessie B.: *Square Dance*. Brown Book Co., 1958, 120 pp.

Fox, Grace I., and Merrill, Kathleen Gruppe: *Folk Dancing*. The Ronald Press Co., 2nd Ed., 1958, $4.50.

Gowing, Gene: *The Square Dancer's Guide*. Crown Publishers, 1957, $3.95.

Hammett, Catherine T., and Musselman, Virginia: *The Camp Program Book.*

The Handy Folk Dance Book. Coop. Rec. Service, $1.00.

The Handy Square Dance Book. Coop. Rec. Service, $1.00.

Harris, Jane A., Pittman, Anne, and Waller, Marlys S.: *Dance Awhile: Handbook of Folk, Square and Social Dances*. Burgess Publishing Co., Revised, 1955, 278 pp., $3.50.

Hunt, Beatrice A., and Wilson, Harry Robert: *Sing and Dance*. NRA., 79 pp., Spiral bound, $2.00.

Kirkell, Miriam H., and Schaffnit, Irma K.: *Partners All—Places All*. E. P. Dutton Co., Inc., 1949, 129 pp., $3.95.

Kraus, Richard: *Play Activities for Boys and Girls.*

Kraus, Richard: *Recreation Leader's Handbook.*

Kraus, Richard: *Square Dances of Today and How To Teach and Call Them*. The Ronald Press Co., 1950, 130 pp., $4.00.

Kulbitsky, Olga, and Kaltman, Frank L.: *Follow the Leader, A Collection of Circle Dances*. American Squares, 13 pp.

Liefer, Fred: *The Li'l Abner Official Square Dance Handbook*. The Ronald Press Co., 1953, 127 pp., $3.25.

McIntosh, David S.: *Singing Games and Dances*. Assn. Press, 1957, 169 pp., $3.00.

Mason, Bernard S.: *Dances and Stories of the American Indians*. The Ronald Press Co., 1944, 269 pp., $5.50.

Ryan, Grace I.: *Dances of Our Pioneers*. The Ronald Press Co., 1939, 196 pp., $4.00.

Schonberg, Harriet: *May I Have This Dance*. Kamin Publishers, 99 pp.

Shaw, Lloyd: *Cowboy Dances*. Caxton Printers, Ltd., Caldwell, Idaho, $5.00.

Skip To My Lou. Girl Scouts, 1958, 32 pp., 25¢.

Stuart, Frances R., and Ludlam, John S.: *Rhythmic Activities, Series I and II*. Burgess Publishing Co., 1955, $2.50 each series.

Tobitt, Janet E.: *Promenade All*. Girl Scouts #23-469, 75¢. (Singing games).

Vannier, Maryhelen: *Methods and Materials in Recreation Leadership.*

Webb, Kenneth B., Editor: *Light from a Thousand Campfires.*

White, Betty: *Betty White's Dancing Made Easy*. David McKay Co., Revised, 1958, 276 pp., $4.50. (Social dance)

World of Folk Dances (Records). Radio Corp. of America, Camden, N.J. (85 dances from 26 countries).

Ziegler, Carl: *Singing Games and Dances for Schools and Playgrounds*. NRA., 64 pp., 80¢.

Leadership and General

Ames, Russell: *The Story of American Folk Song*. Grossett and Dunlap, Inc., 1955, 95¢.

Bucher, Charles A. Editor: *Methods and Materials in Physical Education and Recreation.*

Carmer, Carl: *America Sings: Stories and Songs of Our Country's Growing*. Alfred A. Knopf, Inc., 1950, $5.75.

Carabo-Cone, Madeleine: *Playground Music*. 866 Carnegie Hall, N.Y., 19, $1.00.

Corbin, H. Dan: *Recreation Leadership.*

Eisenberg, Helen and Larry: *How To Lead Group Singing*. Assn. Press, 1955, 62 pp., $1.00.

Eisenberg, Helen and Larry: *Omnibus of Fun.*

Felton, Harold W., *Cowboy Jamboree: Western Songs and Lore*. Alfred A. Knopf, Inc., 1951, $3.00.

Frieswyk, Siebolt H.: *Forty Approaches to Informal Singing*. NRA., 30 pp., 60¢.

Hammett, Catherine T., and Horrocks, Carol M.: *Creative Crafts for Campers.*

Hammett, and Musselman: *The Camp Program Book.*

Harbin, E. O.: *The Fun Encyclopedia.*

Kaplan, Max: *Music in Recreation*. Stipes Publishing Co., 17 Taylor St., Champaign, Ill., 1955, 230 pp., $3.90.

Leonhard, Charles: *Recreation Through Music*. The Ronald Press Co., 1952, 160 pp., $4.00.

Matthews, Paul Wentworth: *You Can Teach Music*. E. P. Dutton and Co., 178 pp., $3.75.

Music and Bugling. Boy Scouts #3336.

Sandburg, Carl: *The American Songbag*. Harcourt, Brace and Co., 1927, $5.75.

Sanders, Mary A.: *Our Songs*. Girl Scouts #23-465, 1942, 75¢.

Thurston, La Rue A.: *Complete Book of Campfire Programs.*

Tobitt, Janet E.: *ABC's of Camp Music*. Girl Scouts or ACA., 1955, 46 pp., 75¢.

Vandevere, J. Lillian: *Sound Sketches with Rhythm Instruments*. Van Roy Publishing Co., 48 pp., $2.00.

Zanzig, Augustus D.: *Starting and Developing a Rhythm Band*. NRA., 24 pp., 50¢.

MAGAZINE ARTICLES

Lushbough, L. E.: *Music Hath Power—If It's Good Music*. C. M., Dec., 1950.

Music Bibliography Notes. C. M., Apr., 1955.

Wagner, Doris: *Let There Be Good Music*. C. M., Dec., 1952.

Song Collections

Beckman, Frederick: *Partner Songs*. Ginn and Co., 91 pp., $1.20.

Best, Dick and Beth: *Song Fest*. Crown Publishing Corp., 1948, $1.95.

Boni, Margaret B., and Floyd, Norman: *The Fireside Book of Folk Songs*. Simon and Schuster, Inc., 1947, $5.00.

Boy Scout Songbook. Boy Scouts #3226, 25¢.

Carmer, Carl: *America Sings: Stories and Songs of Our Country's Growing*. Alfred A. Knopf, Inc., 1950, $5.75.

Felton, Harold W.: *Cowboy Jamboree: Western Songs and Lore*. Alfred A. Knopf, Inc., 1951, $3.00.

Girl Scout Pocket Song Book. Girl Scouts, 1956, 48 pp., 65¢.

Handy Songs. Coop. Rec. Service. Available in ring binder $3.00, or shelf box, $2.00.

Kolb, Sylvia and John, Editors: *A Treasury of Folk Songs*. Bantam Books, 1948, 240 pp.

Leisy, James, *Abingdon Song Kit*. Abingdon Press, 1957, 50¢. (195 songs of all types.)

Let's All Sing. ACA, 1958, 99 pp., 35¢ (quantity discount).

Richardson, Ethel Park: *American Mountain Songs*. Greenberg Publishing Co., 120 pp., $3.50.

Sandburg, Carl: *The American Songbag*. Harcourt, Brace and Co., 1927, $5.75.

Sanders, Mary A.: *Sing High! Sing Low!* Girl Scouts #23-468, 1946, 75¢.

Sing Together. Girl Scouts, 1957, 127 pp., 65¢.

Songs Children Like—Folk Songs from Many Lands. Ass'n. for Childhood Education, 48 pp., $1.00.

Tobitt, Janet E.: *A Book of Negro Songs*. Girl Scouts, #23-470, 60¢.

Tobitt, Janet E.: *The Ditty Bag*. Girl Scouts #23-460, 1946, 184 pp., $1.00.

Tobitt, Janet E., and White, Alice: *Dramatized Ballads*. Girl Scouts #23-413, $2.95.

We Sing. Girl Scouts #23-464, $3.50.

Zander, Carl E., and Klusmann, W. R.: *Camp Songs 'n' Things*. Boy Scouts #3249, 1949, 120 pp., 35¢.

Zanzig, Augustus D.: *Singing America*. NRA. 75¢. (128 songs.)

12

Arts and Crafts

Art is not a thing: it is a way.
ELBERT HUBBARD *"Epigrams"**

IT HAS BEEN SAID that the word "art" is like a woman's mother hubbard; it covers everything, yet touches nothing. The truth of this statement is clearly shown in this book, for nearly all phases of camping have some part which can be classed as art. Tincancraft, nature study and map-making are but a few examples.

Art is where you find it, and in camp it is found right on the campsite by the campers and counselors themselves. The arts and crafts byword might well be, "Stop, look and listen," for far too many of us pass unseeingly by wonderful supplies of native clay and tall reeds and tread upon nuts, acorns and pine cones on our way to mail an order to the nearest craft supply house.

To begin, let us stop for a moment to consider the aims and purposes of arts and crafts in the camping program. Arts and crafts give an opportunity for self-expression, a growing appreciation of beauty in the things of everyday life, a recognition of beauty in the common-place, and a chance to become alertly aware of surroundings. Art is merely the best way of doing a thing which needs to be done, be it scouring the kitchen sink, arranging flowers, setting the dinner table, or laying brick for clay oven.

John Galsworthy said, "In these un-superstitious days no other ideal seems worthy of us, or indeed possible to us, save beauty—or call it, if you will, the dignity of human life . . . the teaching of what beauty is, to all . . . so that we wish

* Reproduced by permission of Elbert Hubbard II.

130

and work and dream that not only ourselves but everybody may be healthy and happy, and, above all, the fostering of the habit of doing things and making things well, for the joy of the work and the pleasure of achievement." * This message indicates the need to find beauty, not only in the things we make and use, but in the relationships we have with one another.

In striving for the ideal through arts and crafts, the foremost idea should be, not to think of what the youngster does to the material with which he works, but of what effect the material has on the youngster.

By now you may be justified in saying, "All this talk and philosophical chatter is fine, but I want to know what to do and how to do it." Of course you do, but you must be patient and try to realize from past experience that you can be told little, but must largely find things out for yourself, and you will see this same principle manifested in the youngsters with whom

you work. The following anecdote illustrates this point and, even though from a formal school situation, is just as likely to occur in a summer camp, where it is equally important to give campers credit for independent thought and having the courage to back up their beliefs.

After a visit to a farm, members of the second grade were asked to paint farm pictures. Brenda had painted a huge barn on the left hand side of her paper with a big fence running horizontally across the paper. Being earnest, if not wise, the teacher suggested that she put a cow in the picture. Some few minutes later the teacher came back to see Brenda and her masterpiece, but still no cow had been added. Thinking that more urging was needed, the teacher commented again on how much a cow would improve the general aspects of the composition. Brenda looked up and flatly stated, "The cow is

*John Galsworthy, *Candelabra*, Charles Scribner's Sons.

(Joy and Camp.)

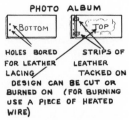

PHOTO ALBUM

BOTTOM   TOP

HOLES BORED   STRIPS OF
FOR LEATHER   LEATHER
LACING   TACKED ON
DESIGN CAN BE CUT OR
BURNED ON   (FOR BURNING
USE A PIECE OF HEATED
WIRE)

A Photo Album.

in the barn." Now anyone would expect this to end the discussion, but not with this persistent teacher, who came back a third time to Brenda and began, "A cow . . ." She got no farther, for Brenda straightened up, propped her hands against her hips, and announced through gritted teeth, "I told you the cow is in the barn and the door is shut!"

Without a basic understanding of children and materials, no creative work will be produced. No set of rules, but only suggestions can be given for working with such highly specialized and individualized beings as children, for it is the counselor's job to point out, guide and expose his group to the possibilities nature has to offer.

The arts and crafts program should stem from the campers, the camp environment and camp situations. The free method of "Here is the material, do whatever you want with it" doesn't work, for some will say, "Do we *have* to do what we want to do today?" Arts and crafts are the most reasonable thing this side of mathematics, and, unless there is purpose in making a thing, the finished product—if it is ever finished—will be only a dead thing.

Nor are arts and crafts limited to the few who can be branded as "talented" or "artistic." Art is for everyone who has eyes to see, ears to hear, or any other of the senses.

The arts and crafts program should be directed as a man drives a wagon. He gives the mule his head and, with reins firm but relaxed, puts the mule on his own, except for a few "gees" and "haws" here and there. It is indeed a rare thing to see a man leading a mule and wagon

and an even rarer one to see them being *driven.* With the same delicacy of touch, the counselor guides his artists and craftsmen to see and use the materials they find in their environment.

In a camping program it is well to avoid the use of such overworked city techniques as craft strip for braiding and media calling for following the directions of others, allowing little opportunity for the child to express his own personality and originality. Keep the program as inexpensive as possible by using indigenous materials and making your own equipment wherever possible. The "back to nature" movement offers a complete stock of arts and crafts materials for the counselor and camper who has "eyes to see" them. Good conservation practices must always be employed, however, being careful to use only what nature can spare and doing as little damage to the environment as possible.

Art has been defined as "order," and a good craftsman is an orderly person who sees to it that there are definite places for supplies, tools and equipment, and that there is adequate space in which to work. Teaching campers an appreciation of these qualities and of the proper use and care of tools is an important phase of instruction in arts and crafts and is a main responsibility of the counselor.

There must be a clear distinction between "busy work" and creative work as determined by (1) the usefulness of the finished product itself and (2) the effect of the making upon the producer.

Making Paste

There are many ways of making paste, one being to mix a half cup of flour with enough water to form a creamy mixture and heat over a low flame for about five minutes, stirring constantly to prevent lumping. If you are not going to use the paste immediately, a few drops of glycerine, oil of wintergreen, or alum will preserve it indefinitely.

Papier-Mâché

Papier-mâché, a gorgeous French word, is a simple arts and crafts medium which adapts itself successfully to all age levels. It is used commercially for figures in window displays, masks, and so on, as seen in the Mardi Gras and the animals prevalent at Easter.

There are almost as many ways to make papier-mâché as there are people to make it. Newspapers torn into small bits, paper towels, or packing excelsior can be soaked in warm water for a few hours until they can be easily mashed into a pulp. Then add enough paste to give the pulp the consistency of clay.

You can use papier-mâché to build animals on a paper armature by applying and shaping the papier-mâché with your hands. When dry, sandpaper the animal, then paint and shellac it.

Relief maps are lovely when made with this medium and, unlike clay, permit pins to be stuck into the surface. They are much lighter in weight than those made of clay and so are more practical for hanging purposes.

When you use white paper as a base, you can divide it into proper proportions and mix with the colors desired for each section. For example, you estimate the amount of material you need for the ocean and mix blue with it, and so on.

Another way to make papier-mâché is to cut bias strips of paper 3 by 4 inches long and 1 inch wide, dipping them into a thin solution of glue, and applying each slightly overlapping the other and carefully smoothing over a thoroughly petrolateumized or oiled mold such as an apple, orange, bowl, jar or bottle with smooth sides. You can also make masks.

Make head puppets by forming a

PAPIER-MÂCHÉ ANIMALS

HAND PUPPET
CHOIR BOY

ARMATURE

Papier-Mâché Figures.

model of clay or plasticine with the neck large enough on the inside to admit the finger with which you manipulate the puppet. Coat the model with some type of lubricant, and apply the strips of paper criss-cross until the entire head and neck are covered. When dry (which takes a varying length of time, according to weather conditions), cut the head in half, remove the clay, and tape the two halves together with strips of paste-covered paper. When the joining is dry, the head is ready to paint and the puppet to dress as desired.

Cows, horses, ducks, in fact the whole animal kingdom, can be made by first crumpling newspapers to form a body and then attaching rolled newspapers for neck, head and legs, tying them securely in place. Then cover this form with strips of paper as previously described. It is an advantage to cut the strips on the bias, since the aim is to keep the paper as smooth as possible when fitting it over the rounded form.

Clay Modeling

Ceramics or clay modeling provides great opportunity for creative work. Clay is found in all parts of the world and ranges from white, yellow, green, gray, and even blues and blacks which result from the presence of such impurities as organic matter or iron oxide. You may often use native clays successfully, and can make the search for them the occasion for an exciting excursion, thus adding materially to campers' sense of achievement. You can construct a potter's wheel and a

kiln inexpensively with the aid of good instructions such as those given in the sources listed at the end of the chapter. They add to the permanent equipment of the camp. Whittle the few tools needed from sticks.

Figurines, animals, tiles and bowls are quickly made and bring out all the creative imagination of the most inhibited. As one child ungrammatically said, "I closed my eyes and seen an angel and made one like I seen it."*

Tops

Tops are fun to make, and play with or give as gifts. Form them from acorns by inserting a match stick about 1½ inch long into the top; fasten the stick with glue, attach a string to the match stick, and dip the acorn into bright-colored enamel, and hang by the string to dry. Vary the color by dipping the top halfway into another color after the first is thoroughly dry.

Portfolios

Portfolios are handy things to have at camp, home and school for keeping correspondence, notes or pictures. You can make one of good size from two pieces of cardboard, each 12 by 9 inches, and a strip of cloth 4 by 16 inches.

Join the cardboards as shown in *A*, with the cloth acting as a hinge. Then turn in the ends of the cloth and paste down the inside as shown in *B*. Cut deco-

* Cole, Natalie Robinson: *The Arts in the Classroom*. John Day Co., 1940, page 39.

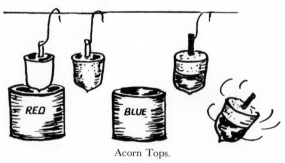

Acorn Tops.

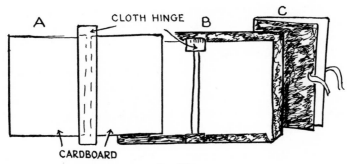

Portfolio.

rated paper (marbelized, finger painted, shadow printed or block printed) 1 inch larger in all dimensions than the cardboard, and spread paste smoothly over its entire surface (wrong side). Then paste to the cardboards to form a cover for the portfolio, and fold the edges in and paste as shown in *B*. Paste a piece of paper ¼ inch smaller in all dimensions than the cardboards inside as a lining. Cut a slit about 1 inch from the outside edges of the cardboards and half way down and insert a piece of tape or ribbon through it to tie the portfolio shut.

To prevent warping, use only the amount of paste actually necessary. Insert a piece of paper between the sides of the portfolio to keep them from sticking together, and press it under a heavy weight until absolutely dry.

Marbelizing paper is fun, because, like finger painting, it completely defeats those who say, "I can't even draw a straight line," for even they can turn out something lovely. Use any kind of paper which is not too absorbent. Mix a little oil paint (any color) with kerosene, turpentine or some other oil and pour onto a large pan of water. Since water and oil do not mix, the oil remains floating on top, and you marbelize the paper by laying it on top of the water. Draw bright, varicolored fish on the paper with wax crayons, scrubbing the colors on vigorously to produce the most highly decorative type of fish imaginable. Make a solution of blue-green oil color and pour on the water, stirring or breathing on it to make it swirl, and dip

the picture in the water. The fish look as though they are in the water and in your imagination you can even hear them swishing about!

Block Printing

Block printing is an old art which appeals to individuals of all ages and is useful in producing personal cards, gift wrapping paper, menus or program covers in quantities. You can use linoleum, cork, soap, scrap rubber, erasers, wash-basin stoppers, dowels, or even potatoes, turnips and apples. Make small designs on the heads of wooden clothes pins and stamp them on cloth with textile paint.

Cut firm, eyeless potatoes or turnips in half and draw a simple design on the flat surface with a brush and water colors. Extend the design to include even the

Block Printing.

edges. Incise the outlines of the design about ¼ inch with a small knife and lift it out of the background.

You can potato print on colored construction paper, wrapping paper, cellophane or tissue paper, but not cloth. Potatoes will not take printer's ink or oils. Paint the embossed design on the potato with a brush, or make a stamp pad by folding a piece of cloth or felt and spread paint on it. Blot out the moisture as much as possible before applying the paint.

INNER TUBE PRINTS.   Make a cut paper design, either bisymmetric or asymmetric, and trace the pieces of the design onto the tubing and cut out with scissors. Use strong vegetable glue to fasten the smooth side of the rubber design to a background of cardboard or wood. Leave almost no wood or cardboard background extending beyond the design, lest it show in the print.

THE BLOCK PRINTING PROCESS.

1. Draw a simple design with definite lines.
2. Transfer the design with carbon or by thoroughly blacking the back of it by tracing over it with a pencil.
3. Remember to make the design on the block in reverse, so that when it is printed it will reproduce the original drawing. This is especially necessary to watch with lettering.
4. Put a portion of printer's ink (comes in oil or water forms) on glass (window pane) or any smooth surface.
5. Use a brayer, rolling pin or smooth bottle (such as an olive bottle) as a roller to roll the paint onto the block.
6. Apply the block to the cloth or paper and press hard with hands or feet to secure a good print.

Chip Carving

Chip carving requires precision and patience and is therefore not suitable for younger campers. Most designs are based upon geometrical patterns, and the "chips" themselves are triangular pieces of wood removed from a board by means of slicing knives; a razor blade may be used as an emergency tool. Chip carving requires a gradual slope and not a gouge. A ruler, compass and pencil are necessary to lay out the design.

Basswood (linden) is best to use because it is soft and workable, yet fine-grained and finishes nicely. Pine or apple wood is also recommended.

The simplest way to finish woodwork is to mix oil paint (burnt umber, burnt sienna, mahogany, walnut) with turpentine and rub it on with a rag which leaves no lint. When the paint is thoroughly dry, shellac it and let dry before again sandpapering and shellacking it. (Sandpaper and elbow grease are important constituents for all woodwork.) A good floor wax makes the best finish. Use chip carving to decorate boxes, albums, scrap books, coasters, trays, letter knives, checkers, belt buckles, costume pins and carved buttons.

Dyeing

Dyeing is an art, not a science. As in other arts, there are several ways to arrive at the same result, but all involve thought, care and patience. Silk, chiffon or cheese cloth are exciting and beautiful when tied and dyed, and curtains and bed spreads or costumes for camp use are easy to make. Natural dyes from berries, bark or roots of plants are soft and attractive and compare favorably with commercial dyes.

Tie Dyeing.

To make vegetable dyes, steep the plants in water overnight and then boil them slowly until you obtain the desired intensity of color.

You must use a large enough container (copper or enamel preferred) to cover the material in the dye bath entirely, and must stir it and move it freely with blunt, smooth sticks.

To insure a good dye job, wash the material thoroughly to remove all the starch. Boil the wet material slowly for an hour in water in which you have dissolved some *mordant* such as alum, cream of tartar or tannic acid (or barks or woods containing it). This mordant is a chemical which helps to fix or charge the color. After boiling, rinse the material well, immerse it in the dye bath, and boil from one-half hour to an hour or until you obtain the desired shade. (Remember that it will appear much darker when wet than after it dries.) Add salt or vinegar to the dye bath to set the color and continue to boil it for another ten minutes. Then remove the material, rinse it and dry it in the shade. Thorough washing and rinsing are most important and must not be neglected. The following are indigenous sources of the principal colors:

Blue:

Hazel roots
Larkspur flowers
Sunflower seeds
Shrub indigo—roots
Red maple—bark, boiled with copper sulphate
Blue ash—boiled with copper sulphate

Black:

Field sorrel leaves
Sumac and gallberry leaves
Maple—inner bark and leaves
Flowering dogwood—branches and bark
Black walnut—roots
Elderberry stems

Brown:

Alder bark
Red oak bark
Maple bark
Hickory bark
Butternut—hulls and bark
Walnut—hulls and bark
Onion skins
Coffee bean—inside

Purple:

Purple flag—petals
Blueberries—berries
Barberries—berries
Maple—rotted wood
Elderberry berries
Sumac berries
Pokeberry berries
Cedar—tips of branches
Red cedar—rootlets

Gray:

Sumac leaves
Butternut bark
Maple bark

Green:

Water scum (algae)—whole plant
Giant arbor vitae—twigs and leaves
Spinach leaves

Red:

Alder—inner bark
Amaranth seeds
Coreopsis flowers
Red dogwood—inner bark
Pokeberries—berries; boil with alum
Cedar—inner bark
Bloodroot—root
Hemlock bark
Beets, boiled with alum
Cleavers—roots, extracted with alcohol or oil
Sycamore—old, half-rotten roots
Red sumac berries

Yellow:

Celandine poppy
Alder—inner bark
Goldenrod flowers
Sassafras bark
Onions and their skins
Balsam—flowers
St. John's wort—flowers
Saffron—dried stigmas
Cottonwood—seed vessels or leaf buds
Thistle—flowers
Sumac roots
Lichen—whole plant
Holly—boiled with alum
Smartweed—boiled with alum
White mulberry—roots and leaves
Black oak—inner bark
Pignut hickory—inner bark
Shiny sumac

Basketry

Basketry is a very old art of which we do not know the origin or native country. Many and foreign-flavored materials such as rattan from India, raffia shredded from a Madagascar palm, hemp from the Philippines, and bamboo from China and Japan are used.

Native to our country are such materials as willow branches, cut in the spring when the sap is running, cattail leaves from low, damp places, flags, rushes, straw, wire grass, sweet grass, sedge, broom wheat, rye, corn husks, and so on. Vines of the honeysuckle and Virginia creeper, when peeled and allowed to dry for two years, work up fast and make an even coil. Wood splints from hickory, ash, oak and maple trees require more experienced hands than those of the average beginner.

Nuts

A hike will disclose large acorns, hazel nuts, and the like, to use in making lapel pins, buttons, bracelets and tops. You may paint a face on an acorn, remembering to place the eyes directly at the center between top and bottom and the mouth half-way between the eyes and chin. Attach a safety pin for fastening with a good grade of airplane or china cement, and complete the decoration with earrings and a hat.

Mammy Doll.

Pine Cones

Pine cones are beautiful in themselves and can be used to make many interesting objects. Large ones with painted tips form lovely tree ornaments to hang by tying a string around the core between

the scales, or by inserting a small screw eye into the cone at the top.

Big cones can be used as candle-stick holders by slicing off the pointed end to make a flat base and inserting a candle in the top.

All kinds of animals can be made from cones, their success depending largely upon the maker, as revealed in the story of the wood carver whose artistic output ran heavily to horses. He carved them swiftly and unerringly from almost any sort of wood, and rough and crude as they were, each had a remarkable individual "horsishness." He explained his gift for carving so easily and quickly by, "I jest look at the piece of wood till I see the horse and then I carve away the wood and there's the horse."

Likewise, you must look at a cone or stick until you clearly see what it is to become. Crafts are logical in that they consist of three steps: (1) thinking of all the possible things which you can make out of a material, (2) choosing the one which seems to fit the material best, and (3) then doing it.

Birds are made by gluing an acorn with eyes painted on it for a head, to the top of a pine cone. Matchstick legs may be glued between the scales in the middle of the cone and stuck in a glob of clay for feet (remember that the clay feet must be made rather big to balance the bird). A feather glued to the cap completes a well-dressed dodo bird.

Woodpeckers are composed of a maple seed, shaped to form a head, a beak, a cone body, a feather tail, and a forked stick tree to peck on. To assemble these various parts, press a pin through the top of the head and into the cone where you removed the stem. A little quick-drying glue around the pin helps fix the head to the body. If any of the pin is left showing, you can snip it off with cutting pliers. The tail is glued on at the proper place.

To mount the bird on a perching twig requires a little care. Press another pin a short distance through the twig or perch

Woodpecker.

cone, the head is an acorn, the neck a twig, and the eyes are beads. Bore holes into the cone to receive the feet and neck, which are held in place with glue. This makes a sturdy turtle which would stand up well in a race with any pine cone rabbit.

A flying fish can be made from a long pine cone with the fins and tail cut from maple wings and glued into slots made in the cone with a pen knife.

Flying Fish.

in an upward, slanting direction. You then rest the head of the pin on a hard surface, and press the body of the bird downward onto the pin point until it has penetrated about ¼ inch or more into the cone. Add glue where the perch and cone meet to strengthen the pin. Snip off the head of the pin with a pair of cutting pliers. Too much pressure may cause the pin to bend; you must then remove it and repeat the process with a fresh pin.

An ordinary cork cut off to ½ inch thickness may be used as a base by boring a hole into its center and filling it with glue before inserting the perch. A clay base can also be used. Eyes for the maple seed head can be painted on, small seeds may be pasted on, or a pin may be inserted through the head and the ends snipped off.

Penguins made with acorn bodies, maple seed heads, and beads for eyes, may be balanced on feet made from the scales of a pine cone.

The difference between making a pine cone and a turtle is a knife, some glue, and a little time and imagination. Cut a slice from the stem end of a large cone (this is a rather difficult job, for it is very tough in texture). The turtle's feet are scales torn from the other section of the

Gallnut people with twig arms and legs can be dressed in all types of fancy gear and made to represent any one from Little Lord Fauntleroy to Little Black Sambo.

An armadillo has a head made of a small chestnut burr, a pine cone body, and a tail and feet made from twigs; it is mounted on a strip of bark.

Shells, bits of sponge, coral, dried seaweed, sharks' teeth or fish fins, when combined with pipe cleaners and liquid glue, make many beautiful and useful objects such as earrings, pins, brooches, hair pins, and designs for boxes, place cards, and so on.

Animals and dolls of all kinds can be created by using various sizes of shells for heads, bodies and legs.

Other camp arts and crafts projects are:

Papier-mâché
    Puppets
    Masks
    Bowls
    Jewelry
    Animals
    Relief maps

Plaster of Paris (see p. 166)
  Plaques
  Tile
  Fossils
  Nature prints
  Sculpture

Silk screen process
  Posters
  Hand bills
  Scarves

Finger painting
Camp furniture
Camping utensils
Archery equipment
Leather work
Terrariums
Fishing flies and lures

ADDITIONAL READINGS

Basketry

Basketry. Boy Scouts #3313, 25¢.

Christopher, F. J.: *Basketry*. Dover Publications, Inc., 1952, 75¢.

Couch, Osma P.: *Basket Pioneering*. Orange Judd Publishing Co., Inc., Revised, 163 pp., $3.50.

Crampton, Charles: *The Junior Basket Maker*. Charles A. Bennett Co., Inc., 1952, 35 pp., $1.00.

Jessen, Bibbi: *How to Work with Raffia*. Bruce Publishing Co., 1955, 64 pp., $1.25.

Block Printing, Stenciling

Kafka, Francis J.: *The Hand Decoration of Fabrics*. McKnight & McKnight Publishing Co., 1959, 199 pp., $5.00.

Kafka, Francis J.: *Linoleum Block Printing*. McKnight & McKnight Publishing Co., 1958, $1.60.

Newick, John: *Making Colour Prints*. Bennett, $4.00. (linoleum block printing)

Polk, Ralph W.: *Essentials of Linoleum-Block Printing*. Charles A. Bennett Co., Inc., 1927, 60 pp., $1.45. (paper)

Tanner, Robin: *Children's Work in Block Printing*. Charles A. Bennett Co., Inc., 51 pp., $2.25.

Braiding and Knotting

Belash, Constantine A.: *Braiding and Knotting for Amateurs*. Charles T. Branford Co., 1936, $2.00.

Craftstrip Braiding Projects. Boy Scouts #3169, 24 pp., 25¢.

Grant, Bruce: *Leather Braiding*. Cornell Maritime Press, 1950, $3.00.

Graumont, Raoul M., and Wenstrom, Elmer: *Square Knot Handicraft Guide*. Cornell Maritime Press, 1959, $3.50.

Leeming, Joseph: *Fun with String*. J. B. Lippincott Co., 1939, $3.50.

Staples, Frank A.: *How To Make a Square Knot Bracelet*. Recreation, Mar., 1955.

Ceramics and Pottery

Dougherty, John W.: *Pottery Made Easy*. Bruce Publishing Co., 1945, 192 pp., $3.00.

Drawbell, Marjorie: *Making Pottery Figures*. The Studio Publications, 1954, 96 pp., $4.50.

Engel, Gertrude: *How To Make Ceramics*. Arco Publishers, 1957, 144 pp., $2.50.

Jenkins, R. H.: *Practical Pottery for Craftsmen and Students*. Bruce Publishing Co., 1941, 204 pp., $2.75.

Kenney, John B.: *Ceramic Sculpture*. Chilton Co., 1959, 302 pp., $7.50.

Kenney, John B.: *The Complete Book of Pottery Making*. Chilton Co., 1959, 242 pp., $7.50.

Lunn, Dora: *Pottery in the Making*. Charles A. Bennett Co., Inc., 1954, 108 pp., $2.25.

Pottery. Boy Scouts #3314.

Priolo, Joan B.: *Ceramics—And How To Decorate Them*. Sterling Publishing Co., 144 pp., $5.95.

Rhodes, Daniel: *Clay and Glazes for the Potter*. Chilton Co., 1959, 219 pp., $7.50.

Seeley, Vernon D., and Thompson, Robert L.: *Activities in Ceramics*. McKnight & McKnight Publishing Co., 82 pp., $1.60.

Taylor, Keith: *Pottery without a Wheel*. Charles A. Bennett Co., Inc., 1953, $1.50. (paper)

Zarchy, Harry: *Ceramics*. Alfred A. Knopf, Inc., 1954, 171 pp., $3.50. (grades 7–11)

Drawing and Painting

Bogorad, Alan D.: *It's Fun To Draw*. Harlem Publishing Co., $1.25. (paper)

Boone, Stephen: *Oil Painting*. D. Van Nostrand Co., Inc., 1956, 85 pp., $4.75.

Cooper, Hal: *Art for Everyone*. Watson-Guptill Publications, Inc., 128 pp., $4.95.

Diller, Mary Black: *Drawing for Young Artists*. Pitman Publishing Corp., 1955, $1.00.

Fabry, Alois: *Oil Painting Is Fun*. The Studio Publications, Inc., 1957, 95 pp., $2.95.

Fabry, Alois: *Sketching Is Fun with Pencil and Pen*. The Studio Publications, Inc., 94 pp.

Garbo, Norman: *Pull Up an Easel—How To Paint for Enjoyment*. A. S. Barnes and Co., 1955, 244 pp., $3.75.

Gasser, Henry: *How To Draw and Paint*. Dell Publishing Co., 240 pp., 50¢.

Hill, Adrian: *Beginner's Book of Oil Painting*. Emerson Books, Inc., 76 pp., $2.95.

Leidl, Charles: *How To Draw Animals*. Greenberg Publishing Co., 1953, 63 pp., $1.00.

Olsen, Herb: *Watercolor Made Easy*. Reinhold Publishing Corp., 109 pp., $7.50.

Painting. Boy Scouts #3372, 25¢.

Zaidenberg, Arthur: *The Joy of Painting*. Hanover House, 190 pp., $4.95.

Flood, Dorothy R.: *A Nature Mural.* Recreation, Mar., 1959.

Flood, Dorothy R.: *An Ideal Outdoor Art Studio.* C.M., Jan., 1958.

General Crafts

Allen, Opal, and Ready, Mrs. Henry M.: *Through the Year with Crafts.* Bruce Publishing Co., 1958, 128 pp., $2.50.

Baillie, E. Kenneth: *Homespun Crafts.* Bruce Publishing Co., 160 pp., $3.00.

Bale, R. O.: *Creative Nature Crafts.* Burgess Publishing Co., 1959, 121 pp., $2.50.

Benson, Kenneth R.: *Creative Crafts for Children.* Prentice-Hall, Inc., 1958, 106 pp., $3.95. (ages 6–11)

Brod, Fritzi: *Decorative Design.* Pitman Publishing Corp., 1949, 46 pp., $1.00.

Build-It-Yourself Book for Boys. By editors of Popular Mechanics, 192 pp., $2.95.

Carlson, Bernice Wells: *Make It and Use It.* Abingdon Press, $1.60.

Carlson, Bernice Wells: *Make It Yourself.* Abingdon Press Paper, $1.35.

Champion, Paul V.: *Creative Crate Craft.* Bruce Publishing Co., 1942, 110 pp., $1.25.

Coffey, Ernestine S., and Minton, Dorothy F.: *A Leader's Guide to Nature and Garden Fun.* Hearthside Press, 1957, 127 pp., $2.75.

Corbin, H. Dan: *Recreation Leadership.*

Cox, Doris, and Warren, Barbara: *Creative Hands.* John Wiley and Sons, Inc., 2nd Ed., 1951, 381 pp., $5.95.

Craft Projects for Camp and Playground. NRA, 31 pp., 50¢.

Dryad Handicrafts, Handicrafts for Children. Charles A. Bennett Co., Inc., Revised, 1957, $6.25.

Exploring the Handcrafts. Girl Scouts, 128 pp., 65¢.

Gottshall, Franklin H.: *Craftwork in Metal, Wood, Leather and Plastics.* Bruce Publishing Co., 1954, 160 pp., $4.00.

Grimm, Gretchen, and Skeels, Catherine: *Crafts for School and Home.* Bruce Publishing Co., 1956, 128 pp., $2.95.

Griswold, Lester: *Handicraft: Simplified Procedures and Projects.* Prentice-Hall, Inc., 9th Ed., 1951, 480 pp., $4.15.

Haines, Ray E., Editor: *The Home Crafts Handbook.* D. Van Nostrand Co., 1948, $6.95.

Hammett, Catherine T., and Musselman, Virginia: *The Camp Program Book.*

Hammett, Catherine T., and Horrocks, Carol M.: *Creative Crafts for Campers.*

Hening, Viola: *Fun with Scraps.* Bruce Publishing Co., 1947, 185 pp., $3.00.

Hofsinde, Robert: *Indian Games and Crafts.* William Morrow and Co., Inc., 1957, 127 pp., $2.50.

Howard, Carolyn: *Easy Hand Crafts for Juniors.* Zondervan Publishing House, 1957, 60 pp., $1.00.

Hunt, W. Ben: *Indian and Camp Handicraft.* Bruce Publishing Co., Revised, 1945, 180 pp., $3.00.

Hunt, W. Ben: *Crafts and Hobbies.* Golden Books, 1957, 112 pp., $1.95.

Ickis, Marguerite: *Folk Arts and Crafts.* Assn. Press, 1957, 269 pp., $5.95.

Ickis, Marguerite, and Esh, Reba Selden: *The Book of Arts and Crafts.* Assn. Press, 1953, 275 pp., $4.95.

Jaeger, Ellsworth: *Easy Crafts.* The Macmillan Co., 1947, $2.95.

Jaeger, Ellsworth: *Nature Crafts.* The Macmillan Co., 1950, 253 pp., $2.95.

Lacey, John: *Make Your Own Outdoor Sports Equipment.* G. P. Putnam's Sons, Inc., 1955, 128 pp., $2.75.

Madden, Ira C.: *Creative Handicraft.* The Goodheart-Willcox Co., Chicago, 1955, 224 pp.

Moore, Frank C., et al.: *Handcrafts for Elementary Schools.* D. C. Heath and Co., 1953, $6.00.

Mulac, Margaret E.: *Hobbies.* Harper and Brothers, $3.95.

Nature Crafts for Camp and Playground. NRA, 32 pp., 50¢.

Norbeck, Oscar E.: *Book of Indian Life Crafts.* Assn. Press, 1958, 253 pp., $5.95.

Perry, Evadna Kraus: *Crafts for Fun.* William Morrow and Co., 1940, 289 pp., $4.00.

Price, Elizabeth: *Adventures in Nature.* NRA, 1939.

Robinson, Jessie: *Things To Make from Odds and Ends.* Appleton-Century-Crofts, Inc., 1945, $2.00.

Sabine, Ellen S.: *American Folk Art.* D. Van Nostrand Co., 1959, 132 pp., $6.95.

Shanklin, Margaret E.: *Use of Native Craft Materials.* Charles A. Bennett Co., Inc., 1947, $2.45.

Vannier, Maryhelen: *Methods and Materials in Recreation Leadership.*

Zarchy, Harry: *Creative Hobbies.* Alfred A. Knopf, Inc., 1953, 303 pp., $3.50. (age 12 and up)

Zarchy, Harry: *Let's Make a Lot of Things.* Alfred A. Knopf, Inc., 1948, 156 pp., $3.25. (grades 5–9)

Bacon, Eleanor T.: *Preparation and Careful Inventory Will Help You Determine Craft Shop Needs.* C.M., Nov., 1952.

Bresser, Bettye: *Let's Make Something.* C.M., May, 1953.

Camp-made Sculpture Material. C.M., June, 1954.

Howenstine, Alice: *Fungus Etching as a Summer Craft.* C.M., June, 1954.

Meixner, Mary: *Art in the Camp Environment.* C.M., April, 1953.

Tinsley, Eleanor: *How To Get More from Your Craft Program.* C.M., May, 1950.

Van Norman, Betty: *Crafts With Natural Materials.* Recreation, Mar., 1959.

Victor, Marllys: *Music and Crafts Can Go Hand in Hand.* C.M., Nov., 1950.

Homemade Games

Champion, Paul V.: *Games You Can Make and Play.* Bruce Publishing Co., 1950, 128 pp., $2.50.

Games To Build. Boys Clubs, 96 pp., $2.00.

Howard, Vernon: *Easy To Make Toys and Games.* Zondervan Publishing House, 32 pp., 50¢.

Leathercraft

Bang, Eleanor E.: *Leathercraft for Amateurs.* Charles T. Branford Co., $2.00.

Cherry, Raymond: *General Leathercraft.* McKnight & McKnight Publishing Co., 4th Ed., 1958, 144 pp., $1.60.

Christopher, Frederick J.: *Leather Work.* Dover Publications, Inc., 1953, 75¢.

Cramlet, Ross C.: *Fundamentals of Leathercraft.* Bruce Publishing Co., 1939, 64 pp., $1.50.

Dean, John W.: *107 Leathercraft Designs.* McKnight & McKnight Publishing Co., 1958, $2.00.

Dougherty, Betty: *Your Leatherwork.* Charles A. Bennett Co., Inc., 1947, $2.75.

Griswold, Lester: *Handicraft—Simple Procedures and Projects.* Prentice-Hall, Inc., 9th Ed., 1951, 480 pp., $4.15.

Groneman, Chris H.: *Leathercraft.* Charles A. Bennett Co., Inc., Revised, 1958, $1.95. (paper)

Groneman, Chris: *Leather Tooling and Carving.* D. Van Nostrand Co., 1950, $3.20.

Leathercraft Methods. Boy Scouts #3167, 20 pp., 25¢.

Leatherwork. Boy Scouts #3310, 25¢.

Leeming, Joseph: *Fun with Leather.* J. B. Lippincott Co., 1941, 91 pp., $3.00.

Lewis, Roger: *Leathercraft.* Alfred A. Knopf, Inc., 1953, 44 pp., $1.75. (ages 7–11)

Mannel, Elise: *Leathercraft Is Fun.* Bruce Publishing Co., 1952, 96 pp., $2.50.

MAGAZINE ARTICLES

Garbee, Eugene E.: *Leathercraft.* C.M., April, 1957.

Metal Work

Becker, William J.: *Metalworking Made Easy.* Bruce Publishing Co., 1942, 136 pp., $2.50.

Birdsall, G. W.: *Do It Yourself with Aluminum.* McGraw-Hill Publishing Co., Inc., 1955, 136 pp., $3.95.

Bollinger, J. W.: *Simple Bracelets.* Bruce Publishing Co., 80 pp., $2.50.

Bollinger, J. W.: *Fun with Metalwork.* Bruce Publishing Co., 1958, 184 pp., $4.75.

Hobbs, Douglas B.: *Working with Aluminum.* Bruce Publishing Co., 126 pp., $2.50.

Hunt, W. Ben: *Indian Silversmithing.* Bruce Publishing Co., 160 pp., $5.50.

Kramer, Karl R. and Nora: *Coppercraft and Silver Made at Home.* Chilton Co., 1957, 175 pp., $4.50.

Larom, Marom: *Enameling for Fun and Profit.* David McKay Co., Inc., 1954, 96 pp., $3.00.

Lewis, Roger: *Metalcraft.* Alfred A. Knopf, Inc., 1953, 48 pp., $1.75.

Make It with Aluminum. Arco Publishing Co., 1955, 144 pp., $2.50.

Metalwork. Boy Scouts #3312A, 25¢.

Untracht, Oppi: *Enameling on Metal.* Chilton Co., 1957, 199 pp., $7.50.

Watts, Harold W.: *Copper Enameling.* Rural Research Institute, 500 5th Ave., N.Y. 36, 28 pp. (free)

MAGAZINE ARTICLES

Staples, Frank A.: *Enameling on Copper—Earrings and Pins.* Recreation, June, 1955.

Mosaics

Hendrickson, Edwin: *Mosaics: Hobby and Art.* Hill and and Wang, Inc., 1958, 111 pp., $4.95.

Hendrickson, Edwin: *Mosaic Patterns.* Hill and Wang, Inc., 1958, 95 pp., $4.95.

Jenkins, Louisa, and Mills, Barbara: *Art of Making Mosaics.* D. Van Nostrand Co., 1957, 132 pp., $5.95.

Young, Joseph L.: *Course in Making Mosaics.* Reinhold Publishing Co., 60 pp., $3.50.

MAGAZINE ARTICLES

Staples, Frank A.: *How To Make A Mosaic.* Recreation, Oct., 1957.

Miscellaneous Techniques

Baranski, Matthew: *Mask Making.* Davis Publications, 1954, 101 pp., $5.50.

Bayley, Thomas: *The Craft of Model Making.* Charles A. Bennett Co., Inc., Revised, $4.50.

Betts, Victoria Bedford: *Exploring Papier Mâché.* Davis Publications, 134 pp., $6.00.

Biggs, Raymond H.: *Building a Ship in a Bottle.* Bruce Publishing Co., 64 pp., $1.00.

Bolton, Eleanor Reed: *Dried Flowers with a Fresh Look.* D. Van Nostrand Co., 1959, 210 pp., $6.95.

Champion, Paul V.: *Birdhouses.* Bruce Publishing Co., 96 pp., $2.25.

Clegg, Helen, and Larom, Mary: *Jewelry Making for Fun and Profit.* David McKay Co., 1951, 162 pp., $3.25.

Fowler, H. Walker, Jr.: *Kites.* The Ronald Press Co., 1953, $1.95.

Hardin, F. E.: *Weathervane Silhouettes.* Charles A. Bennett Co., Inc., six patterns, 35¢ each or 6 for $1.00.

Hofsinde, Robert: *Indian Beadwork.* William Morrow Co., Inc., 122 pp., $2.50.

How To Make and Play a Shepherd Pipe. NRA, 32 pp., 60¢.

Hunt, W. Ben, and Burshears, J. F.: *American Indian Beadwork—Designs and Methods.* Bruce Publishing Co., 1951, 64 pp., $5.50.

Hunt, W. Ben, and Metz, John: *The Flat Bow.* Bruce Publishing Co., 1936, 72 pp., 90¢.

Indian Beadwork. X-acto.

Ishimito, Tatsuo: *The Art of Driftwood and Dried Arrangements.* Crown Publications, 1953, 143 pp., $2.95.

Johnson, Lillian: *Papier Mâché.* David McKay Co., 1958, 88 pp., $3.95.

Johnson, Pauline: *Creating with Paper.* U. of Washington Press, Seattle, Wash., 1958, 208 pp., $6.50.

La Berge, A. J.: *Boats, Airplanes, and Kites.* Charles A. Bennett Co., Inc., Revised, 1950, 131 pp., $2.80.

Laklan, Carli: *The Candle Book.* M. Barrows and Co., Inc., 190 pp., $3.50.

Leeming, Joseph: *Fun with Beads.* J. B. Lippincott Co., 1954, 96 pp.

Leeming, Joseph: *Fun with Paper.* J. B. Lippincott Co., 1939, 152 pp., $3.25.

Leeming, Joseph: *Fun with Shells.* J. B. Lippincott Co., 92 pp., $3.00.

Leeming, Joseph: *Fun with Wire.* J. B. Lippincott Co., 1956, 96 pp., $3.00.

Mandell, Muriel, and Wood, Robert S.: *Make Your Own Musical Instruments.* Sterling Publishing Co., 1957, 128 pp., $2.95.

Miller, J. V.: *Paper Sculpture and Construction.* Charles A. Bennett Co., Inc., 1957, 56 pp., $1.50.

Moritz, La Verne: *Papier-Mâché.* La Vee Studio, 1953, 48 pp., $2.00.

Paper Arts and Crafts. T. S. Denison and Co.

Perry, L. Day, and Slepicka, Frank: *Bird Houses.* Charles A. Bennett Co., Inc., 1955, $1.75.

Richardson, Nancy: *How To Stencil and Decorate Furniture and Tinware.* The Ronald Press Co., 1956, 186 pp., $6.00.

Schaffer, Florence M.: *ABC of Driftwood for Flower Arranging.* Hearthside Press, 128 pp.

Schutz, Walter E.: *How To Build Birdhouses and Feeders.* Bruce Publishing Co., 145 pp., $2.95.

Sculpture. Boy Scouts #3322, 25¢.

Squires, Mabel: *The Art of Drying Plants and Flowers.* 258 pp., $4.50.

MAGAZINE ARTICLES

Howenstein, Alice: *Nature Crafts Year Round—Cattail Leaf Mates.* Recreation, Sept., 1957.

Murphy, Stella: *Driftwood.* Recreation, June, 1958.

Staples, Frank A.: *Bone Carving.* Recreation, Mar., 1957.

Staples, Frank A.: *Books for Nature Prints or Pictures.* Recreation, Apr., 1954.

Staples, Frank A.: *Carving with Plaster of Paris.* Recreation, May, 1957.

Staples, Frank A.: *Decorative Painting on Wood.* Recreation, Feb., 1957.

Staples, Frank A.: *How To Make a Banjo.* Recreation, June, 1957.

Staples, Frank A.: *Lacquer Batik.* Recreation, Jan., 1957.

Staples, Frank A.: *Modeling with Sawdust.* Recreation, Nov., 1956.

Staples, Frank A.: *Parchment Lamp Shades.* Recreation, Mar., 1956.

Staples, Frank A.: *Screen Print on Paper or Cloth.* Recreation, Sept., 1955.

Staples, Frank A.: *Shepherds' Pipe.* Recreation, Oct., 1956.

Staples, Frank A.: *Terrariums You Can Make.* Recreation, Apr., 1956.

Plastics

Bick, A. F.: *Plastics for Fun.* Bruce Publishing Co., 104 pp., $3.25.

Cherry, Raymond: *General Plastics: Projects and Procedures.* McKnight & McKnight Publishing Co., 1948, 160 pp., $1.80.

Cope, Dwight: *Cope's Plastics Book.* The Goodheart-Wilcox Co., Inc., 272 pp., $4.50.

Edwards, Lauton: *Making Things of Plastic.* Charles A. Bennett Co., Inc., 192 pp., $3.75.

Groneman, Chris H.: *Plastics Made Practical.* Bruce Publishing Co., 315 pp., $4.50.

MAGAZINES

Staples, Frank A.: *A Cigarette or Jewel Box.* Recreation, Feb., 1955.

Weaving

Alexander, Marthann: *Weaving Handcraft.* McKnight & McKnight Publishing Co., 1958, 96 pp., $1.60.

Allen, Edith Louise: *Weaving You Can Do.* Charles A. Bennett Co., Inc., 1947, 118 pp., $3.00.

Atwater, Mary Meigs: *Byways in Hand-Weaving.* The Macmillan Co., 128 pp., $8.50.

Black, Mary E.: *New Key To Weaving.* Bruce Publishing Co., Revised, 1957, 594 pp., $12.00.

Blumenaw, Lili: *The Art and Craft of Hand Weaving.* 136 pp., $2.95.

Brown, Harriette J.: *Hand Weaving.* Harper and Brothers, 1952, $4.95.

Cherry, Eve.: *Teach Yourself Handweaving.* Roy Publishers, $2.50.

Christopher, Frederick J.: *Handloom Weaving.* Dover Publications, Inc., 1954, 128 pp., 65¢.

Clifford, Lois I.: *Card Weaving.* Charles A. Bennett Co., Inc., 40 pp., $1.25.

Coates, Helen: *Weaving for Amateurs.* The Studio Publications, Inc., 2nd Ed., 1946, $4.50.

Davenport, Elise G.: *Your Handweaving.* Charles A. Bennett Co., Inc., 1950, $2.75.

Gallinger, Osma Couch: *Joy of Hand Weaving.* D. Van Nostrand Co., 1950, $5.20.

Gallinger, Osma Couch, and Benson H.: *Hand Weaving with Reeds and Fibers.* Pitman Publications Corp., 1948, 199 pp., $3.95.

Hooper, Luther: *Hand Loom Weaving.* Pitman Publications Corp., 1948, $4.95.

Lewis, Roger: *Weaving.* Alfred A. Knopf, Inc., 1953, 48 pp., $1.75. (ages 7–11)

Simpson, Lillian E., and Weir, Marjorie: *The Weaver's Craft.* Charles A. Bennett Co., Inc., Revised, 1957, 221 pp., $5.75.

Thorpe, Heather G.: *Handweaver's Workbook.* The Macmillan Co., 1956, 179 pp., $4.50.

Worst, Edward F.: *Foot Power Loom Weaving.* Bruce Publishing Co., Revised, 1924, 278 pp., $7.50.

Woodworking and Use of Tools

Alber, Doris: *Sunset Wood Carving Book.* Lane Publishing Co., 1952, 95 pp., $1.75.

Anderson, H. S.: *How To Carve Characters in Wood.* U. of New Mexico, 77 pp., $1.50.

Barocci, Louis: *Wood Projects You Will Like.* 126 pp., $3.95.

Dank, Michael C.: *Creative Crafts in Wood.* Charles A. Bennett Co., Inc., 1945, 200 pp., $2.95.

Gottschall, Franklin H.: *Woodwork for the Beginner.* Bruce Publishing Co., 1952, 162 pp., $4.00.

Gottschall, Franklin H., and Hellum, Amanda Watkins: *You Can Whittle and Carve.* Bruce Publishing Co., 1942, 96 pp., $3.00.

Gross, Fred, Editor: *How To Work with Tools and Wood.* Pocket Book.

Hayward, Charles H.: *The Complete Book of Woodwork.* J. B. Lippincott Co., 1955, 344 pp., $3.95.

How To Use Hand Tools. Popular Mechanics, 1955, 160 pp.

Hunt, W. Ben: *Indian and Camp Handicraft.* Bruce Publishing Co., 1945, 180 pp., $3.00.

Hunt, W. Ben: *More Ben Hunt Whittlings.* Bruce Publishing Co., 1947, 108 pp., $2.50.

Hunt, W. Ben: *Whittling with Ben Hunt.* Bruce Publishing Co., 1959, $3.50.

Klenke, William: *Things To Make for the Camp and Game Room.* Charles A. Bennett Co., Inc., 1938.

Lacey, John: *The Audubon Book of Wood Carving.* McGraw-Hill Book Co.

Leavitt, Jerome E.: *Carpentry for Children.* Sterling Publishing Co., Inc., 1959, 96 pp., $2.50.

Leeming, Joseph: *Fun with Wood.* J. B. Lippincott Co., 1942, 111 pp., $3.00.

Lewis, Roger: *Woodworking.* Alfred A. Knopf, Inc., 1952, $1.75. (grades 2–6)

Lincoln, Martha, and Torrey, Katherine: *The Workshop Book.* Houghton Mifflin Co., 1955, 214 pp., $5.00.

Maintenance and Care of Hand Tools. U.S. Gov't Printing Office.

Mankin, Victor J.: *Modernistic Chip Carving.* Bruce Publishing Co., 1942, 72 pp., $1.25.

Scharff, Robert: *Easy Ways To Expert Woodworking.* McGraw-Hill Book Co., 1956, 185 pp., $3.95.

Soeteber, Lyle P., and Moore, Paul R.: *Making Things of Wood.* Charles A. Bennett Co., Inc., 1956, $3.50.

Sowers: *Woodcarving Made Easy.* Bruce Publishing Co., 1950, 96 pp., $2.25.

Upton, John: *The Art of Wood Carving.* 130 pp., $5.50.

Waltner, Edna and W. H.: *Carving Animal Caricatures.* 1958, 104 pp., $1.00.

Woodwork. Boy Scouts #3316A, 25¢.

Wyatt, Edwin M.: *Puzzles in Wood.* Bruce Publishing Co., 1928, 64 pp., 75¢.

MAGAZINE ARTICLES

Cassell, Sylvia: *Try Hiking Sticks.* C.M., Mar., 1952.

Jaeger, Ellsworth: *Making Belts and Necklaces From Twigs.* C.M., Jan., 1950.

Victor, Marllys: *Campers Love Cedar Jewelry.* C.M., Mar., 1952.

13

Literature
in Camp

You cannot tell a good story unless you tell it before a fire. You cannot have a complete fire unless you have a good story teller along.

DR. G. STANLEY HALL

AMONG its many and varied possessions, a camp ought to have a good collection of books available to both campers and staff members. First, there should be books for pure enjoyment, about Indians, animals, legends, folk tales, travel, biography, science, or almost anything under the sun that interests people. These books are for picking up and reading singly or in groups during rest hour, under a shady tree by the brook, on rainy days, in the evening while the corn's a-popping and there's a camp fire blazing merrily, or for tucking in with other duffel for odd moments on a trip.

Then there's another big class of reading material we might call "How to do it books." To these, the counselor can turn for help in handling his group, enabling him to stride forth on the morrow and strut his stuff as an expert as he leads his group in constructing a bridge across the brook, identifying a raccoon track, making a tent or wigwam, portaging a canoe, or braiding a lanyard. Here, too, the camper can turn to find a recipe for ring-tum-diddy, for improving his water skiing, for waterproofing his tent, or for making some plaster casts.

The above implies that, though there should be some central spot as a home base for the books and maintaining a record of what is available, really functional books won't remain on the shelf long enough to need dusting, but instead will be part of a "travelling library," operating right on the job when the person needs it, wherever he may be. Thus,

145

(Joy and Camp.)

there should be some sort of card catalogue of all the books in camp and a record of the whereabouts of each so that a much needed one won't be as good as lost for the camp season because some one carelessly tossed it aside behind his discarded duffel bag the second day of camp. Often, one counselor assumes the responsibility of the library with the help of several campers.

Various systems are used to acquire the necessary aggregation of books. Camp directors usually furnish a backbone assortment and supplement it in various ways. Local, county or state libraries will often lend selections for a whole or part of the summer. In other camps, one of the initial letters to campers may suggest that they bring in a favorite book or two to exchange with others during the summer; they often leave them as permanent additions to the camp collection. An appeal through the local press or radio may also bring in some very worthwhile contributions.

Book or poetry discussion periods may well find a nook in the camp program now and then so that natural book worms can share their interests and perhaps draw others to appreciate this wonderful leisure time pursuit.

STORY TELLING

An Ancient Heritage

The art of story telling is probably almost as old as man, for history tells us that from the advent of speech, primitive peoples loved to cluster about one of their most esteemed and beloved members, the story teller. From 8000 B.C., when the blind bard Homer was recounting the Iliad and Odyssey, down through the Minnesingers, troubadours and traveling minstrels, men have loved to gather to hear again the oft-repeated tales of courage and adventure which doubtless lost nothing in the telling under the golden tongue of the skilled narrator. The American Indians, likewise, made much of story telling, their legends serving to entertain, carry on tradition, and instruct the younger members of the tribe in geography, history and biography. What golden spells must have been woven by their tales of bravery and daring!

To this day, the fat, the lean, the dark, the fair, in fact everyone from the toddler to grandfather and grandmother loves a well-told tale. Though television, radio, movie and "funny" book may have largely impaired the interest and ability of both "teller" and "listener" in the home and in other gathering places, not so in the summer camp, where "Tell us a story" is just as frequent and fervent a plea as ever. True, some campers may need to be encouraged to participate the first few times the story hour comes along, for it is often an entirely new experience for them, but a few sessions will usually convert them into just as avid listeners as the old-timers.

No counselor worthy of his hire will fail to have a few good stories up his sleeve for that inevitable moment when nothing else will quite fill the bill. None worth his salt will meet a request by saying, "Oh, I can't tell stories." Almost anyone can learn to be a "good" story teller, even though not all of us may become supercolossal spinners of yarns.

The Why

There are numerous reasons for telling stories in camp; here are four of the most important:

ENJOYMENT.   Hearing a *good* story is fun, and that is important enough in it-self to warrant its inclusion in the program. It is hard to think of anything we can do that could bring boys and girls more lasting happiness than teaching them to enjoy good literature, for it is foolish to content oneself with trash when so much worth-while writing exists that we could never read all of it if we devoted a lifetime to the task.

RELIVING GREAT MOMENTS.   Who among us does not thrill to the adventures of the pioneers or the doings of such heroes as Paul Bunyan, Robin Hood, Johnny Appleseed, John Henry or Robinson Crusoe? Campers also become much more interested and appreciative of their camp community when they learn of the daily lives of the Indians and early settlers who once lived there, of famous battles or underground railroads located near, or the founding of towns and cities of the area. Such information is usually available from local historical associations or the clipping files and catalogued books of the local library. W.P.A. State Guide Books are also valuable sources of such information and may lead to enthusiastic planning for a gypsy trip to a nearby locality to see what the campers have read about.

GAINING NEW FRIENDS.   Though we are not privileged to know Benjamin Franklin, Gulliver, Huck Finn, or Abraham Lincoln in person, we can form their intimate acquaintance through the story teller. What child can fail to develop a kinder feeling toward animals as he lives in the realm of Albert Payson Terhune, Ernest Thompson Seton, or Uncle Remus and his stories?

MORAL AND CHARACTER VALUES. Since youth is the age of hero worship, there is no better way to teach that "virtue has its own reward" and "crime does not pay" than through the stories of the great and good of all ages. Fortunately, this can come about in a perfectly painless way without the sticky sentimentality or lecturing which may bring resentment and rebellion instead of the desired results.

The When and Where

Almost any time is "story time," but there are occasions which just seem to beg for a story. A campfire, a lovely hilltop at sunset, or a peaceful dell are "naturals," and a circle of blanket-rolled listeners under a starlit sky forms a perfect setting for star study and retelling the same star myths heard by Indian, Greek and Roman boys and girls of many centuries ago. A rainy day seems less dreary when there's an open fireplace and an exciting tale. Camp disappointments and minor tragedies fade under the spell of a Kipling adventure, and dishwashing and other chores seem almost to do themselves when there's a good narrative in the air. A well-chosen story will often keep restless youngsters relaxed during the rest hour or put them in a mood for going to sleep quickly at night. Here, also, the counselor may find a happy solution when unsocial attitudes or conduct have been manifested in his cabin and it also affords a pleasant interlude for restless infirmary inhabitants.

The Who

Though everyone likes to hear stories, not everyone likes the same story, for the teen-ager is bored beyond words with the adventures of Billie Goat Gruff or Jimmie the Jumping Frog; consequently, it is best to have listeners of approximately the same age. If there are differences, select a story appropriate to the older ones in the group for being "talked down to" is particularly obnoxious to all of us.

It should be understood from the very start that there is to be no disturbance of any sort until the story is finished; therefore, "it's all right to sit with your pal as long as you don't bother anyone, and you must save any questions and comments until the story is finished." Encourage campers who "don't like stories" to sample them a few times. If you choose appropriate ones and tell them well, few will fail to succumb to their charms.

The What

There are a few sure-fire stories which appeal to almost everyone, but, in general, "the group dictates the story," and what would be adored by one gathering may fall perfectly flat with another. You must learn to know your group and pick your story for *them*. Suit it to their general intelligence and background.

Boys and girls ordinarily like the same stories until they are about ten, when the boys begin to crave real he-man stories and disdain "kid" or "sissy stuff." Tales of Indians, cowboys, pioneers, pirates, airplanes, sports, and science, now appeal. Girls are not quite so exclusive, being satisfied with many of the stories previously liked as well as some of those now chosen by boys.

A good story teller paints a mental picture of peoples, places and action for his listeners; he must deal, therefore, in things familiar to them or must acquaint them with the unfamiliar. When well done, the listener will visualize each character, the house he lives in and all the scenes and activities mentioned will appear vivid and real to him. Small children, six to ten, like stories containing alliteration and nonsensical jingles as well as those about animals and people they know. They are particularly fond of the ludicrous and illogical, such as "Cora-

Dulcimer Duck.

belle Cow Who Goes Shopping on Roller Skates," or "Dulcimer Duck Who Carries a Pink Silk Umbrella and Wears Green Spats When She Goes to the Beach." They revel in fantasy and make believe and so are particularly fond of folk tales, fairies and such. Special favorites are stories "spun out" of the imagination of a counselor and involving the antics of such characters as Wooly, the caterpillar, Honey, the bear, or Porky, the porcupine.

Older children, ten to fourteen, demand something a bit more challenging to their growing judgments and like to draw their own conclusions from well-constructed but more hidden plots. Stories of Indians, animals, legendary heroes, and such interest them.

Still older campers are even more discriminating and present a real challenge to the story teller for their tastes are now approaching, but are not yet quite ready for, adult literature.

Youngsters of all ages have a good sense of humor, though what strikes them as funny may seem silly or flat to adults, and vice versa.

You may tell several short stories at one sitting, particularly if they vary in style and subject matter, but one long story may be enough, since the story period should never exceed twenty to thirty minutes for small children and forty-five to sixty minutes for older ones. A book or long story may be condensed by an expert, but it is risky business for an amateur. He had better divide it into parts, like a serial, each ending at some natural break which temporarily satisfies his listeners,

yet leaves them curious about what will happen next. Remember Scheherazade who was able to prolong her life 1,001 nights while she held her fickle husband, Sultan Schariar, entranced to see what would happen next in the stories she purposely abandoned at the most exciting spot each night. That is really story telling! Books, long stories or stories depending on the style of the author for their effectiveness are most successful when read rather than told. Reading a story, however, is most effective when the reader so familiarizes himself with it that he can read with gestures and real expression and frequently glance up at his listeners.

For the novice at choosing, many lists are available which classify stories as to type and age appeal. Some such lists will be found in the sources given at the end of the chapter. Another safe way of picking a story is to recall one of your own childhood favorites and, as you read for your own pleasure, be ever on the lookout for stories which would be good to tell.

Not every story that makes good reading is equally good for telling. Rapidly moving action stories without long descriptions of people or situations are usually best. Poetry written especially for children is definitely popular with them and should be included. The Bible is an excellent source of good stories, beautifully written and full of action and general interest.

The inevitable cry, "Tell us a ghost story," sometimes poses a problem, for there are bound to be some campers in almost any group who want nothing else. Certainly no one can question the mental indigestion possible from a diet of gruesomeness and horror, and it may even prove quite upsetting to some of the more sensitive campers. There are *some good* ghost and mystery stories which may be used to quench the thirst for the mysterious and supernatural, and the best procedure is perhaps a gradual wean-ing process brought about by interspersing a *good* ghost story occasionally among stories of other types. They should, of course, never be told just before going to bed.

The How

After you have selected your story, read it carefully for general plot and action and decide upon the best method of presenting it. Then read it again several times, even as many as ten or fifteen, until you are on the verge of memorizing it, for there is much more danger of failing through not knowing your story well than of going "stale" through knowing it too well. Nothing is so disconcerting to listeners as a faltering "er" interjected to give you time to think of what comes next, or an "Oh, I forgot to tell you," as you go back to insert something you should have told five minutes before. Practice telling the story to yourself until you are positive of every character and bit of action.

When the fateful moment arrives, gather your little group of not more than twenty-five or thirty about you, minimizing squirming and wiggling by seeing that all are comfortably seated. Have all located where they can see and hear you clearly; a semi-circle is usually best.

If the setting is to be an open fire, build it of hardwood sufficiently early to let it die down to coals. Appoint one person to inconspicuously keep it going, for a spluttery, smoky fire or one throwing out alarming sparks provides too much competition for any teller.

If your listeners are excited or full of pent-up energy, try bringing them to an attentive mood by playing a quiet game or two. Compel attention with your very first sentence by saying, for example, "Do you know how the rabbit got his powder-puff tail?"

Since your voice is the center of attention, try to make it pleasant and enunciate clearly. A low tone forces close attention, but use care to have your voice loud enough to be audible to those on the outskirts. Check this by asking them if they can hear you. Straining your voice, shouting, and using poorly chosen words and trite phrases detract much.

A sing-song manner with no variation in tone or timing soon becomes monotonous so vary your tone; get excited when the story calls for it; talk in a tired or dispirited tone if that is the nature of the person speaking. Learn the value of a pause to rouse anticipation and put your hearers in a mood for what is to follow. Pick a story you thoroughly enjoy, so that your enthusiasm and natural facial expressions and gestures attract your listeners. Change your voice or turn your head to indicate when different characters are speaking and pause subtly for effect or change your timing to suit the action of the story and build up suspense. Mimicry and dialect, where indicated, add much if you can do it without sounding stilted or forced. Overdramatizing and such mannerisms as dandling something in your hands or slicking down your hair divert attention from the story to you and are therefore undesirable.

Look at your listeners and talk to them instead of mumbling down your shirt collar. Watch the listeners' faces for their reaction, mentally noting the effectiveness of various techniques. If one or two of your audience seem inattentive, bring them back by talking directly to them. Quell disturbers with a sharp glance.

Dressing in costume or accompanying an Indian story with the rhythm of a tom-tom help. Draw a map in the dirt or with a crayon on a large piece of wrapping paper, or use construction paper cut outs on a flannel board to show the homes of the characters and the locations of various scenes.

If your story has a moral, do not over-stress it; it is better to pay your hearers the compliment of letting them grasp it by their intuition. When you reach the climax, conclude with as few words as possible. If they ask, "Is it true?" answer them honestly.

Encourage your campers to use the camp library by telling them selected bits from a chosen book and suggesting that they read the rest of it for themselves. It is often enjoyable for a small group to set aside a certain time each day for the continuation of a long story, with each member of the group taking a turn at telling it. It is also fun to construct a group story with each suggesting developments in the plot or action. Another too seldom appreciated activity is group reading of a play with members reading and perhaps following stage directions for different parts.

There is no secret formula for telling a story, for all good story tellers develop their own techniques. The novice should never miss an opportunity to study a skillful performer or gain experience for himself, for he improves each time and finds that the technique of telling stories is like a piece of good leather; it improves with use.

CREATIVE WRITING

Writing Creatively

I would rather be the author of one original thought than conqueror of a hundred battles.

—W. B. CLULOW

To be creative you must take some old material and fashion it, through your own imagination and personality, into an entirely new and unique product. If you would foster creative work of any sort in others, you must use a cautious and sensitive touch, for dictatorial methods and too many unwanted suggestions soon crush the spark of originality. Your role as a counselor is one of encouraging, giving aid where needed, and in general setting the yeast which in the hands of the camper will foam and bubble over into a true creative product. Hammett

and Musselman* emphasize that writing is but putting words together to show how you think and feel and that there are just three steps to it: (1) see it, (2) feel it, (3) write it down.

Campers are often inclined to dismiss with a shrug the suggestion that they compose a poem or do a piece of creative writing, for some of them have been discouraged by insistence in school upon such mechanical details as neatness, legibility, exact diction, spelling and punctuation. Though these things are admittedly important, original thought and self-expression are the things most to be desired in creative work. Do not expect youngsters to attain adult standards though, as always, they should try to do their best. Mrs. Cumming tells of a seven year old who, after insisting that he could not write anything, chattered on in the following soliloquy which she, unknown to him, recorded as he talked.

I hear echoes when I walk around hiking.
All the pretty voices I hear in places I go.
I see all the pretty flowers around the lake, in the
    forest and the mountainsides.
You have a good time in camp.
I wish I could stay at camp a long time,
And see all the pretty trees around with pretty leaves
    on them,
And see the tadpoles in the lake.
I have a good time going in swimming, and have a
    good time horseback riding.
All these things I have fun doing.
I like the cute birds in the trees;
They whistle at me, and I whistle at them.
The bees are funny things;
They sting some children, but not me.
Sometimes they sting me!
There are very funny things around camp.

---

*Hammett and Musselman: The Camp Program Book.

Some voices sound hummy, and people act very funny
   sometimes.
The mountainside sometimes just sings by itself, and
   no one else makes a noise.
The falls make a pretty noise;
There are rocks at the bottom of the falls.
Then you sit down and think about it, and you want
   to write a poem about it.*

Encourage every camper to jot down his thoughts for his own benefit if not for sharing with others, and recognize him by posting it on the bulletin board, reading it at the campfire or publishing it in the camp newspaper when he does something especially well. Encourage him to write poems, plays, pageants, diaries, letters, and accounts of things seen and done and to illustrate them with simple line drawings.

The Camp Paper

It is advantageous to have a camp paper, for it (1) serves to encourage and recognize creative writing, (2) keeps campers and staff as well as parents and friends informed of the doings of the whole camp, (3) fosters good camp morale and (4) serves as a souvenir to recall many pleasant memories of the summer.

Camp papers vary greatly as to frequency of publication. Some put out a page or two every day while others go to the opposite extreme and publish only one or two during the entire summer with an occasional "extra" to celebrate some special camp event. A few camps print their paper but most mimeograph

or spirit duplicate them. This provides the satisfaction of achievement to campers of different talents as they read and edit copy, make up the dummy, do the art work, type, cut stencils, run off the copies, and assemble and staple the papers. Colored inks and paper add variety and allow for artistic expression. Some type only one copy to be read at a campfire or other occasion but most supply a copy for each camper.

An interested counselor usually heads a staff of campers with one of them selected or elected as editor-in-chief. Other staff writers may be unit and general reporters, reporters for various activities as waterfront, riding, riflery, campcraft, arts and crafts, etc. Anyone not officially on the staff should be encouraged to submit contributions.

To avoid inaccuracies, sloppy appearance and last minute rush, non-current material should be written, cut on stencils, and run off ahead of time. Have a staff meeting soon after each issue appears in which staff members can critically evaluate the issue and plan for the next one. Post assignments for future issues as early as possible, and run everything in a business-like fashion appropriate to a juvenile newspaper office. Include poems, jokes, news flashes, honor achievements, stories, editorials, special features, puzzles, interviews, gossip column, or anything else you and the campers wish.

Make a point of including each camper's name frequently in some connection and give "by lines" to those who write articles to stimulate high standards and give recognition where it is due.

Keep the staff representative of the whole camp, and avoid letting the paper fall into the hands of a little clique. Wholesome, kindly humor adds immeasurably, but anything that might hurt or serve as a personal "axe to grind" is strictly taboo. Although the camp paper is a very worth-while activity, do not let

* Conversation of Charles Mitchell, recorded by Mrs. Ely C. Cumming of Mary Gwynn's Camp, Brevard, North Carolina.

campers become so engrossed in it that they neglect general camp participation and their wonderful opportunity for outdoor living that won't be available back home.

Camp Log

The Camp Log is put out at the end of the summer as a sort of camp annual. It may be mimeographed or otherwise reproduced, or it may take the form of a scrap book, compiled by a central staff or by each individual camper. In it go photographs, programs, invitations, pressed flowers or leaves, place cards, a few pages for autographed messages, poems read at special events, or almost anything else a camper wants to take home to display to friends and relatives and treasure in future years. The cover may range from a simple mimeographed sheet to a leather or wooden portfolio form, constructed and decorated in the arts and crafts shop.

ADDITIONAL READINGS

FOR THE LEADER

Adams, Bess Porter: *About Books and Children*. Henry Holt and Co., Inc., $6.00.

Aids to Choosing Books for Your Children. Children's Book Council, 50 W. 53rd St., New York 19, N.Y., 5¢.

Breen, Mary J.: *For the Story Teller*. NRA, 36 pp., 85¢.

Brown, Jeanette Perkins: *The Storyteller in Religious Education*. Pilgrim Press, 1951, 165 pp., $2.00.

Cheley, J. A.: *Stories for Talks with Boys and Girls*. Assn. Press, Revised, 1958, 380 pp., $3.95.

Cundiff, Ruby Ethel, and Larkin, Webb: *Story Telling for You*. Antioch Press, 1957, 103 pp., $2.00, paper $1.00.

Eisenberg, Helen and Larry: *Fun with Skits, Stunts and Stories*. Assn. Press, 1955, 256 pp., $2.95.

Hammett, Catherine T., and Musselman, Virginia: *The Camp Program Book*.

Musselman, Virginia: *Story Telling*. NRA, 28 pp., 50¢.

Sawyer, Ruth: *The Way of the Story Teller*. The Viking Press, 1942, $3.50.

Thurston, La Rue A.: *Complete Book of Campfire Programs*.

Tooze, Ruth: *Story Telling*. Prentice-Hall, Inc., 1959, 268 pp., $3.95.

MAGAZINE ARTICLES

Cumming, Elizabeth Chandler: *Creative Reading at Camp*. C.M., May, 1954.

Walp, Esther Spargo, and Walp, Russell Lee: *The Wonderland of Books*. C.M., April, 1953.

Materials To Read or Tell

Barrows, Marjorie, Editor: *One Thousand Beautiful Things*. Hawthorne Books, Inc., $4.95.

Beck, Earl Clifton: *They Knew Paul Bunyan*. U. of Mich., 1956, 255 pp., $4.75.

Botkin, B. A.: *Treasury of American Folklore*. Crown Publications, 1944, $5.00.

Cavanagh, Frances, Editor: *Family Reading Festival*. Prentice-Hall, Inc., 1958, 326 pp., $5.95.

Chase, Richard: *Grandfather Tales*. Houghton-Mifflin Co., 1948.

Cheley, J. A.: *Boy's Book of Campfires*. W. A. Wilde Co., 1925.

———: *Campfire Yarns*, W. A. Wilde Co., 1922.

———: *Little Campfires*. W. A. Wilde Co., 1938.

Coatsworth, Elizabeth, and Barnes, Kate: *Horse Stories*. Golden Books, 30 pp., $1.00.

Darton, Harvey: *The Wonder Book of Beasts*. J. B. Lippincott Co., 1946.

Eschmeyer, R. W.: *True-to-Life Stories for Campers*. Fisherman Press, Inc., $1.00 each, hard cover, 50¢ paper.

Felton, Harold W.: *Legends of Paul Bunyan*. Alfred A. Knopf, Inc., 1947, $5.00.

Field, Rachael: *American Folk and Fairy Stories*. Charles Scribner's Sons, 1929.

French, Marion N.: *Myths and Legends of the Ages*. NRA, 319 pp., $4.75.

Goodman, Jack: *Fireside Book of Dog Stories*. Simon and Schuster, Inc., 1943, $4.95.

Graham, Kenneth: *The Wind in the Willows*. Charles Scribner's Sons, 1948.

Grey, Hugh, and McCluskey, Editors: *Field and Stream*. Henry Holt and Co., Inc., 351 pp., $5.00. (Adventure stories by Zane Grey, Stewart Edward White, James Oliver Curwood, etc.)

Grinnell, G. B.: *Pawnee Hero Stories and Folk Tales.* Charles Scribner's Sons, 1932.

Grover, Edwin Osgood, Editor: *The Nature Lover's Knapsack.* Thomas Y. Crowell Co., 1947, 294 pp., (Poetry)

Hamilton, Charles, Editor: *Cry of the Thunderbird.* The Macmillan Co., 1950, $4.50.

Harris, Joel Chandler: *Uncle Remus, His Songs and His Sayings.* Appleton-Century-Crofts, Inc., 1928.

Hazeltine, Alice Isabel, Editor: *Children's Stories To Read or Tell.* Abingdon Press, 1949, $2.50.

Hazeltine, Alice Isabel, Editor: *Selected Stories for Teen-Agers.* Abingdon Press, 1952, $3.00.

Hazeltine, Alice Isabel, Editor: *We Grew Up in America.* Abingdon Press, $2.95. (Autobiographies of famous Americans.)

Jaeger, Ellsworth: *Council Fires.* The Macmillan Co., 1949, 253 pp., $2.95.

Johnson, Edna, et. al.: *Anthology of Children's Literature.* Houghton-Mifflin Co., Revised, 1959, $7.50.

Judd, M. C.: *Wigwam Stories.* Ginn and Co., 1942.

Kennedy, Howard: *The Red Man's Wonder Book.* E. P. Dutton and Co., Inc., 1931.

Kipling, Rudyard: *Just So Stories.* Doubleday and Co., Inc., 1932.

Lantz, J. Edward, Editor: *Stories To Grow By.* Assn. Press, 1953, $2.95.

Leach, Maria: *Rainbow Book of American Folk Tales and Legends.* The World Publishing Co., 1958, 319 pp., $4.95.

Lotz, M. M., and Monahan, Douglas: *Twenty Tepee Tales for "Y" Indian Guides.* Assn. Press, 1950, 75¢. (boys 7–9)

Lucas, Mrs. Edgar: *Fairy Tales of the Brothers Grimm.* G. P. Putman's Sons, Inc., 1949.

Mason, Bernard S.: *Dances and Stories of the American Indians.* The Ronald Press Co., 1944, 269 pp., $5.50.

Ressler, Theodore Whitson: *Treasury of American Indian Tales.* Assn. Press, 1958, 310 pp., $3.95.

Rugoff, Milton: *A Harvest of World Folk Tales.* The Viking Press, 1949, $4.50.

Sanderson, Ivan: *Animal Tales.* Alfred A. Knopf, Inc., 1946, $7.50.

Shedlock, Marie L.: *Eastern Stories and Legends.* E. P. Dutton and Co., Inc., 1935.

Sloan, Gertrude: *Fun with Folk Tales.* E. P. Dutton and Co., Inc., 1942.

Smith, Lillian: *Books for Boys and Girls.* Ryerson Press, 1950.

Stern, James: *Grimm's Fairy Tales.* Pantheon Books, Inc., 1944.

Stevens, James: *Paul Bunyan.* Knopf, Revised, 1948, $4.00.

Thomas, Lowell: *Tall Stories.* Blue Ribbon Book Co., 1931.

Watson, Katherine: *Tales for Telling.* The H. W. Wilson Co., 1950, 267 pp., $2.75.

Wiley, Farida, Editor: *Ernest Thompson Seton's America.* The Devin-Adair Co., 1954, 413 pp., $5.00. (Collection of his animal and nature stories.)

MAGAZINE ARTICLES

Zapl, Arthur Lewis: *The Story Teller at Camp.* C.M., Feb., 1957.

Creative Writing

Burack, A. S., Editor: *The Writer's Handbook.* Boston, The Writer, Inc., 1954.

Hammett, Catherine T., and Musselman, Virginia: *The Camp Program Book.*

Hyde, G. M.: *Journalistic Writing,* Appleton-Century-Crofts, Inc., 1946.

Journalism, Boy Scouts #3812, 25¢.

Kerr, Walter: *How Not To Write a Play.* Simon and Schuster, Inc., 1955.

Wood, Clement: *The Craft of Poetry.* E. P. Dutton and Co., Inc., 1929.

MAGAZINE ARTICLES

Jeffries, David L.: *Publishing a Camp Paper.* C.M., April, 1948.

Newman, Arlene L.: *A Camp Newspaper Is Worth The Effort.* C.M., February, 1959.

The Columbia Scholastic Press Association Columbia University, Box 11, Low Memorial Library, New York 27, N.Y., has a number of inexpensive pamphlets on journalism.

14

Nature and Conservation

Conservation Pledge

I GIVE MY
PLEDGE AS AN AMERICAN
TO SAVE AND FAITHFULLY TO
DEFEND FROM WASTE THE
NATURAL RESOURCES OF
MY COUNTRY — ITS SOIL
AND MINERALS, ITS
FORESTS, WATERS,
AND WILDLIFE

This pledge originated in a national competition conducted in 1946 by *Outdoor Life Magazine* and is reprinted through their courtesy.

A RETURN to the simple life and its intimate contact with nature has always been a stated purpose of camping, but the methods used have not always brought the love of nature hoped for. Campers have victoriously displayed badges and ribbons won by learning the scientific names of twenty insects or mounting twenty flowers, and have returned to the city bearing such live pets as squirrels, turtles, grasshoppers, snakes and even skunks to foist upon long-suffering parents or let die of neglect and mistreatment. Only an occasional camper acquired enough interest in nature to make it a lifelong hobby, for, like human friends, plants and animals become friends only through long and personal acquaintance. Learning a name or viewing a still, cold corpse impaled upon a mounting pin will never bring about such a result.

It may bolster one's ego to identify a giant dragon fly as *Epiaeschna heros,* but it cannot compare with the enchantment of watching this evil-looking, blood-thirsty creature zoom and bank through the air, using its basketlike undercarriage of legs to scoop up flies, mosquitoes and other insects which it later crams into its capacious mouth. Its appetite is enormous, and it has been known to bolt down forty-two flies topped off with large quantities of its own tail which had been bent around and fed into its mouth. Its needle is only an elongated stomach, and its huge eyes have 30,000 facets which enable it to see in all directions. These, with its fierce expression, give it a truly sinister look, but it is quite harmless to

155

Dragon Fly.

man and does not merit its common names of devil's darning needle, horse killer, and snake feeder. Perhaps it is unfortunate that its long "darning needle" does not have its reputed power to sew up the lips of liars.

Nature in camp should not be conducted as an isolated class, for it is at its best only when made a part of each child's experience in the out-of-doors. It can be interwoven with all phases of the indigenous program and should be thought of as what one experiences by touch, taste, smell, sound and sight. It should consist of studying nature's creatures as they carry on their normal activities in their natural habitats, and not of studying dead, dried-up skeletons.

Nature lore should not be knowledge acquired to pass tests or pose as a walking encyclopedia, but should come rather as the inevitable result of widened visions and deepened appreciations. Specimens are not the smelly laboratory variety nor the foreign imports of zoo and circus, but are those things which we encounter every day, but have failed to notice up to now. Aided by such inexpensive pieces of equipment as a homemade butterfly net and a little pocket microscope, the field of exploration is unlimited.

Instead of being bookish or formal, nature should be an active, doing process in which children venture forth to look at whatever lies beside the path, under the rocks, in the trees, or at the bottom of the pond. Campers should unite minds, hearts and hands to explore, uncover,

mount specimens, make insect dip nets, splatter prints, and indigenous arts and crafts projects. If their group is building an outdoor campsite, they must never become too absorbed to stop and watch the antics of a venturesome squirrel or listen to a noisy jay. A night of restless slumber under a quaking aspen creates a real interest in seeing how the flat, wide stem is set "on edge" against the broad leaf so that the least breeze keeps stirring, producing the very disturbing rain-like patter the previous night. Like opportunity, nature experiences often knock but once and we must seize them whenever they appear. We cannot schedule them for definite times and places, for Mother Earth's children are too busy carrying on their daily activities to be amenable to manmade schedules. Let us not be like the poor, misguided nature counselor who said, "Now children, come away from that porpoise washed up on the beach! Remember, we're studying birds today and won't get around to porpoises until two weeks from Tuesday."

A child's feeling of confidence and security in the out-of-doors increases as he learns that nearly all animals are timid and much prefer to stay out of his path and sight, attempting to harm him only if cornered or frightened. He makes friends with chipmunks, squirrels, toads and birds as he discovers that nearly all woodland creatures readily respond to kindly overtures. His appreciation makes him enjoy doing a good turn for smaller, weaker woodfolk instead of tormenting or killing them just for the fun of it. His spiritual self gets uplift from the wonders and beauties of nature and since love comes from the feelings rather than the mind, the result is a genuine and abiding "love" for all living creatures.

Tests and ranks depend on information secured by first-hand observation rather than learned from a book. Books, though, are important, as they answer queries about things the camper has seen but doesn't understand or better prepare him for a future excursion.

Conservation

Campers need to comprehend the interdependence of all forms of life. All living things are dependent upon plants, for every animal, including man, either dines directly upon some form of plant life or upon some other animal which, in the final analysis, does so. Everything looks like a delectable dietary tidbit to something else, so that each is simultaneously engaged in a struggle to secure its own food and avoid becoming the food of another. Each has its own means for securing food, and some methods are unique and most interesting. The opposite leaves of the teasel are joined into a small cup at the stem which catches water and drowns minute ants for its banquet dish. The rare Venus's flytrap has a hairtrigger mechanism which causes the sharp teeth along the edges of its leaves to instantly interlock and trap

any insect unlucky enough to merely brush against them.

Everything has a way of protecting itself. Deer can outrun most of their enemies, and cats climb trees to evade dogs. Porcupines pursue their leisurely way, secure in the knowledge that their barbed quills will deter most attackers; skunks make amiable and affectionate pets, but nature has given them the power to exact a fiendish revenge on whatever frightens or attacks them. The chameleon changes color, the rabbit "freezes," the rosebush has thorns, and the thistle has prickles to help protect it against its enemies.

Nature provides each variety of life in abundance, so that, though some may become food or succumb to disease, wind, flood or unfavorable climatic conditions, there will always be enough left to carry on the species. The female frog lays 20,000 eggs, but only 200 develop into adult frogs, while the other 19,800 lose their lives by accident or become food for fish and water insects. Nature, if left to her own devices, keeps all species in balance, so that they neither die out nor become so numerous as to overrun the earth, and every single form of life has its own role in maintaining this balance. Enough birdlings are created to spare a few for the snake, just as enough lettuce, green beans, and pork chops grow to supply our needs. We must rid our minds once and for all of the idea that certain forms of life are more worthy than others, for man's efforts to kill out what he considers an unworthy species has sometimes backfired in a most unfortunate way. A concentrated drive to eradicate "chicken-killing" hawks, for instance, may bring about a huge oversupply of rats, mice, snakes and frogs which really constitute over 90 per cent of their diet in contrast to the occasional chicken they eat.

Almost everything we do affects plant or animal life in some way. Picking berries in the fall cuts down on the supply of winter food for some bird or animal, and squirrels lose out when we gather nuts. Draining a swamp to provide more farm land kills thousands of plants and animals which cannot survive without a wet environment. Spraying trees kills the insects and grubs which provide food for certain birds. Killing squirrels will eventually mean fewer trees, for dead squirrels cannot bury nuts to sprout and grow into future forest monarchs.

Man, in his greediness to sell beaver pelts, thinned out these little animals until no more beaver dams were built in certain areas. When hard rains came, water rushed down the open streams, causing floods to destroy both property and life; between rains, the creek bed dried out so that water life could not survive, and land animals went thirsty.

Man has used the rivers as garbage tanks and open sewers, and as drains for the various chemicals and waste products of manufacturing; as a result, they are no longer fit for swimming, and even plant and fish life sometimes cannot survive in them.

Man has cut down the trees and shrubs which used to provide food and shelter for animals and birds. He has shot and trapped so many animals for food, furs or sport that some, such as the buffalo, are scarce, while the great auk and passenger pigeon are extinct.

Forest preserves, the requiring of hunting and fishing licenses, open and closed seasons, bag limits, and the nurturing and "planting" of young birds, fish and animals are making feeble strides toward preserving the remnants of our natural heritage, but the understanding and loyal support of thousands of persons are needed if satisfactory progress is to be made. Camping can do much by spreading information and enlisting the cooperation of the youngsters who will be the citizens of tomorrow.

One of man's most myopic perspectives has been with regard to the conservation of the soil upon which all plant and animal life depends. Topsoil consists of a mixture of minerals and the remnants of animals and plants and is admirably suited for plant growth. It lies above the nonfertile subsoil, and varies from a depth of a few inches on hill tops to several feet in the valleys. When on the floor of the forest, it is known as *humus*.

When our ancestors came to America, they were delighted with the rich topsoil they found after they had cleared away the trees and shrubs. When they had quickly worn out the land, through replanting the same crop over and over again, they cared little, for more land could be had for the taking, so that they simply moved on to repeat the same process all over again. Progressive farmers now plant crops in rotation so that one crop helps to restore the fertility lost to the previous one.

Vegetation keeps soil porous and loose, enabling it to absorb and hold large quantities of water which is gradually absorbed by the plants and returned to the air by evaporation. Without plant growth, rains quickly run off down sloping surfaces, forming ever-enlarging gullies and carrying off large quantities of the topsoil. When the farmer makes his plow lines straight up and down the hillsides, he but adds to this wastage so that every year 25,000,000 cubic feet of our richest topsoil are being washed away and eternally lost for cultivation. This is not a cheering picture when we stop to think that from 500 to 1000 years are required to create an inch thickness of fertile topsoil.

The rapidly draining slopes cause swollen streams and eventual floods which menace the plant and animal life along the banks. Campers will be interested in making a tour of their own camp site to find examples of erosion and plan for its elimination.

The topsoil in dry areas, where there are no roots of vegetation to hold it in place, is carried away as dust, leaving behind whole areas of infertile and desolate dust bowls. Many farmers still burn off their land each year in an attempt to kill off weeds and get the ground "ready" for spring crops, but this practice damages their precious topsoil.

Testing the soil and supplying needed chemicals, rotating crops, planting cover crops to hold moisture and prevent erosion, and using terraced and contour plowing on hillside areas are valuable steps in soil conservation.

True conservation is based upon an appreciation of the value of each living thing in maintaining the balance of the whole. It tells us that we are free to use the surplus which nature lavishly supplies, but that we must always carefully leave enough of everything to insure its continuance for our own future use and that of coming generations. We may liken this to an investment at the bank where the interest always continues to come as long as we leave the principal intact. When man, in his infinite short-sightedness, sets himself up to decide which varieties of life are worthy to continue, he is likely to upset nature's nicely poised

balance in ways difficult to foresee. It is much wiser to take the attitude that any wanton destruction of wild life is extremely undesirable.

THE NATURE COUNSELOR

Each counselor must, in a sense, be a nature counselor if camp is to make an appreciation and understanding of the out-of-doors a vital part of camp living. This does not mean that each is expected to be an authority on nature lore, but rather that the individual counselor will be interested in it and willing to start with whatever meager knowledge he has and add to it as he learns with his campers. He need not be ashamed to admit he doesn't know all the answers, for even experts at one time started with absolutely no knowledge in their chosen field. He will gradually need to say, "I don't know, but let's find out" less and less often as he explores with his campers and consults the nature counselor or

(Courtesy of The Philadelphia Evening Bulletin.)

source books about what campers cannot learn by observation.

Nature, like happiness, lurks in most unexpected places, disclosing itself most often to those alert enough to notice, rather than to those who go out consciously seeking it. A ten-mile hike may end up a hundred yards from the cabin as a fascinated group watches a spider weave its web or a trip to gather wood for camp construction turns into a study of different woods and their uses, and who can say that these side excursions are not more valuable than the original objectives?

The main requirements for you if you want to help with a real nature program are curiosity, enthusiasm, and an insight into the possibilities for integrating nature with many camp experiences and, most of all, interest in and love of *human* nature. You must not let nature study become a boresome, tedious thing, but must keep it ever a pulsating, vibrant answer to your campers' query of how, when, where and why?

A trip offers a wonderful opportunity to acquire information about the world in which we live. What camper is not interested in nontechnical information about the different terrains and soils and their effect upon flora and fauna, and about watersheds, rivers, drainage, currents, water life, and the hundreds of displays Dame Nature has set up along the way? When carried on with naturalness and enthusiasm, you can make nature study one of the most interesting activites in camp. Carry it on in the out-of-doors under the sun and skies and winds and rain of nature's own laboratory whenever possible.

Such pieces of equipment as microscopes, pocket magnifying glasses, butterfly nets and attractive nature books stimulate youngsters to want to use them. Hands and imaginations occupied in making cages, arranging bulletin boards, mounting displays, and planning museums and nature trails result in interested, happy campers. They may keep such

creatures as frogs, salamanders, ants, nonpoisonous snakes or larvae as pets for a few hours if they know how to make them comfortable. This provides an opportunity to observe them closely.

Many excellent slides and movie films are now available free or at nominal cost, and there is a multitude of good literature now on the market.

NATURE WALKS

Nature walks are not hikes, but must be taken leisurely enough to allow time to look, listen, smell, taste, touch and investigate. Keep the group small (six to eight) and travel slowly and quietly so that you do not scatter your wild friends in terror. Proceed with your back to the sun so colors will show up more brightly.

Take pocket magnifying glasses, binoculars, sacks or boxes for bringing back unusual "finds," a few good indentification books, and a notebook and pencil to jot down points of interest.

COLLECTING

Though making collections still has its place, it does not occupy the pinnacle it once did. One reason for this is that previous collectors, in their zeal to get "just one more specimen," all but annihilated some of our rarer species of wildlife. Before picking a flower or other specimen, apply the principles of conservation by glancing about to see that there are ample quantities left to carry on the species.

Collections also sometimes become ends in themselves, with the collector heaving a satisfied sigh each time he has corralled another specimen, fastened it on paper and labeled it with a polysyllabic title. He neither knows nor cares anything about Exhibit X beyond having a mere nodding acquaintance with its name; in fact he may completely overlook it the next time he pursues his one-track search for some new victim to add to his store.

This sort of collecting becomes busy work, contributing nothing whatsoever toward furthering a real love of nature.

When properly regarded, collections of rocks, minerals, flowers, leaves, seeds, insects, shells, ferns, mosses, and the like, add to a nature program. Accompany each mounting with its name date, locale, your name as collector, and chatty data concerning its life and place in the balance of nature and its commercial value to man to help you achieve real nature appreciation. Be sure to practice good conservation in all you do.

Reproducing actual specimens with water color or sketching, or taking photographs with the aid of a camera portrait attachment, is even better than mounting actual specimens.

Pressing Plants

It is easy to make a press to prepare leaves, ferns, and flowers for mounting. One 10 by 12 inches will meet ordinary needs and should be constructed so as to simultaneously dry and flatten the plants. Two pieces of board, approximately 10 by 12 inches and about ½ inch thick, are needed for the outside covers. Cut a dozen or more sheets of blotting paper and half as many sheets of corrugated cardboard from packing boxes to fit and complete the outfit with two web or leather straps.

Place each plant between sheets of blotting paper (or newspaper) and separate from the others by the sheets of corrugated paper. Place the covers on the top and bottom, draw the straps tight to hold the whole thing compact, and leave for several days while the plants dry and flatten. If desired, a weight can be placed on top of the press. Beware of picking rare specimens or large quantities of even the plentiful. A hundred campers make a serious inroad if each picks only one leaf. It is usually better to learn to look at nature's exhibits as they grow, leaving them intact for the pleasure of others.

MUSEUMS

Camp museums may be located in the nature house, under a tree near camp, or along a nature trail. You may use them to display such camper activities as a nature bulletin board, mounted specimens, indigenous arts and crafts projects, trail maps, creative writing on nature topics, papier-mâché relief maps, live pets, weather predictions and equipment, knot display boards, friction sets made from camp materials, mats and baskets woven of native materials, articles fashioned from local clay, and so forth.

The craft house itself should be supplied with guide books, displays, tools, storage facilities, working space at tables, and other things. A fireplace provides a cheery environment on damp days. Campers should plan and keep up all

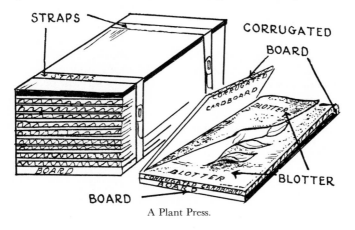

STRAPS   CORRUGATED BOARD

BOARD   BLOTTER

A Plant Press.

(Courtesy of The Philadelphia Evening Bulletin.)

exhibits themselves with all on the look-out for interesting materials. Maintain a "What Is It?" shelf or corner for un-identified curios with the name of the person who first correctly identifies them given a place of honor on the bulletin board. Change the display frequently so that campers do not pass it by because "it's just the same old thing." Make a terrarium and stock it with such inhabit-ants as frogs, toads and salamanders.

Useful Plants

Collect samples of medicinal and other useful plants and label them with their names and uses. It is interesting to gather and serve a meal composed exclusively of wild foods, but be sure you get expert help to avoid eating something harmful or poisonous. Use native dyes, and make elderberry wine, blueberry pie or wild strawberry shortcake.

Raising Wild Things in Camp

A fernery or wild flower garden, an insect cage, an aquarium for water life, or a terrarium for things that live on land may be made. Make outdoor feed-ing stations to attract wildlife where you can watch firsthand.

MAKING A NATURE TRAIL

Laying a nature trail is an interesting and educational experience, for it requires careful consultation and planning to in-clude as many worth-while things as pos-sible. Ideally, the trail should be narrow and about one-half to a mile in length and should include sections of a meadow, woods, a stream or pond, and the edge of a swamp to bring in a variety of life. You may indicate such interesting side trips as a visit to a rare flower, a spring or a beaver dam.

Make all labels brief but interesting and informative. If a lot of information is desirable, it is best to distribute it on sev-eral short labels, for people will not bother to read anything at all if they are discouraged by undue lengthiness. Bristol board tags or pieces of filing card are satisfactory for temporary use, but when more durable labels are called for, you can use bits of tin, enameling them and printing on them with India ink and then protecting them with a coat of shellac or Valspar. Short poems, photographs, bulletin boards, displays, and trailside museums add interest. The changing season calls for new labels and a rerouting of the trail every now and then.

You can sharpen the campers' observations by giving them sheets to fill out as they move along the trail. Invitations to listen, taste, smell or feel help to bring all the senses into play.

You may need to clear the trail somewhat for easy passage, but be sure to keep it woodsy and natural. You can lay flat stepping stones or brush across wet places, or even construct a rustic bridge across a stream. Be careful not to make your trail so that erosion results.

BIRDS*

Bird study has a larger following than any other phase of nature, and these projects for carrying it on are suggested.

Birdwalks—best carried on in early morning or late evening when the birds are most active. Learn to identify by nest, color, sound, and manner of flight. Move slowly and quietly.

Attract birds by planting shrubs and trees near camp to provide food and cover. Supply short pieces of string or yarn (three to four inches) for nesting material during the nesting season. Bird houses placed this summer will attract birds next spring for next summer's camp. Bird baths and feeding trays also help.

Collect feathers. Collect old nests (no birds except hawks use them a second time) and dissect them to see what materials were used in their construction. Place modeled eggs painted the proper colors in whole nests and display them on branches arranged to resemble trees.

Contrast the bills and feet of birds to see how they are adapted to their diet and habits. Listen to the bird's song and watch its pattern of flight.

Take a bird census or keep a record of all the birds you see in camp.

Make a bird scrapbook of pictures, stories, anecdotes and poems.

Make plaster casts of tracks in mud or at the beach.

PLANTS

Make a wild flower garden or fernery. (Ferns and wild flowers will only grow with soil and other conditions similar to those of their natural habitat.)

Draw or paint pictures of wild flowers, adding name, date, where found, and such information as native country, seeds and their dispersal, pollination and uses (medicinal, dyes, and so on). In mounting specimens, use small pieces of Scotch tape or dip the specimens in a mixture of glue and vinegar spread evenly on glass, and transfer them to heavy paper.

Study seeds and their dispersal by barbs, parachutes, or other means. Collect some and keep them for making a wild flower garden. Glue some on mounting boards and label.

Make a plant gall collection.

Study lichens, mosses and ferns. Look at them through a microscope.

Identify nut-bearing bushes and trees. Learn when the nuts ripen.

Study flower arrangement for indoor decoration.

Identify poison ivy, oak and sumac.

Identify different types of mushrooms, particularly the morels which are safe to eat. Do not trust other kinds, for even experts have difficulty in distinguishing the poisonous ones.

Learn which plants are edible; prepare and eat some of them (be sure to get expert advice).

* Write to the National Audubon Society, 1000 Fifth Avenue, New York 28, N.Y., for information about the Audubon Junior Clubs for Summer Camps.

TREES

Identify trees by contour, color, leaf, bark, flower, seed and wood structure. Then learn all you can about them: what they are used for, how they burn, and so on.

Press and mount leaves, using methods suggested for flowers.

Photograph trees; make sketches or water colors of them.

Carry on a tree conservation program, thinning out dead, diseased and crowded ones, and pruning off dead or diseased branches as close to the trunk as possible and covering the scar with paint (brown or green blend in well). Clear out obstructing brush and vines which are choking young trees.

Learn how individual trees serve for shade, beauty, coil conservation, firewood or commercial products. Learn their early uses by the Indians and pioneers. Identify the kinds found in camp furniture, walls, and so forth.

Study stumps to learn the life history of the tree such as its age, injuries, insect damage, favorable and unfavorable seasons, and the like.

Learn the uses of different kinds of woods in fire-building (tinder, kindling, heat, light, fire dogs, and others). Which ones are best for whittling? Notice how the growth of trees is affected by those surrounding them.

INSECTS

Learn the distinguishing characteristics of insects, spiders, bees, wasps, grasshoppers, bugs, beetles, flies, moths, butterflies and the like. Identify the various sorts and learn their habits, food, life cycles, and use or destructiveness. Watch them in their native habitat.

Make sketches of common varieties.

Prepare and mount specimens, adding pertinent information about them.

Raise families of butterflies, moths, ants, insects.

Photograph spider webs and other photogenic things.

Watch an ant colony at work.

ROCKS AND MINERALS

Distinguish between minerals and rocks.

Visit a quarry, a fresh road cut, a dried-up stream bed, or a mine opening.

Gather specimens, using a geology hammer (a regular hammer will serve) to prepare uniform sizes (about 1½ by 2½ inches) for collections. Wash carefully and label. Keep the specimens in boxes with compartments of cardboard; mount small samples on a mounting board or in plaster of Paris. Enter dates, places and interesting facts about the find.

Study the characteristics of rocks, determining which are best for use in fireplaces, as kettle supports, and so on.

FISH

Make your own poles, baits (flies and lures), and lines.

Learn to recognize the different species and learn their life histories.

Prepare and mount an especially good specimen.

Learn about state fishing laws, fish hatcheries and efforts at conservation.

Learn to clean fish and study their structures as you are cleaning them.

ANIMALS

Keep an animal a *short* time (not over twenty-four hours) for observation. Be sure you know how to feed and care for it.

Take close-up photographs. Use a portrait attachment.

Make plaster casts of tracks.

Make a wildlife sanctuary. Put out some foods animals like to attract them, never frighten them and see how tame they get.

Play stalking games.

Stalk animals with a camera (takes patience and skill). Lie or sit still and watch them. If you wait long enough you may be able to discover where they live.

STARS

It is best to study stars on a clear evening when there is no moon to detract from their brightness.

Use the beam of a focusing flashlight to help point them out.

Learn the folklore regarding the stars and constellations.

Paint diagrams of the heavens on dark blue or black paper with luminous paint so you can use them at night.

Take time exposures of stars with your camera.

Binoculars make the observation of stars more interesting.

MAKING PRINTS

There are several methods of printing flowers, leaves and ferns. Better results are obtained if you first press the specimens flat. Use them to decorate your memory book, place cards, invitations and stationery.

Ozalid and Blue Prints

These give beautiful results, but are slightly more expensive than other prints and require some skill to make well.

Crayon Prints

Place a leaf, vein side up, on a flat surface, cover it with a sheet of unlined paper and, holding leaf and paper firmly in place, rub a soft crayon over the paper with parallel strokes until the edges and veins stand out clearly. Outline the edge with a firm black line and cut out the print and mount it or use it for decorating menus or stationery.

Ink Pad Prints

Lay a leaf, vein side down, on an ink pad, cover with a layer of newspaper cut to fit the ink pad, and rub thoroughly. Transfer the leaf, inky side down, onto a piece of paper, cover it with a fresh newspaper, hold it firmly in place, and rub until the ink pad print appears clearly on the paper.

Printer's Ink Print

Spread a small quantity of printer's ink of any desired color on a piece of glass and run a rubber photographic roller through it until it is thinly and evenly spread. Place the leaf, vein side up, on a newspaper and rub the inky roller over it, transferring a uniform coating of ink. Reverse the leaf, place it on a fresh sheet of paper, cover with newspaper and, holding it firmly in place, rub over it with a clean roller until the transfer is completed.

Smoke Print Stationery.

Smoke Prints

Many consider smoke prints the most attractive of all. Candles (plumber's are best) and some grease such as lard or petroleum jelly are necessary. Spread a small quantity of grease evenly over a fourth of a sheet of newspaper and pass it through the candle flame (being careful not to let it get close enough to burn) until it is uniformly coated with carbon. Then lay it on a flat surface, place the leaf, vein side down, on it, cover with a clean piece of newspaper, and rub over the newspaper, holding the leaf firmly in place. Transfer the leaf, carbon side down, to a fresh sheet of paper, again cover with newspaper, and rub until the smoke print is transferred.

A Spatter Print.

Spatter Prints

An old tooth brush and some India ink or diluted poster paint are necessary for this method of printing. Protect the scene of operation by spreading newspapers about, and place the leaf on a plain sheet of paper. Pin the edges flat so that no paint can get under them and slant the heads of the pins slightly toward the center of the leaf. Dip the toothbrush into the paint to get a thin but uniform coating on it. Holding the brush at a 45-degree angle and about 2 inches from the paper, use a knife, nail file or thin, flat stick, to scrape *toward you* across the tooth brush. Continue the process until a sufficiently heavy "spatter" has been deposited around the leaf. Do not remove the leaf until the paint is dry.

PLASTER CASTS

Inexpensive plaster casts of flowers, animal tracks, leaves, and the like, are simple to make and are quite attractive when used as paper weights, book ends or wall plaques. They may be tinted in natural colors if desired. Plaster of Paris may be purchased at the hardware or drug store and should be mixed in an old container such as a tin can, using a stick for stirring. (It is practically impossible to remove the plaster from anything with which it has come in contact.) Estimate the amount of plaster needed for the cast desired and place three-fourths of that amount of water in the container. Pour in as much plaster of Paris as will sink to the bottom, then add a trifle more for good measure. Put in a pinch of salt to hasten setting and stir thoroughly. A good mixture has about the consistency of pancake batter.

If an animal track is to be cast, dust it lightly with talcum powder and place a circular or rectangular collar of cardboard of the size desired for the finished cast around it. Pour in the plaster of Paris and let it harden. Then lift the cast carefully, remove the cardboard collar, and scrub it well with water. Plaques should have a screw eye or paper clip for hanging inserted in the edge before they are dry.

To make a positive cast (with the track in relief), powder the negative cast lightly, place a collar about it and pour in more plaster of Paris. When dry, carefully separate the two casts.

To make casts of leaves, ferns, flowers, seeds, and so forth, pour the plaster of Paris into a mold, dampen the specimen and place it on the plaster of Paris, brushing it with a paint brush to make a tight contact over its entire surface. When about half dry, remove the leaf and let the plaster continue to harden.

Obviously, superfluous plaster of Paris should never be poured down the drain.

NATURE GAMES

STARVATION HIKE. Go out and cook a meal, using only things found growing in the woods. Be sure you *know* what is safe to use.

NATURE QUESTS. See who can bring in and identify a square stemmed plant; a lady beetle; a piece of wood that is shaped like an animal; and such. Be careful not to cause harm or destruction.

NATURE TREASURE OR SCAVENGER HUNT. Give each group, person or pair a list of nature objects to bring in, such as leaves of certain trees, common flowers, certain kinds of rocks, and so forth. The first back with the correct and complete list wins. Some of the items should be easy to find, others hard. Avoid poor conservation practice by not tramping over and collecting items which should be conserved.

NATURE QUIZ PROGRAMS. Carried on like "Information, Please," with small prizes for winners.

LEAF RELAY. Give each team a list of trees. The first one in line runs to get a leaf of the first tree on the list, returns, and gives the list to the second in line, who then reads the second kind of tree and runs to get a sample, and so on. The first group through wins.

IDENTIFICATION. Have pictures of animals, trees, birds, insects, and the like, pasted on cards. Flash them. The first person who correctly identifies the picture receives the card. The person with the most cards at the end of the playing time wins.

TOUCH, TASTE, SMELL IDENTIFICATION. Blindfold players and pass around objects for them to identify, designating whether they are to do so by tasting, smelling, or feeling.

TREE IDENTIFICATION. Make a tour, stopping at various trees, so that each person can fill in the name of the tree on his numbered chart. The person with the most correct indentifications wins. When first learning, participants may take their tree identification books along and be given three or four minutes to identify the tree with the assistance of the book. Ferns, flowers, birds, sea shells, animals, or any other kind of wildlife desired may be identified in this game.

TRAILING. "It" walks carelessly through the woods, making no effort to conceal his footprints or avoid breaking branches. Ten minutes later, a small group or an individual tries to follow his trail and spy him where he is hiding beside it. A variation is to have two persons walk in single file through the woods. At a given signal, they reverse, and the one originally in the rear tries to lead the way back over the same trail. He may be given a start of twenty-five points, with two deducted each time he wanders off the trail and one each time he hesitates more than a minute in determining the correct course.

NATURE SOUNDS. Each listens for five minutes, listing all the nature sounds heard and identified. This is a particularly good game to play at night.

UPSIDE DOWN HIKE. Turn rocks and large sticks over to see what is living underneath. Be sure to restore them without harming any living inhabitants.

WHAT IS IT? Have a number of clues describing a nature object written on a card, with the least well-known first. Read them one at a time until someone is finally able to guess the object and receives the card as his reward. A variation is to let campers take turns, giving oral clues until a fellow camper is able to guess what he has in mind.

WHAT'S WRONG WITH THIS PICTURE? Announce that a certain nature object is to be described, and that, although most of the characteristics given will be true, a few erroneous ones will be included. See how many can detect the incorrect ones.

QUIET, PLEASE! The members of one group sit blindfolded with some designated object located about 6 feet in front of them. The idea is for the second group to creep stealthily in and steal the object without being detected. When members of the blindfolded group hear an opponent approaching and point directly at him, he is eliminated. A variation is to have only one member blindfolded while the others are scattered in various directions and at different distances from him. They take turns whistling, rustling leaves, or stamping a foot, and so forth. If he can judge the direction and point directly to the person, the two exchange places.

ADDITIONAL READINGS

Animals

Anthony, H. E.: *North American Mammals.* G. P. Putnam's Sons, Inc., 1928, 674 pp., $3.95.

Barker, Will: *Familiar Animals of America.* Harper and Brothers, 1956, 300 pp., $4.95.

Bauer, Margaret J.: *Animal Babies.* Abbott Publishing Co., 1949, $2.50.

Berrill, Jacqueline: *Wonders of the Woodland Animals.* Dodd, Mead & Co., Inc., 1953, $2.75.

Brown, Vinson: *How To Understand Animal Talk.* Little Brown and Co., 1958, $3.00.

Burt, William H., and Grossenheider, Richard P.: *A Field Guide to the Mammals.* Houghton Mifflin Co., 1956, 200 pp.

Burton, Maurice: *Curiosities of Animal Life.* Sterling Publishing Co., 1959, 136 pp., $3.95.

Devoe, Alan: *This Fascinating Animal World.* McGraw-Hill Book Co., Inc., 1951, $4.00.

Devoe, Alan, and Devoe, Mary Berry: *Our Animal Neighbors.* McGraw-Hill Book Co., Inc., 1953, 278 pp., $4.00.

Hegner, Robert W.: *Parade of the Animal Kingdom.* The Macmillan Co., 1942, 675 pp., $6.95.

Hogner, D. C., and Hogner, Nils: *The Animal Book.* Oxford U. Press, 1951.

Lane, Frank W.: *Nature Parade.* Sheridan Publishing Co., 1954, 333 pp., $5.00.

Moore, Clifford B.: *Ways of Mammals—In Fact and Fancy.* The Ronald Press Co., 1953, 273 pp., $3.50.

Palmer, Ralph S.: *The Mammal Guide.* Doubleday & Co., Inc., $4.95.

Pinney, Roy: *Wild Animal Pets.* Golden Books, 1959, 68 pp., $1.95.

Portmann, Adolph: *Animal Camouflage.* U. of Mich. Press, Ann Arbor, 111 pp., $4.50.

Sanderson, Ivan T.: *How To Know the American Mammals.* Little Brown and Co., 1951, $3.50.

Seton, Ernest Thompson: *Wild Animals I Have Known.* Charles Scribner's Sons, $3.50.

Zim, Dr. Herbert S., and Hoffmeister, Dr. Donald F.: *Mammals.* Golden Books, 1955, 160 pp., $2.50. paper $1.00.

Magazine Articles

Des Grey, Dr. Arthur H.: *Making Friends with Raccoons.* C.M., June, 1959.

Birds

Alexander, W. B.: *Birds of the Ocean.* G. P. Putnam's Sons, Inc., Revised, 1954, 408 pp., $7.50.

Allen, Arthur A.: *Book of Bird Life—A Study of Birds in Their Native Haunts.* D. Van Nostrand Co., 1930, $6.00.

Bird Study. Boy Scouts #3282, 25¢.

Chapman, Frank M.: *Color Key to North American Birds.* Appleton-Century-Crafts, Inc.

Forbush, Edward Howe: *Natural History of the Birds of Eastern and Central North America.* Houghton Mifflin Co., 1939, 400 pp., $2.50.

Griscom, Ludlow: *Modern Bird Study.* Harvard University Press, 1945, $3.00.

Hausman, Leon, A.: *The Bird Book.* Arco Publishing Co., 1955, 159 pp., $2.50.

Mathews, F. Schuyler: *Wild Birds and Their Music.* G. P. Putnam's Sons, Inc., 325 pp., $4.50.

Pearson, Thomas Gilbert: *Birds of America.* Doubleday & Co., Inc., 1936, $6.95.

Peterson, Roger Tory: *A Field Guide to the Birds.* 3rd Ed., Houghton Mifflin Co., 1958, 290 pp., $3.95.

Peterson, Roger Tory: *Bird Watcher's Anthology.* Harcourt, Brace and Co., 1957, 401 pp., $7.50., limited Ed., $18.50.

Peterson, Roger Tory: *Birds over America.* Dodd, Mead, and Co., 1948, $6.00.

Peterson, Roger Tory: *How To Know the Birds.* Girl Scouts #23-545, 50¢.

Pettit. Mary P.: *My Hobby Is Bird Watching.* Hart Publishing Co., 128 pp., $2.95.

Pough, Richard H.: *Audubon Bird Guide: Eastern Land Birds.* Doubleday and Co., Inc.

Pough, Richard H.: *Audubon Water Bird Guide.* Doubleday and Co., Inc., Revised, 1949, $3.95.

Pough, Richard H.: *Audubon Western Bird Guide.* Doubleday and Co., Inc., 1957, 316 pp., $4.95.

Rand, Austin L.: *Stray Feathers from a Bird Man's Desk.* Doubleday and Co., Inc., $3.75.

Saunders, Aretas A.: *The Lives of Wild Birds.* Doubleday and Co., Inc., $3.50.

Saunders, Aretas A.: *A Guide to Bird Songs.* Doubleday and Co., Inc., 1959, $3.50.

Schutz, Walter E.: *How To Build Bird Houses and Feeders.* Bruce Publishing Co., 1955, $2.95.

Simon, Hilda: *The Amazing Book of Birds.* Hart Publishing Co., 128 pp., $3.75.

Zim, Herbert S.: *Owls.* William Morrow and Co., Inc., 1950, $2.50.

Zim, Herbert S., and Gabrielson, Dr., I. N.: *Birds.* Golden Books, 1949, 157 pp., $2.50.

Caves

Hamilton, Elizabeth: *The First Book of Caves.* Franklin Watts, Inc., 1955, 62 pp., $1.95.

Longsworth, Polly: *Exploring Caves.* Thomas Y. Crowell and Co., 1959, 175 pp., $2.75.

Conservation

Bathurst, Effie G., and Hill, Wilhelmina: *Conservation Experiences for Children.* Dept. of Health, Education, and Welfare, Washington 25, D.C.

Conservation Activities for Young People. U.S. Forest Service, Washington 25, D.C., 1959, 21 pp., Free.

Conservation Education in American Schools. Am. Ass'n. of School Administrators, 29th Yearbook, 1951, 527 pp.

Conservation in Camping. (A Workshop on Conservation.) ACA, 1952, 25 pp.

Conservation Magic for Boy Scouts. Boy Scouts, 1957, 64 pp.

Fox, Adrian C., and Potter, George R.: *Soil and Water Conservation.* Christopher Johnson Publishers, 1958, 64 pp.

Gabrielson, Ira N.: *Wildlife Conservation.* The Macmillan Co., 2nd Ed., $4.75.

Let's Try It—Conserving Our Natural Resources. Girl Scouts, 20¢.

Neuberger, Richard L.: *Our Natural Resources and Their Conservation.* Public Affairs Press, 28 pp., 25¢.

Soil and Water Conservation. Boy Scouts #3291, 25¢.

Weaver, Richard L.: *Handbook for Teaching of Conservation and Resource Use.* The Interstate 1958, 502 pp., $4.40.

You and Conservation—A Check List for Camp Counselors. A.C.A., 1959, 12 pp., 10¢. (Quantity discounts.)

MAGAZINE ARTICLES

Nickelsburg, Janet: *Conservation Projects for Camp.* C.M., Apr., 1957.

Fish

Breder, Charles M., Jr.: *Marine Fish of the Atlantic Coast.* G. P. Putnam's Sons, Inc., 375 pp., $5.00.

Parker, Bertha Morris, *Fishes.* Row, 1951.

Zim, Dr. H. S., and Shoemaker, Dr. Hurst H.: *Fishes.* Golden Books, 1957, 160 pp., $1.00.

MAGAZINE ARTICLES

Finerty, Jean: *Build An Outdoor Aquarium.* C.M., June, 1959.

Flowers and Plants

Armstrong, Margaret: *Field Book of Western Wild Flowers.* G. P. Putnam's Sons, Inc., 644 pp., $5.00.

Chase, Agnes: *First Book of Grasses.* Smithsonian Inst., 3rd Ed., 150 pp., $3.00.

Durand, Herbert: *Field Book of Common Ferns.* G. P. Putnam's Sons, Inc., 1949, 219 pp., $3.50.

Harrington, H. D.: *How To Identify Plants.* Sage Books, 1957, 203 pp., $3.00.

Hausman, Ethel H.: *Beginners Guide to Wild Flowers.* G. P. Putnam's Sons, Inc., 1955, 384 pp., $3.50.

Mathews, G. Schuyler: *Field Book of American Wild Flowers.* G. P. Putnam's Son's, Inc., 1955, Revised, $5.00.

Medsger, Oliver Perry: *Edible Wild Plants.* The Macmillan Co., 1945, 323 pp., $5.95.

Rickett, H. W.: *Wild Flowers of America.* Crown Publishing Co., 1953, 432 pp., $5.95.

Stefferud, Alfred: *How To Know Wild Flowers.* New American Library, 1950, 35¢.

Zim, Dr. H. S., and Martin, Dr. Alexander C.: *Flowers.* Golden Books, 1950, 157 pp., $2.50, paper $1.00.

Insects (Spiders, Butterflies, etc.)

Clausen, Lucy W.: *Insect Fact and Folklore.* The Macmillan Co., 1954, 194 pp., $3.50.

Crompton, John: *The Life of the Spider.* New American Library, 1954, 35¢.

Duncan, Winifred: *Webs in the Wind, The Habits of Web-Weaving Spiders.* The Ronald Press Co., 1949, 387 pp., $5.00.

Gray, Alice: *The Adventure Book of Insects.* Capitol Publishing Co., $2.95.

Huntington, Harriet E.: *Praying Mantis.* Doubleday & Co., Inc., 1957, 44 pp.

Insect Life. Boy Scouts #3348, 25¢.

Klots, Alexander B.: *A Field Guide To the Butterflies.* Houghton Mifflin, Co., 1951, 349 pp., $3.95.

Lutz, Frank E.: *Field Book of Insects.* G. P. Putnam's Sons, Inc., 510 pp., $3.49.

Needham, James G.: *Introducing Insects.* The Ronald Press Co., 1943, 129 pp., $2.75.

Neurath, Marie: *The Wonder World of Insects.* Lothrop, Lee and Shepard Co., Inc., 1952, 36 pp., $1.75.

Oldroyd, Harold: *Collecting, Preserving, and Studying Insects.* The Macmillan Co., $5.00.

Teale, Edwin Way: *The Junior Book of Insects.* E. P. Dutton & Co., Inc., Revised, $3.75.

Zim, Dr. H. S. and Cottam, Dr. Clarence: *Insects.* Golden Books, 1951, 157 pp., $2.50, paper $1.00.

MAGAZINE ARTICLES

Adventuring with Insects. Recreation, June, 1959.

Miscellaneous

Andrews, Roy Chapman: *Nature's Ways.* Crown Publishing Co., 1951, $5.00.

Brown, Vinson: *The Amateur Naturalist's Handbook.* Little Brown and Co., 1948, 475 pp., $4.00.

Buck, Margaret Waring: *In Woods and Fields.* Abingdon Press, 230 pp., $1.75.

Buck, Margaret Waring: *In Yards and Gardens.* Abingdon Press, $1.75.

Chrystie, Frances N.: *Pets.* Little Brown and Co., 1953, $3.75.

Comstock, Anna Botsford: *Handbook of Nature Study.* 24th Ed., Cornell University Press, 957 pp., $5.00.

Eisenberg, Helen and Larry: *Omnibus of Fun.*

First Aid to Animals. Boy Scouts, #3318, 25¢.

Green, Ivah: *Partners with Nature.* International Textbook Co., 1950, $2.00.

Hood, Mary V.: *Outdoor Hazards Real and Fancied.* The Macmillan Co., 1955, 242 pp., $3.95.

Huntington, Harriet E.: *Let's Go to the Desert.* Doubleday and Co., Inc., 1949, 87 pp., $2.75.

Jaeger, Ellsworth: *Land and Water Trails.* The Macmillan Co., 1953, 227 pp., $2.95.

Jaeger, Ellsworth: *Nature Crafts.* The Macmillan Co., 1950, 128 pp., $2.95.

Jaeger, Ellsworth: *Wildwood Wisdom.*

Jaeger, Ellsworth: *Woodsmoke.*

Johnson, Gaylord, and Bleifeld, Maurice: *Hunting with the Microscope.* Sentinel Books, 131 pp., 95¢.

Jordan, E. L.: *Hammond's Nature Atlas of America.* Slingerland Publishing Co., $7.50.

Kesting, Ted: *The Outdoor Encyclopedia.*

Koller, Larry: *Larry Koller's Complete Book of Camping and the Outdoors.*

Lindholm, Major Mauno A.: *Camping and Outdoor Fun.*

Marx, David S.: *The American Book of the Woods.* Botanic Publishing Co., 1940, $2.50.

Moore, Clifford B.: *Book of Wild Pets.* Charles T. Branford Co., 1954, $6.50.

Morgan, Alfred: *Pet Book for Boys and Girls.* Charles Scribner's Sons, 1949, $2.95.

Nature. Boy Scouts #3285, 25¢.

Palmer, E. Laurence: *Fieldbook of Natural History.* Mc-Graw-Hill Book Co., Inc., 1949, 664 pp., $6.75.

Parker, Bertha Morris: *Natural History.* Golden Books, 1952, $5.00.

Parker, Bertha Morris: *The Golden Book of Science.* Golden Books, 1956, $3.95.

Peterson, Roger Tory: *Wildlife in Color.* Houghton Mifflin Co., 1951, 192 pp., $4.00.

Platt, Rutherford: *Walt Disney's World of Nature.* Golden Books, 1957, 176 pp., $4.95.

Price, Betty: *Adventuring in Nature,* NRA, 1939.

Saunders, John R.: *Nature Crafts.* 1958, 68 pp., $1.95.

Straight, Gerald M.: *Nature Funbook.* Hart Publishing Co., 159 pp., $1.25.

Thompson, Stuart L.: *Outdoor Rambles.* NRA, 147 pp., $3.50.

Vannier, Maryhelen: *Methods and Materials in Recreation Leadership.*

Webb, Kenneth B., Editor: *Light from a Thousand Campfires.*

West, James E., and Hillcourt, William: *Scout Field Book.*

Zarchy, Harry: *Let's Go Camping.* Alfred A. Knopf, Inc., 1951, $3.25.

Nature Program

Brown, Vinson: *How To Make a Home Nature Museum.* Little Brown and Co., 1954, 214 pp., $3.50.

Burns, Gerald P.: *The Program of the Modern Camp.*

Frankel, Lillian, and Godfrey: *101 Best Nature Games and Projects.* Sterling Publishing Co., 1959, 128 pp., $2.50. (age 6 and up)

Green, Ivah: *Partners with Nature.* International Text-book Co., 1950, $2.00.

Hammett, Catherine T., and Horrocks, Carol M.: *Creative Crafts for Campers.*

Hammett, Catherine T., and Musselman: *The Camp Program Book.*

Hillcourt, William: *Field Book of Nature Activities.* G. P. Putnam's Sons, Inc., 1950, 320 pp., $3.95.

Joy, Barbara Ellen: *Camping.*

Squires, Mabel: *The Art of Drying Plants and Flowers.* M. Barrows & Co., Inc., 1958, 258 pp., $4.50.

MAGAZINE ARTICLES

Berka, Bonita L.: *Your Nature Program Can be Fun with this Sensible Approach.* C.M., Jan., 1956.

Breeser, Bettye: *Adventures in Nature Study.* J.H., P.E., and R., April, 1956.

Breeser, Bettye: *Hints for the Nature Counselor.* J.H., P.E., and R., Mar., 1957.

Breeser, Bettye: *Nature Tools.* Recreation, Mar., 1957.

Diamond, Ralph: *Using Nature's Resources.* C.M., May, 1957.

Goellner, William A.: *Boys Can Be Fun.* C.M., Dec., 1957.

Hall, William B.: *Make Your Nature Trail Alluring.* C.M., Feb., 1955.

Hammerman, Donald: *What! Teach Outside the Classroom?* J.H., P.E., and R., Nov., 1954.

Indoor Nature Quiz. New Jersey Section of A.C.A., C.M., June, 1956, p. 15.

Klinger, Herbert F.: *Safari—an Adventure in the Out of Doors.* C.M., Apr., 1957.

Mahan, Harold D.: *Let's Have Nature Enthusiasm After Camp Too!* C.M., May, 1956.

Reptiles and Amphibians

Ditmars, Raymond L.: *Reptiles of the World.* The Macmillan Co., 1936, 321 pp., $6.95.

Morris, Percy A.: *Boys' Book of Frogs, Toads and Salamanders.* The Ronald Press Co., 1957, 240 pp., $4.00.

Morris, Percy A.: *A Boys Book of Snakes, How To Recognize and Understand Them.* The Ronald Press Co., 1948, 185 pp., $4.00.

Morris, Percy A.: *Boys Book of Turtles and Lizards.* The Ronald Press Co., 1959, $4.50.

Morris, Percy A.: *They Hop and Crawl—Reptiles and Amphibians of the U.S.* The Ronald Press Co., 1944, 253 pp., $4.50.

Parker, Bertha Morris: *Toads and Frogs.* Row, Peterson & Co., 1951.

Pope, Clifford H.: *The Reptile World.* Alfred A. Knopf Inc., 1955, $7.50.

Pope, Clifford H.: *Turtles of the United States and Canada.* Alfred A. Knopf Inc., 1939, $5.75.

Reptile Study. Boy Scouts #3813, 25¢.

Savage, Jay M.: *An Illustrated Key to the Lizards, Snakes, and Turtles of the West.* Naturegraph Co., 32 pp.

Schmidt, Karl P., and Davis, D. Dwight: *Field Book of Snakes.* G. P. Putnam's Sons, Inc., 1941, 365 pp., $3.50.

Smith, Hobart M.: *Snakes As Pets.* Slingerland, Publishing Co., 50 pp., $1.25.

Wright, Albert Hazen and Anna: *Handbook of Frogs and Toads of the United States and Canada.* Cornell University Press, $6.50.

Zim, Dr. H. S., and Smith, Dr. H. M.: *Reptiles and Amphibians.* Golden Books, 1953, 157 pp., $2.50.

Rocks and Minerals

Allan, David, and Brown, Vinson: *An Illustrated Guide To Common Rocks.* Naturegraph Co., 1956, 32 pp.

Cormack, Maribelle B.: *The First Book of Stones.* Franklin Watts Inc., 1950, $1.95.

Crowell, V.: *Activities in Geology for Children.* State Teachers' College, Trenton, N.J.

Geology. Boy Scouts #3284, 25¢.

Irving, Robert: *Rocks and Minerals and the Stories They Tell.* Alfred A. Knopf Inc., 1956, $2.95. (ages 8–12)

Jensen, David E.: *My Hobby Is Collecting Rocks and Minerals.* Hart Publishing Co., 1955, 122 pp., $3.95.

Pearl, Richard M.: *How To Know the Minerals and Rocks.* McGraw-Hill Book Co., Inc., 1955, 192 pp., $3.75.

Pearl, Richard M.: *Rocks and Minerals.* Barnes & Noble, Inc., 275 pp., $1.95.

Pough, Frederick: *A Field Guide To Rocks and Minerals.* Houghton Mifflin Co., 1954.

Reinfeld, Fred: *Treasures of the Earth.* Sterling, 160 pp., $2.95.

Shannon, Terry: *Among The Rocks.* Sterling Publishing Co., 48 pp., $2.50. (ages 8 up)

Shuttlesworth, Dorothy: *The Story of the Rocks.* Doubleday & Co., Inc., 1956, 56 pp., $2.95.

Williams, Henry Lionel: *Stories in Rocks.* Henry Holt and Co., Inc., 1948, 151 pp., $3.00.

Zim, Dr. H. S., and Shaffer, Dr. P. R.: *Rocks and Minerals.* Golden Books, 1957, 160 pp., $1.00.

MAGAZINE ARTICLES

Shulman, Gerry and Will: *The 'How—To' of Mineral Collecting.* Recreation, June, 1954.

Seashells

Abbott, R. Tucker: *American Seashells.* D. Van Nostrand Co., 1954, 541 pp., $13.75.

Dudley, Ruth H.: *My Hobby Is Collecting Seashells and Coral.* Hart Publishing Co., 1955, 127 pp., $2.95.

Hausman, Leon A.: *A Beginner's Guide to Seashore Life.* G. P. Putnam's Sons, Inc., 1949, 128 pp., $2.25.

Hutchinson, W. M.: *A Child's Book of Seashells.* Maxton Publishers, New York, N.Y., 1954.

Hylander, Clarence J.: *Sea and Seashore.* The Macmillan Co., 1950, $3.75.

Johnstone, Kathleen Yerger: *Sea Treasures—A Guide To Shell Collecting.* Houghton Mifflin Co., 242 pp., 1956, $4.00.

Martin, Curtis: *The Story of Shells. A Guidebook for Young Collectors.* NRA, 97 pp., $2.95.

Morris, Percy A.: *A Field Guide to Shells of our Atlantic and Gulf Coasts.* Houghton Mifflin Co., 2nd Ed., 1951, 236 pp., $3.95.

Verrill, A. Hyatt: *The Shell Collector's Handbook.* G. P. Putnam's Sons, Inc., 1950, 260 pp., $4.00.

Stars

Astronomy. Boy Scouts #3303.

Baker, Robert H.: *When the Stars Come Out.* The Viking Press, Revised, 1954, $3.50.

Bernhard, H. J., et al.: *New Handbook of the Heavens.* New American Library, 50¢.

A Dipper Full of Stars. Girl Scouts #23-543, $2.95.

Edmund, N. W., and Brown, Sam: *Homebuilt Telescopes.* Edmund Scientific Corp., 35 pp., 40¢.

Hausman, Leon A.: *Astronomy Handbook.* Arco Publishing Co., 1956, 143 pp., $2.50.

Kingston, H. R.: *An Easy Pocket Guide for Beginners.*

Maloney, Terry: *The Sky Is Our Window.* Sterling Publishing Co., 1959, $3.95.

McKready, Kelvin: *Beginner's Guide to the Stars.* G. P. Putnam's Sons, Inc., Revised, 1947, 86 pp., $2.00.

Neely, Henry M.: *A Primer for Star-Gazers.* Harper and Brothers, $5.00.

Olcott, W. T.: *Field Book of the Stars.* G. P. Putnam's Sons, Inc., 4th Ed., 1954, 482 pp., $5.00.

Pocket Planetarium. Girl Scouts #23-542. 35¢. (4 sky charts that glow in the dark)

Reed, William Maxwell: *Patterns in the Sky.* William Morrow and Co., Inc., 1951, 125 pp., $2.75. (grades 4–6).

Reed, W. Maxwell: *The Stars for Sam.* Harcourt, Brace and Co., $4.00.

Rey, H. A.: *Stars.* Houghton, Mifflin Co., 1952, $5.00.

Schneider, Herman and Nina: *You among the Stars.* Scott Foresman & Co., 1951, $3.00.

Texereau, Jean: *How To Make a Telescope.* Interacial Publishers, 250 5th Ave., N.Y. 1, 191 pp.

Wooley, R. van der: *A Key to the Stars.* Philosophical Publishing Co., 3rd Ed., 144 pp., $4.75.

Zim, Dr. H. S., and Baker, Dr. R. H.: *Stars.* Golden Books, 1951, 157 pp., $2.50, paper $1.00.

Trees

Cater, Ruth Cooley: *Tree Trails and Hobbies.* 324 pp., $2.50.

Collingwood, G. H., and Brush, Warren D.: *Knowing Your Trees.* Am. Forestry Ass'n., 1955, 328 pp., $6.00.

Collis, John Stewart: *The Triumph of the Tree.* Sloane William Associates, Inc., 1954, $3.50.

Cormack, M. B.: *The First Book of Trees.* Franklin Watts, Inc., 1951, $1.95.

Forestry. Boy Scouts #3302, 25¢.

Grimm, William C.: *Pocket Field Guide to the Trees.* Stackpole Co., $1.50.

Harlow, William.: *Trees of the Eastern and Central United States and Canada.* Dover Publications, Inc., 1957, 288 pp., $1.35.

Hylander, Clarence J.: *Trees and Trails.* The Macmillan Co., $3.00.

Lane, Dr. Ferdinand C.: *The Story of Trees.* Doubleday & Co., Inc., 1952, $5.00.

Marx, David S.: *Learn the Trees from Leaf Prints.* Botanic, $1.75. (Nearly 200 trees)

Mathews, F. Schuyler: *Field Book of American Trees and Shrubs.* G. P. Putnam's Sons, Inc., 465 pp., $3.95.

Peattie, Donald Culross: *Natural History of Western Trees.* Houghton Mifflin Co., 1947, $6.00.

Platt, Rutherford: *A Pocket Guide to the Trees.* Pocket Books, 1952.

Ponderdorf, Illa: *The True Book of Trees.* $2.00.

Symonds, George W. D., and Chelminski, Stephen: *The Tree Identification Book.* M. Barrows and Co., Inc., 1958, 127 pp., $10.00.

Teale, Edwin: *The Lost Woods.* Dodd, 1945, $5.00.

Zim, Dr. H. S., and Martin, Dr. Alexander C.: *Trees.* Golden Books, 1952, 157 pp., $2.50, paper $1.00.

Water Life

Buck, Margaret W.: *In Ponds and Streams.* Abingdon Press, 1955, $3.00.

Buck, Margaret W.: *Pets from the Pond.* Abingdon Press, $1.75. (How to keep them in an aquarium)

Carr, Marion R.: *Sea and Shore.* Golden Books, 1959, 57 pp., $1.50.

Carson, Rachel: *The Edge of the Sea.* Houghton Mifflin Co., 1955, $3.95.

Fisher, James: *Wonderful World of the Sea.* Doubleday & Co., Inc., 1957, 68 pp., $3.45.

Hausman, Leon A.: *Beginner's Guide to Fresh-Water Life.* G. P. Putnam's Sons, Inc., 1950, 128 pp., $2.50.

Hausman, Leon A.: *Beginner's Guide to Seashore Life.* G. P. Putnam's Sons, Inc., 1949, 128 pp., $2.25.

Huntington, Harriet E.: *Let's Go to the Brook.* Doubleday & Co., Inc., 1952, 89 pp., $2.75.

Huntington, Harriet E.: *Let's Go to the Seashore.* Doubleday & Co., Inc., 1941, 88 pp., $3.00.

Hylander, Clarence J.: *Sea and Shore.* The Macmillan Co., 1950, $3.75.

Miner, Roy Waldo: *Fieldbook of Seashore Life.* G. P. Putnam's Sons, Inc., 1950, 630 pp., $7.50.

Morgan, Alfred: *An Aquarium Book for Boys and Girls.* Charles Scribner's Sons, 180 pp., $2.95. (Diet, etc.)

Morgan, Anne Haven: *Field Book of Ponds and Streams.* G. P. Putnam's Sons, Inc., 448 pp., $5.00.

Zim, Dr. H. S., and Ingle, Dr. Lester: *Seashores.* Golden Books, 1956, 160 pp., $2.50, paper $1.00.

15

Aquatics

I wish that I'd been born a fish
So I could swim when'er I wish.
Then mother would not have to say
It is too cold for you today.

THE EAVESDROPPER

The Waterfront Is Versatile

Water bears a natural fascination for people and the waterfront and its surroundings provide the locale for many of the happiest camp occasions. Water-front activities can usually be integrated with the whole camp program since there are so many possibilities either in, on, or close to water. A beautiful waterscape provides an unparalleled setting for a campfire, story telling, spiritual or other program as well as sketching, painting and photographing. Music floating across the water is particularly effective between groups on opposite shores, boat and shore or between two boats; rounds, antiphonal singing, answer and response and echo songs are particularly appropriate.

Wildlife in and around water is fascinating, too, for here one finds quite different birds, trees, flowers, fish, insects, shells and plants to observe. In addition to the usual swimming and boating activities, flutterboards, swim fins and surfboards provide possibilities, and excursions can be made by kayak or raft. Water goggles make a study of underwater life even more exciting and some camps have constructed glass bottomed boxes or boats to further this activity.

Even though no large body of water is available in a camp, there are many "fun" things to do in a small brooklet such as wading, searching for pebbles, trying to catch minnows with the hands, constructing dams or making and sailing small boats.

173

Program Trends

Although water activities have always been popular in camp, a tremendous increase is now in progress in both swimming, boating and allied phases; this is probably due to their increased popularity outside of camp. There is also a conscious attempt to promote these activities as management seeks to cut down the unnecessary loss of lives everywhere by water activities and to give campers instruction in activities which will carry over into the later lives of a large majority of them. There is more interest in swimming and diving in general as well as in synchronized and competitive swimming. Some camps may even carry on intercamp competition. Movie frogmen and other forms of publicity have apparently aroused quite a lot of interest in underwater swimming though most camps show reluctance to accept scuba diving except for counselors or very able campers.

All forms of camp boating are increasing markedly as might be expected from the tremendous sale of small craft now sweeping the country. Rowboats, though still popular, are often supplemented or supplanted by outboards which bring with them a corresponding increase in fishing and water skiing. The ever popular canoe is more than holding its own, as canoe trips for from one night up to several weeks gain in favor. Sailing, too, is showing a decided upswing with such exciting events as sailing regattas on the agenda. Many camps, though possessing natural bodies of water, are turning to swimming pools as a solution to pollution and other waterfront problems.

Since most people at some time in their lives venture into or on the water, it is an excellent thing for them to learn correct techniques, for both pleasure and safety increase in direct proportion to the skill and confidence of the participant. Many of the 7,000 to 8,000 deaths which occur each year in water accidents could be prevented by proper instruction in water skills and safety procedures.

The Camp Program

Waterfront activities are naturally popular and little artificial motivation is needed to enlist the whole-hearted participation of campers. The aquatic program ordinarily consists of these divisions: (1) swimming (instructional and recreational), (2) diving, (3) life saving, (4) boating (canoeing, sailing, rowing, surfboarding, and the like), and (5) trips by water.

THE WATERFRONT STAFF

The Waterfront Director

All waterfront activities are in charge of the waterfront director. ACA standards call for a person at least twenty-one years old with a minimum of a year of camp waterfront experience and a current Water Safety Instructor's certificate in swimming and lifesaving skills from the American Red Cross or an organization with similar standards. The waterfront director is responsible for classifying the abilities of his staff of assistants and for seeing that they are used to best advantage in carrying out a well-planned program which is also coordinated with the entire camp program. All activities using the waterfront such as boat trips or fishing must clear through him.

He also sees that campers are tested and classified for a well-planned program of instruction. He trains and supervises his staff which includes instructors in all waterfront activities such as swimming, diving, life saving, scuba and skin diving, water skiing, canoeing, rowing, outboard boating, and sailing. He assigns responsibilities and checks on their successful completion, and sees to the making of suitable reports on the progress of his department and that of individual campers. He sees that all equipment is adequate in quantity and quality and that the highest type of safety precautions are carried out. He also makes out appropriate seasonal reports and recommendations for the following season.

Although his many duties usually exempt the waterfront director from cabin responsibilities, he should be a trained camper and in sympathy with all phases of camp life so that he sees the waterfront in its proper perspective to the total program. He must know his subject matter thoroughly and must constantly strive to learn while on the job, for he has one of the biggest tasks in camp and is at one time or another likely to be responsible for the life of every member of the personnel. He must have presence of mind, sound judgment, and the ability to remain calm, even when faced with an emergency.

The waterfront director is also responsible for staff use of the waterfront. Usually, during precamp training, he tests and classifies staff as to their swimming and boating abilities and sets up procedures for their instruction and use of equipment. He assigns areas during periods set aside especially for staff as well as during their time off. He also acquaints them with swimming hazards and safety measures and the general rules and procedures for camper use of the waterfront.

Waterfront Assistants

Waterfront assistants should have at least a Senior Life Saving Certificate, although counselors with Junior Certificates are sometimes used as auxiliary staff. They may or may not have cabin responsibilities, and their waterfront duties are determined by the waterfront director in accordance with their various abilities in swimming, diving or boating. All water-

(Courtesy of The Evening Bulletin, Philadelphia.)

front personnel should be trained and interested in the whole camp program and should consider their activities as integral parts of it. All should cooperate willingly in helping out with general camp program on rainy days and when waterfront duties permit.

General Counselors

A cabin counselor should accompany his campers during their periods at the waterfront for it provides still another opportunity to observe them in a different situation and thus understand them better. Since waterfront activity is a favorite for many of the campers, they enjoy feeling that their cabin counselor is interested in it.

Cabin counselors with skills in waterfront activities may be asked to help out during the peak periods of the day or when their group is participating. Waterfront rules must be kept inviolate and counselors should set a good example and impress this important fact on campers.

Counselors who wish to participate in waterfront activities will need to pass classification tests as the campers do. Though it is sometimes possible for staff to receive instruction from waterfront personnel, you must remember that this is a privilege and is possible only when it can be carried on without interfering with your regular duties or those of the waterfront staff.

THE SWIMMING, DIVING, AND LIFESAVING PROGRAM

Early in the camp season, all campers are tested and classified as nonswimmers, beginners, intermediates, swimmers or lifesavers, according to their proficiency in the water. Instructional periods, ordinarily a half hour in length, are usually scheduled in the morning, and in camps where the decentralized or unit system is in operation, they are carried on by unit

Why Not Build a Rustic Bridge?

groups. Those in different classifications separate upon arrival at the dock and each goes to his respective area for instruction. Each group is under the supervision of a senior lifesaver, who has enough assistants to make a ratio of approximately one waterfront staff member for each ten campers. Recreational periods, also a half hour in length, are customarily held in the afternoon.

WATER SAFETY DEVICES

Vigilance every single moment is necessary, for one accident during the summer can cause untold grief and so damage a camp's reputation as to force it into bankruptcy. Three safety devices are in common use:

THE BUDDY SYSTEM. The buddy system provides a companion of about equal ability for each swimmer. The two enter and leave the water together and stay near each other at all times; thus, it is impossible for one of them to disappear or get into difficulty without its immediately being known to the other. When the signal is given for "buddy call" (about every ten minutes), they quickly raise their joined hands in the air. Failure to stay close to and watch over a buddy means prompt banishment from the water for the rest of the day or even longer.

THE CHECK BOARD SYSTEM. As each swimmer enters the water, he turns over a tag bearing his name on the check board so that the red side is uppermost. When he leaves the swimming area, he turns it back to expose the white side again. Station a counselor near to see that no tag is forgotten. Some camps use

(Courtesy of The Evening Bulletin, Philadelphia.)

pegs with the camper's name to insert into a peg board in a similar manner.

COLORED CAPS. Colored caps denote swimming ability so that waterfront staff can immediately spot a camper out of his proper swimming area or one taking hazardous chances for his ability. The following color system is suggested:

> Nonswimmer—red (danger)
> Beginner—yellow (caution)
> Intermediate—green
> Swimmer—blue
> Lifesaver—white

HINTS FOR THE USE OF
THE WATERFRONT

Waterfront counselors must keep their eyes and attention on swimmers at all times; knitting, chatting, reading, or basking in the sun are definitely out of place. When on duty, the counselors never enter the water except to rescue a swimmer (and this is recommended only as a last resort) or when necessary, for some particular phase of teaching. Docks are not lounging places; use them only as directed by the waterfront staff.

Sunburn is even more of a danger for waterfront staff than others since they must spend long hours exposed to the sun's rays; wear long trousers and long sleeves, at least during a portion of the hours on duty. See that campers also take precautions. Recent studies indicate that constant exposure to the sun and heavy tanning permanently harm the complexion and may even predispose to cancer.

As in all camp activities, informality and fun are of supreme importance, but waterfront rules must be rigidly enforced, for there is too much at stake to brook even minor breaches of discipline. Campers readily respond if shown the importance of this requirement. Instructions from a lifeguard must be obeyed immediately with no quibbling.

Wait for at least an hour or two after eating before going into the water. Never swim when tired or overheated.

Campers and counselors never go swimming alone or at times when the waterfront staff is not on duty. On trips, they swim only in approved areas and when at least one Senior Lifesaver is on guard. Never dive into unknown waters which have not been thoroughly investigated for sufficient depth and hidden obstructions. Visitors use the waterfront only when they meet the requirements set up for staff and campers.

Campers enter the water only on signal and come out again promptly on signal. Natural resentment at mandatory orders can be overcome by a warning such as "one more dive and out" instead of a "sudden death" blast announcing the immediate end of the period.

Wear shoes and robes to and from the bathing area. Do not loiter in a wet suit but hurry back to the cabins and take a brisk rub down to avoid chilling. Dry between the toes and sprinkle with talcum to discourage athlete's foot. Hang wet suits and towels out to dry immediately.

Thunderstorms are a particularly serious menace to those near water, and all who are swimming or out in boats must immediately get on shore.

For sanitary reasons, we do not take soap and water baths in the swimming area, nor permit such animals as horses or dogs to swim or drink there.

Night swimming is rarely if ever permissible and then only under the careful arrangement and supervision of the waterfront staff. Powerful, focusing beam flashlights and white swimming caps help to reduce hazards.

Do not overestimate your ability for that is one of the chief causes of swimming catastrophies. Unexpected fatigue can overcome even experienced swimmers.

Before-breakfast dips, if permitted, should be optional, for not everyone reacts favorably to them.

Distance swimming is allowed at the discretion of the waterfront staff, and only when each swimmer is accompanied by his own rowboat, oarsman and senior lifesaver.

Whereas swimming in moderation is one of the best forms of exercise known, too frequent or long periods are debilitating and lay the foundation for colds, sinus infections and other ailments. Two half-hour periods a day, even less if the water is cold, are usually enough. Campers with open sores, skin infections, or colds should not go into the water, and those who develop blue lips or nails or a pale face, who shiver or whose teeth chatter must come out immediately.

BOATING (also see pages 382–386)

The popularity of boating almost equals that of swimming. It not only gives pleasure in itself but also provides transportation to outlying regions on fishing or other trips, and is a means of rescuing those in distress.

Contrary to popular opinion, properly constructed and maintained boats do not capsize when used with common sense and some degree of skill. Most catastrophies result from boats in poor condition or from such misuses or indiscretions as overloading, travelling in dangerous or rough water, fooling around, standing up, rocking the boat, or changing positions improperly. All small craft should be tested for seaworthiness and steadiness, and only those who have passed appropriate tests, including practice in recovering from capsizing and swamping in shallow, safe water, should use them.

Always keep the center of gravity in a canoe low; remove the seats and kneel on a light kneeling pad on the bottom rather than sit on the seats. Some prefer to kneel on the paddle-side knee and rest the back against a thwart with the other leg stretched out in front and braced against a rib of the canoe. Sitting on the floor or even lying flat in the canoe will further increase stability if you should inadvertently be caught in rough water. Step, sit, or kneel in the exact center of the canoe to keep your weight balanced. In two-man paddling, the bowman uses a straight stroke while the stern man, who is responsible for steering, paddles on the opposite side with a "J" stroke.

Rowboats are least likely to upset; canoes rate second place; and sailboats are trickiest of all. All tipped over boats, usually even if submerged, will not sink to the bottom and will continue to support their occupants; therefore, if you are thrown into the water, swim to the boat and hang on until help comes instead of striking out for shore. This explains why endurance and the ability to tread water and float occupy such a prominent place in boating tests.

Before boaters venture far from shore, they should learn to interpret weather signs for it is imperative to head for the nearest land as soon as indications of an approaching storm appear. Stay close to shore on trips, even though you must cover more distance than on a straight course. To change positions in a boat, stay low and keep one or both hands on the gunwale for balance. It is safest to pull into shallow water before attempting the transfer.

Neither visitors, counselors nor campers use boating equipment unless they have passed appropriate tests and have been granted specific permission each and every time by the waterfront staff. Even then, they must state their exact destination and departure time as well as the expected time of return. Boating after dark is permissible only in case of emergency or for an occasional moonlight cruise under the immediate supervision of the waterfront staff.

Those who do not swim well enough

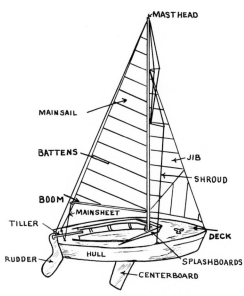

Sailboat Nomenclature.

to qualify as boaters often find the waterfront a tantalizing but forbidden temptation. Camps sometimes permit an occasional excursion under the careful surveillance of the waterfront staff and with one senior lifesaver and a life belt for each nonswimmer.

Stow all waterfront equipment neatly away; never leave it carelessly lying about to be stumbled over or misused. Keep it in good repair and teach campers to respect such equipment as they would fine tools, repairing damage themselves or instantly reporting it to the proper person. Thoroughly ground campers in the care of boats, giving practice in launching them and taking them from the water, entering and disembarking, and so forth. Never drop or drag canoes over the ground to launch them or to remove them from the water. Carry them when on land, and wade in shallow water to keep from dragging them on the bottom. Real boaters are not satisfied to just splash about any old way but pride themselves on neat and exact manipulations performed with perfect timing and skill.

ADDITIONAL READINGS

Swimming, Diving, and Life Saving

Aquatic Games, Pageants, Stunts. Book Dept., Beach & Pool, Revised, 36 pp., $3.00.

Aquatic Program. Boy Scouts. Revised 1957, 70 pp.

Aquatics, ARC. Doubleday and Co., Inc., 1956, 445 pp.

Armbruster, David A., Sr., Allen, Robert H., and Bruce, Harlan: *Swimming and Diving.* C. V. Mosby Co., 3rd Ed., 1958, 373 pp., $5.00.

Bucher, Charles A., Editor: *Methods and Materials in Physical Education and Receration.*

Butler, George: *Outdoor Swimming Pools.* NRA, 1956, 75¢.

Cureton, T. K., Jr.: *Fun in the Water.* Assn. Press, 1957, 143 pp., $4.00.

Curtis, Katherine Whitney: *Rhythmic Swimming.* Burgess Publishing Co., 1942, 140 pp.

Easy Steps to Safe Swimming. The Art Craft Play Co., 60 pp., $1.25.

Friermood, Harold T., Editor: *YMCA Water Safety and Life Saving.* Assn. Press, 1957, $3.00.

Friermood, Harold T.: *New YMCA Aquatic Workbook.* Assn. Press, 1958, $11.50.

Gibbs, Howard G.: *Aquatics Program for Boys' Camp.* Boys' Club, 24 pp.

Hammett, Catherine T., and Musselman, Virginia: *The Camp Program Book.*

Karpovich, Peter J.: *Adventures in Artificial Respiration.* Assn. Press, 1953, $7.50.

Kiphuth, Robert: *Swimming.* The Ronald Press, 1942, 100 pp., $2.95.

Kiphuth, Robert, and Burke, Harry M.: *Basic Swimming.* Yale U. Press, 1950, 125 pp., $3.00.

Life Saving. Boy Scouts. #3278, 25¢.

Life Saving and Water Safety. ARC, 1956, 303 pp.

Lipovetz, Fred John: *The Teaching and Coaching of Swimming, Diving and Water Sports.* Burgess Publishing Co., Revised, 1950, 172 pp.

Lukens, Paul W.: *Teaching Swimming.* Burgess Publishing Co., 1948, 40 pp., $1.75.

McAllister, Evelyn Ditton: *Easy Steps to Safe Swimming.* Vantage Press, Inc., 1959, 83 pp., $2.95.

Mitchell, Elmer D., Editor: *Sports for Recreation.*

Moriarty, Phil: *Springboard Diving.* The Ronald Press, 1959, $4.00.

Pohndorf, Richard H.: *Camp Waterfront Programs and Management.*

Safety-Wise. Girl Scouts, 86 pp., 20¢.

Silvia, Charles E.: *Lifesaving and Water Safety Instruction.* Assn. Press, Revised, 1958, 195 pp., $4.50.

Smith, Ann Avery: *Skillful Swimming.* Edwards Brothers, Inc., 1954, 228 pp., $3.50.

Swimming. Boy Scouts #3299, 25¢.

Swimming and Diving. ARC., 1956, 266 pp.

Teaching Beginners To Swim. NRA, 34 pp., $2.50.

The Outdoor Swimming Pool. Conference for Nat'l Cooperation in Aquatics. A.A.H.P.E.R., 1956, 42 pp., $1.00.

The Science of Skin and Scuba Diving. Conference for National Cooperation in Aquatics. Revised, Assn. Press, $4.95.

Y.M.C.A. *Swimming Manual. From Beginner to Master Swimmer.* Nat'l Council of Y.M.C.A.'s of Canada, 15 Spadina Road, Revised, 1956, 72 pp., 50¢.

MAGAZINES

Bullock, Doris: *Some Basic Skills in the Water.* J.H., P.E. and R., Jan. 1957.

Daviess, Grace B.: *Lead-Up Steps to Advanced Diving.* J.H., P.E. and R., May–June, 1958.

Davis, Jack F.: *Will Your Swimming Classes Make Them Water Safe?* J.H., P.E. and R., April, 1959.

Decker, Gene W.: *A Program of Swimming for Handicapped Persons.* J.H., P.E. and R., Nov.–Dec., 1956.

Flotation Device for Teaching Swimming. C.M., June, 1954.

Gabrielson, Bramwell W.: *Information on Drownings.* Recreation, Sept., 1957. (Summary of doctoral study)

Hasenfus, Joseph L.: *Expand Your Waterfront.* C.M., Jan., 1953.

Masilionis, Jeannette: *The Elementary Backstroke for Beginners.* J.H., P.E. and R., Mar., 1955.

Miller, Norman R.: *Care of Aluminum Diving Boards.* C.M., June, 1957, page 23.

Miller, Norman R.: *Helps in Selecting Swimming Pool Equipment.* C.M., April, 1959.

Taylor, Thomas William: *Float Skills for Beginning Swimmers.* J.H., P.E., and R., April, 1957.

Weber, Elizabeth Ann: *Care of Waterfront Equipment.* C.M., Nov., 1952.

Wilford, Stanford: *Improving Diving Classes.* J.H., P.E. and R., Jan.–Feb., 1957.

Williams, John H.: *Coaching Methods in Springboard Diving.* J.H., P.E. and R., May–June, 1957.

Sychronized Swimming, Water Games, Etc.

Aquafun, Water Games and Water Carnivals, NRA, 1953, 30 pp., 50¢.

Aquatic Games, Pageants, Stunts. Book Dept., Beach & Pool, Revised, 36 pp., $3.00.

Donnelly, Richard J., Helms, William G., and Mitchell, Elmer D.: *Active Games and Contests.* The Ronald Press Co., 2nd Ed., 1958, 172 pp., $6.50.

Empleton, Bernard E., Editor: *Science of Skin and Scuba Diving.* Assn. Press, 1957, $4.95.

Hyde, George Gordon: *Water Stunts.* Boys Clubs, Revised, 1956, 28 pp.

Spears, Betty: *Beginning Synchronized Swimming.* Burgess Publishing Co., Revised, 1957, 151 pp., $3.00.

Yates, Fern, and Anderson, Theresa A.: *Synchronized Swimming.* The Ronald Press Co., 2nd Ed., 1958, 144 pp., $5.00.

MAGAZINE ARTICLES

Bullock, Doris Layson, and Sanders, Joan: *How to Present a Water Show.* Recreation, June, 1959.

Du Bois, Betsy: *Water Dramatics for Young Swimmers.* Recreation, Mar., 1957.

George, Roland J.: *Add to Your Waterfront Program With Surfboards.* C.M., April, 1955.

Gundling, Beula: *Synchronized Swimming and the Y.M.C.A.* J.H., P.E. and R., May–June, 1954.

Hendrick, Myron N.: *Synchronized Swimming—A New Sport.* Recreation, Jan., 1955.

Nicholls, C. P. L.: *Directions for Constructing Surf Paddleboards.* Beach and Pool, April, 1941.

Spears, Betty: *How To Start Synchronized Swimming.* Recreation, Jan., 1955.

Tillman, Al: *Recreation Goes Underwater.* Recreation, Feb., 1955.

Tjaarda, Stephen H.: *Underwater Swimming: A New Addition to Our Aquatic Program.* J.H., P.E., and R., Jan.–Feb., 1954.

Try Water Basketball. C.M., June, 1954.

Why Not Try a Camp Water Carnival. C.M., Feb., 1958.

Water Skiing, Etc.

Andresen, Jack: *Skiing on Water.* The Ronald Press Co., Revised, 1954, 182 pp., $4.00.

Bartlett, Tommy: *Guide to Water Skiing.* Chilton Co., 118 pp., $1.95.

Kesting, Ted: *The Outdoor Encyclopedia.*

Prince, Walter N.: *Water Skiing for All.* Chilton Co., 1956, $3.50.

MAGAZINE ARTICLES

Cramer, Allen: *Give Your Campers the Thrill of Water Skiing.* C.M., April, 1959.

Gore, Harold M.: *Guideposts for Safe Water Skiing.* Recreation, Mar., 1957.

Gore, Harold M.: *Water Skiing Comes to Camps.* C.M., Mar., 1958.

Leedy, Everett: *How Surfboards Can Spark Your Aquatics Program.* C.M., Feb., 1959.

Small Craft

Aymar, Gordon C.: *Start 'Em Sailing.* The Ronald Press Co., Revised, 1959, 128 pp., $4.00.

Bloomster, E. L.: *Sailing and Smallcraft Down the Ages.* U.S. Naval Institute, 1957, 280 pp., $6.50.

Boat Launching Ramps. Outboard Boating Club, 1955, 18 pp., Free.

Bowman, Hank W.: *Outboard Boating Handbook.* Fawcett Publishing Co., 1956, 146 pp., $2.50.

Bucher, Charles A., Editor: *Methods and Materials in Physical Education and Recreation.*

Calahan, H. A.: *Learning To Sail.* The Macmillan Co., Revised, $5.75.

Calahan, H. A.: *Sailing Technique.* The Macmillan Co., $8.75.

Canoeing, ARC., 1956, 436 pp. $1.25.

Canoeing. Boy Scouts, #3298, 1952, 25¢.

Canoeing Manual. A.C.A., 4th Ed., 1958, 96 pp., $2.00.

Canoeing Standards and Graded Classifications. New England Section of A.C.A., 1947.

Carter, Samuel III: *How To Sail.* Sentinel Books, 95¢.

Coles, Adland, and Phillips-Bert, Douglas: *Sailing Yachts.* John De Graff, Inc., 1958, 64 pp., $1.25.

Elvedt, Ruth: *Canoeing A-Z.* Burgess Publishing Co., Revised, 1953, 43 pp., $1.50.

Fisher, John: *Sailing Dinghies.* John De Graff, Inc., 1958, 63 pp., $1.25.

Fisher, John: *Starting To Sail.* John De Graff, Inc., 1958, 64 pp., $1.25.

Fisher, John, and Phillips-Bert, Douglas: *Sailing, Handling and Craft.* John De Graff, Inc., 1958, 200 pp., $3.00.

Goodrich, Lois: *Decentralized Camping.*

Handel, Carle Walker: *Canoe Camping.* The Ronald Press Co., 1953, 192 pp., $3.00.

Handel, Carle Walker: *Canoeing.* The Ronald Press Co., 96 pp., $2.95.

Henry, Porter, and Allard, William: *Handbook of Outboard Motorboating.* McGraw-Hill Book Co., Inc., 1948, 252 pp., $5.00.

Holden, John L.: *The Canoe Cruiser's Handbook.*

Hutchinson, James: *All about Boats.* Popular Mechanics, 1958, 156 pp., $2.95.

Jaeger, Ellsworth: *Land and Water Trails.*

Joy, Barbara Ellen: *All-Weather Canoe Shed.* Camp Publications #11, 2 pp., 25¢.

Joy, Barbara Ellen: *Caring for Boats in Camp.* Camp Publications #1, 2 pp., 15¢.

Kesting, Ted: *The Outdoor Encyclopedia.*

Lineaweaver, Marion: *The First Book of Sailing.* Franklin Watts, Inc., 1953, 72 pp., $1.75.

Lynn, Gordon: *Camping and Camp Crafts.*

Mitchell, Elmer D., Editor: *Sports for Recreation.*

Moorehouse, Lanore, and Fancher, Leonard: *Know Your Canoeing.* American Canoeing Ass'n., 1950, 40 pp.

Nightingale, Geoffrey: *Dingy Sailing for Boys and Girls.* John De Graff, Inc., 1956, 120 pp., $2.50.

Outboard Handling. Outboard Boating Club, 1958, 32 pp., Free.

Pohndorf, Richard H.: *Camp WaterFront Programs and Management.*

Porter, Mary: *Canoeing . . . A Canadian Heritage.* Ontario Camping Ass'n., 1957, 6 pp., 15¢.

Proctor, Ian: *Racing Dinghy Maintenance.* John De Graff, Inc., 3rd Ed., 1954, 157 pp., $3.50.

Pulling, Pierre: *Principles of Canoeing.* The John Macmillan, Co., 1954, 217 pp., $3.95.

Rowing. Boy Scouts, #3392, 1952, 25¢.

Rutstrum, Calvin: *The New Way of the Wilderness.*

Sail Boating (Mechanics Illustrated). Arco Publishing Co., 1959, $2.50.

Sailing Standards and Graded Classifications. New England Section of A.C.A., 11 pp.

Scharff, Robert: *Complete Boating Handbook.* McGraw-Hill Book Co., Inc., 1955, 250 pp., $4.95.

Seamanship. Boy Scouts, #3332, 1940, 25¢.

Swanson, William E.: *Camping for All Its Worth.*

Varney, Russel F., and Margaret A.: *A Manual of Sailing.* Burgess Publishing Co., 1953, 39 pp.

Wold, Enid: *A-Boating We Will Go.* McGraw-Hill Book Co., Inc., 1958, 320 pp., $5.50.

Zarchy, Harry: *Let's Go Boating.* Alfred A. Knopf, Inc., 1952, $3.25.

MAGAZINE ARTICLES

Capen, Edward K.: *Common Sense for Fun on the Water.* J.H., P.E., and R., May–June, 1959.

Claussen, W. Van B.:*Camp Seamanship.* C.M., May, 1945.

Flinchbaugh, Elizabeth: *Points to Consider in Improving or Developing Camp Boating Programs.* C.M., May, 1957.

Johnson, Jo Ann: *Your Smallcraft Program—Its Needs and Potentials.* C.M., Nov., 1956.

Keeping Canoes in Good Repair. Old Towne Canoe Co., C.M., June, 1957.

Riggs, Maida L.: *Learning to Canoe Can Be Fun.* C.M., Feb., 1958.

Sailing in Camp. Recreation, Mar., 1958.

Sanborn, Marion A.: *Shaking Out An Aluminum Canoe.* C.M., June, 1955.

Schellberg, Ruth: *Canoe Caravan.* J.H., P.E. and R., June, 1954.

Van Claussen, W.: *Boating Mooring Methods.* C.M., Mar., 1951.

Van Claussen, W.: *How to Choose Your Oars.* C.M., April, 1951.

16

Spiritual Life

God of the sea, the winds, the tides, we praise thee for the greatness of thy power and the certainty of thy laws. We see careless picnickers throw their litter to be carried far out into the sea by the outgoing tide, but the next morning it lies stranded on the beach where the high tide has left it.

So it is, our Father, in our lives. We throw out a careless word, an unkind thought, and it comes back to us in resentments and friendlessness. A selfish act, a yielding to temptation, or a deed left undone comes back as a haunting memory, another's failure, or a missed opportunity.

Help us, our Father, to cast only good upon the waters that good may come back with the tide. Amen.

DOROTHY WELLS PEASE*

ALTHOUGH CAMPS have different practices in regard to the spiritual life of campers, they almost without exception feel deeply their obligation along this line and have as an important aim the furthering of spiritual growth through an appreciation of the higher values of life.† Most camps have daily or weekly all-camp periods of devotion supplemented by various cabin or unit endeavors highlighting a deeper sense of spiritual values as expressed in all phases of daily living.

Such experiences ordinarily consist of some combination of the following: (1) grace before meals (oral, spoken in unison, sung, silence maintained during an appropriate musical selection, or a period of silent prayer); (2) outdoor vespers, or serious programs of some sort; (3) sunrise services or morning watch; (4) cabin devotions or meditations just before taps; (5) Sunday services in neighboring churches of the individual's choice or on the campsite in a "Woodland Chapel" and conducted by visiting members of the ministry or by camp personnel; (6) group discussions on Christian ethics; (7) singing of spirituals and other appropriate songs.

DIFFERENT FAITHS TOGETHER

In many camps, those of various faiths are encouraged to attend and live in a

---

* From *Meditations under the Sky*, by Dorothy Wells Pease, and published by Abingdon Press, 1957.
† *Camp Leadership Courses for Colleges and Universities*, ACA., page 9,IIB.

183

(Joy and Camp.)

spirit of broad-minded tolerance, and appreciation of each other and of the right of each to worship as he chooses. There should be no attempt to indoctrinate, but, on the other hand, each should be encouraged to become a better member of his own faith. In nonsectarian camps, it is customary to hire counselors of different faiths. If you accept a job in such a camp, it is most important that you believe in and practice whole-heartedly this attitude of tolerance and understanding. Encourage each of your campers to observe such practices as he is accustomed to, such as a moment of silent grace before meals, Catholic children making the sign of the cross before eating, and individual prayers before retiring. Your personal conduct in respect to your fellow men and a constant attitude of kindliness, tolerance, fairness to and respect for every individual in camp best typify your own spiritual convictions.

In a large camp it is customary to arrange separate services for the three major groups, Catholic, Jewish, and Protestant. The following remarks concerning each are extracted from a more detailed discussion in a free booklet, *Suggestions for Camp Directors*.*

Catholic

Each Catholic child is required to attend Mass on Sunday and Holy Days (the only Holy Day falling within the usual camp season of June to September is the Feast of the Assumption of the Blessed Virgin Mary on August 15). It is forbidden by the laws of the church that Catholic children participate in nonsectarian services or religious services of

* *Suggestions for Camp Directors.* The National Conference of Christians and Jews, 381 Fourth Avenue, New York 16, N.Y.

other faiths. A priest should be sent for in case of serious accident to a Catholic camper.

Camps usually take their Catholic campers and staff to the nearest Catholic church for Mass, but arrangements are sometimes made to celebrate Mass at the camp if a priest is available and the Bishop of the diocese approves. Arrangements should be made for Catholics to go to confession and receive Holy Communion at least once a month. Catholics eat no meat on Fridays and other days of abstinence.

Jewish

Those of the Jewish faith observe Saturday, the seventh day of the week, as Sabbath, the day of rest. The Jewish Sabbath begins at twenty minutes before sunset on Friday evening and ends about thirty minutes after sunset on Saturday. Sabbath candles should be lit at or before the beginning of the Sabbath and the service usually follows immediately. Personnel may attend a nearby synagogue or the services may be conducted by a counselor or other lay-leader who understands the spirit and mode of Jewish worship.

Campers of Jewish faith who come from homes of traditional observances will want to adhere to the Jewish dietary laws. No pork in any form should be served; if meat or fowl is on the camp menu, there should be an alternative menu of vegetables, salads, eggs or fish (not shellfish) for those who wish it.

The Jewish Holy Day, *Tishoh B'ab,* usually falls during the camp season; the date varies each year. Those from homes where there is strict traditional observance will wish to observe it as a fast day and will refrain from swimming and festive activities.

Protestant

There are three ways of providing Sunday worship services for Protestant campers: (1) taking them to a nearby Protestant church which meets with the approval of their parents, (2) inviting a local minister to conduct service at camp, or (3) having a worship service conducted by a lay-person or by staff and campers. Camp personnel often enjoy choosing and constructing their own "Woodland Chapel" or "Woodland Cathedral." Most worship services include:

1. Invocation   4. Prayer
2. Hymns   5. Talk
3. Scripture   6. Benediction

Few Protestant denominations observe dietary restrictions although some abstain from eating meat on Fridays. There are no Protestant Holy Days during the camp season.

Informal Worship

Spiritual experiences, of course, are not all confined to formally arranged times or places. Instead, we might think of them as times of the day when our thoughts and very souls rise to unusual heights as we contemplate the way in which some power almost beyond human comprehension has arranged this wonderful universe. Sometimes it may be simply a deep and abiding appreciation of the real goodness and kindliness of our fellow men as we see a companion do a truly noble and unselfish deed or as we note a perfect stranger extend a helping hand to someone younger or weaker or "down on his luck." Occasions for sharing our deeper and more serious thoughts with others may come most unexpectedly as when sharing a brief time off with a fellow counselor, as you look out over the countryside from a vantage spot high on a hill, or as a small camper slips a hand trustingly into yours and confides some inner thought or small trouble (but not to him). Other experiences may be quiet periods of meditation as you lie flat on your back and enjoy the beauties of a sky full of stars or the call of a lone whip-

poorwill in the distance. How true that "The Heavens declare the Glory of God; and the firmament showeth his handiwork."

CAMP SERVICES

Having a special committee of campers and counselors plan a camp spiritual program is a democratic procedure and one most likely to insure whole-hearted camper interest and participation. Make the program acceptable to all the creeds that will attend and alter the procedures at different times so campers will never know quite what to expect. Gear any service planned for campers to their age level and couch it in simple, understandable language with illustrations and events common to their experience. Think of spiritual experiences as brief respites from the busyness of the day which offer a chance for quiet, thoughtful consideration of the deeper meanings of life.

Campers often like to search for some special nook for spiritual occasions and many feel that an out-of-door setting in some natural amphitheatre under a grove of trees or overlooking a beautiful expanse of water is ideal. After dark, a campfire outside, or candlelight or a lantern inside, lend an appropriate atmosphere. Sometimes the entire program is planned and carried out by campers and staff, or, if there is to be an outside speaker, camp personnel may contribute such

parts of the service as Scripture readings, special prayers, a short dramatization of a Bible story or antiphonal reading. Music always adds an enjoyable part and may consist of special music by a choir, a selection sung by a living unit, or vocal or instrumental solos, duets, quartets, or octets. A survey of best loved hymns reveals that a surprising number are based upon God's handiwork in nature and other topics fitting to the camp and outdoor situation. Choral reading is appropriate, particularly when practiced with the intent to read with feeling and comprehension.

There are also many good Bible plays to be acted out or pantomimed to a narrative background. Group discussions of appropriate topics of Christian ideals and how to put them to work in daily living are one of the most enjoyable and worth-while camp activities.

Representative topics are kindness to animals, the high ideals and objectives of the organization sponsoring the camp, true democracy which realizes the worth of *all* individuals regardless of appearance, talent, race, or creed and the application of the golden rule to camp life as shown by consideration for others, generosity, helpfulness, and the like.

Above all, keep the program short and to the point. Since it is hot at the usual church hour, camp worship services are often held in the cool of the early morning or evening. If a collection is taken, it is usually designated for some charitable purpose.

SUNDAY IN CAMP

"Sunday is the golden clasp that binds together the volume of the week."

—LONGFELLOW

Sunday is a "special" day in camp; the regular program is dispensed with and campers are given much free time to engage in quiet, restful activities, although tennis courts, boats, waterfront and other facilities are available to those who want them. Breakfast is usually served a little later than usual and may consist of some extra touch such as eating in a special place, eating in pajamas, or with service cafeteria style. It is a day for dressing in best camp clothes and for spending time together as a cabin group listening to music, singing, holding discussions, telling stories, or writing letters. It is often designated as Visitor's Day with the camp playing host to parents and friends. A cold supper or outdoor cooking is sometimes customary to give the kitchen staff extra time off; this also provides opportunity for small groups to enjoy eating together in a secluded spot of beauty.

Sunday can and should be the most cherished day in the week. In planning for it, we must remember to look at it through the eyes of youth, for if we fill it with taboos, stuffy pursuits, unnatural quiet, and lengthy talks, we will build up rebelliousness, distaste and entirely unchristian attitudes. Campers should know it as a day especially devoted to renewing strength of mind and spirit for the coming week. Observing Sunday in the wrong way can do a great deal of harm to their developing spiritual consciousness.

"God of the open air, we kneel reverently in this temple not made with hands. The tall pines lift our thoughts above us to the Source of all this beauty. The singing of the feather-throated choir puts a melody in our hearts, a song of joy and praise and trust. All the discordant notes of the world are muted; all the problems of life are forgotten. We are filled with an inner peace and know that here we have found Thee. As we leave this hallowed spot, may the reality of Thy presence go with us to give us courage and strength for our daily tasks. Amen."

—DOROTHY WELLS PEASE*

God's Out-of-Doors. The ceaseless march
Of sun and stars from night to dawn
Trace for our eyes the dome's high arch,
Show us what it is builded on,
Hymn, anthem and recessional
The shouting storm in grandeur pours.
Mute worshipers, we hear His call
In this great house of Out-of-Doors.

—AUTHOR UNKNOWN

ADDITIONAL READINGS

Auch, Myrtle: *Adventuring Together as Christians.* Judson Press, $1.25.

Bowman, Clarice: *Spiritual Values in Camping.* Assn. Press, 1954, $3.00.

Bowman, Clarice: *Worship Ways for Camp.* Assn. Press, 1955, 182 pp., $3.50.

Britten, Rodney: *Adventure into Friendship.* Judson Press, $1.25.

Brown, Helen A., and Heltman, Harry J.: *Great Bible Stories for the Verse Speaking Choir.* Westminster Press, 1958, $1.00.

Cheley, J. A.: *Stories for Talks with Boys and Girls.* Assn. Press, Revised, 1958, $3.95.

Edgar, Mary S.: *Under Open Skies.* Clarke, Irwin & Co., Ltd., 103 St. Clair Ave., West, Toronto 5, Canada, 1955, $2.50.

Ensign, John and Ruth: *Camping Together as Christians.* Knox Publishing Co., 1958, $2.95.

Gilbert, Clark R.: *Devotions for Youth.* Assn. Press, 1943, $2.00.

Spiritual Life

Hayward, Percy R.: *Young People's Prayers.* Assn. Press, 1945, $2.00.

Idol, Vera: *Paths of Shining Light.* Abingdon Press, 1956, $2.50.

Kruse, Lenore: *Outdoors with God.* Judson Press, $1.25.

Mattoon, Laura I., and Bragdon, Helen D.: *Services for the Open.* Assn. Press, 1947, 211 pp., $2.50.

Pease, Dorothy Wells: *Altars under the Sky.* Abingdon Press, 1942, 159 pp., $1.50.

Pineo, Caroline C., Blankenship, Lois, and Whitmore, Martha J.: *We Work with God.* Judson Press, 1949, 119 pp., $1.25.

Suggestions for Camp Directors. National Conference of Christians and Jews, 381 Fourth Ave., New York 16, N.Y., 12 pp., Free.

Webb, Kenneth B., Editor: *Light from a Thousand Campfires.*

Woodall, William L.: *Devotions for Boys and Girls.* Assn. Press, 1953, $2.00.

Woodall, William L.: *100 Devotions for Boys and Girls.* Assn. Press, 1957, $2.00.

*From *Meditations under the Sky,* by Dorothy Wells Pease, and Published by Abingdon Press, 1957.

MAGAZINE ARTICLES

Bowman, Clarice M.: *Spiritual Values Begin With Persons.* C.M., Jan., 1955.

Bronstein, Dr. Arthur J.: *The Meditation Period in Camp.* C.M., May, 1955.

Hazzard, Lowell B.: *Spiritual Values in Camp.* C.M., June, 1952.

Holroyd, A. Waldie: *Learning Spiritual Values in Camp.* C.M., Jan., 1950.

MacMillan, Rev. A. M.: *Spiritual Values in Every Camp.* C.M., June, 1952.

Munson, Howard E.: *Can Religion be Handled in Camp.* C.M., Nov., 1950.

Webb, Kenneth: *Ways Your Camp Program Can Inspire Spiritual Values.* C.M., May, 1958.

IV

Camp Craft and Woodcraft

CAMP SMOKE

There's a ripple on the water,
 There's a frost tang in the air,
Now the maple trees are red beside the stream.
 And I see our empty campground,
 With the spruce trees for a background
And the birches bending o'er it, in my dream.

On the ridge the bucks are pawing,
 Where the beeches spread their branches,
And the brush above is all fresh hooked and clean of
 bark.
 There are doe tracks in the valley,
 Made where moonbeams dance and dally,
When the waxing hunter's moon drove back the dark.

There's an old cock partridge drumming
 In the black growth thicket yonder,
Where old bruin left his foot prints in the moss,
 Where he reached and scratched the highest,
 Scratched the spruce bole much the highest,
Just to tell the thicket dwellers he was boss.

There's a snowshoe rabbit sitting
 Where my fir bough bed was piled,
And a "quilley-pig" is grunting round the spot
 Where the cook fire mulled and glimmered
 And the tea pail slowly simmered
While the bacon in the fry pan sizzled hot.

From the blackness of the spruces,
 Where the shadows fall the thickest,
Comes a hoot owl's mournful calling through the
 night;
 And the balsam laden breezes,
 Stealing softly through the reaches,
Soothe the drowsy woodland camper in their flight.

Ah, the woodland trails are calling!
 Load the old canoe with duffle,
I must pitch my tent again beside the spring.
 Bring the pole and six-foot paddle,
 Far up river we will travel
To the campground where the yellow birches swing.

To that same old sheltered campground,
 With the spruce trees in the background,
Where the hoot owl breaks the silence of the night.
 Where the snowshoe rabbit crouches
 We will make new balsam couches,
In the shadows of our campfire's smoky light.

There's a ripple on the water,
 There's a frost tang in the air
And the maple trees are red beside the stream.
 All the old wood trails are calling,
 While the browning leaves are falling,
Where I see the camp smoke curling, in my dream.

—HERMAN H. HANSON

17

Some Camp Pests

Get him while he sleeps.

Black bugs in the water,
Red ants everywhere,
Chiggers round our waistline,
Sand flies in our hair—
But the dust of cities
At any cost we shun,
And cry amid our itchings,
"Isn't camping fun?"

ALICE ARMIGER SKEEN

POISONOUS PLANTS

POISON IVY, poison oak and poison sumac are the three plants poisonous to touch which are most bothersome to campers. It is interesting to note that they do not affect animals other than man, although cases have occurred from contact with the fur of dogs or other animals which have rubbed against the plant. Symptoms of itching and burning with the appearance of little white blisters may occur from a few hours to as long as five days after exposure. Some people continually travel the woods without ever contracting a case, but they can never be confident, for, after years of apparent immunity, some suddenly become susceptible. The best prevention is to learn to recognize these plants, then watch where you go to avoid contact. Wear long sleeves and trousers when hiking in likely areas. Scrub yourself thoroughly with soap immediately upon returning from a hike (some deny the worth of this) and also wash the clothing worn, for the plant oils can remain virulent for weeks.

Poison Ivy

Poison ivy is perhaps the most widespread of the three poisonous plants and is potent at any season, for cases have occurred from mere contact with the smoke as it is being burned in winter or early spring. For this reason, you should be especially careful not to get it mixed in with your firewood. However, poisoning from it occurs most frequently from

191

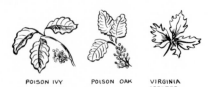

POISON IVY   POISON OAK   VIRGINIA
                                    CREEPER

May to August when it is actively spreading. This may be partly due to the fact that more people are out-of-doors, tramping around where they encounter it during these months.

The ivy plant may climb as a vine or stand as an erect shrub, two to three feet high, and is found in woods, open fields or pastures. It has three shiny, greenish-white leaves and is often confused with the harmless Virginia creeper, or woodbine, which has five leaves. An easy way to distinguish the two is to remember the saying, "Leaflets three, let it be." In the fall, poison ivy bears clusters of white berries, and its leaves turn beautiful colors. It is more poisonous than poison oak, but less so than poison sumac. The plant sweats or bleeds its poison, which may be carried for some little distance through the air. Its sticky, oily droplets adhere to the skin and start their deadly work if not removed very soon. Rid your campsite and more frequented trails of it by using a good commercial spray.

Langs* reports that Aqua-Ivy tablets, taken orally, produced immunity for the entire summer in 95 per cent of the U.S. Coast Guard personnel who took them and that similar results were obtained by giving them to campers. The treatment should be given one to three months prior to the poison ivy season.

If symptoms of poisoning appear, you should immediately consult the camp physician or nurse. There is no magic cure but measures can be taken to minimize the discomfort. You may get some relief on a trip by applying one of the following:

Ferric chloride, calamine lotion, weak solution of potassium permanganate, photographic hyposulfite, or wet dressings dipped in a solution of Epsom salts.

Some advocate applying hot cloths, or exposure to a heat lamp or the sun's rays. For an extensive irritation, it helps to soak the infected part in a vessel of water in which a mixture of baking soda and cornstarch has been dissolved.

Poison Oak

Poison oak is not an oak at all but receives its name from the fact that its leaves resemble those of some oak trees. It is largely found west of the Rocky Mountains along the Pacific slope. It bears three leaves and is an erect shrub. Prevention and treatment are the same as for poison ivy.

Poison or Swamp Sumac

Poison or swamp sumac is the most poisonous of the three plants and is found growing in boggy soil all over the Eastern half of the United States. It grows as a shrub a few feet high, and its leaves turn to a beautiful scarlet in the fall, to the undoing of many who are poisoned when they pick them for inside decoration. Poison sumac is easy to con-

* Langs, Robert J., M.D.: *Poison Ivy-Oak Prevention Discussed.* Camping Magazine, March, 1959.

POISON SUMAC   STAGHORN   DWARF SUMAC

fuse with harmless staghorn sumac, which gets its name from the fact that its branches are covered with a fuzzy velvet like the new horns of a deer. A little study of the characteristics of the two makes it easy to distinguish them.

Poison or Swamp Sumac	Staghorn Sumac
Branches	
Smooth	Covered with fuzz
Leaflets	
Not so pointed	Acutely pointed
Edges smooth	Edges serrated (toothed)
7–13 in number	11–35 in number
Berries	
White or greenish-gray	Scarlet
Found	
Marshy ground	Dry uplands

SNAKES

There are probably no more feared or despised creatures in the world than snakes, yet of the hundred or more varieties living in the United States, only four are poisonous. All are helpful to man, particularly to farmers, for they live on mice, rats and other pests which destroy crops. The nonpoisonous varieties, which are infinitely more plentiful, should therefore never be killed. A snake wants most of all just to be let alone so that he can go about his own business and will not bite a person unless he is frightened or cornered. The bite of the nonpoisonous varieties is no more dangerous than any other puncture wound and needs only the usual treatment to prevent infection.

Snakes do not charm birds, none have "stingers" in their tails, nor do they swallow their young to protect them against an approaching enemy. Their forked tongue is entirely harmless and is protruded as a sort of antenna to detect the presence of an intruder by "feeling vibrations." Snakes are covered with perfectly dry scales and are neither slick or slimy.

Three of the four poisonous varieties (the *rattlesnake,* the *copperhead* and the *cottonmouth moccasin*) are known as *pit vipers* because they have two deep pits,

(Harold M. Lambert.)

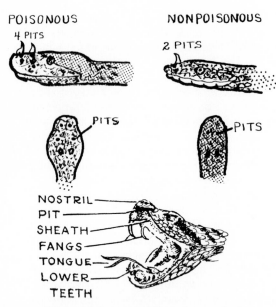

POISONOUS

4 PITS

NONPOISONOUS

2 PITS

PITS

PITS

NOSTRIL
PIT
SHEATH
FANGS
TONGUE
LOWER
TEETH

Heads of Poisonous and Nonpoisonous Snakes.

located one on each side of the face between the nostril and eye, making them appear to have four nostrils. The pupil of the eye is upright and elliptical; and the head is angular and somewhat wider than the narrow neck with a definite angle where the two join. These snakes have two hollow fangs in the upper jaw which they use like hypodermic needles to inject poison into their victims. These ordinarily rest flat against the roof of the mouth, coming to an erect position only when the snake strikes. If the fangs are extracted or broken off, new ones grow within a few days, for several half-grown substitutes are always present. Harmless snakes have no pits; they have round pupils and teeth but not fangs; their heads gradually taper off into necks.

The fourth variety of poisonous snake, the *coral snake,* is like the nonpoisonous varieties in that it has neither pits nor an angle where the head and neck join. Its fangs remain always erect and it must get a good hold on its victims and chew instead of striking as other poisonous varieties do.

Miraculous tales as to the ability of a snake to leap through the air and fasten its fangs into its victim are untrue, for no snake, even when coiled, can strike for more than one-third to one-half its length; and when not coiled, none can strike accurately or very far. It is claimed that the strike of a snake is so swift that no creature can dodge it.

Though there are only four varieties of poisonous snake, they are so widespread that there is probably no state without at least one variety of them.

The Coral or Harlequin Snake

The coral or harlequin snake is long and slender, with a *black* nose and bright colored scarlet and black bands, separated by narrow yellow ones. Although there are several varieties of harmless snakes with similar bright-colored bands, they can be readily distinguished by their *pink* or *yellow* noses. The coral snake is a Southern snake, found only as far north as North Carolina and the lower Mississippi Valley.

The coral snake is rarely seen, for it

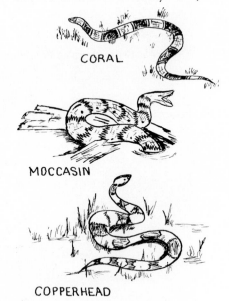

CORAL

MOCCASIN

COPPERHEAD

Poisonous Snakes.

stays in the shade during the day, coming out for food only in the cool after a rain or at twilight.

Its venom affects the nervous system, whereas the poison of the pit vipers affects the circulatory system. Although serious and painful, its bite is fatal to only about 20 per cent of those bitten, even when no treatment is given.

Water or Cottonmouth Moccasin

The cottonmouth moccasin is usually found in swampy territory or in the trees and bushes overhanging streams and marshes. It is three to six feet long and has a dark muddy or olive-brown color with eleven to fifteen inconspicuous dark bars on its short, thick body. It is also a Southern snake, found only as far north as Southern Illinois and West Virginia.

The name cottonmouth comes from the fact that the snake "threatens" before striking by opening its mouth to show the ugly white "cottonmouth" interior.

The Copperhead

The copperhead (also called the Northern moccasin or pilot snake) is found chiefly in the Eastern and Southern states, being present from Massachusetts to Florida and west as far as Illinois and Texas.

It is hazel or pinkish-brown in color, with cross markings of darker reddish-brown in the form of an hourglass or short-handled dumbbell, and its head has a distinct copperish tinge. It is two to four feet long and usually prefers rocky, wooded terrain.

Rattlesnakes

It is estimated that there are sixteen to twenty-six varieties of rattlesnakes in the United States, with nearly all of the fifty states having at least one type. They range in size from the little eight-

RATTLESNAKE

inch Pygmy rattlers to the giant diamond backs. They are variously marked and colored, but all have the characteristic rattle on the end of the tail, with which they usually warn their victim before striking. The tail and rattles vibrate so rapidly that they can scarcely be seen, making a unique sound like the ticking of an alarm clock or the sound of a locust. It is not true that you can tell the age of a rattler by the number of rattles on its tail, for it sheds its skin as often as two to five times a year, leaving a little cap of the skin near its tail each time to harden into another "rattle."

Preventing Snake Bite

Snakes are said to be so shy that they will inevitably try to slither away unseen if they note a person approaching, striking only when surprised or cornered; you may very likely camp for weeks or even months without ever seeing one. Therefore, when traveling in snake country, carry a stick and make a slight noise with it to avoid frightening a snake or sneaking up on it while it is asleep. Boots ten inches or more in height give at least partial protection for 70 per cent of bites are on the foot or leg. When climbing ledges, be careful where you put your hands, for snakes often hide out or sun themselves in crevices or on rock surfaces. Use care in striding over logs if you cannot see what is on the other side and keep your eyes open and watch where you step and sit.

Treatment of Snake Bite

Not many cases of snake bite are reported each year, and few of these prove fatal when proper treatment is given immediately. Ross Allen, famed expert, reports the following percentage of fatalities from snake bites: cottonmouth moccasin, 5 per cent; timber rattler, 4 per cent; copperhead, 1 per cent.* Someone has said that there is more danger of choking to death from eating popcorn in a movie than of dying from snake bite and more people die annually from the stings of bees and wasps than die from this source. Nevertheless, any group hiking through "snaky" territory should take along a snake-bite kit consisting of a tiny steel scalpel, a piece of rubber tubing, a rubber suction pump, and an antiseptic.

If bitten, try to recognize the snake or at least tell if it is poisonous, for, if so, you must start treatment immediately; the poison will spread through your system by way of the blood stream within a few moments. The venom of a poisonous snake instantly causes a painful, burning sensation which is quickly followed by discoloration and swelling. One or two deep fang marks will probably show, whereas only a round set of teeth marks characterize the bite of a nonpoisonous snake.

If the first aider has a companion, he should start in search of a doctor or nurse right away. Have the patient lie down and keep still, for movement of any sort stimulates the circulation and spreads the poison faster. Do not permit him to see his injury or the treatment given, for the shock may prove detrimental.

Direct your efforts toward (1) keeping the poison from spreading (2) getting as much of it out of the system as possible and (3) treating for shock. Speed is essential, for every second counts.

Apply a tight bandage a couple of inches above the wound, using the rubber tubing from your snake kit, a bandana, or other strip of cloth folded to about a two-inch width. Do not twist the bandage with a stick, for it should not stop circulation but merely slow it down enough to cause the veins to distend. Loosen the bandage for a few moments every thirty minutes; if the swelling moves up, move the bandage up ahead of it. Do not give stimulants of any sort, particularly alcohol, for they do no good whatever and may prove harmful by speeding up the circulation and causing the poison to spread faster.

Just as soon as possible, sterilize a razor blade, sharp knife or the scalpel from your kit in alcohol or flame and slash an "X" about ½ inch long and ¼ inch deep through each fang mark. Take care not to cut across an artery or tendon, but make the cut deep enough to produce free oozing of blood and lymph. Then apply the suction cup to the cut for at least twenty minutes; and keep the wound open and draining freely for several hours in order to get rid of as much of the venom-containing blood as possible. When you have no suction pump, it is best to suck with your mouth if there are no lesions or open sores in it. If the swelling and discoloration move to a new location, it indicates the poison has moved there; make a new incision and apply the suction cup. Replace the bandage up ahead of the new swelling.

The superior treatment for snake bite is, of course, to introduce antivenom into the body of the victim to counteract the poison. Make an attempt to get this treatment just as soon as possible, for it greatly minimizes the pain and discomfort of the patient as well as possibly saving his life.

* Byron, Dalyrymple: *Fishing, Hunting, and Camping.* Pocket Books, New York, 1950, page 330.

INSECTS AND SUCH

There are many insects which prove to be quite bothersome and some are even serious when a person is bitten or stung by a large number of them; others are dangerous because they may carry serious diseases such as tularemia, Rocky Mountain spotted fever, and such.

Fortunately, the old repellents, such as unpleasant smudge fires and "dopes" containing citronella and creosote, have been supplanted by modern drug store preparations which are more effective and also more pleasant in that they do not stain the clothing and are not irritating or unpleasant to smell. Some of these are effective for five to twelve hours when applied to the skin; still others can be sprayed around the tent and quarters to provide relief while sleeping.

If you must go through territory where obnoxious insects are abundant, cover yourself with clothing and wear a head net of mosquito netting or bobbinet which can be tucked down inside your shirt collar.

Local symptoms are usually swelling, itching and pain and can usually be relieved by applying household ammonia or a solution of baking soda and water. Avoid scratching the bites lest they become infected.

Woodticks

These blackish or reddish-brown insects cling to tall grass or shrubs and brush off on people or animals as they pass by. These are unpleasant, and the danger is that they sometimes transmit Rocky Mountain spotted fever and other serious or even fatal diseases. Fortunately, they do not usually burrow for from six to eight hours after getting on you and so can be found and removed by a careful tick inspection (by someone else) twice a day. When discovered, do not try to pull them off for the head will remain embedded; do not crush them between your fingers and thus get the infective material on you. Touch a heated wire or recently extinguished match to the tick and it will back out in a hurry.

Chiggers (Chigoes, Jiggers or Red Bugs)

These tiny, red, spider-like creatures are the larvae of a tiny mite, and constitute one of the worst nuisances for the camper, especially in the Southern states. Use the usual prevention and treatment.

Bees, Wasps, and the Like

The bites of these insects are not serious unless you are unfortunate enough to be stung by a large number of them. Avoid going near a nest of them and if one "buzzes" you, walk *slowly* away from it and do not try to swat at it for it is more likely to sting when frightened.

Spiders

The only really dangerous spider is the female black widow. She can be identified by her shiny black body resembling a shoe button, the bright red hourglass spot on her under side, and her distended, round, oversized abdomen. You should get to a doctor immediately if bitten, for a bite can make you seriously ill and about one in twenty ends fatally. There are likely to be systemic as well as local symptoms in ½ to two hours with shock (paleness, weakness and rapid pulse, cold skin, and unconsciousness), nausea, vomiting, and great thirst; there may also be muscle cramps. Apply a tourniquet between the heart and the bite and have the patient lie quietly. Give the usual treatment for shock.

Underside of a Black Widow Spider.

Kissing Bug or Assassin Bug

This little bug is largely found in the Southern states. Its bite, often blamed on a spider, may, at times, make the victim quite ill. The symptoms are the usual itching, burning and swelling. In more severe cases, red blotches occur, followed by nausea, rapid breathing and palpitation of the heart. Get the patient to a doctor or nurse right away.

Centipedes and Scorpions

These are particularly dangerous in the Southwest. The scorpion stings with its poison tail and the centipede bites with its poison fangs. Be sure to inspect your bedding well before retiring and fresh shoes and clothing thoroughly before donning them. Give first aid treatment as for a spider bite and get the patient to the doctor as soon as possible.

Caterpillar (Larva) of Io Moth

This beautiful and showy specimen can be identified by its light-green coat with two pink and white stripes zigzagging down each side. Its back is a wilderness of spines which give off a substance poisonous to touch. The sting causes pain, irritation and swelling.

ADDITIONAL READINGS

Burke, Edmund H.: *Camping Handbook.*
Des Grey, Arthur H.: *Camping.*
Henderson, Luis M.: *The Outdoor Guide.*
Hood, Mary V.: *Outdoor Hazards, Real and Fancied.*
Jaeger, Ellsworth: *Land and Water Trails.*
Kesting, Ted: *The Outdoor Encyclopedia.*
Lindholm, Major Mauno A.: *Camping and Outdoor Fun.*
Lynn, Gordon: *Camping and Camp Crafts.*
Reptile Study. Boy Scouts #3813, 1944.
Safety-Wise. Girl Scouts, 86 pp., 20¢.
Weaver and Merrill: *Camping Can Be Fun.*
West, James E., and Hillcourt, William: *Scout Field Book.*
Whelen, Townsend, and Angier, Bradford: *On Your Own in the Wilderness.*

MAGAZINE ARTICLES

Carlson, Dr. A. E.: *Licking Those Weed and Brush Problems.* C.M., Mar., 1952.
Grigsby, B. H.: *Control of Poison Ivy.* C.M., May, 1957.
Langs, Robert J., M.D.: *Poison Ivy-Oak Prevention Discussed.* C.M., Mar., 1959.
Meisel, Albert G.: *The Scourge of Summer: Poison Ivy.* Reader's Digest, Aug., 1958.
Millard, Reed: *Jiggers—The Chiggers!* Coronet, July, 1957.
Poison Ivy—Its Prevention and Treatment. Consumer Reports, Apr., 1960.
Schwardt, H. H.: *First Line of Defense against Insects.* C.M., May, 1954.

18

Ropes and Knotcraft

The healing fragrance of the wood; the beauties of lake and of coastline; the open air; the clean blue skies—these belong to all people, and the right to enjoy them is the heritage of every child.

CAMPING FOR CRIPPLED CHILDREN*

Why Learn to Tie Knots?

From time immemorial man has needed some medium to join things together. Early man made his "rope" from such native things as thin strips of bark and small branches and the Indians applied wet thongs made from the skins of animals which contracted and became tight as they dried. When commercially-made rope is unattainable or the campers want to be really "woodsy," they can still use bark, vines or withes as these early inhabitants did. You will find a knowledge of how to tie a few simple, serviceable knots indispensable for such tasks as repairing a broken shoestring, lashing camp furniture, suspending a lighted lantern between two trees, tying a bedroll, making a temporary clothesline, pitching your tent, or tying up your boat.

ROPE

How Rope Is Made

A close inspection of a rope shows that it consists of many individual *fibers* twisted to the right to form *yarns,* a few yarns twisted to the left to form *strands,* and three or more strands twisted together to the right to form the *rope.* This twisting in alternate direction keeps the fibers compact when stress is applied but it may cause a new rope to curl and be hard to handle.

* Permission by The National Society for Crippled Children and Adults, Inc.

(Courtesy of The Evening Bulletin, Philadelphia.)

Most commonly used rope is made of sisal, which comes from Central America. Manila hemp rope (named after its chief city of export in the Philippines) wears better, though it is stiff, heavy and more expensive. Inexpensive Indian jute or cotton rope is also used. Campers usually prefer Nylon or Fiberglas ropes since they do not rot or shrink when exposed to moisture and are easier to handle when wet. These qualities especially enhance their value as tent guy lines and for use around boats and water. The size of a rope is usually expressed as its diameter except by sailors who express it in terms of the circumference.

A Camper's Rope

For ordinary purposes around camp, a camper finds a rope about five to six yards long and ⅜ inch in diameter most useful. You will need additional pieces, smaller in diameter, to practice knot tying and lashing.

Alternate wetting and drying greatly shorten the life of your rope so do not expose it unnecessarily. Keep it in a neat, compact roll when not in use. If your rope breaks, learn how to splice it instead of knotting the two ends together. A good splice makes the rope almost as strong as ever.

Knots

There are said to be about 4,000 different kinds of knots in existence, but many of them are used only for very specialized purposes and a camper will find the few presented here adequate for his ordinary needs.

How to Carry Your Rope.

Relaying a Rope.

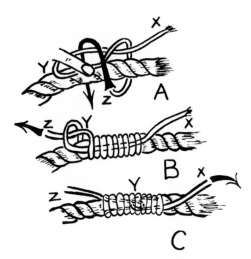

Whipping the End of a Rope.

Relaying a Rope

A rope which has not been whipped sometimes untwists and must be relaid before it can be whipped and put back in good condition again. To do this, hold the rope in your left hand, twist the fibers of strand one tightly and pull them in place with your right hand; move your left thumb up to hold them firmly in place as you twist strand two and pull it up into place. Now twist and pull strand three into place, then strand one again, strand two, and so on, until you have the whole thing back in order. Whip the rope immediately so it won't unravel again.

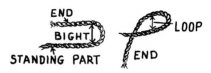

Some Rope Terms.

SOME TERMS USED

End—the short part of the rope with which you lead in tying knots.

Standing Part—the remainder or long end of the rope.

Bight—made by bending an end back to lie parallel to its standing part.

Overhand Loop—made by crossing an end *over* its standing part.

Underhand Loop—made by crossing an end *under* its standing part.

WHIPPING THE END OF THE ROPE

Whip the end of a rope to keep it from untwisting or unravelling. You will need a piece of grocery string or twine about one to two feet long. Lay one end of it back along the end of the rope in a loop, Y, as shown and hold it in place with your left thumb; wind the standing part, Z, in tight spirals around the rope and bight, starting about ½ inch from the end as in B. Continue winding until only a short end of the string remains, Z, and insert it through the end of loop, Y, as in B. Now grasp end X and pull gently until the point where X and Z cross is about midway under the spirals as shown in C. Snip off ends X and Z fairly close to where they emerge from the spirals. Test the whipped end for permanence by trying to push it off over the end of the rope.

CHARACTERISTICS OF A GOOD KNOT

A good knot should (1) be easy to tie, (2) do its job well, and (3) be quick and easy to untie.

Packages are often tied with inefficient knots which slip at the wrong time and are so complicated that the average person snips them in two rather than exercise the patience necessary to untie them and so ruins the cord for future use. Whereas this may be satisfactory in city life, a camper finds cord and rope useful to him in so many ways that he saves every bit of it to use again and again. It therefore behooves him to be able to tie a knot which he can easily untie when he is through with it.

STOPPER OR END KNOTS

Stopper or end knots are used to enlarge the end of a rope so that it will hold in a hole or ring or will provide a good handhold.

Overhand Knot.

The Overhand Knot

For this simple knot, make a loop, push the end down through it and pull the whole thing tight. If you want a larger knot, pass the end through the loop several times before you tighten it. It holds well but tends to jam and is hard to untie after stress has been put on it. It is sometimes substitued for whipping on the end of a rope, but this should be done only temporarily until you can whip the end properly.

Figure-of-Eight Knot.

Figure of Eight Knot

This knot is similar in use to the overhand, but is slightly larger and easier to untie. An additional use is for attaching a line to a fish hook. Its name comes from its appearance. To untie, loosen it by pushing on the end so that you can easily pick it apart.

KNOTS FOR JOINING TWO ROPES

Square or Reef Knot

This knot is excellent to join two ropes of equal size, to tie up a package, or to finish off a first aid bandage. Make a bight in rope B and pass end A down through it, up across both the standing part and end of B and bring it up through the bight in B again. Tighten it by grasping end A and its standing part in one hand and B and its standing part in the other and pulling simultaneously. Notice that end A and its standing part lie parallel *above* the bight in B, while end B and its standing part lie parallel *below* the bight.

Square or Reef Knot.

To untie the knot, loosen it by a hard simultaneous pull sidewise on end A and its standing part; then pick it apart. Can you see how the square knot gets its name from its appearance?

Granny Knot.

When tying a square knot, avoid tying a *granny*, which is quite useless since it pulls loose whenever stress is applied. Note that in the granny, an end comes out on the opposite side of the bight from its standing part.

Sheet Bend (Weaver's Knot or Becket Bend)

This is the best knot for joining two ropes together, particularly when they are of unequal size. Make a bight in the larger rope, A, and bring B up through and around behind it and slip it under its

Sheet Bend.

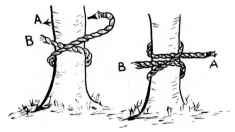

A Clove Hitch.

own standing part where it enters the bight. Leave both ends A and B long. Hold bight A in your left hand and pull both the end and standing part of B tight about it. Notice that one end of the small rope B is on top of the bight in A and the other is below it. Pull on end A and its standing part simultaneously to loosen the knot. This knot is quickly tied, holds securely as long as there is stress on it, and is easily picked apart when the stress is removed.

Clove Hitch

This is one of the simplest and most useful knots known for such purposes as fastening a rope to a tree or your boat painter to the dock. Most lashing is also started and finished with it. Bring end A around the tree and pass it over its own standing part in an overhand loop, then around the tree again and slip it under its own standing part.

To pick it apart, push simultaneously on end A and its standing part B.

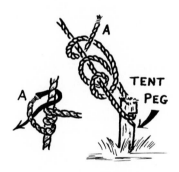

Taut Line Hitch.

Two Half Hitches.

KNOTS FOR ATTACHING A ROPE TO AN OBJECT

Taut Line Hitch

This is an excellent knot to use to tie guy lines to tent pegs for you can tighten or loosen the rope by simply pushing the knot up or down. Thus you can quickly loosen your guy line to allow for shrinkage of tent and rope when it rains and tighten it when they dry out. To make a taut line hitch, bring the end A of the rope around the standing part, making two full turns. Then bring end A up and around above the turns and tuck it under its own standing part.

The Half Hitch and Two Half Hitches

Half hitches (several for maximum security) provide the easiest and quickest way to fasten a rope to a post as when stringing up a rope clothesline.

Slippery Hitch

This is a novelty knot to provide a temporary fastening, for it can be *cast off* (untied) in a hurry, even though under tension at the time. Gather up the standing part of the rope to make bight B (Step 1); then gather up the rope again and take it around the post and up through bight B to make bight C (Step

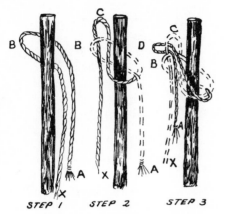

STEP 1   STEP 2   STEP 3

A Slippery Hitch.

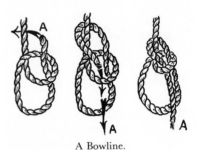

A Bowline.

This little saying may help your campers remember how to tie it:

The rabbit jumped out of the hole,
Ran around the tree and
Jumped back into the hole again.
—ORIGIN UNKNOWN

2). Tighten bight B by pulling end A and again gather up the rope and pull it through bight C to make bight D. Pull tight and the hitch will hold, but a yank on end A undoes the whole thing in a jiffy. It is also called the Highwayman's Hitch for supposedly it enabled him to untie his horse in a jiffy and be off with his loot to get a head start on pursuers.

KNOTS FOR MAKING A PERMANENT LOOP IN A ROPE

Bowline (bō-lin)

The bowline is so named because it was originally used to tie a rope or line to the bow of a ship. A bowline will neither slip nor jam and its noose remains the same size regardless of how much stress you put on it. It is useful in the end of a boat painter, in a bedroll rope or any place where you want a more or less permanent loop to drop over a post or nail and lift off again in an instant. It also has an important use in mountain climbing, for rescues from fires, or for throwing a line to someone in trouble out in the water. It is easy to untie when you are through with it.

Make an overhand loop in the rope and pass end A up through it, then around behind the standing part and down through the loop again and draw it tight.

It is an added accomplishment to learn to tie this knot with one hand as sailors do while holding on to the ship's rigging with the other.

KNOTS FOR SHORTENING A ROPE

Sheep Shank

A sheep shank shortens a rope, may be left in as long as desired, then quickly untied, leaving your rope the original length and completely undamaged.

Fold your rope to the desired length (Step 1). Make an underhand loop with

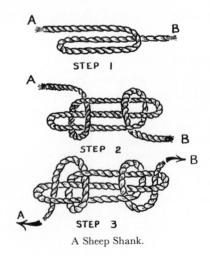

A Sheep Shank.

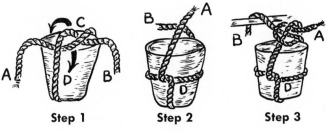

Step 1   Step 2   Step 3

A Barrel Hitch.

end A around one folded-over portion (Step 2); repeat with end B. Pull the loops tight and your rope will hold as long as there is stress on both ends of it.

For a more permanent shortening, pass ends A and B down and up respectively through the bights in the folded portion of the rope (Step 3).

KNOTS FOR SUSPENDING AN OBJECT

Barrel Hitch

When you want to suspend a handleless object, such as an outdoor cache or a container with no bail, a barrel hitch will do the job nicely.

Set the object on your stretched-out rope and bring the two ends up and knot them loosely above (Step 1); then spread the knot as indicated by arrows so that one side goes down on each side of the object (Step 2); bring both the end and standing part up on top of the bucket and join them tightly with an overhand knot (Step 3). The weight of the bucket and its contents keeps the knot secure as you suspend it by standing part, B.

LASHING

Lashing provides a way to fasten various objects, such as sticks or poles, together. It will hold better if the sticks are first notched to make them fit more compactly together. Lashing is used when no nails are available, when it would be objectionable to mar or damage the objects by driving nails into them, or when you need only a temporary joining.

Any kind of cord that is heavy and strong enough to hold securely is suitable. *Binder twine* is recommended for ordinary use, for it is tough, cheap and easily obtained. In lashing, you manipulate the standing part of the rope instead of the end as in knot-tying. Start all lashing with a clove hitch around one or more of the objects and finish off with another clove hitch.

Frapping is a method of tightening lashing by wrapping the end of the cord around its own turns and is the secret of a good, firm piece of work.

Square Lashing

Use square lashing to join sticks together at right angles. Make a clove hitch

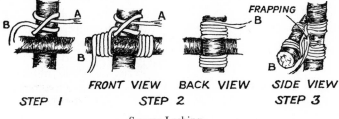

STEP I   FRONT VIEW   BACK VIEW   SIDE VIEW
          STEP 2   STEP 3

Square Lashing.

around one of the sticks (Step 1); bring the standing part, B, across the horizontal stick, around behind the vertical stick and up across the horizontal stick again, then around behind the vertical stick (Step 2); repeat the whole process as many times (usually four or five) as needed and tighten with frapping (about three turns) between the two sticks (Step 3). Finish off with a clove hitch around one of the sticks.

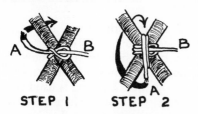

STEP 1   STEP 2

Diagonal Lashing.

Diagonal Lashing

Diagonal lashing joins sticks which cross at other than a right angle in the form of an X. Start with a clove hitch around the two sticks (Step 1); make about four turns around the joining in one direction, then four in the opposite direction (Step 2). Frap it tightly with about three turns between the two sticks and finish off with a clove hitch.

Tripod Lashing

Use tripod lashing (p. 376) to fasten three sticks so they will stand alone and make a foundation for a washstand, etc. Place the sticks close together, fasten the cord by a clove hitch to the outside stick and make four or five rather loose turns about all three sticks. Frap loosely between the sticks and finish off with a clove hitch. Spread the poles apart to form your base.

Shear Lashing

Shear Lashing is used to bind together two poles so that they can be spread apart like "shears" or scissors. Place the

two poles side by side, make a clove hitch around one near the top and take about four or five turns rather loosely about both poles. Frap loosely between the poles and finish with a square knot or clove hitch. Stand the poles up, spread them apart and use as a support for a tent as shown in B, (page 301) and H, (page 297).

Round Lashing.

Round Lashing

Round lashing consists of several lashings, each made like the shear lashing described above except that the turns and frapping are pulled quite tight to prevent movement between the two poles.

Pole Splice

A *pole splice* repairs a broken pole or unites two poles of approximately the same diameter into one long one. Place the two pieces end to end and place long splints, A and B, of smaller sticks or pieces of board along the joint, letting them extend well beyond the joints on both sides. Make a clove hitch around the whole at the top, and wrap the cord

A Pole Splice.

tightly about the joint for some distance. Finish off with the usual square knot or clove hitch. Repeat at two other places along the splints.

Malay Hitch

A *malay hitch* quickly joins wisps of grass, reeds, and the like, into mats for a cabin floor, table, or outdoor mattress or makes a "curtain" for in front of a latrine.

A Malay Hitch.

Continuous Lashing

Continuous lashing enables you to lash small sticks of bamboo, lathe, or such materials into a table top which you can roll up for transporting (p. 72). For a structure which can't be rolled up, notch two long sticks to receive the short sticks at desired intervals. Use short sticks of the same length and approximately the same diameter.

Anchor the middle of a piece of string about four times the length of the long pole by making a clove hitch around it just above the first notch. Bring one end of the string diagonally across the back of the long pole and up and across the first short stick. Carry it tightly around behind the long pole again and up and over the second short stick on the opposite side of the long stick. Continue until all of the short sticks have been anchored. Repeat with the other end of the string, anchoring the short sticks on the opposite sides of the long stick and tie the two ends of the string with two half hitches. Note that the bends in the ends of the string lie parallel to the long stick in front and cross each other in the back. Now lash the other ends of the short sticks to the other long stick and your table top is complete.

You can use lashing in many ways around a campsite, to fashion all kinds of simple furniture and camp "fixin's."

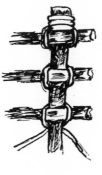

Continuous Lashing.

ADDITIONAL READINGS

Campcraft Skills. Flip Charts (Lashing). Girl Scouts #15-01, $6.00.

Day, Cyrus L.: *Art of Knotting and Splicing.* U.S. Naval Inst., 2nd Ed., 1955, 224 pp., $5.00.

Graumont, Raoul M.: *Handbook of Knots.* Cornell Maritime Press, 1945, $1.50.

Hammett, Catherine T., and Horrocks, Carol M.: *Creative Crafts for Campers.*

Jaeger, Ellsworth: *Land and Water Trails.*

Knots and How To Tie Them. Boy Scouts #3166, 56 pp., 10¢.

Know Your Knots. Boy Scouts #1057, 15¢.

Lindholm, Major Mauno A.: *Camping and Outdoor Fun.*

Lynn, Gordon: *Camping and Camp Crafts.*

Pioneering. Boy Scouts, 1942, 64 pp., 35¢.

Rutstrum, Calvin: *The New Way of the Wilderness.*

19

The Weather

"Whatever the weather may be," says he,
"Whatever the weather may be,
It's the songs ye sing, an' the smiles ye wear,
That's a makin' the sun shine everywhere."
JAMES WHITCOMB RILEY*

MOST OF US are almost completely oblivious to the thrilling drama taking place about us daily as the various forces of nature carry on their roles of causing our weather, whatever it may be. We go along with our noses to the ground, often entirely oblivious to the serene beauty of the blue, cloudless sky above us or the many varieties of clouds moving about in patterns seldom exactly the same. There is often a truly dramatic spectacle taking place as they rush hither and thither to eventually bring us clearing skies, a gentle, refreshing rain or, an occasional terrifying summer thunderstorm with lightning and all the trimmings. A missed opportunity for beauty and wonder, yes, but to the camper there are even more practical considerations, for nearly everything he does depends on the weather. His plans for a cookout, a nature hike or an evening campfire program may be completely upset by it. On a trip, it may be even more serious unless he can interpret weather signs for he will not be able to flip the dials on the radio or TV set to bring in the latest report from the weather bureau.

Indeed, he needs warning far in advance of the first wind or raindrops, for he will need time to search for the nearest suitable campsite, throw up the best shelter he can and lay in a supply of dry wood to make himself as snug as possible. This is doubly important if he is out on the water in a boat for his very life as

* From *Pipes O'Pan at Zekesburg*. Published by The Bobbs-Merrill Co.

209

well as his boat and duffel may be at stake.

A professional meteorologist has many complicated instruments at his command and, by exchanging information with thousands of other meteorologists through-out the world, can pretty well predict what is in store for the local scene al-though even he usually protects himself by plenty of "probablies" and "possiblies" in his forecasts. Even so, a camper with some knowledge and inexpensive and readily obtainable equipment, can make reasonably accurate forecasts from 60 per cent to 80 per cent of the time and have a lot of fun in doing it. However, he must acquire some knowledge of at-mospheric conditions for he will need something a bit more scientific than how Uncle John's rheumatism is today, whether Aunt Sophronia's bunion is giv-ing her pain, or the cat is sitting with its tail to the fire. Weather is "made" by the interaction of heat, pressure, moisture, and wind and all must be watched and interpreted properly to come up with a worth-while forecast.

Atmosphere

What we know as the earth is a globe suspended in space extending outward in all directions for at least 700 miles. At-mosphere near the earth consists of invis-ible gases, about 20 per cent *oxygen* (necessary for animal life), 0.3 to 0.03 per cent *carbon dioxide* (necessary for plant life), some 78 per cent *nitrogen,* 0 to 5 per cent water in the form of vapor, and minute quantities of other gases. How-ever, these gases thin out rapidly as one goes farther from the earth until they eventually approach "nothingness." Even air must respond to the law of gravity, however, and thus gases near the earth are concentrated by the pressure or weight of the succeeding layers of gases above them. Thus, 50 per cent of the at-mosphere is compressed into a 3½ mile area immediately surrounding the earth

and 97 per cent of it is within an eight-een mile radius.

As the air ascends, it cools rapidly at the rate of 1 degree for each 300 feet so that the temperature is down to a chilly 50 degrees at a height of two miles and 20 degrees below zero at five miles; this is about the height of our highest moun-tains, Mont Blanc and Mt. Everest, and explains why they are usually capped with snow throughout the year. It is the nature of gases to expand as much as outside forces let them so that the "air" spreads out thinner and thinner as it gets farther from the earth and the tempera-ture drops to 68 degrees below zero eight miles up.

Air Movements

What we know as "weather" exists only in a comparatively narrow band of atmosphere five to eight miles high which immediately surrounds the earth and the clouds are confined within it; that is why airplanes can safely escape storms by fly-ing above them. The sun shines through the air without warming it, to strike the earth which it does warm; the earth then reflects the heat back to warm the air above it. As the air heats, it expands and becomes lighter which causes it to rise to a new low pressure area where the lack of outside pressure allows it to expand still further. This process of expanding and rising continues indefinitely. Expan-sion is a cooling process (about 5½ degrees for each 1,000 feet) and, as the warm air near the earth rises, air which has previ-ously been cooled in the upper atmos-phere rushes in to take its place, to be heated by the reflected heat from the earth and begin in turn to expand, rise and grow cooler. Thus it is evident that the air is in constant motion upward and downward in what is know as *air currents.* The expansion of the air sideward pro-duces horizontal movements resulting in *wind.* We see air currents in action when a piece of paper, thistle-down or a winged seed is picked up and borne aloft. Spiders on their silken threads have been observed where air currents have carried them as high as five miles. This process, however, is not as simple as it seems for the movements are far from uniform or predictable; one reason for this is that the earth, and consequently the air above it, are not warmed uniformly. For instance, dark plowed soil absorbs heat from the sun's rays much more readily than does a grassy meadow, and land of almost any sort absorbs heat faster than does a body of water; consequently, the air around them is correspondingly heated to different degrees and at different rates. At night, the opposite occurs for the water and grassy meadow retain their heat longer and consequently heat the air above them less rapidly. This air, then, expands and rises more slowly and also expands sideward less rapidly resulting in an area of relatively "still air." Thus, we see that air movement may vary from none at all in one area to a good breeze, or even a stiff gale in another.

Air Pressure

Though the expression "light as air" conveys the impression that air has no weight, this is not true for air commonly presses in all directions including downward with a pressure of about fifteen pounds per square inch at sea level; this is caused by the tendency of gases to expand and the "flattening out" effect as all of the air above presses down upon that below. When you draw inward on

Drawing Liquid through a Straw.

the straw in your Coca Cola, you draw out the air and create what is known as a *vacuum*. Since there is no air in the straw, there is also no air pressure and the downward pressure of the air outside on the surface of the Coca Cola forces some of the liquid up into the vacuum in the straw and eventually into your mouth.

The weight or pressure of air varies according to the amount of moisture it contains in the form of *vapor*. We see evidence of this vapor in the steam that rises from a teakettle or in our breath exhaled on a cold winter morning.

Humidity

The amount of moisture in the air is called *humidity* and it comes about through the evaporation of water from the rivers, lakes, oceans, soil, and even trees and other vegetation. A perpetual interchange takes place, with the air drawing moisture from the earth to form clouds which eventually pour it back again onto the earth as rain or snow.

We are seldom aware of the moisture in the air except on a hot, muggy day when the humidity is so high that the air is said to be *saturated* (has absorbed all the moisture it can hold at its given temperature) and consequently the perspiration cannot evaporate from our bodies. We speak of such a day as a *humid* one.

The humidity of the air, and particularly whether it is rising or falling, is very important to us in predicting the weather and we use an instrument called a *barometer* to measure it. Odd though it may seem, air is heavier when it has a low moisture content (low humidity) and lighter when the humidity is high.

Aneroid Barometer.

Several types of barometers are available, the commonest being the aneroid barometer (meaning without liquid), which consists of a hand or needle that is moved around a marked dial by the pressure of the air on a sensitive box within it. This type of barometer is accurate but rather expensive.

A *mercury barometer* consists of a column of mercury which rises or falls in a graduated tube. The tube, closed on top, has a vacuum (no air) above the column of mercury. Its open bottom end is immersed in a vessel of mercury and as the air pressure on the surface of the mercury

Mercury Barometer.

varies, it causes a corresponding rise or fall in the level of the mercury in the tube. Inexpensive barometers operating on this same principle, but using water instead of mercury, are available, or you can make one yourself.

Most commercial barometers bear such notations as "change," "fair," "stormy," and so on, which are based on the rising or falling of the barometer. In general, a reading of 30 or over may be considered high; below 30, may be considered as low.

To make a clipper ship model barometer (page 213) accurate enough for camp purposes, fit a bottle with a tight cork and insert a piece of rubber tubing through the cork as shown, sealing it in with melted paraffin or candle wax to make it air- and water-tight. Fill the bottle almost full of water, and invert it, making sure that no air is allowed to get into the top.

Suspend the barometer out of the sun's direct rays and fasten it so that it will not be jostled by strong winds or people passing by. After it has remained stationary a day or two to adjust itself, it is possible to estimate changes in humidity by the rise or fall of the liquid level in the bottle. When the air is dry or heavy, it presses down forcibly on the water in the rubber tube, pushing the liquid back up into the bottle. When the humidity is high, it exerts little pressure and the liquid rises and, in extreme cases, may even come out of the tube.

A changing barometer indicates a change in the weather; if falling, the air is light because it is filled with moisture and rain is likely to follow; if rising, there is little moisture and fair weather is indicated.

Water Condensation

Just as in a teakettle, heat causes water to change into vapor which is light enough to be picked up and carried about in the air. The relative amount of moisture in the air in comparison to what it could contain at that temperature (saturation point) is called *relative humidity*. This amount varies with the temperature for the warmer the air the more moisture it can carry; at ground level, a rise in temperature of 20 degrees doubles the amount of moisture that can be borne. When the *saturation point* or *dew point* is reached, the relative humidity is 100 per cent and, if the temperature continues to drop, the air can hold no more moisture and the excess condenses and becomes clouds, dew, or frost. Therefore, at night, if the humidity is high, since the trees and grass cool off more rapidly than the ground, the moisture laden air which comes in contact with them also cools and so can no longer hold all of its moisture. This excess condenses on the trees and grass as dew. The same phenomenon is seen when moisture condenses on contact with a cold pitcher of water or a cold window pane. Higher up, as the warm air from the earth rises and cools,

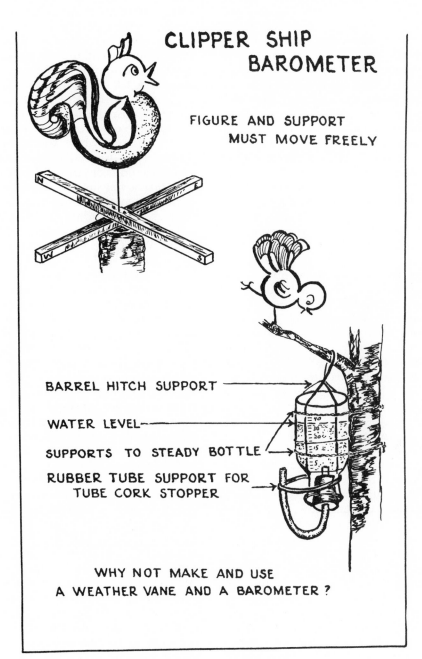

Weather Vane and Clipper Ship Barometer.

it can no longer hold all of its moisture and the excess condenses into *clouds; fog* is like a cloud except that the condensation has taken place near the earth and our difficulty to see far ahead is due to the millions of infinitesimal droplets of water suspended in the air. These reflect back automobile lights or the rays of a flashlight just as though they were millions of little mirrors. *Smog* is a combination of fog and smoke or other particles found near industrial areas.

We have observed the countless bits of dust floating in the air as they are caught in a ray of sunshine under certain conditions. Similar particles of dust high in the air are what ordinarily give the sky its blue appearance and, when especially numerous, produce a gray or hazy effect. They are the substances upon which moisture condenses into droplets. If the moisture laden air is carried still higher, it continues to cool and still more moisture condenses into droplets. They may eventually become electrified and attract each other, forming into increasingly larger droplets. Eventually they become so heavy that they can no longer be air borne and fall to earth as raindrops, each consisting of from one to seven million droplets.

Snow is rain which has come from a cold, upper region where the droplets have been frozen into icy crystals, hundreds or even thousands of them uniting in the beautiful design of a snowflake.

Sleet results when snow is partially melted as it falls through a layer of warm air, then freezes again in a layer of cold air just above the ground.

Glaze results when freezing takes place just as the half-melted snow hits the ground.

Hail occurs when rain from a rather low-lying cloud is caught in a strong up-rush of air and tossed back up into a high, freezing area where it is coated with snow. As it descends again through the low-lying cloud, it gathers more moisture; again it is swept up into freezing air to acquire another layer of ice and snow. This process may be repeated many times until the rain finally becomes too heavy to be carried upward by air currents and so crashes to earth as hail. It is claimed that hail stones as big as baseballs with twenty-five layers of ice and snow fell at Annapolis, Maryland, on June 22, 1915. Hail is a freak which insolently disregards the calendar, for it is said to be most common in June.

Frost occurs when the temperature drops below freezing under conditions which would ordinarily produce dew.

A *halo* or *ring* around the sun or moon occurs when their light is seen shining through a surrounding ring of ice crystals.

Lightning. Mythology explains lightning as the War God, Thor, sending bolts of fire to paralyze the earth people, but we know from the experiments of Benjamin Franklin that it is really electricity. It usually passes harmlessly from one cloud to another, but occasionally comes from a cloud to the earth with enough power to kill men or animals, start fires or uproot trees. The safest place to be during an electrical storm is in a cave or ravine between two hills or embankments. The most dangerous places are near a fence, on a high hill, or under a tree which is especially tall or is standing alone. Water is a good conductor of electricity, so that anyone swimming or boating should get on land as quickly as possible.

Thunder, although alarming, is perfectly harmless and is thought to result from the rapid expansion of air as it is heated by the passage of lightning through it. It is possible to estimate roughly the distance of lightning by counting the time between its flash and the sound of the thunder, for the flash appears almost instantaneously, while sound travels only about 1100 feet per second. Therefore an interval of five seconds would indicate that the lightning was about a mile away (since there are 5280 feet in a mile).

A *rainbow* occurs when we see the sun's

rays through rain which is falling over at one side. The water, like a prism, breaks the rays into the colors of a rainbow.

CLOUDS

The sky, nature's roof, forms a backdrop for the clouds. Cloud names are of Latin derivation and there are four basic types of them with nine combinations of these types.

Basic Forms or Families of Clouds

1. *Cirrus* are the "lock" or "curl" clouds and are the highest of all clouds (5 to 10 miles). They are always white, composed entirely of ice crystals, and are sometimes called "witch's broom" or "mare's tail." If the sky is bright blue above and the wind is from the north or northwest, they indicate fair weather for twenty-four to forty-eight hours. However, if the sky is gray-blue, and they are moving swiftly, especially from the west, they will likely turn to *cirrostratus* clouds and rain or snow may follow.

2. *Stratus* or "spread sheet" clouds are a horizontal overcast of "fog" high (about 2100 feet) in the air. They are always a shade of gray, sometimes being dark enough practically to conceal the sun or moon. Rain usually, but not always, follows.

3. *Cumulus* are the "heap" or "wool pack" clouds which are dark on the bottom and rise to a high, dome-shaped mass of white. They are the lowest of all, being only about a mile above the earth, and usually indicate fair weather, except that on a hot, muggy day, if massed near the horizon or becoming increasingly larger, they may indicate rain.

4. *Nimbus* clouds are the low-lying "umbrella" clouds. They are dark with ragged edges and no definite shapes and usually indicate steady rain or snow. *Scud* clouds are the small, ragged pieces frequently seen traveling rapidly across the sky below them.

Cirrus Clouds—U.S. Weather Bureau—R. H. Curtis

Stratus Clouds—R.A.F.

Cumulus Clouds—U.S. Weather Bureau—ANSCO.

Cirrostratus Clouds—U.S. Weather Bureau.

Cirrocumulus clouds—U.S. Weather Bureau
—R. H. Curtis.

Variations and Combinations

Alto means high: *fracto* means broken by the wind.

5. *Cirrostratus* clouds are whitish and veil-like and form a milky, tangled-web sheet over the sky (about 5½ miles up). They sometimes mean nothing in the morning, but, when they persist or appear in the afternoon, they are likely to be a sure forerunner of rain or snow within twenty-four hours, particularly if they started as *cirrus* clouds and are coming from the west.

6. *Cirrocumulus* clouds, or "mackerel" sky, have a rippled appearance somewhat like sand on the seashore and are about four miles up. They usually indicate fair weather.

7. *Altocumulus* are small, high, white clouds which may lie close together in rows or lines giving a dappled appearance to the sky. They are also called "sheep" clouds and usually indicate fair weather.

8. *Stratocumulus* are the dark-colored twist-shaped clouds (about 1 mile up) which ordinarily thin to *cumulus* or *fracto-cumulus* later on and seldom bring the rain they threaten. They are likely to be accompanied by high winds, especially in the fall.

Altocumulus Clouds—U.S. Weather Bureau

Stratocumulus Clouds—U. S. Weather Bureau.

Altostratus Clouds—U.S. Weather Bureau.

9. *Altostratus* are thin, gray, curtain-like clouds (about 3 miles up) and often show a bright patch where the sun or moon hides behind them. They are sometimes followed by squally weather.

10. *Fractonimbus* clouds follow nimbus and generally break up to disclose patches of blue sky indicating clearing weather.

11. *Fractostratus* clouds follow on the heels of *fractonimbus* and commonly clear into a blue sky with *cirrus* tufts scattered about.

12. *Fractocumulus* are *cumulus* clouds which have been broken into somewhat thinner clouds of irregular appearance. They usually indicate clear weather.

13. *Cumulonimbus* are the "thunderhead" clouds, which are most spectacular of all. They have dark bases and light tops and tower into the air like mountains. When they appear in the west, a thunderstorm will likely occur within a few hours.

Clouds moving in different directions at various levels foretell rain.

Fractocumulus Clouds—U.S. Weather Bureau.

PREDICTING THE WEATHER

Man has always been concerned with weather. Sailors, especially in the days of sailing vessels when no progress could be made without a wind to fill the sails and when severe storms meant possible shipwreck and death, grew expert at foretelling the weather.

Cumulonimbus Clouds—U.S. Weather Bureau.

The multitude of proverbs about the weather bear mute testimony to man's interest in it. Many of these sayings were, of course, mere superstitions, but others are of actual value, for they are based on factors which really "cause" the weather to be whatever it is. The following seem to be somewhat reliable. Can you explain why?

Red sky (or rainbow) in the morning, sailors take warning.
Red Sky (or rainbow) at night, sailor's delight.

Evening red and morning gray,
Sets the traveler on his way;
Evening gray and morning red,
Brings down rain upon his head.

A red sky has water in his eye.

(Raindrops are caused by the condensation of water around a grain of dust, and humidity allows the red rays of the sun to pass through and be more clearly seen.)

Rain before seven, clear before eleven.

(Rains seldom last longer than five hours anyway.)

When dew is on the grass
Rain will never come to pass.

When grass is dry at morning's light,
Look for rain before the night.

When the stars begin to huddle,
The earth will soon become a puddle.

(Mist forms over the sky and causes the smaller stars to cease to be visible. The brighter ones shine through dimly with a blur of light about them, each looking like an indistinct cluster of stars. This, therefore, indicates an increase in humidity.)

Sound traveling far and wide
A stormy day will betide.

The higher the clouds, the finer the weather.

Mackerel scales and mare's tails
Make lofty ships carry low sails.

When the wind's in the south, the rain's in his mouth.
When the smoke goes west, good weather is past.
When the smoke goes east, good weather is next.

The weather will clear when there is enough blue sky to make a pair of Dutchman's breeches.

A ring around the moon means rain;
The larger the ring, the sooner the rain.

(Cirrostratus clouds are around the moon and are the forerunners of unsettled weather.)

WIND DIRECTION

The direction and force of the wind are important in weather prediction. A wind from the east or southeast usually brings rain within twenty-four hours. If from the northeast, the rain will be chilly and the temperature cool. A wind from the west or northwest will probably be followed by fair weather. The stronger the wind, the more likely it is to bring the weather indicated.

TEMPERATURE

Temperature is measured by means of a thermometer (coming from Greek words meaning "heat" and "measure"). Thermometers are inexpensive and are indispensable to the amateur weather forecaster. If possible, place your thermometer facing north and out of the direct sunlight. A rising temperature accompanied by other favorable signs, indicates stormy weather. A thunderstorm never occurs when the temperature is below 60°, is possible between 60° and 70°, and extremely likely above 70° F. if other signs of rain are present.

A drop in temperature to 40° or 50° F. at the end of a calm, clear day in spring or fall when no wind or clouds are present indicates a probable frost before morning.

You can rather accurately determine the temperature if it is between 45° and 80° by catching a cricket and counting

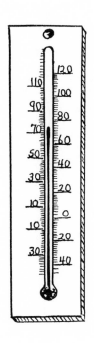

Thermometer.

INDICATIONS OF STORMY WEATHER

Wind lacking to moderate, and from southeast or east.
No dew at night.
Atmosphere muggy and sticky.
Temperature 70° F. or above, especially if rising.
Falling barometer.
Smoke not rising straight up in the air.
Crickets and other sounds seeming extra loud (the atmospheric conditions cause sounds to travel farther).
Rapidly moving cirrus clouds, especially from the west.
Dark clouds gathering on the horizon to the west.
Cumulus clouds in masses near the horizon.
Stratus, nimbus, altostratus, cirrostratus, or cumulo-nimbus clouds.
Clouds moving in different directions at various heights.
Clouds becoming more numerous and nearer the earth.
Red sunrise.
Gray or dull sunset.

INDICATIONS OF FAIR WEATHER

Gentle winds, especially from the west or northwest.
Heavy dew at night.
Fog in the morning.
Temperature below 70° F., especially if falling.
Steadily rising barometer.
Smoke rising straight up.
Spiders spinning new webs (if they continue spinning during a shower, it indicates clear weather soon).
Cloudless skies.
Cumulus clouds or stationary cirrus clouds.
Stratocumulus, altocumulus, cirrocumulus, fracto-nimbus, fractostratus or fractocumulus clouds.
Red sunset (sun goes down like a ball of fire).

the number of times he chirps for his rate increases in almost exact proportion to the rise in temperature. Count his chirps for 15 seconds, add 37 and you will know just about what the temperature is.

No one sign is infallible when predicting the weather; note all and take an average when making a prognosis.

WEATHER FLAGS

INDICATES FAIR WEATHER

INDICATES LOCAL SHOWERS
OR SNOW FLURRIES

INDICATES RAIN OR SNOW

INDICATES A COLD WAVE

THE BLACK TRIANGULAR TEMPERATURE
ABOVE ANY OTHER FLAG MEANS "WARMER";
BELOW, COLDER

IT'S FUN TO HOIST A WEATHER FLAG
INDICATING YOUR PREDICTION OF THE WEATHER.
WEATHER FLAGS CAN BE MADE OF BUNTING
AND SHOULD BE ABOUT 12" SQUARE.

MAKE AND FLY WEATHER FLAGS.

D A T E	T I M E	WIND DIR.	VEL.	CLOUDS	T E M P.	BARO METER	WEATHER SAYINGS OR OTHER SIGNS	PREDICTIONS	WHAT WAS IT ?

CHART FOR RECORDING WEATHER PREDICTIONS

ADDITIONAL READINGS

General

Des Grey, Arthur H.: *Camping.*

Fisher, Robert M.: *How To Know and Predict the Weather.* Harper and Brothers, Revised, 1958, 172 pp.

Kesting, Ted: *The Outdoor Encyclopedia.*

Laird, Charles and Ruth: *Weathercasting. A Handbook of Amateur Meteorology.* Prentice-Hall, Inc.; 1955, 163 pp., $3.95.

Lehr, Paul E., Burnett, R. Will, and Zim, Herbert S.: *Weather.* Golden Books, 1957, 160 pp., $1.00.

Longstreth, T. M.: *Understanding the Weather.* The Macmillan Co., 1953, 118 pp., $2.50.

O'Brien, James E.: *Something about the Weather.* Western Pa., Section of ACA. 200 Ross St., Pittsburg 19, Pa., 15¢. (helpful in setting up a weather station).

Rubin, Louis D.: *Cloud Charts.* The author, Box 8615, Richmond 25, Va., 50¢ and 25¢. (35 color photographs of clouds and how they fortell the weather)

Rubin, Louis D.: *How To Forecast the Weather.* (address as above)

Schneider, Herman, and Bendick, J.: *Everyday Weather and How It Works.* McGraw-Hill Book Co., 1951, $3.00.

Sloane, Eric.: *How You Can Forecast the Weather.* Fawcett Publishing Co., 1957, 150 pp., 35¢.

Spilhaus, A.: *Weathercraft.* The Viking Press, 1951, 64 pp., $2.00.

Tannehill, Ivan Ray: *All about the Weather.* Random House Inc., 1953, 148 pp., $1.95.

Weather. Boy Scouts #3816, 1952, 25¢.

West, James E., and Hillcourt, William: *Scout Field Book.*

Williams, Lou: *Weather Handbook.* Girl Scouts #19-503, 62 pp., 25¢.

MAGAZINE ARTICLES

Staples, Frank A.: *Make a Weather Station for Home—Camp—Playground,* Recreation, March, 1954.

The following are available from Superintendent of Documents, U.S. Government Printing Office, Washington 25, D.C.

The Aneroid Barometer. 15¢.

Cloud Code Chart. 10¢.

Instructions for Climatological Observers, (Circular B). 55¢.

Instruments Used in Weather Observing. 5¢.

Manual of Cloud Forms and Codes for States of the Sky, (Circular S). 30¢.

Weather Forecasting. 25¢.

The American Meteorological Society, 45 Beacon Street, Boston 8, Mass., has a number of free publications concerning the weather.

20

Getting About in the Out-of-Doors

Afoot and light-hearted, I take to the open road,
Healthy, free, the world before me,
The long brown path before me, leading wherever I choose.
                                —WALT WHITMAN*

IF YOU are planning to travel much in the out-of-doors, you will need to know how to use a compass. There are many types available to suit every taste and need. A compass is sometimes located in the end of a waterproof match box or fitted with a leather strap to be worn like a wrist watch. Commoner models are designed to be kept in the pocket and are fitted with a ring for attaching them by a chain or strap to the clothing so they won't be lost or misplaced. Some compasses are enclosed in a metal case like a hunting watch to keep moisture from entering. Moisture inside causes the needle to catch or bind and necessitates drying the compass out with *gentle* heat before it will work again.

The Parts of the Compass

The *compass housing* or case has a circular dial or *compass card* which is divided into *quadrants* (or fourths) designated by the abbreviations for the *cardinal points,* N (North), E (East), S (South), and W (West). These quadrants are likewise divided into fourths as N, NNE, NE, ENE, E, ESE, and so on. NNE designates a point lying midway between North and North East; NE is midway between North and East; ENE is midway between North East and East, and so forth.

* From *Leaves of Grass.* Permission by Doubleday and Co., Inc.

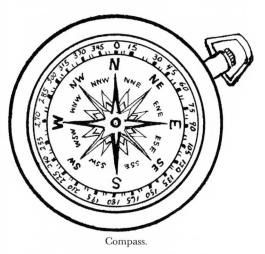

Compass.

the compass card. The needle is now pointing North. Any metal near your compass, such as a metal belt buckle, knife blade, hatchet, outboard motor, or metal bridge, will distract the needle and cause it to read inaccurately.

Inexpensive models popular for camp use are the various Silva compasses, most of which feature the usual compass housing mounted on a movable transparent base marked off in inches to use when measuring distances on a map and marked with a *Direction of Travel Arrow.* To *take a bearing* or *azimuth* (degree reading) on an object, orient your compass as above and turn the moveable base until the direction arrow points directly toward the object and read off the degrees where the arrow crosses the compass card. With a compass which has no such base, orient it as usual and hold a thin object such as a twig, the edge of a card or a piece of string across the housing pointed directly toward the object, and read off the degrees on the compass card where the card crosses it.

For convenience, it is now more common to mark a compass card with the 360 degrees of a circle, starting with North at the top at 0° or 360° and rotating clockwise with E(ast) at 90°, S(outh) at 180°, and W(est) at 270°.

The magnetic needle is freely suspended above the compass card so that its magnetized end (designated by red or blue color or by an "N") will always turn to point toward magnetic North regardless of how the compass faces. There is, however, another type of compass, the *floating dial compass,* which acts in the reverse fashion with the needle fixed and the compass card moving beneath it to indicate the direction; this type is larger and bulkier and consequently not so well suited to ordinary camping use.

Your compass may have an adjustable stem which may be tightened to hold the needle motionless when not in use and thus prevent injuring it by jostling about. If this is the case, you must loosen the stem to allow the needle to swing freely when you want to use it; tighten it again when you are through with it.

Using a Compass

You must first *orient* your compass. To do this, hold it level about waist high so that the needle swings freely and turn it until N on the needle rests along N on

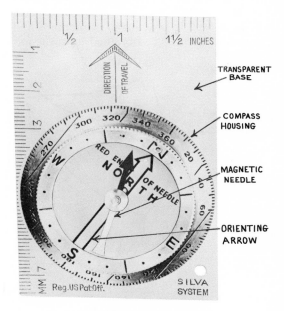

A Silva Compass.
(Courtesy of Silva, Inc., Laporte, Ind.)

If you want to travel in a given direction such as one indicated on a map, orient your compass as before, hold the card or point the *direction needle* in the desired direction as indicated on the compass card and pick out a readily distinguishable object such as a rock or tree directly in line with it. Then put your compass away and start moving toward the chosen landmark. When you reach it, take a new bearing, pick out another landmark and proceed as before, repeating the process as you reach each new landmark.

A simple game to test your ability to read and follow directions is called the "Silver Dollar Game." To play it, place a can lid or other small object on the ground. Pick a compass bearing of less than 120° and walk 100 feet in that direction; then add 120° to the original bearing and again walk 100 feet; for the third time, add 120° and walk another 100 feet. Place a marker where you land; if your readings and measurings have been accurate, you will have walked around an equilateral triangle and should be back exactly where you started. Many other games and activities which give fun as well as practice in using maps and compasses may be obtained from the following sources: Silva, Inc., La Porte, Indiana; The National Park Service, U.S. Dept. of the Interior, Washington 25, D.C.

True North and Magnetic North

Over most of the United States, a compass needle does not point to *True North* but instead to *Magnetic North,* which is a region about 1400 miles south of the North Pole along the northern edge of Canada. The only place where *True North* and *Magnetic North* coincide and the needle therefore actually points to *True North* is along a wavering, wandering line, beginning approximately at Mackinac Island in Lake Michigan and passing diagonally downward across the United States just a little east of Florida. This is called the *Zero* or *Agonic Line.* In regions west of this line, as indicated on the map, the needle points increasingly east of North, while in regions east, it points west of North. The angle between *True North* and the direction in which the needle points is called *declination* and the angle increases as we go farther from the *Agonic Line,* to as much as 20 degrees in the extreme Northeastern and Northwestern sections of the country. The compass declination

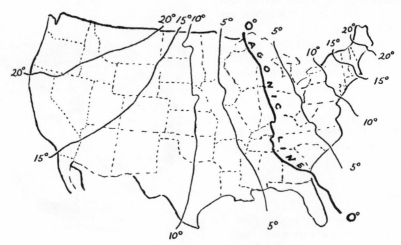

The Agonic Line and Compass Declination.

of a region is usually indicated on a map by including two arrows, one pointing to *Magnetic North,* the other to *True North.* In camp trail mapping, you can ordinarily ignore the difference, using *Magnetic North* as you read it on your compass, and indicating on your map that you have done so.

MAPS

A map is a bird's eye view of an area as you would see it from the air and there are many kinds, ranging from the complicated and detailed road maps of the leading oil companies, to rough, homemade sketch maps to guide a person through relatively rough and unsettled country.

It is easy to understand how early peoples, even before they had any system of writing, made crude maps, for, in the main, they were migratory hunters who moved on to a new location when they had exhausted the available supply of food in the area. Indians, particularly the Aztecs of Mexico, made such rough maps.

The most complete maps are those published by the Topographic Division of the United States Geological Survey; they are inexpensive and are excellent for all who travel on foot, on horseback or by canoe, for they give a graphic picture of what will be seen on a specified trip. They tell us where the hills are and how steep and high they are. They show streams and it is possible to determine the direction of their flow quickly since water always flows from small tributaries into larger main bodies of water; in fact, by reading the changes in elevation as the steam progresses, we can even estimate how swiftly the water will be flowing. They show canoe routes and where it will be necessary to portage; marshlands are indicated so that one can avoid camping near them and their mosquito inhabitants. Timber areas and every

valley and lake, as well as many man-made "improvements" as houses and bridges are depicted. Maps of an area are often available at local resources; if not, write to the United States Geological Survey, Department of Interior, Washington 25, D.C. (If west of the Mississippi, address your request to Geological Survey, Federal Center, Denver 15, Colorado.) Ask for a free "Index to Topographic Maps" of the state in which the area is located. This will show the various regional maps available so that you can select the one you want and send the small sum necessary (usually about 30 cents) to purchase it. Regional maps come on sheets approximately 30 by 38 inches.

The Coast and Geodetic Survey* supplies similar maps for water travel, each showing about forty miles of the seacoast. Some of the larger inland bodies of water such as the Ohio and Mississippi Rivers have also been mapped.

Interesting maps are usually available from National Parks† and National Forests‡ and sometimes from State Parks. State Highway Departments often have detailed country maps. Other sources of hiking maps are given below.§

Learning to Read a Map

A map usually contains a *legend* or summary of information in the lower right hand corner which includes such items as the following:
1. *Name or title* of the region depicted.
2. *Name of the person or firm* who made

* United States Coast and Geodetic Survey, Washington 25, D.C.
† National Park Service, U.S. Dept. of the Interior, Washington 25, D.C.
‡ Forest Service, U.S. Dept. of Agriculture, Washington 25, D.C.
§ For hiking trails, write to the Appalachian Trail Conference, 1916 Sunderland Place, N.W., Washington 6, D.C. or the Pacific Trail Conference, Pasadena, California. For Canadian Canoe routes and waterworks, write Canadian National Railways, General Tourist Agent, Montreal.

the map and *date* made. (This is important, particularly in well-settled regions, where construction may entirely change the appearance of a locality within a few years.)

3. *Compass direction* (Maps are ordinarily laid out with North at the top, but the particular contour shown, or the shape of the area sometimes makes it more convenient to do otherwise; there will usually be two lines, one indicating *True North* and the other *Magnetic North.*)

4. *A scale of distances* (The usual scale ranges from ½ mile to the inch to 20 miles to the inch, depending on the map. It may be given by (1) words and figures, as 1 inch = 24,000 feet; (2) in the form of a ratio, as 1:24,000; or (3) as a fraction, 1/24,000. For making your own camp trail map, a ratio of 200 to 1000 feet to the inch is satisfactory. The scale is usually given also as a graphical scale or measuring bar; this is convenient, for you can quickly transfer the scale to a scrap of paper and lay it on the map to estimate distances between points.)

5. *A key* to the meaning of the various symbols used on the map.

Following a Map

When you want to reach a certain destination on a map, you must first *orient* the map or place it so that N on the map coincides with N as indicated by your compass. To do this, lay the map flat on a table or the ground; place your compass above it; orient the compass and then turn the map until the arrow and line indicating *Magnetic North* on the map lies parallel with N on your compass. Find your present location on the map and, translating the symbols given, plan the best route to your proposed destination, giving due consideration to any impassable or undesirable barriers that lie along the way. Estimate directions and distances of the path you have chosen and indicate them on the map or on a separate piece of paper. When you are

ready to set out, place your *Direction of Travel Arrow* at the degree reading of the first leg of your trip, stand squarely facing along it and pick out a distinct landmark directly ahead and start toward it; then repeat the process as described before.

If your chosen route calls for travelling a certain distance in one direction, then a distance in another and so on, you will have to learn to estimate distances as will be explained later on, or you will have to carry a *pedometer*. This is a small instrument, like a watch in appearance, which, when freely suspended as from your belt, will be jostled at each step and so register the distance you travel. It is adjustable so that the person wearing it can "set" if for the length of his step and thus get an accurate reading. As you proceed, check your progress by the landmarks you pass such as hills, fire towers, telephone lines, rivers, and so forth with the map. Practice will quickly increase your skill at finding your way by use of map and compass.

Making a Map

A person who draws or makes maps is known as a *cartographer;* campers often enjoy becoming amateur *cartographers.* Before starting, it is wise to make a brief study of the principles of map making; get several types of maps and study them carefully. Map study is a fascinating hobby which many enjoy.

ROUGH-SKETCHING YOUR MAP. When making a map, it is more interesting to travel cross-country, choosing a route not more than a mile or two in length which provides a variety of things to show along the way. Take a compass, a pencil and notebook, or a pencil and a few sheets of paper tacked onto a piece of thin board, or held on a clip board, to make a rough sketch map as you hike over the route. Quadrille or cross-section paper is convenient, since each square could represent a certain number of feet or strides. You should take ample notes as you go along to help you convert your rough trail map into an accurate and attractive finished product when you return to headquarters.

The usual way to measure distances for a trail map is by counting strides, which, when you know the length of your average stride, can be easily converted into feet or yards.

A *step* and a *pace* are the same thing, and a *stride* consists of two steps. In counting strides, then, you need count only each alternate step as each time your left foot hits the ground.

To determine the length of your stride, use a string exactly twenty or twenty-five feet long to lay off a distance of 100 yards. Then, starting with your toe at the starting line, count each one of your strides as you walk along in the normal pace for a cross-country hike; try it several times and take the average. Now divide 3600 (the number of inches in the 100 yards) by the number of strides to obtain the number of inches you cover at a stride. Some advocate cultivating a step of exactly a yard to simplify arithmetical calculations but such a pace proves unnatural and fatiguing for many and so scarcely seems worth the effort.

To avoid having to count in high numbers, start with a counted number of pebbles and throw one away each twenty to fifty strides so you need count only the remainder to find the number of strides you took. Another way to estimate distances is by the time elapsed, having previously determined how long it takes you to cover a mile or half-mile at average pace.

When estimating distances, you must remember to allow for the fact that your step is shortened when going up or down hill, particularly if the hill is steep.

When you are ready to rough draft your map, mark your starting point on the paper; pick out an object some distance away on your path; take a compass bearing on it and start out, counting your strides as you go. If you see features

or landmarks you want to include along the way, jot them down on your sketch map, making any notes you think will be helpful later on. When you reach the object sighted, pick out another; take the new compass bearing and proceed as before.

When you want to show an object off at the side, such as the old deserted house, C, take a compass bearing some distance from it, at A; count strides to B, and take another bearing. By projecting the two

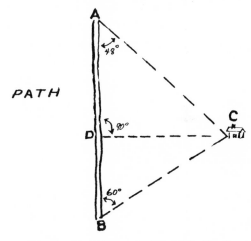

Locating an Object at the Side of the Road.

angles on the map and properly plotting distance AB to scale, you can locate the old house at C, where the lines intersect. If you want to know how far back from the path the old house sits, you need only measure perpendicular distance, CD, on the map and translate it by scale.

MAP SYMBOLS.   Certain symbols are in general use on maps and make it possible for one person to understand maps made by others. These symbols are of four types:

1. *Culture*, or the works of man, such as bridges, houses, dams, and so forth, shown in black.

2. *Relief*, or relative elevations and depressions above or below sea level, (hills and valleys) are drawn in brown. Hills are indicated by *contour lines*, explained in

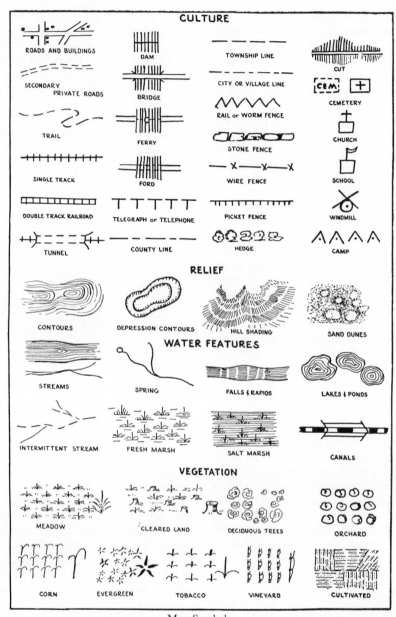

Map Symbols.

the legend in the lower right hand corner of the map. All points on a single contour line are the same elevation or height above sea level, usually indicated by a number printed along the line, each line indicating a rise or fall of a certain number of feet (from 5 to 250 feet, depending on the map). To estimate the height of a hill, count the number of contour lines to the top and multiply by the number of feet represented by the distance between each two lines. When contour lines are widely spaced, they indicate a gradual slope; when close together, a steep one; lines falling practically on top of each other indicate a cliff or mountainside.

Widely spread contour lines over the countryside signify that the whole region is rolling. It may help you get a better concept of how the land would actually appear if you think of the lines as left by water which once covered the hill and which has completely receded.

3. *Water features,* such as lakes or rivers, are drawn in blue.

4. *Vegetation,* such as woods and crops, are shown in black, blue, or green.

For convenience, maps are often drawn entirely in black instead of colors. Common maps symbols are simple and usually

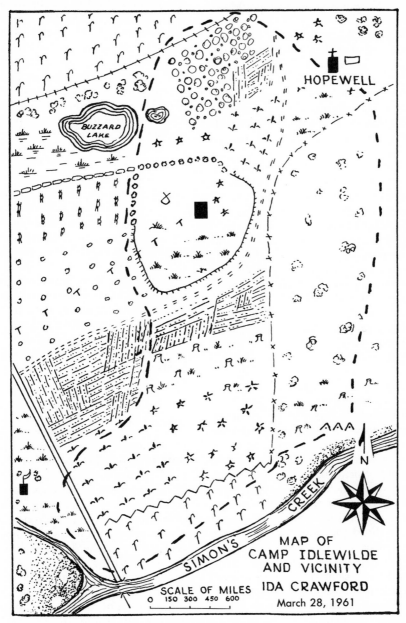

A Trail Map. (Scale in Feet.)

roughly resemble what they depict. You may have to invent symbols for unusual objects; make them bear likeness to what they represent and explain them in your legend. Just for practice, start in the lower right corner and take an imaginary trip around the path indicated in Camp Idlewilde. Write out what you would see along the way.

MAKING THE MAP. When you have completed your rough sketch map, translate it to your completed trail map as soon as possible while the details are still fresh in your memory. Use a ruler, compass and protractor to insure accuracy and don't worry if the point at which you finish on the map fails to exactly coincide with the point from which you started; such a deviation is common with the crude instruments and measurements used and is called the *error of closure*. Keep your symbols small. Use black India ink, supplementing it with colors if you wish.

Keep the purpose of your map in mind. If it is intended for others to follow, too many details will only be confusing. If it is to be principally a decorative wall map, make it a gaily colored "romance" or picture map. You can give the map a parchment-like appearance by daubing it lightly with a bit of linseed oil or painting it with yellow shellac. If your map is to see hard use on the trail, you will want to make it especially durable. Fold it to a convenient size for carrying, then open it flat and cut it in pieces along the creases. Glue the pieces to each other and in proper sequence onto a piece of unbleached muslin or other strong cloth. Spray it all over on both sides with clear shellac or make a case for the folded map of clear plastic sheets, sewing or cementing them shut along three sides. Fold the map with the area of current interest uppermost, slip it into the case and seal the fourth side with Scotch or Mystic tape. You can now read the map right through the transparent cover and can take it out and refold it to a new area as needed.

Making a Relief Map

A *papier-mâché* relief map for use in camp can be quite decorative and provides an even more realistic picture of the area in question. Start with a large piece of thin board, plywood, or stiff cardboard and lay off the area to scale, indicating the locations of rivers, woods, houses, and other things you want to show. Tear up a quantity of old newspapers or paper towels in small scraps and soak them for several hours in hot water. Knead and manipulate them until they become a "gooey" mixture; press as much water out of them as possible; and mix in a quantity of library paste. Now cover the base with this mixture, building it up to the proper height and contour for hills, and scooping it out for rivers, valleys or other depressed areas. When dry, paint it and draw in details in the proper colors using tempera paint or India and colored inks. Add trees made of twigs and bits of sponge; "grass" can be made of sawdust dyed green and placed on a thin layer of glue. Sand sprinkled over glue makes good bare ground and buildings may be fashioned from twigs or cardboard and finished in appropriate colors. Making a model of your campsite is a good project and will keep your campers busy and happy for hours.

Orienteering

Orienteering is a sport which originated in Sweden several years ago and provides fun and valuable experience in using map and compass for the over 40,000 Swedish boys and girls who compete annually for proficiency pins. It is also currently attaining a much deserved popularity in the United States. There are many forms of it to appeal to everyone from the youngest beginner to rugged experts. They compete for best time over rugged terrain, using a compass, a topographic map and their good common sense and training to pick the best and quickest way to cover the course. They check in at designated stations along the way. Full details concerning games, instructive materials, and films may· be obtained by writing Silva, Inc., LaPorte, Indiana.

FINDING YOUR WAY WITHOUT A COMPASS

Those experienced in woods travel seldom become lost for they have learned many tricks of the trade to help themselves along. One of the most important requirements is to become observant and to mentally note surroundings as you proceed, occasionally looking back over your shoulder to see how things will appear as you approach them on your return trip; you must learn to observe keenly. When beginning, you will usually want to take careful, written notes but, as you gain experience, you may largely dispense with this as you store the information in your mind.

An essential piece of equipment for travel in any strange surroundings is your compass; don't start out without it. But remember that your compass is of no use to you *after* you are lost for you can't know what direction to take to return if you don't know from what direction you came. You must use it as you go out, then reverse directions to return.

There is no Sixth Sense of Direction

Most people become confused when trying to retrace their way and maintain a straight course without a compass and no well-marked trails or with several trails, each looking equally inviting and "right." The harder you look, the more confused you become, for your intense scrutiny now causes you to see details you didn't even notice in your casual glance as you first came along.

Many seasoned explorers and wilder-

ness guides claim to have developed a sixth sense of direction which instinctively tells them how to go. Rutstrum* refutes this by describing how a certain Southern university proved that none of a goodly sample of explorers, guides, seamen and others could actually keep on a straight course without the use of their eyes. When blindfolded they, without exception, followed a more or less circular course, some circling to the right, others to the left, with none able to walk directly to the target as he had claimed. Some attributed this circling tendency to the fact that nearly everyone has one leg slightly shorter than the other, which would naturally cause him to circle toward the shorter leg, but the same circling persisted when they swam, drove a car, or directed the driving of a car from the back seat. Thus it appears that their ability to find their way probably depends on their unconsciously noting such things as the direction of the sun and the lay of the land as they move along.

This inability to tell directions without using your eyes shows up in the old game in which a blindfolded person is turned about and then told to walk up to and "pin the tail on the donkey," which he previously saw up in front of him. The poor donkey usually ends up with his tail fastened to most unlikely parts of his anatomy.

Woodsmen have long observed this tendency of a person lost in the woods to circle about for days, gradually coming back to his approximate starting point. To avoid this, they advise that, after choosing the direction in which you want to go, you pick out two trees or other landmarks, walk straight toward them, and pick out another in line with them before you reach the first so that you always have three objects in line ahead of you in the chosen direction.

* Rutstrum, Calvin: *Way of the Wilderness*, The Burgess Publishing Company, Revised, 1952, pages 5–6.

If Lost in the Woods

To prevent being separated, hiking groups sometimes have at least the leader equipped with a whistle to call back any strays. If you should inadvertently stray from your group while wandering in the woods, don't get panicky but stop and calmly think the situation over. Remember there is probably no real emergency, so use your head and save your legs. Climb a high hill or tree and try to recognize landmarks to orient yourself again. If that doesn't help, follow a creek or river downstream, or a telephone or electric light line and you will surely come to human habitation before long. Look for smoke for it will indicate that there is someone nearby. Go downhill rather than uphill. If it is getting dark don't wander around but settle down as comfortably as possible to wait for morning. If you have a compass, knife, matches, and a flashlight along, you can undoubtedly spend several days without coming to any real harm. If you don't have food and water, your previous training should enable you to purify water and get emergency food from nature. It is often advisable to calmly sit down and wait for the group to hunt you out, signalling as described later on, to speed your rescuers on their way. If you decide to move on, mark your campsite conspicuously and leave a note to tell them in what direction you've gone.

Danger or Distress Signals

Three of anything has been long and widely known as a signal of danger or distress. Three rocks placed on top of each other, three clumps of grass, three blazes on trees, three smudge fires, three steamboat whistles, or three gunshots are examples. Note that the Morse code applies this principle in its call for help, SOS, which consists of three dots, three dashes, and three dots.

Make a *smudge* fire as a smoke signal for help by placing three fires just far enough apart to be distinguishable at a distance. Build a good fire and get it going well. Then pile noninflammable materials such as green or rotten wood or wet leaves on it to make it "smudge" or smoke. Friends in camp or the ever-watchful fire warden in his fire tower will soon see the signal and send help. Never give a distress signal just for fun, lest it be ignored in time of real need like the plea of the little boy who cried "wolf" too often.

For those who lack a compass, old Mother Nature gives directions if we can but understand her language.

Using Your Watch as a Compass

We know that, roughly speaking, the sun rises in the East and sets in the West, but we can use a watch and the sun to tell directions even more accurately. Stand with your left shoulder toward the sun and hold your watch flat in your palm. Point the hour hand directly toward the sun. South is now located halfway between the hour hand and 12 o'clock. Use the shortest distance, clockwise in the morning and counterclockwise in the afternoon. If you are on Daylight Saving Time, south will be located halfway between the hand and one o'clock. On a cloudy day when the sun isn't evident, stand a knife blade or match up along the side of the watch and move them

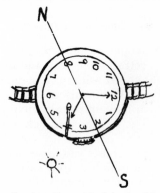

Finding South at Four o'clock in the Afternoon.

about until the shadow of the match falls directly along the hour hand; the hour hand is now pointed directly at the sun and you can proceed as before. Incidentally, you can set your watch fairly accurately by using a compass and reversing this process.

Telling Directions by the Stars

The stars are our oldest and most faithful guides to direction. When ancient literature speaks of "being guided by a star," it doubtless refers to the *North Star,* which is an even more accurate guide to direction than a compass, for it never varies more than one degree from True North no matter where you are in the United States.

To locate the North Star, find the *Big Dipper* and *Little Dipper* in the sky. Forming the front edge of the Big Dipper are two stars known as the *Pointers* because they point directly to the North Star (also called the *Pole Star* or *Polaris*) in the tip of the Little Dipper's handle. The North Star is always due north and the Little Dipper makes a complete circle about it every twenty-four hours while the Big Dipper circles around the Little Dipper in the same length of time. The bowls of the two Dippers face so that they always seem to be pouring into each other.

There are many interesting myths about the stars. One version tells us that many years ago a tribe of Indians was living happily in the midst of good hunting and plenty until an extremely large mother bear and her cub came to the vicinity and frightened away all the small game. This brought famine to the Indians and they decided to send out their best hunters to kill the bears. After being hotly pursued through many miles of wilderness, the bears finally fled to the top of a tall mountain, where the mother bear leaped in desperation into the sky and was followed by her cub. The hunters began to shoot, and finally pierced the cub's tail with an arrow, fastening it in the northern sky. This arrow is the North Star. The cub began running around its tail, and has continued to do so ever since, making one complete circuit each day. The mother bear's wounds show as the seven stars of the Big Dipper, and she remains to this day in the sky, run-

Finding the North Star.

ning around her cub and likewise making one complete circuit a day. The Indians called the Big Dipper the Big Bear (Ursa Major) and the Little Dipper the Little Bear (Ursa Minor).

The Moss on Trees

Everyone has no doubt heard that moss grows on the north side of a tree, but we must not take the saying too literally. This sign does have a grain of truth in it, but, to rely on it, we must first be sure not to mistake the gray-green lichen commonly found growing on rocks and trees for true moss.

We must also learn to select the trees we inspect, for we can certainly not rely on every tree. Moss grows on any side of a tree where conditions are favorable, that is, where the tree holds moisture. Therefore, we must not depend on trees that are leaning or broken over or those with unusually rough spots on their bark. We must consider only straight trees with a fairly smooth bark and not located in a heavily wooded section where they are shaded on all sides. The trees we examine must be normal ones where the moss tends to grow on the north side because the sun's rays reach it there for only a short time each day. Still we must not be satisfied until we have inspected several, taking the average and being careful not to be influenced by the bottoms of the trunks, where the moss grows more or less all around the tree.

N ᴛᴏ NE

Annual rings are usually wider and bark is thicker on the North side of a tree.

Tree Growth

A tree usually grows thickest and most luxuriantly on the south or sunny side and, in general, the annual growth rings on a stump are wider and the bark

thicker on the north or northeast side, but here again we must take the average of several stumps.

The Tips of Pines

The tip-top branches of pines, hemlocks and spruces ordinarily point slightly southeast (toward the rising sun), but this is not necessarily true when they grow in deep valleys or on windswept hill tops where strong winds may distort them. No one sign of nature is infallible, but the average of a number of them is reasonably reliable.

MEASURING INACCESSIBLE DISTANCES

Measuring the Height of a Tree or Cliff

Mark your own height prominently on a tree or cliff or have a friend whose height you know stand against it. If you have a ruler, hold it upright at arms length in front of you with the bottom at eye level and step back away from the tree until ½ inch on the ruler covers the distance from the ground to the mark or the top of your friend's head on the tree as you sight across it with one eye closed. Sight the top of the tree across the ruler, note the number of half inches on the ruler and multiply them by your own height or that of your friend. If you do not have a ruler, you can use a straight stick, noting the height on the tree with

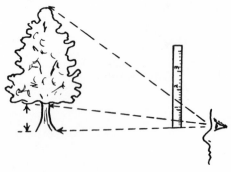

Measuring the Height of a Tree.

your thumb; locating the top of the tree on the stick; finding the number of times the height of the mark goes into it and multiplying by your own or your friend's height as before.

An Indian method, not quite so accurate, but giving as exact a figure as is usually needed is to walk away from the object you want to measure until you can just see the top of it as you look through your legs while bent over with your hands on your ankles. The height of the object, XY, is, roughly, the same distance as YZ.

Indian Method of Measuring Heights.

Measuring the Width of an Object

To measure the width of an object such as a river or gorge, select a landmark easily distinguishable on the other side, such as tree, Z, and mark spot X at a 90-degree angle directly opposite it. Now walk down the river bank until you reach a compass bearing of 45 degrees with the tree and mark spot Y. You have now outlined an isosceles triangle with XY equal to XZ and can determine the width of the river by measuring XY.

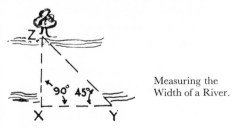

Measuring the Width of a River.

Measuring Depth

You can determine the approximate depth of a river, lake or chasm by drop-ping a rock from just above the water's surface and timing it until it hits bottom. Multiply the square of the number of seconds that elapse by 16, and the result is the approximate depth in feet.

Learning to Estimate Measurements

Many boys and girls are notoriously poor at judging distances and heights, probably owing more to lack of practice than to any innate inability to do so. It is handy to be able to make such estimates, and the best way to acquire skill is by estimating simple things you can actually weigh or measure to check on your accuracy. Practice should give you ability to judge within 10 per cent of the correct answers most of the time.

In judging long distances, it sometimes helps to divide them mentally into short, well-known distances and then count the number of shorter distances in the long one. For instance, use a mental image of a yardstick to estimate the number of "yards" in an unknown distance.

In making rough estimates, it is useful to know some of your own measurements such as:

1. The length of your ordinary hiking pace.

2. The length of your foot in the type of shoe you ordinarily wear.

3. Your exact height and the distance from finger tip to finger tip with both arms outstretched. (These distances are usually approximately the same, so that you can use one for measuring vertical heights, the other for horizontal ones.)

4. A finger joint that is exactly an inch long.

TRAILS AND SIGNALS

Trails are as old as mankind, for it is impossible for any creature to go through wooded territory without leaving some trace. Such obscure signs as a track in the mud or sand, a branch accidentally broken off, or a vine carelessly torn by the foot, though easily overlooked by the tenderfoot, are quite obvious to one skilled and practiced in following trails.

The first trails were made by the big game animals when going to and from their favorite feeding grounds, water holes or salt licks. The Indians, then pioneer trappers and explorers on foot or on pack horse, and, finally, covered wagons and stagecoaches followed these same trails making them ever wider and easier to follow. We still find many of them preserved in the routes of our railroads and highways.

Original paths seldom passed through valleys but rather kept to the ridges in hilly or mountainous country where there were few streams to ford and the traveler could command a wide view of the surrounding countryside and thus protect himself from a surprise ambush.

Blazes

The favorite pioneer method of marking a trail through the wilderness was by *blazing* or periodically using an axe or sheath knife to take a chip out of a tree thus exposing the white surface which was easily apparent from some distance.

There were several ways to blaze trails. One, called the *line blaze,* faced the traveler so that, as he came to one blaze, the next was apparent ahead of him. An extraordinarily long slash indicated a change in direction. The line blaze was used when the "blazer" wanted others to be able to follow him. If he wanted to be able to retrace his path without having others follow him, he merely reversed the process, making the blazes on the far sides of the trees as he went along. This was known as a *blind trail.*

Another form is seen in the *lop sticks* of the Northland, where the lower branches of tall, straight trees are cut away, leaving peculiar, top heavy specimens which stand out at great distances. Blazes are still used in certain sparsely settled regions.

When our forefathers came to America there were so many trees that they were regarded as a nuisance and the main thought was to get rid of them as quickly and completely as possible. Of course it would be unthinkable to use these blazes today in regions near organized camping, for trees are far too precious to be mutilated in this way. We now know that any wounds in the bark of a tree are just as injurious as cuts or breaks in our own skin, for they make openings for parasites and disease to initiate their damaging, perhaps even fatal attacks on the trees.

Modern Methods of Laying Trails

BRUSH BLAZES.   The brush blaze was a favorite Indian way of trail marking. It consisted of breaking a branch of a shrub every hundred yards or so, leaving it still attached but with the lighter, under sides of its leaves exposed to attract attention. The branch was left pointing in the direction to be taken. An abrupt change in direction was indicated by breaking the branch completely off and laying it so that its butt end pointed in the new direction, perhaps supporting the butt in the fork of a crotched stick to make it still more evident.

It is still permissible to use this method in regions where the underbrush is heavy and a few broken branches will never be missed but this is also unlikely to be true near the average organized camp.

GRASS.   In prairie regions, where fairly long grass is abundant, wisps of grass can be used as a cord to tie other clumps of grass together, leaving the heads straight up if the trail lies straight ahead, and inclining them in the correct direction if a change is to be made.

ROCKS.   Along the seashore or in bare regions, use rocks to mark a trail. A small rock on top of a large one indicates "this is the trail"; a smaller rock placed at one side of these two means turn in the direction of the smaller rock. Pebbles are sometimes placed in the form of a V to show direction.

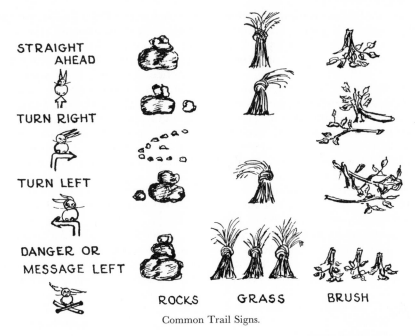

STRAIGHT
AHEAD

TURN RIGHT

TURN LEFT

DANGER OR
MESSAGE LEFT

ROCKS   GRASS   BRUSH

Common Trail Signs.

SIGNALING

OTHER WAYS. Paper, weighted down with stones, is sometimes used, but in order not to mar nature's beauty, those following the trail should be instructed to gather them as they come along. Direction arrows may be made on bare ground or chalk marks may be made on trees to mark a temporary trail. Paint may be used for a more permanent marking.

It is fun to have a progressive supper hike with the trail blazers and cooks going ahead to lay the trail while the rest of the group follows later to find first course, main dish, dessert and finally the rendezvous for program. Use codes or the above methods of laying a trail as you wish or prepare cards, giving compass directions and distances which the group, best kept small, must follow accurately to find their suppers. Plan alternate routes and divide the group if there are many members, having them converge at a common meeting place at the end if desired.

The Morse Code

The most universally used and understood code is the International Morse Code which uses dots and dashes to spell out messages. It may be adapted to many

Alphabet

A	.-	N	-.
B	-...	O	---
C	-.-.	P	.--.
D	-..	Q	--.-
E	.	R	.-.
F	..-.	S	...
G	--.	T	-
H	....	U	..-
I	..	V	...-
J	.---	W	.--
K	-.-	X	-..-
L	.-..	Y	-.--
M	--	Z	--..

Numerals

1	.----	6	-....
2	..---	7	--...
3	...--	8	---..
4	....-	9	----.
5	.....	0	-----

International Morse Code.

means of communication giving the dot by a short (held while you count "one") flash or sound and the dash by a long one (held while you count "one, two, three").

Wireless telegraphy uses this system, and you may also send messages with a lantern, flashlight, automobile horn, flags, torch, whistle, drum, or a mirror used to reflect the sun's rays. When using a smudge fire for transmitting smoke signals in Morse code, two persons hold a blanket above the fire, removing it periodically to allow large billows of smoke to rise and spell out the message. At night, you can signal by holding a blanket in front of your blazing campfire, tucking up the edge of it to reveal the fire, then letting the edge drop to conceal it.

Pause and count three to indicate the end of a letter; count five at the end of a word, and pause still longer for the end of a sentence. Work for accuracy and clearness rather than speed. When first

practicing receiving the Morse code, it is best to use two persons, one to call out the dots and dashes as they come in, the other to write it down for later decoding. Practice signaling from short distances at first; then increase the distance until you are finally so far away that you need field glasses to read the message. It's not only fun to do but may save steps or help in an emergency when you want to get a message to a group at some distance away.

Written Codes

It is fairly simple to work out a secret code for a cabin or group of campers to use in writing messages which cannot be interpreted by others. Here are three examples of codes; use your ingenuity to make up your own original one.

You can write an invisible note to a friend, using pure lemon juice. The paper is apparently blank and only he knows how to bring it out by pressing over it briefly with a warm iron.

	1	2	3	1	2	3	1	2	3	1	2	3	1	2	3
Message	S	H	A	L	L	W	E	S	L	E	E	P	O	U	T
Code	T	J	D	M	N	Z	F	U	O	F	G	S	P	W	W

Add one, two or three letters in sequence as indicated to each letter of the real message.

	−1	+1	−1	+1	−1	+1	−1	+1	−1	+1	−1	+1	−1
Message	W	I	L	L	W	E	H	I	K	E	O	U	T
Code	V	J	K	M	V	F	G	J	J	F	N	V	S

Alternately subtract one letter, then add one, to the real meassage.

Angle Code. (From Gibson: *Recreational Programs for the Summer Camps,* page 51.)

ADDITIONAL READINGS

Burke, Edmund H.: *Camping Handbook.*
Compass and Maps. Girl Scouts, 48 pp., 25¢.
Compass and Maps. Girl Scouts #15-04, Flip Charts, $6.00.
Des Grey, Arthur H.: *Camping.*
Greenwood, David: *Down to Earth Mapping for Every-body.* Holiday House.
Henderson, Luis M.: *The Outdoor Guide.*
Jaeger, Ellsworth: *Tracks and Trailcraft.* The Macmillan Co., 1948, $3.95.
Jaeger, Ellsworth: *Wildwood Wisdom.*
Kesting, Ted: *The Outdoor Encyclopedia.*
Koller, Larry: *Larry Koller's Complete Book of Camping and the Outdoors.*
Lindholm, Major Mauno A.: *Camping and Outdoor Fun.*
Mustard, Major C. A.: *By Map and Compass—An Introduction to Orienteering.* Silva, Inc., 1950, 64 pp., 75¢.

Rhodes, Glenn and Dale: *Camping Maps, U.S.A.; A Booklet of Maps.* Authors, Box 162, Upper Montclair, N.J., $1.95.
Rutstrum, Calvin: *The New Way of the Wilderness.*
Signaling. Boy Scouts #3237, 25¢.
Surveying. Boy Scouts #3327, 25¢.
The Pathfinder Orienteering Area. Silva, Inc., 10 pp., 50¢.
Weaver, Robert W., and Merrill, F.: *Camping Can Be Fun.*
Wells, George and Iris: *The Handbook of Wilderness Travel.*
Whelan, Townsend, and Angier, Bradford: *On Your Own in the Wilderness.*
West, James E., and Hillcourt, William: *Scout Field Book.*

MAGAZINE ARTICLES

Baker, Mary Jane: *Orienteering with the Silva Compass.* C.M., Dec., 1954.
Brainerd, John and Barbara: *Maps, Important Material for Program and Conservation Plan.* C.M., Dec., 1958.

21

Hiking, Trailing, and Stalking

There are camp fires unkindled and songs unsung,
And the untraveled miles of the trail.
There are unbroken dreams 'neath whispering trees,
Till the stars of the morning grow pale.

CHART PITT*

HIKING is fun and almost everyone enjoys it, whether for the purpose of reaching a certain destination, exploring a historical or otherwise interesting spot, or just taking a ramble like the bear's trip over the mountain "to see what he could see." It is also one of the best ways to get and keep in condition. The wise hiker wears clothing which is both comfortable and appropriate to the season, time, and place.

How to Hike

CARE OF YOUR FEET. Since each of your feet comes down and momentarily bears your weight about a thousand times for each mile, feet deserve a maximum of care and attention. Never start on a long hike without having gradually toughened yourself to it by a series of shorter hikes.

Blisters result from friction between your shoes and skin, and it is far more satisfactory to prevent than try to cure them. Avoid wearing darned socks or new shoes, put a coating of moist soap on the backs of your heels and inside heels of your socks and dust your feet and the insides of your socks with talcum or foot powder before you start out. At the first sign of redness or soreness at any point, apply a piece of adhesive tape to absorb the friction and save your skin. However, never apply tape after a blister has started to form. Keep your toe nails cut fairly short and straight across so the corners won't dig into your skin.

* From *Field and Stream.* Romany Road.

240

(H. Armstrong Roberts.)

USING YOUR BODY.   Walk with a rhythmic swing of your whole body, not with a city sidewalk swing from your hips as you hold your upper trunk motionless. Point your toes straight ahead (Indian style) or even slightly pigeon toed, not out like a duck in a way both fatiguing to you and hard on your arches. When you toe out, you shorten your stride by an inch or more and so have to take several hundred extra steps on a five-mile hike. Lean slightly forward from your hips and glide along smoothly with a minimum of sideward and upward movement.

Do not make a hike a speed or endurance contest; what you do and see along the way is far more important than how far you go. Strike a steady pace that you can maintain indefinitely and rest five or ten minutes out of every half-hour on a long hike. Avoid resting too long lest your leg and back muscles stiffen, but relax completely, lying flat on your back with feet propped up on a convenient rock or tree so that the blood which has collected in your legs and feet will drain away.

Three miles an hour is a good speed for maintained hiking. The Scout's *pace*, which consists of dog trotting for a certain number of paces (thirty to fifty), then walking the same number of paces, eats up the miles steadily and rapidly. You can cover a mile in ten to twelve

Walk like an Indian, not like a Duck.

minutes in this fashion without undue fatigue. Although swift Indian runners were said to cover one hundred or more miles between dawn and dusk, fifteen or twenty will usually be sufficient for even the oldest and most seasoned hikers in an organized camp. Unless you are really trying to cover a certain distance in a limited time, it's more fun to hike at a moderate pace, allowing time to stop and examine anything that looks interesting along the way.

When hiking with campers, one of the counselors should head the line as a pace setter, striking a medium pace which all can maintain without undue hardship. Another counselor should bring up the rear. Groups are most successful when composed of those of approximately the same age and physical stamina, so that the strong do not have to wait for the slow or the latter overdo in an effort to keep up.

A good woodsman never steps on anything such as rocks or logs which he can step over or go around and thus avoids undue fatigue and sprained ankles. "Watch your step" as you proceed for you'll really handicap yourself and your companions if you injure yourself and can't continue under your own power. Hold aside low-hanging branches so they won't snap back into the face of the person following you and warn them of dangerous holes or other hazards along the way.

Where to Hike

Stay off main highways whenever possible for by-path or cross-country hiking is less dangerous and the soft ground and grass of field and forest are less fatiguing on your feet. It is more interesting to ramble off the beaten path where nature's handiwork is unmarred by man.

If you must travel on a busy highway, divide into twos or threes and spread out in single file or walk not more than two abreast and entirely off the pavement on the left side of the road facing oncoming

traffic. Walking on a highway at night is particularly dangerous; avoid it except in emergency and then wear something white, or tie a white strip of cloth about one leg, and carry a lighted lantern or flashlight to alert approaching vehicles. It is dangerous to walk along a railroad track and perfectly foolhardy as well as illegal to walk over a railroad trestle.

Hitchhiking is, of course, taboo for hikers. Not only is riding with strangers extremely dangerous and even against the law in some states, but, if you are a red-blooded camper, you will want to be independent enough to go the whole way on your own two feet.

When hiking cross-country show due respect for the property of others, for every stick, stone, flower and fruit tree is someone's property and he may feel about it like the old farmer who said of his wife, "She ain't much, but she's mine!" Respect "no trespassing" signs; they have likely been put up because of damage done by previous travelers and may be assumed to mean just what they say. Close gates behind you if you found them that way, and avoid climbing fences for it is easy to break them down and permanently damage them. If absolutely necessary to climb a fence, do so next to a post where you will do the least damage and carefully restore any portions you may have bent out of shape.

Do not walk across cultivated fields, but stay close along the edges where no crops have been planted. Pick fruit or flowers only when given express permission to do so.

Protect Yourself

To remain in perspiration-soaked clothing is just as dangerous as to stay in rain-soaked clothing insofar as bringing on a cold is concerned. When on a trip of any length, always carry a change of clothing with you and do not hesitate to take time to slip into it if you get wet. This applies particularly to wearing wet socks and wet shoes for, in addition, they will

make your feet sore and tender. If no change is possible, it is well to stop, build a fire, and dry out thoroughly before proceeding.

Thirst

Thirst is often due to a drying out of the tissues lining your mouth rather than to any real need for water, and so is best relieved by merely rinsing your mouth instead of gulping down large quantities of liquid. Candy eaten along the way is sure to induce thirst; munching raisins or other dried fruit or sucking on a fruit pit or clean pebble is preferable. Carry your own canteen of water unless you know there are *safe* sources at frequent intervals along the way.

Make the Miles Fly

Think of interesting things to do to make the miles go faster. A continuous round-robin story with each unexpectedly called upon to take up the story at a given signal, singing merry hiking songs, marching in strict "military fashion" for variation, and playing hiking games serve this purpose. Sing sweetly and talk quietly; don't annoy others by loud, boisterous conduct.

Kinds of Hikes

Even old, familiar trails take on a new glamour when there is a definite purpose for following them. Have a certain objective in mind but do not become so engrossed that you can't stop for something of unusual interest that comes up. Here are some possible types of hike:

1. *Carefree Hike:* to some interesting or beautiful spot where you cook an outdoor meal, hold a program, or carry on some other project.
2. *Breakfast Hike:* to a good vantage point to see the sun rise and to cook breakfast.
3. *Star Hike:* to a hill on a clear evening to study the stars and their legends. Take your blanket rolls for an overnight sleep-out.
4. *Fishing Trip:* to fish in a nearby stream or lake. Take a lunch which you may hope to supplement with fresh fish.
5. *Bee Line or Crow Flight Hike:* follow a compass bearing as closely as possible to see what interesting scenery you encounter on the way.
6. *Historical Hike:* to some historical place about which you have previously briefed yourself by reading or consulting local people.
7. *Moonlight Hike:* to see how entirely different nature folk live at night.
8. *Camera Hike:* to see who can snap the most interesting photographs.
9. *Nature Hike:* to study interesting flowers, trees, animals, insects, and the like, along the way. See who can collect the most interesting pieces of driftwood, sea shells, or other items for use in the craft shop or nature collection.
10. *Map Hike:* use a compass and map and collect notes for use in constructing a trail map or try to follow a trail map someone else has constructed.
11. *Rain Hike:* waterproof yourselves thoroughly and go out to see how animals and plants conduct themselves in the rain.
12. *Creek's or River's End Hike:* follow a creek or river to its origin or mouth.
13. *Overnight Hike:* find a good place to spend the night, cook breakfast, and return to camp.
14. *Sealed Orders Hike:* give the group a set of sealed directions with a new one to be opened each time the previously designated spot is reached. Give the clues in poetry form or in riddle or code so that the group must decipher them but do not make them so difficult that the hikers

lose interest or lose their way completely. It is best not to have more than five or six in a group. If desired, the orders may be hidden along the route, for instance, the first might read, "Go 30° for 250 yds. and look under two rocks piled on top of each other to the right of the path." There the followers might find a second direction, "go straight east 200 yds., and look in hollow tree," etc.

15. *Progressive Supper Hike:* lay a nature trail which hikers must follow in order to find their suppers. Serve different courses progressively along the way, with dessert at the last station where the evening program is held.

16. *Trail Clearing Hike:* find and clear a new trail and establish an outpost camp at the end. Leave a supply of wood for the next group.

17. *Hare and Hound Hike:* the "hares" start out, leaving some not too conspicuous trail signs (see pp. 236–237) along the way. The "hounds" leave later at a specified time and try to follow the trail of the "hares." The object is to spot the hares, who may hide any place within 50 feet of the trail. If a hare is able to stay out of sight until all the hounds have passed him on the trail, he gets in "free." Hares seen are "caught." Use small groups, separating them and laying several trails if there are too many for one.

18. *Hold the Front:* the participants draw for places and assume that order in single file. The object is to get and maintain the position at the head of the line. The leader asks the head to identify a nature object seen along the way; if he does it correctly, he holds his position; if not, those behind him are given a chance in turn to identify it, the one who finally does so moving up past all those who failed. The leader then asks a new question of the person just behind the one who answered correctly. If he misses, those behind him have a similar chance to advance to his place in line. The person at the head of the line when the game ends, wins.

19. *Roadside Cribbage:* give each player the same number of counters (ten to twenty acorns, pebbles, or such). Then give each a list of objects, such as specific kinds of birds, trees or flowers. As they hike along, each looks for the specified objects, and the first to see one calls "pegs" and throws away one of his counters. The player who first gets rid of all his counters wins the game. If a player doubts that the one who called "pegs" really saw the object he claimed, he can challenge him; if wrong, the challenger must accept the other's counter; if not, the player takes back his counter and also receives one from the challenger.

20. *Hike to Another Camp:* this would be done, of course, only by invitation or previous arrangement.

21. *Ride out by Bus or Camp Truck:* then hike back.

22. *Conservation Hike:* discover places where erosion or other examples of poor conservation are taking place. Return and remedy them later.

23. *"What Is It?" Hike:* give each member of the group a prepared list of objects that might be seen along the way such as a particular kind of bird, tree, moss or flower. Designate a certain number of points for each according to its rarity. The hiker who first sees and correctly identifies anything on the list scores the allotted number of points for himself or his team.

No matter what kind of a hike you take, do not let it degenerate into a prosaic walk. Cloak it in an aura of glamour and adventure for small children by pretending they are a band of giants, little elves, colorful gypsies or bold, swaggering pirates. Whatever the realm of fancy of the campers, it is much more fun to hike in the land of "let's pretend." You must, of course, adapt your methods to the age of the group. Plan your hike, no matter how short it is. Meet as a group to decide where to go, what to do, what to wear, and what equipment to take, how to pack it, and how to divide up the jobs on the way and at your destination. Avoid returning over the same territory, if you can.

Be on the lookout for interesting places you may want to come back to for a cook-out, an overnight hike or to make an outpost camp. Perhaps you may see a new source of clay for your pottery kiln, some tall reeds that are just right for basket weaving or a high hill ideal for a supper cook-out and overnight bivouac to study stars.

TRAILING AND STALKING

Have you ever seen a whippoorwill sitting lengthwise on a closely matching limb in a effort to make you think he is only the stub of a rotten limb or a possum feigning death in hopes you'll pass him by with scarcely a glance. To see such interesting episodes of nature, you'll have to train your five senses to be alert. Learn to move quietly and inconspicuously for nearly all animals and birds are exceedingly timid and will be gone to the four winds without so much as letting you catch sight of them unless you do. If hiking with others, work out signals such as a finger on lips for "freeze where you are," or a beckoning hand for "come closer."

Sharpen your powers of observation by practice. A good game to play back at camp is to group twenty or more objects on a table or have pictures of them mounted on a poster. Give each observer a minute to study the array, then have him turn his back and write down as many as he can remember, scoring one point for each success.

Tracking and Stalking

It's great fun to learn to trail some animal through the woods or fields and, if skillful at it, you may be able to creep up close and watch him as he goes about his daily activities. But you'll need to be very observant to follow his tracks. Start out by studying human tracks along a sandy beach or the edge of a river or lake where they are easy to see. Learn to tell whether the person was walking, running, carrying a heavy object, or perhaps walking backward to fool you. Learn to estimate how fresh the tracks are; those newly made will have sharp edges and no debris will have yet blown into them.

Now try your hand at studying bird or animal tracks, learning to identify them from some of the good source books available. Look for other traces such as droppings, bits of hair left on bushes, or signs of feeding. Do not look down at your feet as you follow but keep looking ahead for signs of the trail such as a darker path made as the undersides of leaves were turned upward, etc. This will enable you to follow at greater speed, and so increase your chances of catching up with your quarry. If you lose the trail, mark the last spot you were sure of and prospect around in an ever widening spiral until you pick it up again.

Getting really near will test all your ingenuity and skill, for animals have highly developed senses of smell and hearing and sometimes sight, and will quickly flee for parts unknown at the least sign of an intruder. Learn to move slowly and silently and avoid stepping on dry twigs which may snap like the crack of a rifle.

Be ready to "freeze" if the animal looks your way. *Stalking* is the name given to this ability to move along completely unseen and unheard by any other two- or four-legged creature. Step with toe down first on grass and bring your heel down first on hard ground.

You may want to copy the commandos and camouflage your costume to blend in with the surrounding terrain. Avoid bright colors and fashion dull overgarments of some such material as burlap sacks. Metal may reflect the sun's rays so avoid belt buckles and such and use green branches to cover your face. They help you blend in with the background. Since most animals have a well-developed sense of smell, approach them by moving *into* the wind even though it means making an entire half-circle to do so.

Survey the landscape for natural hiding places such as bushes, large rocks and trees and plan how best to take advantage of them. Remember that you will show up very clearly when silhouetted against the sky so stay very low. Use every bit of shelter available if you have to cross a ridge. Quick movements attract attention; use them only when sure the animal is looking in another direction. Wild animals must constantly guard against their natural enemies for their very lives depend upon it; hence, instinct and practice have given them an uncanny wariness and ability to detect the unusual and *you* are definitely "unusual" in their forest home. When near, drop into a cat creep on all fours or even wriggle along on your stomach. Infinite patience and skill are needed to make close-up photographs and real-life studies but it will be worth your effort.

Tracking and Stalking Games

TRAIL THE DEER. A leader starts out ahead wearing shoes with a peculiar heel plate or arrangement of brads; others try to trail him. Hob nails or upholstery nails can be inserted into rubber heels and later removed without damaging them.

DEER STALKING. One player, the "deer," places himself in an environment providing some covering such as grass, bushes and trees. Others scatter out about 100 yards away and each tries to approach him without being seen. Anyone the "deer" sees and can identify is eliminated; the one closest to the "deer" at the end of a designated time wins and can be the "deer" for the next game.

FREEZE. "It" is in front with the others lined up about 100 feet away. As "It" turns his back and counts to ten, the others move toward him as rapidly as possible. At the end of the count, "It" shouts "freeze" and quickly turns around; he calls out the name of any person he sees making the slightest motion. That person must go back to the starting line again. First person to touch "it" or cross the finish line wins and becomes the new "it".

TOUCH THE RABBIT. "It" sits on the ground with eyes closed while others gather around in a circle. Leader points to one player who tries to sneak up to "It" and touch him without being heard. If "It" hears him and points directly to him, he must return to place. Anyone able to come in and touch "It" without being detected, wins and becomes the new "It".

CAPTURE THE FLAG. Each team occupies its own territory, separated by a path, a line on the ground or markers of some sort. Each team erects its own flag about 100 to 200 yards behind the separation line. The object is to enter the opponents' territory and capture their flag without being caught. Color guards for the flag may be designated but they must not approach within twenty-five steps (marked off by a circle) of the flag unless in pursuit of an opponent who has entered the circle. Anyone in the opponents' territory may be captured by catching him and holding him long enough to pat him on the back three times (if this proves too rough, rule that he is caught when his opponent merely touches him). Prisoners are put in "prison," an area about twenty steps back of the separation line and may be released only by being touched by a teammate. Any prisoner rescued gets a "free trip" home with his rescuer but a player who captures the flag becomes a prisoner and must replace the flag if he is caught before he is safely back in his own territory. Set a time limit, as a half hour, and the winning team is the one with the most prisoners if neither has captured the other's flag by the end of that time.

A variation is to widen the area and include trees, rocks, bushes, and natural hiding places which may be used for concealment when trying to approach the flag or release prisoners. The time may be extended to hours or even a half day without having the players lose interest. Choosing a good terrain is the secret of success in this game.

ADDITIONAL READINGS

Hiking

Francis, Godfrey: *Mountain Climbing*. Sportshelf, 192 pp., $2.50.

Geist, Roland C.: *Hiking, Camping and Mountaineering*.

Hammett, Catherine T., and Musselman, Virginia: *The Camp Program Books*.

Hiking. Boy Scouts #3380, 25¢.

Hiking—In Town and Country. Girl Scouts #19-641, 1952, 48 pp., 30¢.

Kesting, Ted: *The Outdoor Encyclopedia*.

Rutstrum, Calvin: *The New Way of the Wilderness*.

Wells, George and Iris: *The Handbook of Wilderness Travel*.

West, James E., and Hillcourt, William: *Scout Field Book*.

Whelan, Townsend, and Angier, Bradford: *On Your Own in the Wilderness*.

Tracking and Trailing

Henderson, Luis M.: *The Outdoor Guide*.

Jaeger, Ellsworth: *Land and Water Trails*. The Macmillan Co., $2.95.

Jaeger, Ellsworth: *Tracks and Trailcraft*. The Macmillan Co., 1948, $2.95.

Mason, George F.: *Animal Tracks*. William Morrow and Co., 1943, $2.50.

Pocket Field Guide to Animal Tracks. Stackpole Co., 1954, $2.50.

West, James E., and Hillcourt, William: *Scout Field Book*.

22

Tincancraft

First the thought, and then the act,
Before the dream becomes a fact.

H. S. WALTER*

The Versatile Tin Can

A tin can is one of the most versatile objects in existence. Washed, it can be used for a cup or cooking utensil; turned upside down, it acts as a stove; flattened out, it becomes a tray, a shade or anything that your creative mind designs. So, the next time you start to throw away a tin can, stop to consider how very easily a little time and effort could convert it into a useful object.

The tools you need for working with tin are few and inexpensive, and so common that most homes or camps already have them. Tin snips, cotton gloves, pliers, hammer, file and nails or nail sets are all that are really essential. If decorative articles are your goal, you will need steel wool to polish the metal and "duck billed" tin snips to help cut curved surfaces neatly.

It is possible to purchase sheet tin at a hardware store, but it is simple to get your own free tin by cutting and straightening out a tin can of suitable size. Incidentally, tin cans are really misnamed for they consist of only about two per cent tin, used as a thin covering on both sides of a layer of steel. You can make handy and attractive things from tin cans, and they also provide preliminary training in using tools and patterns preparatory to working with such relatively expensive metals as copper, aluminum, silver and brass. If you make a mistake, you can simply throw it away and begin

* Permission by The Indianapolis News.

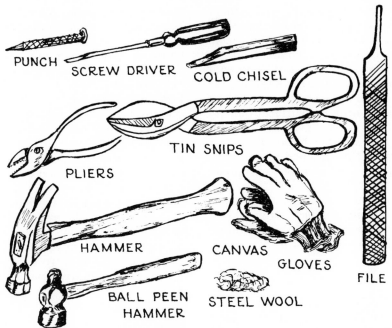

PUNCH   SCREW DRIVER   COLD CHISEL   TIN SNIPS   PLIERS   HAMMER   CANVAS GLOVES   FILE   BALL PEEN HAMMER   STEEL WOOL

Tools for Tincraft.

again with the loss of nothing more serious than a little time. Scrap wire for handles is free for the picking up in neighboring scrap heaps.

Tin cans are available in almost any shape and size desired, varying from the small, flat tobacco tins to large oil cans. The standard sizes used for canning fruits and vegetables are as follows:

#1—large evaporated milk cans
#2—most canned vegetables
#3—canned tomatoes
#5—twice the size of a #3 can
#10—gallon size, available from restaurants, dormitories, camps, and elsewhere.

Safety

Always wear cotton gloves when working with tin, for there is great danger of cutting yourself on the jagged, sharp edges, and also of getting blisters from the unaccustomed use of heavy tin snips.

When making an object from a flattened tin can, first make a paper pattern, adjusting and altering it until it meets your complete approval. Trace it on the tin with a pencil and begin to cut. Work slowly and carefully to insure a better product and avoid injuring your hands. Smooth jagged edges with a file or snip back the edge a short distance every ¼ to ⅛ inch. Place a circle of wire tightly around the can to stiffen it, roll back the snipped edge around and under the wire with a pair of pliers and keep working until you attain a very smooth rounded edge. Then place the object over a wooden post or butt of a small log and pound the turned over edge flat with a hammer.

General Hints

To pierce holes, place the article over a tree stump or block of wood, and use a hammer and nail set, ice pick or other sharp object of appropriate size. Neater holes may be made with a hand drill, resting the object on a soft piece of wood for the drill to enter as it pierces the metal. Use holes for decoration, for inserting a wire handle, or for suspending the object from a nail.

Hammering or using rough methods to convert a tin can into a flat sheet leaves dents and marks on the metal. This is sometimes objectionable and can be avoided as follows: cut off both ends and remove a strip of tin containing the side seam; place the concave surface of the can down on a flat surface; pick up one edge and press the metal flat with the heel of your other hand. To form a cylinder from the flattened piece, shape it around a round stick of appropriate size.

Pieces of metal may be joined by riveting, nailing, soldering or leaving tabs on one piece to insert into slits in the other, bending them over as shown (p. 251).

Cooking Utensils

You can make a complete set of nested cooking utensils by choosing tin cans of appropriate sizes as shown in A in the figure on page 252. Be sure to equip them with detachable handles so that they will nest compactly. Other useful camp "fixings" are also shown in the drawings.

Kettles, stew pans, plates, and frying pans are best made from number 10 or gallon tin cans, cut to appropriate depths. Cups are made from number 2 or number 2½ cans, while number 2½ or number 5 cans are about right for cereal bowls. Before using tin-can cooking or eating utensils, heat them and scrub them thoroughly with hot water and a good scouring powder to remove the lacquer usually present on them. Use only cans that have contained food, not paint or oil, for cooking utensils. Make a ditty bag (page 307) of denim or other strong material with a draw string top to fit around your nested cooking outfit. Always be sure to dry out tin utensils thoroughly, immediately after using them for they rust very quickly. Use a plastic scouring pad rather than steel wool to clean them.

Hobo Stoves

Hobo stoves (C, page 252) are handy little cooking devices that will heat up in no time at all with just a handful of twigs for fuel. If you want to cook directly

(H. Armstrong Roberts.)

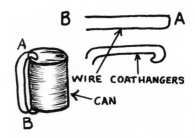

Snap-on Handle Made from Coat Hanger.

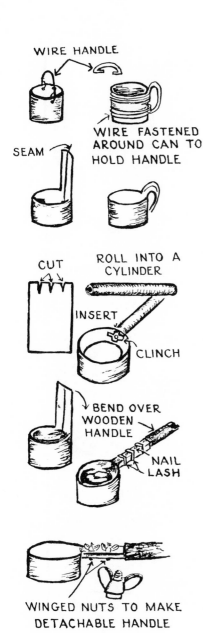

Ways of Adding Handles.

on their tops, first heat them and thoroughly scrub the tops to remove the lacquer. An excellent stove, large enough to support several pots and pans, can be made from an old wash tub or wash boiler (N, p. 252).

You can make a compact hobo stove* by cutting off the top of a number 10 tin can and slicing the sides into three or four strips which will pack almost flat; when ready to use it, merely stick the sides solidly into the ground and balance the top over them.

Other Articles

To make a useful and decorative set of kitchen containers, select tin cans of the right size and enamel them (two coats, for permanence) in any color scheme desired. Paint the name of the contents on the outside, and further decorate them with decalcomania designs. If you wish, you can buy glass or wooden knobs at the variety or hardware store. Waxing or painting the outside with clear lacquer further preserves the containers.

For a bright metal finish, burnish the outside with steel wool. Another method of finishing is to hold the object over the fire until it assumes a cloudy dullness, then quickly burnish it with a brush and a good scouring powder.

To make an anchor for the candle in a candle holder, cut an "X" in the bottom of the tin can and bend the edges up until they are the right size to fit snugly around the candle.

*Suggestions for Improvised Camping Out Equipment. Camp Publications.

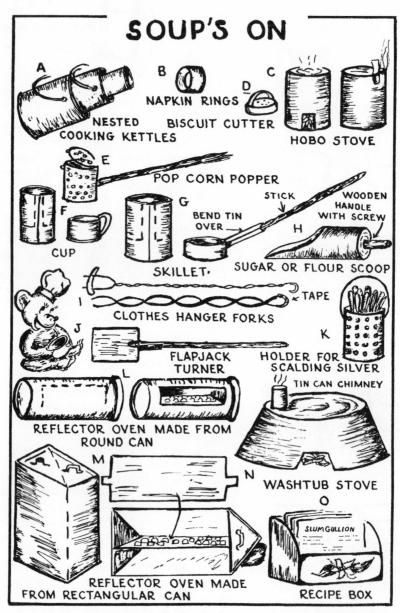

Cooking Devices.

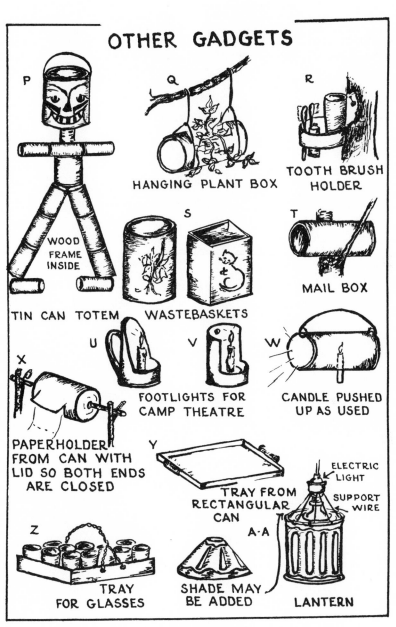

OTHER GADGETS

P

Q HANGING PLANT BOX

R TOOTH BRUSH HOLDER

WOOD FRAME INSIDE

TIN CAN TOTEM

S WASTEBASKETS

T MAIL BOX

U V FOOTLIGHTS FOR CAMP THEATRE

W CANDLE PUSHED UP AS USED

X PAPERHOLDER FROM CAN WITH LID SO BOTH ENDS ARE CLOSED

Y TRAY FROM RECTANGULAR CAN

Z TRAY FOR GLASSES

A-A SHADE MAY BE ADDED

ELECTRIC LIGHT

SUPPORT WIRE

LANTERN

Tin Can Utilities.

ADDITIONAL READINGS
(See also page 142)

Bell, Enid: *Tin-Craft as a Hobby*. Harper and Brothers. (out of print)

Groneman, Chris H.: *Ornamental Tin Craft*. Bruce Publishing Co., 1949, 160 pp., $1.65.

Hammett, Catherine T., and Horrocks, Carol M.: *Creative Crafts for Campers*.

Jaeger, Ellsworth: *Wildwood Wisdom*.

Lindholm, Major Mauno A.: *Camping and Outdoor Fun*.

Lukowitz, Joseph J.: *55 New Tin Can Projects*. Bruce Publishing Co., 1958, 80 pp., 90¢.

Lynn, Gordon: *Camping and Camp Crafts*.

Mason, Bernard S.: *Junior Book of Camping and Woodcraft*.

23

Knifemanship and Toolcraft

The Yankee boy, before he's sent to school,
Well knows the mysteries of that magic tool,
The pocket-knife. To that his wistful eye
Turns while he hears his mother's lullaby;
His hoarded cents he gladly gives to get it,
Then leaves no stone unturned till he can whet it;
And in the education of the lad
No little part that implement hath had.
His pocket-knife to the young whittler brings
A growing knowledge of material things.

JOHN PIERPONT

THE KNIFE, along with the gun and the axe, was an important tool of the pioneer. It is equally important to a camper, for its usefulness ranges from making fuzz sticks or clumps to start a stubborn fire and handy gadgets to use around the campsite, to making such decorative articles as totem poles, lapel pins, and so forth. Girls become quite as skilled as boys in its use when carefully taught and enthusiastically encouraged. Extremely young children, say under nine, may lack the hand-eye coordination necessary to make the use of a knife safe, but older campers can easily acquire the necessary skill. All of us have seen the promiscuous carving of initials and designs in places where they don't belong. This indicates that the charm of using a knife is very appealing and should be well channeled toward constructive rather than destructive lines.

Selecting a Knife

A knife on the order of the Boy or Girl Scout knife with multi-purpose blades is usually best for general camp use. It should be strong and fit well in your hand and, though a certain amount of roughness on the handle is necessary for a firm grip, too much may cause blisters. A brightly colored handle is helpful since it is easier to find if you should happen to drop your knife into the duff.

A cheap knife is poor economy in the long run, for it is usually poorly constructed and the steel in the blade is soft

255

Framework for a Tarp Shelter (H. Armstrong Roberts.)

and won't hold a sharp edge. On the other hand, blades of extremely hard steel will chip easily.

Keep the *reamer* on your scout knife sharp, for it is used to bore holes in leather and other materials.

Since the usual camp knife has only one blade suitable for whittling, an advanced whittler may prefer to supplement it with a special whittling knife with two or three blades of various shapes and sizes which are better adapted to intricate carving. However, the work a skilled workman can do with an ordinary jackknife is amazing.

Caring for Your Knife

A knife is a high-class tool and, as such deserves the best treatment. Keep it clean and dry at all times, and immediately remove all rust and stain with scouring powder or ashes from your campfire, dampened with a little water. Always dry the blade after it has had moisture on it.

Never use your knife to poke in the fire or to stir hot food, for extreme heat ruins the *temper* of the blade, making it soft, and it will never again hold a sharp edge. Warm the blade on a cold day by holding it in your hands a few moments so that it will not chip.

Never leave a knife lying carelessly around. Keep it in your pocket, fastened by a chain, leather thong or stout cord long enough to permit using the knife without detaching it.

The blades on a new knife are often stiff and difficult to open. Apply a few drops of lubricating oil to the stubborn springs and repeatedly open and close the blades, using some sort of metal pry for the purpose. They will gradually loosen up with continued use.

Opening and Closing Your Knife

To open a blade, grasp the knife between your left thumb and index finger, insert your right thumbnail in the notch of the blade and pull it open. Be careful never

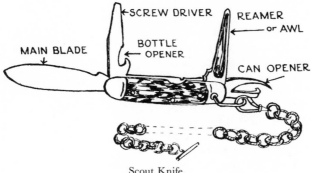

Scout Knife.

to lay the fingers of your left hand across the slot into which the blade fits for the spring on the blade of a new knife is often strong enough to snap the partly opened blade back shut again with disastrous results to any finger that happens to be in the way. Close your knife the same way, again being careful not to get your fingers across the slot at any time during the process.

Sharpening Your Knife

Surprisingly enough a new knife has often been purposely left dull so that the new owner can sharpen it to suit his own particular taste and needs.

The edge on the blade is called the *bevel* and it should be of medium thickness for ordinary camp use, extending only a short way back from the edge of the blade to prevent weakening it. If the bevel is thinned too much, it weakens the blade which may chip; if too rounded, the knife is dull.

A new blade may be rough-shaped on the fast-grinding surface of a file or hand-turned grindstone. Unless experienced, never use a power grindstone for it cuts away too fast and is likely to overheat the blade and spoil its temper. A blade with a nick in it must be ground even with the nick and can best be done in the same way.

Finish sharpening your blade on an oilstone or *carborundum stone, (whetstone)*. The latter is more convenient since the water used with it is always available,

unlike the oil needed for using an oilstone. The usual carborundum stone has a coarser side for preliminary, fast grinding and a finer side for putting on the finishing touches or *honing* the blade. If you are using a rectangular stone, hold it in your left hand with the coarse side up; grasp your knife in your right hand and place it crosswise of the stone with the back of the blade raised to a twenty-degree angle. Keeping this angle uniform, draw the back of the blade toward you across the stone with a straight stroke, then turn the blade over and push it away from you. Continue this alternate stroking. Keep the stone moist with water to offset the heat created by the friction. If you are using a circular stone, hold the knife blade still and apply the stone to it in a circular fashion. When both sides are finished, polish it off by stroking it on both sides on a piece of leather such as a razor strop, belt, or leather shoe sole to remove the *wire edge* or hooked roughness.

A sharp blade is much safer than a dull one, for it bites into the wood instead of sliding off and cutting the user. Test the sharpness of the blade by drawing it downward with a sliding stroke

Twenty Degree Angle for Sharpening.

across a sheet of paper held up vertically between thumb and forefinger. If sharp, it will cut the paper cleanly and easily; if dull, it will tear it or not even penetrate at all. You will need much practice to learn to sharpen a knife quickly and well.

Keep your knife in good condition after each use by stroking it a few times on the fine side of a carborundum and finishing off on a piece of leather. You should never need to use the file and coarse side of the carborundum again unless your knife is misused or gets a nick in its blade. A well-kept knife is a matter of pride to a good camper.

There is an unwritten law among campers that one never asks to borrow another's knife, for one way to quickly sever a fine friendship is to return a knife dull and full of nicks.

Using Your Knife

Find some softwood and practice whittling. Hold and use your knife at all times so that you cannot possibly cut yourself or anyone else, *even if it should slip*. Keep your thumb around the handle, never on the back of the blade, for if the knife should slip off to the side of the object you are cutting, the pressure of your thumb would close the blade right on your fingers.

Cut *away* from yourself with a sliding stroke and never let the knife slip over to one side as you cut. Cut slowly and deliberately and pride yourself on being a safety artist. Carelessness and overconfidence cause accidents.

You will soon graduate from whittling for the sake of whittling, and will be able to turn out such useful articles as fuzz sticks and fuzz clumps. These are excellent to have ready to start a fire in a hurry when firewood is damp from a recent rain or good timber is scarce. When you can make them with fine, close-cut "curls," each just as long as possible, without severing it from the stick,

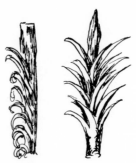

Fuzz Stick.   Fuzz Clump.

you can really be proud of your skill. Never try to cut through knots for this will soon dull any blade.

Close your knife if you are going to walk about for even two steps; bad accidents have occurred from tripping while carrying an open knife in the hand. Never hand an open knife to another; close it first.

Splitting Kindling with a Knife.

You can make fine kindling by gripping a small piece of wood or twig in your left hand as shown and pressing the blade down through the wood to split it. Note how your fingers are kept out of the path of the knife. Take care not to pry or twist with your knife or you will sooner or later chip the blade.

At the first sign of redness or other symptom of an approaching blister on the index finger or other part of your knife hand, apply a piece of adhesive tape, a Band-aid or a leather finger-stall to prevent friction.

Apply a pad to prevent blisters.

Some Things to Make

You are now ready to attempt something a little more difficult. Some "gadgets" are simple and can be made by anyone who has a little persistence and an average amount of skill. Advanced whittlers use additional tools such as crooked knives, sloyd knives, chisels, wood carving tools, vises, jigsaws, coping saws, eggbeater drills, and so on, to save time and produce more finished work.

Many woods are adaptable to carving, but some are naturally more suitable than others. You can find good wood lying about in almost any wooded area, or can pick up bits of scrap lumber at building sites or from carpenters or cabinetmakers. If you want an especially fine piece, purchase it at the lumber yard.

The best wood for whittling is soft enough to cut well, yet has enough "body" to hold it together; it should split straight and smooth, yet not be so soft as to split ahead of the knife when you don't want it to. Avoid brittle woods and those which will not hold together when large sections have been cut away; porous wood is usually too coarse-grained for good whittling. Experimenting will soon enable you to choose what you want. White pine, oak, white ash, white or yellow poplar, red cedar, basswood, butternut, maple and holly are all recommended. Prunings from fruit trees such as cherry or apple are also good. Whittling wood should be well seasoned, dried for at least a year before use. Perhaps you'll want to select some green wood this summer and lay it aside to use next season.

A hiking staff (page 311) for use over rough or hilly country is both useful and interesting to make. Choose a fairly straight, sturdy stick about chest high and an inch or a little more in diameter. Decorate it by cutting away sections of the bark, leaving the natural wood exposed in any pattern of initials, faces, figures or spirals your taste dictates.

Enamel or paint add to the decorative effect, and a coat of clear varnish or lacquer applied over the whole stick helps to protect the colors and keep the bark intact. Bark carving is best done in the summer or fall, for bark is inclined to peel off in the spring when the sap is running. Proceed slowly and patiently; nothing is quite so discouraging as to ruin a "masterpiece" on which you have spent hours of labor by a careless or hasty miscut just as you are adding the finishing touches. Finish it with a coat of wax, rubbed in well. Your staff will become dearer each time you take it on some pleasant expedition and you will find it of real help in making your way over difficult terrain.

Campers and staff members often like to have a name tag to wear to help everyone learn names, especially during the first few days of camp. The "woodsy" way is to make your own tag from a small twig about 2 to 2½ inches long and as big around as your index finger. Flatten one side of it with your knife and sandpaper it smooth. Then print your camp name on it with India ink, burn it in with a woodburning set or carve around it with your knife so it stands out in relief. Gouge out a small groove above center on the back, and fasten a safety pin in it with plastic wood or household cement. Apply a thin coat of wax to the whole pin or rub it well with clean hands until it shines from the natural oil of your skin. Make clothespins from pieces of green wood, leaving the bark on the tops or shaping them into heads, birds, or other decorative designs.

Use a small-saw to cut off thin slices of hardwood of interesting cross section and

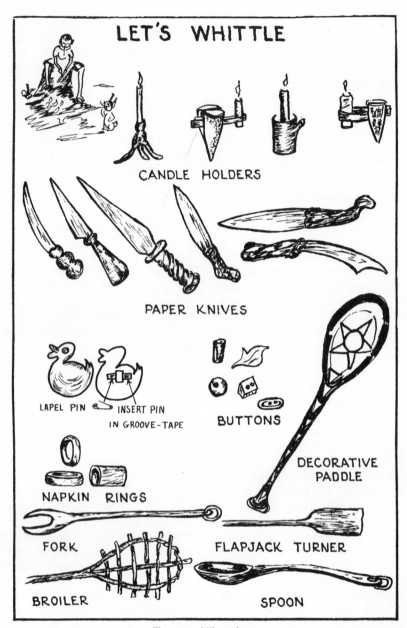

LET'S WHITTLE

CANDLE HOLDERS

PAPER KNIVES

LAPEL PIN — INSERT PIN IN GROOVE-TAPE

BUTTONS

NAPKIN RINGS

DECORATIVE PADDLE

FORK

FLAPJACK TURNER

BROILER

SPOON

Try your skill on these.

use your knife to shape them into pins or buttons. Finish as described on page 262. Make holes in the buttons with a small drill or by driving a small nail through them.

Clothes pegs can be lashed to trees or tent poles as shown or you can make pegs and shape them to fit into holes bored in the wood, securing them with plastic wood or glue. There are many other whittling projects scattered throughout the book and you can dream up still others out of your head.

To get campers whittling, just casually

Clothes Pegs.

let them see you working on some interesting project during rest hour or at odd
moments as when listening to someone
read aloud or tell stories. They'll soon be
joining you and you can all have fun
together.

Making a Noggin

A *noggin* is a rustic drinking cup made
from a hollowed-out burl of a tree and is
designed to be worn on the belt. Making
one provides a good many hours of enjoyment for those who like good hard
work.

A Noggin.

A burl is a scar on a tree and results
from an injury by insects, animals or
man, usually when the tree was young.

The first step in making a noggin is to
locate a tree with a suitable burl about
five inches in diameter. Investigate the
burl by removing the bark from its apex
to see if the defect at its base has gone all
the way through and so would result in
a leak in your finished noggin.

If the burl is satisfactory, saw it off,
covering the exposed area on the tree
with paint to protect it from the attack
of insects. Include enough of the tree for
a handle on the end of the noggin. You
must now laboriously gouge out the inside of the burl with a bit, a chisel or
some similar sharp instrument. Continue
hollowing with a sharp knife until a shell
not more than ⅛ to ¼ inch thick remains.

Removing a Burl from a Tree.

Remove the bark from the outside and
briskly sandpaper both outside and inside until the burl is very smooth. To
prevent your noggin's splitting or check-
ing as it dries out, keep it submerged in
a vessel of linseed oil, grease or bacon fat
whenever you are not working on it.
Drill a hole in the handle; attach a
leather thong or strong cord; polish the
wood with a woolen cloth, and your
work of art is complete. Pioneers made
bowls and plates from wood, too. Make
a bowl just as you do a noggin but omit
the handle.

Making a Whistle

To make a whistle out of willow, butternut, or basswood, you must remove a
section of the bark intact so that you can
later slip it back into place; whistles are
therefore most successfully made in the
spring when the sap is running and the
bark is easy to loosen.

Select a straight, smooth shoot, without knots or other blemishes, and about
6 to 9 inches long and ¾ inch thick.
Slant end A (which will be the mouthpiece) and cut notch B through the bark
and into the wood on the small end of
the stick. Then cut a ring through the
bark and around the shoot at C, and roll
and beat the bark from C to A with the
back of your knife, and "work" it until it
is loose enough to slip over end A as you
exert a twisting pull. The beautiful, smooth
white surface exposed readily explains the
origin of the term "clean (or slick) as a

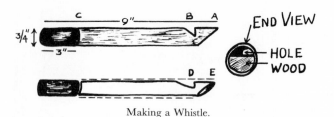

Making a Whistle.

whistle." Enlarge B as shown at D and thin the area between D and end A. Replace the bark on the wood and your whistle is ready for use and should emit a clear, shrill tone.

You can make a two-toned or multi-toned whistle by continuing depression D down almost to ring C, and making one or more round holes in the bark between B and C. By placing your fingers over these various holes, singly or in combination, you can produce various tones.

You can also make a whistle from a piece of elderberry branch. Remove its pithy center with a long, stiff wire or an ice pick and whittle a piece of softwood to partially fill the center at the mouthpiece end. Whittle another piece to completely close off the opposite end. Cut holes along the top of the whistle for as many tones as you want and it is ready for use.

Making a Model Totem Pole

Some camps make huge totem poles similar to those of the Indians of long ago with smaller models for camp villages or units. Individuals may whittle out miniature models (a few inches to a foot tall). These provide several hours of fascinating pastime and reward your efforts with an interesting souvenir.

Carefully work out your design on paper and transfer it to a piece of scrap wood of appropriate size and texture, and you are ready to start. To give the totem pole a real Indian flavor, keep the design merely a rough outline, bizarre in effect, and with no attempt to cut away the wood to show intricacies or details.

You can best bring out details with enamel or paint. Cut such protruding parts as tails or beaks separately and glue them to the main pole.

Finishing a Wooden Article

Use straight strokes of fine sandpaper or plain sand held in a piece of leather to smooth the wood to satin finish. Many feel it more "woodsy" and attractive to leave the article the color Mother Nature gave it; some, however, prefer to add decorative touches of color. Keep whatever you do simple and let it blend rather than clash with nature. Avoid gaudy paints and enamels. The soft tints of water colors give a delightful effect if you use plenty of paint and let it soak in well so that one coat will do. It is still more interesting to use plant dyes as the Indians did. (See pages 136–137.) Pleasing effects can also be obtained by rubbing in shoe polish, or various other household commodities as strong coffee or tea.

Bark carving, as described for making a walking stick (page 259), is another appropriate method for finishing an article.

An Indian method which gives a pleasing effect is to smoke the design on by rubbing the object well with grease, then holding it over the fire until it has become a dark brown; burnish it while still warm with a piece of cloth. Then cut out any design you want and it will stand out in white relief. You can obtain a similar result by applying a mask of adhesive tape, cut in the shape of the design before you smoke the wood, and then removing it when finished.

To produce a dark design on a natural wood background, leave all of the bark on the wood and cut the design down into the wood; hold it over the fire until the design has been charred or has turned as brown as you wish. Then remove the rest of the bark to leave the design standing out in an attractive dark shade.

The Sheath or Hunting Knife

A sheath or hunting knife served many purposes and was an indispensable piece of equipment to the pioneer. The average camper, however, is likely to use it only for heavy carving or for such menial

Totem Poles.

A Sheath Knife.

kitchen tasks as slicing bread, peeling potatoes, cutting up meat, and so on; thus it provides a handy but not essential supplement to his jackknife.

There are many styles, sizes and shapes of sheath knives, but one of fairly small size with the blade moderately thin and not over 4 to 5 inches long is most suitable for camp use. Most modern handles are made of some sort of composition, although those of horn, hair or leather are still sometimes found. Between the handle and the knife blade is an upright guard to keep your forefinger from slipping forward onto the blade as the knife is used.

Sharpen and care for a sheath knife like a pocketknife, and keep the blade safe in its sheath; wear it on your belt

just back of your hip. (See page 268.) The rivets along the sides and bottom of the sheath are to keep the sharp blade from cutting through.

TOOLS

When simple tools are easily available, most campers enjoy using them for repairing and constructing camp furniture and "fixin's." Each living unit should have a set of skeleton tools, painted with the unit's colors or design so that straying ones can be spotted at a glance. Tools are easily lost or mislaid, and a tool board helps to prevent this, and keeps them orderly and where they can be readily found.

Lay a suitable board down and arrange the tools on it in the order you want them. Pound in nails at the proper points to support the tools when the board is hung upright. Paint an outline of the tool underneath each so that a missing tool

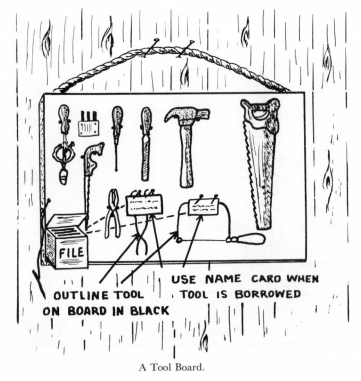

FILE

OUTLINE TOOL ON BOARD IN BLACK

USE NAME CARD WHEN TOOL IS BORROWED

A Tool Board.

can be immediately spotted. Keep a card file near the board with a card for each tool on which a camper or counselor can sign his name and substitute it for the tool when he removes it from the board. When he returns it, he can replace the card and cross off his name. It is an imposition to expect the camp handy man to lend his own tools; separate ones should be provided for campers and counselors to use.

Remember that a "workman is known by his tools" so learn to care for yours and keep them in good condition at all times. Hold each camper responsible for returning a tool in the same excellent condition it was in when he took it. A thorough reconditioning of the tools makes a good rainy-day project.

Cheap tools are usually inferior and will prove a poor investment in the long run. A wide assortment of tools should be available in the camp with a skeleton supply in each unit. Here is a suggested list:

Claw hammer
Shovel
Saw and saw files
Cold chisel (⅜")
Machine oil can and oil
Bucksaw and sawbuck
Plane
Hand drill
Files
Sandpaper (assorted)
Rakes
Tin snips
Post hole digger
Cord

Plastic wood
Tube of all-purpose cement
Camp axe (20")
Coping saw
Rope for lashing
Brace and bit
Screw drivers (4" and 8")
Grindstone
Binder twine
Pliers with wire cutter (6" or 8")
Assortment of nails, tacks, screws, brads and the like
Ice pick
Wheelbarrow
Thin copper or other wire
Needles
Strong shoe thread

ADDITIONAL READINGS
(See also pages 143–144.)

Des Grey, Arthur: *Camping.*
Jaeger, Ellsworth: *Wildwood Wisdom.*
Kesting, Ted: *The Outdoor Encyclopedia.*
Knife and Axe. Girl Scouts, 40 pp., 25¢.
Lynn, Gordon: *Camping and Camp Crafts.*
Maintenance and Care of Hand Tools. U.S. Gov't Printing Office.
Mason, Bernard S.: *The Junior Book of Camping and Woodcraft.*
Rutstrum, Calvin: *The New Way of the Wilderness.*
Tobitt, Janet E.: *Program in Girl Scout Camping.*
Toolcraft. Girl Scouts #15-05, Flip Charts, $6.00.
Whelan, Townsend, and Angier, Bradford: *On Your Own in the Wilderness.*
Whittling is Easy. Boy Scouts #3165, 16 pp., 25¢.
Whittling is Easy with X-Acto. X-Acto, Inc., 48 Van Dam St., Long Island City 1, N.Y., 40 pp.
Woodcarving. Boy Scouts #3315, 25¢.

MAGAZINE ARTICLES

Cassell, Sylvia: *Make Whittling Worthwhile.* C.M., June, 1954.
Cassell, Sylvia: *Try Hiking Sticks.* C.M., Mar., 1952.
Jaeger, Ellsworth: *Making Belts and Necklaces From Twigs.* C.M., Jan., 1950.

24

Axemanship

Camp is the smooth grip of an axe handle,
The clean bite and the white chips flying.
OUR AMERICAN HERITAGE

THERE ARE many varieties of axes available, perhaps a throwback to early days when they were made by the community blacksmith to suit his own particular taste or that of his customers. Each axe was named for the region from which it came as the Maine axe, the Hudson's Bay axe, the Kentucky axe, and so on. Many varieties are still in existence and this is perhaps justified since axes are used for many purposes.

Axes range in length from the little 13½ inch scout axe, intended to be used by one hand, to the 33 inch axe of the lumberjack and experienced woodsman, and they vary correspondingly in weight.

Double-bitted and Pole Axes

Axes are of two general types: the double-bitted and the pole. A *double-bitted* axe is usually full size and is distinguished by having two blades, one at each side of the head. It is attributed to that legendary hero of the Northwoods, Paul Bunyan, who, of course, wouldn't have been content to chop like ordinary people but had to have an axe with which he could chop "both coming and going." One edge is ordinarily ground thin and sharp for felling trees, the other thick and strong for splitting *down* wood. The champions of the double-bitted axe claim that it is better balanced and easier to handle than the pole axe. However, it has no place in the organized camp for it is too dangerous for any but the experienced to use.

266

A *pole axe* has only one edge and comes in a wide variety of styles and sizes. The pole is the flattened side opposite the *edge* or *bite* and can be used for such tasks as pounding a tent peg into the ground. We shall discuss only the two most commonly used in the organized camp, the *scout axe* and the *camp axe*.

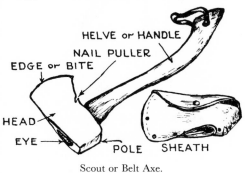

HELVE or HANDLE
NAIL PULLER
EDGE or BITE
HEAD
EYE
POLE   SHEATH

Scout or Belt Axe.

The Scout Axe

This short 12–13½ inch axe weighs only 1 to 1¼ pounds and is recommended for general camp use. It is sturdy and rugged, inexpensive, light, easy to handle, and will meet almost every need from preparing firewood to doing light camp construction. It is meant to be held in one hand (hence it is sometimes called a *hand axe*) and can be carried in its sheath on your belt just back of your hip (which accounts for another name, the *belt axe*).

SELECTION.   Scout axes vary in weight but the lighter models are best suited for the inexperienced. Don't try to economize, for cheap axes are poorly balanced and constructed, and the steel is often inferior and won't hold an edge. Grasp the axe by the head and sight along it to see that the head is in direct alignment with the handle. The grain of the wood should run along parallel with the handle. The parts are named as indicated in the figure. Some axes have wooden handles of tough hickory. In others, the head and inner core of the handle are a continuous piece of metal so that the head can't come loose, with an extra grip of wood

or composition around the handle to provide a secure hold. The bump at the end of the handle is to prevent its flying from your hand when the axe is in use.

The Camp Axe

A *camp* or *three-quarter axe* is small and light and can easily be handled by counselors or older campers. It has an eighteen to twenty-two inch handle and a head slightly larger and heavier than the scout axe. Its greater weight and longer handle provide more power for chopping but the inexperienced should leave it alone for it is potentially dangerous. It should be fitted with a good sheath with metal rivets or a metal lining which the edge cannot cut through. Though quite useful for heavy-duty chopping around camp, its length makes it unwieldy for back packing where a scout axe will usually do all the work needed anyway; in fact, some take no axe at all on a short trip where plenty of wood for cooking or for building a campfire can be gathered and broken by hand or under the foot.

Caring for Your Axe

Regard your axe as the fine tool that it is and keep it in good condition all of the time, sharp and ready for use. Like a knife, a good camper neither lends nor borrows an axe; you will understand why when you have once gone through the arduous task of putting your edge in top-notch condition.

The end of the *helve* or handle must fit tightly into the eye and is kept so by means of (1) a wooden wedge (2) a steel wedge or (3) a series of screws. However, no matter how tightly the head fits when new, it will eventually dry out and must then be tightened immediately for you can easily see how dangerous a loose head on a swinging axe could be.

You may be advised to soak your axe overnight in a pail of water to tighten it

How To Wear Your Sheath Knife and Hatchet.

but this is only a temporary measure and the head will be looser than ever when it dries out again. Soaking it in oil is a little better for the oil causes the head to swell and thus it lasts a little longer but the only really satisfactory method is to insert a new wedge.

Never leave an axe lying about for someone to cut himself on or stumble over. Either drive it into a dead tree or stump (never a live tree) or replace it in its sheath and lay it up, hang it on a nail, or replace it on your belt. When on a trip, many prefer to keep it handy in their pack instead of wearing it on a belt.

If it is necessary to carry an unsheathed axe for even a short distance, grasp the handle close to the head and with blade down so it can't cut you if you trip or catch it on underbrush. When handing it to another, extend it head first for him to grasp and be sure he has hold of it securely before you let go.

Sharpening Your Axe

Since axes serve so many different purposes, the manufacturer purposely leaves the edge dull so that the new owner can sharpen it according to his wish. If you are inexperienced, it is usually best to get an experienced person to put the axe in shape for you the first time. If you are going to sharpen it yourself, you must first thin an area as indicated in the picture. However, be sure to do it just right

AREA TO BE SHARPENED ON GRINDSTONE

Sharpen an area like this.

for, if too stubby, the edge will not cut at all and if too thin, it will lack strength and may chip. The preliminary work is usually done on a hand grindstone. The job can be done with a file but is slow and laborious. For a scout axe, the thinned area should be 1 to 1½ inches wide at the widest portion. Leave the corners of the blade, which enter the wood first, somewhat thicker and more durable so they'll withstand the harder work they have to do. Support the axe against a log or block of wood laid on the ground or a table and use a seven to eight inch *flat* or *mill* file. It is all important to apply the file to the edge or bite

Sharpening an Axe with a Mill File.

at the proper angle. Use the coarse side of the file and, starting at the edge, stroke back toward the pole with a long, straight stroke. After you finish one side, turn the axe over and repeat on the other. Repeat the process with the fine side of the file.

If you are sharpening a large axe, place it alongside a solid log of such size that the edge of the blade extends slightly above it, and anchor it solidly against the log with two stakes, one near the head and the other near the end of the handle. Kneel on one knee with the file handle in one hand and the other hand resting on top near the tip of the file to guide it over the axe at the proper angle. Use the coarse side of the file first, then the fine.

When you have sharpened the axe as much as possible with the file, you are ready to *hone* it with a *carborundum* or *sharpening* stone, holding the axe between your knees and rubbing the stone over it with a circular motion. This removes the *burr* or *wire edge* left by the file.

Keep your axe sharp enough to bite, not chew, into the wood for it saves much work and is also less dangerous since the edge bites into the wood instead of glancing off and perhaps striking you or someone else nearby.

Using an Axe

Always use a good, solid and broad chopping block, from one to two feet high. If it has a tendency to roll, anchor it with solid stakes driven into the ground tight against it. Level off the top and make a slight depression to hold the wood. Aim every stroke so that your axe will enter the block as it severs the wood, never into the ground where it would be nicked or dulled by contact with sand or pebbles.

Inspect your surroundings carefully to see that there is no one near you and no brush or overhanging branches to catch your axe head to deflect it on the backswing. Wet hands are slippery so see that your hands are dry.

Cut at a forty-five degree angle.

If using a scout axe, kneel on one knee, grasp it in one hand near the end of the handle; take a good backswing bringing the axe down so that the edge enters the wood at a 45 degree angle. Never chop directly across the grain for you will make little progress and it will quickly dull your axe. Chop around, not through, knots for they also dull and chip your axe. *Direct the blow toward the chopping block, not toward any part of yourself.*

If using a camp axe, stand with your feet comfortably spread and solidly placed on the ground, with no pebbles or sticks underneath which might slide or roll with you. You will need both hands. Your left hand remains near the top of the handle throughout the stroke. Place your right hand fairly well down the handle for the backswing and slide it up toward the left as the axe descends. Hands are close together as the axe bites into the wood. Continue sliding the right hand down to help lift and control the axe during the backswing, then back to meet the left as the axe descends. Learn to coordinate all your muscles in a rhythmic swing of your whole body, using in particular the powerful muscles of your back, shoulders and hips. Remember that effective chopping is more a matter of skill and timing than muscle and that power comes from long, rhythmic strokes attained by getting a good backswing and letting the weight of your axe head add power as it descends. Avoid the short, ineffectual "peckings" of the novice who slowly removes wood by chewing it out instead of taking out relatively large chips, usually one for each two strokes, as a good woodsman does. Work steadily and diligently but not excitedly and keep your eye on the spot you want to hit. Try to strike it everytime, and stop and rest if you get tired; fatigue brings loss of control and coordination and a bad accident may result.

Cutting a Log in Two

If the log is small enough to be turned over easily, chop out large chips to form a V on one side about half way through, turn the log over and repeat from the other side until the V's meet. Make the top of each V approximately equal to the thickness of the log and cut at an angle of 45 degrees. A common mistake is to make the V too narrow at the top so that you do not chop halfway through the log and must then go back and widen it from the top. If your axe sticks in the wood, press down on the handle to loosen the blade before you try to remove it.

Take out a chip with each two strokes.

Chop alternately from right to left, with well-aimed decisive blows, twisting your axe slightly at the end of the stroke to loosen the chip so that you take out a sizeable chip with each few strokes. Remember that the better the axeman, the fewer the chips. If you have a long log which you want to cut in several shorter pieces, cut all of the V's on one side before you turn it over for the weight and length of a long log makes it steadier and less inclined to roll.

Severing a Log.

When a log is too large to turn over, stand to one side of it and cut a fairly wide V on the opposite side; then step across the log and repeat from the other side. If the V's are the proper width, you can finish the job with a few well aimed blows. An experienced woodsman stands directly on top of a large log and cuts a V between his feet but this is taboo for the novice whose inaccurate strokes might easily gash his feet or legs.

Felling a Tree

It is often essential to cut down a small sapling for campsite construction, and you will want to do a clean, quick job of it. You can usually sever small saplings by bending them over to strain the fibers and giving one or two good blows from the hatchet on top of the bend. For a larger sapling, make *kerfs,* nearly straight across at the bottom, and sloping at the top so that the stump left will be flat and less dangerous to passers-by. Continue your kerfs until they nearly meet, then a gentle push will send your sapling to the ground. Never do this with anything but a very small tree for the butt might slide back to hit you and injure you seriously.

Felling a Small Tree.

If the top of the tree is surrounded by overhanging branches so that there is danger of the tree's getting caught as it falls, you must decide in which direction there will be less entanglement and make your first kerf, A, on that side. Then make kerf, B, on the opposite side a little higher. When the kerfs nearly meet, the trees will topple over toward side A; watch for it and stay well out of the way so you won't be struck by branches or the butt end as it falls.

Use dead, diseased, crooked, or crowded trees for cutting whenever possible, not live, sound ones. It takes but a moment for you to destroy what will take nature years to replace.

Chopping Small Sticks.

Limbing a Tree.

Lopping Branches

Lopping branches or limbing a tree means removing the branches close to the side of a down tree. To do it, stand on one side of the trunk and lop the branches from the other side, chopping upward toward the top of the tree as you keep the trunk between you and your swinging hatchet so that you can't hit yourself. Start at the butt end and proceed to the top, severing the branches as close to the trunk as possible. Then cross over to the other side and remove the remaining branches.

Cutting Small Sticks

One of the best methods is the *contact* method where you place your axe at an angle of 45 degrees on the stick, raise both axe and stick and bring them down simultaneously against the chopping block.

Another method is to grasp the stick in your left hand and slant it down with the spot you want to sever resting solidly against the block. Then swing the axe down with good momentum, severing the stick so that it falls close to the block in-

stead of flying dangerously through the air. Keep your left hand high, well out of the way of the axe, and direct the axe so that it will enter the block, even if you miss the stick. If the stick isn't severed with the first blow, give it a half turn and try it again. Give a large stick a quarter turn and use four strokes.

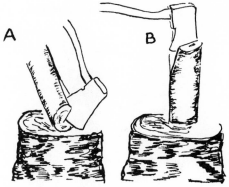

Splitting Kindling.

Splitting Kindling

Since split wood burns much better than whole sticks with the bark intact, it is time well spent to keep some kindling and larger split wood on hand. Standing at one side of the chopping block, grasp the piece of wood in your left hand, place the axe on top of it, and bring wood and axe down simultaneously on the chopping block (contact method) several times, if necessary, until you have made a split clear across the end of the wood. With your hatchet still in the split, turn your hatchet face down, remove your left hand, stand the wood upright, and bring both hatchet and wood down against the chopping block until the wood splits all the way down. Split these segments into still smaller pieces if you want finer kindling. Notice again that, when correctly done, the hatchet is directed toward the chopping block so that it cannot possibly hurt you.

If a stick is too large to be split by this method, stand it upright on the chopping block, place your axe on it and drive it into the wood by pounding on it with a stick of wood. Never use another axe for this purpose for there is danger of breaking one or both of them.

Be wary about holding a stick up against the chopping block with your foot; this practice is dangerous unless you are sure your axe is aimed directly toward the chopping block and can't possibly glance off and hit your foot.

Stake Sharpening.

Sharpening a Stake

To sharpen a stake such as a tent peg or other pole you want to drive into the ground, hold it upright on the chopping block and sharpen it on four sides. You can make a four-sided point more quickly and it will drive better than a round point.

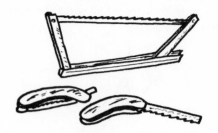

Collapsible Bucksaw and Folding Saw.

SAWS

Most woodsmen prefer a saw to an axe for cutting through large pieces of wood or felling anything larger than a sapling. There are a number of folding and collapsible saws available which are light and compact and suitable even for taking on long trips, for preparing firewood and helping with construction as at an outpost camp. To cut up a log for firewood, saw it into twelve inch lengths and then split them with your axe. Stumps left by sawing are less dangerous to passers-by since they are flat on top instead of having wicked pointed tops.

ADDITIONAL READINGS

Des Grey, Arthur H.: *Camping*.
Toolcraft. Girl Scouts #15-05 Flip Charts, $6.00.
Henderson, Luis M.: *The Outdoor Guide*.
Jaeger, Ellsworth: *Woodsmoke*.
Knife and Axe. Girl Scouts, 40 pp., 25¢.
Lynn, Gordon: *Camping and Camp Crafts*.
Mason, Bernard S.: *The Junior Book of Camping and Woodcraft*.
Pioneering. Boy Scouts #3382, 25¢.
Rutstrum, Calvin: *The New Way of the Wilderness*.
Swanson, William: *Log Cabins*. The Macmillan Co., 1948, $2.95.

25

Fires and Fire Prevention

Each color or tint that a tree has known
  In the heart of a wood-fire glows
Look into the flames and you will see
  Blue dusk and the dawn's pale rose,
The golden light of the noonday sun,
  The purple of darkening night,
The crimson glow of the sunset,
  The sheen of the soft moonlight.
Fire brings forth from the heart of a tree
Beauty stored there in memory.

MARY S. EDGAR*

FOREST CONSERVATION

Why the Need

Times do change and we can see no clearer example of it than in our altered attitude toward our forests. When the first settlers came to America, they could not have imagined that it would ever be necessary to think of conserving trees for they were surrounded by a seemingly endless expanse of them and their main desire must have been to cut them down to make room for building homes and planting the crops necessary to sustain themselves. Forests also sheltered Indians, some of whom were naturally resentful of the white man's intrusion and "taking over" policies, and wild animals that sought to fill their stomachs by raids on precious livestock. At the same time, the forests proved a real boon, for they furnished fuel for fires, lumber for homes and barns, and posts for fencing in possessions. Lumber was used to build stockades against the unfriendly Indians and animals. In addition, the forests provided food and herbs, and sheltered fish and wild game that supplied a welcome variety to an otherwise monotonous diet.

Soon these hard working, resourceful people found that there was an eager market in England and other foreign countries for wood products. This gave them a means of procuring the ready cash necessary to buy the finished products youthful America was not yet

* From *Wood-Fire and Candle-Light*. Permission by The Macmillan Company, Ltd. of Canada.

273

(Joy and Camp.)

equipped to produce. Consequently lumbering became a business, probably the first big industry of the United States and the loggers expanded their operations in ever widening circles, establishing logging camps, which eventually became the towns and cities of young America.

But what of the effect of all this on the forests? The practice of the money-minded logging companies was to cut down everything in their paths and this "clean cutting" philosophy took with it the young saplings as well as ripe trees, leaving a desolate waste of stumps behind which would take nature from thirty to 100 years to replace. It seemed that few citizens were far-seeing enough to even glimpse what a continuation of these practices would eventually lead to, though William Penn, as early as 1653, made an unsuccessful plea to "save one acre of forest for every one that was cut."

What Progress is Being Made

Modern times, however, have revealed some very hopeful signs of progress in appreciating and trying to save our priceless heritage of forest land. One evidence is in the development of the science of *forest management* or careful planning to make the best possible use of our forests for both present and future generations. It includes, among other things, the study and control of insects, diseases, and destructive grazing which are harmful to tree growth, and the prevention and extinguishing of the ever threatening forest fires which continue to wreck immeasurable damage. Tree farming is now a scientific occupation with trees considered as a crop which must be planned for, nurtured, and harvested with all the care and thought accorded any other crop. Highly trained specialists select the mature trees which have attained their maximum growth and consequently are ready for harvesting and, at the same time, plan how to promote a continuous stream of new growth to replace what is taken. These commercially promoted areas, together with the 161 national forests scattered over forty states and twenty-nine national parks, usually also provide shelter and at least some degree of protection for birds and other wild life.

Nevertheless, our trees are still disappearing far too rapidly and this loss can be stopped only as more and more people become aware of the problem and are willing to help.

How Forests Help Us

Trees and woodlands serve us in many more ways than we can possibly mention here. One of most concern to us in camping is that they furnish the natural background for thousands of summer camps where youth can assemble to seek relaxation and fun in a cool, pleasant atmosphere and see animal and plant life in its natural habitat. These same benefits are available for thousands of others who are increasingly learning the joys of taking to the woods for hiking, picnicking, swimming, boating, family or group camping, hunting, fishing, and so forth. Nearly one-third of the land area in the United States is still covered by wild growth and three-fourths of this is devoted to commercial usage. New uses are constantly being found for lumber so that 70 per cent of a felled tree, including even the bark and sawdust, can now be used in such diversified products as lumber for building, furniture, pulp and paper, fuel, charcoal, plastics, drugs, and pressed wood.

Trees also furnish us with maple syrup, resins, fruit, nuts, turpentine, chemicals, and even the trees to make our Christmas merry. Standing timber also protects our watersheds and minimizes erosion. Its underlying carpet of grass, shrubs, debris and underbrush holds back the rain so that it can be absorbed into the soil and gradually returned to the air in a steady stream as it is drawn up through the wide spreading roots and eventually evaporated through the leaves. Without

vegetation on our hills and slopes, downpours of rain and the melting of winter snows would cascade unimpeded down hillsides into swollen streams, causing them to overflow their banks and leave behind the destruction, waste, and heartbreak of a flood.

FOREST FIRES

Destruction Caused by Fire

In spite of modern scientific forestry, fires continue to engage in "clean cutting" and still occur at an average rate of over 500 a day, destroying the growth on millions of acres of land annually, or an area larger than the state of Maine. They leave ugly, blackened wastelands in their wake, which will take nature from 50 to 100 years to restore.

In addition to this aesthetic loss, there is no longer vegetation to catch and hold the rainfall so that we have set the stage for floods and erosion which rob the soil of its rich, productive top layers and cause plants and animals, including man, to be uprooted from their homes and possessions. Back in the forest where the fire raged, countless wild animals of every description fled in terrified panic in a fruitless attempt to escape the raging inferno, for a forest fire in full stride travels fast enough to overtake the fleetest animal, or a man on horseback. In addition, fire burns off the decayed and decaying twigs and other vegetable matter and depletes the minerals so that the resulting soil is no longer fertile and productive. Trees which are not killed outright are left scarred and weakened and they become easy preys to insect and disease or are so loosened that they are blown over by the next strong wind.

What Causes Forest Fires

Though such forces as lightning or trees rubbing together in a high wind may start occasional fires, the chances are nine out of ten that man was directly or indirectly responsible. The largest number of fires (31 per cent) are incendiary in origin for, strangely enough, some people purposely start fires to "get even" with a neighbor or cover up the evidence of a misdeed, and children or maladjusted adults do it just for the sake of excitement. The next largest number (21 per cent) results from smokers who toss away still burning matches or cigarette butts as they hike or ride through the forests in their automobiles. The third most frequent cause (17 per cent) is the spreading of fires set by people who use poor judgment or poor methods in burning off wastes or debris or who still follow the destructive practice of "burning off" their land in the spring in the mistaken belief that it will help get rid of unwanted weeds, insects, or other pests. Ignorant or careless campers who build wrong fires in wrong places or leave fires untended or without properly extinguishing them cause 4 per cent of fires. The other 27 per cent result from lumbering, railroads or miscellaneous and unknown causes.

Types of Forest Fires

Forest fires are classified into three types: (1) *Surface fires* are commonest and travel along just above the ground, consuming the forest floor or *duff* (litter of grass, leaves, twigs, and underbrush). They are usually the beginning form of the other two types of fires. (2) *Ground fires* burn along below the surface in the decayed and decaying vegetable growth there and often continue unnoticed for days, since there is ordinarily no flame and little smoke. When conditions are right, they may break out on the surface and soon turn into a raging inferno and, even while still underground, they are very hot and do serious damage. (3) A *crown fire* results when a high wind whips a surface fire upward into the tree tops where it gallops along at breakneck speed and often proves heartbreakingly

hard to stop. Since it is often combined with a surface fire, the destruction is thorough and devastating. Full fledged crown fires may easily cross such natural barriers as open fields and sizeable rivers as the wind picks up flaming embers and sweeps them along high in the air.

Fire Prevention*

Man has not been caught napping in his never-ending attempt to stem the wanton destruction of fire. Efforts are devoted to preventing fires, detecting them as early as possible and having trained men and special equipment on a stand-by basis to put them out as rapidly as possible.

Since 90 per cent of forest fires are caused by man, obviously the most hopeful approach is to try to develop in people a widespread realization of the problem and a spirit of cooperation in solving it. To this end, wonderful progress has been made through newspaper and magazine articles radio and television programs, public talks, posters, exhibits, colored slides, and motion pictures. Groups such as the American Red Cross, the Boy and Girl Scouts, civic and community organizations and thousands of teachers have given unselfishly of their time and efforts in this behalf.

In 1945, a poster of a bear dousing a campfire with a pail of water captured the public fancy and "Smokey" has appeared time after time since then as a symbol of fire prevention. In 1950, an actual bear cub rescued from a New Mexico forest fire was named "Smokey" and has since become the symbol of forest safety to thousands.

Evidence that this campaign has had a worth-while impact is seen in the fact that there were 15,000 fewer fires annually

*Much of the information in this section has been secured from the publications of the American Forest Products Industries, Inc. and Forest Service, U.S. Dept. of Agriculture.

in the years 1946–50 than occurred in a similar period before World War II.

In addition, forcible measures have been taken, such as a requirement in some states that no one may build an outdoor fire who has not procured a license by demonstrating his knowledge and ability to do so safely. Many public areas now allow fires only in designated, safely constructed fireplaces and fire sites, with careful patrol and supervision from rangers. Fire towers or lookouts are scattered throughout forest areas, equipped with maps and powerful detection instruments and with short wave radio and telephone for communicating with other areas. Thus, beginning fires are quickly pinpointed and man power and equipment dispatched over fire roads to control them while still in the "baby" stage. Some fire towers are manned constantly by trained personnel while others can be called into use when dry weather and high winds make conditions especially hazardous. Other watchers patrol on foot, on horseback or by airplane.

Modern fire fighters no longer rely on the brute force of such tools as pails, axes, and shovels. The whole process has been increasingly mechanized with men and specialized equipment quickly conveyed by jeep, truck, airplane or helicopter. Chemicals and many improved methods have been pressed into use. The United States Forest Service is responsible for protecting some 210 million acres of privately and publicly owned land.

What You as a Camper Can Do

1. Be careful with fire and observe all the hints for its safe use discussed in this book; instruct others and encourage them to do likewise.
2. Report any fire you see just as quickly as you can.
3. Plant trees and help protect useful timber.

Never cut a living tree when a dead one will do. If a green one is indispensable, pick out the least desirable specimen that will serve your purpose. Select one that is crooked, diseased, of a less desirable species, or in a thicket where none have a chance to grow because of overcrowding.

CHOOSING THE SITE FOR YOUR FIRE

You must be sure, above all things, that your fire will not spread, so choose your site carefully; if on someone's private property, always secure permission first.

No matter how pleasant and romantic a fire in a deeply wooded area seems, it is always dangerous, for there are usually dry branches on the bottom of even live trees and a roaring fire underneath may dry out green branches and set them on fire. It is much safer to build your fire out in the open or where there is a clearance of at least twenty-five or thirty feet up to the lowest branches.

If you must build a fire on top of a grassy area, you may restore its appearance by removing the sod with a spade and replacing it after the fire is out and the ground is cool again.

The floor of the forest is usually covered with a litter of dead leaves, broken branches, and other debris called *duff* and underlying organic matter of the soil in the form of leaf mold and decomposing branches called *humus*. These are combustible and fire may smoulder and break out in them hours after your campfire is forgotten. Clear away all such material down to hard ground for an area of at least eight to ten feet before you build your fire. Use special caution with the soil known as "peat" or "muck" for this itself is combustible, and fire may creep along it and break out even as long as several days later. Surround your fire site with rocks, if available. (See p. 283.)

GREEN STICK POKER →

FIRE TONGS →

WATER →

SHOVEL →

Tools for the Campfire.

It is best to lay a foundation of sand, gravel or flat stones first. Avoid using shale and limestone which may crack and fly like shrapnel when heated. Rocks near water or in creek beds have often become so water-logged that heating creates enough steam to burst them. If you dry them out *gradually* by *gentle* heat, you may eventually find them satisfactory to use.

Never build a fire against a tree, for, if dead, it might catch on fire; if green, you will injure or perhaps kill it.

FIRE CONTROL

Before lighting a campfire, make preparations to (1) handle it quickly if it starts to spread, and (2) put it out when through with it.

Certain tools are useful for this purpose. A shovel or spade is handy for clearing off combustible debris before building your fire and for smothering it with dirt if it starts to spread. It also serves to move coals into the exact position needed for baking or other cooking and to push blazing firebrands over to one side where they will not burn or smoke your food. Lastly, you can use it for burying garbage and extinguishing the fire.

It is well to have a special container of water near to use in case of emergency; do not use it for any other purpose and, if not needed for this, it will be available to put out your fire when you are through with it.

Minimize the danger of having your fire spread by keeping an orderly campsite with all equipment neatly in place and all debris promptly cleared away and disposed of.

Never leave a campfire unattended for even a few moments, for it can spread and get completely out of control in that brief time.

If a Fire Starts to Spread

When a fire starts to run wild, immediate action is important, for every instant counts and a fire that you alone could easily control may get completely out of hand in a short time. Send or go for help unless you are sure you can handle it by yourself.

To extinguish a fire, you must either (1) deprive it of oxygen, for no fire can burn without it, or (2) deprive it of fuel. To smother it, douse it with water, beat it with a broom, a green switch of evergreen with top branches remaining, or a wet burlap bag or any heavy material saturated with water, or cover it with sand, dirt or gravel. Beat into the wind so that you will not simply be fanning the fire and spreading sparks ahead of you. To deprive it of fuel, go up far enough ahead in a windward direction to allow time to dig a trench, twelve to eighteen inches wide and deep enough to reach mineral soil; throw the inflammable material *away* from the path of the fire so that the fire will simply starve to death for lack of fuel. Watch over the area long enough to be sure the fire is really out.

SELECTING CAMPFIRE MATERIALS

General Hints

A fire out of control is a dreadful thing, yet nothing is quite so helpful to a camper as a controlled campfire, for it cooks his food, warms him when he is cold, destroys his unwanted rubbish, allows him to send messages, and, most important of all, cheers him and keeps his morale high with its bright, friendly glow. One of your most poignant memories of camping days will be of the time spent in pleasant camaraderie and genuine fellowship around a campfire.

The disappointment and discomfort experienced by a new camper when no one in a group can produce more than a smudge fire are enough to sour him on camping forever. A camper is known by his campfire; therefore you must know enough about fires to be able to build the right one in the right place at the right time.

Three components enter into building a successful fire: (1) good *tinder* to catch immediately when you apply the match and burn long enough to ignite (2) the kindling, which in turn sets fire to the (3) *firewood,* which will burn long enough and with sufficient force to provide the heat, light or atmosphere you want. You must carefully select, prepare and arrange each of these three components to get a "just right" fire. A skillful fire builder does not carelessly pick up any old wood, toss it into a hit-or-miss pile and apply a match. He works quickly and deftly, each movement made for a definite purpose; he carefully selects each bit of fuel to do just what he wants it to do. A fire which is balky and refuses to burn briskly or which coughs spasmodically a few times and then quietly dies in the middle of the meal preparation is most likely composed of the wrong sort of wood or the wood is arranged in the wrong way.

You must know the wood of your particular region so that you can make the best selection from what is available. It isn't enough to be able to glibly recite the names of trees when in full leaf, for campers use dead, dry wood which has no leaves and must be identified by its bark and the character of the wood itself.

Tinder

Many things are suitable for tinder, that highly inflammable material that ignites at the touch of a match. The white birchbark of the Northland is the general favorite since it burns well, even when wet or rotten. Never strip it from a living tree. Use the plenteous quantities usually available which have peeled off and fallen to the ground or use *dead* curls that can be removed without harming the tree.

Pieces of fat pine, dry evergreen cones, last year's dry weed stalks, dried goldenrod, grape or honeysuckle vines, Queen Anne's lace, old birds' or squirrels' nests, milkweed silk, sagebrush, dried cactus, corn stalks and dry corncobs make excellent tinder. The bark of the elm, hemlock or cedar is good when "fuzzed" up a bit.

Three fuzz clumps or fuzz sticks, pyramided together at the base of a fire, make good tinder, but, as a matter of fact, woodsmen seldom use them for they take too much time to prepare when so many natural tinders are readily avail-

Fuzz Clump.

Fuzz Sticks.

First a curl of birch bark, as dry as it kin be,
Then some twigs of soft wood, dead, but on the
  tree,
Last o' all some pine knots to make the kittle
  foam,
An' thar's a fire to make you think you're settin'
  right at home.
                              —ERNEST THOMPSON SETON

able. Shavings, if thin and curly, also serve adequately.

A handful of twigs, each hardly bigger than a match, and broken in the middle, make good tinder and burn even more readily if the twigs are split.

Such things as oiled bread paper, excelsior, or newspapers are good if incidentally taken along as food wrappings, but no camper should ever become dependent on them and take them along just to build fires.

Dry grass and leaves make poor tinder for, though they blaze brightly, they do not last long enough to set fire to anything heavy.

Kindling

You will need kindling which will catch readily from the tinder and burn briskly and long enough to ignite the firewood; it should be small in size, ranging from the size of a match stick to about the size of your little finger. Fat pine, cedar, or paper birch are best, but all the birches are satisfactory. Split evergreen, basswood, tulip, sumac, white and nearly all other kinds of pine, spruce, balsam or box elder and the frayed bark of cedar or hemlock are all good.

FIREWOOD

Firewood is divided roughly into two types, hardwood and softwood, and each has its special uses to a camper.

Soft Woods

The lumbering industry considers only the *evergreens* or *conifers* as soft woods and all the broad-leaved trees (*deciduous,* or those which shed their leaves annually) as hard woods. Campers, however, consider as soft wood all wood which is actually softer and weighs less for its size. This includes the evergreens and also some of the broad-leaved trees.

To distinguish between soft woods and hard woods, pick up samples and test their comparative weights in your hand; hard woods are more compact and consequently weigh more. Soft woods burn quickly and furiously and so are prized as kindling, to provide quick flames for rapid boiling or baking or to blaze brightly and spread cheer and light for council fires. They are of little use for maintained heat or elaborate cooking since they quickly burn down to dead ashes with few good coals.

The soft woods include alder, quaking aspen, balsam, basswood (linden), buck-

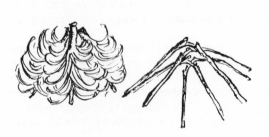

Fuzz Sticks, Broken
Sticks and Fuzz Clumps
Pyramided as Tinder.

eye, cedar (red or white), chestnut, cottonwood, soft or silver maple, pine (jack or
Labrador and white or loblolly), pitch pine
(fine for kindling, but, even when burning
brightly, emits a resin which taints food
and coats utensils), spruce, sycamore,
tamarack, and tulip (yellow poplar).

Hard Woods

You will want hard woods for most
cooking and warmth. They kindle slowly
and require a hot fire of softwood to get
them started, but, when once ablaze, are
long-lasting and burn down to a bed of
glowing coals which continues to throw
out steady heat for a long time. Hickory,
oak and maple are usually considered
best for cooking. However, apple, white
ash, beech, all the birches, dogwood,
holly, hornbeam (ironwood), locust, mulberry, pecan, yellow pine, and tamarack
(lodge pole pine) are also good.

Spitfire Woods

These are woods which, in general,
burn well enough, but tend to spit and
make alarming noises. A still worse feature is their tendency to throw sparks
which may start a forest fire or burn
holes in tents or blankets. Soft woods in
this class are alder, arbor vitae (white
cedar) balsam, basswood (linden), box
elder, red cedar, chestnut, hemlock, all
the pines, sassafras, spruce, tamarack,
tulip (yellow poplar) and willow (this is
also undesirable because it imparts an
unpleasant taste to food cooked over it).

Slow-Burning Green Woods

These are woods which, when green,
will scarcely burn at all and so are good
for neither cooking nor for warmth but
this very fire resistance greatly enhances
their value as firedogs, backlogs and fire
banks. The following belong in this class:
black ash, balsam, basswood (linden),
box elder, buckeye butternut (white wal-

nut), chestnut, cypress, hemlock, red
(scarlet) maple, red and water oak, per-
simmon, pine (black or pitch and white),
poplar (aspen), sassafras, sourwood, sycamore (plane tree or buttonwood), tamarack, tulip (yellow poplar) and tupelo
(sour gum).

SELECTING WOOD

You must use discrimination when
selecting firewood, for just any old wood
won't do. Green wood, because of its
moisture content, seldom burns well, but,
on the other hand, wood that is extremely
old has lost some of its most valuable
heat-producing qualities. A little intelligent experimentation will help you
select the best.

The *duff* of the forest usually consists of
a layer of dead and decaying leaves and
twigs on top of rich, black soil of partially
decomposed vegetable matter called
humus. This varies from a few inches to a
foot or two in depth. This forest carpet
tends to hold moisture so that, even in
dry weather, branches lying on the
ground in contact with it are often half
rotten and more or less damp, at least on
the underside. Therefore, picking up
branches from the ground is sometimes a
poor way to get firewood. As the trees in
a heavily wooded area grow, each constantly struggles to reach above its neighbors to absorb more of the sunlight. Thus,
the lower branches are too shaded to
thrive and eventually die, and make
especially good firewood when they have
hung on long enough for the bark to dis-
integrate, for the free circulation of air
about them keeps them relatively dry.
They seem to have been greatly prized
as fuel even in feudal times when all of
the land belonged to the lord of the
manor. The peasants were not permitted
to cut trees, but could use only such firewood as they found on the ground or
could reach in the trees with their pruning hooks and shepherd's crooks (an

ingenious way for the lord to keep his trees free from underbrush). It is easy to imagine how they invented devious methods to obtain more than was rightfully theirs—thus the expression "by hook or by crook." Branches extending up into the air on downwood also provide dry fuel, and dry, weathered roots and knots make excellent, long-lasting fuel.

You can test wood for dryness by trying to break it, for small, dry sticks will break cleanly with a snap, while wet or green ones bend and finally break with jagged edges. Large dry sticks feel firm and heavy in the hand and will usually snap if hit sharply on the edge of a rock; if two dry sticks are tapped together, they emit a clear, sharp sound rather than the dull, muffled one of wet or green sticks. Sticks that crumble or break up too easily when given a sharp blow are rotten and would only smoulder and smoke if put on the fire.

Wood picked up from the ground is called *squaw wood* and should not be ignored, for, when well chosen, it makes a valuable contribution to any fire. The Indians likely used little else for they had no implement comparable to our sharp hatchet for chopping and splitting. Modern campers differ as to just how much to use a hatchet in preparing firewood. It is only common sense and not at all unwoodsman-like to break sticks by hand or underfoot instead of chopping when you can do so easily. You may also avoid chopping by laying long pieces of wood

across the fire to burn apart. On the other hand, the ability to use a hatchet skillfully is a big asset, particularly for splitting wood. Walt Whitman said, "We are warmed twice by wood; once when we cut it and again when we burn it." All pieces of wood over two inches in diameter should ordinarily be split before placing them on the fire.

Storing Wood

If you are going to stay at a campsite for any length of time, it is worthwhile to arrange your wood in stacks, ranging in size from large sticks for the council fire down to kindling and tinder, each stack kept in place by stakes driven into the ground. Arrange the stack where it will be convenient yet not in the way of proceedings around that popular spot, the fire site. Wood gatherers for a meal or other activity should leave enough prepared wood to replace what has been used. Throw a tarpaulin or poncho over your woodpile to keep it dry or, if none is available, place a small emergency supply of materials under your sleeping tent.

LAYING A FIRE

A good camper collects a big handful of tinder, about twice as much kindling, and enough firewood to maintain his fire for some time before he applies the

A Woodpile.

Foundation for a Fire.

LIGHTING THE FIRE

match, for no self-respecting fire builder wants to have to scamper about to get fuel to keep his fire going after it is once started. Gather plenty of fuel and have it near.

Lay your foundation for a fire by crossing three small sticks as shown, each with one end resting on top of another so the air can get underneath. Then pile a quantity of tinder loosely within them leaving a little tunnel at the bottom on the *windward* side (side from which the wind is blowing) through which to apply your match, so that the flame will be carried upward and into the center. Surround this with loosely pyramided kindling, preferably split. This is what is known as a *basic fire-lay* and is the foundation for any type of fire you want. Now lay on still larger pieces, leaving ample air spaces, for burning consists of *combustion* (the uniting of fuel and oxygen) and many fire failures are caused by dumping the fuel on too compactly.

Fire burns up, only material directly in the path of the flame will ignite, and squatty fires lack enough air to draw well and so are smoky and balky. Keep adding still larger pieces of wood loosely until you have a substantial amount to ignite from that below.

Matches

Use wooden *kitchen* or *torch matches*, for safety or book matches are practically worthless for camp use.

Matches are so essential that, when going on a trip, you should separate your supply, placing the bulk of them in a waterproof container kept in a well-protected spot in your pack and carrying a small-day-by-day supply in a waterproof container on your person. Several containers are illustrated: A is a metal box such as a typewriter ribbon or bouillon cube box and is not waterproof so that, for trip use, you must waterproof the matches themselves. B is a glass bottle with a screw-on top or tight-fitting cork and is, of course, subject to breakage. C represents a common type of metal case which you can purchase inexpensively from a supply house or equipment store. It is water-tight and equipped with a screw top which is anchored on to prevent loss. D, also waterproof, is made of hard black rubber or composition; it has a compass in its screw top and sometimes a magnifying lens in the other end. Both C and D will float if accidentally dropped

Some Match Cases.

in the water. You can also keep matches dry by crimping a cover of aluminum foil around them.

WATERPROOFING MATCHES. The commonest method of waterproofing matches is to coat them with melted paraffin, which forms a waterproof covering as it hardens. You can purchase paraffin at a grocery store. To melt it, place a quantity of it in an old tin can and immerse it in a can of water placed over the fire. Do not cover it or place it directly over flame for it is inflammable and might catch on fire. Only counselors or older, very responsible campers should handle it for it causes nasty burns if spilled on oneself while hot. Never pour it down a sink for it would stop up the drain when it hardens.

Remove the can of paraffin from the water and pour the liquid paraffin over the matches in their box or remove them and separate them into bunches, tying a long string around each far enough back from the heads to leave air spaces; dip each bunch into the hot paraffin (not too hot or they may burst into flame). When needed, pick a match out of its bed of paraffin and scrape off a little of the excess; the remaining paraffin will but make the match burn more ardently.

You can also waterproof matches by dipping them in a thin solution of shellac, varnish, fingernail polish, or collodion.

Applying the Match

Pride yourself on laying your fire so well that you need only one match to start it. Only a greenhorn, with poorly selected and arranged material, ends up with a collection of burned matches around him, making his fire site resemble a game of "pick-up-sticks."

Kneel on the windward side close to the little tunnel in the tinder and select one match, closing your container to protect the other matches. Grasp the match part way down the shaft to lessen the chance of breaking it and strike it,

immediately shielding it from the wind with your cupped hands. Hold the match head down so that the flame will run up the shaft and wait until it is burning through at least a third of its length before *slowly* inserting it through the tunnel to the *bottom* of the tinder.

If you have chosen your material well and arranged it properly, you will need do nothing more than stand by to apply more fuel as needed; avoid smothering the fire by putting on too much wood or applying it too compactly. On the other hand, be sure to keep plenty of loosely arranged wood on the fire to keep it going. If the flame fails to take hold after two or three attempts, don't keep striking more matches, for the trouble is obviously in the fire-lay and you'll save time in the long run by tearing it down and starting all over again. Don't toss away burning matches; drop them in the fire or break them and stick the heads in the ground.

Some General Hints About Fires

A novice builds a fire large enough to roast an ox when his menu consists of only a few little, insignificant wieners. The Indian expressed his disdain for such practices by saying, "White man big fool; make big fire, can't go near; Indian make little fire and sit happy."

A skillful camper can cook a simple meal over a fire no larger than his hat. Big fires take more work, are hot and wasteful of fuel, burn the food, or cook it too rapidly, and create a dangerous fire hazard. They are called *bonfires* to distinguish them from proper campfires. If many people are to be served, it is better to divide them into small groups for cooking or build several small fires to use for various items on the menu.

Cook over coals, not flames, so that your food cooks slowly and clear through instead of being burned and sooty on the outside and raw on the inside. Coals are also more comfortable to cook over, and they do not cover your kettle with a black, sooty mask. Good cooking coals result from a brisk *hardwood* fire, ignited well in advance and kept going until it burns down to a thick bed of glowing embers.

Heavy, large sticks burn better if you elevate them on slow-burning green fire-dogs (see p. 286) which admit air and fire from below. This helps especially on damp, muggy days.

To control the smoke and channel it away from people, create a partial vacuum on the side toward which you want the smoke to go. Do this by building the fire in front of a cliff or other noninflammable barrier, inverting your canoe on its side facing the fire, or suspending a poncho or blanket on a stick framework.

A forked green stick *fire poker* three to four feet long is excellent for rearranging fuel and embers to better advantage. You may use a shovel instead, but should allow the hot coals to rest on it only momentarily lest the heat ruin its temper.

Fire tongs (see p. 278) help in rearranging fuel or moving hot rocks about (see p. 340 for directions for making them). *The inspirator,* attributed to Steward Edward White, is an indispensable device for encouraging a stubborn fire. Make it from a piece of rubber tubing of small diameter and about two feet long. When applied to strategic spots *at the bottom* of the fire and blown gently, it supplies the extra oxygen needed to make a smoky, smouldering fire burst into flame. It is well worth its slight weight for you can coil it up and carry it inside a cooking kettle.

Using an Inspirator.

You may resort to the old-fashioned method of blowing directly on a fire by mouth but turn your head each time you breathe in, for inhaling smoke is a mighty unpleasant experience.

KINDS OF FIRES

Wigwam or Tepee Fire

This is a quick burning fire, for, being tall and slender, the flames climb right to the top and soon have the whole thing ablaze. Hence a small tepee fire provides a good basis for many other types of fire. Start with a foundation fire and place the fuel in tall tepee style with plenty of air spaces between.

It burns with a brilliant, cheerful flame and is consequently a favorite for a small campfire when a few friends gather to chat or hold a short program, but its rapid burning demands frequent fuel replenishment and it does not furnish the coals and steady, long-lasting heat needed for most cooking. Its quick, strong flame is fine for cooking one-pot dishes or bringing water to a boil in a hurry. Keep it small, six inches high or less, when using it as the basis for other fires; make it about eighteen inches high for a campfire.

Wigwam or Tepee Fire.

Indian Fire, Star Fire or Lazy Man's Fire

This fire serves about the same purposes as the wigwam fire, but its struc-

Indian, Star or Lazy Man's Fire.

ture makes it slower-burning and longer-lasting. Start with a small wigwam fire and use long poles, preferably small, as fuel. Overlap the poles in the center to provide better ventilation and radiate them in a wide circle at the outside.

The name "lazy man's fire" comes from the fact that you use long poles which require no chopping and, as their ends burn, you simply push them farther into the fire with your foot. Extinguish the fire by pulling the poles back out of the flame and dousing their ends with water. You can use the unburned portions again another time.

Hunter-Trapper Fire

This is one of the most thoroughly satisfactory cooking fires. Use two fire dogs of green, slow-burning wood; lay them at an angle with the wide end about fifteen to sixteen inches apart and fac-ing the wind. Separate them at the narrow end to a width just broad enough to support the smallest cooking vessel. Flatten the tops to provide a steadier support for your kettles.

Build a small wigwam fire between the firedogs and keep it burning until you have a supply of coals to distribute under the cooking vessels. Lay sticks of green wood, flattened on top, across the firedogs to support the utensils if desired, but they will eventually burn in two and must be watched and replaced when necessary. You can keep part of your fire burning brightly at one spot for quick boiling, and for furnishing new coals to pull over to the other end of the fire for

Stone Hunter-Trapper Fire.

Hunter-Trapper Fire.

sustained heat for frying or broiling.

The firedogs act as reflectors to collect all the heat and throw it up under the vessels, making this an excellent fire when fuel is scarce or the weather hot. Damper sticks under the logs on the windward side help to get the fire started and keep it burning more briskly. You can convert this into a reflector fire (page 288) by slanting some sticks into the ground and piling logs against them. Non-popping stones may be substituted for the wooden firedogs.

Log Cabin or Criss-Cross Fires

A log cabin fire is also an excellent cooking fire, especially when you need a

Log Cabin Fire.

good bed of coals. The small wigwam fire on top quickly burns down and sets the framework of hardwood sticks ablaze. Its loose structure provides plenty of ventilation, so that it quickly burns down to a long-lasting bed of coals. Use sticks of not more than 1 inch in diameter so that they will burn quickly.

Fire-in-a-Hole

This is an efficient fire for preparing a quick, one-pot meal. Build it in a small hole about one foot wide and six to ten inches deep. The walls of the hole reflect all the heat onto the kettles, which are supported on two or more green sticks laid across the top of the hole. This conserves the heat very well and only small sticks need be used for fuel. Place the

Fire-in-a-Hole.

dirt removed from the hole on the leeward side of the fire. There it will not interfere with a free draft and can be replaced in the hole as soon as the cooking is finished. This is a good fire for hot weather or a windy day. If you dig the hole deep enough, it can be used as an imu (see page 358).

Trench Fire (Picture on p. 288.)

This is another good fire for a hot, windy day. It is a long fire and provides room for a much more elaborate menu than does the fire-in-a-hole. Dig a trench about a foot wide at the windward side and narrow it to one half foot at the opposite end. Slant the trench downward from ground level at the windward end to a depth of eight to twelve inches at the leeward end. Support your cooking vessels directly on the sides of the trench or on green sticks laid across it. Spread your coals and fire along as needed for individual items on the menu and be sure that enough air can enter at the front end to keep the fire burning briskly. This fire is also so efficient that you need use only twigs or small pieces of wood for fuel.

If you want to use the trench for more than one meal, it is worth-while to line it with nonpopping stones to reflect the heat rays.

The Automatic Stew Fire

Like the other types of fire-in-a-hole, this is particularly good on a hot or windy day. Its particular advantage is that the sticks, which are two to three

Trench Fire.

feet long, stand slanting downward into the hole, dropping farther down and automatically feeding the fire as they burn. It is not an extremely hot fire, but is excellent for slow, steady heat over a long period of time. You can make it hotter by mixing in a few sticks of softwood with the hardwood and adding a lining of nonpoppable rocks to reflect the heat upward.

Wood Reflector Fire.

Automatic Stew Fire.

An automatic stew fire will pretty much look after itself while you busy yourself with other chores. A glance at it every now and then to see that it is burning satisfactorily and that the food has enough water on it is about all that is necessary.

The Reflector Fire

A reflector fire gives steady heat for baking with a reflector oven or for reflecting heat into an open tent in cold weather. Make a *fire bank* of big stones or

three or four logs stacked up against a couple of uprights driven into the ground about four feet apart and at an angle of 75 degrees. Cover the whole front with dirt so that you can build the fire close to it without danger of the wood's catching on fire.

Place the reflector on the leeward side of the fire, to draw the smoke and flames away from the food with only the heat reflected back to the food or the sleepers basking in their tent.

A reflector fire can be very easily made from a piece of aluminum foil. Drive two forked sticks into the ground and wrap

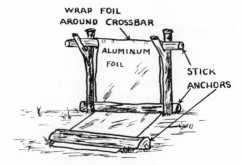

Aluminum Foil Reflector.

one end of the aluminum foil a few times around a cross bar supported in the crotches of the sticks about two feet above the ground. Bring the aluminum foil down to ground level, and hold it taut at the bottom by another stick placed back of the forked sticks. Extend the end of the aluminum forward and anchor the front corners with some rocks or a heavy stick.

The Altar Fire

An altar fire is a convenient labor-saving device for a more or less permanent camp site; it eliminates stooping and bending to tend the fire and it is also safer since there is no danger of the fire spreading through the duff. First construct a hollow base or altar at a convenient height for those who use it; 1½ to 2 feet high for children, 2½ feet or more for adults. Make the hollow base by cementing rocks together or by notching logs and fitting them together log cabin style. Fill the center with noninflammable material such as flattened tin cans, sand or rocks. An alternate base which does not need to be filled in can be made as follows: make a framework by placing sticks between the crotches of four forked sticks driven into the ground; cover the top of the framework with a "floor" of sticks laid closely together, then a sheet of aluminum foil, followed by a layer of sand, water packed earth, or inverted pieces of sod, sloped gently inward toward the center to hold the fire. Cranes and lug poles may be used as with any fire, and an excellent reflec-

tor fire results if one side of the altar is extended upward a couple of feet.

Council Fires

When a group meets in the summertime for an evening program around the campfire, they want a maximum of light and cheer with a minimum of heat. Keep the size of your fire consistent with the size of the group so that all are comfortable. Avoid using varieties of wood which crackle and pop for they are dangerous and distract attention from the program. A careful blending of softwoods for light and cheer with hardwoods for long-lasting qualities gives best results and a plentiful supply of well-placed tinder, kindling, and split larger pieces interspersed among the logs will soon be blazing merrily. Some prefer to get a more spectacular effect by first dousing the materials with kerosene (never gasoline); be extremely careful if you use this latter method. Gather the materials and lay the fire well ahead of time. The average campfire program seldom lasts more than an hour and a well constructed fire should burn that long without further attention but extra fuel may be placed near in case it is needed.

LOG CABIN FIRE. (See page 287.) This is a favorite for campfire programs. Make a base from two logs, about 3 feet long and 5 to 6 inches thick placed about 2½ feet apart. Then build up five or six layers of successively smaller and shorter

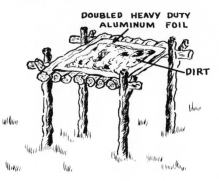

Altar Fires.

logs, laid parallel and with small spaces between. On top, build a foundation fire which, when lit, will burn brightly and soon drop hot embers down to set the whole thing ablaze.

WIGWAM FIRE. As previously mentioned, a small wigwam fire is excellent for a small group. A tall bonfire, towering high in the air, though spectacular, is hazardous, for no matter how well it is wired or otherwise fastened together, there is always danger that the long poles may work loose or burn in two and fall perilously close to the people about it. It is also usually too hot for comfort in summer.

EXTINGUISHING YOUR CAMPFIRE

Water is the best thing to use to extinguish your campfire. Scatter any remaining embers thin and *sprinkle* the water on by hand to make it go as far as possible and yet be sure that each bit of living fire is thoroughly drenched. Carefully pull aside all blazing pieces and give them a special dousing, saturating them or immersing them in a nearby stream or lake bed. Stir the fire bed repeatedly and keep sprinkling on water. Be sure your fire is *dead out;* test it by placing your hand at various spots on the ground to see that no heat remains. It's not safe to leave if there is a single trace of heat, flame, smoke or steam.

If water is unattainable, smother the fire with sand or gravel but choose the soil carefully for some types contain enough vegetable matter to smoulder for days and then eventually break out into a full-fledged forest fire. Never place hot ashes on inflammable material, but wet them down thoroughly and deposit them at a fireproof spot if they must be moved.

WET-WEATHER FIRES

The novice at fire-making has enough trouble getting a bright, steady flame in clear, dry weather, but that is as nothing compared to his difficulties when the heavens have been pouring buckets of rain for hours and everything is squashy under foot. Then comes the real test for now a camper needs a fire more than at any other time. It is quite as important psychologically as physically to send everyone to bed with warm dry clothing, hot food in their stomachs, and memories of fun and fellowship about a cheerful blaze. Going to bed on a dismal night without these comforts is enough to quell anyone's ardor for camping.

If you are a wise counselor you will be prepared for such an emergency. Amidst the deluge you can calmly produce your waterproofed matches and some good tinder you have put aside for the occasion, and capably set to work. Whenever you are in camp, always keep a supply of kindling and firewood under a tent or tarpaulin. If caught without it, search for it under overhanging rocks, fallen trees, or on the dead bottom limbs of standing trees. The dampness of any wood is usually confined to its outer layers so that you can reach dry wood by stripping off the bark or shaving off a few layers. Splitting large sticks will reveal an inner core of dry wood for kindling and you can even make fuzz clumps or fuzz sticks from it.

Trench Candles

Trench candles, carried in a waterproof tin box, are excellent for starting a fire on a rainy day. Make them by tightly rolling and twisting six to ten sheets of newspaper around a strip of cloth or thick cord. Tie pieces of string tightly about the roll at intervals of two to four inches, leaving an end long enough to suspend them. Sever the roll midway between each two strings and pull out the center cloth or cord of each segment to serve as a wick. Suspend the pieces for a couple of minutes in melted paraffin or old candle wax, bring them out to harden

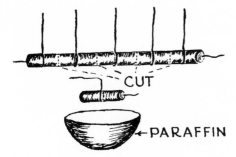

CUT

← PARAFFIN

Making Trench Candles.

slightly, and re-dip them several times to collect additional coats of wax.

Trench candles are almost impervious to rain and wind and burn long enough to start a fire under nearly any conditions. A plain candle stub or, better still, a plumber's candle serves in the same way but isn't nearly as good. Trench candles will provide enough heat for cooking on a hobo stove or furnish a fairly adequate light when burned flat in a dish or other container.

Peas

Barbara Ellen Joy and Jeanne Bassett* describe a method for making "*peas*" which are also good for starting wet-weather fires. Mix ashes from a softwood fire with kerosene and roll them into small balls about the size of large peas. Let them dry and carry them in a tin box. They will burn brightly enough to start any stubborn fire.

Laying the Fire

A fire built on sopping-wet ground can produce enough steam to smother itself. Scoop away the wet top ground and build a little platform of bark, stones or sticks for a base.

A wigwam fire is best on wet ground. Lay the fire with even more care than usual, using only fuzz sticks or good tinder and kindling at first and adding other fuel gradually as your fire gains momentum. Damp fuel dries out with

surprising rapidity if you lean it gingerly up against already flaming sticks and you can keep other wood drying out by placing it close to the fire.

An inspirator is especially helpful for wet-weather fires.

If moisture is falling, suspend a piece of tarpaulin or an extra poncho on a framework of sticks at least five feet above the fire until you get it going well. Anchor the corners with guy ropes if there is much wind. Since this usage is rather hard on the material, some camps set aside a few pieces for this specific purpose. If there is an especially strong wind blowing, build a windbreak of branches or a tarpaulin on the windward side.

ADDITIONAL READINGS

Burke, Edmund H.: *Camping Handbook*.
Des Grey, Arthur H.: *Camping*.
Fire Building. Girl Scouts #15-02, Flip Charts, $6.00.
Firemanship. Boy Scouts #3317, 25¢.
Forestry. Boy Scouts #3302, 25¢.
Hammett, Catherine T. and Musselman, Virginia: *The Camp Program Book*.
Jaeger, Ellsworth: *Council Fires*.
Jaeger, Ellsworth: *Wildwood Wisdom*.
Jaeger, Ellsworth: *Woodsmoke*.
Joy, Barbara E. and Bassett, Jeanne: *Wet Weather Fires and Artificial Tinders*. Camp Publications, (#66), 7 pp., 35¢.
Lindholm, Major Mauno A.: *Camping and Outdoor Fun*.
Lynn, Gordon: *Camping and Camp Crafts*.
Mason, Bernard S.: *The Junior Book of Camping and Woodcraft*.
Rutstrum, Calvin: *The New Way of the Wilderness*.
Thurston, La Rue A.: *Complete Book of Campfire Programs*.
Watson, Jane Werner: *The True Story of Smokey the Bear*. Golden Books, 1955, 28 pp.
West, James E., and Hillcourt, William: *Scout Field Book*.
Whelan, Townsend, and Angier, Bradford: *On Your Own in the Wilderness*.

MAGAZINE ARTICLES

Hensler, P. C.: *Make it a Fire-Safe Summer*. C.M., Mar., 1952.
Reimann, Lewis C.: *Don't Wait for Fire to Strike!* C.M., April, 1955.

* Barbara Ellen Joy, and Jeanne Bassett: *Wet Weather Fires*. Camping Magazine, April, 1939.

26

Tents
and Shelters

*Aloft I raise my Shield; the pelting Rain
And rattling Hail assault my Slope in vain.
The burning Sun, the Weight of Winter Snow
Alike I scorn—then rest secure below.*

FROM MOTTOES*

CAMPERS often go out for an overnight trip, curling up in jungle hammocks, sleeping bags, or blankets when the weather report is favorable or they are near enough to a shelter to pick up their duffel and go inside if a sudden storm menaces. In fact, many prefer to be unhampered by tent walls and roof so that they may be lulled to sleep by the sound of gently lapping waves and a distant eerie hoot owl under a star spangled canopy of sky overhead. Nevertheless, in order to enjoy longer trips or be carefree when the forecast is for "possible thunderstorms," some other shelter is necessary; don't fool yourself that you can remain snug, dry and happy for long with a "waterproof" sleeping bag and ground cloth. In addition, tents have a fascination for youngsters who may be disappointed if none are available even though the weather be fine.

The ideal tent would be quick and easy to set up and take down, light and compact to carry, absolutely rainproof, bugproof, and reptile proof, and easily heated in winter or cool nights, yet well ventilated and cool for summer. Unfortunately, it is impossible to combine all these qualities in one tent, for, as the old farmer said, after several hours of gazing steadfastly at the giraffe in the zoo, "There jest ain't no setch animal." These desired qualities largely account for the many varieties of tents, each with particular features adapting it to certain situations yet making it unsuitable to others.

* Permission by Western Brick Company.

(Courtesy of The Philadelphia Evening Bulletin.)

Fortunately, however, new designs, construction and materials have produced a wide array of tents, unbelievably compact and light weight, from which to choose one that best suits your needs with particular attention to climate and means of transportation. Therefore your choice will differ depending on whether you are going by canoe, automobile, truck, horseback, or on foot and whether you will be making a one-night stop or a long term camp.

TYPES OF TENTS

Most tents can be classified roughly into three types, according to their general shape, but a few do not fall clearly into any one category, for they combine features of two or more types.

Conical and Pyramidal Tents

These, in general, are tall tents, erected with a center pole, which often gets in the way like a sore thumb, and with sides which taper down abruptly and are kept in position by tent pegs. They are suited for open-plains living where the sudden and severe storms characterizing such regions quickly drain down their steep sides like water off a duck's back. They are substantial and hold firm against anything less than a severe windstorm.

Their bulk and weight usually make them impractical for light-trip camping. They work nicely for a permanent or semipermanent camp, for the large sizes bed down several campers, lying with feet toward the center pole and bodies radiating like the spokes of a wheel.

TEPEE.   The tepee of the plains Indian is an example of a conical tent with no bothersome pole in the center. Campers often make their own by lashing together the tops of five to twenty poles and spreading their ends out in a broad circle to form a framework. A covering of canvas (the Indians used birch bark, buffalo hides or deer skins) is then spread over

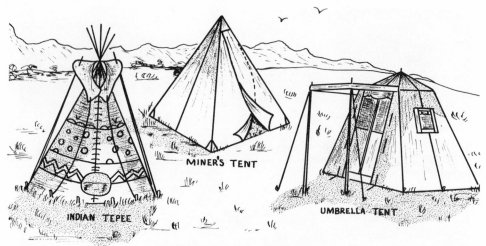

Conical and Pyramidal Tents.

the framework. One of the advantages of the tepee in cool weather is the smoke flaps which can be adjusted to allow the smoke to escape so that it is possible to have a small fire on the inside for warmth and cooking. The steep pitch of the walls makes the tepee shed water well without too much waterproofing.

MINER'S TENT.   This old favorite can be pitched easily with one pole or suspended from a tree limb. Its sharp slope makes it shed water well. The usual size accommodates two to three campers who can stand up comfortably in it but its bulk and weight usually rule it out for light trip camping.

UMBRELLA TENT.   This is one of the best tents for family camping, or long trips where the campers stay put for some time. It has ample head room and its front flap affords a front porch for light cooking. The usual sizes will accommodate three to five campers inside and side flaps added to the canopy admit two to three more. It is supported by a center pole with attached umbrella arms.

Wedge or "A" Tents

Wedge or "A" tents are favorites for light camping for many of them are light and convenient to carry, easy to pitch and provide a crawl-in type of shelter which is all that is really essential for the trip-camper who is out-of-doors most of the time. Their steep roofs shed rain well, and the absence of excess guy ropes and heavy poles in the smaller models

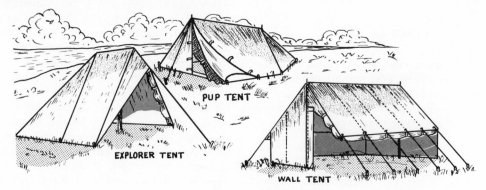

Wedge or "A" Tents.

makes them particularly adaptable to forest country where they can be lashed to trees, or tent stakes can be quickly fashioned. Some larger models are high enough to permit standing.

Pup Tent.   The familiar pup tent has long been a stand-by, particularly for overnight trips. It is just large enough to accommodate two and their duffel for crawl-in sleeping but proves rather inadequate during a prolonged rain unless other facilities are available. When made of light materials, it may weigh as little as three to five pounds and comes with collapsible aluminum poles which can be dispensed with if ropes are used. Models are available with front flaps, floor and screen door. The *mountaineer* tent is a similar type in a slightly roomier size.

Explorer Tent.   The explorer tent is a favorite for canoe, pack animal or automobile camping. It is amazingly roomy, and has enough head room to stand erect. It can be pitched with one inside "T" pole or with outside shear poles which can be cut on the spot. It is easy to pitch and strike and sometimes has a screened window in the rear to improve ventilation. It is similar to the *forester* tent and can be adapted for winter camping.

Wall Tent.   This perennially popular tent is most likely to be found at the main camp or where camp is to be set up for several weeks. There is plenty of head room and the sides can usually be rolled up for free ventilation. They come in all sizes to fit various needs but are usually too heavy for light trips.

Lean-to Tents

Lean-to tents, with an open front for receiving heat from a reflector fire, are favorites for cold-weather camping as well as summer use. They have a sloping ceiling to catch and reflect the heat rays down onto the sleeping occupants and are sometimes available in light models suitable for medium or even light-weight camping.

Camper Tent.   The Camper tent has a short ridge and a front porch. It requires two poles for pitching it, and is often used in light-trip camping.

Baker Tent.   This is a much favored tent for middle-weight camping. Though not very satisfactory in continued high winds, it is adaptable to both summer and cold-weather use. The porch accommodates a small fire for cooking in wet weather or for reflecting heat from a reflector fire down onto the sleepers in cool weather. It is a favorite for automobile or station-wagon camping where the canopy can be suspended over the vehicle to provide added privacy and space. It is really half of a wall-tent with a flap which serves as an awning in sun-

Lean-to Tents.

(Abbott and Hammond.)

shiny weather, can be lowered over the front when rain comes, or thrown back over the top when you want a reflector fire in front of it.

Tarp Shelters

The tarp (tarpaulin) is a versatile piece of equipment almost worth its weight in gold for it can be used as a ground cloth, converted into almost any type shelter desired, used to cover one's duffel, or erected as a dining porch or cooking area. It comes with grommets around all four sides for anchoring it with guy lines and often has snaps along the edges so that two or more tarpaulins can be joined to provide a larger surface. Some have a number of strategically placed tie tapes to increase the possibilities. It is available in almost every size, material, and weight one could want and a piece 10′ x 10′ will shelter two, yet weighs only a pound or so when made of feather-weight material and can be folded into a surprisingly small package. A poncho bears much similarity to a tarpaulin, and, though usually smaller, serves the

same purposes as well as substituting for a raincoat. Oilcloth furnishes a cheap substitute but will not stand up under continued use.

In cold or stormy weather, a blanket, a piece of old tent, or another tarp or poncho can be folded and erected across the ends of a tarpaulin to give added protection.

For a frequently used spot, such as an outpost camp, you may want to erect shelter frames so that incoming trippers need only throw their tarps across them and tie them securely into place.

Blanket Folded and Used as End for a Tarpaulin.

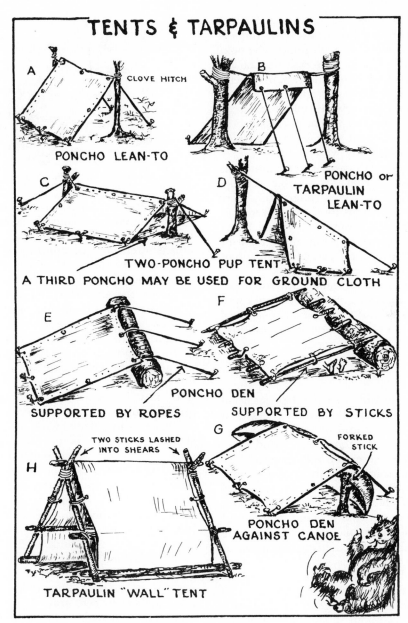

TENTS & TARPAULINS

A — CLOVE HITCH — PONCHO LEAN-TO

B — PONCHO or TARPAULIN LEAN-TO

C

D — TWO-PONCHO PUP TENT

A THIRD PONCHO MAY BE USED FOR GROUND CLOTH

E — PONCHO DEN — SUPPORTED BY ROPES

F — SUPPORTED BY STICKS

G — FORKED STICK — PONCHO DEN AGAINST CANOE

H — TWO STICKS LASHED INTO SHEARS — TARPAULIN "WALL" TENT

Tarpaulin and Poncho Shelters.

TENT FEATURES

Materials

The standard material for tents used to be closely woven duck or canvas which, though excellent in many situations, has certain serious drawbacks for light-trip camping. It is heavy and bulky to pack and carry and is not in itself waterproof but must be treated by some process which adds additional weight and bulk.

Back-packers, especially, will probably prefer a tent of one of the new lightweight materials such as balloon cloth (Egyptian cotton), airplane cloth, sailcloth, nylon or other trade marked substances. Though more expensive, most of these are mildew and rot resistant. Bear in mind, of course, that extremely light materials may be less sturdy in a high wind and require careful handling in order to prevent pinhole openings that let a steady or violent rain seep through. A tent fly, poncho or tarp erected above such a tent may be necessary to make it completely waterproof.

Outfitters sell various tent materials by the yard so that it is possible to make your own tent. Lynn (page 303) gives complete directions for making a tent as well as a tarp, using only your home sewing machine. If your material isn't already waterproof, you can waterproof it as described later on.

Weights of tents vary immensely depending upon size, materials used, ropes and number and type of tent poles, and whether they are made of aluminum, hard wood, or heavy metal.

Size

The size of tent you need depends upon whether you merely want a crawl-in shelter for the night or will spend daylight hours in the tent and so need room for cooking, recreation and general "living." One solution is to provide small, crawl-in type shelters for sleeping and additional, more ample space under tarps or accessory tents for cooking, dining and recreation. Floor space needed for sleeping can be estimated by figuring that a youth-size sleeping bag measures about 32 inches by 70 inches and there must be some allowance for space between inmates and for sheltering their gear so that you should allow about thirty square feet per camper. A two-camper tent, then, should be about 7½' x 8' and six feet high if it is to permit standing up. Adults require somewhat more space.

Quality and Color

An extremely cheap tent is likely to prove a headache and an expensive one

Frame for a Tarpaulin, Poncho or Ground Cloth Shelter.

in the long run, for it will be short-lived and give poor service. It is liable to be made of leaky, nondurable material and is often not cut squarely, so that it can never be pitched quite right. The seams may be poorly constructed, failing to brace the material and give it the added strength they should, or they may be sewed with that abomination, the "chain stitch," which ravels out as soon as one thread is broken. The *grommets* are metal rings sewed in to serve as reinforcements for attaching ropes (D, p. 301) and may be so poorly inserted as to quickly pull out when any stress is put on them, as in a strong wind or after tent shrinkage. It may be possible to get an inexpensive tent which will fulfill ordinary camp needs, but the inexperienced should not attempt to select one without expert advice. If you are buying a "surplus" tent, inspect it carefully, for if it has been folded and stored for long, it may be leaky at the folds.

Tents formerly came in white or very light shades, but new tents in light colors are rarely seen now. The modern trend is toward a soft brown, gray or green which blends in well with its forest home, and will not collect sun or moon glare, will not soil as easily nor silhouette the occupants at night, and will not attract bugs and insects as much. If you have a white tent, you may find it worth-while to dye it with a good cloth dye. Some tents, particularly those intended for family camping, now stand out in bright shades of blue, yellow and such.

Ventilation and Insect Screening

Important features in any tent for summer use are the amount and type of ventilation provided. At one extreme is the tarpaulin shelter and the old-style pup tent, open at both ends and obviously admitting plenty of breezes as well as various flying and crawling creatures, to enjoy a free lunch at the expense of the occupants. Do not think of going on an overnight trip, particularly in malaria country, without adequate protection against these blood-thirsty creatures—no trip can be fun with them as tentmates. You can often make out in them comfortably if you will douse yourself with a good insect repellant and spray around your tent with an insecticide. You may also erect some sort of insect shield about your bed (pages 329, 331), but the best way is to have screened doors and windows in your tent.

Three types of materials are commonly used for insect-protection. (1) Mosquito netting is cheap and easy to drape over tent openings, but is fragile and so coarsely woven as to admit some of the smaller insects such as the pestiferous punkies or "no-see-ums." (2) Double layers of cheesecloth screen insects out but at the same time keep out some of the cooling breezes. This material is more durable and less expensive than mosquito netting. (3) Bobbinet, though the most expensive of the three, seems to be best as it is fairly durable and finely woven enough to be effective, yet admits plenty of air. The illustration shows a way to provide more ventilation in a tent. The rain flaps should overlap the windows so that there will be no leaks and should be arranged so as to lower from the inside when bad weather sets in. Windows should be at least twelve by eighteen inches in size.

You can fashion doors in the same way with a center slit for an entrance, bordering it with tape and zipper. Weight down the bottom with stones, logs, or, better still, equip it with short tapes which you

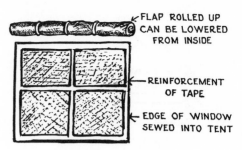

FLAP ROLLED UP CAN BE LOWERED FROM INSIDE

REINFORCEMENT OF TAPE

EDGE OF WINDOW SEWED INTO TENT

Bobbinet Window with Flap.

can fasten to small pegs driven into the ground.

In an emergency, you can drape bobbinet or other material from a forked stick framework over the whole tent, holding it tight to the ground with stones or logs.

Flooring

Some tents are pitched on a wooden framework with a regular wooden floor and a wall extending part way up. This is quite suitable for tents which remain more or less permanently in one spot.

Tent with Side Rails, Pitched on a Wooden Floor.

Every tent without a wooden floor should be fitted with a *sod cloth,* which is a strip of material six to eighteen inches wide sewed to the bottom of the tent wall and arranged to be turned in toward the center so that drafts and insects cannot get in under the bottom of the tent. Weight in down on the inside with rocks, wood blocks, or pieces of duffel.

A floor cloth is also highly desirable and, when laid on top of the sod cloth,

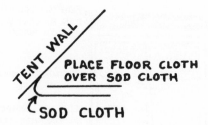

Sod Cloth in Place inside Tent Wall.

Tent Pegs.

removes the danger of invasion by things that fly, crawl and creep as completely as is possible with the movable type of tent. The floor cloth is sometimes sewed directly to the tent wall, making the sod cloth unnecessary, but this is undesirable since it cannot be taken out for cleaning.

Tent Flies

These are extra strips of tent material stretched above the regular tent as an added protection against rain and are almost a necessity with large canvas tents which are often far from waterproof. A very light tarp erected above a light-weight tent may serve the same purpose without adding materially to the pack load. A fly also keeps a tent cooler in hot weather by deflecting some of the direct sun's rays as well as keeping it warmer when the weather is cool. They are fastened by guy ropes to the regular tent pegs or to their own tent pegs.

Tent flies are a perfect nuisance unless anchored tightly, for the slightest breeze sets them flapping and booming so that even a dog-tired hiker cannot sleep. When not needed for protection against rain, they may be removed and used as an extra tarp to provide a dining or kitchen area.

Tent Pegs

Pegs should be twelve to eighteen inches long and 1½ inches in diameter and sharpened on four sides. Shape the notch for fastening the rope as shown and smooth it on the inside to prevent excessive wear on the tent rope. Make an additional upper notch if you want to attach a tent fly. Insert pegs at a 60 degree angle, sloping them away from the tent wall.

If the ground is too soft or sandy to hold pegs or is so rocky or hard that pegs cannot be driven in, fasten the guy ropes to logs, stones, or surrounding bushes. Pegs will hold in soft or sandy soil by bracing them with another peg as shown, or you can pound long pegs in at a right angle to the line of pull of the rope to make them hold better.

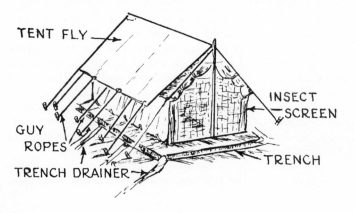

Wall Tent with Tent Fly.

Anchoring a Tent Peg in Soft or Sandy Soil.

Tent Ropes

Nylon or Fiberglas tent ropes are best since they do not shrink and have to be loosened when wet and are resistant to mildew and rotting. Number five manila or sash cord are satisfactory and may be somewhat waterproofed by periodically rubbing them with beeswax or melted candle. Tent ropes need not be large but must be strong to withstand the stress of wind and storm.

Large tents with guy ropes are usually supplied with sliding fasteners, which permit you to quickly tighten or loosen them. If not, use a taut-line hitch to attach the rope to the tent peg so that you can tighten or loosen it by merely slipping the knot up or down on its standing part. Use two half hitches or a figure-of-eight knot to hold the rope secure in the grommet at the other end. You may reverse this, making your taut-line hitch in the end of the rope and placing a bow line in the other end, thus leaving both knots tied to cast the bow line end over the tent peg quickly and have your tent up in a jiffy.

Use your camp rope to anchor light tents as in A, B and D. This saves having to carry extra poles or chop them at the campsite. E shows a method of support by means of a pole and two forked sticks. Use bushes or standing trees whenever you can to save the extra work of chopping and also practice good conservation.

PITCHING AND STRIKING A TENT

Pride yourself on having a neat, correctly pitched tent—one that stands taut

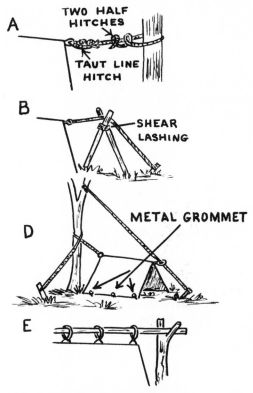

Tent Ropes and Supports.

and shipshape. New tents usually come with complete directions for *pitching* (putting them up) and *striking* them (taking them down). Here are some general directions that can be adapted for manipulating most tents.

Pitching

1. Close the front door flaps and fasten them with their zipper or tapes.

2. Peg down the two front corners so the tent will be facing the way you want it.

3. Peg down the rear corners so that all corners are lined up at right angles to each other.

4. Put the front tent pole in place, raise the front of the tent, and peg down the front guy line, using a taut-line hitch.

5. If there is a second pole, put it in place and peg down the guy line in the same way, stretching the tent ridge between the two poles.

6. Peg down all the other guy lines and adjust them with their taut-line hitches and shape the whole tent up taut and trim.

7. Adjust the sod cloth inside the tent and lay down your ground cloth if your tent doesn't have a floor.

Striking

1. Close the front door and fasten it.
2. Loosen all the guy lines and pull out the pegs.
3. Fold the door flaps in and bring all the guy lines to the center.
4. Fold the tent to the size of your tent bag.
5. Place poles and pegs in their bags and roll them up in the middle of the tent (be sure the metal is padded so it won't damage the tent fabric.)
6. Place the tent in the bag.

Ditching

Don't ditch around your tent if weather reports are favorable or you are located on rather porous soil which will quickly absorb rain, for ditching may start serious erosion, but don't take a chance if you feel a ditch is necessary. Make it about four inches deep and four inches wide with a straight inside edge coming just under the tent edge and the outside wall slanting outward as shown. Remove the sod carefully, placing it to the outside of the ditch so that you can replace it and tamp it down firmly after you strike your tent. Place "drainers" at low spots to drain the water away from the tent (page

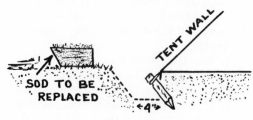

Ditching a Tent.

300). If your tent is pitched on slightly sloping ground, you will need to trench only on the upward side of the tent.

USE AND CARE OF TENTS

Your tent will give longer life and better service if you care for it properly. Fold it neatly along the seams to take the wear, roll it tightly and carry it in a bag. (A gunny, flour, or feed sack equipped with a drawstring will do.) Leave the tent pitched to dry out thoroughly, for canvas and duck tents, in particular, tend to mildew and rot if packed while damp. Never carry your tent so it will rub against metal objects.

Don't even lightly bump or rub the inside of a tent surface when it is wet, for this will break the air seal and cause a leak which you can't stop until the tent dries out again.

When rolling your tent flaps, roll them with the edges inside so they won't catch and hold the rain. Unroll them and air them occasionally to prevent mildew and discourage field mice and other unbidden guests from building nests in them.

If a tent is to stay in the same position for several days, open it as wide as possible and air it thoroughly every sunny day.

Pitch your tent in a tight and workman-like manner to give a neater appearance and to prevent its whipping badly in a stiff breeze. You will need to tighten the ropes occasionally for they have a tendency to sag. Always loosen guy ropes slightly before a storm, for they and the tent shrink when wet, subjecting them to great strain and sometimes even tearing the tent wall itself or pulling the grommets right out of it. This effect is greatly minimized if your tent and ropes are made of nylon or most of the other new fabrics.

Never use pins or nails to attach additional ropes, for they make holes which leak and may later develop into rips and tears. Be sure there are no clothes poles or other objects near enough to the walls or roof to wear holes in them by rubbing during a wind. When you need more ropes on a tent, have a good tent or awning maker insert steel grommets for anchoring them.

Waterproofing

You can waterproof tent material when making your own tent, or you can re-waterproof a tent that has started to leak. One method is to use paraffin. Lay the material flat and go over it painstakingly with a cake of paraffin (or candle wax), rubbing carefully until every fiber is evenly and thoroughly coated and the whole surface has a white appearance. Then, with a *warm* (not hot) iron (a flat iron is superior to an electric iron which heats too rapidly), rub over the material, melting the wax and causing it to permeate the fibers. This method keeps out moisture by coating the whole surface with wax and will be effective for ordinary rains, but adds materially to its weight and "bunglesomeness." You must keep material so treated away from the heat of a fire, or from long exposure to the direct rays of the summer sun for these will melt the paraffin.

Another method of waterproofing consists of melting thin shavings of beeswax or paraffin in turpentine (one pound to a gallon) and painting the surface of the tent with it. Dissolve the mixture by immersing a vessel containing it in hot water, changed as rapidly as the water cools. This coating is rather dangerous since it may catch fire if direct heat or flame is placed near it. The alum-sugar of lead method of waterproofing is not desirable because it is poisonous. Many patented preparations for waterproofing are available at outfitting stores, some to be sprayed on the pitched tent with a spray gun.

Before starting out on a trip with an old tent, pitch it and test it for leaks by pouring buckets of water on it or spraying it with a hose for an hour or two. Mending leaks on a trip is annoying, for they seem never to be noticed until a big juicy drip goes "splotch" in your ear just as you are blissfully drifting off to dreamland. Leaks in canvas or duck can be temporarily mended with adhesive tape.

To make a more permanent repair, draw the edges of the tent around the leak together with a large needle and thread, taking alternately long and short cross stitches. Waterproof the mend as previously described. An application of paint will temporarily mend nylon and compounds for waterproofing it and other materials more permanently may be purchased from outfitting stores.

Building a Shelter

Brush shelters are romantic and interesting, even though not very watertight, and are often a convenience at an outpost camp. Weave them from leafy branches overlapped like shingles, and thatch them at the ends if desired. Indian tepees are easy to build and fun to decorate and can be made quite livable. Campers may even aspire to build their own lean-to or log cabin. Directions for doing all these things can be found in the sources given at the end of this chapter.

ADDITIONAL READINGS

Burke, Edmund H.: *Camping Handbook.*
Des Grey, Arthur H.: *Camping.*
Geist, Roland C.: *Hiking Camping, and Mountaineering.*
Hammett, Catherine T., and Mussleman, Virginia: *The Camp Program Book.*
Henderson, Luis M.: *The Outdoor Guide.*
Jaeger, Ellsworth: *Wildwood Wisdom.*
Jaeger, Ellsworth: *Woodsmoke.*
Kesting, Ted: *The Outdoor Encyclopedia*
Koller, Larry: *Complete Book of Camping and the Outdoors.*
Lindholm, Major Mauno A.: *Camping and Outdoor Fun.*
Lynn, Gordon: *Camping and Camp Crafts.*
Mason, Bernard S.: *The Junior Book of Camping and Woodcraft.*
Peterson, Doris T.: *Your Family Goes Camping.*

Rutstrum, Calvin: *The New Way of the Wilderness.*
Swanson, William E.: *Camping for All It's Worth.*
Weaver, Robert W., and Merrill, Anthony F.: *Camping Can Be Fun.*
West, James E., and Hillcourt, William: *Scout Field Book.*
Whelen, Townsend, and Angier, Bradford: *On Your Own in the Wilderness.*

MAGAZINE ARTICLES

Choosing Tents for Camping Out. C. M., April, 1953.
Cohen, Harold, and McBride: *Modern Tents for Campers.* C. M., Nov., 1957.
Saloman, Julian H.: *One Vote for Tents.* C. M., Nov., 1950.

27

Duffel for Camping and Trips

Follow the trail to the open air
Alone with the hills and sky;
A pack on your back, but never a care,
Letting the days slip by!

AGATHE DEMING*

SELECTING CAMP DUFFEL

THE NEWCOMER to camp usually brings with him all sorts of unnecessary *duffel* (camp jargon for your equipment), which lies collecting dust and taking up valuable space. When he goes on a trip out of camp, he likewise drags along things which he doesn't really need and which add much to his discomfort, for everything taken, even though not carried on your back, has to be handled and moved about many times.

The secret of camping, particularly trip-camping, is to take only what you actually need for health, safety and happiness. Yet it is just as grave an error to take too little and try to live like an animal of the woods with only what you wear or can procure from the fields. The ultimate in camping is expressed by the title of Elon Jessup's book, *Roughing It Smoothly,* and its attainment should be the ideal of every camper. Making a wise choice of what to take is a major project; start making a list well ahead of time so you can continually revise it before the time for departure arrives.

Any sort of trip limits the amount of equipment that can be taken, particularly by adolescent boys and girls, who should never plan to carry heavy packs for more than a short distance. Transportation by canoe, pack saddle or wagon allows a little more latitude, though lightness and compactness are still highly desirable. Some camps minimize the

* Reproduced by permission of Miss Deming.

(Harold M. Lambert.)

problem on long trips by sending such heavy materials as food and bedding ahead by auto, truck or pack horse, leaving the campers to bring only such light equipment as they can readily manage. You can also lighten your trip load by replenishing food supplies at farm houses and stores along the way and by shipping supplies ahead by parcel post or express. Fresh clothing may be supplied in this way and the soiled sent back to camp.

No matter what your means of transportation, keep your outfit just as compact and light as possible without omitting anything you really need. Whenever the temptation to pack some questionable piece of gear arises, recall that "each ounce weighs a pound" and it is truly the straw that breaks the camel's back on a long trip. What you need depends on the season, the nature of the terrain, and the length of the trip.

Camps and counselors should not foster extended expeditions into the woods unless there is enough equipment of the right sort to do it comfortably. However, no great outlay of money is necessary, for you can improvise much of the equipment at home. Make your poncho, ground cloth, tent, packsack and sleeping bag from waterproof material or waterproof them by the paraffin method. Make a paper pattern and adjust it until it is "just right" before cutting into your goods. You can make or assemble cooking utensils, mess kits and many other pieces of equipment.

Cut down on both weight and expense by finding ways to make one piece of equipment serve several purposes and by fashioning what you can at the campsite. For instance, it may be more sensible to use sticks for toasting and make tent stakes or small tent poles as needed instead of carrying them along.

Mark each article of equipment, including clothing, with your name, either by name tape or with India ink or marking pen. Burn labels into wooden articles such as hatchet or shovel handles with a wood-burning set.

Keep such leather parts as axe sheaths, knapsack straps and sheath-knife covers clean and soft by oiling them with neat's-foot oil or a good shoe polish.

Ditty Bags.

Ditty Bags

A good camper doesn't place a single thing loose in his pack; he collects things of a similar nature together and puts them in a small *ditty bag*, then places all his ditty bags inside his pack so that he has only to take out the appropriate bag and not turn everything topsy-turvy while searching for some small object which has dropped to the bottom or been overlooked and left behind at the last stop.

The number of ditty bags you need depends on the length of your trip and the amount of duffel you will take. A minimum is one for toilet articles, one for clothing, one for mess kit, and one for first aid equipment. You may want others for tools and other repair materials, shoes, articles of food, and so on.

You can purchase ditty bags of light vinylite or heavy cloth from outfitters or, by saving the plastic bags that many articles now come in, you can secure an assortment of almost every size you need. Bear in mind that some plastics are quite inflammable and must be kept away from open fire, however. It is easy to make bags from waterproof material or strong cloth such as denim or un-bleached muslin which you then water-proof. In reality, you can get by without waterproofing them if you carry them in a waterproof packsack. To determine the size you need for an individual bag, gather all the items you want to include and make a paper pattern to surround them, allowing extra width for double-stitched seams and extra length for a wide hem with a draw string at the top. Ditty bags with round bottoms, such as the case for "toiletries," will stand open and upright while in use, though these are not as simple to construct as those made by simply sewing two straight pieces of cloth together. Make the bags of distinguishing colors and draw a rep-resentative picture on them or letter the name of the contents on the side with enamel for permanence, with wax crayon which will wash out, or mystic tape for temporary use. Long narrow bags can be slipped upright into your pack and found quickly without disturb-ing the rest of the contents if clearly marked on top. Regular cloth shoe bags are handy for carrying various pieces of equipment in your pack and may be tied in a jiffy to a tree or the foot of your bed where they serve as woodland "dresser drawers."

Shoe Bag Hold-All.

PACKING FOR A TRIP

Even though "camp" is only a few feet from your cabin, take pride in your ability to pack well, for no worthy camper ever forgets part of his duffel. Be systematic and make a check list of what you will need. Then gather everything together and double check it, going through it item by item to see how many things you can get along without. Place what you have left on the scales and actually weigh them; does this encourage you to eliminate still other things? Women and youths should not try to carry more than twenty to twenty-five pounds; mature men thirty to thirty-five pounds. Thirty pounds is good for canoeing, cycling or horseback trips.

You are now ready to start stowing your gear into your pack sack but do it logically. For instance, pack the things you might need in a hurry (camera, rain wear, first aid kit, map, canteen, sunglasses and so forth) on top or in easily accessible pockets. Food for lunch, matches and knife come next, and so on.

Do not include breakables or crushables unless they are well-padded, and carefully plan every detail, putting heavy things and those not needed until night at the bottom of your pack. Fit things in compactly, so that there is nothing jiggling or making a noisy clatter.

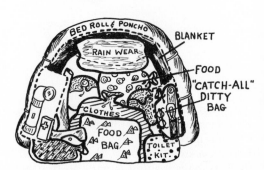

Packing Your Packsack.

(Joy and Camp)

Place only a few small, especially needed things in your pockets, which should be deep and built for service. Things lost along the trail have an uncanny way of hiding among the brush and leaves so that you cannot find them even if you can take time for backtracking. Fasten these items to your pocket with a safety pin; pin your whole pocket shut; or attach them to a buttonhole or belt loop by a stout cord or chain which is long enough to permit you to use them without detaching.

BACK PACKING

Traveling on foot with your bedding, food, and clothing on your back offers the ultimate in freedom for it is only when you get off the beaten path and learn to walk unobtrusively through the forest that you experience the wonderful world of wildlife.

Stow all of your equipment in some form of a packsack, even though you're only going out for a sightseeing tour or a simple lunch. In that way you'll be able to take extras that you might want such as your knife, binoculars, containers for gathering interesting specimens, camera, and so forth; you won't lose precious gear as you lay it down to examine something you find along the way; and you'll have your hands free for pushing aside underbrush, for examining or for helping you climb. Only a rank beginner trails along with objects dangling and flapping from his waist and bulging out of his pockets, making him look like a veritable porcupine. Objects suspended from your belt pull heavily on your waist unless you can tuck them away in a pocket, and equipment hanging from one shoulder is but little better.

Even a light pack may bother you at first but day-by-day use will strengthen your muscles until you will scarcely notice it at all and would indeed feel ill-equipped without it.

PACKSACKS

KNAPSACK.   A knapsack is a small bag which, though not large enough to carry blankets and other gear necessary for overnight stays, is nevertheless handy for younger campers or for daylight jaunts and cook-outs.

HAVERSACK.   A haversack is suitable for adolescents on light trips for it will hold the things needed for an overnight stay by attaching extra bedding to the rings around the top and sides in the shape of an inverted "U". In fact you

KNAPSACK

HAVERSACK

RUCKSACK

Various Packsacks.

may even be able to find room for your sleeping bag inside if you get one of the extremely light models which fold up into a package scarcely larger than a long loaf of bread. It usually has two or more pockets for storing odds and ends or things you want to keep readily available.

RUCKSACK.   This is a favorite for light camping with your bedding again attached as a "U" around the top and sides. The name is of German origin and means "back sack." A distinguishing feature is that the shoulder straps come close together in the back, thus making it hug your shoulders and ride comfortably on them with weight low where it is borne mostly by your hips as it should be. A rucksack has several handy pockets and several models come with a light aluminum frame which makes them still easier to carry and keeps them away from your back so the air can circulate freely. The Norwegian "Meis" pack is a deservedly popular model with a built in aluminum pack frame, a belt for fastening it snugly at the hips, several pockets and a draw string at the top.

ADIRONDACK PACK BASKETS.   The Adirondack pack basket is a heritage from the Indians of the North East and many campers prefer it, for its construction of oak or ash protects the contents. It is rigid enough to keep canned goods and other hard objects from gouging your back. It is shaped to fit the back and is equipped with straps for carrying it. Though not waterproof itself, the Adirondack pack basket usually comes with a protective canvas waterproof cover. Bedding can be arranged in a "U" over the top and sides and it is available in several sizes. Among its disadvantages are: it is awkward to fit into a canoe or automobile; it may catch on brush and trees as you pass through the woods; and it takes up the same amount of room whether full or empty.

DULUTH PACKSACK.   This is one of a variety of big sacks or bags capable of hauling a large supply of food and cloth-

Adirondack Pack Basket.

ing. They are favorites with husky men but are too heavy for adolescent campers to handle.

Improvised Packsacks

(Note that none of these are waterproof and you will therefore need to cover them with a poncho or piece of plastic if this quality is needed.)

SHOULDER STICK PACK.   The most picturesque and romantic way to carry your possessions is to tie them in a big bandanna, hang it on the end of a stick, tramp-style, and jauntily stride along with it perched over your shoulder. Unfortunately, your jaunty feeling lasts only a short time for this is in reality a most uncomfortable way to carry your gear.

BLANKET ROLL.   You may roll your supplies in a blanket, secure it with three inch horse blanket pins and a short rope, and wear it in a "U" around your shoulder. This works well enough for a short trip, but the roll becomes hot and sweaty and catches on every tree and branch along the way, making it ill-adapted for any but short trips. Use your poncho or ground cloth as the outside layer to render it waterproof.

Blanket Roll.

Slack Pack.

BLUE JEANS OR SLACK PACK. Jaeger* describes a novel way to make a pack-sack out of blue jeans or slacks. Tie your duffel into a secure parcel and slip it into the body of your slacks; secure it by running a rope through the belt loops and up around the crotch. Convert the legs of the slacks into pack straps, bringing them up across your shoulders and under your arms; fasten them about two inches apart at the center, not the edges, of the pack so it hugs your shoulders snugly and centers the weight well down on your back.

BURLAP BAG PACK. You can convert a burlap bag or flour sack, four pebbles, and a strong rope about 2½ to 3 feet long into a pack. Place a pebble in one corner of the sack and tightly fasten the rope, slightly off center, around the corner with a clove or timber hitch. Place another pebble in the other lower corner and again fasten the long end of the rope around it. You should now have left the two ends of the rope of equal length; now bring them up and fasten to the upper two corners with pebbles in them, leaving enough slack to slip your arms through and use as carrying straps for the sack. Pad the ropes where they cross your shoulders with old socks or impro-

vised padding as described later on. Pin the top of the bag shut with large safety pins.

Selecting a Packsack

There are many varieties of packsacks available, so search around until you find one that suits your needs. A wide top which can be closed with a draw string is convenient. Choose as small a one as will hold what you need and make sure the shoulder straps are attached about two inches apart at the back. Straps should be at least two inches wide and of sufficiently heavy material not to wrinkle and thus cut into your shoulders. The sack should not touch any part of your back except your shoulders and hips, and should be well sewed and made of tough, long lasting, waterproof material. The center of gravity, when the pack is loaded, should be fairly low on your back. If it is too high, it will make you top-heavy and unsure of your footing; if it is too low you will have to lean forward to carry it and this is very fatiguing.

Pack Frames

These adaptations from the Indians are very useful devices for supporting your pack, for making it ride comfort-

* Jaeger, Ellsworth: *Wildwood Wisdom,* page 54.

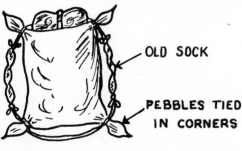
OLD SOCK

PEBBLES TIED IN CORNERS

Burlap Bag Pack.

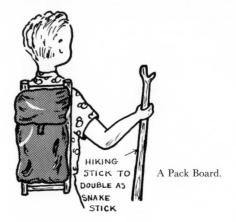
HIKING STICK TO DOUBLE AS SNAKE STICK

A Pack Board.

ably, and for keeping it away from you so that the perspiration can evaporate. They come in many varieties and are usually made of lightweight aluminum (weighing as little as 20 ounces) or plywood. You can make your own pack frame from pieces of orange crate or lightweight scrap lumber, padding it where it contacts your back.

Some are already equipped with a light canvas carrying case to serve as a pack but you can easily remove it if you prefer to use your own. The average pack can be attached by slipping its shoulder straps over the frame. If you prefer not to use a packsack, you can place all of your duffel on the ground on a poncho or tarp, and tie it into a parcel, lashing it to the frame with a diamond hitch. There are also pack harnesses available to fasten around a bundle and convert it into a pack with shoulder straps.

When buying a pack frame, there are several points to bear in mind. Get a light, durable one of appropriate size and with adjustable straps. Try it on your pack to see that it rides comfortably. The upper cross strap or bar should be level with your shoulder blades; the lower one should be just below your belt line and only as wide as your hips.

Improvised Shoulder Pads

Narrow straps across your shoulders or those made of flimsy material which wrinkle, soon cut and become uncomfortable. You can buy pads to slip over the straps or you can make your own. Use a strip of leather, webbing or other heavy material 2 inches to 2½ inches wide for the frame work, padding it with foam rubber or thick felt. Fasten the padding to the straps or arrange it so the straps can be slipped through it.

Tump Line

Shoulder straps alone are used to support most packs, but experienced foot travelers who make a practice of carrying heavy packs day after day use a *tump line* in conjunction with them. This consists of a narrow strip of leather or webbing, 16 to 20 feet long and widened to 2½ to 3 inches at the center where it rests at about your hairline just above your forehead. Its most important use is as a safety measure for climbing steep mountains or crossing swift streams where the footing is precarious; here you can support your pack only by the tump line so that a mere flick of your head will release it if you start to fall, thus relieving you of the heavy pack. It also serves to rest you, for, when used with your shoulder straps, it distributes the weight between your head, neck, and shoulders; and, when used alone, it shifts all of the weight to your shoulders.

Though impractical for most girls, it may be a welcome adjunct for older boys and men who carry heavy loads over long distances. It is possible to improvise one from two 7 inch lengths of rope attached to your pack with an old sock or other strong material anchored in the center to serve as a cushion over your forehead.

A Shoulder Pad.

A Tump Line.

A Duffel Bag.

DUNNAGE BAGS

There are various types of large bags and boxes available for transporting large quantities of equipment to and from camp. The duffel bag is one of the most widely used. It is made of waterproof material and is designed for shipping equipment by automobile, wagon, train, pack horse or canoe, but not for carrying on the back except for short distances. If sending a dunnage bag by train or common carrier, buy a lock to protect the contents if it does not already have one. The most convenient model has a zipper running down one side so that you can easily obtain anything in it without having to remove a lot of things first. Some prefer wooden lockers with partitioned shelves which can also be used as storage spaces or tables on arrival at camp.

THE GOOD OLD PONCHO

The poncho, a waterproof cloth available in a variety of sizes, is a perfect example of a piece of equipment which pays its way by serving many purposes. It has a hole near the center large enough to slip your head through so that you can wear it as a large waterproof cape, and many come with a hood already attached. There are overlapping flaps to cover the hole and make it waterproof for use as a flat piece. There are snaps along the edges so that you can fasten it around blankets arranged as a bed roll where it serves both as a waterproof cover and ground cloth. The metal *grommets* along the sides are for inserting ropes to convert it into a shelter or lean-to (see page 297) and it is also useful to shield a fire when you must build it in the rain or in a strong draft. Some varieties have

A Poncho Worn as a Raincoat.

snaps along the sides so that two of them can be snapped together to form a large piece for a tent, a fly over a light tent, or as a dining porch in rainy weather. They come in a variety of materials: vinyl plastic weighing only twelve ounces, treated nylon weighing nineteen ounces, and so on; the feather weight ones can be folded almost to the size of a bandanna.

GROUND CLOTH

A ground cloth is similar to a poncho, but does not have a center hole for wearing it as a rain cape. It is even simpler to construct and takes about four yards of material.

In making either a ground cloth or a poncho, allow for wide seams which won't pull out, and use double or triple stitching throughout. Snaps and grommets (not less than ½ inch in size) may be purchased and inserted. Many water-repellant or waterproof materials are available for making either a poncho or a ground cloth. Among them are nylon, Egyptian cotton, duck, and vinyl plastic (the lightest of all).

WHAT TO TAKE

Clothing

Take only plain, serviceable, snag-resistant, washable clothing. Camp is not the place for fragile or dressy things, for your clothing must wear well and protect you from the weather, be it windy, sunny, cold or hot. It must fit snugly and comfortably, yet loosely enough to permit active use of your body when hiking, climbing or canoeing. It should be loosely woven to permit rapid evaporation of perspiration and should have plenty of deep, secure pockets for holding equipment. Nylon, Dacron, and Orlon are excellent materials, and rayon, seersucker, and cotton jersey are also good.

SHIRTS.   Cotton shirts with open throat and short sleeves make satisfactory camp apparel or for hiking in open country on a sunny day, but light, loosely woven wool flannel shirts are preferable for trip-wear in most climates. Although flannel shirts sound hot and uninviting for summer, they are in reality quite comfortable, for they readily absorb perspiration and just as readily let it evaporate. Cotton shirts absorb moisture until they reach saturation point, then lie like a chilly wet wash, bringing on chills and summer colds. Take at least one extra flannel shirt to wear as a jacket or provide for a change if you become perspiration soaked or are caught in the rain. Long sleeves are advisable for woods-travel to prevent scratches and contact with poison ivy and oak, and deep, buttoned pockets are useful.

SWEATERS.   Sweaters make pretty poor outer attire, for they collect every burr in sight, snag on bushes, stretch out of shape, and become soggy and heavy when wet. Their best use is as a bed jacket or for extra warmth when worn under a more serviceable shirt or jacket.

JACKET.   A waist length windbreaker jacket of closely woven, water-repellent poplin is desirable to provide additional warmth.

TROUSERS.   Blue jeans are the preference of many for general camp wear. They are inexpensive, comfortable, serviceable and washable, and provide ample pockets for storing various items of camp gear. Slacks should be of smooth, tough, hard-surface cotton material that will not pick up burrs or snag on branches. When going through the woods, roll the legs down for protection from branches, poison ivy and insects. Get them without cuffs and cut them off if they are too long instead of rolling them up for cuffs collect dirt and duff and catch on brush and protruding rocks to trip you. Taping the legs tightly around your ankles helps to keep out sand and insects. A pair of shorts provides a cool change for wear around the campsite and in a canoe. Riding breeches or jodhpurs make very poor camp attire for they are too tight about the knees for comfort when hiking or stooping around the campsite.

BELT.   If you want to wear your hatchet or other equipment, you will need a strong belt with clips or safety thongs for your knife, compass, small match box, and similar equipment. Most campers, however, prefer to carry these items in the pockets or near the top of their pack where they will be handy.

HAT.   A hat with a fairly wide brim will protect you from the sun, wind, cold and rain, and a strap or tie strings for anchoring it under your chin in windy weather is helpful. A duckbill visor cap is also good.

PAJAMAS.   Always take pajamas for sleeping. Do not sleep in your hiking clothes for they will be cold and clammy from the day's perspiration.

UNDERWEAR.   Take at least one change of underwear. Wash them out at night so that you will always have a dry set in case you get caught in the rain.

SOCKS.   Socks are one of the most important items for a trip-camper for they can completely make or mar your comfort and happiness. Lightweight wool socks are the most practical, for they cushion your feet, absorb perspiration and let it evaporate quickly, and also help to prevent blisters. If your skin is sensitive to wool, wear a thin pair of cotton socks underneath; this will also make them wear longer. Socks with nylon reinforced toes and heels give better service. Socks should fit well, for, when they are too large, they chafe and cause blisters; when they are too short, they cramp your feet just as ill-fitting shoes do. You will need socks that are a full size larger than usual.

Wash them out each night and put on a clean pair in the morning. Give your feet a treat by washing them and putting on dry socks at noon if the hiking has been rough and the weather hot. Avoid mended socks, for, no matter how skillfully darned, they almost invariably irritate and cause blisters. Slipping into an extra pair of wool socks on cold nights is almost equivalent to having an extra blanket.

SHOES.   You will need at least two pairs of shoes; a heavy pair for general woods wear and a light pair for resting your feet in the evening around the campfire, for canoe wear, or for wearing if your others get wet.

For general woods hiking, select strong, sturdy shoes with fairly thick, flexible soles. Get a full size larger than usual to allow for heavy wool socks and the swelling of your feet which invariably accompanies hiking long distances in hot weather. Get rubber or composition soles, heavily corrugated or with rubber cleats, and heels that are broad and low. Smooth rubber or leather soles and heels are treacherous in the woods where there is always some moisture.

Many prefer light boots coming just above the ankle. These give some protection in snake-country and your trouser legs can be tucked into them to prevent snagging on underbrush or letting sand and insects in. Boots higher than this are a nuisance for they are usually stiff, clumsy, and hot and often cause blisters on feet and ankles.

Moccasins are a popular choice for the light pair and many will have nothing else when hiking in dry woods. They are thin and pliable and traveling in them is almost like going barefoot, yet you have the added protection of a thickness of leather with the heavy wool socks you wear with them. For hiking, use double soled moccasins with a layer of leather on the inside and a layer of rubber or composition on the outside. Moccasins permit "feeling" your way along the trail with sureness and ease. However, if you have never worn them, your feet will be used to the support of hard city shoes and you must accustom yourself to them around camp and on short hikes. They are excellent when in a canoe, though some prefer to slip them off and paddle in their socks. It is easy to make your own moccasins using the many patterns and kits available.

Rubber sneakers are restful around the campfire or in a canoe but are not very satisfactory for hiking, for, unless well constructed, they give little foot support, won't hold up over rough terrain, and become water logged on exposure to dew or rainy weather. Some like slipper socks for campfire wear.

Tie your shoestrings by moistening them and then pulling one loop through the knot a second time before tightening it. This prevents the strings from coming untied in a dangerous or bothersome way along the trail.

You cannot actually waterproof shoes with any degree of permanency and wouldn't want to if you could for it would make them heavy and airtight and cause your feet to become steamy and tender. However, it is a good idea to apply a light application of neat's-foot oil or a good shoe polish now and then to keep the leather in good condition and make it water-resistant.

When your shoes get wet, dry them slowly with gentle heat, stuffing them with clothing, dried grass, or moss to preserve the shape. Rapid drying with intense heat cracks and utterly ruins leather.

Have you ever thought what the word "tenderfoot" means? A good camper avoids being one by giving proper care and attention to his feet and footwear. New shoes never make good companions on the trail and old rundown ones give little support and may fall to pieces on the way, leaving you in a predicament.

CLOTHING FOR RAINY WEATHER. *Getting wet* will not cause a cold or any ill effects whatsoever but *staying* wet likely will, so stop immediately, change into dry clothing, and get thoroughly warm in front of a blazing fire. Better yet, don't get wet! A wise camper always goes prepared for rain. He carefully packs his own waterproofing, uses waterproof packsacks and bedrolls or carries extra tarpaulins or ponchos to cover any duffel not so protected.

Keep your own rainwear near the top of your pack where you can find it in a hurry when you need it. There is little agreement as to the best rain protection but none disputes the inadequacy of the gossamer, oiled-silk cape with hood which is nice for town-wear. Town raincoats usually prove more or less unsatisfactory.

The general preference is for a loose fitting, knee-length "rain shirt" or combination poncho and raincoat with loose raglan-type sleeve and a wide bottom which can be spread to cover your duffel when in a canoe. These are now available in new lightweight materials and can be folded up quite compactly; nylon is probably the best material.

A regular poncho is also a favorite (page 313). Rain pants and shirt are good if made of material strong enough to stand up under rough treatment.

Raincoats which are too long are a pure nuisance, for they flap about in your way at every step, tripping you when you climb hills, and constantly flying open to expose the lower part of your body to the elements. They are usually hot and binding and cause profuse sweating.

Unless you have an attached hood to keep your head dry, get a sou'wester or light waterproof hat with a medium brim (which will also serve as a sun hat) and strings to tie under your chin.

You may want light rubbers to fit over your shoes or moccasins. Rubber boots are clumsy and tiring to walk in and are recommended only for actually wading through water.

BANDANNA. A large-sized bandanna is another piece of equipment which adapts itself to many purposes. You can use it to handle hot pans around the cooking fire, to tie up a home-made mess kit, to hold specimens gathered along the way, to double for a triangular bandage or tourniquet, to shield your neck and face from sunburn and insects, to wear around your forehead to keep the perspiration out of your eyes or to place folded under your tump line or the straps on your packsack to keep them from cutting. Carry it in your hip pocket or wear it around your neck cowboy fashion, ready for instant use.

CANVAS GLOVES. Cheap, washable canvas gloves are a very important part of your equipment. They are a wonderful aid when handling cooking pots and pans and when building fires or working with brush. They protect your skin from abrasions and keep your hands clean for actually working with food. They must be small enough to fit properly, for large ones are awkward and tend to slip, making them dangerous to use.

SWIMMING SUIT AND CAP. You will need these for refreshing dips or for bathing purposes when other facilities are not available.

Toilet Articles

Carry a few well-chosen toilet articles in a ditty bag approximately 9 by 19 inches or in a specially constructed case. The case shown is particularly handy, for you can wear it around your waist while using it, tie it at the foot of your bed, or roll it up and place it in your pack en route. Fashion it from strong material such as unbleached muslin or denim. Spread out all the articles you want to include in logical sequence and make a paper pattern to fit, allowing enough space for hems and turning up six or seven inches of the material for pockets; be sure to allow enough fullness to accommodate the thickness of the objects. An ordinary toilet kit which rolls up can be adapted by attaching tie strings to it.

For a short trip, you need take only small quantities of toilet supplies (a small piece of soap instead of the whole bar, a small quantity of tooth powder instead of the whole can, and the like). Pack them in unbreakable containers. Such

planning is the secret of successful *Go Light* trips. You may sometimes have to pack such articles as your toothbrush, toilet soap, washcloths and towels wet so it is best to fit them with individual oiled-silk or plastic ditty bags. You need take no great supply of washcloths and towels for you can wash them out and hang them up to dry overnight. A small metal mirror is superior to the breakable type.

By carefully saving and washing out the plastic bottles and bags that home products commonly come in, you can soon accumulate almost all the containers and bags you need.

MISCELLANEOUS EQUIPMENT

Include a few tools in your trip-outfit. If several campers are going, you need not burden each member of the party with duplicates. Two axes will serve a whole party, for few will be using them at the same time; one would be inadequate owing to the danger of loss or breakage.

A Toilet Case.

Tools

Such tools as a screwdriver, pliers with wire cutter, and so forth, are useful. A compact tool haft is available which consists of a hollow handle filled with various attachments for converting the tool into a hammer, a screwdriver, an awl, etc. Carry a trowel or small shovel with detachable handle for trenching your tent, digging sanitary facilities, and manipulating and putting out fires.

AXE, KNIFE AND SHEATH KNIFE.   The choice of an axe, knife and sheath knife has already been discussed.

Always keep your axe in its sheath, and wear it on your belt or pack it with your duffel where you can find it quickly.

Carry your knife in your pocket, attached to your belt or belt loop, or in a "catch all" ditty bag in one of the pockets of your packsack.

One or two sheath knives for the group are convenient to use as cooking knives or as strong knives for heavy work.

TOOLS FOR SHARPENING.   Include at least one file and one sharpening stone for party use.

Adhesive Tape

Adhesive tape serves many functions in addition to its first aid use in applying bandages and supporting sprains. It will stick to almost anything that is dry, especially if pressed on with a little heat as from a heated spoon or frying pan. You can use it to mend a leaky tent or canoe temporarily, or to mend a rip in clothing, or a leak in a bucket or kettle. It will also secure a cork in a bottle, fasten the lid on a box or tin can, and even make hinges for a lid.

Camera

Only a really good camera and equipment will give superior results in nature photography, for you must take shots where you find them, often in the shade or in other difficult situations. Keep your camera where you can snatch it up and use it in the brief period nature poses. Be sure to take extra films along and have a small plastic cover or ditty bag to cover your camera in case of a sudden rain.

Purse and Money

You may need a small amount of money for supplies along the way and for emergency use. Pin it fast in your pocket, keep it in a secure place in your packsack, or wear it in a money bag around your waist.

Watch

At least two people in a group should have watches. Luminous dials are an advantage at night.

Glasses

On long trips, campers with poor vision should take along an extra pair of glasses in a strong case.

Maps

Even though you may not actually need a map to find your way, a topographical map of the region will be very interesting and will help you choose the most intriguing path. Prepare it for hard use on the road as described on page 230.

Compass

You will need a compass for following or making a trail map. Slip it into your shirt pocket and secure it with a strong cord or thong.

Stationery

Never take ordinary ink for it is likely to leak and ruin valuable duffel, and anything written with it runs and becomes indecipherable when it gets damp.

Prestamp your postal cards or envelopes and write with a hard pencil or ball point pen.

Notebook and Pencil

Always keep a small (about 3¾ inches by 6¾ inches) loose-leaf notebook, opening on the side, and a pencil in your pocket. A hard pencil is best, for it will not smear as the pages of the book rub together. An excellent habit to form is to jot down and file anything you run across which might be of later help. Games, stories, songs, bits of nature lore, and so on are veritable gold mines during counseling days and may be stored in a file box or large-capacity notebook cover for ready reference. Select a few choice items to take on a trip for "program" and include a few blank pages for making notes along the way.

Protection from Sunlight

You will need a broad-brimmed hat, long sleeves and full-length trousers, a bandanna for your neck, a *good* pair of sunglasses and some sun-tan oil if you are to be much in the open, particularly on water. Carry sunburn ointment, too, in case someone is foolish enough to overexpose himself. Avoid cheap sunglasses for their faulty lenses often cause eye strain. Wear them in bright sunlight to protect your eyes but don't get in the habit of wearing them so that you keep them on indoors, in shade, or on cloudy days.

Protection from Insects

Take a good insect repellent to apply to your face, neck, and hands, a head net, and insect protection for your tent. Many good sprays are now available which will aid greatly in keeping your campsite free from irritating insects though science is still debating and experimenting, for the use of some is dangerous under certain conditions. Before purchasing or using them, get expert advice and be sure to follow directions carefully.

Bed Roll

This includes a poncho or ground cloth, rope, a sleeping bag or a bed roll of blanket pins and rope. Extra socks, underwear, towels, and the like in a ditty bag, make a satisfactory pillow.

Sit-Upons

These inventions of the Girl Scouts are useful when sitting on damp ground and also make good pillows. Make them by placing a few layers of newspaper between two pieces of oilcloth about a foot square and binding the edges together with a blanket stitch. You may paint your name on your sit-upon. Roll it up and tie it with a string for carrying.

Tents

Tents or extra tarpaulins and ponchos are necessary in case of rain.

Flashlight

Take a good flashlight with extra bulbs and batteries. The type with the head on the side is especially good since it can be hung up to serve as a lantern. Each camper should have his own flashlight.

A Good Type of Flashlight.

Binoculars

Good, lightweight binoculars are valuable for nature study and for such purposes as giving or receiving messages from a distance. The *power* of binoculars, usually printed on them as 6X, 8X, 10X, and so on, indicates the number of times they magnify. For instance, 8X glasses make an object a half-mile away seem as though it were only ⅟₁₆ mile away because they magnify it to eight times normal size.

You might naturally assume that it is best to get the highest powered glasses available, but this is not necessarily true, for glasses magnify what you do not want to see as well as what you do. Thus they intensify haze, smoke, the trembling of your hands holding them, the movements of the boat, or even a gnat that happens to cross your line of vision. Also, the higher the power, the narrower the field of vision —in other words, you see more and more of less and less. You will usually find it desirable to get a clear view of a fairly wide field, and so your choice will be a 6X or 8X pair. Wear the glasses suspended just below your collar, ready for instant use. Models are available with adjustable lens protectors, which can be slipped on or off in a jiffy so that you need not carry them in a case.

Canteen

If you are not sure there is pure water along your route, purify an adequate supply once a day and carry it in individual canteens or large group containers.

Aluminum canteens are best for they are lightweight and neither taint the water nor rust. They are ordinarily covered by thick layers of felt and flannel which, when kept wet, cool the contents by evaporation. An outer covering of canvas keeps the felt from drying out too rapidly. To sterilize water in the canteen, remove its outside coverings and boil the water for twenty to thirty minutes. Rinse out your canteen occasionally with boil-

Home-made Canteen.

ing water. You can make a canteen from a flat quart bottle, fitting on tight covers of flannel, felt, adhesive tape, or an old wool sock and an outer layer of canvas over the lower two-thirds of it; attach carrying straps. The coverings make the bottle less breakable. Some prefer desert bags for carrying their water supply.

Pedometer

This is an interesting instrument to record the distance you cover on foot. (See page 226.)

Mending Kit

Pack mending equipment in a tin box or canvas bag and include such items as needles (laced through a small piece of cardboard), both straight and safety pins, a few yards of thread wound on a piece of cardboard, small pointed scissors, buttons, patches of cloth and leather, assorted rubber bands, adhesive tape, twine, strong waxed linen thread, nails, tacks, strong wire, glue, and canoe and tent repair kits.

Thread Holder.

Fishing Gear

Fresh fish make a welcome addition to your camp menu.

Toilet Paper

Books and Pamphlets

Sources for songs, games, nature identification, poetry, or stories are welcome.

Candles

Short, fat plumbers' or miners' candles are best for they burn long enough to start even a wet-weather fire and also give off quite a bit of light.

Matches

Include a large reserve supply and a small daily supply, either waterproofed, in a waterproof container, or wrapped in aluminum foil.

Equipment for Building Fires in Wet Weather

Trench candles (page 290), "peas" (page 291) or plumbers' candles and bits of dry tinder will come in handy. An inspirator (page 285) coiled up in one of your cooking kettles is worth its weight in gold for starting fires in wet weather.

Extra Paddles

Include one or more extra paddles when traveling by canoe in case one is lost or broken.

Water Purification Equipment

Carry some means of purifying water (page 377) unless you are going to boil it or camp where you know there is a safe source.

Whistle

At least one person in the group should wear a whistle on a cord or lanyard to use in emergencies.

Individual Mess Kit.

Cooking and Eating Outfits

Nested cooking kits are most economical of weight and space and come in sizes serving up to twelve persons. They usually have their own canvas carrying case but, if you find it too tight for easy handling, transfer them to a home-made cotton bag or an old flour or sugar sack with a draw string. Aluminum is perhaps the best lightweight material although lightweight stainless steel has less tendency to cause food to stick and burn. Porcelain will chip with trip-usage.

Aluminum drinking cups burn your lips when filled with hot liquids. Enamel cups, especially with handles open at the bottom, stay cool enough to hold comfortably, and tin ones will do. Best of all are unbreakable, lightweight plastic cups for they are poor conductors of heat and keep the contents hot yet don't burn your lips. You may want a collapsible metal cup or noggin for water-stops along the way. Plastic is considered by many to be the best material for plates and other dishes and sectional plates are available. Pie tins also make good unbreakable plates.

You can make your own cooking or mess kits or assemble them at a variety or hardware store, using the trial and error method to insure compact nesting. Carry your cooking kit in a home-made bag and tie your individual mess kit up in your bandanna or place it in a ditty bag.

Wire bail handles for cooking pots are best for they serve to suspend them over the fire and can be folded flat for nesting. Fold down rings on lids instead of knobs and shallow spouts and bail ears also aid in compact nesting. Pot covers should fit tightly to keep the heat and juices in and dirt and ashes out. Low, broad utensils heat faster and are less liable to upset than high ones. Knives, forks, and spoons can be placed inside the kettles or carried inside a bag made on the order of a toilet kit (page 317). Use the largest pail, which fits outside your kit, for a water bucket so that it will always be clean for contact with the cloth cover. Some never wash the outsides of their cooking kettles, claiming that the accumulation of carbon improves their heat-retaining properties. If you follow this practice, you will need to pack them between layers of newspapers.

Your reflector oven should fold flat. A Dutch oven is a big convenience, but is cumbersome to transport.

Careful planning of your menu will facilitate your utensil problem, for you can cook many things as one-pot meals, or dispense with cooking utensils entirely by cooking in aluminum foil or on sticks or woodland broilers fashioned at the campsite. If you take individual mess kits, the Boy or Girl Scout kits are as good as any.

First Aid Kits

Be safety conscious so that you will have little need for first aid treatment. Nevertheless, every trip going out of camp should carry along a first aid kit complete enough to care for minor ailments and injuries, assembled in a compact container to protect the contents. A flat tobacco tin makes a satisfactory individual kit, and a small-sized lightweight tackle box with its several compartments is excellent for a larger kit. Aluminum kits are light in weight. You can make a

First Aid Kit.

canvas cover with a carry strap for carrying over one shoulder. Another convenient way to make a kit is with pockets to hold various items. Put contents in unbreakable plastic containers or wrap them with corrugated cardboard, sponge rubber, several layers of tissues, or heavy blotters. You can buy first aid kits, but they are more expensive and often do not contain exactly what you want. You may prefer to plan your own with the help of your camp doctor or nurse.

You need take only small quantities of each medication and can buy small plastic vials for liquids and ointments at the drug or variety store or you can use well rinsed ones that commercial products come in. Some medications are available in ampules just large enough for a single treatment. The camp doctor or nurse will advise what supplies to take but the following are suggested:

Instruction book (American Red Cross suggested)
Triangular bandage (a clean bandanna will do)
Absorbent cotton
Adhesive tape
Band aids
Gauze squares—roller gauze
Aromatic spirits of ammonia—for bites, stings, and fainting
Boric acid solution—for minor eye irritations
Aspirin
Baking soda—for bites, stings, indigestion, or sunburn.
Oil of cloves—for toothache
Tincture of iodine (2% solution), Zephiran Chloride or Merthiolate for open cuts and abrasions (ampules provide the most convenient form)
Tannic acid (jelly or powder) or picric acid—for burns
Tweezers (sharp pointed)
Ferric chloride (5% solution) or calamine lotion—for poison ivy or oak
Snake bite outfit
Small scissors

Emergency Crutch.

paper or sand held in a piece of cloth or leather, and padded with sponge rubber, gauze or some folds of soft cloth bound on with adhesive tape.

Safety pins
Insect repellent

You can make a temporary crutch as illustrated. The top, which rests under the armpit, should be smoothed with sand-

CHECK LISTS FOR PACKING EQUIPMENT

Select from the following to make out your own check list. Then check and recheck it to eliminate everything not really essential. Revise it on the basis of your experience when you return, and keep it handy for use the next time.

PERSONAL EQUIPMENT

ESSENTIAL

Wearing Apparel

Extra trousers and shirt
Shorts
Sun glasses
Moccasins or extra shoes
Wool socks (3 pairs)
Swim suit
Wide brimmed hat or duckbill visor cap
Pajamas
Rain wear
Heavy canvas gloves
Bandanna
Extra underclothes
Windbreaker or wool shirt

OPTIONAL

Wearing Apparel

Swim cap (for girls)
Insect head-net or mosquito netting
Leather belt for hatchet, knife, etc.
Light rubbers

Toilet Articles

Toilet soap in plastic box
Towels and washcloths
Pocket mirror (metal preferred)
Toothbrush and paste
Comb
Sun-tan lotion
Insect repellant
Sanitary napkins (girls)

Toilet Articles

Shaving kit (men)
Kleenex
Lotions for hair or skin

For Food

Canteen
Mess kit, including fork and spoon

For Food

Collapsible drinking cup or noggin

PERSONAL EQUIPMENT (Continued)

ESSENTIAL

Tools

Knife
Waterproof match box and matches
Flashlight, extra bulb and batteries
Packsack
Waterproofed matches

Miscellaneous

Maps
Pocket notebook
Hard pencil
Bed roll with ground cloth

OPTIONAL

Tools

Hatchets or saws
Tump line
Fishing equipment and license
Whistle
Pedometer
Mending kit

Miscellaneous

Compass
Money
Binoculars
Camera and film (in waterproof bag)
Nature books, poetry, games
Air mattress and pillow
Stationery (already stamped)
Musical instrument
Song books
Extra eyeglasses in case
Tent
Watch

GROUP EQUIPMENT

ESSENTIAL

Tools

Axes or saws
Repair kit for mending tents, air mattresses, etc.
Nails, twine, etc.
Adhesive tape
Tarpaulins, ponchos or pup tent
    for sheltering equipment, dining porch, etc.
Spade or shovel
File and sharpening stone
Can opener
Electric lantern

For Food

Menus and recipes
Paper napkins
Tablets for purifying water
Aluminum foil
Cooking forks, spatula, spoons
Cooking utensils
Water pail (plastic or canvas folding)
Paraffined cloth or plastic food bags
Salt and pepper in shakers (fit piece
    of waxed paper inside tops)
Food (carefully checked against check list)

OPTIONAL

Tools

Extra paddles
#10 tin can buckets, etc.
Candles
25 or 50 feet of strong cord
A few lengths of wire

For Food

Hobo stoves, reflector oven,
    Dutch oven
Paper towels
Light chain with hooks on both
    ends for supporting pots over
    the fire

GROUP EQUIPMENT (Continued)

ESSENTIAL

Fires and Sanitation

Extra supply of waterproofed matches
Toilet paper
Insect repellent
Wash pan or canvas wash basin
Dishcloths, towels
Yellow soap or detergent
Metal or plastic sponge for
  cleaning pans

Miscellaneous

Check list of equipment
Mending kit (buttons, thread, etc.)
First aid kit

OPTIONAL

Fires and Sanitation

Inspirator, "peas," trench
  candles, etc.
Long-handled dish mops

Miscellaneous

Maps of area
Old newspapers
Extra shoelaces (twine will do)

ADDITIONAL READINGS

Burke, Edmund H.: *Camping Handbook.*
Des Grey, Arthur H.: *Camping.*
Henderson, Luis M.: *The Outdoor Guide.*
Jaeger, Ellsworth: *Wildwood Wisdom.*
Joy, Barbara Ellen: *Camp Assembled First Aid Kit.* Camp Publications, 2 pp., 15¢.
Joy, Barbara Ellen: *Camp Craft.*
Joy, Barbara Ellen: *Camping.*
Joy, Barbara Ellen: *Suggestions for Improvised Camping-Out Equipment.* Camp Publications, 6 pp., 35¢.
Koller, Larry: *Complete Book of Camping and the Outdoors.*
Lindholm, Major Mauno A.: *Camping and Outdoor Fun.*
Lynn, Gordon: *Camping and Camp Crafts.*
Mason, Bernard S.: *The Junior Book of Camping and Woodcraft.*
Rutstrum, Calvin: *The New Way of the Wilderness.*
Swanson, William E.: *Camping for All It's Worth.*
Tobitt, Janet E.: *Program in Girl Scout Camping.*
Wells, George and Iris: *The Handbook of Wilderness Travel.*
West, James E., and Hillcourt, William: *Scout Field Book.*
Whelen, Townsend, and Angier, Bradford: *On Your Own in the Wilderness.*

MAGAZINE ARTICLES

Good Idea. C.M., Mar., 1946.

SOURCES OF CAMPING EQUIPMENT

Abercrombie & Fitch Co., Madison at 45th St., New York, N.Y.

Alaska Sleeping Bag Co., 309 S.W. Third Ave., Portland 4, Oreg.
Barnard Guards, 2183 Hendon Ave., St. Paul 8, Minn.
Boy Scouts of America, National Supply Service Division, New Brunswick, N.J.; 231 S. Green St., Chicago 7, Ill.; 485 Brannan St., San Francisco 7, Cal.
Camp and Trail Outfitters, 112 Chambers St., New York 7, N.Y.
Charles Bradley Wood, 40 Niles Hill Road, New London, Conn.
Corcoran, Inc., Stoughton, Mass.
David T. Abercrombie Co., 97 Chambers St. New York 7, N.Y.
F. Chapman and Sons, 440 N. Orleans St., Chicago 10, Ill.
Fisler Sales Co., 1329 Main St., Kansas City, Mo.
Gerry Mountaineering Equipment, Ward, Colo.
Girl Scouts of the U.S.A., National Equipment Service, 155 East 44th St., New York 17, N.Y., 1824 Washington Ave., St. Louis 3, Mo.; 770 Mission St., San Francisco 3, Calif.
Holubar, P.O. Box 7, Boulder Colo.
Hudson's, 105 Third Ave., New York 3, N.Y.
L.L. Bean, Inc., Freeport, Me.
Martin J. Wilburger & Co., 1352 Wagner Ave., Philadelphia 41, Pa.
Mor-San Sales, 10–21 50th Ave., Long Island City 1, N.Y.
The Smilie Company, 536 Mission St., San Francisco 4, Calif.
Trailwise, 1615 University Ave., Berkeley, Calif.
Woodward and Lothrup, Washington, D.C.

28

Sleeping in the Open

"I've got to get up. I need the rest."

With never a thought of danger, he lies in his blanket bed,
His coat of canvas the pillow supporting his drowsy head
As he watches the white clouds drifting through limitless
*   azure seas*
Where only the stars can find him as they peep through the
*   sheltering trees.*

JAMES BARTON ADAMS

SINCE A THIRD or more of a camper's time is spent sleeping, his bed is deserving of much of his thought and attention. A good night's rest with at least eight hours of sleep for adults and even more for youngsters is a "must" for those on a trip.

If you are going by covered wagon or if the camp truck is to transport the heavy baggage, bulk and weight are not of tremendous importance. But when you travel entirely on your own two feet with all your possessions on your back, it is really a problem to provide a comfortable bed that will weigh little and not be cumbersome to handle. Canoe bedding, too, must be kept light and compact, although it is possible to take a little more than when back-packing.

One of the most difficult jobs in all the world would be to try to get a crowd of experienced campers to agree on which type of outdoor bed is best. One reason for this is, of course, the difference in circumstances and localities in which they have camped. Obviously, a person who has always bedded down in the cold Northland, often in the dead of winter, will have entirely different standards from those that would be applicable or desirable for the organized summer camp.

A good bed should provide warmth, a reasonable degree of softness, smoothness and freedom from bumps, and protection from wind and rain; you must attain these qualities according to the nature of the particular terrain in which you sleep. Taking into consideration your means of transportation, you must select from the several types of beds available.

Since we are accustomed to sleeping on a mattress which needs practically no attention, most of us are inclined to ignore what is under us and think only in terms of what to use for cover. As you scamper about gathering your duffel in a packsack ready for an overnight, the sun is shining, warmly and cheerfully; it is hard to realize that it will go to bed long before you and that the air will get increasingly colder as night progresses. The uninitiated will really travel light, but experience will teach you that you need as many or more blankets under you as over you. The ground is always more or less damp and the earth is an efficient conductor of heat away from your body so that you will likely spend a chilly night no matter how high you pile the blankets over you if you place too few underneath.

To rest, you must relax, and it's a little difficult to imagine an iceberg relaxing. Incidentally, the padding of the extra blankets underneath isn't at all objectionable, either.

WHAT TO USE

Blankets

The finances of the boy or girl in an organized camp may make the purchase of a sleeping bag or other fancy sleeping equipment out of the question. Blankets are the answer in this case. Indeed, some prefer them to a sleeping bag, for they are more adaptable to changes in temperature and are simple to spread for airing and cleaning thoroughly from time to time. Air and sun your blankets on a bush or drape them over a rope between two trees every day to get rid of the night's accumulation of perspiration, for dry blankets are much warmer than clammy ones. Blankets for outdoor beds should be of a dark, neutral shade which won't easily show soil.

Blankets of 100 per cent virgin wool are much to be preferred, for their loose weave and long nap create pockets to imprison dead air and act as insulation against the loss of body heat. They thus cut down on weight without sacrificing warmth. One wool blanket is the equivalent of several of part-wool or cotton blankets. Many so-called wool blankets, however, have a percentage of cotton mixed in. Cotton blankets are usually adequate in summer but serve poorly in cool, damp weather, for they gather and retain moisture from the body as well as from the air and ground.

Single blankets are easier to manipulate and two relatively thin blankets are warmer than one thick one since they trap a layer of insulating dead air between them. Hudson's Bay blankets or blankets of llama or camel's hair are the warmest of all and are the choice of Northwoods hunters and trappers. However, they are expensive and provide more warmth than a summer camper needs. Quilts and comforters are bulky and too fragile for trail requirements.

Making a Bed Roll

Some people simply roll up in their blankets and claim to sleep in perfect comfort throughout the night. This is unlikely to be the case for we don't truly go to bed and "sleep like a log," but actually turn frequently to lie in many different positions before the night is over. Consequently we are likely to find parts of our anatomy exposed several times during the night and end up with an unhappy, restless time of it.

It is easy to make an envelope or Klondike bed roll using four 3-inch blanket pins and as many blankets as you want, all of the same size. First, lay your poncho or, ground cloth on the ground, and place the blankets you want outside (blanket number 3) with its edge at the middle of the poncho. Next, place the edge of blanket number 2 at the

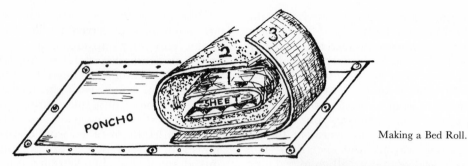

Making a Bed Roll.

center of blanket number 3. Lay down as many blankets as you want in this fashion, the edge of each placed at the center of the one under it. Place your sheet on top and fold it in half lengthwise. Now fold your blankets over, in reverse order, beginning with number 1 on top, then number 2, and so on; when

BOWLINE KNOT
TWO HALF HITCHES
(PULL TIGHT)

Tying a Bed Roll.

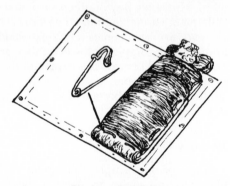

Pinning a Bed Roll.

all are folded, pin through *all* the blankets along the sides and bottom with your blanket pins, two along the sides and two across the bottom. Make your bed roll wide enough to let you turn during the night since confinement in narrow quarters seriously interferes with rest. Roll and tie your bed roll for carrying.

To wrap up in an envelope bed made from one blanket, lay a third of it down, lie down on it, bring the other two-thirds across you and turn over slightly so you can tuck the edge in under you. Then lift your legs and tuck the bottom in under your feet and you're all ready for the night. With two blankets, place them down with the edge of one at the center

of the other, lie down on top of the two thicknesses and fold the other halves across you, lift up your legs and tuck the bottoms under them. To use three blankets, lay the third one down just above the first and wrap yourself up in them as before. Don't make the envelope too tight; allow yourself room to move.

Sleeping Bags

A sleeping bag consists of an outer shell of water-resistant material with an inside compact arrangement of insulating substances. The best ones fasten with a strong, heavy duty zipper extending along one side and across the bottom so that they are easy to get into and can be opened out flat for a daily sunning and airing.

Bags intended for bedding-out in very cold weather come with attached hoods and have a filler of eiderdown, duck or goose down, any one of which gives much warmth with little weight. This warmth is unnecessary and even undesirable for summer camping. Dacron is one of the new materials which is proving highly satisfactory since it is light in weight, as

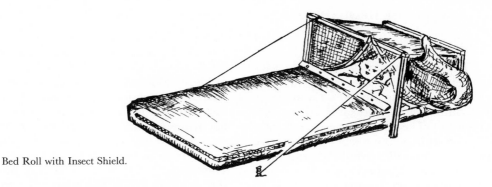

Bed Roll with Insect Shield.

warm as wool, about 70 per cent as warm as down, impervious to moths and mildew and fewer people are allergic to it than to some of the other materials. The old favorite linings of wool and kapok are now falling into disfavor, especially for light camping for they are both heavier and more bunglesome to transport. The inner filler of a bag should be fastened down with a quilting stitch so that it will not become lumpy or matted. Some bags intended primarily for cold weather answer a double purpose in that they consist of a bag within a bag which can be separated to provide two light ones suitable for summer use. *Mummy bags* taper down toward the feet and thus conserve heat and cut down on bulk and weight but some find that they tend to turn over with the sleeper and are too confining for comfort.

Sleeping bags have several points in their favor. There are no waste corners to add bulk and weight and you are zippered in so that you remain covered, an important point for youngsters who are often restless sleepers.

Most of them have an adjustable awning to shelter your head; the awning is supported by four sticks and sometimes guy ropes. Although this protection may be effective against dew, be assured that you will need a tent or other shelter over you in case of rain for a bed roll itself is only water-resistant, not waterproof, nor would you want it to be, for your bed will become clammy and uncomfortable unless your perspiration can evaporate.

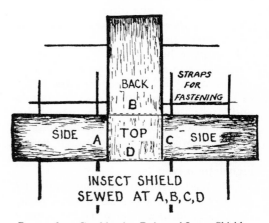

Pattern for a Combination Rain and Insect Shield.

Some bags have pockets for inserting an air mattress; however, this is not worth its extra weight for a back-packer.

If your bed roll doesn't have a thin washable inner lining which can be removed for frequent laundering, you should provide one. Nylon is best for it allows free movement with a minimum of friction. Make it by sewing up one side and the bottom of a piece of nylon, a sheet, or piece of unbleached muslin and anchor it to the inside of the bedroll with snaps or tie strings so it can't bunch up under you. Use a poncho or ground cloth under your sleeping bag to keep out the moisture from the ground. In hot weather, you may want to sleep on top of your bag, using it for cushioning, and wrapping yourself up in extra sheets or a light blanket.

LAYING THE GROUNDWORK

Sleeping on the Ground

"Trippers" often make one-night trips or even longer ones sleeping in their bed rolls with only the ground for a mattress. Pollyanna might find some advantages in this sort of bed, for there are no squeaking bed springs, the sleeper may be sure that the slats will not fall out, and there is no danger whatsoever of falling out of bed. But even Pollyanna would have to admit that softness is not one of its virtues and this type of sleeping probably fostered the expression "making mountains out of molehills."

It helps to hollow out depressions for your hips and shoulders, repeatedly trying them for "fit." If spending the night in this fashion, get down on your hands and knees and go over every inch of the surface where your bed is to lie, removing each twig, acorn and tough weed. Arrange to sleep with your head slightly higher than your feet.

One way to soften a ground bed is to gather such things as pine needles, moss, leaves, dry ferns on dry grass for a mattress. To keep them from spreading as the night progresses, wrap them up in your tarp or poncho. Hay makes a good mattress and can often be purchased cheaply from a neighboring farmer. Fern and hay "mattresses," however, hold the heat and so are often not too desirable in summer.

If the night is particularly cold, build a reflector fire so that you can snuggle down between the fire and reflector with the fire to warm you on one side and the reflector on the other. A layer of newspapers under the bed roll will serve as effective insulation. If there is a cold wind, seek the shelter of a clump of bushes or a thick growth of trees.

In snaky country, it may be worthwhile to investigate the possibilities of using a jungle hammock to hang between two trees.

Mattresses

A bed sack weighing only a pound or a little over and about 2½ feet wide and 4½ feet long can be made of bed ticking, unbleached muslin, an old blanket, canvas, drill, burlap or grain sacks. Equip one end of it with snaps, safety pins, or tie strings so that you can open it and stuff it with dry leaves, grass, ferns, hay or whatever is available at the campsite. Pack it just full enough to let your body sink restfully into it; if it's too full, you'll roll off the sides. Waterproof the under side of the bag or use it on top of a tarpaulin, ground cloth or poncho. A mattress of these dimensions is long enough to support the upper three-fourths of your body, which is really all that is necessary. Air mattresses of light plastic are quite inexpensive and longer lasting ones of rubberized cloth cost only a little more. They are fine for those who want luxury and don't object to the extra weight. Inflate them with a small hand inflater or with a special tip arrangement on your inspirator (page 285) but avoid overinflation; leave them "soft" enough to conform to the shape of your body when you lie down. Carry a tire patching outfit for mending small leaks for the extremely light ones can be punctured by a chance sharp stick or stone.

Stretcher Beds

A comfortable and light form of mattress is the stretcher bed. Make it of a 36 inches x 8 feet strip of canvas, drill, bed ticking or a double thickness of burlap or grain sack. Allow a four-inch seam on each side for inserting sticks to support it on logs, rocks, or forked sticks about ½ to 1 foot above the ground; pound in stakes just inside the four corners to keep them from rolling toward the center. The waterproof canopy with a *bobbinet* insect shield shown previously can be used with this bed.

Stretcher Bed.

Browse Beds

Beds of balsam, hemlock or spruce boughs sound romantic and are no doubt comfortable when skillfully made, but the camper in an organized camp will seldom be in a region where trees are plentiful enough to be trimmed for bedding. Making a comfortable one is tricky so be sure to learn from an expert if you should have occasion to make it. It is definitely not done by just piling up an assortment of boughs in haphazard fashion—such would be worse than sleeping on the bare ground.

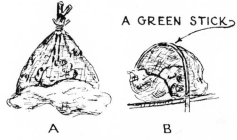

A GREEN STICK

A   B

Other Varieties of Insect Shields.

SOME EXTRAS

Insect Shields

The rain canopy over the stretcher bed consists of a top and three flaps to roll up when the weather is nice and lower and tie around the supporting framework when it rains. The best material for the

insect shield is bobbinet. Fasten it along the four sides of the top of the rain canopy and leave the sides long enough to tuck in around the sleeper under the bed roll. (See pattern on page 329.)

Pillows

Inflatable air pillows are available and air mattresses sometimes come with pillows already attached. You can make a light, soft pillow which costs practically

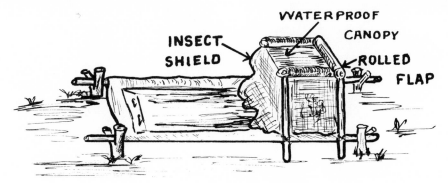

Stretcher Bed with Rain and Insect Shield.

nothing by stuffing a bag with the soft down from milkweed pods or with cat-tail heads picked when nearly ripe in the late summer or early fall. Such a pillow is also suitable for use as a kneeling pad in a canoe. However, as a matter of fact, on the trail, campers usually dispense with a pillow, and use a packsack (with hard objects removed) or a rolled-up coat or sweater instead.

Night is a dead monotonous period under a roof; but in the open world it passes lightly, with its stars and dews and perfumes, and the hours are marked by changes in the face of nature.

—ROBERT LOUIS STEVENSON
in *Treasure Island*

ADDITIONAL READINGS

Burke, Edmund H.: *Camping Handbook.*

Des Grey, Arthur H.: *Camping.*

Geist, Roland C.: *Hiking, Camping and Mountaineering.*

Jaeger, Ellsworth: *Wildwood Wisdom.*

Kesting, Ted: *The Outdoor Encyclopedia.*

Lindholm, Major Mauno A.: *Camping and Outdoor Fun.*

Lynn, Gordon: *Camping and Camp Crafts.*

Mason, Bernard S.: *The Junior Book of Camping and Woodcraft.*

Rutstrum, Calvin: *The New Way of the Wilderness.* $4.50.

Swanson, William S.: *Camping for all It's Worth.* $2.49.

Weaver, Robert W., and Merrill, Anthony F.: *Camping Can Be Fun.*

Whelen, Townsend, and Angier, Bradford: *On Your Own in the Wilderness.*

29

Keeping Food
Cool and Safe

Then after a day filled with pleasure and work,
As you trudge back to camp with your trout,
The smell of bacon that's cooking up there,
Is the sweetest of odors, no doubt.

F. K. BERRY,
Cooking in Camp

"OH, THIS IS THE LIFE," you say, as you sink back with a few of your pals on the first night away from permanent camp. Just a handful of friends, a delicious supper under your belt, dishes all washed up and put away, and nothing to do but gather around the campfire and enjoy yourself until time to turn in for the night, away from civilization for a few days with no danger of outsiders crashing in.

You may be right insofar as human intrusion is concerned, but do you realize that hundreds of forest eyes are, or soon will be, focused upon your camp? Friendly eyes, to be sure, but also curious, and wanting to investigate this strange assortment that has established itself in the midst of their forest home. These creatures are hungry, too, and willing to nibble on anything and everything they can find after you have gone to bed.

Unless you are camping in wild country well toward the borders or outside of the United States, you are extremely unlikely to be visited by such animals as wolves, foxes or bears which constantly plagued the lives of the early settlers of the country. But such animals as chipmunks, squirrels, roving dogs, pack rats, and field mice are likely to be your neighbors. In some regions, porcupines are numerous and may prove troublesome, for their sharp teeth can be very destructive. Anything with a salty taste has a fatal attraction for them, and perspiration-soaked paddles, axes, shoes, belts, bridles and saddles must be kept well beyond their reach.

PROTECTION FROM INSECTS

You must anticipate the ever-present flies, ants and other tiny crawling or flying creatures that love to sample your food and literally get in your hair. To protect food from ants and other crawling insects, erect a water barrier by placing the food on a table with each leg resting in a small container of water or insert a strong piece of wire such as a straightened-out coat hanger through a small hole in a shallow tin can and solder the joint to make it watertight; then turn back both ends of the wire to form hooks, hang the food on one, suspend it by the other, and keep the cup filled with water. A sprinkling of common moth flakes or moth balls around the legs of a table or placed on the path ants would have to take to reach food is also effective.

To keep out flying insects, place the food in jars or cans with tight-fitting suction or screw-on lids or plastic covers, wrap it in cloth, mosquito netting, cheesecloth or waxed paper, or place it in plastic bags, sealed at the top with a warm iron.

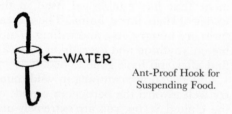

Ant-Proof Hook for
Suspending Food.

PROTECTION FROM ANIMALS

The type of marauders expected will, of course, determine the kind of cache or protection you must provide. Even tin cans are not safe, for some animals, including dogs, can pierce them with their teeth and suck out the contents. The usual method of caching food is to suspend it about fifteen to twenty feet above the ground and at such a distance from overhanging branches that neither jump-ing nor climbing animals can get to it. Attach a rope and throw it across a tree limb to provide a pulley for quickly raising and lowering it.

The Green Sapling Cache

One method sometimes used to cache food is to bend a small green sapling over, attach the food among its branches, and then let it fly back into place. This gives adequate protection from dogs and other land animals, but spreads a bounteous feast for ants and tree-climbing animals unless you place the food in containers which protect it.

The Peeled-Stick Cache

This is an easily made cache which provides satisfactory protection from any animals likely to be encountered. Peel the bark from a stick so that its smooth surface will provide poor footing for climbing animals, and use a forked stick to hoist it into place between the crotches of two trees. Fasten the food to the end of a rope, throw the free end over the pole and draw the food up as high as desired. Fasten the free end around one of the trees with a couple of half hitches.

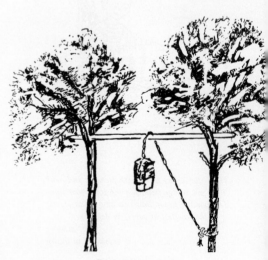

Peeled Stick Cache.

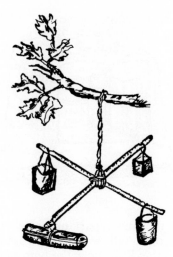

St. Andrews Cross Cache.

St. Andrews Cross Cache

An even safer cache for several packages is provided by the St. Andrews cross support. It consists of two poles lashed securely together at right angles with the various packages of food suspended from the four ends of the poles. Try to balance the amount of weight hanging from each arm. This keeps the packages safe from prowling animals and its tendency to sway in the breeze even discourages ants and such creatures.

Cupboard Cache

Make this convenient cupboard from an oblong box such as an old orange crate and insert appropriate shelves in it. Fit it with an insect-proof covering of plastic and a protective front of canvas, oilcloth or cheesecloth with tabs to tie into eyes, or loops to slip over hooks placed around the bottom and sides of the crate. Suspend the box by a rope fastened in large screw eyes along its top edge or by overhand or figure-of-eight knots in holes in the box. This cupboard is awkward to take on a hiking trip, but is excellent on a wagon or canoe trip. It is a practical refinement to leave at an outpost camp.

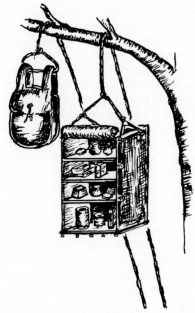

Cupboard Cache.

Construct a similar cupboard, to fold or roll up, from canvas, leaving wide hems at the top for inserting stick supports upon arrival at the campsite.

KEEPING FOOD COOL

One of the main problems when trip camping is keeping such perishable foods as butter and milk cool. You can keep milk for twenty-four hours or a little longer, and butter will remain sweet and relatively firm for two weeks or more if stored in an airtight container.

As with most things in camping, the particular method you use will depend largely upon what is available and convenient and your ingenuity will be called into play to make the most of the possibilities.

Cooling with Ice

Though not practicable when backpacking, it is entirely feasible to take ice for cooling when transporting supplies by

automobile or truck. A fifty-pound cake
will last four days when properly cared
for and a hundred-pound cake will last
correspondingly longer.

As soon as possible after you arrive at
the campsite, dig a hole big enough for
the ice and food you want to pack with
it. Line the bottom and sides with small
rocks or gravel and a layer of grass or
leaves. Insulate the ice by wrapping it
tightly with several layers of newspaper
and an outside covering of burlap. Thoroughly moisten the insulation and place
the package in an old cardboard box or
tin can with holes punched in it to allow
the ice water to drain off. Pack the food
in close to the ice and lower them into
the pit. Shovel wet sand or gravel in all
around and cover the whole thing with
wet burlap or dampened tree branches
and the like.

Plan your cooking program so that you
need open your "refrigerator" as seldom
as possible and the ice will last surprisingly well.

Cooling with Running Water

When water from a stream or lake is
available, you can devise several varieties
of satisfactory coolers. Where the water
is disturbed as by strong waves, swift current or boats, weight the food down with
rocks or anchor it to trees or rocks on the
shore so that it can't be overturned or
washed away. Place it in waterproof containers to keep impure water from con-
taminating it.

A SPRING BOX. A large box or barrel
can be sunk at the water's edge, weighting it down with heavy rocks to keep it
immersed. By feeling the water in a lake,
you can often locate one of the underground streams which feeds it and will
find the water quite cool there. Place
your cooler under trees or shade it with
a framework of branches kept wet by
frequently dousing it with water. Insert a
shelf large enough to hold all your food
which is not in watertight containers.

Spring Box.

Leave the under part unshelved to accommodate tall watertight containers.
Make large holes near the bottom of the
barrel to promote a free flow of water
through it.

Anchor the box or barrel in the water
under some shade and cover it with a
piece of burlap with ends dangling in the
water to absorb moisture and cool the
contents by evaporation.

IMMERSING DIRECTLY IN WATER. You
may place your food in a large watertight container such as a five-gallon milk
can and submerge it in a cool spot in the
lake or stream, using rocks to weight the
container down, if necessary. Place it in
the shade and cover it with a piece of
burlap and brush framework as described
for the spring box.

If you have no large container, lash a
stick framework, sink it in the water and
anchor it with heavy rocks or drive stakes
into the stream bed at the inside corners
of the framework. Fit food in watertight
containers into the spaces in the
framework.

Cooling by Evaporation

Cooling by evaporation is effective,
particularly on a hot day when there is a
fairly good breeze. Putting salt in the
water will hasten the evaporation and so
make it more efficient.

AN ORIOLE CACHE. This provides one
of the best all-around methods for stor-

Framework for Immersing Food in the Water.

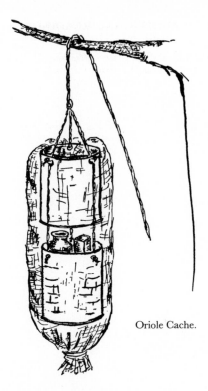

Oriole Cache.

ing food, for it cools as well as protects it from animals and insects.

Make three or four holes near the tops of two buckets or number 10 tin cans, spacing them evenly so that the cans will hang straight. Join the cans with rope as shown with enough space between them to insert food into the lower one.

Keep the upper can filled about two-thirds full of water and use small rocks to weight down the center of a piece of cheesecloth large enough to cover both cans with it. Bring the cheesecloth down under the cans and fasten it tightly to form an insect-proof cover.

The cheesecloth absorbs water from the top can and the resulting evaporation keeps the contents cool. Hang the cache in the shade in a fairly strong breeze. Swing the rope over a limb and raise the contents where it will be safe as explained for the peeled-stick cache.

OTHER COOLING DEVICES.   Another

way to cool food is to place it in a cupboard cache or a bucket or pan and immerse it in a vessel of water. Place all in the shade, and cover the food container with cheesecloth or burlap long enough to extend down into the water.

If you dig a shallow pit in a bank close to a lake or stream, it will usually quickly fill with underground water which is even cooler than that in the lake or stream. Place food in suitable receptacles in the pit and shade the top of it as previously described.

Dig a hole in a shady place under a tree and line it with rocks, gravel, leaves or grass. Place the food in it and surround the top and sides with dampened leaves or grass, redampened frequently.

Keep your drinking water cool by suspending it in the breeze in a desert bag; the water seeps out slowly through the canvas and cools the contents by evaporation.

ADDITIONAL READINGS

Burke, Edmund H.: *Camping Handbook.*
Des Grey, Arthur H.: *Camping.*

Rutstrum, Calvin: *The New Way of the Wilderness.*

MAGAZINE ARTICLES

Joy, Barbara Ellen: *Care of Food and Equipment on Trips.* Camp Publication, 10¢.

30

Cooking Devices

None is so poor that he need sit on a pumpkin; that is shiftlessness.

HENRY THOREAU

A GOOD CAMPER is able to adapt himself happily to whatever media for camp life he finds plentiful in his particular region. If wood is scarce or you are prohibited from cutting green saplings to use as kettle supports, there may be ample quantities of nonpopping rocks which will do beautifully. A dump yard in the vicinity may provide flat or odd-shaped bits of metal, old stove parts, and the like, which you can convert into cooking devices and other gadgets for use around the campsite. Ingenuity and skill will aid you in improvising cooking devices, and your satisfaction is greatly enhanced by knowing the origin of your creation "from the ground up."

THE CROTCHED STICK

Few things are more valuable around a camp site than the good old crotched stick; there are a thousand-and-one uses for it. When seeking one, there is no use wasting time in searching for the variety shown in B in the illustration, for it is rare and is unsatisfactory anyway, since it is quite likely to split when you try to drive it into the ground. If it is ever necessary

The Crotched Stick.

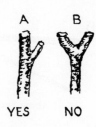

to drive one, lay another stick through the crotch to pound on, but even then your chances of driving it without splitting are meager. A forked stick like A in the illustration will serve the purpose just as well, is much easier to find, and eliminates most of the danger of splitting the crotch, since you pound on the main part of the stick to drive it. For easy driving, give the stick a four-sided point.

CAMPFIRE PARAPHERNALIA

A camper disabled through carelessness is about as welcome around camp as a rainstorm. It is well to take time to prepare properly for work.

Canvas work gloves and a big bandanna are useful when handling hot objects around the fire and keep the hands clean for cooking. A green forked-stick fire poker and a shovel are indispensable for manipulating the hot rocks, burning embers and glowing coals into more advantageous positions for cooking.

Fire Tongs

Hot rocks are often used for cooking or heating purposes and, if no shovel is available, they are best moved between a forked stick and another stick, as in B.

Figure A shows a pair of fire tongs made by taking a strong green sapling of hickory or other suitable wood, about two

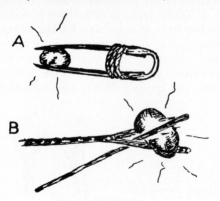

Green Stick Fire Tongs.

to three feet long, and shaving away part of it near the center so that you can bend it around in the form of a "U." It bends more easily if you heat it over the fire while working with it. Lash the two ends of the stick into position. These fire tongs are excellent for shifting firebrands about and may even be used for lifting small heated rocks.

Tin Can or Hobo Stove

A hobo stove is made from a number 10 tin can and provides a fine little stove for frying bacon and eggs or other quickly cooked foods. Cut a three-inch hole at the bottom for building a fire and a one-to-two-inch hole on the opposite side near the top for a smoke vent. A fire of small twigs is all you need to heat it; in fact, you must use care to keep the fire small enough not to burn the food. Lay the fire and place the hobo stove in position over it, making sure that the stove is level so the food won't spill. A trench candle can be used under it instead of wood to furnish heat.

Hobo Stove.

Paraffin Stove or Buddy Burner

The little paraffin stove or buddy burner is excellent for quick cooking, for it will burn several minutes, throwing out enough heat to cook simple dishes.

Make it by melting about two-thirds of a medium or small-sized can of paraffin or old candle stubs. When the wax begins

Paraffin Stove or Buddy Burner.

to harden, insert a piece of cardboard or corrugated paper which has been wound in a loose spiral, making sure to leave the edges extending a little above the wax to act as a wick. You can use a paraffin stove in your cooking fireplace just like a small fire. When through with it, smother it by putting a lid over it and save it to use another time. You can also use a buddy burner for light or for starting a stubborn fire.

SUPPORTS FOR THE KETTLE

Self-reliant campers find many ways to support their cooking utensils over the fire. As previously mentioned, you can build supports of nonpopping stones or green, slow-burning wood, or lay small green sticks across a pit or other support to form a sort of grate.

Scrap heaps often yield iron bars for grates and large pieces of sheet metal for stove tops. An old metal washtub makes an excellent stove when a door for fuel is cut at the bottom of one side and a small hole for a chimney and cross ventilation is placed at the top of the other (N, page 252). A piece of gravel screen makes a fine grate on which to roast steaks and such foods directly over the coals.

Single Pot Holders on Dingle Sticks

When you have only one kettle to heat, a variety of *dingle sticks* or *single pot holders* are now available. Several types are shown here, and others can be devised from whatever materials you have at hand. The Indian *waugan* is one of the simplest, especially if you have a large rock or stump available to use in place of the forked upright stick, for you will then need only a long notched stick for suspending the kettle. The adjustable crane, attributed to Stuart Thompson, is a clever arrangement by which you can raise or lower a kettle over the fire by simply winding or unwinding the string by which it is anchored. The *spygelia* and *brush crane* illustrate other single pot holders.

INDIAN WAUGAN

THE SPYGELIA

ADJUSTABLE CRANE

BRUSH CRANE

Single Pot Holders.

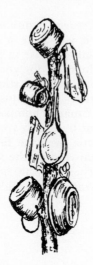

A Pan Tree.

Pan Tree

Make a handy pan tree by cutting the branches off a dead but solid tree for convenient pegs; then anchor the shaft of the tree into the ground near the fire or work table.

Kitchen Cabinet

Make a kitchen cabinet of any desired shape and design, combining forked sticks and lashing to suit your own particular taste and needs. Store your dishes on it with a waterproof covering over them to keep them clean and dry for the next meal.

Chippewa Kitchen

This is another variety of kitchen cabinet which features shelves and protruding ends for suspending things. Make it any size desired, ranging from a small tripod for a few persons to the fairly commodious size shown in the picture. If desired, you can build your fire right under it, suspending your pots by means of a lug pole across the lower levels of the kitchen as shown.

The Standard Crane

The standard crane is a favorite for suspending several kettles simultaneously. It consists of a lug pole supported by two forked sticks about three to four feet above the fire. Hang pot hooks of various lengths on the lug pole to provide for varying the distance of your kettles from

A Kitchen Cabinet.

A Chippewa Kitchen.

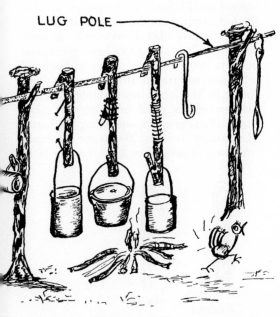

LUG POLE

The Standard Crane.

the fire. After the meal is over, remove the lug pole and build up the fire for the evening program.

The Victor Auer Crane (page 344)

The Victor Auer crane serves the same general purposes as the standard crane, but its peculiar method of construction enables the cook to swing the arm and kettles to one side when the food is ready to serve. The arm of the crane is branched, and one branch ends in a long strip of bark which you bring around the upright and lash back to the main stick; the other arm is a forked stick with its crotch resting against the upright. The crane will turn about on the upright so that you can place it in any position you want.

Pot Hooks

Keep several pot hooks of varying lengths available to permit choosing one

The Victor Auer Crane.

Gib Used as a Pot Lifter.

to suspend your food at just the right height above the fire.

The *gib* is made by splicing two sticks together with their forks facing each other, so that one can be used to hold the handle of the kettle, and the other to anchor the *gib* across the lug pole. Fasten the two sticks together with nails, lashing or a combination of the two. A *pot hook* has a notch cut in it which slants downward and is deep enough to hold the handle of the kettle securely. *Wire pot hooks* must be made of rather heavy material which will not straighten out when supporting a weight. A *gallows crook* is made by leaving a long strip of tough bark to bring up and around and lash down to form a handle. It is the least convenient of the lot, for you cannot remove it from the fire without lifting the end of the lug pole to slip it off. The *hake*

uses a large nail for a kettle support. Any of these pot hooks can be used to lift hot kettles from the fire.

CLAY OVENS

The various sorts of clay ovens are interesting to construct and, if properly made, give excellent results when roasting meats and vegetables, or baking pies, cakes and cookies. They must be made of clay of a good cohesive quality which will bake hard if they are to be durable and satisfactory. No one except an earthworm would want little pieces of clay oven dropping into his food as it cooks.

Satisfactory clay is available in most regions. Consult published geological surveys or persons in the neighborhood who are interested in geology to help locate it. If such is unavailable, seek the clay in cellars, road cuttings, and other places of excavation, and along the banks of running streams. Test it for cohesiveness and workability by allowing it to

Pot Hooks.

GIB   POT HOOK   WIRE POT HOOK   GALLOWS CROOK   HAKE

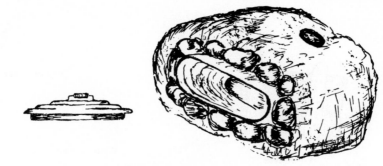

Clay Wash Boiler Oven.

NO. 10   TIN CAN CHIMNEYS

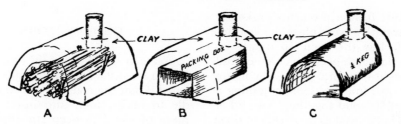

Other Varieties of Clay Ovens.

dry out for a little, then knead it thoroughly and curl it around your finger. If you can curl and uncurl it without breaking or cracking it, it will probably be satisfactory.

Dig enough clay to make your oven, using care not to mix any dirt with it. Allow it to dry for a while and then work and knead it until it is quite pliable. If it does not seem to stick together well, weave a little hay or grass into it to give added body.

To make a clay oven from an old wash boiler such as you can pick up in a junk heap, cut a hole in the top for a chimney, and build up a platform of clay or rocks for it to rest on. Lay a layer of rocks over the sides, ends and back of the boiler and cover it with clay to the depth of about a foot, making sure to leave the chimney hole uncovered. Bake the clay in the sun for a couple of days, and then build a slow-burning fire of partly green wood inside it and keep it going for two or three hours to bake it hard and firm; the

fire must not be too hot or it will cause cracks to appear.

There are other forms over which to build a clay oven. One form is of small sticks bound into a round bundle of the desired size and shape, another uses a wooden packing box, and a third uses a half-keg. Make the chimney hole by inserting a tin can with both ends removed or by inserting a small wooden box or a bundle of sticks of the appropriate size. Cover the forms with clay and bake as previously described, with the fire inside burning out the wooden form as it hardens the clay. If cracks appear, fill them with new clay and let it harden the next time you use the oven. Make the oven just large enough to accommodate the baking for the group it is to feed.

When ready to bake, build a hot fire in the oven, and keep it going until your oven is as hot as desired. If the fire does not burn well, you can improve the ventilation by raising the wood on rocks or green stick firedogs. When the proper

Oven Door.

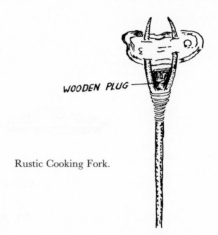

WOODEN PLUG

Rustic Cooking Fork.

temperature has been reached, rake out the fire from the oven, place the food inside, and close the oven up tightly by placing a flat stone over the chimney and fitting a tight door into place. The figure shows how to make a door by joining a few pieces of wood together. The lid of the wash boiler makes an excellent door for a wash boiler oven and a large flat stone also works well.

COOKING FORK

You can make a handy cooking fork from a sweet-tasting stick of fire-resistant wood. Point the end, split down the middle to make tines, and insert a small piece of wood to keep the tines apart. Lash the fork for a short distance below the split to keep it from splitting too far.

(Abbott and Hammond.)

ADDITIONAL READINGS

Burke, Edmund H.: *Camping Handbook.*
Des Grey, Arthur H.: *Camping.*
Jaeger, Ellsworth: *Wildwood Wisdom.*
Jaeger, Ellsworth: *Woodsmoke.*
Lindholm, Major Mauno A.: *Camping and Outdoor Fun.*
Mason, Bernard S.: *Junior Book of Woodcraft.*
Rutstrum, Calvin: *The New Way of the Wilderness.*

Swanson, William E.: *Camping for All It's Worth.*
West, James E., and Hillcourt, William: *Scout Field Book.*

Magazine Articles

Bassett, Jeanne, Young, Monroe, and Joy, Barbara Ellen: *Device For Barbecuing.* C.M., April, 1942. (or Camp Publications, 2 pp., 15¢.)
Joy, Barbara Ellen: *Care of Food and Equipment on Trips.* C.M., June, 1956.

31

Foods and Outdoor Cooking

CAMPER'S STEW

'Case cookin' lak religion is—
Some's 'lected, an' some aint,
An' rules don't no mo' mak a cook
Den sermon's mek a saint.

HOWARD WEEDEN

PLANNING AND PACKING FOR TRIPS

Planning the Menu

No MATTER how much other fun there is in camp, nothing can quite take the place of good, nourishing food, tastily prepared and attractively served. With the variety of mixes and dehydrated foods now on the market, there is no excuse even on long trips for serving dull, monotonous meals. All that is required is a little imagination, a pinch of good common sense, some forethought and planning, and a good outdoor recipe book. Then even the inexperienced can turn out a tasty meal.

Young beginners should start out by planning simple *nosebag* or *poke* lunches such as sandwiches, fruit and a cold drink to be packed at main camp and taken out and eaten, burning the paper bags at the campsite. The next step might be cooking a one-pot meal for a supper cook-out, then an aluminum-foil menu with meat and vegetables all cooked together in a package, followed by cooking in hot coals, and so on through the whole category of wonderful cooking methods available in primitive surroundings. It is usually best to add only one new item or method each time you cook so that the whole meal won't be ruined if the new technique doesn't turn out the way it was supposed to. Then, when you're ready for trips of several days duration, preparing and serving complete meals will be simply following a more or less familiar routine in a new setting. Some more elaborate dishes and methods of cooking are very challenging and interesting when you have an unlimited amount of time on your hands but on a trip it is usually better to stay away from "trick" cookery and concentrate on simple yet substantial meals which won't detain you for long at the campsite so that you can eat and be on your way again without undue delay. By all means, let the campers help cook; half the enjoyment of any feat is in the satisfaction of knowing *you* helped bring it about.

Whatever type of outdoor meal you plan, you ought definitely to steer clear of the inevitable and indigestible picnic menu of wieners, buns, pickles and marshmallows which apparently constitutes the average American's idea of the only possible outdoor menu. It is important from the psychological as well as the health standpoint that meals in the out-of-doors be just as nutritious, well-cooked and attractively served as those indoors. The fact that vigorous exercise and breathing large quantities of fresh air produce ravenous appetites is not an adequate excuse for serving half-raw, half-burned conglomerations.

Let campers help plan their own menus, learning the elements of good nutrition as they do. This automatically leads them to greater appreciation of the importance of a well-balanced diet and often results in their eating and eventually learning to like foods previously spurned. If possible, make an appointment with the dietitian ahead of time to help on this.

If you want youngsters to learn something of budgeting as well, give them a definite allowance for each meal, day or trip and a standard price list as furnished by the dietitian. Many books and pamphlets containing camp recipes are available, and you can use regular cook books by adapting cooking methods to out-of-door facilities. The numerous barbecue cookbooks now available, though primarily intended for cooking with charcoal, are easily adapted to wood cookery. Working closely with one or more counselors, campers plan menus and figure out proportions of the food-stuffs needed. Take into consideration (1) time needed for cooking, (2) utensils needed (each item adds bulk and weight to the pack), (3) bulk, and (4) keeping qualities of the food. These criteria explain why *one-pot meals* for which the various ingredients for the whole meal are cooked together in a single pot are so well adapted to trip menus. Intriguing names such as "blushing bunny" or "egg-in-a-nest" add glamour to a prosaic dish.

When campers have computed menus and proportions, make triplicate copies, one to be retained by the counselor in charge, the others to be turned over to the camp director and dietitian. Camps often supply forms for doing this which have blanks for entering the names of the personnel going, the date and time of leaving, destination, number of days and meals of the trip, menu and proportions of foodstuffs, and cooking vessels and other supplies needed. When the list has been approved, the representatives of the group who are to serve as *marketers* meet with the dietitian or trips counselor to measure out and pack the food and equipment. Many camps have a custom of letting all living units cook out at least one day a week so that the kitchen help can enjoy time off.

If many campers are to participate, it is best to divide them into small groups of six to eight with one or two counselors, and let each group plan its own menu and cook it individually.

Packing Food

Any kind of trip, but particularly one in which the group travels on foot, presents a challenge to plan menus requiring food which is not too bulky and cumbersome to carry.

Obviously, it is wise not to take most

things in their original packages, which are usually crushable and too flimsy to stand the wear and tear of a journey. Instead, measure out just enough for the trip and place it in sturdy containers kept on hand for the purpose. Mark the contents of all packages clearly on both sides and tops so that you can quickly locate what you want en route. Print labels for frequently used staples with indelible ink on metal-rimmed tags, or on gummed paper labels or adhesive tape protected and held secure with Scotch tape.

Avoid taking things which may spoil or become soft and those that may be mashed or broken by rough handling.

DRY MATERIALS.   Dry materials may be packed in a plastic bag which is sealed with a warm iron or in a plastic bag inside a cloth bag; this serves the double purpose of protecting the contents from moisture and keeping out insects. Another method is to pack them in fabric bags which you can purchase from an outing supply store. It is easy and cheap to make them of sailcloth, waterproofed with paraffin, double stitched at all seams, and with a wide hem and draw string at the top long enough to tie with a half hitch for use as a handle. Make them short and broad with round bottoms (see page 307) so they'll stand upright with minimum danger of tipping over. Label the contents with wax crayon which will wash out or with India or indelible ink for permanence.

LIQUIDS.   Do not take liquids in glass bottles which are heavy and may break. Instead, place them in plastic bottles or in light aluminum cans with screw-on or press-in tops. You can purchase such containers from outfitting companies but it is easy to acquire enough by saving them from various commercial products.

Carry water in canteens, thermos bottles, jugs, or in one- or two-gallon kerosene or gasoline cans with pour spouts

kept for the purpose. Desert bags keep the contents cool by evaporation and five-gallon milk cans provide quantities for large groups.

Carry semiliquid materials, such as jam and peanut butter, in heavy, round cardboard cartons with tight-fitting lids such as ice-cream cartons or oatmeal boxes lined with waxed paper.

OTHER PACKING NOTES.   Carry eggs in heavy, cardboard egg panniers, wash and bury them in such dry materials as flour or cornmeal or wrap them well and carry them in tin cans.

Flavorings add much to the taste of food and it is worth-while to take small quantities of several varieties. Pack them tightly in small metal, glass or plastic containers so they won't rattle. Salt draws moisture and will eventually rust out a tin container. Make a rust-proof salt and pepper shaker by fitting corks into the ends of a section of bamboo with a division in the middle or carry them in plastic containers.

Use adhesive tape to secure doubtful corks or lids.

For a short, one-meal trip, you may simply carry your food in a cooking kettle, a number 10 tin can stove or a water bucket. For longer trips it is best to pack all in waterproof knapsacks or duffel bags, each bearing a metal-rimmed tag listing its contents. Some like to collect all the crushables and breakables in one bag for special handling. Each time you cook, place the supplies for your next meal on top so that you need not unpack everything to get what you want.

Use bread wrappers or waxed paper freely in packing, and pad breakables liberally with newspapers or other padding.

LIGHTENING THE LOAD.   When going on a long trip, it may be possible to send a part of your food supplies and other equipment ahead by camp truck, parcel

CORK [] SALT = PEPPER [] CORK   Bamboo Salt and Pepper Shaker.

post or express or you may plan a rendezvous with the camp truck for replenishment. Another possibility is to lay in fresh supplies from grocery stores and farm houses along the way.

Many varieties of dehydrated foods are now available and most of them are very good substitutes for the fresh product. They are usually somewhat more expensive but make a great saving in space and weight since 95 per cent of the water content of the foods has been removed. For instance 100 pounds of regular potatoes weigh only seventeen pounds in powdered form thus saving the excess baggage of twenty pounds of peelings and sixty-three pounds of water.

WHAT TO TAKE

Vegetables and Soups

Such fresh vegetables as carrots, cabbage, beets and onions keep pretty well on a trip, even as long as several weeks, if you sprinkle a bit of water on them, seal them in waxed paper and then wrap a layer of other paper tightly about them. Clean them and remove tops and roots before starting.

Dried beans and peas are light and keep well, but must be soaked overnight and so require too long a cooking time to be practical on most trips. Rice is a light and versatile food, for you can use it as breakfast food, dessert, or the main dish of any meal. Coarse-grained cereals are "musts" in every day's menu.

Canned vegetables and soups are bulky and heavy because of the large amounts of water canned with them so it is well worth-while to substitute the light compact dry preparations even though they may cost somewhat more. Add extra noodles or precooked rice to give them more staying power. The following dehydrated vegetables are now available from outfitters or your grocer's shelves: beets, celery, tomatoes, okra, beans, sweet corn, cabbage, onions, carrots, spinach,

turnip and mustard greens, sweet and Irish potatoes, and mixed vegetables. Those dehydrated by modern methods require only about thirty minutes of soaking.

Eggs and Dairy Products

Fresh eggs stay usable for some time but powdered forms are lighter and prove quite suitable for use in cakes and other forms of cooking and some even find them palatable when scrambled with bacon or ham. A tablespoonful of powdered egg added to two tablespoonfuls of water gives the equivalent of one fresh egg. They are highly perishable after being mixed with water and should be cooked immediately and eaten while still warm.

Butter packed in air-tight cans and cooled under primitive refrigeration methods, keeps quite well but oleomargarine keeps even better. Canned butter in ½ or 1 pound cans will last indefinitely without refrigeration. Cheese, when wrapped in a damp cloth and placed in a plastic bag, will then keep well for a long time.

Fresh milk will not keep long, and it is not safe to buy from untested herds along the way. You can use evaporated or condensed milk for all cooking purposes, and most people find it palatable to drink.

Powdered Milk

Powdered milk has the water removed and one cup of it added to 3½ cups of water produces the equivalent of a quart of fresh milk. On long trips, powdered skim milk is better than whole milk for it does not have as much tendency to get rancid and is quite pleasing to drink when one once gets accustomed to it. Note that powdered skim milk supplies fewer calories since the fat has been removed. *Pream* is a good dehydrated substitute for cream.

Breadstuffs

Bread, particularly rye, remains fresh for some time if it is double-wrapped in waxed paper, but it is hardly worth the bulk and weight on long trips, for you can easily bake cakes, fresh biscuits, muffins, flapjacks, cinnamon rolls, and shortcake in a reflector oven along the way. You can make them from prepared mixes, but it is cheaper and just as satisfactory to mix your own dry ingredients before you leave camp. Whole-wheat or graham flours are particularly healthful. Date, nut, and brown breads are available in canned form which keep indefinitely but they are heavy to carry.

Fruits and Desserts

Canned fruits contain large quantities of water and so weigh too much and take too much space to be practical for long trips. Dried apples, prunes, peaches, raisins, pears, black figs, dates, apricots and fruit mixtures weigh little and may be mixed into bread stuffs, put on cereals, or simply eaten as fruit. To prepare them, cover with cold water, bring to a boil, then simmer until tender, adding more water and sugar if needed.

Puddings made from powders add variety to the diet. Tinned nuts are an exceptionally rich source of energy and can be munched along the way or used with desserts or in cooking.

Supply quick-energy carbohydrates in ample quantity in candy bars or hard candy, jams, jellies, marmalades and occasional sweet desserts. Saccharine has less bulk than sugar for sweetening purposes but does not supply any calories for energy needs.

Wild strawberries, blackberries, dewberries, blueberries and huckleberries ripen during camp season and add a new taste to muffins, flapjacks, shortcake or pies. Campers also enjoy picking them.

Meats

Do not take fresh meats for more than the first meal out unless you have ice; cool it on the way out with plastic bags of water, sealed with a warm iron and frozen solid in the refrigerator. Bacon keeps a little better, particularly if bought in the chunk and sliced off as used. Several foreign types of balogna and sausage are more or less dry and keep almost indefinitely; dehydrated stews, chili with beans, beef minestrone, hash, and ground beef are now available. Of course there are many canned meats available if you don't object to their extra bulk and weight. You may get fresh fish, clams, crabs, frog legs, turtles for soup, and the like, along the way according to the region you are in.

Bacon fryings or fats from cooking other meats furnish the fat you need for cooking, but you may prefer vegetable fats since they do not soak into your food as much.

Other Beverages

You can make good trip-beverages from malted-milk tablets or powders, hot-chocolate powders, and canned, condensed juices such as tomato, lemon, lime, orange, grape, etc. These are also available in even more compact dehydrated powder form. You can dehydrate your own juice by extracting fresh juice, mixing it with sugar, and then letting it dry.

Instant coffee and tea bags are lightweight and suitable for older campers and counselors.

OUT-OF-DOOR COOKING

Only a few of the more woodsy recipes are included here. For further details about outdoor cooking and additional recipes, consult the references at the end of the chapter.

Some General Notes About Cooking

For general camp cooking, regular kettles with wire handles which can be hung over lug poles or on pot hooks are recommended.

Always coat the outside surfaces of kettles with a thick paste of detergent mixed with water or rub a moistened bar of laundry soap over them until they are completely covered before using them over an outdoor fire. The soap rinses off easily when the utensil is washed, taking the smoke and soot with it.

When preparing vegetables, do not leave them standing in water longer than necessary, for it removes some of their precious vitamins. Add them to rapidly boiling salted water and cook quickly, using as little water as possible. Avoid overcooking, keeping them on just long enough to tenderize them without destroying their crispness. Add them to water below the boiling point only if you want to extract their flavor as in making soups or stews.

You can skin tomatoes quickly by scalding them with boiling water or holding them over the flames until their skins crack. However, it is more healthful to wash the skin well and eat it too.

Use a glass bottle or tin can when you need a rolling pin.

Grease the vessel in which you melt chocolate or measure molasses to keep them from adhering to the sides.

Test eggs for freshness by dropping them into water. If they sink quickly, they are fresh; if they sink slowly, proceed with caution, for they are doubtful; if they float, don't use them at all, for they are ancient.

Put a container of water over the fire when you first light it and you'll have hot water all ready for your main cooking by the time the fire burns down to coals.

When a recipe calls for sour milk, you can produce it immediately by adding two tablespoonfuls of lemon juice or a few drops of vinegar for each cup of sweet milk.

You can improvise double boilers for cooking rice and other cereals by placing the food vessel, supported on three or four small stones, inside a larger vessel partly filled with water.

Line your frying pan with aluminum foil before cooking meat or other hard to remove food; then burn off the aluminum foil in the campfire and dispose of it and you'll have no difficult pans to scrub.

A little vinegar and water boiled inside the utensils in which fish has been cooked removes the fishy odor.

When cooking meat, use a low or moderate heat. This requires more time, but the meat will not shrink so much and will be much more palatable and tender. When you want to draw the juices and flavor out of meat, as in making soup or stew, start it in cold water and cook it with low heat. If you want to seal the juices and flavor in, drop it into boiling water or sear it on all sides over a hot fire, then cook it over low or moderate heat. Do not season meat until it is nearly done, for seasonings draw out juices. Neither overcook nor undercook fresh meat, but cook pork especially thoroughly because of the danger of trichina.

Frying is frequently overused in camp cookery and, when incorrectly done, results in an unappetizing and indigestible dish. The chief drawback comes from letting fried foods absorb too much fat as they cook. To avoid this, have the food as dry as possible and heat the grease to just under the smoking stage before you put the meat in. The hot grease sears the food, sealing the juices in and the grease out. Drain fried foods on a paper napkin to remove excess grease. When frying in a skillet over an open fire, avoid high flames lest they set fire to the grease in the pan.

Pan broiling is a healthful and highly recommended form of frying, pouring off the excess grease as it forms and leaving barely enough in the pan to keep the food from sticking. Turn the meat several times.

Broiling is cooking by direct exposure to the heat from glowing coals. Build a fire of hardwood well in advance of cooking time so that it will burn down to a good bed of coals. Place the meat over the flame to sear it quickly on both sides and then place it over the coals; watch it carefully. Beware of dripping fat for it ignites into a hot flame which may burn the meat. Avoid using resinous or strong-tasting woods lest they impart a disagreeable flavor to the food.

Wilderness cookery is cooking without utensils and includes cooking in ashes or coals, in an imu or beanhole, or on a stick or spit. It is fun to plan a whole meal using only wilderness cookery, and it is surprising what a variety of tantalizing menus you can serve.

COMMON MEASURES

3 teaspoons (tsp.) = 1 tablespoon (T)
16 T = 1 cup (C)
1 C = ½ pint (pt.)
2 pts. = 1 quart (qt.)
4 qts. = 1 gallon (gal.)

#½ can = 1 cup
#1 can = 1½ cups
#2 can = 2½ cups
#2½ can = 3½ cups
#3 can = 4 cups
#5 can = 5 cups
#10 can = 1 gal. (12 cups)

2 T butter = 1 oz.
2 C butter or lard = 1 lb.
4 T flour = 1 oz.
4 C flour = 1 lb.
2 C granulated sugar = 1 lb.
3–3½ C brown sugar = 1 lb.
3–3½ C powdered sugar = 1 lb.
4 C cocoa = 1 lb.
3½–4 C cornmeal = 1 lb.
2 C rice = 1 lb.
2–2½ C dry navy beans = 1 lb.

OUTDOOR RECIPES

ONE POT MEALS

These are stews or mixtures which, as the name suggests, are cooked in one kettle and furnish a whole meal in themselves. They may be served hot on rice, toast or crackers. Cook over flames or coals.

Slumgullion (Serves 5)

6–10 slices of bacon
2 onions, diced
1 #2 can tomatoes
¼–½ lb. cheese, diced
2 C meat, already cooked
½ tsp. salt

Cut the bacon into small pieces and fry the onion with it; drain off part of the fat, and add the tomatoes, meat, and salt. Cook for about 20 minutes; then add the cheese and continue cooking until it is melted.

Irish Stew (Serves 5)

5 onions, sliced
1 lb. meat cut in 1 inch cubes
5 potatoes
Other vegetables such as carrots, etc. as desired
Salt and pepper

Melt a little fat in a kettle and fry the onions and meat until brown. Cover them with cold water and bring to a boil. Cook slowly for 1½ hours, add the potatoes, and continue to cook slowly until they are tender. Season to taste.

Ring Tum Diddy (Serves 5)

6 slices bacon, diced
2 onions, sliced
¼ lb. cheese, diced
1 #2 can tomatoes
1 #2 can corn
Salt and pepper

Fry the bacon and onions until brown, and pour off part of the fat. Add them to the tomatoes and corn and bring to a boil. Add the cheese and cook slowly until it is melted. Season to taste.

Komac Stew (Serves 8)

1 small can tomatoes or 4 fresh tomatoes (diced)
1 green pepper
2 onions, diced
3 eggs
4 T butter
Salt and pepper

Melt the butter and fry the onions until brown. Wash and dice the pepper and add to the tomatoes and onions and cook slowly for ½ hour, stirring frequently. Season to taste and add the eggs one at a time, stirring meanwhile. Avoid cooking over a fire which is too hot, for it will make the mixture curdle and look unappetizing even though not impairing the taste or quality.

Stick Cookery

For stick cookery, peel and sharpen a green stick about two feet long. Resinous woods and willow impart an unpleasant taste, but sugar maple, sassafras, black birch, hickory or various other woods are satisfactory; if in doubt about the suitability of the wood, peel the end and bite it. Cook over coals, not flames. You can support the stick above the fire laying it

Bread Twister or Doughboy.

across a rock or forked stick and weighting the handle end down with a rock or forked stick.

1. *Bread Twister or Doughboy.* Mix regular biscuit dough, using just enough water to make it sticky, roll it out flat about ¼ to ½ inch thick and cut into long strips about 2 inches wide. Remove the bark from the end of a stick about twice the size of your thumb, heat the end, flour it and wind a strip of dough spirally around it, leaving a slight gap between the spirals. Bake for 10 to 15 minutes over coals, turning it so that all sides bake evenly. It will come off the stick in the form of a cylinder closed at one end. When filled with jam, jelly or cheese, it is known as *a cave woman cream puff.*

2. *Pig in a Blanket.* Cook a wiener or long sausage on a stick, then cover it with biscuit dough and bake.

3. *Bacon Twister.* Cook a piece of bacon thoroughly, cover it with dough and bake like a pig in a blanket. You can use sausage instead of the bacon.

Pioneer Drumsticks (Serves 5)

1¼ lbs. beef, chopped fine
¾ C cornflakes, crumbled fine
1 egg
Onion (if desired)
Salt and pepper

Thoroughly mix the ingredients and wrap a thin portion tightly around the peeled end of the stick and squeeze firmly into place. Toast it slowly over coals, turning frequently, and serve in a roll. Some prefer to put the cornflakes on after the meat has been placed on the stick, so that they form a sort of crust over the outside.

5. *Angel on Horseback.* For each serving, thread one slice of bacon on the sharpened end of a stick, and partially cook. Then wrap the bacon tightly around a 1-inch square of cheese, and hold over the fire until the bacon is done and the cheese melted. Serve with lettuce in a bun.

Angel on Horseback.

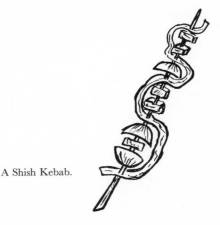

A Shish Kebab.

6. *Shish Kebabs.* Lace a slice of bacon in and out among alternate one-inch squares of steak, chops, slices of onion, oysters, small tomatoes, green peppers, and so forth, as desired, impaled on a stick. The bacon will serve to baste them. Broil over gradual heat from coals. The shish kebab got its name from two Turkish words, "shish" meaning skewer, and "kebab" meaning "broiled meat."

7. *Cooking on a Forked Stick.* A forked stick or a wire fork (I, page 252) may be used for cooking steaks, oysters, wieners, sausages, bacon, toast, green corn, apples, parsnips, marshmallows, chops, or toasting sandwiches. When cooking meats, toast, and like foods, run the tines into the food lengthwise or lace them through the food several times to hold the food securely so it can be turned to cook evenly on all sides.

8. *Date Dreams.* Make these by alternating pitted dates with halved marshmallows on a stick and toasting slowly over the fire.

A Forked Stick Fork.

Cooking in Ashes or Coals

The secret of cooking in ashes or coals is to build a hardwood fire early and let it burn to coals. If flames are needed for some item of the menu, draw the coals over to one side and replenish them as needed from the fire on the other side. Parsnips, fish (wrapped in clay), oysters (in the shell) and squash may be cooked in this way.

1. **Potatoes.** Scrub Irish potatoes, sweet potatoes, or yams of medium size and without blemishes well, and place them on hot coals in a single layer with none touching another; cover to a depth of about one inch with coals, frequently replenishing them. They are done when a sharp stick will penetrate them easily (45 to 60 minutes, depending on their size). Jab a small hole in each end to let the steam escape. Some like to coat potatoes with skins on with a thick layer of wet mud or clay before roasting; both skins and mud will come off cleanly when they are done. Cook fish in the same way.

2. **Onions.** Cook them as you cook potatoes.

3. **Eggs.** Prick a small hole through the egg shell (but not the membrane) on the large end of the egg and another through membrane and all at the small end (these holes are to let the steam escape and so keep the egg from bursting). Balance the egg carefully on its large end close to the fire where it will get moderate heat; avoid too much heat lest the egg explode. The eggs should be ready to eat in five to twelve minutes, depending on whether you want them hard or soft. Some prefer to wrap the egg in wet leaves, wet mud or clay before baking.

4. **Little Pig Potatoes.** Slice the end off a potato and hollow out enough of the center to permit the insertion of a small, thin sausage (cheese, bacon or raw egg may be used instead). Replace the end of the potato and fasten it with slivers of wood and bake it as previously described.

5. **Roasting Ears.** Turn back the husks from young, tender roasting ears and clean the corn and remove the silks. Sprinkle lightly with salt, replace the husks, soak the whole thing in water a few moments, and bake in the same way as you bake potatoes.

6. **Roasted Apples.** Core the apple and fill the cavity with raisins, brown sugar, nuts, and the like. Bake them as you bake a potato.

7. **Ash Bread.** Build a hardwood fire, preferably on top of a large rock, at least a half hour before baking. Rake the embers aside and place the loaf of bread, well floured and rolled out to a thickness of ½ to ¾ inches, on the hot surface. Cover it with ashes and a layer of coals, replenishing them as they cool. It is ready to eat when a sliver of wood inserted in it comes out without dough's adhering to it. Unlikely as it seems, the loaf will emerge quite clean and any adhering ashes can be quickly brushed away.

You may use any bread dough, but baking powder biscuit dough is preferred because of the short baking time necessary. If desired, raisins, nuts, berries or fruit may be mixed with the dough.

Baking Potatoes in a Number 10 Tin Can

Scrub the potatoes well and wrap each in a layer of waxed paper, covered by damp newspaper. Pack them in wet dirt or sand inside a number 10 tin can so that none touches another or the sides of the can. Place the can among hot coals and leave about forty-five minutes, adding additional glowing coals as needed. Keep the dirt in the can moist by adding more water if necessary.

Baking in a Reflector Oven

Reflector ovens are very useful cooking utensils and should be a part of every outdoor cooking kit. Make them from tin cans (L and M, page 252) or purchase them from outfitting companies. They fit into a canvas carrying case and are compact and easy to carry if made with hinges which allow them to fold flat. A

WIND

Baking in a Reflector Ovens.

reflector oven made from aluminum foil also works well.

Set the reflector oven about 8 inches to 12 inches away from the fire and on the windward side so that the ashes and flames will be blown away from the contents; its efficiency is greatly increased by placing a reflector wall of rock or wood on the leeward side of the fire. Make the fire as high and wide as the oven and add fuel to keep the flames about even with the oven shelf. When the shelf is hot enough to sizzle when you sprinkle water on it, place the food directly on it or in a baking pan set on the shelf. The sloping top and bottom catch and reflect the heat onto the food from both above and below, insuring thorough cooking and even browning, but the metal must be kept bright and shiny to do its job well. Handles on the oven permit you to adjust it easily just far enough from the fire to insure the right amount of heat. Prop it up so that the shelf is level.

1. *General Baking.* Rolls, biscuits, pies, cakes, cookies, meat and small birds such as chickens can be baked to a turn in a reflector oven.

2. *Sweet Potato Soufflé* may be baked in hollowed-out orange peels (be sure to remove all the bitter lining) or in scooped-out apple peels.

3. *Eggs Baked in Orange Shells.* Prepare the orange peel as above and break an egg into it; season, and set in the reflector oven to bake.

4. *Potatoes.* Scrub Irish potatoes, sweet potatoes or yams. Grease their jackets with butter or bacon fat to keep them tender. Bake them in a reflector oven for 45 minutes and test them to see when they are done.

5. *Some Mores.* Make a sandwich of a marshmallow and a piece of a chocolate candy bar between two graham crackers. Press gently together and place in a reflector oven to bake.

6. *Banana Boats.* Peel back a narrow strip of peeling from the inside curve of a banana, scoop out part of the inside and fill with marshmallow, chocolate, nuts or raisins. Replace the strip of peeling and bake in a reflector oven.

Baking in a Skillet

Support the skillet on rocks or green sticks over coals, or prop it up in front of a fire.

Cooking on a Skillet.

1. **Bannock** is a traditional woodsman's bread and is made by baking biscuit dough in a floured skillet on the windward side of the fire; its efficiency is likewise increased by a reflector wall on the leeward side of the fire. Turn the loaf over when done on one side, and both sides will be ready in about fifteen minutes. Coals shoveled out and put behind the pan hasten the baking of the under side.

2. **Pancakes (Flapjacks).** Grease skillet lightly and brace as described. Use only moderate heat from a small fire or from coals, and heat the skillet just under the smoking point before dropping the batter from a spoon. Turn the flapjacks as soon as bubbles appear on top. Avoid too much heat for they are easily burned. Add blueberries or other ingredients for variety.

3. **Darn Goods.** Fill a frying pan half full of fat and heat just short of the smoking stage (it is hot enough when a piece of bread dropped into it browns in forty-five seconds). Pat biscuit dough with no shortening into little biscuits about ¼ inch thick, and cut a few slashes in each to allow the grease to come up through. Place them in hot fat, turning them when the bottoms are brown; cook for a total of approximately ten minutes. Drop in a few at a time in order not to cool the grease so that the biscuit dough will absorb it. Drain off the excess grease by laying the darn goods on paper towels or a soft cloth.

4. **French Fries.** Dry potato strips by wrapping them in cloth or absorbent paper. Test the temperature of the fat as described for darn goods and drop the potatoes in gradually so as not to cool the fat. When done, drain them on absorbent paper or soft cloth.

Hush Puppies (Serves 4)

1 T flour
1 C cornmeal
1 egg, well beaten
1 tsp. baking powder
½ C milk
¼ onion, diced fine

Sift the cornmeal, flour, baking powder and salt together and add the onion. Stir the milk and egg with them into a batter stiff enough to form little balls. Drop them from a spoon into hot grease and cook like darn goods.

A Dutch Oven.

Cooking in a Dutch Oven

The Dutch oven has been a favorite for everything from roasting to baking since the days of the early pioneers. It is made of heavy cast iron with a tight-fitting lid of the same material to keep all the heat and steam in and allow none of the succulent flavors to escape. Its weight, of course, rules it out for light-trip camping.

When intended for outdoor use, a Dutch oven has a flat cover with a turned-up flange around the edge so that hot coals can be placed on it. Its three sturdy legs raise it far enough off the ground to provide room for a few hot coals under it. However, they must not actually touch it or the food inside will burn.

A Home-made Dutch Oven.

You can improvise a Dutch oven by inverting a *heavy* skillet tightly over a *heavy* kettle. Support this legless oven on green sticks or rocks to provide a little space for coals underneath.

1. **Pot Roast.** Put bits of fat meat or other fat in the bottom of the kettle. Sear all sides of the roast over an open fire, and put it in the kettle, with such vegetables as onions, parsnips, carrots, turnips, Irish or sweet potatoes added with the meat or about a half hour before it is ready to serve. This provides a delicious meal in itself, and you can make gravy from the stock left in the bottom if desired. A five-pound piece of meat requires about three hours to cook. This is a good way to cook tough meat, for it combines frying, baking and steaming, and the long exposure to even, moderate temperature tenderizes almost any cut. If the meat is quite lean, rub it with fat or lay a few strips of bacon across it to baste it as it cooks.

2. **Baking.** A Dutch oven is excellent for baking corn bread, biscuits, rolls, pies, cookies, potatoes in their skins, chicken; in fact, almost anything to be baked will come out cooked to a turn.

The Imu or Pit Barbecue

This is another splendid method of cooking by steam, which supplies a moderate even heat. It is really a variety of fireless cookery, and justifies the long cooking time required by the excellent results obtained. About three hours are necessary to cook a chicken, about a half-day for a ten-pound roast, and as much as fifteen or sixteen hours for anything as big as a whole sheep.

To begin the *imu*, dig a hole about two to three times as large as the food to be cooked and line the sides and bottom with nonpopping rocks; build a good hardwood fire in it and keep it going for an hour or two until the rocks are sizzling hot and there is a good bed of coals. Get all the food ready and place it in the pit just as rapidly as possible so that no more

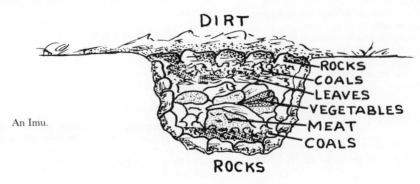

An Imu.

heat than necessary will escape. Remove part of the coals and hot rocks, place the food in the pit, and pack the hot rocks and coals back in around and over it. Then shovel on about 6 inches of dirt to make a steamproof covering (if you see smoke or steam escaping, shovel more dirt over the leak). You can now forget the food until you dig it up ready to eat three to twenty hours later. You can cook green corn, parsnips, carrots, onions, ham, clams, potatoes with meat, and so forth, in this way.

A preheated Dutch oven makes the best container for the food, but if none is available you may wrap the meat and vegetables in damp butcher paper, damp paper towels, damp grass or seaweed, or damp nontasting leaves such as lettuce, cabbage, sassafras or sycamore. Bitter resinous leaves and burlap bags may be used if kept several layers away from the food.

Bean Hole Beans

¾ lb. (2C) dry navy beans
½ lb. salt pork or bacon, diced
1½ tsp. salt
⅛ C sugar
⅛ C molasses
2 onions, chopped fine

These are excellent when cooked in a Dutch oven inside an imu or a bean hole made like an imu. Wash the beans and soak them overnight until their skins start to crack. Then mix all the ingredients and place them in a bean hole and let cook for six to eight hours. This cooking time can be shortened several hours by first cooking the beans in water over an open fire until they are soft, then pouring off the water and mixing in the ingredients before placing them in the *imu*.

Cooking on a Stone Griddle

Prop a large, flat, nonpopping rock on green sticks or stones, leaving plenty of room underneath for draft. Build a fire both on and under the stone, which has been well scrubbed, and when it is sizzling hot, clean off the top, grease it well with a swab and fry such food as bacon and eggs or flapjacks on it.

A Stone Griddle.

Barbecuing

There are several ways to barbecue meat; you can hold it directly over coals (never flames) or place it a short distance away at the side of the fire. Barbecuing is a satisfactory method for cooking anything from a small chicken to large cuts of meat or even whole animals.

1. **Barbecuing on a Spit over the Fire.** Dig a pit and build a good hardwood fire in it and let it burn down to coals. Place the meat on the *spit* and fasten it

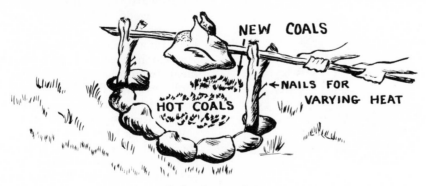

Barbecuing on a Spit.

firmly in place so that it will turn as the stick does and so cook evenly on all sides. The coals will cool off and need to be replaced frequently, so keep a separate fire at one end or side of the pit to provide a constantly fresh supply.

When barbecuing a chicken, select a young, tender bird, commonly known as a springer or broiler. One weighing two pounds serves two people and you can cook several side by side on the same spit. Clean the chicken well and insert the spit firmly from tail to neck. Protect the wings and legs from burning by pinning them close to the body with wooden slivers. Rotate the spit slowly over the coals, and baste the bird every ten minutes with melted butter, bacon fat or other shortening applied with a swab made from cloth tied around the end of a stick.

Make the handle of the spit long so that you can stay well back from the fire and place notches at varying heights for adjusting the spit to the proper distance above the heat. You can use a peeled green stick for a spit, but a metal rod with a nonheating handle does a better job since it conveys the heat into the meat and cooks it from the inside as well as the outside. Cook roasts of beef or pork, ducks, turkeys and small game in this way.

2. **Barbecuing on a Wire Grill.** Fit a wire grill or piece of gravel-screen on a framework of green wood or metal poles over a pit. Build a fire of hardwood and

Wire-Grill Barbecuing.

let it burn to coals; place the food to be cooked (wieners, chickens, spareribs, chops, steaks, and the like) on the grill over at one side of the pit. Two persons, using garden forks or similar tools, can anchor them in the food-laden grill and draw it into position over the coals. Use a long-handled spatula, further lengthened by tying a long stick to the end of it, to turn the meat. Do not prick the meat with a fork for holes will allow juices to escape. Baste the meat with a cloth swab to keep it from drying out.

Barbecuing at the Side of a Fire.

3. **Barbecuing at the Side of the Fire.** For this style of cookery, suspend the meat by a cord or wire from a lug pole five to six feet above the ground and on the leeward side of the fire. Insert a flat piece of wood or flattened number 10 tin can about half way down the string. Even on a seemingly still day, the tin can will catch enough breeze to keep the meat turning automatically so that it cooks evenly. Prepare the chicken as described for cooking over the fire and reverse the lug pole and meat periodically to cook both sides. Set a pan under the meat to catch the drippings, and baste it every ten or fifteen minutes. A reflector wall on the leeward side speeds up the process.

REINFORCE WITH WIRE

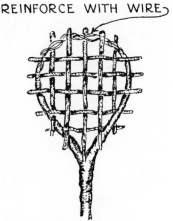

A Tennis-Racket Broiler.

Cooking on a Rustic or Tennis Racket Broiler

Lace a broiler of green sweet-tasting branches securely together, strengthening them with wire if necessary, and cook such foods as wieners, steaks, and some mores, on it. Use green branches so that they won't burn through and let the food drop into the fire.

Aluminum Foil Cooking

Aluminum foil is a very versatile material for you can waterproof matches or food with it, line cooking utensils to save hard scrubbing, make a reflector oven and dishes from it; you can fashion cooking utensils from it and then eat right out of the utensils. The foil is disposable so that you have no dishes to wash or carry. Since foil will not burn, place it in the fire to burn off the food after use, then crumple it into a ball and bury it or take it home with you. If you want to save the foil, you can wash it off and use it again.

An Aluminum Foil Package.

How to Cook Pressure-cooker Style

Heavy-duty foil is best for outdoor cooking for it is about twice as thick as ordinary foil. To prepare a meal in it, tear off a piece large enough to surround the food and leave two to three inches on the three open sides. Lay the food on one half of the piece, bring the other half over and fold the edges up in at least two ½ inch folds and crimp them to make an airtight envelope; the all important thing is to make it absolutely airtight so that no steam can escape, carrying away with it the juices and wonderful flavor. If you have ordinary, rather than heavy-duty foil, use two layers, wrapping them around in opposite directions.

Cook in a good bed of coals from a hardwood fire made well ahead of time. Round out a depression in the coals big enough for the food, place the package in it, and pull the coals back over and around it. Turn the food over half way through the cooking process. When it is done, rake it out carefully, let it sit a minute to cool and then make a slit down the center or open the ends and eat it right from the foil.

When cooking vegetables, wash them just before you wrap them in the foil and the moisture will provide the necessary steam to cook them. When cooking meat which has little fat, put in a slight amount of butter, cooking fat or oil or a few strips of bacon. Add very little, if any, water and salt and pepper to taste.

What to Cook

To cook a hamburger meal, place a patty in the foil along with strips of potato, green pepper, onions, carrots, tomato, etc. Flavor with a pinch of salt and cook fifteen minutes.

Lamb or pork chops, steaks, fish, and chicken can be cooked in this way, surrounding them with such vegetables as sliced carrots, turnips, potatoes, onions, or green beans. Wet a roasting ear thoroughly, leaving it in its husks, wrap a hot

(Courtesy of The Philadelphia Evening Bulletin.)

dog in biscuit dough, core an apple and fill the hole with brown or white sugar, cinnamon and raisins and cook similarly. You can wrap the ingredients for several meals before you start out, labeling them so that you can select the right one and toss it into the coals when ready to eat. Of course you will have to be careful about taking perishable foods without adequate refrigeration. If you want to take extra foil with you, tear off a strip and roll it around a small stick; folding it might cause holes at the creases.

COOKING TIME.   Cooking time will depend on such factors as the size of the package and the heat of the coals; if necessary, peep into the package to see if it is done but be sure to seal it up air-tight again before replacing it in the coals. When cooking several things to-gether, you must, of course, allow enough time for the slowest one to cook. The fol-lowing are suggested cooking times:

Meats

Chicken (cut up)	20–30 minutes
Fish (whole)	15–20 minutes
Fish (fillets)	10–15 minutes
Shish kebab	14 minutes
Beef cubes (1 inch)	20–30 minutes
Frankfurters	10–15 minutes
Pigs-in-blanket	15–17 minutes
Lamb chops	20–30 minutes
Pork chops	30–40 minutes

Vegetables

Corn (silks and husks removed)	6–10 minutes
Potatoes (Irish)	60–70 minutes
Potatoes (sweet)	45–50 minutes
Carrots (sticks)	15–20 minutes
Squash (acorn)	30 minutes

Miscellaneous

Apple (whole	20–30 minutes
Banana (whole)	8–10 minutes
6–10 minutes	
Biscuits (wrap loosely in foil to allow for rising)	6–10 minutes
Stew (1 inch meat chunks, potato cubes, onions, carrots, salt, etc.)	20 minutes

Cooking Utensils

Foil makes a good reflector oven for a trip. Make a framework of lashed sticks and fasten a piece of foil across level for a shelf. Then take another twenty-four inch piece of foil, place the center of it behind the stick at the back and wrap it around other sticks to form the top and bottom of the oven. The oven will be still more efficient if you place other pieces of foil at the ends of it. Lightly grease the top of the shelf and place two inch circles of biscuit dough on it, spacing them some distance apart. Keep the flames from the fire about shelf high and your biscuits should cook thoroughly in about ten minutes. You can use this oven for cookies, rolls, pies or almost anything else you want to bake.

Fashion stew pans and frying pans from a double layer of heavy-duty foil, fastening the top securely around a loop formed by lashing the tips of a forked stick together and shaping the middle portion of the foil into whatever sort of vessel you want. Let the butt end of the forked stick extend backward for a handle. Fry in the frying pan or make soup, cocoa or anything else you want in the stew pan. You can also make the framework from a coat hanger, twisting the top into a long handle with a loop at the end to form the basis for the body of the utensil.

ADDITIONAL READINGS

Foods and Outdoor Cooking

Beard, Jim: *Complete Book of Barbecue and Rotisserie Cooking.* The Bobbs-Merrill Co., Inc., 1954, $2.75.

Beard, Jim: *New Barbecue Cookbook.* Random House, Inc., 1958, 128 pp., $2.95, Maco Magazine Corp., 1958, paper, 75¢.

Better Homes and Gardens Barbecue Book. Meredith Publishing Company, Des Moines, Iowa. 1956, 162 pp., $2.95.

Breland, J. H.: *Chef's Guide to Quantity Cooking.* Harper and Brothers, 1947, 470 pp., $6.50.

Burke, Edmund H.: *Camping Handbook.*

Carhart, Arthur Hawthorne: *The Outdoorsman's Cookbook.* The Macmillan Co., Revised 1955, 211 pp., $2.95.

Cooking. Boy Scouts #3257, 25¢.

Des Grey, Arthur H.: *Camping.*

Hammett, Catherine T., and Musselman, Virginia: *The Camp Program Book.*

Henderson, Luis M.: *The Outdoor Guide.*

Hildebrand, Louise, and Hildebrand, Joel: *Camp Catering, or How To Rustle Grub.* Stephan Daye Press, 1941, $1.75.

Jaeger, Ellsworth: *Wildwood Wisdom.*

Jaeger, Ellsworth: *Woodsmoke.*

Jones, Bob: *The Outdoor Picture Cookbook.* Hawthorn Books, Inc., $2.95.

Joy, Barbara Ellen: *Camp Craft.*

Joy, Barbara Ellen: *Camping.*

Joy, Barbara Ellen: *Menus for Outdoor Breakfasts, Suppers, and Lunches, and Wilderness and Crowd Cookery.* Camp Publications, 6 pp., 35¢.

Joy, Barbara Ellen: *Outdoor Cookery for Crowds.* Camp Publications, 4 pp., 25¢.

Joy, Barbara Ellen: *Progressive Suppers.* Camp Publications, 4 pp., 25¢.

Joy, Barbara Ellen: *Special Foods for Trips.* Camp Publications, 6 pp., 35¢.

Joy, Barbara Ellen: *Tried and Tested Outdoor Recipes.* Camp Publications, 24 pp., 80¢.

Joy, Barbara Ellen: *Wilderness Cookery for Everybody.* Camp Publications, 5 pp., 30¢

Koller, Larry: *Complete Book of Camping and the Outdoors.*

Let's Start Cooking. Girl Scouts, #23-355, $1.50.

Lindholm, Major Mauno A.: *Camping and Outdoor Fun.*

Lynn, Gordon: *Camping and Camp Crafts.*

Mason, Bernard S.: *Junior Book of Camping and Woodcraft.*

O'Connor, Hyla Nelson: *Barbecue Cook Book.* Arco Publications, Ltd., 1954, 144 pp., $2.50.

Outdoor Cooking with Reynolds Wrap. Reynolds Metal Company, Richmond 19, Virginia, 1950, 32 pp., Free.

Rutstrum, Calvin: *New Way of the Wilderness.*

Smith, E. Evelyn: *Quantity Recipes for Quality Foods.* Burgess Publishing Co., 1950, $3.00.

Staff Home Economists of Culinary Arts: *The Hungry Man's Outdoor Grill Cook Book.* Spencer Press, Inc., 1953, $1.50.

The Hungry Man's Outdoor Grill Cookbook. Grossett & Dunlap, Inc., 1953,

Treat, Nola and Richards, Lenore: *Quantity Cookery.* Little Brown and Co., Revised, 1951, 628 pp., $4.95.

Weaver, Robert W., and Merrill, Anthony F.: *Camping Can Be Fun.*

West, James E., and Hillcourt, William: *Scout Field Book.*

Whelen, Townsend, and Angier, Bradford: *On Your Own in the Wilderness.*

Wilder, James Austin: *Jack-Knife Cookery.* E. P. Dutton and Co., Inc., 1929, $2.75.

Native Foods and Survival Methods

Burke, Edmund H.: *Camping Handbook.*

Coon, Nelson: *Using Wayside Plants.* Author, P.O. Box 287, Watertown, Mass., 1957.

Fernald, Merrit L., and Kinsey, Alfred C.: *Edible Wild Plants of Eastern North America.* Harper and Brothers, Revised, 1958, 452 pp., $6.00.

Hood, Mary V.: *Outdoor Hazards, Real and Fancied.*

Jaeger, Ellsworth: *Woodsmoke.*

Medsger, Oliver Perry: *Edible Wild Plants.* The Macmillan Co., 1945, 323 pp., $5.95.

Ramsbottom, John: *Mushrooms and Toadstools.* The Macmillan Co., 1953, 306 pp., $6.25.

Some Common Edible and Poisonous Mushrooms. U.S. Dept. Of Agriculture, No. 796.

Smith, Alexander H.: *The Mushroom Hunter's Field Guide.* U. of Michigan, 1958, $4.95.

Thomas, William S.: *Fieldbook of Common Mushrooms.* Putnam's Sons, Inc., Revised, 1948, 320 pp., $5.00.

V-Five Association of America: *How To Survive on Land and Sea.* U.S. Naval Institute, Annapolis, Maryland, 2nd Ed., 1958, $4.00.

Zarchy, Harry: *Let's Go Camping.*

MAGAZINE ARTICLES

Craig, Orval B: *All-Camp Outdoor Cooking Program.* C.M., Dec., 1950.

Doermann, Marie C.: *Menu Planning.* C.M., April, 1952.

Hicks, Marjorie: *Packet Foods Encourage More Camp Outings And Better Meals On The Trail.* C.M., March, 1953.

King, Mary: *The Mixes Are Made For Campers.* C.M., May, 1952.

Kough, Blanchford: *Successful Cook-Outs.* C.M., Jan., 1953.

Walsh, Margaret M.: *Good Nutrition, A Camp Obligation.* C. M., Feb., 1954.

32

Trip Camping

TRIPS AND TRIP CAMPING

MONOTONY is a thing repugnant to all of us, and youth most of all craves excitement and ever new experiences. Boredom may set in with camp routine and one of the best ways to relieve it is to gather up one's food and bedding and take to the by-paths in search of new things to see and do. Some camps have always sponsored a liberal supply of trips out of the main camp, and fortunately, increasing numbers are broadening this worth-while phase of their program. When campers eat only meals prepared by the kitchen crew, served inside the familiar four walls of the dining room, interspersed with an occasional trip a few yards away to eat already prepared menus at a nearby campsite, they might almost as well be back in town engaging in the usual town picnics. Some readers may doubt that such camp programs exist today, but there are still far too many camps which fail to utilize their natural heritage to any appreciable extent, actually qualifying only as glorified summer resorts in a not too rustic setting. How much more fun it is for a camper to get away from his city pursuits and really learn to be at home in the out-of-doors. He makes rapid strides toward growing up and becoming a self-reliant citizen as he helps plan what will be needed on a trip and assumes responsibilities for packing his own duffel in addition to doing his share of the group work. Here he has opportunity for a down to earth lesson in applying what he has learned of campcraft as he makes himself comfortable, happy, and healthy in a woodland nook. Now he sees how such skills as using a knife, ax and spade, lashing, tent pitching and striking, fire building, cooking, packing duffel and countless other skills all fit together to make a "home away from home." If trips are well-planned with due consideration for the fun element, they become the highlight of the summer; they are something to look forward to and work enthusiastically toward as the child masters the necessary skills for advancing to progressively harder ones.

There are several reasons why some camps are still hesitant about including this type of activity in their programs. As mentioned, many organized camps have not practised trip-camping on an extensive scale, and directors who have had experience as counselors or as campers in such camps, or those who have not experienced camping at all as children are understandably reluctant to promote or even permit trip-camping for their precious charges, the campers. They are strengthened in this feeling by the fact that some parents are unenthusiastic, if not actually averse to the idea. Even the campers, themselves, who have never known the thrill of sleeping out with only the stars for a roof, are backward about going, for who among them has not heard wild, if completely unauthenticated, tales of attacks by wild animals, snakes crawling in bed with unwary sleepers, and the like? If such things ever *really* happened, they have surely been multiplied and exaggerated thousands of times for each occurrence.

Some counselors are squeamish about trip-camping, and many are completely untrained for it. Some colleges offering camp counselor training courses cannot or do not find the time and facilities to include such trips in their programs, thus leaving prospective counselors with only book knowledge and none of the experi-

ence and confidence necessary to sponsor trips safely and enthusiastically. The precamp training period is usually far too short to permit giving more than a nodding acquaintance with real trips. It is to be hoped that we will rapidly overcome this dearth of trained counselors and that every camp in the near future will have at least one trained staff member designated to train fellow counselors and supervise trips of appropriate length and ruggedness so that every physically able boy and girl in camp has the opportunity to go on several during the summer.

To be safe and comfortable, of course, campers must have the proper equipment for living in the open. In some camps, where campers are financially able to do so, they furnish their own personal equipment, while the camp supplies such group equipment as tents, nested cooking outfits, and so forth. In others, where the children are less well-off, the camp owns the equipment and lends or rents it to the campers. Personal and group trip-equipment can be made at home, as has been described elsewhere, so that much can be accomplished even though finances are limited.

Values

When a trip has been well-planned for and led up to, it usually becomes one of the most pleasant experiences of the summer. As a counselor, you must be just as enthusiastic as your campers in planning and looking forward to it, for your attitude is indeed "catching." Cloak the whole trip in the blanket of romance and adventure which strongly appeal to the imagination and love of make-believe, inherent in every child.

What better way can there be for instilling in a youngster a real love of nature and the out-of-doors than to let him spend all of his sleeping as well as waking hours in it for a few days or weeks? In addition to the planned experiences, no person with open eyes, ears and mind can fail to respond to the unforeseen and unplanned-for events that are sure to crop up along the way.

People are brought more closely together when working, playing, and sleeping together on the trail, for a trip-group is a little world unto itself where fast friendships quickly sprout and blossom. On the other hand, a camper who is selfish, lazy, or a rationalizer is quickly spotted by his peers and promptly subjected to one of the most effective treatments known—the failure of his own group to approve of and accept him.

You, as a counselor, will gain a clear insight into the true nature of your campers as they chatter informally about everything under the sun in busy group-living. If you are responsive, you can usually get much help in understanding what makes them "tick" and gain real knowledge to help you figure out how to tune their "ticks" to ways more acceptable to themselves and society.

Campers on trips learn to be independent and self-reliant, yet the working and planning together bring about the true feeling of "we-ness" which is so essential for good group-living.

How to Lead Up to Trips

Perhaps you doubt the wisdom of such an enthusiastic promotion of trips for everybody. This skepticism should disappear when you consider how broad the meaning of the word "trip" is. For the very young, inexperienced camper, it may mean only a simple lunch or supper cook-out followed at a later time by making a bed roll, packing up a few belongings, getting the provisions for a simple meal or two and hieing himself off to spend the night in the open a few feet from his cabin door. Nevertheless our neophyte will be gaining experience as he helps to plan what supplies and equipment will be needed and uses a check list to see that nothing is omitted. Perhaps the group will want to pretend

that they are part of a covered wagon train bound for Californ-i-a and will be so far from camp that they will just have to get along without whatever has been forgotten. See that a camper's first overnight is really fun with only simple cooking and clean-up chores to do, with lots of time left over for things that rate "tops" with him. Sew the whole evening all up with a good program around a cheery fire and an extra treat such as marshmallows to toast or popcorn to pop. If your campers are really young and very frightened, you may want to consider leaving a lighted lantern in full view of all to give confidence through the night. If his debut to trip-camping has been sufficiently successful, our camper's appetite will be whetted for returning to the main camp and working feverishly toward the additional skills required for more difficult expeditions.

A good camp trip-program will include successively longer and more difficult trips on its agenda to be held out as reward in succeeding summers as skills become greater and experience and stamina grow. Older campers sometimes rebel if they return summer after summer to repeat what they have already done and which they may consider "kid stuff." Long trips of several days duration to entirely new territories may solve the problem beautifully and serve to maintain enthusiasm and contentment. However, trips of such a rigorous nature are *not* recommended for young campers.

How and Where Shall We Go?

Many camps are fortunate enough to have widespread acreage which provides for almost any sort of trip that might be wanted. For them, it is merely a matter of selecting and developing a variety of campsites to meet the need. This project can well be undertaken by campers and will afford challenging activity ("program," if you please) for days or weeks as each camper group forages about searching for what it considers the "perfect spot," and then plans and carries out the work necessary to develop it to the fullest. Several groups may vie with each other in a friendly manner to see which can do the best job of constructing an outpost camp to be its own unit camp, clearing the necessary area, erecting the camp "fixings" for comfortable living, picking a meaningful name and perpetuating it in a rustic sign, and finally marking a trail with its own unique signs so that others may come to admire the architectural masterpiece and attend the christening services. Soon you'll have a whole set of these outpost camps at your disposal (the camp maintenance force may have to help younger campers with more difficult construction) and it may become a tradition for each succeeding group which uses the site to add some new convenience to the set-up. It will all have been so much fun that you may want to tear the new campsites down at the end of the season so that next year's crop of campers can enjoy the experience all over again.

For the camp which has only limited acreage available or which has older, experienced campers who have pretty well explored the native haunts, there are many possibilities away from home grounds. Perhaps arrangements may be made with a nearby farmer to camp on his property; most people enjoy having well behaved youngsters around and will cooperate 100 per cent if assured that the group understands outdoor manners and safety and will turn out to be cooperative neighbors and tenants. Even though the owner may want a small fee for the use of his property, it may be well worth it.

It may be possible to travel to a distant shore by canoe, sailboat, rowboat or even raft where there are sites available for cook-outs or overnight stops. Bicycles offer another neglected possibility for covering surprising distances in a short time; stay off main highways and seek the interesting back roads. Both campers and bicycles may be transported to suitable points of departure if such roads are not available in the immediate vicinity, returning to pick them up at a scheduled time and place when the trip is over.

Nearly every camp will find public lands offering camping facilities somewhere in the vicinity, so again it is a problem only of getting the campers there by bus, train or camp facilities. Some enterprising camps such as Camp Wakeela* have arranged for eleven and twelve year old campers to procure an unused farm wagon and, with a framework of saplings, soaked to make them more pliable, and an old tent, convert it into a covered wagon. A neighboring farmer supplied the "horse power" to pull the wagon loaded with the duffel while the campers took turns riding and walking pioneer style. Other camps convey heavy equipment to outlying districts by pack animals, jeep, camp truck or station wagon. Horseback trips are always a favorite.

Good possibilities, too seldom used by organized camps with limited facilities, exist in the national, state, county and local parks, forests, and wildlife refuges where arrangements may often be made to camp and explore the well-marked trails. It is best to avoid the popular areas which are too crowded for privacy. Most of them have restrictions about cutting timber and building fires and sometimes even make it mandatory to cook only with charcoal or canned heat. These are minor difficulties and actually give the camper experience in situations he will meet as an adult citizen. Trail maps, guide books and professional personnel are usually available to help.

It may be possible to affiliate with the AYH (American Youth Hostels) (page 16) and secure maps of their trails and hostels. The Appalachian Trail is a 2,050 mile footpath leading from Mount Katah-

* Segal, Harvey G.: *Westward Ho*. Recreation, March, 1957, page 82.

din in Maine to Mount Oglethorpe in Georgia and winding through beautiful scenery in the Green and White Mountains, the Berkshires, Alleghenies, Catskills, Blue Ridge and Smokies. The Pacific Coast Trail Way of about 2,150 miles leads from Canada to Mexico through the Cascades, Sierra Nevada, and Sierra Madre Mountains. Though both of these trails contain rugged sections suitable only for seasoned trippers, other areas can be reached by automobile or public transportation and are quite suitable for young, inexperienced groups under good leadership. Both offer some campsites and temporary shelters at convenient stopping places. The reader can gain further information by contacting the sources listed at the end of the chapter and his attention is particularly called to the excellent book by George and Iris Wells (page 387) which describes available wilderness areas in forty-seven of the original forty-eight states.

How Rugged Shall the Trip Be?

Always remember that no trip is good camp practice or fun when it degenerates into an endurance contest or a race against time. Tens miles a day may be enough for average hikers or even five if the going is rough, while seasoned "trippers" might well go twice as far or more. Those going by canoe may well cover twelve to twenty miles or more a day, while cyclists may count on going thirty to sixty miles. Allow plenty of opportunity for seeing, exploring and just plain having fun, for it's not "how far" but "how much" that counts when evaluating a trip. On long excursions, it is wise to take it easy the first day or two as the group warms up. Later, allow for a "lazy day" now and then when the "trippers" can sleep at the previous night's campsite and have time to catch up on laundry or mending, or spend the day exploring the countryside, playing games, fishing, singing, enjoying cheerful banter, or "just settin'" as the mood dictates. "Trippers" should return alert and rested, not mentally and physically fagged out so that they must spend the next few days in recuperation.

It is best, whenever possible, to have some of the counselors, and possibly a particularly able camper or two, go over a new route before taking a group of campers on it. Interested individuals may want to make a trail map of it for use by those who are to folow. Provide enough variety to offer a new possibility for each trip even though there are several during the summer and plan to return over new territory.

At the end of a frequently used route or at overnight stops along the way, it is a good idea to establish an *outpost* or *primitive camp,* equipping it with rustic furniture and camp "fixin's" to save time and make "trippers" more comfortable during their stay.

Make every trip a safe one, for danger is not at all essential to fun and adventure and has no place at all in the organized camp.

Who Should Go On Trips?

The best size for a trip group is six to ten campers with two or three counselors, depending on the age of the group; the ratio on long trips should not exceed five campers to each counselor. Have at least two counselors in every group, no matter how small, so that, in case of emergency, there will be one adult to stay with the campers while the other goes to use the telephone or secure help. The only safe exception might be with seasoned trippers who are sixteen years old or over. At least one counselor must be trained and experienced in trip-camping, having learned by practice as well as through training courses and extensive reading. At least one should have had training in first aid and preferably hold a current American Red Cross certificate.

An Outpost Campsite.

Campers should be of approximately the same age, strength and experience, lest the young and inexperienced wear themselves out or be unjustly called "lazy" or "tenderfoot" while trying to keep up with the others.

Every person going on a trip should have a physical check-up and "O.K." from the camp nurse or physician. Knowing that they will have to pass such a test may stimulate those going on the trip to get plenty of rest and sleep and put themselves in tip-top physical condition beforehand.

It is wise to set up a progressive set of skills in campcraft and woodcraft which campers must pass before being allowed to go on a trip. The list should be short and easy for the first trips with additional skills added as the trips grow more difficult. A chart on which a camper can check himself off as he passes a test keeps him aware of his status and shows him exactly what he must do to win the coveted right to go on a longer trip. As a preliminary to passing tests, include practice and instruction in the many skills of campcraft and woodcraft as a regular part of the program, just as canoeing, arts and crafts, or swimming are. Set up an exhibit of such techniques as

fire building, lashing, knot tying, building outdoor fireplaces, and so forth at the campsite as a model for those attempting to perfect their own skills and pass tests. Bulletin board material and an ample supply of books and pamphlets should be available at all times.

A set of tests would include appropriate skills in such techniques as the following:

A demonstrated knowledge of good manners in the out-of-doors
Use and care of knife and hatchet
Selection of fuel and firebuilding; uses of various types of fires
Conservation and proper extinguishing of campfires
Outdoor cookery
Making a bedroll and having experience in sleeping out-of-doors
Trip equipment and proper packing of duffel
Pitching a tent and ditching it properly
Camp sanitation and proper disposal of garbage
Knowledge of weather and weather prediction
Lashing and tying various useful knots
First aid
Experience in one-meal camping, then in all-day and overnight hiking and camping out.
Paddling, horseback or bicycle riding if the trip is to involve such methods of transportation.

Such requirements give real impetus to learning and perfecting camping skills. In addition, they insure that the participants will likely be safe, happy and comfortable on the trip. Joy (page 390) sets up sample specific requirements as well as complete plans for carrying on a trip-program.

The Trips Counselor

Many camps appoint one person, known by some such title as "Trips Counselor," in charge of the entire trip-program and he may have one or more assistants to help him as needed. Such persons often set up the program of "enabling skills," variously known as *campcrafts, pioneering, wildlife craft, woodcraft,* and so forth, for the whole camp and either direct the program itself or work with the unit counselors who in turn administer the programs to their groups.

The trips counselor should be a mature, seasoned person who is thoroughly versed in his field through wide experience as well as through reading and instruction. He should be level-headed, resourceful, completely dependable and most of all enthusiastic about the possibilities of his program. He must be an expert with map and compass as well as in campcraft skills and the various ways of constructing campsite refinements and makeshift devices. He must be a good organizer, tactful yet forceful, for he must coordinate the whole program, working with counselors, campers, and indeed the whole camp personnel. He must be able to arouse enthusiasm and have a sense of fairness and see that all have equal opportunity to use the camp equipment, trails, and camping-out spots.

One of his big responsibilities will be to see that there is enough equipment of the right type on hand and that it is kept in good repair and supplemented with new when necessary. He must arrange for storing equipment efficiently and safely in appropriate bins, shelves, racks and hangers in the equipment room or rooms. He must keep endless lists as he checks it out and in for troops leaving and returning

to camp. Though each trip-group should be responsible for seeing that their own gear is returned dry, clean and in good condition for storage, the Trips Counselor must act as the final authority on such matters. He must know how to keep leather goods, tents and other gear in A-1 shape. He will be expected to keep his equipment inventory up-to-date, adding anything acquired during the summer and turning in an accurate closing inventory as he oversees the packing away of the gear for the winter. The trips counselor's responsibility is very important, for all personnel must be kept aware of the fact that trip equipment is one of the more expensive items on the camp budget and that all must cooperate to see that it lasts as long as possible; each item lost or ruined through neglect or misuse means that much less money is available for additional needed items or for other phases of the camp program.

The trips counselor must be available as advisor to campers and counselors in unit groups who are planning outings and he often accompanies a group on some of the more rugged trips.

Preparations

PRELIMINARY PLANNING.   Much of the enjoyment of a trip consists of anticipation as campers and counselors coordinate in planning for it. First the group must decide how to go, where to go and how long to stay. Next will come the job of making lists of personal and group equipment and food. Some of the items to consider in decision making will be:

The experience and age of the group going;

The probable temperatures that will be encountered and the ever present possibilities of rain;

The means of transportation. Count every inch an ounce when selecting gear which must be carried on the back. Fortunately, the wonderful new developments in materials, types of equipment, and concentrated and dehydrated foods have greatly simplified this problem.

Are there stores or farm houses along the way from which you can replenish food supplies? Are you *sure* that you can count on supplementing your diet with fish caught and wild berries picked along the way or are you just hoping?

What is the type of terrain? Will the going be rough or relatively easy?

Is ample wood available for cooking and camp construction or will you need to carry charcoal and a charcoal stove or some form of canned heat?

Is there ample water available for drinking, cooking, and cleanliness? Is the water from a tested source or will it have to be purified? Remember that dehydrated foods require lots of water for cooking.

How much time do you want to take out for cooking? Some foods require elaborate preparations and long cooking time. Others are very simple and therefore are especially good for lunches. Other good quick lunches consist of sandwiches supplemented with a quickly prepared hot drink or soup.

How many and what type of cooking utensils do you have available and how many do you want to bother with? You can cut down by planning items that you can cook in aluminum foil, in used tin cans, or on rustic broilers or sticks. Recall that frying pans are heavy, and many think too many fried foods not particularly healthful anyway. One-pot meals also conserve on utensils.

Are permits needed to camp, build fires, or fish?

Are good maps of the area available? Only experienced groups with a leader, experienced in using map and compass, should venture into areas without well-marked trails.

What is available in the way of telephone, physicians, and helpful inhabitants and forest rangers in case of emergencies?

GROUP ORGANIZATION. Campers like to help plan their trip and enjoy doing the preparatory work under the watchful eye of their counselors. Each moment of hard work increases their proprietory feeling for the trip as it becomes "ours" rather than "yours." Resentment or at best indifference results when campers are merely dragged along on an expedition set up and planned by someone else. How much help they can give will, of course, depend on their age and experience but a counselor is definitely not showing good leadership when he makes a work-horse of himself while the bored campers merely look on. Someone has said that "work is only work when you would rather be doing something else"; work turns into engrossing fun when it is what a camper has set up for himself to do.

Try out the power of suggestion by a judicious use of "let's" or "wouldn't it be fun to" or "how shall we?" Ask the campers to help you solve problems; you'll be surprised at the good ideas they come up with and the willing, cooperative spirit it engenders. Do not mistake this to mean, however, that *everything* should be left in their hands; instead, you must temper it always with your more mature judgment where dangerous or foolish practices are involved. It is the test of the really talented leader to *guide* the group into desirable decisions without their even realizing that the whole thing was not their own idea. See how skillful you can become but never, *never* let them suspect what you are doing. If you can't succeed any other way, however, you must have the courage to say "NO" and stick to it when it is a case of safety, good common sense, or good camping practice.

A good method is to set up appropriate committees for food, program, personal and group equipment, etc.; better cooperation results when campers are allowed some choice in their areas of work.

THINGS TO DO. Menus must be planned, and proportions and food lists computed and turned in through the proper channels to allow ample time to measure out staple items and get any special ones called for. This should usually be done in cooperation with the camp dietitian, whose advice and knowledge will prove of inestimable value. Each camp usually has its own procedure to follow, and you as a counselor should find out what it is and carefully adhere to it.

A list of personal equipment must be worked out and given to each camper or posted in his cabin for him to check against as he packs, for leaving behind a single necessary item can be a minor or even major catastrophe for the person involved. Cut the list to those things absolutely essential for comfort, health and safety as discussed in chapter 31. For instance, small campers need only small size sleeping bags and packsacks and this will cut down on the weight they have to carry. Bear in mind that an air mattress isn't really necessary for a child and ample firewood is often available without axe or saw; at least, only two (in case of loss or breakage) will suffice for the group.

Determine such group equipment as tents, cooking outfits, and the like and prepare a list in duplicate, keeping one copy to check against along the way and leaving the other with the trips counselor to check against on the return. You must lay out a definite route and set up a definite time schedule. Leave a copy at the main camp so that they can quickly locate you should it become necessary.

Make out a "kapers" chart or schedule of trip duties before leaving, rotating them so that no one will feel he has been unfairly burdened. Place different combinations of campers working together at various times to prevent the development of cliques and pet animosities. Outline duties clearly so that none can fail to do what he is supposed to because he misunderstood; this also makes it more difficult to get by with shirking.

Pool all money and divide it between two or three responsible persons. Usually only money for an emergency need be taken for good hiking country usually lies away from towns. If campers should have occasion to go to town, set a limit (say ten or fifteen cents) for each to spend; this prevents stuffing on sweets and other appetite spoilers or "showing off" by those with greater allowances. A good trip menu will include all the sweets necessary or advisable for participants to have.

Select one or two campers as trip scribes to keep a trip diary. If they have the ability to see unusual or funny events and put them into words, it will be much enjoyed. Reading the diary furnishes good program around the campfire in the evening and it may later be made into a little booklet, adorned in the arts and crafts department, and presented to each member of the trip soon after his return to camp. Such a diary is much treasured, for it recalls many a funny happening and poignant memory long after camp days are over.

Give a good deal of thought to "program" on a trip, and include in your duffel ideas for games, songs, stunts, poems, and the like for use at odd moments. A spelling bee, a nature quiz or a round-robin story may be just the thing for a rest period along the trail when you slip off your pack and take a breather. They also come in handy around the campfire just before crawling into your *downy soft* bed rolls. Likewise, a serious discussion of a topic of interest to all or a devotional program, at times, does much to improve group morale.

Pack your equipment with care. Systematize it, with like things such as tools, equipment for fires and sanitation, cooking utensils, extra tarps, etc. in separate bags, each labeled or of a distinctive color so that it can be quickly located when needed. Also, number each one conspicuously and attach a strong tag, listing the exact contents. The list is used to check against each time the bag is repacked after use; the counselor in charge of equipment carries a list of all bags and contents so that he can locate what is needed in a jiffy.

Distribute equipment equitably, taking into consideration the strength of the hiker and don't hesitate to make changes en route if conditions warrant it. For instance, if there is an unusually heavy bag of camp gear for one camper to tote, another with no group equipment might relieve him of part of his personal duffel. The watchword of any successful trip must be "one for all and all for one." Entrust important or perishable items only to responsible campers or counselors.

A minor but very important point is to discuss with the group the importance of sticking together at all times so that no one gets lost. Each counselor should have a whistle with perhaps a few extra for campers who must leave the group for water or firewood. Agree upon the exact procedure for both group and camper in case someone should become separated.

ON THE ROAD

Choosing a Campsite

It is well to begin looking for a good campsite at least an hour or two before sundown, for you will be tired and thankful to have supper over, the dishes washed, and everything made shipshape for the night well before dark, since camp lighting is usually somewhat inadequate for such chores.

When you wish to camp on other than camp property, it is not only illegal but discourteous to do so without the owner's permission. An explanation of the nature of your group and what you are doing with an assurance that you will be careful with your fire and leave behind a neat campsite usually secures willing permission. Remind your group that it represents *camp* and that the camp's continued good name depends on their observance of all the rules of consideration for others and out-of-door courtesy

and good conservation practices. If others are sleeping near, you must be careful not to keep them awake or make yourselves obnoxious in any way.

In choosing a campsite, consider a number of points. It will probably be impossible to find one combining all of the following good features, but you can at least look for one embodying as many as possible.

Privacy, a certain amount of isolation, and a beautiful view are much to be desired. Good drinking water and water for cooking and bathing are, of course, a big advantage, but you should take no chances, always sterilizing water in some way if there is any doubt. Good firewood and a safe place to build a fire are always essential, and wood, for camp construction is a convenience.

Select an elevated gentle slope with fairly porous soil to ensure good drainage in case of a storm; if well-chosen, you may not even have to ditch your tents. Avoid a place covered with a growth of lush grass, for it indicates that the ground is water-soaked and too damp for good sleeping or sitting. Sand is undesirable, for it permeates everything you eat and wear. The ground should be smooth enough for good sleeping.

The Indians, always wise in matters of camping, usually pitched their tepees on open fields or plains where they were not endangered by falling trees and branches during a storm. Stay clear of a lone or unusually tall tree for it is particularly likely to attract lightning. Though trees may give some shelter during a deluge, they will continue to drip on the tent for hours after the rain is over. An open spot just at the edge of a woods is most desirable, for firewood is handy, yet you do not have to sleep under trees. Nearby bushes and high grass are undesirable since they shut off the breeze and tend to harbor bothersome insects.

Dry stream beds and the banks of streams are risky, for a sudden storm may catch your camp in the midst of a flash flood and an island may be completely inundated during a storm. Look for high water marks before deciding to camp on such spots.

Rock piles may harbor snakes and ant hills; old, rotten trees infested with ants bring hordes of uninvited bedfellows to get into your food and make you miserable.

Mosquitoes also make mighty uncomfortable camp mates. A spot not too near water or high grass and exposed to a good breeze is usually relatively free from them, but it may prove to be a somewhat dangerous place to build a fire. Mosquitoes are so small that they rarely fly far against the breeze, and the leeward side of a lake or stream some distance away is therefore usually fairly safe. A fairly dense growth of trees between camp and their breeding places also serves as pretty good protection.

Making Camp

When a campsite has been chosen, everyone, after consultation with the work chart, should fall to and do his allotted share of the work as quickly as possible. Systematized chores get done quickly and leave a maximum of time free for doing more pleasant things. The following procedure is suggested:

Take a short dip if not too hot or tired, if you have a qualified waterfront person along, and if you know the water is free from pollution. First make sure there are no deep holes, hidden snags or swift currents.

Bring up all the duffel and deposit it in orderly fashion. Line up the numbered bags in order so that needed tools, utensils or other items may be quickly found. Shelter them with an extra tarp or tent if it looks like rain.

Put perishable supplies to cool.

Dig a latrine.

Get drinking water, taking steps to purify it if not sure of its source.

Pitch tents and dig trenches around them if there is any possibility of rain. It is best to pitch them facing

north or northeast if weather signs point to a storm, since most violent summer storms come from the southwest (thus the sailor's name "Sou'-wester," for his hat). If fair weather is indicated, you may want to face the tents southeast to catch the early morning sun.

Make beds, clearing away all pebbles, sticks and lumps of grass first. It is usually best to arrange the beds rather close together for a feeling of security and companionship. Get out the personal equipment you will need. If you are going to unpack or rearrange large quantities of your duffel, spread it out on your poncho or other solid surface so that small pieces can't lose themselves in the duff.

Take care of such general camping equipment as boats, canoes, lanterns, and so forth.

Dividing Trip Duties

It is ordinarily best to divide the campers into committees for each meal, with duties assigned somewhat as follows:

1. Cooks.

Get the menu just after the previous meal and figure out methods and approximate cooking time, type of fire and fireplace needed, and so forth.

Tell the fire builders the kind of fire and fireplace you want and where and when to build them.

At the proper time, get the food and measure out the proportions, covering the remainder so that it will not be contaminated by insects and dirt.

Soap the entire outsides of the kettles and cook the food. Take pride in seeing that everything is palatable and well-seasoned.

Get out the eating utensils and set the table or arrange to have the food served cafeteria style.

Act as hosts or hostesses and serve the food. As soon as everyone has finished eating, put left-over food away and replace unused portions.

2. Fire Builders.

Equip yourselves with axe, knife, gloves and matches. Have handy a fire poker, shovel and equipment in case the fire should start to spread.

Consult the cooks and build the type of fire and fireplace wanted. Build it early enough to let the fire burn down to coals by the time the cooks are ready.

Gather enough wood to last through the meal, chopping or breaking it up into appropriate sizes and arranging a neat woodpile convenient to the fire, but not in the way or where sparks might be blown into it.

Keep the fire going, at least one person standing by constantly to replenish fuel, rearrange coals, and so forth, at the direction of the cooks. Keep up the fire long enough to heat dishwater.

Completely extinguish the fire as soon as all are through with it and leave the fireplace neat, with enough fuel to start the next meal if it is to be eaten there.

If breakfast will be the next meal or if there are signs of rain, gather some tinder, kindling and firewood and put them under a tent or extra tarpaulin.

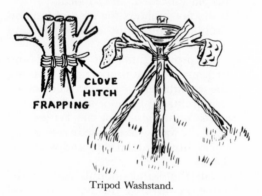

CLOVE HITCH
FRAPPING

Tripod Washstand.

3. Clean up and Sanitation.

Dig and line a grease pit.

Arrange a refrigerating or cooling system for perishable foods.

Put dishwater on to heat as soon as the cooks are through with the fire and there are large containers available for it. Heat enough for sterilizing, too.

Wash all dishes and sterilize them. Wipe them out first with dry leaves, napkins, or paper towels before immersing them in the dishwater. Fill one pan with hot soapy water, another with hot water for rinsing and sterilizing. Sand or wood ashes make good substitutes for scouring powder.

Dishes can be sterilized by placing them in a net bag or one made from a double thickness of cheesecloth and immersing it in boiling water for two minutes; then hang bag and all up to drain and dry. Silverware can be immersed in a tin can device (K, page 252).

Wash out dishcloths and towels and hang them out to dry. Scald them after the evening meal.

Bury and cover all garbage.

Burn out, flatten and bury tin cans.

Be sure there is enough water properly sterilized and on hand for drinking purposes.

Making a Latrine

Make some sort of latrine whenever two or more campers are staying away from camp. An easy one to make is the *straddle trench,* dug two to three feet deep, downhill from camp and at a distance of at least 100 feet. Pile the dirt along the sides where a quantity of it can be kicked back into the trench or shoveled in with a homemade tin can shovel after each use. Make the shovel by compressing the ends of a forked stick and flattening a tin can over them or by splitting a stick, inserting a flattened tin can in the slit, nailing it fast and lashing the stick to keep it from splitting further. If you use the trench for several days, purify it peri-

Latrine with Tin Can Shovel, Seat, and Toilet Paper Holder.

odically by covering it with a layer of chloride of lime, creosote or ashes, or by burning a fire over it.

Tin Can Shovel.

Keep toilet paper nearby on a forked stick and covered with a number 10 tin can or a one-pound coffee can with a detachable lid (X, page 253) as a shelter from wind and weather. Cut a slot down one side to pull the paper through. Make holes in both ends of it and place it on a stick supported across two forked sticks driven into the ground.

The latrine should be close enough to the campsite for convenience and easy and safe to get to at night, yet is must not be near the source of drinking water and must be far enough away to provide privacy. If no natural screen of bushes or underbrush is available, build one of brush or canvas like the one on page 105. Arrange facilities for handwashing nearby.

Making Drinking Water Safe

The only way to be absolutely sure that water is safe for drinking and cooking or washing dishes is to chemically test it; if this has not been done, you must sterilize it, no matter how clear and sparkling it looks, for it may carry serious diseases such as typhoid fever. It is best to bring water from camp in clean canteens or thermos jugs or fill them from *safe* sources along the way. When that is impossible, use one of the following methods to purify it:

1. Boil it for ten to twenty minutes (time it from when it actually starts to boil). This causes the water to taste flat because the air has been removed but you can restore its good flavor by stirring it vigorously with a spoon or pouring it back and forth several times from one container to another.
2. Use one to two drops of iodine or Halazone or Globaline tablets according to the directions printed on the container. A few drops of lemon juice will make it taste better.
3. Use one part of chlorine to 100 parts of water. Let stand thirty minutes.
4. Use one to two drops of Clorox per gallon and aerate as in method 1.

When water is available at an outpost or frequently used campsite, it is worthwhile to send a sample to the state board of health for testing so that you won't have to bother to sterilize it. Directions for doing this can be secured from your state or county board of health or the camp director.

During very hot weather, you may want to add a little salt to your drinking water to prevent heat cramps and possible prostration. Consult the camp doctor or nurse about this.

Food

Make an earnest attempt to serve all meals on time and maintain high standards for cooking, serving and eating them. The practice of subsisting on a diet of fried foods or on partially raw, overcooked, or poorly seasoned food is both unnecessary and inexcusable. Never let campers make a practice of hanging around munching on bits of this or that while they're waiting for the main course to be ready. If it is long overdue or they're really quite hungry, give *everyone* something such as an apple to allay hunger pangs. Every meal should be a ceremony with all participating in a silent, spoken, or sung grace and sitting down to eat together in pleasant surroundings. Improve your dining table with interesting wild grasses, leaves or the like. An invariable custom should be to eat only with clean hands and face and neatly arranged hair just as if dining at home or back at the main camp. Singing well loved songs or playing an interesting game makes time pass faster for those waiting for the meal and workers may be able to join in too.

Garbage Disposal

Keep your campsite neat and clean, and dispose of all garbage immediately in an appropriate way, for slops and rubbish dumped about a campsite look unsightly, draw flies and other pests, and may even give off offensive odors.

MAKING A GREASE PIT. To make a grease pit for disposing of liquid wastes dig a hole on the downslope from camp and line it with small stones or gravel. Cover it with a framework of small branches topped with dry leaves to act as filters as you pour your dishwater and other liquid slops, waste fats, and the like into it. Burn it out periodically, using paper or kerosene to kindle a quick-burning fire. Replace the branches and leaves to use it again.

DISPOSING OF SOLID WASTES. Carry bits of fruit and vegetables which would make good food for wild animals out well away from camp. Other solid wastes should be dried out on a frame of screening or green branches as shown until it becomes dry enough to burn, in a brisk

Drying Kiln for Solid Wastes.

fire. Do not bury it for some prowling animal will be sure to dig it up. Such wastes as aluminum foil, banana, orange and apple peelings will not burn, and should be carried back to camp with you unless you are on an extended trip in which case they should be burned clear of food and then buried at some distance from camp. Remove both ends from tin cans and place them in the fire to burn out the inside contents and soften the solder so that you can mash them flat under your foot. Carry them back home with you if you are on a short trip (after all, they won't be nearly so heavy to carry back empty as they were to bring out). On an extended trip, bury them for the burning causes them to rust quickly to powder in the ground, and the flattening makes them require less space and keeps animals from getting claws, hoofs,

or heads caught in them. Never leave tin cans lying around to catch rainwater and become mosquito breeding places.

Twist paper to be burned tightly and burn it a little at a time, holding it down with a green stick poker so that the gases produced will not cause it to fly into the air and become a potential source of forest fire. Tear cardboard boxes into bits and feed them to the fire a little at a time.

Bedding Down for the Night

Cache all food safely (as illustrated in Chapter 29) against roving dogs and other animals. Turn pots and kettles upside down and stow everything neatly away for the night. See that your fire is completely out and safe from spreading.

Many animals like to chew on candles, soap, and the like; securely hide them or suspend them from tree limbs so that they are inaccessible. Porcupines, in particular, crave salt and consequently may chew and completely ruin articles which have been perspiration soaked, such as axe, paddle, or oar handles, saddles, and so forth. They too, should be suspended from ropes.

Turn your shoes upside down as a protection against rain or heavy dew and place them close beside your bed roll where you can locate them quickly if you need them in the night. If you wear glasses, place them in their case inside your shoes or in a packsack to avoid losing or breaking them.

Keep your flashlight nearby where you can instantly locate it in the dark.

If mosquitoes or other insects prove bothersome, a good spraying of tent and surroundings with a good insect repellent will usually insure a restful night.

In Case of Rain

Trippers should be experts at reading weather signs for it's much better to foresee a rain coming in time to prepare for it than to have to do everything in the rain. If you decide to pitch your tent for the night, there are some things you should do a little differently from the usual. Many of these have already been discussed. If you do have to continue in the rain, a poncho is better than a raincoat for it is ample enough to cover a good bit of duffel in addition to yourself.

If you have tents with front flies, you can make a connecting porch between two of them by pitching them to face each other and just far enough apart for the flies to slightly overlap. Slant them downward toward the tent so the water will run off down over the roof. This provides a "breezeway" in which you can actually do a little *light* cooking but keep your fire very small and put it out if your tent flies dry out lest they catch on fire.

If you expect to be rained in for an evening or several daylight hours, it will be more sociable to pitch your tents in a semicircle so that you can sit in your tent doorway and have the cheeriness of a campfire in the middle. You can cook under a tarp.

Stake down guy wires deeper than usual and dig a ditch around your tent if the ground isn't right for rapid drain off.

Tents with Breezeway.

A good tent, when properly pitched, will stay put through anything less than a hurricane. Remember to face your tents properly with backs to the wind and rain. Loosen guy wires enough to prevent shrinking and pulling out, leaving you with a wet tent around your neck.

Place all of your duffel under tents, tarps or ponchos and do not unroll your bed roll until you are ready to get into it so it won't collect dampness.

Health on Trips

Keep yourself and your clothing clean. Stay in camp a half day or day occasionally on a long trip to wash out your clothing or stop at a nearby town; several can wash their clothes very cheaply at a laundromat.

All the rules of health and sanitation are doubly important on a trip where the illness or incapacity of a single person is most annoying to all. A stimulating and refreshing bath or sponge off every day is a "must." Wash well before each meal, and use strong soap immediately after a possible exposure to poison ivy.

Never sleep in the clothes you have worn all day. A change to clean pajamas is restful and stimulating and permits you to wash out your soiled clothing and hang it up to dry over night. It is particularly important to wash out your socks each night.

Take care of minor ailments, which clearly fall within the realm of first aid, on the trail; they may turn into major ones if neglected. Take anyone who shows signs of a serious ailment back to camp or to the nearest physician immediately. One counselor who is best trained in first aid should administer all treatment except in emergency when he is not available; this counselor should keep an exact record of everything he does. He must be careful to avoid doing the wrong

Clothes Lines.

thing and should never try to play doctor or nurse.

If a camper shows symptoms of appendicitis (nausea and vomiting, abdominal pains which may be general at first but eventually become localized, inability to straighten the leg comfortably while lying down or to stand up straight) *do not apply heat or give a cathartic under any circumstance.*

You can make a good emergency hot-water bottle by wrapping a heated stone, canteen or plastic bottle filled with hot water in a towel or flannel shirt. If you need a stretcher, button up two coats, insert two saplings through their arm-holes, and lash in spreaders to keep them apart. A blanket and safety pins can be used in the same way. Improvise a crutch as shown on page 323.

Digestive disturbances can be very "upsetting" so observe the principles of moderation and good nutrition. Many such cases can be traced to rancid food particles and germs left on dishes not thoroughly washed and sterilized.

Leave wild animals strictly alone and don't try to pet or make friends with them.

Strenuous days on the trail necessitate a maximum of rest and sleep. This means an early bedtime for the sun is an early riser and is likely to shine rudely right into your eyes and will be as disturbing as birds and other wildlife, which will be noisely searching for an early breakfast.

Be on guard against blisters, sunburn, and exposure to poison ivy; carrying a packsack on sore shoulders can be pure torture. Summer colds are also miserable so change wet clothing immediately and be especially careful to keep your head, shoulders, and feet dry.

Breaking Camp

Pack your food with the makings for lunch, usually an easily prepared meal, on top of the packsack where it will be readily available.

Burn out your latrine and cover it.

Burn out and cover your grease and garbage pits. (Don't dump grease over an open fire; the blaze might cause severe burns.)

If you have ditched your tent, replace the sod or fill in the ditch so it won't start erosion.

Leave your campsite even neater than it was upon arrival. Remove all traces of human habitation, restoring it to nature's beauty.

Take a last look around your campsite to see that you are not leaving any personal or group equipment behind.

Your fire should be "dead as a mackerel."

> Let no man say,
> And say it to your shame,
> That all was beauty here
> Until *you* came.
>
> —Author Unknown

BACK AT THE MAIN CAMP

Each camper and counselor should have a physical check-up by the physician or nurse within twenty-four hours after arriving back in camp. All should return in the pink of condition, and cases of poison ivy, sunburn, indigestion, overfatigue, and the like, are unforgiveable for they usually indicate poor planning and poor management of the trip.

Have a weeding out party: unpack all gear, both personal and group, and carefully sort it into three piles: (1) used many times, (2) used occasionally and, (3) never used. See how many items from piles (2) and (3) you can strike off your equipment list and leave home next trip.

Repair, air-out, and store all personal equipment and check-in unused food with the dietitian.

Check all group equipment against the inventory you made at the beginning of the trip and care for any needing repairs. Air and clean all equipment thoroughly and return it to its proper place.

"Trippers" should take it easy for a day

or two after returning from a hard journey, taking time for laundry and getting personal effects in order. You may want to complete copies of your trip-log; write up your adventures for the camp newspaper; or dramatize episodes for yourselves or for your fellow campers at a subsequent campfire program.

Within a short time after returning, call a group meeting to evaluate the trip, noting both the good and bad points in preliminary planning and preparations, the suitability of the food, morale of the group, and so on. Carefully write down all suggestions and use them to improve future trips. You may want to relay your ideas on to the director and trips counselor for possible help to others.

CANOE TRIPS

Canoe trips are favorites, especially with senior campers, for travel is relatively easy and proportionately greater loads of equipment and food can be taken than by any other mode of travel except wagon, automobile, or truck. A person must be a triple-threat man, however, to undertake long trips safely for he must be a good camper, an excellent swimmer, and skilled in canoeing. He should also have toughened himself by short trips. Camps nearly always have rigid standards or tests set up which a camper must pass before he can qualify; they usually include passing the American Red Cross Intermediate swimming test or its equivalent as well as tests to cover the other two phases.

You can cover three or four miles an hour on a lake and even more when traveling with the current of the river. However, on long voyages, plan to lay over one out of every three or four days for a rest and variation from the constant paddling.

Equipment

A sixteen foot cruising model canoe seems to be the general favorite for camp

(H. Armstrong Roberts.)

(Joy and Camp)

trips and you can choose from among canvas covered, fiberglas, plywood, aluminum or other new materials entering the market. Each type has its adherents but aluminum canoes seem to be gaining in favor, for they are strong and durable, yet light in weight, an especially important consideration when portaging must be done. They need very little upkeep; with care they should last for years; and usually dent instead of puncturing when encountering obstacles at moderate force; and they have built-in air chambers which make them float and even right themselves when overturned.

Carefully choose your trip-canoe for strength, stability in the water and lightness if you will need to portage. For lake travel, choose a canoe with a slightly rounded bottom and width that continues well out to the ends. A flat bottom, shoe-type curved keel, giving higher and slim ends, is better. Though long, tapered ends give more speed, a flatter bottomed boat gives more stability in the water.

Put your canoe in first class repair and equip it with a painter and proper thwarts. Most people like to remove the seats and kneel on the bottom of the canoe with knees well apart and buttocks resting against a thwart for paddling; others prefer to leave the seats in for a change of position in calm water. Kneeling is the safest position since it keeps the center of gravity low; it also helps you advance more rapidly, and it keeps the canoe steadier and well under control. You will need a light waterproof kneeling pad which will float and so act as a life preserver in an emergency; it will also serve as a pillow at night or to sit upon on damp ground around the camp fire. Buy one or make it from two layers of sponge rubber inserted inside an inner tube.

The sternman should select a paddle which reaches up to his chin when he stands it up on the ground; the bowman needs one about three inches shorter. Maple paddles are best for trips since they are springier and less likely to break. Print your name with India ink on a piece of adhesive tape and attach it to the paddle so that you can always use the one you are accustomed to. Place an extra paddle on the floor of each canoe in case one is lost or broken. Pack a repair kit of the proper kind for the type canoe you are using.

You will need your dark glasses and a map of the route and should have light moccasins or low rubber sneakers for paddling though some prefer to slip off their shoes and paddle only in their socks.

Take a piece of mosquito netting to weight down around you if you want to sleep in your canoe. When planning the rest of your duffel, follow the same principles as for any other trip.

On the Water

The usual ratio for a trip is two people and their duffel to a canoe though a large craft can carry three. An experienced paddler, well versed in the "J" stroke, should be in the stern for he is responsible for steering the canoe. The bowman, paddling on the opposite side, sets the rhythm of the stroke and keeps a sharp lookout for half-hidden rocks or snags and must master the "draw" stroke to pull the canoe away from suddenly revealed obstacles. Distribute your personnel so that each craft is manned by a crew of equal strength and stamina; canoes should keep together, not more than two or three canoe lengths apart, for companionship and help in case of trouble.

Some prefer to pack their duffel in boxes made especially to fit into a canoe but you may use regular packs or duffel bags. All the gear to go in a canoe should be assembled and packed while the canoe is entirely afloat.

Packers can wade along the side to stow it if the canoe is in shallow water. It is very important *to trim your load* by keeping the weight balanced crosswise and toward the center of the canoe so that both bow and stern are as light as possible. Place heavy things on the bottom and leave three to four inches of *freeboard* or clear space below the gunwales. Pack your duffel under the thwarts, if possible, and tie it so it can't slip about and throw the canoe off balance and so you won't lose it if you should capsize. The weight should be distributed so that, with passengers and duffel aboard, the bow rides about an inch or two higher than the stern; take the canoe, loaded with both duffel and crew, out a little distance from

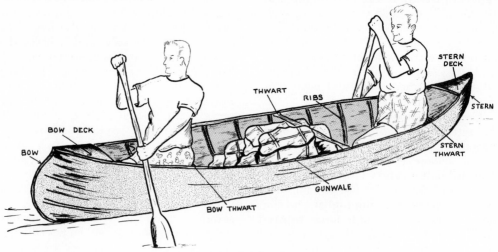

A Loaded Canoe.

shore and test it before you start on the trip. Pack the things you might want in a hurry on top.

When you are ready to take-off, the bowman steadies the bow between his legs while the sternman walks down the *exact center* of the canoe with his weight low and both hands on the gunwales. His weight in the stern raises the bow so that the bowman can push off as he enters to get the canoe into the clear and set it in motion.

Beware of sunburn; it is easy to get a bad case which will incapacitate you without realizing it, for the chances are you won't be traveling close enough to shore to have any shade whatsoever and you won't begin to feel sunburn until it's too late. Keep well covered and use a good sun tan lotion.

Keep your eye out for a good stopping place in the middle of the day and take several hours out to lunch and to refresh yourselves in the shade. Confine a large share of your paddling to the cool of early morning and evening. When putting in to shore, ease yourself in slowly for rocks or snags can do serious damage. Before disembarking, be sure your canoe is well-supported throughout its length either by beach or water; secure the canoe well by its painter if possible, so it won't be washed away. Never leave a canoe moored very long in the water, especially in a breeze or waves for lashing about on pebbles or rocks can soon damage it or even wear a hole through it and it may be washed away. Bring it onto the shore and carry, don't drag it, to position. Turn it upside down well away from shore so it won't be blown back into the water and lost.

An experienced and prudent canoeist should be chosen to be in the lead-canoe as the group progresses down the water with the second most experienced acting as "tail" man. A system of hand signals should be worked out to convey messages and all should understand that they are to be immediately and implicitly obeyed.

Safety

A canoe is, for its size, one of the safest means of water travel for it won't capsize if you use it properly, and even if it should, you are in no danger *if* you'll hang on, for, even when filled with water, a canoe will support three or four people. The main thing is to swim to it, catch hold and stay with it, for it is just as foolish to abandon it and try to swim to shore as it would be to throw away a life preserver. Hang on with one hand and paddle to shore with the other; in fact, if there's a wind or current, you'll probably be carried there without any effort on your part. If you've fastened your duffel to the canoe, it will be coming right along with you. This is all fine and dandy but it is still better not to capsize in the first place; here are some hints to help prevent it.

Never paddle in unknown water after dark unless an emergency necessitates it.

Change seats only in shallow water and, if you must move around, keep your weight as low as possible and right in the center of the canoe with your hands on both gunwales. Move slowly and deliberately. Save your horse play for land—a canoe is no place for it!

On large bodies of water, stay close to shore. Learn to anticipate changes in the weather. (In some circumstances you might even want to carry a small portable radio for getting weather reports.) Get *off* the water if a storm is approaching. It is particularly dangerous to remain on water during squalls or lightning as well as winds. If necessary to continue paddling during a light sprinkle, raise your duffel a little off the floor, if possible, and cover it with an extra tarp or ground cloth. If you should ever be so unfortunate as to be caught in rough water, sit on the floor to keep your weight low and keep paddling for you must maintain your canoe at an angle to the waves instead of letting it get crosswise to minimize the danger of shipping water and swamping. If you should lose a paddle, kneel and paddle with your hand. In a real emergency, you can use two poles crosswise to lash two canoes broadside; lash them exactly parallel to make them more seaworthy.

Never wear heavy or tight clothing or weight yourself down with knives, axes, heavy shoes or rubber boots lest you suddenly be thrown into the water and have to swim for it. Avoid overloading your canoe.

If it comes to a question of whether to portage or paddle through white water, don't hesitate; portage! It will give you a chance to stretch your legs as well as insure your safety. Recall our red brothers' saying, "No Indian ever drowned on a portage." You had also better portage than proceed through rock strewn waters for you can easily do irreparable damage to your canoe. For a two-man portage, invert your canoe and place one person at the bow who supports the canoe above his shoulder and chooses the path, while his companion gets under the canoe, supports it over his head and follows. For a short portage, you can carry the canoe upright with one person at each end grasping it underneath. Counselors and senior campers will probably prefer the one man carry.

> Thus the Birch Canoe was builded
> In the valley by the river,
> In the bosom of the forest;
> And the forest's life was in it,
> All its mystery and its magic,
> All the lightness of the birch tree,
> All the toughness of the cedar,
> All the larch's supple sinews;
> And it floated on the river
> Like a yellow leaf in Autumn
> Like a yellow water lily.
>
> LONGFELLOW,
> *The Song of Hiawatha.*

ADDITIONAL READINGS

Brower, David R.: *Going Light—With Backpack or Burro.* Sierra Club, 1953, $3.00.

Burke, Edmund H.: *Camping Handbook.* Arco Publications.

Camping. Boy Scouts #3256, 25¢.

Cycling. Boy Scouts #3277, 25¢.

Des Grey, Arthur H.: *Camping.*

Henderson, Luis M.: *The Outdoor Guide.*

Joy, Barbara Ellen: *Camp Craft.*

Joy, Barbara Ellen: *Care of Food and Equipment on Trips.* Camp Publications, 10 pp., 40¢.

Joy, Barbara Ellen: *Organization of the Camp Craft Program in the Camp.* Camp Publications #55, 4 pp., 25¢.

Joy, Barbara Ellen: *Overnight Trips—Yes and No.* Camp Publications #56, 12 pp., 45¢.

Joy, Barbara Ellen: *Packing Food for Trips.* Camp Publications #59, 4 pp., 25¢.

Joy, Barbara Ellen: *Progressive Scale of Skills for Trip Requirements.* Camp Publications #60, 6 pp., 35¢.

Koller, Larry: *Complete Book of Camping and the Outdoors.*

Lindholm, Major Mauno A.: *Camping and Outdoor Fun.*

Lynn, Gordon: *Camping and Camp Crafts.*

Peterson, Doris T.: *Your Family Goes Camping.*

Rutstrum, Calvin: *The New Way of the Wilderness.*

Tobitt, Janet E.: *Program in Girl Scouts Camping.*

Weaver, Robert W., and Merrill, Anthony F.: *Camping Can Be Fun.*

Webb, Kenneth B., Editor: *Light From a Thousand Campfires.*

Whelen, Townsend, and Angier, Bradford: *On Your Own in the Wilderness.*

MAGAZINE ARTICLES

Cumbee, Frances: *Basic Campcraft Skills.* J.H., P.E., and R., June, 1951.

DeWitt: *Your Camp's Overnight Hikes.* C.M., June, 1950.

Hake, Margaret L.: *19 Campers and How They Grew.* C.M., May, 1953.

Harris, Frank W.: *Hosteling—It's Place in Your Camp Program.* C.M., Mar., 1957.

Joy, Barbara Ellen: *Care of Food and Equipment on Trips.* C.M., Jan., Feb., 1941.

Joy, Barbara Ellen: *Consistent Careful Maintenance of Equipment Leads to Successful Campcraft Program.* C.M., Nov., 1952.

Ohberg, Mrs. Hjordis G.: *A Successful Tripping Program.* C.M., Jan., 1958.

Paxson, C. G.: *Po-Tiki On a Budget.* C.M., May, 1952.

Thompson, George: *Well Planned and Coordinated Trail Trips Teach More Then Skills.* C.M., Feb., 1959.

Thompson, George: *Your Campers Can Go Camping.* C.M., March, 1956.

Thompson, Millicent: *A Camp Dietitian Looks at Trips.* C.M., April, 1952.

Canoe Trips

(See also pages 181–182)

Bucher, Charles, Editor: *Methods and Material in Physical Education and Recreation.*

Handel, Carle W.: *Canoe Camping:* A Guide to Wilderness Travel. The Ronald Press Co., 1955, 288 pp., $3.00.

Henderson, Luis M.: *The Outdoor Guide.*

Holden, John L.: *The Canoe Cruiser's Handbook.*
Jaeger, Ellsworth: *Land and Water Trails.*
Jaeger, Ellsworth: *Wildwood Wisdom.*
Lloyd, Douglas: *Some Thoughts on Canoe Trip Camping.* Ontario Camping Ass'n., 4 pp.
Pohndorf, Richard H.: *Camp Waterfront Programs and Management.* Assn Press, 1960, 266 pp., $7.50.
Primitive Camp Sanitation. Girl Scouts, Flip Charts #15-03, $6.00.
Rutstrum, Calvin: *New Way of the Wilderness.*
Wells, George and Iris: *The Handbook of Wilderness Travel.*

MAGAZINE ARTICLES

Olson, Sigurd F.: *Let's Take a Canoe Trip.* Recreation, Feb., 1954.
Simone, Irwin: *Careful Plans Make Canoe Trips Fun.* C.M., Mar., 1959.
Van Wagner: *Planning A Canoe Trip Program.* C.M., Jan., 1957.

SOURCES OF INFORMATION CONCERNING CAMPING AND HIKING AREAS

American Youth Hostels, Inc., National Headquarters, 14 West Eighth St., New York 11, N.Y.
Appalachian Trail Conference, 1916 Sunderland Place, Washington 6, D.C.
Canadian Parks. Canadian Government Travel Bureau, Ottawa, Canada.

Ford Treasury of Station Wagon Living. Golden Books, VOL. I, 1300 Camping Grounds in United States; VOL. II, Canadian Camping Grounds, $2.95 each.
Pacific Crest Trailway. Pacific Crest Trailway Conference, Pasadena, Calif.
Recreational Areas of the U.S. Rand McNally and Co., Map 34" x 52". Key guide containing addresses of state and national agencies from which obtain information on Campsites in United States and Canada. Obtain from Times Week Magazine, P.O. Box 239, Radio City Station, New York 19, New York, $1.00.
Rhodes, Glenn and Dale: *Camping Maps, U.S.A.; A Booklet of Maps.* Authors, Box 162 Upper Montclair, New Jersey, $1.95. Indicates major camping sites in each of the 48 states.
Superintendent of Documents, United States Government Printing Office, Washington 25, D.C.
Camping Facilities of the National Park Service. (15¢)
Campsites in United States National Parks and National Forests.
National Forest Vacations. (30¢)
Wells, George and Iris: *The Handbook of Wilderness Travel.* Harper and Brothers, 1956, 306 pp., $4.00. (Contains general information and also information concerning some 300 wilderness areas and 1,000 trails over the entire United States.)
Wilderness Trails. Boy Scouts #3585, 1956, 59 pp., 75¢. Most famous trails in each state; where to start and finish, length, food and wood supply, shelters, whom to contact, etc.

Selected
General Bibliography

Benson, Reuel A., and Goldberg, Jacob A.: *The Camp Counselor*. McGraw-Hill Book Co., 1951, 337 pp., $5.50.

Berg, B. Robert: *Psychology in Children's Camping*. Vantage Press, Inc., 1958, 156 pp., $3.00.

Bucher, Charles: *Methods and Materials in Physical Education and Recreation*. The C. V. Mosby Co., 1954, 432 pp., $4.00.

Burke, Edmund H.: *Camping Handbook*. Arco Publishing Co., 1955, 144 pp., $2.00.

Burns, Gerald: *Program of the Modern Camp*. Prentice-Hall, Inc., 1954, 320 pp.

Corbin, H. Dan: *Recreation Leadership*. Prentice-Hall, Inc., 1953, 465 pp., $6.50.

Des Grey, Arthur H.: *Camping*. The Ronald Press Co., 1950, 171 pp., $4.00.

Dimock, Hedley S.: *Administration of the Modern Camp*. Assn. Press, 1948, 294 pp., $5.00.

Dimock, Hedley S., and Statten, Taylor: *Talks to Counselors*. Assn. Press, 1939, 75¢.

Doherty, J. Kenneth: *Solving Camp Behavior Problems*. Assn. Press, 1944, 62 pp., $1.00.

Doty, Richard S.: *The Character Dimension of Camping*. Assn. Press, 1960, 192 pp., $4.75.

Eisenberg, Helen and Larry: *Omnibus of Fun*. Assn. Press, 1956, 625 pp., $7.95.

Geist, Roland C.: *Hiking, Camping and Mountaineering*. Harper and Brothers, 1943, (Out of Print).

Goodrich, Lois: *Decentralized Camping*. Assn. Press, 1959, 256 pp., $4.75.

Hammett, Catherine T., and Musselman, Virginia: *The Camp Program Book*. Assn. Press, 1951, 380 pp., $5.00.

Hammett, Catherine T., and Horrocks, Carol M.: *Creative Crafts for Campers*. Assn. Press, 1957, 431 pp., $7.95.

Harbin, E. O.: *The Fun Encyclopedia*. Abingdon Press, 1940, 1,000 pp., $3.95.

Henderson, Luis M.: *The Outdoor Guide*. Stackpole Co., 1950, 350 pp., $5.00.

Hood, Mary V.: *Outdoor Hazards, Real and Fancied*. The Macmillan Co., 1955, 242 pp., $3.95.

Holden, John L.: *The Canoe Cruiser's Handbook*, John L. Holden, 2530 Salem Ave., Cincinnati 8, Ohio.

Hunt, W. Ben: *Indian Crafts and Lore*. Golden Books, 1954, 112 pp., $1.50.

Hurlock, Elizabeth B.: *Adolescent Development*. McGraw-Hill Book Co., 2nd Ed., 1955, 590 pp.

Irwin, Frank L.: *The Theory of Camping—An Introduction to Camping in Education*. The Ronald Press, Co., 1950, 178 pp., $3.75.

Jaeger, Ellsworth: *Council Fires.* The Macmillan Co., 1949, 253 pp., $2.95.

Jaeger, Ellsworth: *Land and Water Trails.* The Macmillan Co., 1953, 227 pp., $2.95.

Jaeger, Ellsworth: *Wildwood Wisdom.* The Macmillan Co., 1948, 228 pp., $4.75.

Jaeger, Ellsworth: *Woodsmoke.* The Macmillan Co., 1953, 228 pp., $2.95.

Joy, Barbara Ellen: *Camp Craft.* Burgess Publishing Co., 1955, 86 pp., $2.75.

Joy, Barbara Ellen: *Camping.* Burgess Publishing Co., 1957, 84 pp., $2.75.

Kesting, Ted: *The Outdoor Encyclopedia.* A. S. Barnes and Co., Inc., 1957, 433 pp., $7.50.

Koller, Larry: *Complete Book of Camping and the Outdoors.* Random House, Inc., 1957, 128 pp., $2.95.

Kraus, Richard: *Recreation Leader's Handbook.* McGraw-Hill Book Co., 1955, 312 pp., $4.75.

Laird, Donald A., and Laird, Eleanor C.: *The New Psychology for Leadership.* McGraw-Hill Book Co., 226 pp., $4.00.

Ledlie, John A., and Holbein, F. W.: *Camp Counselor's Manual.* Assn. Press, Revised, 1958, 128 pp., $1.25.

Lindholm, Major Mauno A.: *Camping and Outdoor Fun.* Hart Publishing Co., 1959, 192 pp.

Lynn, Gordon: *Camping and Camp Crafts.* Golden Books, 1959, 112 pp., $1.95.

MacFarlan, Allan A.: *Campfire and Council Ring Programs.* Assn. Press, 1951, 155 pp., $2.50.

Mason, Bernard S.: *Dances and Stories of the American Indian.* The Ronald Press, Co., 1944, 269 pp., $5.50.

Mason, Bernard S.: *The Junior Book of Camping and Woodcraft.* The Ronald Press, Co., 1943, 120 pp., $4.50.

Mason, Bernard S.: *The Book of Indian Crafts and Costumes.* The Ronald Press, Co., 1946, 118 pp., $5.50.

Mitchell, Elmer D., Editor: *Sports for Recreation.* The Ronald Press, Co., 1952, 522 pp., $6.50.

Moser, Clarence: *Understanding Boys.* Assn. Press, 1953, 190 pp., $2.50.

Moser, Clarence: *Understanding Girls.* Assn. Press, 1957, 252 pp., $3.50.

Mulac, Margaret: *The Play Leader's Manual.* Harper and Brothers, 1941, $3.00.

Murray, Janet P., and Clyde E.: *Guide Lines for Group Leaders.* Whiteside, Inc., 1954, 224 pp., $3.95.

Ott, Elmer F.: *So You Want To Be a Camp Counselor.* Assn. Press, 1946, 63 pp., $1.00.

Peterson, Doris T.: *Your Family Goes Camping.* Abingdon Press, 1959, 160 pp., $2.50.

Pohndorf, Richard H.: *Camp Waterfront Programs and Management.* Assn. Press, 1960, 266 pp., $7.50.

Ressler, Theodore Whitson: *Treasury of American Indian Tales.* Assn. Press, 1958, 310 pp., $3.95.

Roberts, Dorothy M.: *Leadership of Teen-Age Groups.* Assn. Press, 1950, 195 pp., $3.50.

Rutstrum, Calvin: *The New Way of the Wilderness.* The Macmillan Co., 1958, 276 pp., $4.50.

Safety-Wise. Girl Scouts, 86 pp., 20¢.

Swanson, William E.: *Camping for All It's Worth.* The Macmillan Co., 1952, 154 pp., $2.49.

Teicher, Joseph: *Your Child and His Problems.* Little Brown and Co., 1953, $3.75.

Thurston, La Rue A.: *Complete Book of Campfire Programs.* Assn. Press, 1958, 318 pp., $5.95.

Tobitt, Janet E.: *Program in Girl Scout Camping.* Girl Scouts, 1959, 277 pp., $1.50.

Vannier, Maryhelen: *Methods and Materials in Recreation Leadership.* W. B. Saunders Co., 1956, 288 pp., $4.25.

Vinal, William G.: *Nature Recreation. American Humane Society.* 180 Longwood Ave., Boston 15, Mass., 1954, 322 pp., $3.50.

Weaver, Robert W., and Merrill, Anthony F.: *Camping Can Be Fun.* Harper and Brothers, 1948, (Out of Print).

Webb, Kenneth B., Editor: *Light From a Thousand Campfires.* Assn. Press, 1960, 384 pp.

Wells, George and Iris: *The Handbook of Wilderness Travel.* Harper and Brothers, 1956, 306 pp., $4.00.

West, James E., and Hillcourt, William: *Scout Field Book.* Boy Scouts, 1948, 540 pp., $1.25.

Whelen, Townsend, and Angier, Bradford: *On Your Own in the Wilderness.* Stackpole Co., 1958, 324 pp., $5.00.

Wittenberg, Rudolph: *Adolescence and Discipline. A Mental Hygiene Primer.* Assn. Press, 1959, 320 pp., $4.95.

Wittenberg, Rudolph M.: *How To Help People.* Assn. Press, 1953, $1.00.

Zarchy, Harry: *Let's Go Camping.* Alfred A. Knopf, Inc., 1951, $3.25.

Directory of
Publishers and Organizations

AAHPER: American Association for Health, Physical Education, and Recreation, 1201 16th St., N.W., Washington 6, D.C.

Abingdon: Abingdon Press, 810 Broadway, Nashville 2, Tenn.

ACA: American Camping Association, Bradford Woods, Martinsville, Ind.

ALA: American Library Association, 50 E. Huron St., Chicago 11, Ill.

Am. Art Clay: American Art Clay Company Indianapolis 24, Ind.

Am. Canoe Ass'n: American Canoe Association, 8224 S. Woodlawn Ave., Chicago, Ill.

Am. Forestry Ass'n: American Forestry Association, Washington 6, D.C.

American Forest. Products Industries, Inc., 1816 N St. N.W., Washington 6, D.C.

American Squares, 1161 Broad St., Newark 5, N.J.

American Youth Hostels, 14 W. 8th Street, New York 11, N.Y.

Antioch: Antioch Press, Yellow Springs, Ohio.

Appleton: Appleton-Century-Crofts, Inc., 35 W. 32nd St., New York 1, N.Y.

ARC: American National Red Cross, 17th and D St., Washington 6, D.C.

Arco: Arco Publishing Co., Inc., 480 Lexington Ave., New York 7, N.Y.

Ass'n. for Childhood Ed.: Association for Childhood Education, 1200 15 St., N.W., Washington 5, D.C.

Assn. Press: Association Press, 291 Broadway, New York 7, N.Y.

Audubon: National Audubon Society, 1130 Fifth Ave., New York 28, N.Y.

Bantam Books: Bantam Books, Inc., 25 W. 45th St., New York 36, N.Y.

Barnes: A. S. Barnes & Company, 232 Madison Ave., New York 16, N.Y.

Barnes & Noble: Barnes & Noble, Inc., 105 5th Ave., New York 3, N.Y.

Barrows: M. Barrows & Company, Inc., 425 4th Ave., New York 1, N.Y.

Bennett: Charles A. Bennett Co., Inc., 2808 Duroc Bldg., Peoria, Ill.

The Bobbs-Merrill Co., Inc., 468 Forth Ave., New York 16, N.Y.

Botanic: Botanic Publishing Company, Box 724, Dept. TLA, Cincinnati 1, Ohio.

Boys' Clubs: Boys' Clubs of America, 381 4th Ave., New York 16, N.Y.

Boy Scouts: Boy Scouts of America, New Brunswick, N.J.

Branford: Charles T. Branford Company, 69 Union St., Newton Center 59, Mass.

Broadman: The Broadman Press, 127 Ninth Ave., North, Nashville 13, Tenn.

Brown: W. C. Brown Co., Dubuque, Iowa.

Bruce: Bruce Publishing Company, 400 N. Broadway, Milwaukee 1, Wis.; 330 W. 42nd St., New York, N.Y.

Burgess: Burgess Publishing Company, 426 S. 6th St., Minneapolis 15, Minn.

Camp Archery: Camp Archery Association, 200 Coligni Ave., New Rochelle, N.Y.

Camp Fire Girls: Camp Fire Girls, Inc., 450 Avenue of the Americans, New York 11, N.Y.

Camp Publications: Camp Publications, 6 High St. Bar Harbor, Maine.

C.M.: Camping Magazine, Published by the American Camping Ass'n., Brodford Woods, Martinsville, Ind.

Capitol: Capitol Publishing Co., 737 Broadway, New York 3, N.Y.

Children's Bureau Publication: Supt. of Documents, Government Printing Office, Washington 25, D.C.

Childrens' Press, Jackson Blvd. and Racine Ave., Chicago 7, Ill.

Children's Theatre Press: Children's Theatre Press, Anchorage, Kentucky.

Chilton: Chilton Co., 56th & Chestnut Sts., Philadelphia 39, Pa.

Citadel: Citadel Press, 222 4th Ave., New York 3, N.Y.

Coop. Rec. Service: Cooperative Recreation Service, Rodnor Road, Delaware, Ohio.

Cornell: Cornell University Press, 124 Roberts Place, Ithaca, N.Y.

Cornell Maritime: Cornell Maritime Press, Cambridge, Md.

Crowell: Thomas Y. Crowell Company, 432 4th Ave., New York 16, N.Y.

Crown: Crown Publishers, 419 4th Ave., New York 16, N.Y.

Davis: Davis Press, Inc., 44 Portland St., Worchester, Mass.

Daye: Stephen Daye Press, Inc., 105 E. 24th St., New York 10, N.Y.

De Graff: John De Graff, Inc., 64 W. 23rd St., New York 10, N.Y.

Dell: Dell Publishing Co., 261 Fifth Ave., New York 16, N.Y.

Denison: T. S. Denison & Co., 321 Fifth Ave. S., Minneapolis 15, Minn.

Devin-Adair: The Devin-Adair Publishing Company, 23 E. 26th St., New York 10, N.Y.

Dodd: Dodd, Mead & Company, Inc., 432 4th Ave., New York 16, N.Y.

Doubleday: Doubleday & Company, Inc., 575 Madison Ave., New York 22, N.Y.

Dover: Dover Publications, Inc., 920 Broadway, New York 10, N.Y.

Dutton: E. P. Dutton & Company, Inc., 300 4th Ave., New York 16, N.Y.

Eastman: Eastman Kodak Co., 343 State St., Rochester 4, N.Y.

Edmund: Edmund Scientific Corp., Barrington, N.J.

Edwards: J. W. Edwards, Publishers, Inc., Ann Arbor, Michigan.

Emerson: Emerson Books, Inc., 251 W. 19th St., New York 11, N.Y.

Exposition: The Exposition Press, Inc., 386 4th Ave., New York.

Fawcett: Fawcett Books, Greenwich, Conn.

Fisherman: The Fisherman Press, Inc., Oxford, Ohio.

Friendship: Friendship Press, 257 4th Ave., New York 10, N.Y.

Ginn: Ginn and Company, Statler Bldg., Boston 17, Mass.

Girl Scouts: Girl Scouts of the U. S. A., 830 Third Ave., New York 22, N.Y.

Golden Press, 630 Fifth Ave., New York 20, N.Y.

Goodheart-Wilcox: The Goodheart-Wilcox Company, Inc., 1332 S. Wabash Ave., Chicago 5, Ill.

Greenberg: Greenberg, Publishers, Inc., 201 East 57th St., New York 22, N.Y.

Hanover: Hanover House, 575 Madison Ave., New York 22, N.Y.

Harcourt: Harcourt, Brace, and Company, 383 Madison Ave., New York 17, N.Y.

Harlem Book Co., 221 Fourth Ave., New York 3, N.Y.

Harper: Harper & Brothers, 49 East 33rd St., New York 16, N.Y.

Hart: Hart Publishing Co., Inc., 670 Fifth Ave., New York 19, N.Y.

Harvard: Harvard University Press, Cambridge 38, Mass.

Hawthorn: Hawthorn Books, Inc., Englewood Clifts, N.J.

Hearthside: Hearthside Press, 118 E. 28th St., New York 16, N.Y.

Heath: D. C. Heath & Co., 285 Columbus Ave., Boston 16, Mass.

Hill and Wang: Hill and Wang, Inc., 194 Fifth Ave., New York 11, N.Y.

Holden: John L. Holden, 2530 Salem Ave., Cincinnati 8, Ohio.

Holiday: Holiday House, 8 W. 13th St., New York 11, N.Y.

Holt: Henry Holt and Company, Inc., 383 Madison Ave., New York 17, N.Y.

Houghton: Houghton Mifflin Company, 2 Park St., Boston 7, Mass.

Interstate: The Interstate Printers and Publishers, 19–27 North Jackson St., Danville, Ill.

Johnson: Johnson Publishing Co., Lincoln, Nebraska.

J. H. and P. E.: Journal of Health, Physical Education and Recreation, published by The American Association for Health, Physical Education, and Recreation, 1201 16th St., N.W., Washington 6, D.C.

Judd: Orange Judd Publishing Company, Inc., 15 E. 26th St., New York 10, N.Y.

Kamin: Kamin Publishers, 1365 Sixth Ave., New York.

Knopf: Alfred A. Knopf, Inc., 501 Madison Ave., New York 22, N.Y.

LaVee: LaVee Studio, 22 E. 29th St., New York 16, N.Y.

Lippincott: J. B. Lippincott Company, 227–231 S. 6th St., Philadelphia 5, Pa.; 521 5th Ave., New York 17, N.Y.; 333 W. Lake St., Chicago 6, Ill.

Little: Little, Brown and Company, 34 Beacon St., Boston, Mass.

Lothrop: Lothrop, Lee & Shepard Company, 419 4th Ave., New York 10, N.Y.

Macmillan: The Macmillan Company, 60 5th Ave., New York 11, N.Y.; 2459 Prairie Ave., Chicago 16, Ill.

McCall: McCall's, P. O. Box 1390, New York 17, N.Y.

McGraw-Hill: McGraw-Hill Book Company, Inc., 330 West 42nd St., New York 36, N.Y.

McKay: David McKay Company, Inc., 55 Fifth Ave., New York 3, N.Y.

McKnight: McKnight & McKnight Publishing Co., 109 W. Market St., Bloomington, Ill.

Maco: Maco Magazine Corporation, 480 Lexington Ave., New York 17, N.Y.

Morgan: Morgan & Morgan, Publishers, Scarsdale, New York.

Morrow: William Morrow & Company, Inc., 425 4th Ave., New York 1, N.Y.

Mosby: C. V. Mosby Company, 3207 Washington Blvd., St. Louis 3, Mo.

National Wildlife Federation: National Wildlife Federation, 232 Carroll At., N.W., Washington 12, D. C.

Naturegraph; Naturegraph Company, P. O. Box 46, San Martin, Calif.

New Am. Lib.: New American Library of World Literature, Inc., 501 Madison Ave., New York 22, N.Y.

New England Camping Association, Inc., 110 Tremont St., Boston 8, Mass.

Northwestern Pr.: Northwestern Press, 315 Fifth Ave., South, Minneapolis, Minn.

NRA: National Recreation Association, 8 W. Eighth St., New York 11, N.Y.

Oceana: Oceana Publications, 80 4th Ave., New York 3, N.Y.

Ontario Camping Association, 93 Yorkville Ave., Toronto 5, Canada.

Outboard Boating: Outboard Boating Club of America, 307 N. Michigan Ave., Chicago 1, Ill.

Pantheon: Pantheon Books, Inc., 333 Sixth Ave., New York 14, N.Y.

Philosophical: Philosophical Library, Inc., 15 E. 40th St., New York 16, N.Y.

Pilgrim: Pilgrim Press, 14 Beacon St., Boston 8, Mass.

Pitman Publishing Corporation, 2 W. 45th St., New York 36, N.Y.

Plays: Plays, Inc., 8 Arlington St., Boston 16, Mass.

Pocket Books, Inc., International Building, Rockefeller Center, New York.

Pop. Mechanics: Popular Mechanics Press, 200 E. Ontario St., Chicago 11, Ill.

Pop. Sci.: Popular Science Publishing Co., 353 Fourth Ave., New York 10, N.Y.

Prentice-Hall: Prentice-Hall, Inc., Englewood Cliffs, N.J.

Public Affairs: Public Affairs Press, 22 E. 38th St., New York 16, N.Y.

Putnam: G. P. Putnam's Sons, Inc., 210 Madison Ave., New York 16, N.Y.

Radio Corporation of America, Camden, N.J.

Random: Random House, Inc., 457 Madison Ave., New York 22, N.Y.

Rec.: Recreation, monthly magazine published by the National Recreation Association, 8 W. Eighth St., New York 11, N.Y.

Reinhold: Reinhold Publishing Corporation, 430 Park Ave., New York 22, N.Y.

Ronald: The Ronald Press Co., 15 E. 26th St., New York 10, N.Y.

Row: Row, Peterson and Company, Evanston, Ill.

Roy: Roy Publishers, 30 E. 74th St., New York 21, N.Y.

Sage: Sage Books, 2679 S. York St., Denver 10, Colo.

Saunders: W. B. Saunders Company, W. Washington Square, Philadelphia 5, Pa.

School Products: School Products Co., 330 E. 23rd St., New York 10, N.Y.

Scott: W. R. Scott, Inc., 8 W 13th St., New York 11, N.Y.

Scribner: Charles Scribner's Sons, 597 5th Ave., New York 17, N.Y.

Sentinel: Sentinel Books, 112 E. 19th St., New York 3, N.Y.

Sheridan: Sheridan House, 257 4th Ave., New York 10, N.Y.

Sierra: Sierra Club, 1050 Mills Tower, San Francisco 4, Calif.

Silva, Inc., Laporte, Ind.

Simon and Schuster, Inc., Rockefeller Center, New York 20, N.Y.

Slingerland: Slingerland-Comstock Company, R. F. D. No. 1, Warren Road, Ithaca 3, New York.

Sloane: William Sloane Associates, Inc., 425 Fourth Ave., New York 16, N.Y.

Smithsonian; Smithsonian Institution, Washington 25, D.C.

Spencer; Spencer Press, Inc., 153 N. Michigan Ave., Chicago 1, Ill.

Sportshelf, 10 Overlook Terrace, New York 33, N.Y.

Stackpole: Stackpole Co., Telegraph Press Bldg., Harrisburg, Pa.

Sterling: Sterling Publishing Co., Inc., 215 E. 37th St., New York 16, N.Y.

Studio: The Studio Publications, Inc., 432 Fourth Ave., New York 16, N.Y.

Studio Crowell: Thomas Y. Crowell Co., 432 Fourth Ave., New York 16, N.Y.

Supt. of Documents: Superintendent of Documents, U. S. Government Printing Office, Washington 25, D.C.

Tandy: Tandy Leather Co., 300 Throckmorton St., Fort Worth, Texas.

U. of Ill.: University of Illinois Press, Urbana, Illinois.

U. of Mich.: University of Michigan Press, Ann Arbor, Michigan.

U. of New Mexico: University of New Mexico Press, Albuquerque, N. Mex.

U. S. Naval Inst.: U. S. Naval Institute, Annapolis Md.

Van Nostrand: D. Van Nostrand Company, Inc., 120 Alexander St., Princeton, N.J.

Van Roy: Carl Van Roy Co., 2917 Ave., R., Brooklyn 29, N.Y.

Vantage: Vantage Press, Inc., 120 W. 31st St., New York 1, N.Y.

Viking: The Viking Press, 625 Madison Ave., New York 22, N.Y.

Vinal: William Vinal, Vinehall, R.D. 2, Norwell, Mass.

Watson: Watson-Guptill Publications, Inc., 24 W. 40th St., New York 18, N.Y.

Watts: Franklin Watts, Inc., 699 Madison Ave., New York 21, N.Y.

Whiteside: Whiteside Press, Inc., 425 4th Ave., New York 16, N.Y.

Wilson: The H. W. Wilson Company, 950–972 University Ave., New York 52, N.Y.

World: World Publishing Co., 2231 W. 110th St., Cleveland 2, Ohio.

X-Acto: X-Acto, Inc., 48–99 Van Dorn St., Long Island City 1, New York.

Y.W.C.A. Publications Services, 600 Lexington Ave., New York 22, N.Y.

Zondervan: Zondervan Publishing House, 1415 Lake Drive, S. E., Grand Rapids, Michigan.

Films and Slides Pertaining to Camping

The number of films and slides which could be used in a camping situation is almost unlimited. No attempt has been made to include an exhaustive list but rather to include only those particularly pertinent to the camping situation.

ABBREVIATIONS USED

AAH, PE and R—American Ass'n for Health, Physical Education and Recreation.
A-D—Avalon-Daggett Productions.
ARC—American Red Cross.
EBF—Encyclopedia Brittanica Films, Inc.
FLM ASSOC—Film Associates.
IFB—International Film Bureau.
IND. U.—Indiana University.
LIFE—Life Camps, Inc.
McGRAW—McGraw-Hill Book Company.
NFB—National Film Board of Canada.
SILVA—Silva, Inc.
S-M—Simmel-Meservey.
TFC—Teaching Film Custodians.
USDA—United States Dept. of Agriculture.
UW—United World Films.
YA—Young America.

The following abbreviations are used to show the age groupings of campers for whom the film will be most useful:

> pri (primary)—ages 6–8
> int (intermediate)—ages 9–12
> jh (junior high)—ages 13–15
> sh (senior high)—ages 16–18
> col (college)—college and adult

Combinations denote that the film can be employed for campers of the first-designated group through those of the last-mentioned category; for example, jh-col means that the film is usable for campers of the junior high through adult group.

PROCURING FILMS

The firm name given is that of the producer of the film who ordinarily sells but does not rent films, but he can often furnish a list of sources for renting them. School principals or equipment dealers can also furnish information, and comprehensive lists of film libraries are issued periodically and may be available at your local library. The most complete list of available sources, classified by state and community, is *A Directory of 16mm Film Libraries*. The H. W. Wilson Co.'s *Educational Film Guide* contains the most complete list of films currently available for sale, rental, and/or free loan.

Arts and Crafts

ABC's of Pottery Making (Coil Method)—11 min., sd., b&w, (jh-col). Making of bowl; use of templet pattern, hand tools, and potter's wheel; finishing; baking. (Bailey).

Adventures in Modern Leathercraft—13½ min., sd., color. (Tandy, free loan).

Adventuring in the Arts—22 min., sd., color. Crayon etching, patchwork pictures, papier-mâché, music, and pantomime. (Girl Scouts).

The Art of Leathercarving—22 min., sd., color. Shows that with today's assortment of stamping tools, you need not be a "born" artist to do satisfactory work. (Tandy, free loan).

Craftsmanship in Clay—4 films, 11 min. each, sd., color. Techniques for using materials that come out of the camp environment. (Ind. U.)

How To Make a Simple Loom and Weave—(pri-col). Making the frame, adding nails for warp string, stringing the loom and weaving with a variety of materials. (EBF).

How To Make Papier Mâché Animals—12 min., color, (pri-col). (Bailey).

Loom Weaving—6 min., sd., color, (jh-col). Art teacher and manual training teacher cooperate to help students build loom out of old broom and a few pieces of wood. Some techniques also shown. (IFB).

Making Indian Mocassins—17 min., sd., color. From selection of hide to first fitting shown by Ben Hunt. (Boy Scouts).

Making a Pack Basket—2 reels, sd., color. "Pop Williams" shows construction of a large pack basket from a green tree. Can be adapted to weaving of commercially prepared materials. (Boy Scouts).

Painting: Learning To Use Your Brush—sd., b&w. Materials and basic brush strokes for the beginner. (YA).

Portage—20 min., sd., color. The making of a birch bark canoe. (NFB).

Pottery Making—11 min., sd., (int-col). Coil method of making Indian bowl from the preparation of the clay to the finished product. (EFB).

Sculpturing is Fun—10 min., b&w. Shows how to make a number of creations from an ordinary bar of soap. (UMF).

Axemanship

Axemanship—9 min., sd., b&w. Peter McLarin demonstrates the use and care of various types of axes. How to chop down a tree, split logs, and cut firewood. (Boy Scouts).

Boating

Boats, Motors and People—30 min., sd., b&w or color. Emphasis on safety. (ARC).

Oars and Paddles—24 min., sd., (int-col). Proper use of rowboats and canoes—launching and getting underway, handling oars, how to save self when boat overturns, boat rescue of swimmers, canoe paddling strokes, etc. (ARC).

Small Craft Safety—14 min., color. Gives common causes of boating accidents and how to prevent them. Also shows rescue methods and life-saving techniques. (Herbert Kerkow, Inc., 480 Lexington Ave., New York 17, N.Y.).

Camping

Adventures at Day Camp—20 min., sd., b&w. Activities of a Brownie, Intermediate, and Senior Scout. (Girl Scouts).

Boy's Day Camp—2 reels, color. Shows rich and varied program possible. (Y.M.C.A. Day Camp program of Rochester, N.Y.).

Camp Time, Any Time!—22 min., sd., color. Camping including nature mobile, rock collecting, clearing a stream, weather station, clay firing, canoeing, waterfront, trail signs, primitive unit, songs, etc. (Girl Scouts).

Camping Slide Films—1959, two slide film units. Campfires, how to fry, bake, and boil meals over red-hot coals. Fundamentals of camp safety. Directed by Betty Staley. (Athletic Institute).

Hosteling Holiday—26 min., sd., color. Story of a group of boys and girls in a youth hostel who bike and hike through New England. (AYH).

Let's Go Troop Camping—20 min., sd., b&w. How a leader works with her troop in preparing for a trip. (Girl Scouts).

The Handicapped Go Camping—10 min., (sh-col). Typical incidents of a camping day. (State College of Wash.).

Counselor Training and School Camping

Camping Education—1947, 35 min., sound, color, (pri-jh-sh-col). Shows one week of camping by a 6th grade. (Loan, Paragon Motion Pict. Corp., 4770 Bancroft St., San Diego).

Camping Education—2 reels, sd., b&w, (col). The program at National Camp for training professional camp leaders. (Life).

Classroom in the Cascades—30 min., sound, color, (sh-col). Shows a well-organized camp program for a high school class. (Central Washington College of Educ., Ellensberg, Wash., loan).

Counselor Training Filmstrips—(Y.M.C.A. Program Services. Set of two, $35). Based on the Y.M.C.A. *Camp Counselor's Manual* by Ledlie and Holbein, Assn Press.

    1. *The V.I.P. in Camping*—85 frame silent cartoon concerning the philosophy and objectives of camping; the importance and functions of the counselor and how he can make his job successful and satisfying. (Assn Press).

    2. *Understanding and Helping the Camper*—87 frame, silent, color cartoon showing how to know one's campers, plan a good program with them and handle various problems with them. (Assn Press).

Education Moves Outdoors—18 min., sd., color. Shows opportunity for use of the out-of-doors as a vehicle for training teachers for pub. schools. (Audio-Visual Services Center, Northern Illinois State College, DeKalb, Ill.).

Life's Summer Camp—1948, 20 min., sound, b&w, (jh-sh-col). Shows training of teachers, administration, and youth leaders. (Life, loan).

School Time in Camp—18 min., sd., color, (int-jh). School camping experience of 5th and 7th grades of New York City. (Life).

Teacher Education in the Out-of-doors—25 min., sd., color. Features the teacher education program developed there. Senior students spent a week teaching children in a school camping situation. (Audio-Visual Center, Northern Ill. U., DeKalb).

Youth in Camps—2 reels, sd., (col). Decentralized, "Camptivity" plan of camping. (Life).

Conservation

Adventuring in Conservation—15 min., color or b&w, 1960, (int-sh). Boys and girls discover nature's community and the relationships among trees, small plants, birds, insects, etc. Results of forest fires, mutilation of trees and small plants, overuse of trails, and littering of camp sites. Conservation of resources emphasized, estinguishing campfires, diversion dams, selection of trees for cutting, planting new trees. Film from all over the United States shows young people in actual camp and conservation activities. (Ind. U.).

Adventures of Junior Raindrop—FS. 8 min., color, 1948, (pri-jh). Animated cartoon and actual scenes showing bumpy welcome to hard-packed earth, and joining other disgruntled raindrops to form torrents, gullies and other flood problems. (USDA, loan).

Conservation of Natural Resources—11 min., sd., (jh-col). Waste in water power, forests, farm lands, etc., with effective steps to control it. (EBF).

Conservation Vistas—17 min., sd., color, (col.), 1958. Classroom and outdoor activities that add interest to the teaching of conservation. (USDA).

Elementary Conservation Series—1954.
    Your Friend the Forest—6 min., color.
    Your Friend the Soil—7 min., color.
    Your Friend the Water—6 min., sd.

Every Man's Empire—18 min., sd., color, 1948, (int-col). The 150 National Forests of the U.S. and how they store water for city water supply, provide range for livestock, food for wild animals and birds, streams for fish, and recreation for people. (USDA).

Heritage We Guard, A—SCS; 50 min., b&w, 1940, (int-col.). Story of important role played by wildlife resources in the early development of the United States; the damage to soil and wildlife that accompanied our westward expansion.

The Meaning of Conservation—11 min., (int-jh). What is being done to maintain our country's resources and natural beauty by limiting hunting and fishing, building dams to control floods, planting trees, and developing new farming methods. (Coronet).

This Vital Earth—11 min., sd., color, (jh-col). Interdependence of plant and animal life and dependence of land on past living forms. (EBF).

Wildlife and the Human Touch—18 min., color, 1952, (int). Forest animals in their natural habitats in our National Forests; improvement of these habitats, and management of forests for the benefit of all who use them. (Loan, USDA).

Woodland Manners—19 min., sound, color, 1952, (int-col). The necessity for keeping forest recreational areas sanitary, attractive, and serviceable. A picnicker or camper should leave his area in as good or better condition than he found it. (Rental, Wash. State College, Pullman, Wash.).

Yours is the Land—20 min., sd., color, (jh-col). Effects of wasting natural resources, balance of plant, animal, and insect life, and dependence of man upon the land. Shows methods of conservation. (EBF).

Fires

The Art of Building a Fire—15 slides. Fifteen slides showing proper sequence of steps in building a fire. (Wards).

Fire Building and Cooking—sd., b&w. Correct techniques shown. (Boy Scouts).

First Aid

Artificial Respiration—6 min. Step-by-step demonstration of the new Back-Pressure Arm-Lift methods. (USDA).

First Aid Fundamentals—10 min., sd., 1953, (jh). Skin-wounds, burns, sprains, bruises. Back-Pressure Arm-Lift method of artificial respiration. (Coronet).

Help Wanted—22 min. Basic principles of first aid and caring for victims before the doctor arrives. Prepared under the supervision of prominent physicians and surgeons. (U.S. Pub. H. Service).

Loopfilms on Artificial Respiration—1959. Mouth-to-mouth, Back-Pressure Arm-Lift with an aid, and modified Sylvester method. (AAH, PE and R).

No Time to Spare—12 min., color, (int-col). Back-Pressure Arm-Lift method of artificial respiration demonstrated by the passer-by on the street as he encounters individuals needing it.

Fishing

Tie Your Own Flies—10 min., sd., (int-col). Shows proper technique. (Hawley-Lord).

Forest Fires

Days of a Tree—28 min., sd., color or b&w, 1956, (int-col). A boy and his dad learn of the disastrous effects of forest fires. (USDA).

It's No Picnic—26 min., sd., b&w, 1948, (int-col). A family enjoys a Sunday afternoon in the woods. The campfire is carefully extinguished but Dad unwittingly is careless with his pipe and the beautiful woods becomes a blackened waste. (USDA).

Little Smokey—FS, 12 min., color, 1953, (pri-col). The famed bear and Hopalong Cassidy tell of Smokey's crusade to prevent forest fires. (USDA).

Men, Women and Children—28 min., color or b&w, 1954. A group of school boys (Smokey Bear's Junior Forest Rangers) sets out to do something about the loss of a school forest through fire. Shows how every day unsafe habits of kindly people can cause devastating forest fires. (USDA).

One Match Can Do It—10 min., sd. Shows how one match can start a destructive forest fire, methods of fighting fire. Barren hillsides then result in floods, creating general havoc. (S-M).

The Frying Pan and the Fire—18 min., color, 1947, (int-col). Two girls, leave their campfire to photograph a deer, the fire gets out of control and destroys their new camping gear and nearly starts a disastrous forest fire. Correct and incorrect ways of fighting forest fires shown. (USDA).

Indians

Hopi Indian Arts and Crafts—11 min., (pri-jh). Weaving, silversmithing, basket making, and pottery making. (Coronet).

Hopi Indian Village Life—11 min., (pri-int). A blending of the old and new ways. (Coronet).

How Indians Build Canoes—10 min., color, (int-col). Algonquin Indians building an authentic birch bark canoe, usiny only materials supplied by the forest. (IFB).

Indian Dances—11 min., sd., color, 1952, (jh-col). Based on the keen powers of observation of the Indian as he portrays four dance patterns: the grouse, an eagle in flight, the buffalo, and the deer. Tom-tom accompaniment. (EBF).

Indian Pow-Wow—11 min., sd., color. Tribes from Southwest arrive for pow-wow by various means of conveyance. Eagle Dancers from Laguna, Devil Dancers of the Apaches, Kiowa War Dancers from Oklahoma, the Yeibechi Dancers from the Navajos. Indian rodeo at Cheyenne, Wyoming. (A-D).

Meet the Sioux Indian—10 min., sd., 1949, (int-col). Tepees erected, meat prepared as pemmican, bead work and quill work, etc. (Deusing).

Navajo Children—11 min., sd., (pri-jh), 1938. A boy and girl moving from their winter quarters to their summer home. (EBF).

The Apache Indian—11 min., (pri-int). Ceremonies, magnificent horsemanship, and love of pageantry in tribal functions. (Coronet).

The Hopi Indian—11 min., (pri-jh). Crops, food, marriage ceremony. (Coronet).

The Navajo Indian—11 min., (pri-jh). Carding, weaving, dyeing rugs, etc. (Coronet).

Smoki Snake Dance—11 min., sd., color. Prayer dances of the Indians of the Southwest. Horsetail Dance of Taos, Feather Dance of Shawnees, and Clown Dance. (A-D).

Totems—11 min., color, (int-col). Against background of tom-toms and traditional chants, shows carved and painted totems of the British Columbia Indians. (NFB).

Woodland Indians of Early Americans—11 min., (pri-int). Life before the European influence. Hunt wild turkey, harvest wild rice, fish, gather at wigwam for evening meal. (Coronet).

Knives

How To Sharpen Your Knife and Use It Safely—12 slides. Twelve slides illustrating correct techniques. (Wards).

Knifecraft—11 min., sd., b&w. Ben Hunt shows how to care for and use a pocket knife as he whittles a Katcina Dool lamp. (Boy Scouts).

Map and Compass

By Map and Compass—26 min., sd. Reading a map and using a compass. A boy and his dad explore the wilderness. Various animals are encountered. (Silva).

Maps and Their Uses—11 min., sd., 1951, (int-col). Use of symbols on maps and the use of special maps and their symbols. (Coronet).

Maps Are Fun—11 min., sd., color, 1948, (int-jh). Story of a boy who prepares a map of a paper route. Brings out how to read legends, scale, grid, color, the types of maps, and how to read a map index. (Coronet).

Reading Maps—11 min., sd., color, 1955, (pri). An introduction to maps. Shows that maps are drawn in a language of signs that stand for physical features, and demonstrates the value of the legend, scale, etc. (EBF).

Sport of Orienteering—20 min., sd., color, (sh-col). Shows Scandinavians participating in this popular game and explains how they use a compass and map. Cross-country running. (Silva).

Photography

Cameras Go to Camp—16 min., sd., color. Show how campers and camp director can use cameras to best advantage. (Eastman).

Let's Take Pictures—13 min., color, sd., 16 mm. Do's and don't's of amateur photography for teenagers. (Riken Optical Industries, 521 Fifth Ave., N.Y. 17, free).

Picture Making By Teenagers—11 min., color, (jh-col). Self-expression and creativeness with some of the problems that face the student artist. (IFB).

Puppets

ABC's of Puppet Making—20 min., sd., b&w. Simple and more complicated puppets from cardboard, cotton, glue, papier-mâché, etc. How to manipulate and stage puppet shows (Bailey).

How To Make a Puppet—12 min., sd., b&w or color, 1955. Use of plasticine, papier-mâché, etc. Several types of puppets shown, and audience is challenged to find original ones to fit their own needs (Bailey).

Riflery

Aim for Safety—15 min., sd., color. (F. P. Jones, Winchester Repeating Arms Co., New Haven 4, Conn.).

Shooting Safety—28 min., sd., color. Proper care and handling of firearms. (The Sporting Arms and Ammunition Manufacturer's Institute in 1951).

Tomorrow We Hunt—14 min., sd., color. An account of a high school Firearms Safety Education Program as set up in N.H. (Sporting Arms and Ammunition Manufacturers' Institute, 250 E. 43rd St., New York 17, N.Y.).

Ropes and Knotcraft

Trick and Fancy Roping—10 min., color. Technique of rope handling, how to make rope for roping. Both children and adults in action.

Useful Knots—23 min., sd. How to tie and use such knots as the overhand, slip, square, sheet bend, two half-hitches, slippery hitch, clove, and rolling hitch. (U.S. Navy).

Story Telling

Paul Bunyan and the Blue Ox—5½ min., sd., (pri-int). Retells this famous story, using puppets as characters. (Coronet).

Swimming

Advanced Swimming—10 min., sd., (int-col). Perfecting the style and strokes of the average swimmer—body alignment, arm and leg action, breathing, etc. Supervised by Fred Cady. (Official).

Aquatic Artistry—9 min., sd. Running front, cutaway somersault, full twist, forward one and one-half, backward one and one-half, forward two and one-half pike, half gainer, half gainer with twist, and front with half twist shown. (TFC).

Begineers Swimming—11 min., sd., color or b&w, 1955. Basic techniques of swimming for beginners. (Coronet).

Diving Fundamentals—10 min., sd., (int-col). Fundamentals of doing many kinds of diving. Supervised by Fred Cady. (Official).

Fundamentals of Swimming—27 min., color, 1950. Especially designed for intermediate swimmers. American Red Cross. (ARC).

Heads Up—24 min., Designed especially for water-safety classes and shows approaches, carries, and releases. Also valuable hints for other swimmers. (ARC).

Learning To Sail—10 min., (jh-col). The technique of sailing expertly demonstrated for beginners. Ship's tackle and sailing maneuvers explained. (Hawley-Lord).

Learning To Swim—11 min., sd., (int-jh). Six steps for beginners in learning the Australian crawl. (YA).

Learning To Swim—30 min., color. Fundamentals of water adjustment, relaxation, and first strokes for beginning swimmers. (ARC).

Loopfilms on Diving—9 loops. Fancy dives by an Olympic champion. Each described and rated by Phil Moriarity. (AAH, PE and R).

Loopfilms on Diving for Girls and Women—9 loops. Nine elementary and intermediate dives, each described and rated. (AAH, PE and R).

Loopfilms on Synchronized Swimming—set A, 7 loops; set B, 7 loops. Demonstrated by June Taylor. (AAH, PE and R).

Matt Mann's Swimming Techniques for Boys—17 min., sd., (int-col). Elementary forms of swimming, crawl, breast, back, and butterfly strokes. (Coronet).

Matt Mann's Swimming Techniques for Girls—10 min., sd., color, (int-col). Crawl, breast, back, and butterfly strokes. (Coronet).

Ornamental Swimming—9 min., 1946. Team of girls show rhythmic patterns such as "submarine," "concertina, and "pinwheel." (Bell and Howell).

Skilled Swimming—27 min., color, 1950. Nine styles of swimming. Emphasis on speed strokes and turns. For advanced swimmers. (ARC).

Springboard Techniques—10 min., sd., color, (jh-col). Shows proper use of springboard with step-by-step analysis in slow motion at a sand pit with a diving belt. Shows lifts, tucks, somersaults, etc. (Coronet).

Swimming Dolphin Butterfly Breast Stroke—16 min., sd., b&w. Directed by David Armbruster. (Bureau of Audio-Visual Instruction, Extension Division, U. of Iowa, Iowa City).

Swimming for Beginners—8 min., sd., (int-col). Instructing a ten-year old child in conquest of fear, breathing, kicking, arm strokes, etc. Supervised by Fred Cady. (Official).

Synchronized Swimming: Basic Skills—20 min., sil., (jh-col). Strokes, stunts, and hybrids from beginning to advanced levels. (Consolidated Film Industries).

The Back Stroke—9 min., (int-jh). Floating on back, leg kick, arm and breathing movements. (IFB).

The Breast Stroke—11 min., (int-jh). Arm movement, breathing, leg kick. (IFB).

The Crawl—11 min., (int-jh). Leg movement and breathing, paddle movement, then correct arm movement. (IFB).

The Sport of Diving—3 films, 10 min. each. Commentary by Lyle Draves with demonstrations by Vicki Draves.

(1) *Fundamentals of Diving*
(2) *Low Board*
(3) *Swan Dive and Front Jack Knife*

Tents and Shelters

Making an Indian Tipi—8 min., sd., color. Step-by-step process shown. (Boy Scouts).

Tincancraft

Tin Can Craft—11 min., sd., color. Ben Hunt bends tin cans into usable cooking equipment. (Boy Scouts).

Trip-Camping

Canoe Country—15 min., sd., color, (ele-col). The Watsons' take a canoe trip along an old fur route. Fishing, swimming, and setting up camp. Keeping matches dry, how to use campfires safely, and how to carry a canoe. (NFB).

Indian Canoeman—10 min., sd., (int-col). Canoeing, portaging, camping and finding food in the wilds of Canada. Two Indians of the Tête de Boule tribe shown. (Hawley-Lord).

Overnight—2 reels, color or b&w, (jh-col). Group and leader plan and enjoy overnight camping trip. All participate in group planning. (Girl Scouts).

Wilderness Day—29 min., color. Canoe and camping trip on the lakes of Northern Minnesota with prep-

aration of shelters, handling fires, cooking, waste disposal, proper canoe handling. (U. of Minn.).

Weather

Clouds—10 min., sd. How movements of clouds cause weather changes and why rain falls. Various types of cloud formations and how layman can forecast weather. (USDA).

Clouds and Weather—11 min., sd. Typical weather cycle, types of clouds accompanying cyclone, factors of barometric pressure, movement of warm and cold air masses, etc. (USDA).

Clouds Above—11 min., b&w or color, (pri). Four main types of clouds and their significance. Absorption of water by air, formation of clouds, precipitation of rain, etc. (Bailey).

Fair Weather Clouds—14 min., sil. Each type of fair weather cloud, nature of fog, and effects of temperature on clouds. (Films of Commerce).

Foul Weather Clouds—15 min., sil. Foul-weather clouds, nature of fog-banks, "undecided" clouds, etc. (Films of Commerce).

One Rainy Day—11 min., sd., 1953, (pri). Children listen to story which explains how storm begins with winds, clouds, thunder and lightning, and how rain helps soil, plants, and people. (Coronet).

Story of a Storm—11 min., sd., 1950, (int-col). Shows how weather moves across country and affects the people who are in its path. (Coronet).

What Makes Rain—9 min., sd., 1946, (int-jh). Explains how and why water moves from earth to sky and back again. Evaporation and condensation. (YA).

Index

A

A CAPELLA, 127
"A" tents, 294–295
Acorn tops, 134
Adhesive tape, 240, 258, 259, 303, 318, 350
Adirondack pack basket, 310
Adirondack shack, 103
Adjustment, personal, 32, 41–42, 51–53
Affection, desire for, 71–72
Age groups, characteristics of, 76–78
Ages of campers, 27
Agonic line, 224
Air, components of, 210
    movements, 210–211
    pressure, 211
Air mattresses, 329, 330
Alcohol, use of, 65, 94
Alibis, 93
Allergies, 61
Altar fire, 289
Alto, 216
Aluminum foil cookery, 361–363
Aluminum foil reflector oven, 288–289
American Camping Association, 23–24, 39, 45
American Forest Products Industries, Inc., 276
American Meteorological Society, 221
American Youth Hostels, 16, 368
Aneroid barometer, 211, 212
Angels on horseback, 355

Angle code, 238
Animals. See *Nature*.
Ant-proof hook for food, 334
Appalachian Trail, 368–369
Appendicitis, 381
Apples, roasted, 356
Aqua-ivy tablets, 192
Aquatics, 54, 60, 173–182
Archery, 111
Arey, Professor, 21
Art songs, 125
Arts and crafts, 130–144. See also *Printing, Plaster Casts,* and *Tincancraft.*
    philosophy of, 130–132
    projects,
        acorn tops, 134
        bark carving, 135–136
        basketry, 137–138
        block printing, 135–136
        chip carving, 136
        clay modeling, 134
        dyeing, 136–137
        nuts, use of, 138–139
        papier mâché, 133–134
        plaster of Paris, 140, 166
        photograph album, 132
        portfolios, 134–135
        relief maps, 133, 227, 230
        whittling. See *Knives*.
Ash bread, 356
Assassin bug, 198
Association of Private Camps, 24
Audubon Society, 15, 163
Automatic stew fire, 287–288
Awards, 25, 57, 69, 103, 110
Axes, 266–272, 317, 318
    care of, 267–268
    selection of, 266–267
    sharpening, 268–269
    using, 269–272
    wedges, 267, 268
Azimuth, 223

B

BACKLOGS, 281
Back-to-nature movement, 27
Bacon twister, 355
Baden-Powell, Sir Robert, 12
Bags, ditty, 250, 307, 317
    duffel, 313
    dunnage, 313
    sleeping, 328–329
Baker tent, 295–296
Baking, 356–358, 361
    in reflector oven, 356–357
    in skillet, 357
    in tin can, 356
Balch, Ernest Berkley, 20
Ball peen hammer, 249
Ballads, 124

Banana boats, 357
Bandana, 310, 316, 321, 340
Bannock, 357
Barbecue pit, 358–359
Barbecuing, 358–360
Bark carving, 259, 262–263
Barometer, 211–212, 219
    clipper ship, 213
Barrel hitch, 205, 213
Basket, Adirondack pack, 310
Basketry, 137–138
Bean hole beans, 359
Beard, Daniel, 9, 12
Bearing, compass, 223
Becket bend, 202–203
Bed making, 54, 57. See also *Sleeping in the open.*
Bed roll, 310, 319, 327–328
Beds, bough, 331
    sack, 330
    stretcher, 330–331
Bedtime, 55, 63, 379
Bedwetting, 73, 96–97
Bee line hike, 243
Belt, 314
    axe. See *Scout axe.*
Bevel, 257
Bibliography, selected general, 389–390
Big Dipper, 233–234
Bight, in rope, 201
Binder twine, 205
Binoculars, 320
Birds. See *Nature*.
Birthright of Children, 31
Black widow spider, 197
Blanket pins, 310, 327–328
Blanket roll, 310, 327–328
Blankets, 327
Blazes, 236–237
Blind trail, 236
Blisters, 240, 258, 315
Block printing, 135–136, 140
Blue jeans, 314
    pack, 311
Blue prints, 165
Boating, 174, 178–179. See also *Canoeing*.
Bobbinet, 299, 330, 331
Boisterousness, 94
Bonfires, 284, 290
Boots, 195, 315
Borrowing, 53, 57
Bowline knot, 204, 301, 328
Boy Scouts, 12
Bread twister, 355
Broiler, rustic, 260, 361
Broiling, 353
Browse bed, 331
Brush blaze, 236
Brush crane, 341
Brush shelters, 303
Buddy burner, 340–341
Buddy system, 176
Budgeting, 349

Bulletin boards, xii, 107
Bully, 94
Bunyan, Paul, 266
Burl, 261
Burlap bag pack, 311
Burlesques, 121
Burr, on axe, 269
Buttons, making, 259–260

C

CABINET, kitchen, 342
Caches, 334–335, 336–337
    cupboard, 335
    green sapling, 334
    peeled stick, 334
    St. Andrews cross, 335
Camp,
    axe, 267, 269
    breaking, 381
    clothing. See Clothing.
    Director, 48, 51–52, 101
        Assistant, 48, 49
    duffel. See Duffel.
    duties, 56–58, 373
    first day of, 53–55, 72–73
    housekeeping in, 56–57
    log, 153
    loyalty, 65–66
    making, 375–380
    morale in, 28, 52–56, 65–66, 124
    names, 54
    organization of, 48–49
    outpost, 27, 303, 335, 366–369, 370
    paper, 152–153
    program. See Program.
    rules, 55
    schedule, 55, 105–106
    site, choosing, 368, 374–375
Camp Arey, 21
    Bald Head, 21
    Becket, 12
    Chocorua, 20
    Comfort, 19
    Dudley, 21
    Gunnery, 19
    Kehonka, 21
    Lowland, 12
Camp Director's Association, 23
Camp Fire Girls, 12
"Camp Smoke," 190
Camper tent, 295
Campers, ages of, 27
Camfire equipment. See Fires.
Camping, agency, 11–12
    Boy Scout, 12, 13
    Camp Fire Girls, 12, 13
    church, 20
    day, 13
    decentralization in, 24–25, 53

Camping, educational stage of, 21, 22
    family, 3–7
    films and slides pertaining to, 395–400
    for girls, 21
    4-H Club, 12
    fresh air, 12
    Girl Scout, 12, 13
    history of, 3–16, 19–28
    municipal, 13
    objectives of, 8–9, 29–34, 68–69, 101
    organized, 7–9
    present status of, 8
    private, 11, 13, 20
    public, 13
    recreational stage, 21–22
    resident, 7, 13
    school, 14–15, 19
    social orientation, stage of, 21, 22
    special types of, 16
    trends in, 24–28, 103–104
    trip. See Trips.
    unit, 24–25, 25–26, 106
    welfare agencies, 12–13
    Y.M.C.A., 13, 21
    Y.W.C.A., 13
Camping Magazine, 24
Campsite, selecting, 368, 374–375
Candles, 165, 321, 379
    holders, 95, 251, 253, 260
Canoeing, 174, 178, 368, 382–387
    choice of equipment, 382–384
    kneeling pad, 332, 383
    paddles for, 383–384
    position for, 383
    requirements for trips, 382
    safety in, 178–179, 383–386
    stowing equipment, 384–385
Canons, 125
Canteen, 320
Capture the flag, 246–247
Carborundum stone, 257, 269
Cardinal points, 222
Cartographer, 226
Casting off rope, 203
Caterpillar of Io moth, 198
Catholic campers, 184–185
Cave woman cream puffs, 355
Caves, 168
Centipedes, 198
Centralized Camping, 24–25
Chair, rustic, 96
Chanteys, sea, 124–125
Character development, 10–11, 32–33, 147
Charades, 121
Charts, kapers, 56, 57, 58, 373, 375
    self-rating, 41–44
    skills for going on trips, 370–371
    weather, 221
Check board system, 176
Check lists for packing equipment, 308, 323–325, 371–373, 381
Cheesecloth, use of, 299

Chiggers, 197
Children, characteristics of, 76–79
Chip carving, 136
Chippewa kitchen, 342, 343
Chopping block, 269, 271
Clay modeling, 134
Clay ovens, 344–346
Clean up and sanitation committee, 376
Cleanliness, personal, 58–59, 380
Clipper ship barometer, 212, 213
Cliques, 53, 94
Clothes line, 380
Clothing, 57, 59, 314–316
Clouds, 214, 215–218
Clove hitch, 203, 297, 376
Coals in cooking, 281, 284–285, 286, 287, 361
Coast and Geodetic Survey, U.S., 225
Codes, angle, 238
    Morse, 237–238
    written, 238–239
Combustion, 283
Compass, 222–225, 283, 318
    bearing, taking, 223, 227
    card, 222
    declination of, 224–225
    floating dial, 223
    housing, 222
    orienting, 223
    using watch as, 232–233
    variation, 224–225
Competition, 25, 69, 72
Condensation, 212–214
Cones, pine, arts and crafts with, 138–139
Conical tents, 293–294
Conservation, 132, 155–159, 242–244, 273–278
Construction, camp, 109–110
Contact method of chopping, 271
Contour lines, 227–230
Cooking, 284–285, 348–364
    aluminum foil, 361–363
    ashes or coals in, 355–356
    baking, 356–358, 363
    barbecuing, 358–360
    broiling, 346, 353–354
    common measures, 354
    devices, 339–347
    Dutch oven, 358–359
    fork, 260, 346, 355
    frying, 353
    in a can, 356
    in an imu, 358–359
    in a skillet, 357
    kettle supports, 340–344
    on a rustic broiler, 361
    on a spit, 359
    on a stick, 354–355
    on a stone griddle, 359
    on a wire grill, 360
    one-pot meals, 322, 349, 354
    outfits, 321–322
    pan broiling, 353
    recipes, 354–362

Cooking, utensils, tin, 250–252, 363
    wilderness, 353, 354, 356
Cooks, duties of, 375–376
Cooling devices for food, 335–338
Copperhead snake, 195
Coral snake, 194–195
Cotton mouth moccasin snake, 195
Council fires, 289–290
Counselor(s), accepting a position, 46
    applying for a job, 45–46
    cabin, 49, 50–51, 53–66
    head, 48
    in-training (C.I.T.), ix, x, 78
    nature, 156, 159–160
    program specialist, 24, 26, 40, 49, 52
    qualifications, xi–xii, 26, 37–44, 46–47, 65–66
    ratio to campers, 26, 103
    rewards of, 45
    time off, 64–65
    training of, ix–x, xiii, 26, 46–47, 78, 366
    trips, 371
    unit assistants, 40, 49
        heads, 48, 49
    waterfront, 174–178
Crafts. See *Arts and crafts.*
Cranes, 341–343
Crayon prints, 165
Creative writing, 151–153, 154
Criss-cross fire, 287, 289–290
Crotched stick, 339–340
Crow flight hike, 243
Crown fires, 276
Crushes, 97–98
Crutch, improvised, 322
Culture, on maps, 227
Cumulus clouds, 215, 219
Cupboard cache, 335, 337

D

DAMPER stick, 286–287
Dancing, 128
Danger signals, 232
Darn goods, 357
Date dreams, 355
Day camps, 13
Day dreaming, 93
Decentralization, 24–25, 53
Deciduous trees, 280
Declination of compass, 224–225
Democratic procedures, 9, 22, 30, 31, 32, 84–86, 88–
    89, 106–108, 371–374
Depth, measuring, 235
Desert bag, 337
Dew, 212, 219
    point, 212
Diet, healthful, 59, 61, 62, 349
Dieters, 61
Digestive disturbances, 381
Dingle sticks, 341
Dining room, 54–55, 57, 60–62

Directions, compass, 222–223, 226
  without a compass, 230–234
Discipline, 28, 69–70, 82–86
Discussions, 87–90
Dish washing, 58, 376
Distances, measuring, 226, 227, 234–235
Ditching of tent, 300, 302, 375, 379–380
Ditty bags, 250, 307, 317, 318, 321
Doll, mammy, 138
Double bitted axe, 266
Doughboys, 355
Dragon fly, 155–156
Dramatics, 86–87, 116–123
Draw stroke, 384
Drying kiln for solid wastes, 378
Dudley, Sumner F., 21
Duff, 276, 277, 281
Duffel, 305–325
  bags, 313
  waterproofing, 303, 315
Duluth pack sack, 310
Dumb Crambo, 121
Dunnage bags, 313
Dutch oven, 322, 358–359
Dyeing, 136–137

E

EATING between meals, 62, 378
Education in camping, 10, 29–31. See also *Camping, school.*
Eggs, 350, 351, 356, 357
  powdered, 351
Emotional maturity, 39, 42–44, 97. See also *Social adjustment.*
Empathy, 87
End knot, 202
Enuresis. See *Bedwetting.*
Envelope bed, 328
Equipment. See *also Duffel.*
  campfire, 278, 340–341
  check list for, 54, 306–308, 323–325, 371, 373, 381
  marking of, 54, 306, 307, 350
  sources of, 325
Erosion, 107–108, 158, 244, 275
Error of closure, 230
Euphoria, 91
Evaporation, cooling by, 336–337
Evasion (withdrawal), 92–94
Evening activities, 54, 62–63, 110
Examination, physical, 26, 51, 54, 59–60, 370, 381
Explorer tent 295

F

FAMILY camping. See *Camping, family.*
Feet, care of, 240, 242–243
Field glasses, 320

Figure-of-eight knot, 202, 301, 335
File, 249, 257, 268–269
Films and slides pertaining to camping, 395–400
Fingernails, 58
Fire banks, 281, 288–289
Fire builders, duties of, 376
Fire dogs, 281, 285, 286–287
Fire poker, 278, 285
Fire tongs, 278, 285, 340
Fire-in-a-hole, 287
Fires, 273–291, 376
  basic lay, 283
  crown, 276
  equipment for, 278, 340–341
  extinguishing, 290
  forest, 65, 275–276
  ground, 276
  kinds, 285–290
  laying, 279, 282–283
  lighting, 275, 283–284
  prevention, 276–279
  selecting wood for, 279–282, 284–285
  site, selecting, 277–278
  smudge, 232, 238
  surface, 276
  wet weather, 281, 290–291, 321
First aid, 54, 240, 380–381
  kits for, 322–323
First days in camp, 53–56, 72–73
Fish. See *Nature.*
Fishing, 111–112
Flapjacks, 357
  turner, for, 260
Flashlight, 319
Floating dial compass, 223
Floor cloth, 299–300
Flowers. See *Nature.*
Fly, tent, 298, 300
Fog, 214, 219
Folk songs, 124–125
Fontaine, Mr. and Mrs. Andre C., 21
Food,
  allergies, 61
  between meals, 62, 378
  cooking. See *Cooking.*
  cooling devices, for, 333–338
  dehydrated, 351–352
  from home, 62
  planning and packing, 348–351, 372. See also *Diet, healthful.*
  protection from animals, 322, 333–335, 379
    from insects, 334
  wild, 162, 163, 169, 352, 364
Forest fires, 65, 275–276
Forester tent, 295
Fork, clothes hanger, 252
  rustic, 260, 346, 355
Fracto, 216
Frapping, 205, 376
Freeboard, 384
French fries, 357
Fresh Air Camps (Farms), 12

Frost, 214, 219
Frying, 353
Fun in camp, 31
Fuzz clumps, 258, 279–280
    sticks, 258, 279–280

G

GALLOWS crook, 344
Games, bibliography of, 112–113
    dramatic, 120–122
    hiking, 243–245, 246–247
    nature, 166–167
Garbage, disposal of. See *Wastes, disposal of.*
Gib, 344
Girl Scouts, 12, 13, 24, 319
Glasses, on trips, 318, 379
    sun, 60, 319
Glaze, 214
Globaline tablets, 377
Gloves, canvas, 249, 316, 340
Good Will Farm for Boys, 20
Gossip, danger of, 51
Granny knot, 202
Grease pit, 378, 381
Grease swab, 359
Green sapling cache, 334
Griddle, stone, 359
Grill, wire, 360
Grommets, 298, 301, 303, 313
Ground cloth, 299–300, 313, 319, 327–328
Ground fires, 276
Grounds keepers, 57
Gulick, Charlotte V. (Mrs. Luther Halsey), 12, 23
Gunn, Frederick William, 19
Gunnery Camp, 19
Guy ropes. See *tents, ropes.*

H

HAIL, 214
Hake, 344
Halazone tablets, 377
Half hitch, 203, 301, 328, 380
Halo (ring), 214
Hammer, ball peen, 249
Hand axe. See *Scout axe.*
Handles, ways of making, 251
Hare and hound hike, 244
Harlequin snake, 194–195
Hat, 314
Haversack, 309–310
Health and safety, 26, 33, 41, 54, 59–60, 242–243, 370, 380–381, 385–386. See also *Mental health.*
Height, measuring, 234–235
Helve, 267
Hemp, Manila, 200
Highwayman's hitch, 203–204
Hiking, 240–247, 315–316, 369
    games, 243–245, 246–247

Hiking, kinds of, 243–245
    orienteering, 230–231
    staff, 259, 311
Hinckley, Rev. George W., 20
Hobo stove, 250–251, 252, 340
Hold the front, 244
Homesickness, 56, 95
Honing, 257, 269
Hoppers, table, 55, 57, 61
Horsemanship, bibliography of, 113
Hot water bottle, emergency, 381
Housekeeping in camp, 56–59
Humidity, 211–214
Humus, 158, 277, 281
Hunter-trapper fire, 286–287
Hush puppies, 357

I

ICE, to keep food cool, 335–336
Imu, 358–359
Indian fire, 285–286
Indians, 9, 113–114, 199, 233–234, 282, 284, 293, 310, 311, 341, 374
Indigenous program, 27, 108, 109, 117–118, 130–132, 155–157, 162
Individual differences, 25–26, 76–79
Inferiority complex, 28, 70–75
Ink pad prints, 165
Inner tube prints, 136
Insects,
    protection from, 197–198, 298, 319, 329, 332, 334–337, 375, 379, 384
    study of. See *Nature.*
Inspirator, 285, 291, 321, 330
Intoxicants. See *Alcohol.*
Irish stew, 354

J

"J" STROKE, 179, 384
Jack Spratt Club, 61
Jacket, 314
Jewish campers, 185
Jodhpurs, 314

K

KAPERS. See *Camp duties.*
Kapok, 329
Kerfs, 270
Kettle, soaping, 353
    supports for, 340–344
Kiln, drying, 378
Kindling, 258, 271–272, 279, 280, 282
Kissing bug, 198
Kitchen cabinet, 342
Kitchen, Chippewa, 342, 343
Klondike bed, 327–328

Knapsack, 309
Kneeling pad for canoe, 332, 383
Knives, 255–265, 318
    care of, 256
    selection of, 255–256
    sharpening, 257–258
    sheath, 263–264, 318
    use, 143–144, 256–263
Knot(s), 200–208
    barrel hitch, 205, 213
    becket bend, 202–203
    bowline, 204, 301, 328
    clove hitch, 203, 297, 376
    end, 202
    figure-of-eight, 202, 301, 335
    granny, 202
    half hitch, 203, 301, 328, 380
    highwayman's hitch, 203–204
    overhand, 202
    reef, 202
    sheep shank, 204–205
    sheet bend, 202–203
    slippery hitch, 203–204
    square, 202
    stopper, 202
    taut line hitch, 203, 301
    weaver's, 202–203
Komac stew, 354

L

Lantern, tin can, 253
Lashing, 205–208, 342, 343
    continuous, 207
    diagonal, 206
    frapping, 205
    malay hitch, 207
    pole splice, 206–207
    round, 206
    shear, 206, 301, 377
    square, 205, 377, 380
    tripod, 206, 376
Latrines, 376–377, 381
Laundry, 59, 315
Lazy man's fire, 285–286
Leadership, 26, 68–90
    autocratic, 82–83
    democratic, 84
    laissez-faire, 83
Leaf relay, 167
Lean-to tents, 295–296, 297
Leather equipment, care of, 307
Legend, map, 225
Leisure time, 31–32
Library, camp, 108, 145–146
Lightning, 178, 214, 275, 374, 385
Limbing a tree, 271
Line blaze, 236
Linoleum block printing, 135
Literature in camp, 145–154

Little Dipper, 233–234
Little pig potatoes, 356
Log cabin fire, 287, 289–290
Log, cutting in two, 270
Lop sticks, 236
Lopping off branches, 271
Lost in the woods, 231–234, 374
Lowe, Juliette, 12
Lug pole, 343

M

Mackerel sky, 216, 218
Magnetic attraction, 223
Magnetic needle, 223
Magnetic North, 224–225, 226
Malay hitch, 207
Manila hemp, 200
Maps, 225–230, 318
    case for, 230
    legend for, 225, 227–228
    orienting, 226
    relief, 133, 227, 230
    symbols, 227–230
    topographic, 225
Marbelizing paper, 135
Marble axe. See *Camp axe.*
Mare's tails, 215, 218
Marionettes, 122, 123, 133–134
Marketers, duties of, 349
Match cases, 283
Matches, 283–284, 321
    waterproofing, 283–284
Mattoon, Laura, 21
Mattresses, 57, 330
    air, 329, 330
Measurements, learning to estimate, 235
Measuring depth, 235
    distances, 226, 227, 234–235
    height, 234–235
    width, 235
Mending kit, 320
Mental health, 32, 41–44. See also *Social adjustment.*
Mercury barometer, 212
Mess kits, 250, 321–322
Metal work, 142. See also *Tincancraft.*
Meylan, George L., 23
Mid-West Camp Director's Association, 23
Milk, powdered, 351
Minerals. See *Nature.*
Miner's tent, 294
Moccasins, 315
Money on a trip, 318, 373
Mordant, 137
Morse code, 237–238
Mosquito netting, 299
Mosquitoes, 375, 379
Moss on trees, 234
Motivation, 25, 103
Mountaineer tent, 295
Mummy bags, 329

Museums, nature. See *Nature museums*.
Music, 120, 124–129. See also *Singing*.

N

NAME tags, 54, 259
National Association of Directors of Girls Camps, 23
National Forests, 4, 225, 275
National Park Service, 4, 13, 224, 225
National Parks, 225, 275
Nature, 27, 33, 108, 155–172, 366–367
    animals, 164, 168
    birds, 163, 168
    casts, 166
    collections, 156, 160–161
    conservation. See *Conservation*.
    counselor, 155–157, 159–160
    fish, 164, 169
    flowers, 169
    games, 166–167
    insects, 164, 169
    museums, 162
    plants, 161, 162, 163, 169
    prints, 165, 166
    reptiles and amphibians, 170
    rocks and minerals, 164, 170–171
    seashells, 171
    stars, 165, 171. See also *Stars*.
    trails, 162–163
    trees, 164, 167, 171
    walks, 160
New experience, desire for, 73
Newspaper, camp, 152–153
Nicknames, 54
Nimbus clouds, 215, 219
Noggin, 261
North, magnetic, 224–225, 226
    true, 224–225, 226, 233,
North Star, 233
Nosebag lunch, 348
No-see-ums, 299
Notebooks, camp, 47, 66, 319
Nuts, arts and crafts with, 138

O

OBJECTIVES of camping, 29–34
Oilstone, 257
One-pot meals, 322, 349, 354
Onions, cooking, 356
Orienteering, 230–231
Orienting a compass, 223
    a map, 226
Oriole cache, 336–337
Outdoor education, 14
Outpost camps, 27, 56, 303, 335, 366–369, 370
Ovens, clay, 344–346
    Dutch, 322, 358–359
    reflector, 252, 288–289, 322, 356–357, 361
    washboiler, 345

Overcompensation, 94
Overhand knot, 202
Ozalid prints, 165

P

PACE, 227
Pacific Coast Trail Way, 369
Pack, basket, 310
    frame, 311–312
        improvised, 310–311
    sacks, 308, 309–311
    shoulder pads, 312
Packing for trips, 305–309, 349–352, 371–374, 384–385
Pacs, 315
Paddles, canoe, 383–384
Painter, 383
Pajamas, 314, 380
Pan broiling, 353
Pan tree, 342
Pantomime, 121
Paper bag dramatics, 121
Paper knives, 260
Paper, marbelizing, 135
Papier-mâché, 133—134, 139, 230
Paraffin, 283–284, 290–291, 303
    stove, 340–341
Parties, 114
Paste, making, 132
"Peas," 291
Pedometer, 226
Peeled stick cache, 334
Pegs, clothing, 260, 261
    tent, 272, 300, 301, 302
Pencil, 319
Photography, 114, 161, 318
Pig in a blanket, 355
Pillows, 331–332
Pilot snake, 195
Pine, fat, 279, 280
Pine cones, arts and crafts with, 138–139
Pins, blanket, 63, 310, 327–328
    wooden, 260
Pioneer drumsticks, 355
Pit barbecue, 358–359
Pit vipers, 193–194
Pitching a tent, 301–302
Plant press, 161
Plants. See *Nature*.
Plaster casts, 166
Plaster of Paris, 140
Plastics, 143
Play acting, 86–87. See also *Dramatics*.
Pointers, 233
Poison ivy, 191–192
Poison oak, 192
Poison sumac, 192–193
Poke lunch, 348
Poker, fire, 278, 285
Polaris, 233

Pole axe, 267
Pole splice, 206–207
Pole Star, 233
Pollyannas, 93–94
Poncho, 291, 297, 306, 313, 316, 327–328
Portage, canoe, 386
Portfolios, 134–135
Pot holders, 340–344
Pot hooks, 343–344
Pot lifters, 344
Pot roast, 358
Potato printing, 135–136
Potatoes, cooking, 356, 357, 361
Pottery, 134, 140
Power, desire for, 72, 83
Precamp training, 50, 59
Primitive camping. See *Outpost camps.*
Printer's ink prints, 165
Printing,
    block, 135–136, 140
    crayon, 165
    ink pad, 165
    inner tube, 136
    nature, 165–166
    ozalid, 165
    potato, 136
    printer's ink, 165
    smoke, 165–166
    spatter, 166
Problem campers. See *Social adjustment.*
Program, camp, 25, 26, 27, 30, 56, 63, 101–115
    director, 25, 48, 49, 101, 105
    indigenous. See *Indigenous program.*
    specialists, 49, 102
    tests of good activity, 108–109
Progressive supper, 236, 244
Protestant campers, 185
Publishers, directory of, 391–394
Punishment, 85–86
Punkies, 299
Pup tents, 295, 297, 299
Puppets, 122, 123, 133–134
Pyramidal tents, 293–294

Q

Quadrants, 222
Quiet, please!, 167

R

Rainbow, 214–215
Rainy day activities, 110–111
Rationalizing, 93
Rattlesnake, 193, 195
Reamer, 256, 257
Recipes, cooking. See *Cooking.*
Recognition, desire for, 73–74
Records and reports, 64
Reef knot, 202

Reflector fire, 287, 288–289
Reflector oven, 252, 322, 356–357, 361, 363
Regression, 94–95
Relationships,
    with campers, 39, 50–51, 53–64, 68–81
    with director, 51–52
    with parents, 55, 64
    with staff, 48–49, 52–53
Relaying a rope, 201
Rest and sleep, 26, 55, 60, 62–64, 326–327, 369, 381
Rest hour, 26, 62, 148
Riflery, 114–115
Ring tum diddy, 354
Roadside cribbage, 244
Roasting ears, cooking, 356, 362
Rock blaze, 236, 237
Rocks and minerals. See *Nature.*
Rocky Mountain spotted fever. See *Woodticks.*
Rope, 199–208
    bight in, 201
    camp, 200
    end of, 201
    guy, 300
    how made, 199–200
    knots. See *Knots.*
    lashing. See *Lashing.*
    loop in, 201
    relaying, 201
    standing part of, 201
    tent, 300, 301, 302
    whipping, 201
Rothrock, Dr. Joseph Trimble, 20
Round lashing, 206
Rowing. See *Boating.*
Ruck sack, 309, 310

S

Safety. See *Health and safety.*
    water. See *Aquatics.*
Sailing. See *Boating.*
St. Andrews cross cache, 335
Salt and pepper shaker, bamboo, 350
Sanitation, 376
Saws, 272
Scavenger hunt, 167
School camping, 14, 15, 19
Scorpions, 198
Scott, Charles R., 23
Scout axe, 267
Scout's pace, 241–242
Scud clouds, 215
Sea chanteys, 124–125
Sealed orders, 121
Sealed orders hike, 243
Security, desire for, 53, 72–73
Seton, Ernest Thompson, 12
Shadow plays, 122
Sharp, L. B., 15
Shear lashing, 206, 297, 301, 377

Sheath knife, 263–264, 318
Sheep clouds, 216
Sheep shank, 204–205
Sheet bend, 202–203
Shelters, brush, 303
Shirts, 314
Shish kebabs, 355
Shoe bag hold-all, 307
Shoes, 58, 178, 240, 315–316, 379
Shoestrings, tying, 315
Shoulder pads for pack, 312
Shoulder stick pack, 310
Shovel, 278, 318
    tin can, 376, 377
Shower, outdoor, 105
Signals, 237–238
Signs, rustic, 109
Silk screen process arts and crafts projects, 140
Silva Company, 223, 224, 231
Silver dollar game, 224
Singing, 60, 61. See also *Music.*
    leading, 125–129
Sisal, 200
Sit upons, 319
Skits. See *Stunts and skits.*
Slack pack, 311
Sleep. See *Rest and sleep.*
Sleeping bags, 328–329
Sleeping in the open, 326–332, 375, 379, 380
Sleet, 214
Slides and films pertaining to camping, 395–400
Slippery hitch, 203–204
Slumgullion, 354
Smog, 214
Smoke prints, 165–166
Smokey the Bear, 276
Smoking, 46, 65, 94, 276
Smudge fire, 232, 238
Snake bite, treatment for, 196
Snakes, 193–196, 330, 375. See also *Nature.*
Sneakers, 315, 384
Snow, 214
Soaping kettles, 353
Social adjustment, 28, 32, 70–98
Sociodrama, 86–87
Sociogram, 79–80
Socks, 240, 314–315, 380
Sod cloth, 299, 300
Some mores, 357
Songs, art, 125
    folk, 124–125
    voyageur, 125
    work, 125
Sou'wester, 316, 375
Spatter prints, 166
Special days, 63, 110
Spectatoritis, 11
Spiders, 197
Spiritual values, 22, 33, 183–188
Spit, cooking on, 359–360
Spitfire wood, 281
Spoon, wooden, 260

Sports in camp, 27
Spring box, 336
Spygelia, 341
Square knot, 202
Square lashing, 205, 377, 380
Squaw wood, 282
Staff manual, 49–50
Staghorn sumac, 192, 193
Stake, sharpening, 272
Stalking, 245–247
Standard crane, 342, 343
Standing part of rope, 201
Star(s)
    lore, 233–234
    North, or Pole, 233
    study, 165, 243. See also *Nature.*
    telling direction by, 233–234
Star fire, 285–286
Starvation hike, 166
Stationery, 165, 318–319
Step, 227
Stew, Irish, 354
    Komac, 354
Stew fire, automatic, 287–288
Stick, crotched, 339–340
    damper, 286–287
    dingle, 341
    fuzz, 258, 279–280
    lop, 236
Stick cookery, 354–355
Stone griddle, 359
Stopper knots, 202
Story telling, 107–108, 146–151
Stoves,
    hobo, 250–251, 252, 340
    paraffin, 340–341
    washtub, 251, 252, 341
Straddle trench, 376
Stratus clouds, 215
Stretcher beds, 330–331
Stretcher, improvised, 381
Stride, 227
Stunts and skits, 108, 115, 116–117, 121
Stuttering, 73
Sumac, 192–193
Sun glasses, 319
Sunburn, 60, 177, 319, 381, 385
Sunday in camp, 186–188
Surface fires, 276
Swab, grease, 359
Swamp sumac, 192–193
Sweaters, 314
Sweet potato soufflé, 357
Swimming. See *Aquatics.*
Symbols, map, 227–230

T

TABLE, outdoor, 72
Tarpaulin, 291, 296–297
Taut line hitch, 203, 301

Teasel, 157
Temper of knife blade, 256, 257
Temperature, 218–219
Tennis racket broiler, 260, 361
Tents, 292–304
 care of, 302–303
 color of, 298
 ditching, 300, 302, 375, 379–380
 dyeing, 298
 floor cloth, 299–300
 flooring, 299–300
 fly, 298, 300
 grommets, 298
 ground cloth, 299–300
 guy ropes, 300
 insect screening, 299
 kinds of, 293–296
 materials, 297–298
 mending, 303
 pegs, 203, 300, 301
 pitching, 301–302, 375, 379–380
 ropes, 300, 301, 302
 sod cloth, 299
 ventilation, 299
 waterproofing, 303
Tepee fire, 285
Tepee tent, 293–294, 303
Thermometer, 218–219
Thirst, 243
Thompson, Stuart, 341
Thunder, 214
Thunderhead clouds, 217
Ticks. See *Woodticks.*
Time off, 64–65
Tin can, cooking in, 356
 disposal of, 376, 378–379
 shovel, 376, 377
 skillet, 252
Tincancraft, 248–254
Tinder, 258, 279–280, 282
Toilet articles, 317
 case, 317
Toilet paper holder, 253, 377
Tongs, fire, 278, 285, 340
Tools, 143–144, 264–265, 272, 317, 318
 board, 264
 for camp fire, 278, 340–341
 for tin craft, 248–249
 haft, 318
Tooth brush holder, 253
Tops, acorn, 134
Totem poles, 253, 262
Tracking. See *Hiking, Stalking.*
Trailing, 167, 245–246
Trails, 235–237
Tree rings, telling directions by, 234
Trees,
 deciduous, 280
 felling, 270–271
 identification. See *Nature.*
 limbing, 271
 moss on, 234

Trench candles, 290–291
Trench fire, 287, 288
Trench, straddle, 376
Trenching of tent, 300, 302, 375, 379–380
Trips, 27, 305, 365–387
 breaking camp, 381
 canoe, 321, 369, 382–387
 counselor, 371
 duties on, 372–377
 equipment for, 366, 371–374. See also *Duffel.*
 food for. See *Food.*
 garbage, disposal of, 378–379
 kinds of, 367, 368–369
 making camp, 374–375
 packing for, 305–309, 373–374, 384–385
 personnel on, 369–370
 values of, 365–367
 where to go, 367–369, 387
Trousers, 314
True North, 224–225, 226, 233
Tump line, 312

U

Umbrella tent, 294
Underwear, 314
Unit camping, 24–25, 25–26, 106
United States Forest Service, 13, 277
United States Geological Survey, 225
Upside down hike, 167
Ursa Major and Minor, 234

V

Vapor, 211
Venus's flytrap, 157
Victor Auer crane, 343, 344
Virginia creeper, 138, 192
Visitors' day, 64
Voyageur songs, 125

W

Wall tent, 294, 295, 297
Wash stand, tripod, 376
Washboiler oven, 345
Washtub stove, 251, 252, 341
Wastes, disposal of, 57, 378–379
Watches, 318
Water, purifying, 377–378
 safety in. See *Aquatics.*
Waterfront. See *Aquatics.*
Waterproofing,
 duffel, 303, 315
 matches, 283–284
 personal, 316
 shoes, 315
 tents, 303
Waugan, Indian, 341

Weather, 209–221
  chart, form for, 221
  flags, 220
  phenomena, 212–215
  predicting, 108, 217–221
  proverbs, 218
Weathervane, 213
Weaver's knot, 202–203
Weaving, 143
Wedge tents, 294–295
Wedges, axe, 267–268
"What Is A Camper?", 67
Whetstone. See *Carborundum stone.*
Whistle, making a, 261–262
  on a trip, 232, 321, 374
White, Stewart Edward, 285
Whittling. See *Knives.*
Width, measuring, 235
Wigwam fire, 285, 290
Wilderness cookery, 354
Wind, 210
  direction, 218
Windward side, 283
Wire edge, 257, 269
Wire grill, cooking on, 360
Wishes, fundamental, 69–75

Wishful thinking, 93
Witch's brooms, 215
Wohelo, 12
Wood,
  down, 266
  for whittling, 259
  hard, 281, 285
  selecting for fire, 279–282
  slow burning green, 281
  soft, 281
  spitfire, 281
  squaw, 282
  storing, 282
Woodbine. See *Virginia creeper.*
Woodticks, 60, 197
Woodworking, 143–144. See also *Knives.*
Wool pack clouds, 215
Work songs, 125
W.P.A. Guidebooks, 147
Writing, creative, 150–153, 154
Writing home, 55

Z

Zero line, 224